On the Opening of the Eyes

Annotated Translation with Glossary of the Kaimoku-sho

by

Nichiren Daishonin

Translated from the Japanese
(Taisho Volume 84, Number 2689)
with annotations and glossary

by

Ryuei Michael McCormick

© Ryuei Michael McCormick

All rights reserved. This book or any portion thereof may not be reproduced or used in any manner whatsoever without the express written permission of the publisher except for the use of brief quotations in a book review.

Printed in the United States of America

First Printing, 2021

Contents

Foreword	5
Translator's Introduction	6
Translator's Note	10
On the Opening of the Eyes, First Fascicle	12
On the Opening of the Eyes, Second Fascicle	49
Abbreviations	96
Notes	98
Glossary	150
Bibliography	399

Foreword

One of my earliest attempts to read some of Nichiren Shonin's writings created quite a quandary for me as I came across a single word that did not seem to fit. It was the word "atonement" and I could not figure out its meaning in the context of the paragraph I was reading. I spent a good bit of time trying to find other words of similar meaning to substitute into the sentence. It did not help and there was no one to whom I could address the question at that time.

This experience convinced me of the need to have a complete library of texts on Buddhist canon, the Lotus Sutra, in particular, and multiple translations of Nichiren Shonin's writings to support my own personal study. Nichiren Buddhism is founded on faith, practice, and study, so all of these books would support deepening my study and subsequent understanding. This library allows me to thoroughly research every passage to make sure I fully understand what I have read.

All translations carry with them the subtle and unaware cultural biases which influence the manner in which meanings are derived. The greater number of translations provide entry into the works which may overcome these biases and open the works to greater understanding.

Ryuei Michael McCormick Shonin has offered this new translation of the *Kaimoku-sho*, one of Nichiren Shonin's five major writings. This translation is fresh and modern. It also includes an extensive Notes section that is quite detailed allowing for the possibility of reading the text without having to bury oneself in a stack of books. The work provides a great entry into the *Kaimoku-sho* in a manner that is supportive throughout one's journey into the text.

This book will be a welcome addition to any collection of translations of the *Kaimoku-sho*, further creating greater accessibility to a most necessary and wonderful text.

Myokei Caine-Barrett
Myoken-ji Temple
Houston, TX

Translator's Introduction

The essay *On the Opening of the Eyes* (*Kaimoku-shō*; 開目抄) is one of the five major writings of Nichiren Daishonin (1222-1282), the progenitor of those Buddhist schools and movements that follow his teachings about the *Lotus Sutra* and practice the chanting of that sutra's "august title" (*daimoku*; 題目) in the form of "Namu Myoho Renge Kyo" (南無妙法蓮華経). In this writing, he reflects upon the course of his life and the nature of the hardships and persecutions that had beset him. In the course of it, he clarifies his mission and renews his determination to work selflessly, even at the cost of his life, for the sake of Japan and by extension all sentient beings whose liberation is guaranteed by the universal promise of Buddhahood conveyed by the *Lotus Sutra*.

On September 12, 1271, Nichiren was arrested by the Hei no Saemon-no-jo Yoritsuna (d. 1293), deputy chief of the board of retainers of the Kamakura shogunate. He was taken to the execution grounds on Tatsunokuchi beach. The traditional story is that he was saved from death when a mysterious ball of light flew through the sky, frightening the executioner and the other samurai. A messenger from the regent arrived soon after with orders that Nichiren was to be exiled, not executed. On October 10, 1271, Nichiren was sent into exile on Sado Island. At first, he lived in a small broken-down shrine in a graveyard called Tsukuhara. It was the hope of his enemies that Nichiren would die in the harsh winter of Sado Island without any adequate shelter or provisions.

Many of Nichiren's followers, like Nisshin and Nichiro had also been arrested and imprisoned. They wondered why they had not received divine protection from such persecution. In order to resolve these doubts Nichiren started writing *On the Opening of the Eyes* in November of 1271. He finished it in February of 1272, after the successful conclusion of the Tsukuhara Debate. This was a debate arranged by Sado Island's deputy constable between Nichiren and several hundred monks from other schools of Buddhism on January 16 and 17. Nichiren addressed *On the Opening of the Eyes* to Shijo Kingo, a samurai in Kamakura who was one of his staunchest followers.

Shockingly, Nichiren wrote that he had been beheaded at Tatsunokuchi and it was his spirit that had come to Sado Island. Such a statement reflects Nichiren's feelings that in a sense he had given up his life at the execution ground and begun a new life. At the same time, he was aware that he could still literally die in the harsh winter on Sado Island or that he might once again face execution. *On the Opening of the Eyes* was intended to be a memento in case of his death. In other words, it was Nichiren's last will and testament, so that he could bestow his most important teachings upon his disciples before it was too late. Throughout the work, Nichiren states that the most important question is whether he really has been acting as the practitioner of the *Lotus Sutra*; and, if so, why he and his followers have not received the blessings and protection of the buddhas, bodhisattvas and other divine guardians of the Dharma.

In the following passage from his autobiographical work, *On Various Distinguished Actions* (*Shuju onfurumai gosho*; 種種御振舞御書), Nichiren describes the circumstances of writing *On the Opening of the Eyes* and his purpose for writing it:

> After everyone had left [following the Tsukuhara debate] I finally finished writing a thesis entitled *On the Opening of the Eyes* in two fascicles, which I had been writing since the eleventh month of the previous year. I wrote it thinking that if I was to be beheaded, I should have recorded the miracles in my life. The gist of this writing is as follows:
>
> The safety of Japan depends solely upon Nichiren. For example, a house cannot stand without pillars, and a person would be dead without a spirit. I am the spirit of the Japanese people. Hei no Saemon, however, has cut down the pillar of Japan. The world will be in turmoil; lies will prevail; fighting will begin among members of the Hojo clan; and moreover Japan will be attacked by foreign forces just as I wrote in my *Treatise on Spreading Peace Throughout the Country by Establishing the True Dharma* (*Risshō Ankoku-ron*; 立正安国論).
>
> Thus I wrote *On the Opening of the Eyes* and gave it to my disciples and lay followers in Kamakura through Shijo Kingo's messenger. It seems that some disciples who were still with me thought it was worded too strongly, but nobody could stop me. (WNS5, adapted, p. 36)

Throughout *On the Opening of the Eyes* Nichiren uses a series of comparisons to show that the teaching of the *Lotus Sutra* can enable all people to attain buddhahood. These comparisons range from the various non-Buddhist philosophies and religions of China and India to all the schools of Buddhism that had been brought to Japan by the thirteenth century. This writing is therefore a survey of the development of world religions, especially of Buddhism, from the perspective of a highly educated Japanese monk of the thirteenth century whose sole concern was to discern which teaching could best liberate people from suffering and enable them to attain the selfless compassion of buddhahood.

Nichiren also shows that the *Lotus Sutra* itself predicted that anyone propagating it in the Latter Age of the Dharma would be bound to encounter the kinds of hardships that Nichiren and his disciples had already faced and would continue to face. Nichiren also discerned that of all the teachers in Japan at that time, he was the only one who was directing people to the *Lotus Sutra* instead of away from it. Having reflected upon these things, Nichiren states his determination in the form of a threefold vow to continue upholding the *Lotus Sutra* for the sake of Japan, no matter what hardships he might have to face:

> …no matter how many great difficulties fall upon me, I will not submit to them until a wise person defeats me by reason. Other difficulties are like dust in the wind. I will never break my vow to become the pillar of Japan, to become the eyes of Japan, and to become a great vessel for Japan.

For the Nichiren Buddhist tradition, this writing is considered Nichiren's testimony regarding his identity as the foremost practitioner of the *Lotus Sutra* (*Hokekyō-no-gyōja*; 法華経の行者) in the Latter Age of Degeneration (*mappō*; 末法). The Latter Age of Degeneration is the era when the true spirit of Shakyamuni Buddha's teachings will be forgotten. Nichiren and his East Asian contemporaries believed that this era had begun in the year 1052. However, as the practitioner of the *Lotus Sutra*, Nichiren believed that he was fulfilling the mission given to Superior Practice Bodhisattva, one of the four leaders of the bodhisattvas appearing from underground in Chapter Fifteen of the *Lotus Sutra*. These bodhisattvas are given the specific transmission to spread the Wonderful Dharma in the Latter Age by the Eternal Shakyamuni Buddha in Chapter Twenty-one of the *Lotus Sutra*. By upholding the *Lotus Sutra* and spreading the practice of the *daimoku*, Nichiren came to believe that he was, at the very least, the forerunner of Superior Practice Bodhisattva. The mainstream of the Nichiren Buddhist tradition in Japan has long considered Nichiren to be the "appearance" of Superior Practice Bodhisattva" and the exemplar of all those who continue to uphold and practice the *Lotus Sutra*.

Translator's Note

This translation of the two fascicles of the essay *On the Opening of the Eyes* has been divided into numbered sections which are not in Nichiren's original. Each numbered section of the translation has a corresponding note. The note for each numbered section will indicate where the passage from *On the Opening of the Eyes* can be found in the Taisho Tripitaka. When possible, I have indicated where quotes from other works can be found in the Taisho Tripitaka.

There will also be explanations of the people, beings, texts, and other things referred to. If a name or term is in bold in the note, that means it has an entry in the glossary. However, the following terms are either so important and/or appear so frequently throughout *On the Opening of the Eyes* that I will list them here rather than in the individual notes for each section:

Names of and terms related to Buddhas: buddha, buddha-nature, buddhas of the ten directions, emanation-body, Mahavairochana, Many Treasures, Shakyamuni, tathagata, and World Honored One.

Terms related to the Dharma: Age of the Semblance Dharma, Age of the True Dharma, Buddha Dharma, Dharma, Latter Age of Degeneration, perfect teaching, skillful means, slander of the True Dharma, sutra, True Dharma, and Wonderful Dharma.

Terms related to the Sangha and Buddhist practitioners: arhat, bodhisattva, great master, monk, nun, privately-awakened one, sage, Sangha, three vehicles, two vehicles, and voice-hearer.

Terms related to Buddhist practice and realization: attain buddhahood, awakening, benefit, cessation, compassion, embracing, enlightenment, faith, generating the thought of awakening, gratitude, mantra, merit, nembutsu, nirvana, precept, subduing, vow, and wisdom.

Names and terms related to Buddhist cosmology: Brahma, cause, dragon, effect, god, evil destinies, heaven, human, *icchantika*, kalpa, ordinary people, ordinary person, pure land, seed, sentient being, and ten directions.

Names and terms related to the *Lotus Sutra*: attainment of buddhahood by adherents of the two vehicles, attainment of buddhahood in the remotest past, Duration of the Life of the Tathagata (The) chapter, forty years or so, lotus flower, *Lotus Sutra*, One Vehicle, Original Gate, practitioner of the *Lotus Sutra*, prior sutras, Sacred Eagle (Mount), stupa of treasures, Sutra of the Lotus Flower of the Wonderful Dharma, three kinds of enemies, three thousand realms in a single thought-moment, and Trace Gate.

Names of other Buddhist sutras: Agama sutras, *Flower Garland Sutra*, *Mahavairochana Sutra*, Prajna sutras, *Nirvana Sutra* and Vaipulya sutras.

Names of Buddhist schools: Dharma Characteristics school, Flower Garland school, hinayana, Mahayana, Mantra school, Nembutsu school, Pure Land school, Three Treatises school, Tiantai school, and Zen school.

Names of the Buddha's disciples and other important Buddhists: Chengguan, Dengyo (Great Master), Devadatta, Honen, Mahakashyapa, Maitreya, Miaole (Great Master), Nichiren, Shariputra, and Tiantai (Great Master).

Names of treatises: *Great Calming and Contemplation*, *Profound Meaning of the Lotus Sutra*, and *Words and Phrases of the Lotus Sutra*.

Other names and terms: brahmin, delusion, Ganges River, greed, hatred, ignorance, ignorant, mind, non-Buddhist scriptures, non-Buddhist teachings, place of awakening, pure, scripture, stupa, suffering, transgression, and wrong views.

If one is not familiar with any of the above terms, I would recommend looking them up in the glossary before reading *On the Opening of the Eyes*.

In the glossary, names and terms that have entries will be in bold upon the first mention in another entry.

It is my hope that, between the notes for each numbered section and the glossary, you, the reader of this translation, will have enough background information to understand what Nichiren is talking about. If you would like to know more about the context and meaning of *On the Opening of the Eyes*, then please consider reading my commentary on this essay entitled *Open Your Eyes: A Nichiren Buddhist View of Awakening*.

On the Opening of the Eyes, First Fascicle

1. All sentient beings should respect these three: rulers, teachers, and parents. Everyone should study these three matters: Confucianism, non-Buddhist teachings, and Buddhism.

2. First of all, in Confucianism, the Three Sovereigns, Five Emperors, and Three Kings of ancient China are called the most respected under heaven. They are regarded as the leaders of all the ministers and a bridge for all the people. Until the time of the Three Sovereigns, people were like birds and beasts who had no idea who their fathers were. However, since the time of the Five Kings, people have acknowledged their fathers and mothers and could discern their filial duty. Zhonghua, for instance, treated his stubborn and ignorant father respectfully, [despite his father plotting to have him killed in favor of his younger half-brother]. The Duke of Pei, [founder of the former Han dynasty,] continued to revere his father even after he became the emperor. King Wu, [founder of the Zhou dynasty,] had a wooden statue of his later father, the Count of the West, carved [and carried it into battle against the last king of Yin]. A man called Ding Lan [of the Later Han dynasty in China] is said to have had a statue of his late mother made [and treated it respectfully as though it were alive]. These are all exemplars of filial piety.

3. It is said that Bi Gan of the Yin dynasty, worrying about the downfall of the dynasty, dared to speak up against King [Zhou Xin, who was his nephew,] and was beheaded. [Returning from a political mission, a man named] Hong Yan of Wei found that his ruler, the Duke of Yi, had been killed. [The northern barbarians had cannibalized the duke, and left only his liver on the road]. Hong Yan picked the liver up, cut open his own stomach to insert it, and died. These are both exemplars of loyal subjects.

4. Yin Shou was the teacher of Yao, Wu Cheng was that of Shun, Grand Duke Wang was that of King Wen of Zhou, and Laozi was that of Confucius. They were called the four sages. Even the most respected under heaven bowed low and all the people respectfully joined their hands together before them. These sages wrote some three thousand fascicles comprising the *Three Records* [*of the Three Sovereigns*], *Five Canons* [*of the Five Emperors*], and *Three Histories* [*of the Three Dynasties*]. However, they explain nothing more than the "Three Mysteries." The "Three Mysteries" mean, first of all, the "mystery of being" which is the philosophy established by such as the Duke of Zhou. The second is the "mystery of non-being," set forth by such sages as Laozi. Finally the "mystery of being and non-being," which is the philosophy of Zhuangzi. Mystery can mean profoundness, but it also can mean

darkness. In explaining how life came to be before there were any fathers or mothers, some of these sages state that it arose from the primordial life force, while others maintain that nobility and ignobility, happiness and suffering, right and wrong, gain and loss, and so forth, are just things that happen to everyone naturally.

5. Exquisite though these philosophies may appear, they actually know nothing of life in the past or in the future. As they are in darkness, their philosophies are obscure. Knowing only the present, they insist that in this present world we must protect ourselves and maintain peace in our country by establishing benevolence and righteousness to avoid bringing ruin upon our families and our country. These wise and holy men are sages, but they do not see the past anymore than ordinary people can see their own backs, and they cannot see into the future anymore than blind men can see before them. They merely maintain that if one manages his household well, performs filial devotions, and practices the five constant virtues in this world, people will revere him, and his fame will spread so widely in the land that a wise king will invite him to be his minister or teacher, or even put him on the throne. Even heaven will come to defend and serve him! For instance, they say, King Wu of Zhou had five elders who served him, and twenty-eight constellations came to assist Emperor Guangwu of the Later Han as his twenty-eight generals. Ignorant of the past and future, however, these sages cannot help in the future lives of their parents, noble rulers, and accomplished teachers. Not knowing their debt of gratitude from the past, they cannot be considered truly holy and wise.

6. Therefore Confucius said, "Truly wise and holy men do not exist in China, but in the land to the west, there is a man called Buddha. He is a true sage." This indicated that non-Buddhist scriptures are an initial gate to the Buddha Dharma. It would be easier, Confucius knew, for the people to understand what is taught in the Buddhist scriptures about morality, concentration, and wisdom if they first learned the fundamental Confucian concepts of propriety and music. He therefore taught the kings' ministers to know who is noble and who is base, children to put a high value on filial piety towards their fathers and mothers, and students to be in accord with their accomplished teachers.

7. Great Master Miaole says [in his *Supplemental Amplifications on the Great Calming and Contemplation*]: "The dissemination of Buddhism in China indeed depended on this [teaching of Confucianism]. Propriety and music came first. Then came the True Way." Great Master Tiantai says [in his *Great Calming and Contemplation*]: "The *Supreme Golden Light Sutra* says that all wholesome teachings in the world are based on this sutra. Those who have a profound knowledge of worldly conditions will know the Buddha Dharma." [Further on in the *Great*] *Calming and Contemplation* [he also] says: "I, [the Buddha], will send three sages to teach the people in China." The [*Supplemental*] *Amplifications* [*on the Great Calming and*

Contemplation by Miaole] says: "The *Practicing the Pure Dharma Sutra* says that Moon Light Bodhisattva was called Yan Hui in that country; Light Purity Bodhisattva, Confucius; and Kashyapa Bodhisattva, Laozi. In India, 'that country,' refers to China."

8. Secondly, in the non-Buddhist teachings of India, the three-eyed and eight-armed Great Freedom God and Vishnu are the two gods who are considered to be the loving father and compassionate mother of all sentient beings, as well as their most honored gods and supreme lords. The masters named Kapila, Uluka, and Rishabha, who lived eight hundred years before the time of the Buddha, are the three hermits. The teachings of these three hermits, sixty thousand in number, are known as the four Vedas. Thus, at the time of the Buddha's birth, six non-Buddhist masters who had studied these non-Buddhist scriptures had become the teachers of kings throughout the five regions of India. Their branch schools numbered in the nineties. Each of these schools were divided into sub-branches. They all took pride in themselves, each claiming to be higher than the Heaven of Neither Perception [Nor Non-Perception], and sticking to their own rock-like contentions. Their teachings are incomparably more profound and exquisite than those of the Confucian masters. They see through not only two, three, or seven lives into the past and future, but also eighty thousand kalpas into the past and future.

9. The highest principles of their various teachings may be summed up as follows: (1) some maintain that effects exists within their causes, (2) while others claim that effects do not exist within their causes, (3) and still others insist that the effects both do and do not exist within their causes. These are the highest principles of the non-Buddhist teachings. Among these non-Buddhist teachings, the wholesome ones observe the five precepts or ten virtuous precepts, practice meditative absorption with outflows, ascending to the form realm and formless realm, and making their way up gradually like an inchworm to the upper realms. They take these for nirvana but as soon as they reach the Heaven of Neither Perception [Nor Non-Perception], they all plunge into the three evil destinies at the bottom. None can remain in these heavens although they believe that those who reach them can remain there forever. The adherents of these schools stubbornly insist on what they inherited from their teachers. Some of them bathe in the Ganges River three times a day in the midst of winter, while others pull out their hair, hurl their bodies against rocks, roast their bodies in fire, burn themselves amid the five fires, or live naked. They sacrifice a number of horses to gain merit, burn grass and trees, or worship every tree.

10. These evil teachings are numerous in number, and their teachers are revered as highly as Shakra is by the gods and an emperor by his subjects. Nevertheless, adherents of the ninety-five non-Buddhist schools, whether they are better or worse, are unable to leave samsara. Those who follow better teachers will

fall into the evil realms in two or three lives, while those who follow worse teachers are bound to plunge there in the next life.

11. Ultimately, the most important thing for the outer way [of non-Buddhist teachings] is to prepare people for the inner way [of Buddhism]. This is why some non-Buddhists maintain that the Buddha will appear one thousand years later, while others insist on one hundred years later. The *Nirvana Sutra* says that what is written in all the non-Buddhist scriptures "is nothing but the teaching of the Buddha." The *Lotus Sutra* says, "They pretend to have the three poisons and wrong views. They save sentient beings with these skillful means."

12. In the third place, the World Honored One of Great Enlightenment is the great leader, the great eye, the great bridge, the great ship captain, and the great field of merit for all sentient beings. The non-Buddhist scriptures and non-Buddhist teachings of the four sages and three hermits, despite their worthy titles, are actually ordinary people who have not yet abandoned the three categories of delusions. Although their names suggest that they are wise, in reality they are as ignorant as infants, who know nothing of the principle of cause and effect. How can we cross the sea of samsara aboard a ship steered by such men? How can we cross over the labyrinth of the six destinies by means of a bridge constructed by such men? Our Great Teacher has already transcended the transmigration with change and advance, not to speak of transmigration with differences and limitations. He has already extinguished the root that is fundamental ignorance, not to speak of delusions of views and attitudes that are the coarse branches and leaves arising from it.

13. The Buddha expounded all of his holy teachings over a period of fifty years, from the time of his attaining the way at the age of thirty until he entered cessation at the age of eighty. Every single character and every single phrase is a true word. Not a sentence or verse is false. Even sages and the wise who taught the non-Buddhist scriptures and the non-Buddhist teachings are true because their deeds are consistent with their minds. How much more so with the Buddha, who was a person of truth since unaccountable kalpas in the past? Therefore, what he expounded for fifty years of his life is the Mahayana when compared to the non-Buddhist scriptures and non-Buddhist teachings, and his words are the true words of a great man. Ever since his attaining the way until the eve of his entering nirvana, he expounded only the truth.

14. Considering the eighty thousand storehouses of the Dharma expounded by the Buddha in various sutras for fifty years, however, we see differences among them, such as those between hinayana and Mahayana, provisional and true sutras, exoteric and esoteric teachings, gentle and rough expressions, true words and false words, or right views and wrong views. The *Lotus Sutra* alone among them represents the right words of Shakyamuni the World Honored One and the true words of all the buddhas of the ten directions and three times. The World Honored

One of Great Enlightenment declared [in the *Infinite Meanings Sutra*] that, although the sutras expounded during the first forty years or so are as numerous as sands of the Ganges River, "[I] have not yet fully revealed the truth." He explained in the *Lotus Sutra* during the following eight years, that he will finally "expound the true teaching." At that moment, Many Treasures Buddha emerged from the earth and attested to his teaching saying, "What you have expounded is all true." Then all the emanation-body buddhas came crowding together from various worlds in the universe attesting it to be true and rejoicing by touching the Heavens of Brahma with their long, wide tongues. The meaning of these words in the *Lotus Sutra* is singly clear - brighter than the sun in the blue sky and the full moon at midnight. Look up and put your faith in it. Prostrate yourself before it and think hard about it.

15. Twenty important doctrines are in the *Lotus Sutra*. Such schools as the Abhidharma Treasury, Completion of Reality, Discipline, Dharma Characteristics, and Three Treatises do not know even their names, while the Flower Garland and Mantra schools plagiarized them to build their own fundamental structure. The three thousand realms in a single thought-moment doctrine is hidden in the depths of the sixteenth, "The Duration of the Life of the Tathagata," chapter in the Original Gate of the *Lotus Sutra*. Although Nagarjuna and Vasubandhu were aware of it, they did not speak of it. It is only our Tiantai Zhizhe who embraced it.

16. The teaching of the "three thousand realms in a single thought-moment" is based on the mutual possession of the ten realms. The Dharma Characteristics and Three Treatises schools established the eight realm teaching. Not even knowing ten realms, how could they know of their mutual possession? The Abhidharma Treasury, Completion of Reality, and Discipline schools, based on the Agama sutras, expound only the six realms, ignoring the other four realms. They insist on the existence of only a single buddha throughout the ten directions, denying the existence of buddhas in each of the directions. It is only natural that they leave out the concept of every sentient being having the buddha-nature. They do not recognize that anyone possesses the buddha-nature. Nevertheless, the Discipline and Completion of Reality schools today speak of the existence of buddhas throughout the ten directions and that sentient beings have the buddha-nature. It must have been that scholars after the cessation of the Buddha plagiarized the Mahayana doctrines to the advantage of their own schools.

17. For instance, non-Buddhist scriptures and non-Buddhist teachings did this. Non-Buddhist teachings [in India] before the time of the Buddha did not hold so tightly to their own views. After the Buddha, however, they seemed to realize their own shortcomings as they learned from Buddhism and cunningly stole Buddhist concepts to make their own wrong views more sophisticated. They are the so-called appropriators and plagiarizers of Buddhism.

18. The same can be said of the non-Buddhist scriptures [in China]. Confucian and Taoist scholars before the Buddha Dharma was introduced to China had been as simple and immature as infants. However, in the Later Han dynasty, when the Buddha Dharma came to China and gradually spread after the initial controversies, some Buddhist monks returned home because they could not keep Buddhist precepts or chose to return to secular life. Some Buddhist monks simply adopted Buddhist teachings into Confucianism and Taoism in collaboration with secular men.

19. It says in the fifth fascicle of the [*Great*] *Calming and Contemplation*:

> Nowadays there are many evil monks who, having abandoned the Buddhist precepts, go back to secular life and, being afraid of punishment, become Taoist teachers. Again, contrary to the Taoist teaching, they would seek fame and profit by boastfully talking about Zhuangzi and Laozi. They would utilize Buddhist concepts in their interpretation of Taoism, forcibly taking the high for the low, crushing the honorable to mix it with the humble, and leveling Buddhism to Taoism."

20. It says in the [*Supplemental*] *Amplifications* [*on the Great Calming and Contemplation*]:

> Some Buddhist monks destroy the Buddha Dharma. Men like Wei Yuansong abandon Buddhist precepts, secularize themselves, and wreak havoc upon the Buddha Dharma as laymen. ... They plagiarize the correct teaching to bolster the erroneous scriptures. ... "Forcibly taking the high for the low" ... means that these men with the heart of Taoist intellectuals forcibly equate the two teachings [of Buddhism and Taoism], mixing up right and wrong. With their shallow background, they plagiarize the just teachings of the Buddha Dharma to back up the erroneous [teaching of Taoism], and forcibly cram the lofty eighty thousand teachings [of the Buddha] in twelve kinds of scriptures into the lowly five thousand words in two volumes teachings [of Taoism] in order to support their false and base teaching. This is what is meant by "crushing the honorable to mix it with the humble."

You had better look at this comment as it is in agreement with what is stated above [in the *Great Calming and Contemplation*].

21. The same thing was happening within Buddhism itself. Introduced into China in the Yongping era (58-75) of the Later Han dynasty, the Buddhist scriptures were seen to be superior to the erroneous scriptures [of Confucianism and Taoism]. Then the three southern and seven northern schools of Chinese Bud-

dhism competed with each other for supremacy as though orchids and chrysanthemums bloomed at the same time. They were all refuted, however, by Great Master Zhizhe of the Chen and Sui dynasties, and the Buddha Dharma was revived by him for the salvation of all beings.

22. Afterwards, the Dharma Characteristics and Mantra schools were transmitted from India and the Flower Garland school was revived [in China]. The Dharma Characteristics school among them was against the Tiantai school doctrinally, both opposing each other like water and fire. Although the Tripitaka Master Xuanzang and his disciple, Great Master Ci'en [of the Dharma Characteristics school], did not go so far as to abandon their own schools, in their minds they seem to have surrendered to Tiantai as they read his interpretations carefully and realized their own fallacies.

23. Next, the Flower Garland and Mantra schools were originally provisional schools based on provisional sutras. Tripitaka masters Shubhakarasimha and Vajrabodhi stole the three thousand realms in a single thought-moment concept from Tiantai using it as the basis for their own school. They added to it the mudras and mantras to appear superior to others. Those scholars who do not know this believe that the *Mahavairochana Sutra* had the three thousand realms in a single thought-moment doctrine from its beginning in India. At the time of Chengguan, the Flower Garland school stole the three thousand realms in a single thought-moment doctrine and read it into the words of the *Flower Garland Sutra* that assert, "Mind is like a skillful painter." People do not realize this.

24. The six schools [of Nara Buddhism] such as the Flower Garland school were brought over to Japan before the Tiantai and Mantra schools. The Flower Garland, Three Treatises, and Dharma Characteristics schools continued to disagree like fire and water. Then, Great Master Dengyo appeared in Japan and not only refuted the wrong views of the six schools but also decisively proved that the Mantra school had stolen the Tiantai interpretation of the *Lotus Sutra* in order to establish its own foundation. Great Master Dengyo cast aside the opinions of the various teachers of the various schools and based his arguments solely on the Buddhist scriptures. He thus won debates against eminent clergy of the six schools - eight, twelve, fourteen, and some three hundred in number - as well as Great Master Kobo. Everyone in Japan without exception surrendered to the Tiantai school, as temples in Nara, The Toji Temple in Kyoto, as well as all the temples in the entire land of Japan came under the spell of Mt. Hiei. It also became clear that the founders of the various Buddhist schools in China had surrendered to Tiantai, which made it possible for them to escape the charge of slandering the True Dharma.

25. Afterwards, as the world degenerated and the understanding of the people deteriorated, the profound doctrine of Tiantai was no longer studied. As other schools became more prosperous their zealotry increased and the Tiantai school

was reduced gradually by the six schools [of Nara Buddhism] and the seventh [Mantra] school until it was no longer equal even to them. It was further reduced by the unworthy Zen and Pure Land schools with lay members moving over to those erroneous schools. The movement was gradual at first, but in the end even the most eminent clergy all left Tiantai for the Zen and Pure Land schools to strengthen them. Meanwhile, the fields and estates donated to the six or eight schools were transferred [to the Zen and Pure Land schools] and the True Dharma was lost. Not having tasted the delicacy of the True Dharma, such great benevolent guardian deities as Amaterasu Omikami, Hachiman, and the Mountain King left the land, leaving room for demons to grow in power. This country is now about to crumble.

26. Now in my humble opinion, there are many differences between those scriptures expounded [by the Buddha] during the first forty years or so and those expounded during the last eight years. However, what scholars consider to be most important, with which I certainly agree, are the concepts of the attainment of buddhahood by adherents of the two vehicles and the attainment of buddhahood in the remotest past.

27. First, [as for the attainment of buddhahood by adherents of the two vehicles,] it is revealed in the *Lotus Sutra* that Shariputra is the future Flower Light Tathagata, while Mahakashyapa will be Light Tathagata; Subhuti, Beautiful Form Tathagata; Mahakatyayana, Jambunada Gold Light Tathagata; Maudgalyayana, Tamalapattracandana Fragrance Tathagata; Purna, Dharma Brightness Tathagata; Ananda, Mountain Sea Wisdom Supernatural Power King Buddha; Rahula, Walking on Flowers of Seven Treasures Tathagata; [two groups of arhats,] five hundred and seven hundred in number respectively, tathagatas named Universal Brightness; two thousand of those who have something more to learn and those who have nothing more to learn, tathagatas named Treasure Form; and Mahaprajapati and Yashodhara will be tathagatas named Gladly Seen By All Beings and Emitting Ten Million Rays of Light respectively in the future.

28. These people appear to be respected [as future buddhas] in the *Lotus Sutra*, but it is disappointing to see that in scriptures expounded before it, they are not so honored. The Buddha, the World Honored One, is a man of true words, and that is the reason why he is called a sage or great man. In the non-Buddhist scriptures and non-Buddhist teachings, wise men, sages, and divine hermits must have been so named because they were men of true words. The World Honored One is called a great man because he is superior to all these people. This great man declares: "This is the one great purpose for which the buddhas appear in the worlds. ... [I] have not yet fully revealed the truth. ... The World Honored Ones expound the true teaching only after a long period. ... I have laid aside all skillful means." These words of the Buddha were attested to be true by Many Treasures Buddha and the various emanation-body [buddhas] who stuck out their long, wide

tongues confirming the truth of these words. Under the circumstances, who can cast doubt on the [Buddha's] assurances that in the future Shariputra will become Flower Light Tathagata and Mahakashyapa will become Light Tathagata?

29. It is also true, however, that prior sutras are also the true words of the Buddha. Among those scriptures the *Great Vaipulya Sutra of the Buddha's Flower Garland* says:

> There are just two places where the Great Medicine King Tree, representing the wisdom of the Tathagata, is unable to grow: the vast deep pit of the unconditioned where adherents of the two vehicles have fallen, and the great flood of wrong views and greed where sentient beings who have destroyed their wholesome roots and are unreceptive [to Buddhism] are drowned.

30. This means that in the Himalayas there is a huge tree named Limitless Root or Great Medicine King Tree; it is the supreme king of all trees in Jambudvipa, measuring one hundred and sixty-eight thousand yojanas in height. All trees and grasses in Jambudvipa have roots in it, bearing flowers in accordance with the condition of the branches, leaves, flowers, and fruits of this giant tree. The Buddha compares the giant tree to buddha-nature while all the trees and grasses represent sentient beings. However, this giant tree cannot grow in a burning pit or in poisonous water. The state of mind of adherents of the two vehicles is like a burning pit, and the hearts of *icchantika* are likened to the water disk [that supports this world]. It means that these two kinds of people will never become buddhas.

31. The *Great Assembly Sutra* says:

> Two categories of people will never be reborn. Therefore, they will never be able to acknowledge and requite their debts of gratitude. These are the voice-hearers and the privately-awakened ones. ... They are like a person who has fallen into a pit, unable to benefit themselves or others. Having fallen into the pit of liberation, they are unable to benefit themselves or others.

32. The non-Buddhist scriptures [of China] in three thousand fascicles are all about explaining these two things: filial piety and loyalty to the ruler. Loyalty also stems from filial piety. To be filial means to be high; heaven is high but not at all higher than being filial. To be filial also means to be deep; the earth is deep but not any deeper than being filial. Both sages and the wise have their origin in filial piety. How much more should we students of the Buddha Dharma acknowledge and requite the four debts of gratitude? As disciples of the Buddha, we must acknowledge and requite the four debts of gratitude.

33. Moreover, adherents of the two vehicles such as Shariputra and Mahakashyapa kept two hundred and fifty precepts, lived a life of dignity in accordance

with the three thousand regulations of deportment, progressively mastered the three kinds of meditative absorption: flavored, pure, and non-outflow, completely studied the Agama sutras, and exhausted all delusions of views and attitudes within the triple world. They should be examples of people who acknowledge and requite debts of gratitude. Despite all this, the World Honored One condemned them for not acknowledging their debts. The reason for this is that it is for the purpose of saving one's parents that one leaves home [to attain enlightenment], but adherents of the two vehicles, seek only their own liberation. Even if they benefit others to a certain degree, they are still to be blamed for not requiting their debt to their parents so long as their mothers and fathers are left wandering on the path with no possibility whatsoever of attaining buddhahood. Therefore, they do not acknowledge their debts of gratitude.

34. The *Vimalakirti Sutra* says:

> Vimalakirti also asked Manjushri: "What are the seeds of the Tathagata?"
>
> ...
>
> He answered, "The dust and trouble [of the defilements] are the seeds of the Tathagata.
>
> ...
>
> [Mahakashyapa said,] "Even those who have committed the five heinous transgressions can generate the thought of awakening."
>
> ...
>
> [Manjushri] also said, "For example, good men, just as the beautiful and fragrant, blue lotus flowers bloom in a muddy field and do not bloom on a dry plateau, [those who have entered the unconditioned will not be able to generate the qualities of a buddha]."
>
> ...
>
> [Mahakashyapa] also said: "Those who have already attained arhatship are unable to generate the thought of awakening and attain the Buddha Dharma. It is just like those who have damaged their sense faculties and cannot enjoy the five [sensual] pleasures."

35. This means that even if the three poisons of greed, hatred, and delusion become the seed of buddhahood; even if the five heinous transgressions, such as killing one's father, become the seed of buddhahood; and even if blue lotus flowers start to grow on a dry plateau, adherents of the two vehicles will never become

buddhas. That is to say, in comparing good deeds by adherents of the two vehicles with evil deeds of ordinary people, although the latter deserve to be buddhas, the former do not. While hinayana sutras chastise the evil and praise the virtuous, this [*Vimalakirti*] *Sutra* slanders the virtuous deeds of adherents of the two vehicles and praises the evil deeds of ordinary people. This sounds like a non-Buddhist teaching rather than a Buddhist sutra. It must have been said, however, to stress the impossibility of ever attaining buddhahood by adherents of the two vehicles.

36. The *Great Expanded Dharani Sutra* says:

> Manjushri Bodhisattva asked Shariputra, "Would you say that withered trees can bloom, streams flow back to their mountain springs, a shattered rock reunite its shards, or scorched seeds germinate again?"
>
> Shariputra answered, "No."
>
> The bodhisattva then retorted, "If these cannot happen, why do you rejoice in asking about attaining awakening in the future?"

37. This means that just as withered trees will not bloom, mountain streams will not flow back into the mountains, shattered rocks will never become whole, and scorched seeds will never germinate, the followers of the two vehicles are likewise as their seed of buddhahood has been scorched.

38. The *Larger Prajna Sutra* says:

> The gods, who have not yet generated the thought of perfect awakening, should do so now. Those who have determined to become voice-hearers will never generate the thought of perfect awakening. Why not? It is because terminating samsara is itself an obstacle.

39. This means that we should not rejoice for adherents of the two vehicles because they will never generate the thought of awakening. We should rejoice for the gods because they will generate the thought of awakening.

40. The *Shuramgama Sutra* says:

> Even those who committed the five heinous transgressions will be able to generate the thought of unsurpassed, complete and perfect awakening and attain buddhahood upon hearing about the samadhi of this *Shuramgama Sutra*. Oh, World Honored One, those arhats who have extinguished the outflows are like a broken vessel. They will never be able to accept and retain this samadhi.

41. The *Vimalakirti Sutra* says:

> ...if those who give alms to you are not sowing in a field of merit, if those who give such offerings plunge into the three evil destinies...

42. This means that those humans and gods who support such sagely monks as Shariputra and Mahakashyapa will never fail to plunge into the three evil destinies. Next in rank only to the Buddha himself, these sagely monks were considered the eyes of humans and gods and leaders of all sentient beings. It was therefore hard to understand why they were repeatedly criticized before a great assembly of humans and gods. Was the Buddha simply trying to punish his own disciples to death?

43. In addition, [the Buddha] compared [bodhisattvas and those of the two vehicles] to cow's milk and donkey's milk, or to golden vessels and earthenware pottery, or to the light of the sun and the light of fireflies respectively, harshly condemning the latter. He condemned them not just in one word or two, or for a day or two, or for a month or two, or for a year or two, or in one sutra or two, but relentlessly for some forty years, in countless scriptures, and before countless great assemblies, without a single word of mitigation. Everyone knows that the World Honored One is a man of truth. You and I and everyone in heaven and on earth know it. It is not one or two people but hundreds, thousands, and tens of thousands of people, gods, dragons, and asuras in the triple world, all those in the five regions of India, the four continents of the world, the six heavens of the desire realm, the form realm, the formless realm, and those humans, gods, adherents of the two vehicles and great bodhisattvas who all gathered together in this world like clouds from the worlds of the ten directions know this. They all heard him condemn adherents of the two vehicles. Upon returning to their own lands, they told everyone what they heard from Shakyamuni Buddha of the Saha world. Therefore, every one of the sentient beings in the countless worlds of the ten directions without exception knew that such adherents of the two vehicles as Shariputra and Mahakashyapa would never attain buddhahood and that they should not give offerings to them.

44. Nevertheless, the Buddha suddenly retracted his words and stated in the *Lotus Sutra*, expounded in the last eight years [of his dispensation], that adherents of the two vehicles could attain buddhahood. How could a large assembly of humans and gods believe this? Not only did they find it hard to believe, they began finding contradictions between the *Lotus Sutra* and earlier sutras. As a result, his teachings over fifty years were about to be judged false. While they were wondering whether or not the Buddha had revealed the truth during the first forty years or so of his teaching and whether it was a heavenly devil appearing to be the Buddha who expounded the *Lotus Sutra* in the last eight years, the Buddha proceeded to announce the names of the buddhas his adherents of the two vehicles would become when they attained buddhahood, as well as the names of the kalpas in

which they would attain buddhahood, the lands they would preside over as buddhas, and the number of the disciples they would have.

45. The Lord Teacher Shakyamuni the World Honored One in effect seemed to have contradicted himself. It was not without reason that non-Buddhists laughed at him as a great liar. Accused of contradiction in his own words by the dumbfounded assembly of humans and gods, Shakyamuni the World Honored One futilely tried to dispel their doubts by one way or another explaining them away. Just when the Buddha was having a difficult time to quiet them, Many Treasures Tathagata of the Treasure Purity world to the east emerged from the ground in front of him within the great stupa of seven treasures, five hundred yojanas high and two hundred and fifty yojanas wide, and ascended up into space. It was as though the full moon appeared over the mountains in the east amid a pitch-black night. From this great stupa of seven treasures, hanging in space without touching the earth or heaven, sounded the Brahma voice [of Many Treasures Tathagata] attesting that [Shakyamuni Buddha] spoke truly.

46. [The *Lotus Sutra* says:]

> Thereupon a loud voice of praise was heard from within the stupa of treasures: "Excellent, excellent! You, Shakyamuni the World Honored One have expounded to this great assembly the Sutra of the Lotus Flower of the Wonderful Dharma, the Teaching of Equality, the Great Wisdom, the Dharma for Bodhisattvas, the Dharma Upheld by the Buddhas. So it is, so it is. What you, Shakyamuni the World Honored One, have expounded is all true."

It also says:

> Thereupon the World Honored One displayed his great supernatural powers in the presence of the assembly, which included not only the many hundreds of thousands of billions of bodhisattva-mahasattvas who had already lived in this Saha world, headed by Manjushri, but also [monks, nuns, laymen, and laywomen, gods, dragons, yakshas, gandharvas, asuras, garudas, kimnaras, mahoragas,] human and non-human beings. He stretched out his long, wide tongue upwards until the tip of it reached the Heavens of Brahma. Then he emitted rays of light with an immeasurable variety of colors from his pores. The light illuminated all the worlds of the ten directions. The buddhas who were sitting on the lion-shaped thrones under the jeweled trees also stretched out their long, wide tongues and emitted innumerable rays of light.

It also says:

[Thereupon Shakyamuni Buddha,] wishing to send back to their home worlds the emanation buddhas of the ten directions, [said, "May the buddhas be where they wish to be!] May the stupa of Many Treasures Buddha be where it was."

47. When the World Honored One of Great Enlightenment attained buddhahood, the buddhas of the ten directions came to comfort Shakyamuni the World Honored One. In addition, they sent great bodhisattvas to him. At the time of expounding the Prajna sutras the long, wide tongue of Shakyamuni the World Honored One covered a trichiliocosm, attesting to the truth, while one thousand buddhas appeared from the ten directions. When the *Supreme Golden Light Sutra* was expounded, four buddhas appeared in four directions. At the time of expounding the *Amitayus Buddha Sutra*, buddhas appeared in six directions, covering a trichiliocosm with their tongues to testify to its truth. In the case of the *Great Assembly Sutra*, buddhas and bodhisattvas of the ten directions gathered together in the Great Treasure Chamber. These sutras are to the *Lotus Sutra* as yellow rocks to gold nuggets, white clouds to white mountains, ice to a silver mirror, or black to blue. These differences may not be distinguished by the dim-eyed, squint-eyed, one-eyed, or wrong-eyed.

48. As the *Flower Garland Sutra* was expounded first, it had no preceding sutra to compare with; the words of the Buddha could not be contradicted. How could there be any serious doubt about that sutra? Sutras such as the *Great Assembly Sutra*, *Larger Prajna Sutra*, *Supreme Golden Light Sutra*, and *Amitayus Buddha Sutra* were taught to chastise adherents of the two vehicles who attached themselves to the hinayana sutras. The existence of the pure lands in the ten directions was expounded in them to encourage the ordinary people and bodhisattvas to aspire to the pure lands and for adherents of the two vehicles to realize what was wrong with themselves.

49. Because these Mahayana sutras were a little different from the hinayana sutras, they mentioned such things as buddhas appearing in the worlds of the ten directions, bodhisattvas being dispatched from the worlds of the ten directions, the expounding of a particular sutra in the worlds of the ten directions, buddhas gathering together from all the worlds of the ten directions, Shakyamuni the World Honored One covering the trichiliocosm with his tongue, or that various other buddhas did the same. This must have been just to tear apart what was expounded in the hinayana sutras: that there is only a single buddha in all the ten directions.

50. The *Lotus Sutra*, is even more fundamentally different than the Mahayana sutras expounded before and after it, causing voice-hearers such as Shariputra, great bodhisattvas, and humans and gods to wonder about [the Buddha who taught it], "Isn't he Mara in the form of a buddha?" Nevertheless, those poor-sighted fellows of the Flower Garland, Dharma Characteristics, Three Treatises,

Mantra, and Nembutsu schools did not see any difference between their canons and the *Lotus Sutra*. Their eyes must have been dim indeed.

51. During the lifetime of the Buddha there might have been some who cast aside the sutras expounded during the forty years or so of his dispensation and sided, though with difficulty, with the *Lotus Sutra*. After his cessation, however, it must have been exceedingly difficult to open, read, and put faith in this sutra. For one, the prior sutras consist of many words, while the *Lotus Sutra* consists of just a few words. While the former consists of many sutras, the latter consists of just one. While the former are the teachings of many years, the latter is of just eight years. To many, the Buddha is a great liar who cannot be trusted. If they believe in him at all, they might believe in the prior sutras, never in the *Lotus Sutra*. Also, it appears today that everyone seems to put faith in the *Lotus Sutra*, but their faith is superficial and not heartfelt. They willingly put faith in those who do not see any difference between the *Lotus Sutra* on one hand and the *Mahavairochana Sutra*, the *Flower Garland Sutra*, or the *Amitayus Buddha Sutra* on the other, but do not believe those who point out differences between them. Even if they believe in the latter, they do so reluctantly.

52. Nobody believes in me, Nichiren, who is saying that in the seven hundred years since the introduction of Buddhism to Japan, only Great Master Dengyo read the *Lotus Sutra* correctly. It is stated, however, in the *Lotus Sutra*, "It is not difficult to grasp Mt. Sumeru and hurl it to a distance of countless buddha-lands ... it is difficult to expound this sutra in the evil world after my cessation." My stubborn insistence is corroborated by the sutra.

53. It is said in the *Nirvana Sutra*, [a teaching for] the transmission of the *Lotus Sutra*, "Those who slander the True Dharma in the Latter Age of Degeneration are as countless as the soil of the worlds of the ten directions is immeasurable. Those who keep the True Dharma are as few as a bit of soil on a fingernail." What should we think of this? Are the people in Japan just a bit of soil on a fingernail? Is Nichiren the soil of the worlds of the ten directions? Think it over!

54. Reason wins under the rule of a wise king, while injustice gets the upper hand under the rule of a foolish ruler. So, remember it is only in the world of a sage that the true significance of the *Lotus Sutra* is revealed. The sutras expounded before the *Lotus Sutra* appear more powerful than the Trace Gate of the *Lotus Sutra*. If they win over the latter, however, such adherents of the two vehicles as Shariputra will never be able to attain buddhahood. How regrettable it would be for them!

55. Second, [as for the concept of attaining buddhahood in the remotest past,] Lord Teacher Shakyamuni the World Honored One, grandson of King Simhahanu and the heir of King Shuddhodana, was born during the ninth interim kalpa within the kalpa of abiding, when the human life span was gradually decreasing

to one hundred years. As a child, he was called Prince Siddhartha, namely All Aims Achieved Bodhisattva. At the age of nineteen he left home, and he became the World Honored One when he attained enlightenment at the age of thirty. At the Peaceful Place of Awakening, he ceremonially appeared as the lord of the Lotus Treasury World, the Land of True Recompense, whereupon he taught the great Dharma that is sudden, subtle, and wonderful of the ten profound gates, six characteristics, and perfect interfusion. All the buddhas of the ten directions appeared, and all the bodhisattvas gathered like clouds to listen to him. In view of the place, intelligence of the audience, and number of buddhas gathered there, as well as the fact that it was the first discourse, there did not seem to be any reason why any great Dharma should have been concealed.

56. Therefore, it is stated in the [*Flower Garland*] *Sutra*, "[The Buddha] showed his unrestricted power in expounding a sutra of full perfection." This sutra of full perfection in sixty fascicles should be flawless and perfect, every word or dot in it without exception. It is like a single wish-fulfilling gem that can produce as many gems as one might wish, which is as good as having a countless number of them. One gem can pour out as much treasure as ten thousand gems. So, one word in the *Flower Garland Sutra* should be as valuable as ten thousand words. An assertion in the sutra that, "There is no distinction between the mind, the Buddha, and sentient beings," is said to be the doctrinal foundation of not only the Flower Garland but also the Dharma Characteristics, Three Treatises, Mantra, and Tiantai schools. What could be concealed in such a great sutra as this?

57. Nevertheless, it is asserted in this sutra that adherents of the two vehicles as well as the *icchantika* will never attain buddhahood. This seems like a flaw in the gem. In addition, [the Buddha's] attainment of awakening for the first time [under the Bodhi tree] is repeated three times, concealing his attainment of buddhahood in the remotest past as expounded in the "Duration of the Life [of the Tathagata,"] chapter [of the *Lotus Sutra*]. This sutra seems like a cracked gem, a moon hidden by clouds, or a sun eclipsed. This is indeed inconceivable.

58. Compared to the *Flower Garland Sutra*, such sutras as the Agama sutras, Vaipulya sutras, Prajna sutras, and the *Mahavairochana Sutra* are not worth mentioning, although they too embody the honorable teachings of the Buddha. No reason seems to be given why what is not revealed in the former should be revealed in the latter. Consequently, the Agama sutras say, "[When the Buddha] attained enlightenment for the first time…" The *Great Assembly Sutra* speaks of "the first sixteen years after the Buddha attained enlightenment." It says in the *Vimalakirti Sutra*, "The Buddha at first sat under the [Bodhi] tree, striving to overcome Mara." The *Mahavairochana Sutra* says, "I once sat at the place of awakening," while the *Benevolent Kings Sutra* speaks of "twenty-nine years" since his enlightenment.

59. These provisional sutras are not worthy of discussion, but there is something that is astonishing to hear and see. The *Infinite Meanings Sutra* downplayed such profound doctrines as the "Dharma-realm of mind-only" of the *Flower Garland Sutra*, the "Ocean Seal Samadhi" of the Vaipulya and Prajna sutras, as well as the great Dharma of "mutual identification and non-duality," as belonging to the time [when the Buddha] "had not yet fully revealed the truth" or taught [that bodhisattvas had to undertake] "countless kalpas of practice." When [the Buddha in] it states, "Having sat upright at the place of awakening beneath the Bodhi tree for six years, I was able to attain unsurpassed, complete and perfect awakening," it is agreeing with the teaching of the *Flower Garland Sutra* about [the Buddha's] attainment of awakening for the first time [under the Bodhi tree]. This is inconceivable, but perhaps it is because [the *Infinite Meaning Sutra*] is merely the preface to the *Lotus Sutra*, and the main discourse has not yet been given.

60. In the main discourse of the *Lotus Sutra*, wherein is taught the concise and expanded opening of the three [vehicles to reveal the One Vehicle], it states, "Only a buddha together with a buddha can fathom the true reality of all things," "The World Honored Ones expound the true teaching only after a long period," and "I have laid aside all skillful means." Many Treasures Buddha said of [Shakyamuni Buddha's teaching in] the eight chapters of the Trace Gate, "What you have expounded is all true." What then should have been left unrevealed? Nevertheless, the duration of the lifespan [of the Buddha] since the remotest past was not revealed. Instead, [the Buddha] says, "I, for the first time, sat at the place of awakening, gazed on the tree, and walked about..." This is most inconceivable!

61. Thus it is stated in the "The Appearance of Bodhisattvas from Underground," chapter [of the *Lotus Sutra*] that Maitreya Bodhisattva wondered why the Buddha claimed to have taught the great bodhisattvas, who had never been seen before in the last forty years or so, saying, "Then I taught them, and caused them to first generate the thought of awakening." So he asked:

> When you, the Tathagata, were but a crown prince, you left the palace of the Shakyas, sat at the place of awakening not far from the city of Bodhgaya and attained unsurpassed, complete and perfect awakening. It has only been some forty years or so since then. World Honored One! How did you do these great deeds of the Buddha in such a short time?

62. It was at this point that Shakyamuni the World Honored One decided to expound "The Duration of the Life of the Tathagata" chapter in order to dispel such doubts. Referring to what had been said in the prior sutras and in the Trace Gate of the *Lotus Sutra*, he said:

> The gods, humans, and asuras in the world think that I, Shakyamuni Buddha, left the palace of the Shakyas, sat at the place of

awakening not far from the city of Bodhgaya, and attained unsurpassed, complete and perfect awakening.

Then he cleared away the doubts by stating: "To tell the truth, good men, it is many hundreds of thousands of billions of *nayuta asamkhya* kalpas since I became the Buddha."

63. The *Flower Garland*, Prajna, and *Mahavairochana* sutras conceal not only the attainment of buddhahood by people of the two vehicles but also the attainment of buddhahood in the remotest past. Those sutras have two faults. In the first place, as they preserve distinctions, they fail to open the provisional and reveal the doctrine of three thousand realms in a single thought-moment expounded in the Trace Gate. In the second place, they have not yet outgrown the Trace Gate because they fail to reveal the remotest past expounded in the Original Gate. These two great Dharmas are the backbone of the teaching of the Buddha throughout his life, and the essential heart of all the sutras.

64. The second chapter, "Expedients," in the Trace Gate makes up for one of the two faults of the prior sutras by revealing the three thousand realms in a single thought-moment and the attainment of buddhahood by adherents of the two vehicles. Yet, this chapter is not outgrowing the traces and revealing the origin. Its teaching about the three thousand realms in a single thought-moment and attaining buddhahood by adherents of the two vehicles is not fully established. They are like the reflections of the moon in the water or rootless grass floating on waves.

65. In the Original Gate, the attainment of awakening for the first time [under the Bodhi tree] is disproven and the effects of the four doctrinal teachings are thereby eliminated. As the effects resulting from the four doctrinal teachings are eliminated, the causes leading to those effects shown in the four doctrinal teachings are eliminated. Thus, the cause and effect of the ten realms expounded in the prior sutras and the Trace Gate was eliminated and the doctrine of the cause and effect of the ten realms as expounded in the Original Gate was established. This is the doctrine of the original cause and original effect. In this relationship, the beginningless nine realms are all included in the beginningless buddha-realm. This is the true mutual possession of the ten realms, one hundred realms and one thousand aspects, and three thousand realms in a single thought-moment.

66. Seen in this light, [the buddhas of the] ten directions on [lotus] pedestals described in the *Flower Garland Sutra*, the small Shakyamuni [Buddha] of the Agama sutras, as well as the provisional buddhas of the Vaipulya, Prajna, *Supreme Golden Light*, *Amitayus Buddha*, and *Mahavairochana* sutras are all reflections of the Buddha of "The Duration of the Life of the Tathagata" chapter. They are like shadows of the moon in the sky reflected in large or small containers of water. Sectarian scholars, misled by the doctrines of their own schools or not knowing "The Duration of the Life of the Tathagata" chapter of the *Lotus Sutra*, mistake the moon in

the water for the real one; they try to go into the water to grasp this reflection or tie it up with a rope. [In his *Profound Meaning of the Lotus Sutra*,] Tiantai says, "They look at only the moon in the pond, without knowing the moon in the sky."

67. I believe that even with the doctrine of attaining buddhahood by adherents of the two vehicles, the prior sutras seem to have the upper hand. Concerning the doctrine of the attainment of buddhahood in the remotest past expounded in the *Lotus Sutra*, the prior sutras are incomparably stronger. For not only are they stronger, the first fourteen chapters that comprise the Trace Gate of the *Lotus Sutra* also side with them and do not even mention the eternal life of the Buddha. With the exception of two chapters, "The Appearance of Bodhisattvas from Underground" and "The Duration of the Life of the Tathagata," the latter fourteen chapters of the *Lotus Sutra* all describe [Shakyamuni Buddha's] attainment of awakening for the first time [under the Bodhi tree].

68. In the forty-fascicled *Nirvana Sutra*, the [Buddha's] last discourse under the twin sal trees, as well as in various Mahayana sutras expounded before and after the *Lotus Sutra*, not a single word or phrase is said [about the attainment of buddhahood in the remotest past]. Although the Dharma-body has been explained to be without beginning and without end, the origin of the reward-bodies or accommodative-bodies has not been revealed. How can anyone side with only the two chapters, "The Appearance of Bodhisattvas from Underground" and "The Duration of the Life of the Tathagata," while discarding the rest of the Mahayana sutras, including the prior sutras, most of the *Lotus Sutra* including the Trace Gate, and the *Nirvana Sutra*?

69. Now the Dharma Characteristics school of Buddhism originated with Asanga Bodhisattva, a great treatise master who appeared in India nine hundred years after the cessation [of the Buddha]. At night he went up to the inner court of Maitreya Bodhisattva and asked him questions concerning all the holy teachings of the Buddha's lifetime. During the day he spread the Dharma Characteristics school doctrine in the state of Ayodhya. His disciples included great treatise masters such as Vasubandhu, Dharmapala, Nanda, and Shilabhadra. Even King Shiladitya the Great bowed before him and all the people of the five regions of India pulled down their banners and followed him. Tripitaka Master Xuanzang of China spent seventeen years in India visiting some one hundred and thirty states while studying Buddhism. Rejecting all other schools, he chose this school to transmit to China and passed it on to the sage king, Emperor Taizong. He had such disciples as Shenfang, Jiashang, Puguang, and Kuiji, and he resided at the Daci'ensi Temple, spreading the teaching in more than three hundred and sixty states in China.

70. In Japan, during the reign of Emperor Shōmu, the forty-fifth ruler, such monks as Doji and Dosho transmitted this school from China and practiced it at

Yamashina-dera Temple. Thus, this school must have been the primary school of Buddhism in the three countries [of India, China, and Japan]. The gist [of the teachings of the Dharma Characteristics school] are as follows:

> According to all Buddhist sutras, beginning with the *Flower Garland Sutra* and ending with the *Lotus* and *Nirvana* sutras, sentient beings without the nature [for awakening] and those with the determined nature as adherents of the two vehicles will never attain buddhahood. The Buddha is never duplicitous. Once he decides that buddhahood is unattainable, he will never change his mind even if the sun and moon should fall and the great earth is turned upside down. Therefore, even in the *Lotus Sutra* and *Nirvana Sutra* it is not definitely stated that those without buddha-nature and those with a determined nature, who had been rejected in the prior sutras, will ever attain buddhahood.

> Close your eyes and think about it. If it is stated in the *Lotus Sutra* and *Nirvana Sutra* that those with a determined nature and those without the nature [for awakening], will attain buddhahood, why is it that such great treatise masters as Asanga and Vasubandhu, and such tripitaka masters and human teachers as Xuanzang and Ci'en did not find this? Why is it that they did not write about, have faith in it, and transmit it, or ask Maitreya Bodhisattva about it? Although you appear to rely on the words of the *Lotus Sutra*, actually you believe in the biased view of Tiantai, Miaole, and Dengyo and read Buddhist sutras through their bias. This may be the reason why you consider the *Lotus Sutra* and the prior sutras as incompatible as fire and water.

71. The Flower Garland and Mantra schools, which claim to be incomparably superior to the Dharma Characteristics and Three Treatises schools, maintain:

> The doctrines of the attainment of buddhahood by adherents of the two vehicles and the attainment of buddhahood in the remotest past are not limited to the *Lotus Sutra*. They are clearly mentioned in the *Flower Garland Sutra* and the *Mahavairochana Sutra*. Dushun, Zhiyan, Fazang, and Chengguan of the Flower Garland school and Shubhakarasimha, Vajrabodhi, and Amoghavajra of the Mantra school are incomparably more eminent than Tiantai and Dengyo. Furthermore, Shubhakarasimha and others are in the direct line of succession to Mahavairochana Tathagata. How could these people, provisional transformations [of buddhas and bodhisattvas], make mistakes? Accordingly, it is said in the *Flower Garland Sutra*, "It has been immeasurable kalpa since Shakyamuni attained buddhahood." The *Mahavairochana Sutra* states, "I am the

original beginning of everything." How could you say that the doctrine of the attainment of buddhahood in the remotest past is limited to "The Duration of the Life of the Tathagata" chapter? It is speaking like a frog in a well who has never seen an ocean, or a mountain woodcutter who has never visited the capital. Isn't it that you have seen only "The Duration of the Life of the Tathagata" chapter without knowing such sutras as the *Flower Garland* and the *Mahavairochana*? Moreover, do all those in India, China, Silla, and Baekje say that the teachings of attaining buddhahood by the adherents of the two vehicles and attaining buddhahood in the remotest past are revealed only in the *Lotus Sutra*?

72. According to these opinions, although the *Lotus Sutra* expounded in the last eight years is superior to those other sutras expounded in the previous forty years or so, and although it is the rule that when there is a discrepancy between older and newer legal judgments, the newer one takes precedence over the old, the prior sutras seem more influential than the *Lotus Sutra*. Things might have been as they should be while Shakyamuni Buddha was alive, but after his cessation many treatise masters and teachers have been leaning toward the prior sutras.

73. Thus, it is difficult to have faith in the *Lotus Sutra*. Moreover, as we gradually approach the Latter Age of Degeneration, sages and wise people gradually disappear while the confused grow in number. These people are easily deceived by even trivial mundane matters, not to speak of understanding the profound Dharma that is a supramundane matter. Vatsiputra and Vaipulya in India were wise people; yet they were unable to distinguish between Mahayana and hinyana sutras. Vimalamitra and Madhava had sharp capacities but were still unable to differentiate the true teaching from the provisional teaching. It was in India within the first millennia of the Age of the True Dharma, close to the time and place of the Buddha, that errors like these were already occurring. How much more so in countries such as China and Japan, which are far away from the land of the Buddha, where different languages are spoken, where people are of dull capacity, where the life span is shorter, and where greed, hatred, and delusion are redoubled!

74. It has been many years since the Buddha left the world and the Buddhist sutras are misunderstood. Does anyone understand them correctly? The Buddha says in the *Nirvana Sutra*: "Those who uphold the True Dharma in the Latter Age of Degeneration are as few as a bit of soil on a fingernail while those who commit slander of the True Dharma are as numerous as the soil of the ten directions."

75. It is said in the *Decline of the Dharma Sutra*: "Slanderers of Buddhism are as numerous as the sands of the Ganges River, while those who uphold the True Dharma are just a pebble or two." It would be difficult to find even one person upholding the True Dharma in a period of five hundred or one thousand years.

Those who fall into the evil destinies because of mundane transgressions are as few as a bit of soil on a fingernail, whole those who fall there because of crimes against the Buddha Dharma are as numerous as the soil of the worlds of the ten directions. More monks than laymen, more nuns than laywomen fall into the evil destinies.

76. Now I, Nichiren, believe it has already been more than two hundred years since the arrival of the Latter Age of Degeneration. I was born in a remote country place. Moreover, I am a poor monk without social status. While having traversed the six destinies of samsara, I must have sometimes been born a great king in the human or celestial realm, making everyone obey me just as a strong wind sways the twigs of small trees. Still, I could not attain buddhahood then. At other times, I must have studied the teachings of Mahayana and hinayana sutras, going through the outer and inner levels of the ordinary stage of the practice of a great bodhisattva. Having practiced the way of a bodhisattva for as long as one, two, and innumerable kalpas, I was about to reach the state of non-retrogression. However, powerful, evil conditions prevented me from attaining buddhahood. Was I excluded from the third category of people in this world who established a connection to Great Universal Wisdom Excellence Buddha? Or, am I one of those who, [while having listened to the *Lotus Sutra* and sowed the seed of buddhahood] five hundred dust-particle kalpas in the past, have kept retrogressing until today?

77. While practicing the *Lotus Sutra* in this present life and enduring evil conditions, royal persecutions, and accusations by non-Buddhists and adherents of hinayana sutras, I was able to realize that people have been fooled by such men as Daochuo, Shandao, and Honen, who were possessed by devils and appeared to have mastered provisional and true Mahayana sutras. Speaking highly of the *Lotus Sutra* and slighting the capacity of the people, they fooled the people by saying that the doctrine of the *Lotus Sutra* was "too exquisitely profound to understand," that "there has never been anyone who attained [buddhahood through the sutra]," or that "not even one out of a thousand persons [had attained buddhahood through it]." During an innumerable number of past lives, the people have been fooled this way as many times as the number of sands in the Ganges River into believing provisional sutras. From provisional sutras they fell into the hinayana sutras, and then into the non-Buddhist teachings and scriptures, and finally into the evil destinies.

78. I, Nichiren, am the only one who knows this in Japan. If I speak out even one word of this, royal persecutions will never fail to befall my parents, brothers, and teachers. If I do not speak out, however, it would seem that I did not have compassion. Wondering whether or not I should speak out in the light of the *Lotus Sutra*, *Nirvana Sutra*, and others, I came to realize that if I did not speak out, I would fall without fail into the Hell of Incessant Suffering in future lives even if nothing

happened to me in this life. If I spoke out, I realized, the three obstacles and four devils would overtake me.

79. As I was vacillating between the two options [of speaking out or keeping silent] and thereby retrogressing in the face of royal persecutions, I hit upon the "six difficulties and nine easier actions" mentioned in the "Beholding the Stupa of Treasures" chapter [of the *Lotus Sutra*]. It says that even a man as powerless as I can throw Mt. Sumeru, even a man with as little superhuman power as I can carry a stack of hay on his back and survive the disastrous conflagration at the end of the world, and even a man as ignorant as I can memorize various sutras as numerous as the sands of the Ganges River. Even more so, it is not easy to uphold even a word or phrase of the *Lotus Sutra* in the Latter Age of Degeneration. This must be it! I have made a vow that this time I will have an unbending awakening mind and never retrogress!

80. It has already been more than twenty years since I began speaking of this teaching, and persecutions have been increasing day by day, month by month, and year by year. Small persecutions are incalculable while severe persecutions were four in number. Not speaking of two of them, I have already been twice the target of royal persecution and my life is now in jeopardy. Moreover, my disciples and lay supporters, including those laymen who had just come to hear me speak, were punished severely as though they had been rebels.

81. In fascicle four of the *Lotus Sutra* it says, "Many people hate [this sutra] with jealousy even in my lifetime. Needless to say, more people will do so after my cessation." In the second fascicle it says, "Some will slander this sutra, and despise the person who reads or recites or copies or keeps this sutra. They will hate him, look at him with jealousy, and harbor enmity against him." In the fifth fascicle it says, "...many people in the world would have hated it and few would have believed it." It also says, "Ignorant people will speak ill of us, abuse us..." It also says, "...they will say to kings, ministers, and brahmins, and also to householders [and other monks], 'They have wrong views.'" It also says, "Or drive us out of our monasteries from time to time." It also says [in the seventh fascicle], "...people would strike him with a stick, a piece of wood, a piece of tile or a stone."

82. The *Nirvana Sutra* says:

> Thereupon numerous non-Buddhists gathered together and went to see King Ajatashatru of the Magadha kingdom [saying,] "... Now there is a most wicked man, a shramana, who is Gautama. ... all wicked people in the world are gathering around him and becoming his followers, doing nothing good. With the power of his incantations, Gautama converted such men as Mahakashyapa, Shariputra, and Maudgalyayana.

83. Tiantai says [in his *Words and Phrases of the Lotus Sutra*], "Even during the lifetime of the Buddha it was difficult to spread the *Lotus Sutra*. How much more so after his cessation? Because people do not listen to the principle, it is difficult to teach them." Miaole says [of this in his *Notations on the Words and Phrases of the Lotus Sutra*], "Hatred means slavery to delusions, and jealousy means unwillingness to listen to the *Lotus Sutra*."

84. In China, numerous scholars, including the ten teachers of the three southern and seven northern schools considered Tiantai their hated enemy. [In Japan,] Tokuitsu had this to say, "What's the matter with you, [Tiantai]? Whose disciple are you? With your less than three-inch-long tongue, you have slandered doctrine expounded by the [Buddha's] face-covering tongue."

85. The *Dongchun* says:

> A question was asked, "Much hatred and jealousy existed even during the Buddha's lifetime. Why is it that those who expound this sutra after his cessation encounter so many difficulties?" He answered, "As a popular saying goes, a good medicine tastes bitter. This sutra tears down the barriers among the five vehicles and establishes the one profound teaching. Therefore, it reproaches ordinary people and scolds sages, repudiates the Mahayana and breaks down the hinayana, calls heavenly devils poisonous insects, regards non-Buddhists as demons, censures adherents of the two vehicles who stuck to the hinayana as poor and lowly, and disparages bodhisattvas by calling them mere beginners. This is the reason why heavenly devils hate to listen to it; it grates upon non-Buddhists ears; hinayana sages of the two vehicles are alarmed; and bodhisattvas are afraid. All of these fellows make trouble [for those who spread the *Lotus Sutra*]. How can we say that much hatred and jealousy is merely an empty expression?"

86. The *Clarification of the Precepts Treatise* says:

> The archbishops [of the six schools of Nara Buddhism defamed Dengyo in their petition to the Imperial Court], "In the land of Xia to the west [of China] there was the Brahmin Demonic Eloquence, while here in the east there is a shave-pate shramana who spews cunning words. They are in a dark conspiracy to deceive the world." The treatise [refutes this,] saying, "...In the past we hear of Archbishop Huiguang in the time of the Northern Qi dynasty [who was defeated in debate and tried to poison Grand Master Bodhidharma]; now we see six archbishops here in Japan [who, defeated in debate, are trying to persecute Dengyo]. How true is it of the *Lotus Sutra*'s prediction: 'Many people hate [this sutra]

with jealousy even in my lifetime. Needless to say, more people will do so after my cessation.'"

87. The *Outstanding Principles of the Lotus Sutra* says:

As for the time, it is toward the end of the Age of the Semblance Dharma and in the beginning of the Latter Age of Degeneration; as for the land, it is to the east of Tang China and west of the Jie tribe, and as for the people, they live in the time of the five degenerations and engage in constant warfare. It is said in the *Lotus Sutra*, "Many people hate [this sutra] with jealousy even in my lifetime. Needless to say, more people will do so after my cessation." How true it is!

88. A child will inevitably resent being given a moxa treatment by his father or mother. A seriously sick person may grumble at the bitter taste of precious medicine. So it was with the *Lotus Sutra* even during the lifetime of the Buddha. How much more so in the Semblance and Latter Ages of the Dharma and in a remote corner of the land! Just like mountains placed on top of mountains and waves on top of waves, there will be persecution on top of persecution, and injustice on top of injustice.

89. It was Tiantai alone who correctly read the *Lotus Sutra* and all the other sutras during the Age of the Semblance Dharma. Various masters in Northern and Southern China hated him. However, as sagacious rulers of the Chen and Sui dynasties in China clarified who was right through debates in front of their own eyes, his enemies eventually disappeared. Toward the end of the Age of the Semblance Dharma, Dengyo alone in Japan correctly read the *Lotus Sutra* and all the Buddhist sutras. Although the seven major temples in Nara rose against him, nothing happened to him because Emperor Kanmu and Emperor Saga themselves clarified who was right.

90. But now it has been over two hundred years since the beginning of the Latter Age of Degeneration. I have not been allowed to meet opponents in debate; instead, I have been banished and my life put in jeopardy. It proves that the warning in the *Lotus Sutra* about much hatred and jealousy after the cessation of the Buddha is not an empty threat. It also proves that we are in the beginning of endless warfare and in a decadent world of corruption where unreasonableness takes precedence over reason.

91. Therefore, although Nichiren's liberating knowledge of the *Lotus Sutra* is not even one ten millionth of that of Tiantai and Dengyo, I dare say that my endurance of persecutions on its behalf and compassion for the people are beyond these masters. I am sure that I deserve to receive heavenly protection, but there is not even a shred of it. Instead, I have been condemned with heavier and heavier

penalties. Looking back in this light, I wonder whether or not I am a practitioner of the *Lotus Sutra* and whether or not all heavenly benevolent deities have left this land.

92. However, if I, Nichiren, had not been born in this country, the twenty-line verse of the "Encouragement for Keeping this Sutra" chapter in the fifth fascicle of the *Lotus Sutra* would have been in vain and the World Honored One would have become a great liar. The eighty *kotis* of *nayutas* of bodhisattvas [who made a vow to uphold the *Lotus Sutra*] would be accused of committing the same transgression of lying as Devadatta did. The verse says, "Ignorant people will speak ill of us, abuse us … and threaten us with swords or staves." In the world today, is there any other member of the Sangha than me, Nichiren, who is spoken ill of, abused, and threatened with swords or staves on account of the *Lotus Sutra*? If I, Nichiren, were not here, this verse would be a false prediction.

93. Another passage from the sutra says, "Some monks in this evil world will be cunning. They will be ready to flatter others." It also says, "They will expound the Dharma to the white robed lay followers. They will be respected by the people of the world as the arhats who have the six supernatural powers." If there were no Dharma masters of the Nembutsu, Zen, or Discipline schools in the present world, this prediction would also make the World Honored One a great liar.

94. "In order to speak ill of us, in order to slander us in the midst of the great multitude … they will say to kings, ministers, and brahmins, also to householders…" These would be vain words unless members of the Sangha in this world had slandered and exiled me.

95. It is further stated, "Or drive us out of our monasteries from time to time." If I, Nichiren, had not been exiled repeatedly on account of the *Lotus Sutra*, what could we make of the two ideograms that mean "from time to time"? Even Tiantai and Dengyo did not read these two ideograms from experience, not to speak of other people. I alone read them from experience. For I, Nichiren, perfectly fit these golden words about the person spreading the *Lotus Sutra* "in the dreadful, evil world" at the beginning of the Latter Age of Degeneration.

96. For example, the World Honored One predicted in the *Transmission of the Dharma Treasury Sutra* that one hundred years after his cessation there would be a great emperor named Ashoka. It is predicted in the *Maya Sutra* that six hundred years after the cessation of the Buddha, there would be a man named Nagarjuna Bodhisattva in South India, while the *Great Compassion Sutra* says, "Sixty years after the Buddha's cessation, there will be a man called Madhyantika, who will build a base in the Palace of the Dragon King to spread Buddhism." These predictions of the Buddha all came true. Otherwise, who would have faith in Buddhism?

97. The Buddha spoke of the "dreadful, evil world," "the future Latter Age," "the Latter Age when the Dharma is about to be extinguished," and the "fifth five-hundred-year period" in both the *Flowering of the True Dharma Sutra* and the *Sutra of the Lotus Flower of the Wonderful Dharma* as precisely the right time for spreading [this sutra].

98. If there had not been the three kinds of powerful enemies against the practitioner of the *Lotus Sutra* today, who would believe in the Buddha's teachings? If there had not been Nichiren, who would be the practitioner of the *Lotus Sutra* to prove the Buddha's words? Even the three southern and seven northern schools [in China] as well as the seven major temples [in Nara] were among the enemies of the *Lotus Sutra* during the Age of the Semblance Dharma. How can the Zen, Discipline, and Nembutsu schools today escape from being enemies of the sutra?

99. Since the words of the sutra correspond to my bodily experience, the deeper I fall into disgrace with the shogunate, the greater my pleasure is. This is like hinayana bodhisattvas, who have not completely abandoned delusions, vowing to extend their karmic activity [in this world]. That is to say, as he sees his parents suffering greatly in hell, he would intentionally accumulate bad karma in order to go to hell himself, where he would be glad to share their sufferings. I am in a similar situation. Though my sufferings today are difficult to bear, I am happy. For in the future, I will be free from evil destinies.

100. Nevertheless, people doubt me, and I myself wonder why the gods have not come to help me. They made vows to the Buddha to protect a practitioner of the *Lotus Sutra*. I would think, therefore, that they should hurriedly come to his aid, calling him a practitioner of the *Lotus Sutra*, even if they have suspicions about him, and carry out their vows to the Buddha. Yet, none has come to help me. Does that mean that I am not a practitioner of the *Lotus Sutra*? Since this question is the basis of this writing and of cardinal importance in my life, I will take this up again and again in order to find a definite answer.

101. While traveling on official business, Jizha was shown hospitality by the lord of Xu. He sensed that the lord was envious of his treasured sword. Jizha decided to present the sword to the lord on his return journey when his royal mission had been accomplished. However, the lord was already dead when Jizha tried to see him again. Therefore, it is said, he placed the sword on the lord's tomb to carry out what he had promised in his heart. Wang Shou is said to have paid for drinking water from a river by throwing coins in it, while Hong Yan followed his slain ruler in death when he cut open his own stomach to insert his lord's liver in it. These are examples of wise men requiting their debts of gratitude.

102. How much more should great sages like Shariputra and Mahakashyapa requite their debts of gratitude? They were sages who observed the two hundred and fifty precepts and the three thousand regulations of deportment without fail,

abandoned delusions of views and attitudes of the triple world, and were delivered from the triple world. They were the teachers of Brahma, Shakra, and other gods, and the eyes of all sentient beings.

103. Nevertheless, they have been discarded as being unable to attain buddhahood in those sutras taught forty years or so prior [to the *Lotus Sutra*]. By taking the pill of immortality that is the *Lotus Sutra*, they were assured of attaining buddhahood just as though scorched seeds could germinate, a shattered rock become whole again, or a withered tree bear flowers and fruit. Not having formally become buddhas by going through the eight phases of a buddha's life, how could they afford to forget their debt of gratitude to this sutra? If they did, they would be not only inferior to the wise men mentioned above but also similar to those beasts that know nothing about gratitude.

104. A turtle which had been saved by a man named Mao Bao in Jin China is said to have never forgotten his debt of gratitude. Out of gratitude, a large fish in Lake Kunming presented a brilliant gem in the middle of the night to the man who had released him from a hook. Even animals requite their debts of gratitude, not to speak of those great sages.

105. Venerable Ananda was the second son of King Dronodana while Venerable Rahula was a grandson of King Shuddhodana. Born into families of high social standing and having attained arhatship, they both had been considered as having no possibility of attaining buddhahood. During the eight-year expounding of the *Lotus Sutra* on Mt. Sacred Eagle, however, they were granted their names as tathagatas: Mountain Sea Wisdom Supernatural Power King and Walking on Flowers of Seven Treasures Buddha respectively.

106. Had they not been assured of buddhahood, thanks to the *Lotus Sutra*, who would respect them no matter how noble their family blood or how great their sagehood had been? King Jie of the Xia dynasty and King Zhou of the Yin dynasty were the lords of ten thousand chariots who were respected by their subjects. However, when they lost their kingdoms as a result of tyrannical governing, the names Jie and Zhou came to refer to those who are wicked and cruel. Even today, an ignoble person or leper would feel offended if they were called Jie or Zhou.

107. If it had not been for the *Lotus Sutra*, who would know the names of as many as one thousand and two hundred or innumerable voice-hearers? Who would have listened to them? Even if one thousand voice-hearers compiled all the sutras, nobody would read them, not to speak of making portraits and statues of them as a focus of devotion. As they are, those arhats are respected and worshipped today simply due to the *Lotus Sutra*. Without the *Lotus Sutra*, they would be like fish without water, monkeys without trees, infants without breasts, and subjects without a ruler. How can they afford to discard a practitioner of the *Lotus Sutra*?

108. Listening to the prior sutras, the voice-hearers gained the divine eye and wisdom eye in addition to their physical eyes. They also gained the dharma eye and buddha eye by listening to the *Lotus Sutra*. They should be able to see through all the worlds in the ten directions, not to speak of finding a practitioner of the *Lotus Sutra* in this Saha world. Even if I, Nichiren, were so wicked a person to have abused the voice-hearers with a slanderous word or two, or abused and struck them with staves or swords for one or two years, or one, two, one hundred, one thousand, ten thousand, or one hundred million kalpa they would not abandon me so long as I am a practitioner of the *Lotus Sutra*. For instance, do fathers and mothers abandon children who abuse them? It is said that an owl, when grown up, eats its mother, but a mother owl does not give up its baby. A beast called the *hakyō* is said to devour its father when grown up, but its father does not abandon its child. These are acts of animals and birds. How could great sagely voice-hearers abandon a practitioner of the *Lotus Sutra*?

109. The four great voice-hearers, to express their understanding, said:
We are voice-hearers in this sense of the word.
We will cause all sentient beings
To hear the voice telling
Of the awakening of the Buddha.

We are arhats
In the true sense of the word.
All the god and humans
All Maras and Brahmas
In the worlds
Should make offerings to us.

You, the World Honored One, are the great benefactor.
By doing this rare thing,
You taught and benefited us
Out of your compassion towards us.

No one will be able to repay your favors
Even if he tries to do so
For many hundreds of millions of kalpas.
No one will be able to repay your favors
Even if he bows to you respectfully,
And offers you his hands, feet, or anything else.

No one will be able to repay your favors
Even if he carries you on his head or shoulders
And respects you from the bottom of his heart
For as many kalpas

> As there are sands in the Ganges River,
> Or even if he offers you
> Delicious food, innumerable garments of treasures,
> Many beddings, and various medicines,
> Or even if he erects stupas and monuments
> Made of ox-head sandalwood,
> And adorns it with treasures,
> Or even if he covers the ground
> With garments of treasures
> And offers them to the Buddha
> For as many kalpas
> As there are sands in the Ganges River.

110. In the sutras of the first four of the five flavors, the voice-hearers were scolded and humiliated in great assemblies of humans and gods on numerous occasions. Lamenting his lack of aspiration for awakening, for instance, Venerable Mahakashyapa cried out with a loud voice that resounded throughout the trichiliocosm. Told by Vimalakirti that anyone who gives alms to him will fall into the three evil destinies, dumbfounded Venerable Subhuti dropped his alms bowl. Being told that voice-hearers were not entitled to receive alms, Shariputra spit out the food he had in his mouth. Unable to see the intelligence of his audience, Purna was scolded for being as stupid as putting manure in a beautifully decorated vessel. The World Honored One, who praised the hinayana Agama sutras and earnestly urged his disciples to uphold the two hundred and fifty precepts earlier at the Deer Park, now suddenly changed his mind and scolded them as vehemently as this. It was a contradiction hard for them to swallow.

111. In another instance, the Buddha scolded Devadatta for being such a fool and a lickspittle. Devadatta resented the Buddha as if he had been shot through the chest by a poisoned arrow. He said:

> Gautama is not a Buddha, I am the first son of King Dronodana, elder brother of Venerable Ananda, and a member of the Gautama clan. No matter how badly I behaved, he should have told me about it privately. How could he be a buddha or a great man when he put me to such shame in the midst of a large assembly of humans and gods? Formerly, he was my enemy who robbed me of the woman I had loved. Now he is my enemy who insulted me in front of a crowd. He will remain my sworn enemy age after age and lifetime after lifetime.

112. As I contemplate these instances, these great voice-hearers were originally from non-Buddhist brahmin families or leaders of various non-Buddhist religions in India. Therefore, they were believed and respected by kings and lay supporters. Some of them were originally of high social status and from rich families. Giving

up rank and honor and suppressing their pride, they took off layman's clothes to put on shabby saffron robes, discarding their white-haired fly whisks and bows and arrows, symbols of their high social standing. Like beggars, they followed the World Honored One, each with alms bowl in hand, without a shelter from wind and rain, and little food or clothing to sustain their bodies. As all the people in the five regions of India and within the four oceans were disciples and lay supporters of non-Buddhist religions, even the Buddha himself encountered nine great difficulties, including Devadatta rolling a boulder down a hill at him, King Ajatashatru releasing a drunken elephant in his direction, and King Agnidatta giving him only horse feed for ninety days. When the Buddha went to a brahmin village to beg for food, he did not receive any offerings except for a bowlful of rice gruel. It is also said that a brahmin woman named Chinchamanavika who, placing a bowl on her stomach, claimed to have been made pregnant by the Buddha. Even the Buddha was confronted with difficulties such as these, not to speak of his disciples, who had to go through numerous difficulties.

113. Countless members of the Shakya clan were murdered by King Virudhaka of Shravasti, and many more of them were trampled to death by drunken elephants. The nun Utpalavarna was beaten to death by Devadatta, and Venerable Kalodayin was murdered and buried under horse manure, while Venerable Maudgalyayana was beaten to death by a group of non-Buddhists armed with bamboo staves.

114. Moreover, the influential six non-Buddhist masters joined forces in appealing to such powerful kings as Ajatashatru and Prasenajit saying:

> Gautama is the most evil man in Jambudvipa. Wherever he goes, there are three calamities and seven disasters. Just as many rivers flow into an ocean and many trees grow on a huge mountain, many evil men such as Mahakashyapa, Shariputra, Maudgalyayana, and Subhuti gather around Gautama. The primary duties of a man are to be a loyal subject and a filial child. However, they are fooled by Gautama into renouncing their families against parental wishes. They hide themselves in the mountains against the royal ordinance. As such they should not be allowed to stay in the country. It is due to their presence that there are disorders of the sun, moon, and stars in the heavens, while there are many natural calamities on earth.

115. These were difficult enough to bear, but there was more to come, making it hard for them to follow the Buddha. Not knowing what to do upon being scolded and shamed often by the Buddha in front of the great assemblies of humans and gods, they only remained bewildered.

116. The heaviest blow of all hit them [when the Buddha says] in the *Vimalakirti Sutra*: "Those who offer alms to you, voice-hearers, cannot be called those who sow seeds in the field of merit where the seed of buddhahood can germinate and grow. Those who give offerings to you will fall into the three evil destinies."

117. This was when the Buddha was staying in the Amrapali Grove, where a great assembly as immeasurable as the sands of the Ganges River, including Brahma, Shakra, the gods of the sun and moon, the four heavenly kings, the many gods of the triple world, the earth goddess, and the dragons had gathered. Amid this great assembly, the Buddha declared, "Those gods and humans who give offerings to monks like Subhuti will fall into the three evil destinies." How could they, those gods and humans who heard him say this, present offerings to the voice-hearers? After all, it even appeared that the Buddha was trying to kill off those voice-hearers. Right-hearted people felt that he was too severe. Those hinayana sages were barely able to sustain their lives with the offerings given to the Buddha.

118. As I contemplate this, if Shakyamuni Buddha had entered cessation after teaching only forty years or so without expounding the *Lotus Sutra* in the last eight years, who would have given offerings to these respectable people? They would certainly be as though in the realm of the hungry ghosts while still alive.

119. However, just as the great sun in the spring melts away the ice and strong winds shake off all the dew, those sutras expounded in the forty years or so were discredited at once by one statement in the chapter on "Expounding the Dharma" of the *Infinite Meanings Sutra*: "…had not yet fully revealed the truth." Just as a strong wind disperses dark clouds revealing the full moon in the sky and the sun shines in the clear sky, it was made crystal clear that "The World Honored Ones expound the true teaching only after a long period." It was stated in the spotless mirror that is the *Lotus Sutra*, in the indisputable words of the Buddha that are as clear as the sun and moon in the sky, that men like Shariputra and Mahakashyapa could attain buddhahood and that they would be called Flower Light Tathagata and Light Tathagata respectively in the future. That was the very reason why lay supporters among gods and humans after the cessation of the Buddha continued to look up to those hinayana sages as if they were buddhas.

120. When the water is clear, the moon is bound to be reflected in it. When the wind blows, trees and grasses are bound to bend. So, when there is a practitioner of the *Lotus Sutra*, those sages should come to see him even if it means that they must overcome such obstacles as great fires or huge boulders. Mahakashyapa is said to have entered samadhi, but now is not the time for him to do so. I wonder why they have not rushed to rescue the practitioner of the *Lotus Sutra* when his life is at stake. Are we not living in the fifth five-hundred-year period?

121. Are these scriptural words "widely propagated" false? Am I, Nichiren, not a practitioner of the *Lotus Sutra*? Are they protecting those great liars who speak of a "separate transmission outside the sutras"? Are they defending those who say we should "abandon, close, set aside, and cast away" the *Lotus* Sutra, urging that its gate be shut and the *Lotus Sutra* practice halls be closed down? Or is it that the various gods, shying away from the great difficulties in this defiled world, do not descend to help the practitioner of the *Lotus Sutra* in spite of their vow before the Buddha to do so? Both the sun and moon are still in the sky, Mt. Sumeru still exists, the tides of the sea still rise and ebb, and the four seasons come and go in order. Why is it then that no one comes to help the practitioner of the *Lotus Sutra*? This doubt of mine grows greater and greater.

122. Again, it appears that in the prior sutras great bodhisattvas, gods, and humans were guaranteed the attainment of buddhahood in the future. However, that guarantee is merely color and shape without substance, just like trying to grab the moon's reflection in the water or mistaking the shadow for the body. We might say that in those prior sutras they do not owe the Buddha as much as they seemed.

123. Upon reaching enlightenment, the World Honored One did not begin teaching. Instead, some sixty great bodhisattvas such as Dharma Wisdom, Merit Forest, Diamond Banner, and Diamond Repository appeared before Lord Teacher Shakyamuni the World Honored One from the buddha-lands of the ten directions to teach in response to the request of such bodhisattvas as Chief Wise and Moon of Liberation, to explain the doctrine concerning the ten abodes, ten kinds of practice, ten dimensions of merit transference, and ten grounds. They had not learned these teachings from Shakyamuni the World Honored One. The Brahmas of all the worlds of the ten directions and others also came to teach, but what they taught was not what they learned from Shakyamuni the World Honored One. All the great bodhisattvas, gods, dragons, and others in the Flower Garland assembly were great bodhisattvas who had won inconceivable liberation before Shakyamuni Buddha taught. They might have been Shakyamuni the World Honored One's disciples in the past, when he was still undertaking bodhisattva practice. Or, they might have been disciples of those buddhas in the worlds of the ten directions who had previously attained buddhahood. At any rate, they were not disciples of the Buddha who is the Lord Teacher whose attainment of awakening for the first time [was under the Bodhi tree in this world].

124. It was only when the Buddha began teaching the four doctrinal teachings in the Agama sutras, Vaipulya sutras, and Prajna sutras that he began having disciples. These sutras were taught by the Buddha, but his teachings in them were not really his own. Why is that so? It is because the distinct and perfect teachings in the Vaipulya sutras and Prajna sutras were not any different from those in the *Flower Garland Sutra*, which were not of Shakyamuni the World Honored One himself but of such great bodhisattvas as Dharma Wisdom. Those bodhisattvas appear

at first glance to have been the Buddha's disciples, but it is more proper to say they were his teachers. Having listened to them teach distinct and perfect teachings in the *Flower Garland Sutra*, the Buddha learned from them and repeated the teachings when he taught the Vaipulya and Prajna sutras later. Therefore, the distinct and perfect teachings of the Vaipulya sutras and Prajna sutras are exactly like those in the *Flower Garland Sutra*, whose great bodhisattvas are teachers of Shakyamuni the World Honored One. This is the reason why these bodhisattvas were called "good friends," meaning not exactly teachers nor disciples in the *Flower Garland Sutra*. The two teachings of the tripitaka and the shared are merely branches of the distinct and the perfect. Those bodhisattvas such as Dharma Wisdom, who knew the latter, should have known the former as well.

125. The teacher reveals to disciples what they do not know. For instance, all followers of non-Buddhist teachings in India among humans and gods before the time of Shakyamuni Buddha were disciples of the two gods and the three hermits. Although they split into ninety-five schools, their teachings did not go beyond those of the three hermits. Shakyamuni the World Honored One had also been a disciple of non-Buddhist teachings, but while practicing ascetic and peaceful practices for twelve years, he perceived the principles of suffering, emptiness, impermanence, and non-self in all phenomena. Thereafter, he no longer considered himself a student of non-Buddhist teachings and claimed to have won his wisdom without the guidance of teachers. So, humans and gods looked up to him as a great master.

126. Therefore, during the time when the [first] four flavors were taught, Lord Teacher Shakyamuni the World Honored One was not the teacher who revealed what others did not know, but he was rather a student of such bodhisattvas as Dharma Wisdom. Likewise, Manjushri Bodhisattva had been a teacher of Shakyamuni Buddha for nine generations. That is why in various sutras the Buddha said that he "did not expound even a single word."

127. When the Buddha at the age of seventy-two taught the *Infinite Meanings Sutra* on Mt. Sacred Eagle in Magadha, he discredited all the sutras, major as well as minor sutras, expounded in the preceding forty years or so by declaring, "In these forty years or so, [he] had not yet fully revealed the truth." Upon hearing it, great bodhisattvas as well as gods and humans were all shocked and wished to know the true teaching. Although a shred of truth seems to have been revealed in the *Infinite Meanings Sutra*, the truth itself was not yet revealed. It was like the moon on the verge of appearing over the mountains in the east. Its rays shone upon the mountains in the west, yet the moon itself could not be seen.

128. In revealing the concise opening of the three vehicles to reveal the One Vehicle in the "Expedients" chapter of the *Lotus Sutra*, the Buddha briefly expressed the three thousand realms in a single thought-moment doctrine held deep in his heart. Since it was the first time for the Buddha to reveal the truth, it sounded

to his disciples as faint as the voice of a nightingale heard by someone half-asleep or the moon rising half way over a mountain covered by a thin cloud. Surprised by the words of the Buddha, Shariputra and other disciples called on gods, dragons, and great bodhisattvas, and together they petitioned the Buddha: "As many gods and dragons as there are sands in the River Ganges, and the eighty thousand bodhisattvas who are seeking buddhahood, and the wheel-turning noble kings of billions of worlds are joining their hands together respectfully, wishing to hear the perfect way." In other words, they requested him to expound the doctrine that they had never heard of during his teaching in more than forty years of the prior sutras, when he expounded the four flavors and three teachings.

129. As for the perfect way which they wished to hear, the *Nirvana Sutra* says, "The prefix *sad* of *saddharma* means 'perfect'." The *Profound Meaning of the Four Mahayana Treatises* says, "The prefix *sad* in *saddharma* is a Sanskrit word meaning 'six,' which is the perfect number in India." A commentary by Jizang says, "The word *sad* means 'perfect.'" Tiantai says in fascicle eight of his *Profound Meaning of the Lotus Sutra*, "*Sad* is a Sanskrit word translated here as 'wonderful' in Chinese." Nagarjuna Bodhisattva, the thirteenth of the twenty-three successors, the first ancestor of the Flower Garland school and the Mantra school, an emanation of Dharma Cloud Unhindered King Tathagata, a great sage who attained the first ground, states in his one thousand fascicled work, the *Great Perfection of Wisdom Treatise*, that *sad* means six.

130. *Myoho Renge Kyo* is a Chinese translation of the title of the *Lotus Sutra*, which is called the *Saddharma-pundarika-sutra* in India. Tripitaka Master Shubhakarasimha's mantra representing the essential heart of the *Lotus Sutra* is as follows:
Nomaku sammanda bodanan
on a an aku
sarubaboda kino sakishubiya
gyagyanosanshaba arakishani
satsuridaruma fudarikya sotaran
ja un ban koku bazara rakishaman
un sohaku

131. This mantra, representing the essential heart of the *Lotus Sutra*, came from an iron stupa in Southern India. In it, *Saddharma* means the "True Dharma," while '*sad*' can mean "true" or "wonderful." Therefore, the *Lotus Sutra* is called either the *Sutra of the Flowering of the True Dharma* or the *Sutra of the Lotus Flower of the Wonderful Dharma*. Placing the two ideograms used to transliterate *namas* in front of the latter we get "Devotion to the Sutra of the Lotus Flower of the Wonderful Dharma."

132. The ideogram for "wonderful" also means "perfect." "Six" refers to myriad practices subsumed in the six perfections. "Wishing to hear the perfect way"

means wanting to know all the myriad practices subsumed in the six perfections. The Chinese compound for "perfect" is composed of two ideograms, the first can mean "possession" and indicates the "mutual possession of the ten realms," while the second can mean "satisfactory," that is to say, it is satisfactory for each of the ten realms to contain in itself characteristics of the other nine realms. Altogether, each of the sixty-nine thousand three hundred and eighty-four characters of the *Lotus Sutra*, in twenty-eight chapters in eight fascicles, contains the character for "wonderful." Each represents the Buddha with thirty-two marks or eighty minor marks. As each of the ten realms contains in it characteristics of the buddha-realm, Great Master Miaole says [in his *Supplemental Amplifications on the Great Calming and Contemplation*], "Each realm contains the fruition of buddhahood, not to speak of the fruitions of the other nine realms."

133. In response to the request for the teachings the Buddha says [in the "Expedients" chapter of the *Lotus Sutra*], "…the buddhas, the world honored ones, appear in the worlds in order to cause all sentient beings to open the gate to the insight of the Buddha." Here, "all sentient beings," includes Shariputra, the *icchantika*, and all those in the nine realms. Therefore, his vow to save innumerable sentient beings was at last fulfilled. That is what he meant in declaring in the same chapter, "I once vowed that I would cause all sentient beings to become exactly as I am. That old vow of mine has now been fulfilled."

134. Upon hearing this, the great bodhisattvas and gods expressed their understanding by saying, "So far we have heard many teachings of the World Honored One. But we have never heard such a profound, wonderful, and excellent teaching as this." [In his *Essay on the Protection of the Nation*,] Great Master Dengyo says:

> "So far we have heard many teachings of the World Honored One" means that they had listened in the past to such great teachings as the *Flower Garland Sutra* before they heard the *Lotus Sutra*. "But we have never heard such a profound, wonderful and excellent teaching as this" means that they have never heard the One Buddha Vehicle teaching of the *Lotus Sutra*."

That is to say, they said that while listening to various Mahayana sutras as numerous as the grains of sand in the Ganges River such as the *Flower Garland Sutra*, Vaipulya sutras, Prajna sutras, the *Revealing the Profound Secrets Sutra*, and the *Mahavairochana Sutra*, they had never heard of the attainment of buddhahood by adherents of the two vehicles or the attainment of buddhahood in the remotest past, the two doctrines that constitute the essential heart of Buddhism and the backbone of the three thousand realms in a single thought-moment teaching.

On the Opening of the Eyes, Second Fascicle

135. But now, [having listened to the *Lotus Sutra*,] the various great bodhisattvas, Brahma, Shakra, the gods of the sun and moon, the four heavenly kings, and others have truly become the disciples of the Lord Teacher Shakyamuni the World Honored One. In the "Beholding the Stupa of Treasures" chapter, the Buddha treated the great bodhisattvas as his disciples, and sternly admonished them by saying, "To the great multitude, I ask who will protect and keep this sutra, and read and recite it after my cessation? Make a vow before the Buddha to do this!" And so those great bodhisattvas and others followed the Buddha just as a gale sways the branches of small trees or the kusha grass, or rivers flow into the ocean.

136. However, since it had not been long since the expounding of the *Lotus Sutra* had begun on Mt. Sacred Eagle, it seemed to them dream-like and unreal. Then appeared a stupa of treasures that attested to the Buddha's teaching. Referring to all the buddhas who appeared from all the worlds of the ten directions, the Buddha declared that they were all his own emanation-bodies. Shakyamuni Buddha and Many Treasures Buddha took seats side-by-side in the stupa that hung in space, like the sun and moon together in a blue sky. A large assembly of humans and gods appeared in the sky like the stars, while the emanation-body buddhas on the ground sat on lion-shaped thrones under the jeweled trees.

137. Compared to this, when the Lotus Treasury World appeared in the *Flower Garland Sutra*, buddhas with reward-bodies in this world and other worlds in the ten directions stayed in their respective worlds. Buddhas of other worlds did not come to this world to proclaim themselves to be emanation bodies [of Shakyamuni Buddha], nor did [Shakyamuni] Buddha visit the other worlds of the ten directions. Only such great bodhisattvas as Dharma Wisdom came to this assembly.

138. The nine honored ones upon eight lotus petals and the thirty-seven honored ones who appear in the *Mahavairochana Sutra* and the *Diamond Peak Sutra* seemed to be transformation-bodies of Mahavairochana Buddha. They were, unlike the transformation-body buddhas from the past, completely provided with the three bodies. The one thousand buddhas of the *Larger Prajna Sutra* and the various buddhas who appeared in the six directions upon the expounding of the *Amitayus Buddha Sutra*, did not bother to make the long trip to visit this world from their respective lands. Those buddhas who gathered together from the worlds of the ten directions when the *Great Assembly Sutra* was expounded were not emanation-bodies of [Shakyamuni] Buddha. The four buddhas appearing in the four directions when the *Supreme Golden Light Sutra* was expounded were merely transformation-body buddhas. In no sutra, except for the *Lotus Sutra*, are those buddhas

who had attained buddhahood after years of practice and who completely possessed the three bodies referred to by Shakyamuni Buddha as "my emanation-bodies."

139. [In the "Beholding the Stupa of Treasures" chapter of the *Lotus Sutra*,] that is an introduction to the "The Duration of the Life of the Tathagata" chapter, it states that Shakyamuni the World Honored One, whose attainment of awakening for the first time occurred only forty years or so before, called the assembly of buddhas who had attained buddhahood as far back as a kalpa or even ten kalpas, "my emanations." This was against the principle of equality among buddhas and greatly surprised everyone. If the Buddha had attained awakening for the first time only forty years or so before, large assemblies of people in the worlds of the ten directions would not have received his guidance. Even if he were capable of appearing in emanation-bodies to guide them, it would have been of no use. [In his *Profound Meaning of the Lotus Sutra*,] Great Master Tiantai says, "Since there are so many of his emanation-bodies, we should know that he has been the Buddha for a long time." This describes the astonishment of the great assembly.

140. To add to their surprise, great bodhisattvas, as many as the particles of dust of a thousand worlds, sprang up from underground. They looked incomparably superior to Universal Sage and Manjushri, who had been regarded as ranking disciples of Shakyamuni the World Honored One. The great bodhisattvas who had gathered upon the expounding of the *Flower Garland Sutra*, Vaipulya sutras, Prajna sutras, the "Beholding the Stupa of Treasures" chapter of the *Lotus Sutra*, or the sixteen bodhisattvas such as Vajrasattva in the *Mahavairochana Sutra* and other sutras, looked like monkeys waiting on Shakra or woodcutters associating with court nobles compared to these great bodhisattva appearing from underground. Even Maitreya Bodhisattva, successor to Shakyamuni Buddha, did not know who they were, not to speak of those below him.

141. Among those great bodhisattvas, as many as the particles of dust of a thousand worlds, there were four great sages known as Superior Practice, Limitless Practice, Pure Practice, and Steadily Established Practice. Awe stricken by these four, the great bodhisattvas and others on Mt. Sacred Eagle and up in space could not even gaze upon them nor understand who they were. Standing in front of these four who had come from underground, the four bodhisattvas in the *Flower Garland Sutra*, four bodhisattvas in the *Mahavairochana Sutra*, and sixteen bodhisattvas such as Vajrasattva in the *Diamond Peak Sutra* seemed to be like men squinting at the sun or fishermen facing the emperor. These four bodhisattvas from underground were like the four sages such as Grand Duke Wang who lived with the people, or the Four Whiteheads of Mt. Shang who waited on Emperor Hui. Indeed, the four bodhisattvas from underground appeared commanding and awe-inspiring. Apart from Shakyamuni, Many Treasures, and the emanation buddhas of the ten directions, everyone would have looked up to them as "good friends."

142. Wondering who they were, Maitreya Bodhisattva said to himself:

> I know all bodhisattvas in this world, as well as, those great bodhisattvas who have come from the worlds of the ten directions since the time the Buddha was still a crown prince, during the forty-two years of teaching after his awakening at the age of thirty, until today here at Mt. Sacred Eagle. I also know every great bodhisattva in all pure and impure lands in the ten directions where I was sent on errands or visited on my own, but have never seen bodhisattvas like these. I wonder what kind of buddha was he who taught them? He must have been incomparably superior to Shakyamuni, Many Treasures, or the emanation buddhas of the ten directions. When we see a heavy rainfall, we know the dragon who caused it is large. When we see the blossoming of a large lotus flower, we know the pond is deep. I wonder what land these great bodhisattvas come from and what buddha they were lucky enough to meet and what kind of great Dharma they learned and practiced.

143. Maitreya Bodhisattva was speechless, but perhaps with the Buddha's power, he was able to express his doubts and asked:

> We have never seen these many thousands of billions of bodhisattvas. … These bodhisattvas have great powers, virtues, and energy. Who expounded the Dharma to them? Who taught them? Who qualified them to attain [perfect enlightenment]? Under whom did they first generate the thought of awakening? What Buddha Dharma did they extol? … World Honored One! I have never seen them before. Tell me the name of the world in which they lived! I have visited many worlds, but have never seen them anywhere. I do not know any of them. They appeared suddenly from underground. Tell my why?

144. [Restating Maitreya's bewilderment in his *Words and Phrases of the Lotus Sutra*,] Tiantai says:

> Since the time of [the Buddha's] teaching at the Peaceful Place of Awakening until this present assembly, there has always been an inflow of mahasattvas coming from the worlds of the ten directions to listen to him. Their number is illimitable, but I saw them and remember them all through the power of my knowledge as the successor [of the Buddha]. I also made trips to various worlds in the ten directions to see the buddhas in person and became acquainted with their great assemblies. Nevertheless, there is not even one whom I know among these bodhisattvas.

145. [Further explaining in his *Notations on the Words and Phrases of the Lotus Sutra*], Miaole says, "Wise men know the origins of things just as a snake knows what it is to be a snake." The meaning of these words in the sutra and these commentaries are clear, that is to say, nobody had ever seen or heard of those bodhisattvas [who appeared from underground] from the time of [the Buddha's] first attaining enlightenment until today, either in this world or in any of the worlds of the ten directions.

146. The Buddha responded to this question, saying, "Ajita! [I know that] you have never seen these [great, innumerable *asamkhya* bodhisattva-mahasattvas who appeared from underground.] After I attained unsurpassed, complete and perfect awakening in this Saha world, I taught these bodhisattvas, led them, trained them, and caused them to generate the thought of awakening." He continued, "I once sat under the Bodhi tree in the city of Bodhgaya, attained perfect awakening, and turned the wheel of the unsurpassed Dharma. Then I taught them and caused them to generate the thought of awakening. Now they abide in the state of non-retrogression. [They will be able to become buddhas. My words are true. Believe me with all your hearts!] I have been teaching them since the remotest past."

147. Then Maitreya Bodhisattva and other great bodhisattvas had a further doubt. At the time the *Flower Garland Sutra* was taught, numerous great bodhisattvas such as Dharma Wisdom gathered. While wondering who they were, Maitreya and others were told by Shakyamuni Buddha, apparently to their satisfaction, that Dharma Wisdom and other great bodhisattvas were Shakyamuni's good friends. The same thing happened to those great bodhisattvas who gathered at the Great Treasure Chamber and to those who gathered at White Heron Lake upon the teaching of the Prajna sutras. The great bodhisattvas appearing from underground now, however, seemed incomparably superior to them, and it appeared probably that they were teachers of Shakyamuni the World Honored One. Nevertheless, the Buddha declared that it was he who caused them to generate the thought of awakening, as if they were younger people that the Buddha had been teaching and guiding as his disciples. It was only natural, therefore, that they had serious doubts.

148. Prince Shotoku of Japan was a son of Emperor Yomei, the thirty-second sovereign of Japan. When he turned six years old, elderly men coming from Baekje, Goryeo, and Tang China paid homage to the emperor. The six-year old crown prince declared that they were his disciples, and these elderly men holding hands in reverence said that the crown prince was their teacher. It was indeed a wonder. It is also said in a non-Buddhist scripture that a certain man, while walking on a street, came across a young man about thirty years old beating an old man of about eighty. Asked what the matter was, the story says, the young man answered that

this elderly man he was beating was his son. The relationship between Shakyamuni Buddha and the great bodhisattvas from underground is similar to these stories.

149. Therefore, Maitreya Bodhisattva and others asked the question, "World Honored One! When you, the Tathagata, were a crown prince, you left the palace of the Shakyas, sat at the place of awakening not far from the city of Bodhgaya, and attained unsurpassed, complete and perfect awakening. It has been only forty years or so since then. World Honored One! How did you do these great deeds of the Buddha in such a short time?"

150. For forty years or so, starting with the *Flower Garland Sutra*, all the bodhisattvas have asked questions in every assembly to dispel the doubts sentient beings might have had. This, however, is a more crucial question than that asked by Great Adornment and eighty thousand other bodhisattvas in the *Infinite Meanings Sutra* concerning the apparent discrepancy between the teaching, given during the first forty years or so, that it would take countless kalpas of practice to attain enlightenment and the teaching that one could attain it quickly.

151. In another instance, cited in the *Contemplation of the Buddha of Infinite Life Sutra*, it is said that King Ajatashatru, incited by Devadatta, imprisoned his own father, King Bimbisara, and tried to murder his own mother, Queen Vaidehi; but two loyal subjects, Jivaka and Chandraprabha, talked him into sparing his mother. Inviting the Buddha, Vaidehi first asked this question: "For what transgression might I have committed in a past life did I give birth to such an evil son as this? For what causes and conditions, World Honored One, were you born as the cousin of such a wicked man as Devadatta?"

152. Of these two questions, "For what causes and conditions, World Honored One…?" is a profoundly serious doubt. "Wheel-turning noble kings are not born together with enemies. Shakra does not live together with a demon. The Buddha has been a man of compassion from the time of innumerable kalpas in the past. Why was he born related to his greatest enemy? Isn't it because he was not really the Buddha?" Vaidehi might well have wondered. The Buddha did not answer this question. Therefore, those who read and recite the *Contemplation of the Buddha of Infinite Life Sutra* do not understand the real relationship between Shakyamuni and Devadatta unless they read the "Devadatta," chapter of the *Lotus Sutra*. This serious question of Vaidehi was not as serious a question as the one asked by Maitreya.

153. The thirty-six questions asked by Kashyapa in the *Nirvana Sutra* were also not as serious as the one asked by Maitreya. If the Buddha had not squarely answered the question to dispel this doubt, all the holy teachings of the Buddha's lifetime would have appeared to be as worthless as foam on the water, and all

sentient beings would have remained in a web of doubts. Here lies the importance of the "Duration of the Life of the Tathagata" chapter of the *Lotus Sutra*.

154. Thereafter, in the sixteenth chapter of the *Lotus Sutra*, the Buddha explains, "The gods, humans, and asuras in the world think that I, Shakyamuni Buddha, left the palace of the Shakyas, sat at the place of awakening not far from the city of Bodhgaya, and attained unsurpassed, complete and perfect awakening." This declaration in the sutra represents what all the great bodhisattvas had in mind from the time of the teachings given at the Peaceful Place of Awakening until those given in the "Peaceful Practices" chapter of the *Lotus Sutra*. "To tell the truth, good men, it is many hundreds of thousands of billions of *nayuta asamkhya* kalpas since I became the Buddha."

155. The "attainment of awakening for the first time" mentioned in three places in the *Flower Garland Sutra*, the "first attainment" in the Agama sutras, the "first sitting under the Bodhi tree" in the *Vimalakirti Sutra*, the "sixteen years after the first enlightenment" in the *Great Assembly Sutra*, the statement that "I once sat at the place of awakening" in the *Mahavairochana Sutra*, the "twenty-nine years since his enlightenment" in the *Benevolent Kings Sutra*, the statement "I sat at the place of awakening" in the *Infinite Meanings Sutra*, and the statement "I for the first time sat at the place of awakening" in the "Expedients" chapter of the *Lotus Sutra* were all shown to be false by this one declaration.

156. Thus it was revealed that Shakyamuni the World Honored One had long been the Buddha since the eternal past, and it became clear that various buddhas were all his emanation-bodies. In the prior sutras, as well as in the Trace Gate, the various buddhas and Shakyamuni the World Honored One all stood shoulder-to-shoulder, and each practiced Buddhism on their own. Therefore, those who considered various buddhas to be their focus of devotion looked down on Shakyamuni the World Honored One. Now, however, those buddhas on lotus pedestals in the *Flower Garland Sutra,* or the buddhas in the Vaipulya sutras, Prajna sutras, and *Mahavairochana Sutra* all became subordinates of Shakyamuni Buddha the World Honored One.

157. Attaining enlightenment at the age of thirty, the Buddha took over this Saha world, which had been the domain of Great Brahma Heavenly King, the devil king of the sixth heaven, and others. The Buddha now reversed what had been said in the prior sutras and even in the Trace Gate of the *Lotus Sutra* that this world is the impure land whereas other worlds in the ten directions are pure lands. He now declared that this world is actually the original land and what had been said to be pure lands throughout the ten directions are just impure lands that are its manifestations. Since the Buddha is the Eternal Buddha, then those great bodhisattvas who were taught by the transformation-body of the Trace Gate or who came from other worlds are all disciples of the Lord Teacher Shakyamuni the

World Honored One. If the "Duration of the Life of the Tathagata" chapter had not been expounded, it would be like the sky without the sun and moon, a country without a king, mountains and rivers without gems, or a man without a spirit.

158. Nevertheless, seemingly knowledgeable men of such provisional schools as Chengguan of the Flower Garland school, Jiaxiang of the Three Treatises school, Ci'en of the Dharma Characteristics school, and Kobo of the Mantra school tried to extol their own canons by stating: "The lord of the *Flower Garland Sutra* represents the reward-body of the Buddha whereas that of the *Lotus Sutra*, the accommodative-body," or "the Buddha in the 'Duration of the Life of the Tathagata' chapter of the *Lotus Sutra* lives in the region of darkness, it is Mahavairochana Buddha who is in a state of illumination."

159. Clouds cover the moon and slanderers hide the wise. When people slander, ordinary yellow rocks appear to be gold and flatterers seem to be wise. Scholars in this degenerate age, blinded by slanderous words, do not see the value of the gold in the "Duration of the Life of the Tathagata" chapter. Even among those of the Tiantai school some are fooled into taking yellow rocks for gold. They should know that if Shakyamuni had not been the Eternal Buddha, there could not have been so many who received guidance from him.

160. The moon does not shy away from its own reflection, but it cannot be reflected without water. Even though the Buddha hopes to convert sentient beings, he cannot show the eight phases of a buddha's life unless he is able to establish a relationship with them. It is like the voice-hearers, who have reached the first ground [in the distinct teaching] or first abode [in the perfect teaching]. They still must wait until a future lifetime to complete the eight phases of a buddha's life. This is because they have listened only to the prior sutras and only striven for self-control and their own salvation.

161. If the Lord Teacher Shakyamuni the World Honored One's attainment of awakening for the first time were only a short while ago in this world, Brahma, Shakra, the gods of the sun and moon, the four heavenly kings, and others who ruled this world since the kalpa of abiding, would have been the Buddha's disciples only for forty years or so. And those who had only established a relationship to him while listening to his expounding of the *Lotus Sutra* for eight years on Mt. Sacred Eagle could hardly think that the new master had actually been the Buddha from the remote past. It seemed to them that he still did not have precedence over those rulers who had already been in this world for such a long time.

162. But now since the attainment [of buddhahood] in the remote past has been revealed, the bodhisattvas Sunlight and Moonlight, disciples of Medicine Master Tathagata in the world to the east; the bodhisattvas World Voice Perceiver and Great Power Obtainer, disciples of Amitabha Tathagata in a land to the west; the various disciples of buddhas in various lands in the ten directions as well as all the

great bodhisattvas who are the disciples of Mahavairochana Tathagata depicted in the two realms [of the Womb-realm and Diamond-realm mandalas] of the *Mahavairochana Sutra* and the *Diamond Peak Sutra* are now all disciples of the Lord Teacher Shakyamuni the World Honored One. Since the buddhas of the ten directions are all emanation-bodies of Shakyamuni Tathagata, their disciples are of course his disciples. Needless to say, the gods of the sun, moon, and stars, and the other gods that have been in this world since the beginning of the kalpa of abiding are all disciples of the Lord Teacher Shakyamuni the World Honored One.

163. Nevertheless, all Buddhist schools except for the Tiantai are confused about the focus of devotion. The Abhidharma Treasury, Completion of Reality, and Discipline schools make the focus of devotion Shakyamuni the Word Honored One, who attained buddhahood by going through the thirty-four enlightened mental states of overcoming fetters. This is like a crown prince of a world-honored sovereign, who, confused, thinks of himself as a son of a commoner. The Flower Garland, Mantra, Three Treatises, and Dharma Characteristics schools are the four Mahayana schools. Of them, the Dharma Characteristics and Three Treatises schools regard as their focus of devotion a buddha similar to the superior accommodative-body. It is just like a crown prince of a heavenly king thinking of himself as the son of a samurai. The Flower Garland and Mantra schools look down on Shakyamuni the World Honored One and establish Rochana and Mahavairochana respectively as their foci of devotion. It is like a king's son despising his father while respecting a nameless person who acts as though he were the king of the Dharma. The Pure Land school considers Amitabha Buddha, who is merely an emanation-body of Shakyamuni in the pure land to the west, to be the lord teacher of this world and abandons the Buddha who is actually related to us. The Zen school, just like a lowly man of little virtue despising his parents, despises the Buddha and his sutras. They are all confused about the focus of devotion.

164. It is analogous to the situation before the time of the Three Sovereigns, when people did not know who their fathers were and behaved like birds and beasts. Those Buddhist schools that do not know of the "Duration of the Life of the Tathagata" chapter are the same as birds and beasts; they do not know the debt they owe [to the Eternal Buddha]. For this reason, Great Master Miaole, [in his *Five Hundred Questions Treatise*], says:

> In all the holy teachings of the Buddha's lifetime, [except for the
>
> 'Duration of the Life of the Tathagata' chapter,] the duration of the
>
> life of our parent, [the Buddha,] has not been clearly expressed and cannot be known. If one does not know the long lifespan of our father, [the Buddha,] then one will also be confused about the domain he governs. Such a man, no matter how capable he may be, is not at all worthy of being a human.

165. Great Master Miaole was a man of the Tianbao era (742-756) toward the end of the Tang dynasty. Having widely read and deeply contemplated the canons of the Three Treatises, Flower Garland, Dharma Characteristics, and Mantra schools, he concluded that those who do not know the Buddha revealed in the "Duration of the Life of the Tathagata" chapter are like birds and beasts, who may be talented but do not know the land governed by their father. "No matter how capable he may be" refers to men like Fazang and Chengguan of the Flower Garland school and Tripitaka Master Shubhakarasimha of the Mantra school, who were men of talent, but were like children who do not know their own father.

166. Great Master Dengyo, the founder of exoteric and esoteric Buddhism in Japan, has said in his *Outstanding Principles of the Lotus Sutra*:

> The canons of other schools also expound the Buddha's motherly love. However, those sutras have motherly love but no fatherly strictness. Only the Tiantai Lotus school, with both its strictness and love, is the father of all noble ones, those with something more to learn and those with nothing more to learn, as well as of those who are generating the thought of awakening.

167. As for the three steps for attaining buddhahood - sowing, maturing, and harvesting - even those terms are not mentioned in the canons of the Mantra or Flower Garland schools, not to speak of its true meaning. They maintain that one is able to reach the first of the ten grounds and attain buddhahood with one's present body within the present lifetime. However, as provisional sutras they do not expound the sowing of the seeds in the past. Thus, they talk about harvesting without sowing seeds, which is like Zhao Gao or Dokyo illegitimately trying to usurp the throne.

168. These schools of Buddhism quarrel with one another for superiority, but I do not jump into the scramble, leaving the matter to the sutras. Based on the concept of the seeds [of buddhahood] expounded in the *Lotus Sutra*, Vasubandhu Bodhisattva insisted on the "unsurpassed seed" [in his *Lotus Sutra Treatise*]. This later became the three thousand realms in a single thought-moment doctrine of Tiantai. The seed of the various venerables appearing in the *Flower Garland Sutra* and various Mahayana sutras, such as the *Mahavairochana Sutra*, is without exception this three thousand realms in a single thought-moment doctrine. It was Great Master Tiantai alone who perceived this in the history of Buddhism.

169. Chengguan of the Flower Garland school plagiarized this doctrine to interpret the following saying in the *Flower Garland Sutra*, "Mind is like a skillful painter." The canon of the Mantra school, including the *Mahavairochana Sutra*, does not contain any teachings about the attainment of buddhahood by adherents of the two vehicles, the attainment of buddhahood in the remotest past, or the three

thousand realms in a single thought-moment. Tripitaka Master Shubhakarasimha came to China and read Tiantai's *Great Calming and Contemplation*, and thereafter read Tiantai's concept of the three thousand realms in a single thought-moment into such expressions in the *Mahavairochana Sutra* as "the reality of mind" and "I am the original beginning of everything" in order to lay the foundation for the Mantra school. With the addition of mudras and mantras to the teaching, he maintained that the *Lotus Sutra* and the *Mahavairochana Sutra* were equal in principle, but in practice the latter is superior. Where in the *Mahavairochana Sutra* can we find the doctrine of the attainment of buddhahood by adherents of the two vehicles? Where is the mutual possession of the ten realms represented in the two-realm mandalas [of the Diamond-realm and Womb-realm]? This is the most serious falsification of all. For this reason, Great Master Dengyo, [in his *Dependence on Tiantai of Other Buddhist Schools*] says: "The newly transmitted Mantra school has eliminated the fact of its doctrinal transmission [from the former Tiantai monk Yixing]. The Flower Garland school, which had been introduced earlier, hid the influence of Tiantai upon its doctrines."

170. If one had gone to Hokkaido, he might be able to claim this well-known poem by Hitomaro to be his own:
    At the first light of dawn
    A boat leaves the foggy beach of Akashi,
    Disappearing behind an island.

Perhaps islanders would be fooled by such a man. So have the scholars of China and Japan been fooled.

171. The Venerable Liangxu had this to say, "Compared to the *Lotus Sutra*, the teachings of the Mantra, Zen, Flower Garland, and Three Treatises schools are for leading people to the *Lotus Sutra*." It was because of his wrong views that the Tripitaka Master Shubhakarasimha was punished by Yama. It must have been due to his change of heart and submission to the *Lotus Sutra* that he was later released. It was to show their submission to the *Lotus Sutra* that Shubhakarasimha and Amoghavajra thereafter placed the *Lotus Sutra* in the center between the two realms [of the Diamond-realm and Womb-realm mandalas] as if it were the great king served to the left and right by two subordinates, the *Mahavairochana Sutra* of the Womb-realm and the *Diamond Peak Sutra* of the Diamond-realm. In assessing the doctrines of various sutras, Kobo of Japan regarded the *Flower Garland Sutra* higher than the *Lotus Sutra*, the latter being placed on the eighth [of the ten stages of mind] behind the *Mahavairochana Sutra* and the *Flower Garland Sutra*. However, when he transmitted ritualism to his own disciples, Jitsue and Shinga, and to the disciples of Great Master Dengyo, Encho and Kojo, he placed the *Lotus Sutra* in the center between the [mandalas of the] two-realms as mentioned before.

172. In another instance, when Jiaxiang of the Three Treatises school wrote the *Profundity of the Lotus Sutra Treatise* in ten fascicles, he maintained, in contradiction

to Tiantai, that the *Lotus Sutra* was expounded during the fourth, not the fifth, period of Shakyamuni's lifetime, because it was meant to combine the two vehicles into the bodhisattva vehicle thereby eliminating the two vehicles. However, he later submitted to Tiantai and served him for seven years, discontinuing his own lectures, dispersing his own disciples, and even making himself a footstool [so Tiantai could climb up to his teaching platform].

173. Ci'en of the Dharma Characteristics school, in his *Chapters on the Forest of Meanings of the Dharma Garden of the Mahayana* in seven or twelve fascicles, wrote, "The One Vehicle teaching is just a skillful means, while the doctrine that there are four vehicles is the true teaching," as well as many other false concepts. However, in the fourth fascicle of the *Essential Meaning of Praising the Profundity of the Lotus Sutra*, he is said to have maintained that both teachings are true. Although his written statements were ambiguous, his heart was with Tiantai.

174. Chengguan of the Flower Garland school wrote a commentary on the *Flower Garland Sutra*, in which he compared it with the *Lotus Sutra* and seemed to have concluded that the *Lotus Sutra* was only a teaching of skillful means. However, he later wrote that the Tiantai school considered [the three thousand realms in a single thought-moment doctrine] to be true, as did his own school. Isn't it that Chengguan regretted what he had written earlier? So did Great Master Kobo. Without a mirror, one cannot see one's own face. Without enemies, one cannot see one's own faults. Scholars of the Mantra and other schools did not realize their own faults until they met Great Master Dengyo.

175. Therefore, we say that, although the buddhas, bodhisattvas, humans, and gods appearing in various sutras seem to have attained buddhahood through their own respective sutras, in reality they were truly awakened because of the *Lotus Sutra*. The four great vows of Shakyamuni and other buddhas such as saving innumerable sentient beings were only fulfilled by this sutra, in which it is stated, "That old vow of mine has now been fulfilled."

176. Considering this, it is doubtless that the buddhas, bodhisattvas, and gods appearing in such sutras as the *Flower Garland*, *Contemplation of the Buddha of Infinite Life*, and *Mahavairochana Sutra* would protect those who read and practice them. However, if those who read and practice the *Mahavairochana*, *Contemplation of the Buddha of Infinite Life*, and other sutras should become antagonistic to practitioners of the *Lotus Sutra*, those guardian deities would abandon practitioners of those other sutras for those of the *Lotus Sutra*.

177. It is, for instance, like a filial son who would abandon his own father for royal service if his loving father should become an enemy of the king. This is a most filial act, and the same could be said of the Buddha Dharma. I believe that the buddhas, bodhisattvas, and ten rakshasi mentioned in the *Lotus Sutra* will protect me, Nichiren. In addition, numerous buddhas in the six directions and the

twenty-five bodhisattvas mentioned in the canon of the Pure Land school, the one thousand two hundred deities of the Mantra school, as well as all buddhas and guardian deities of the seven schools of Buddhism will protect me, Nichiren. I believe it was in this way that guardian deities of the seven schools of Buddhism protected Great Master Dengyo.

178. I, Nichiren, think that as soon as the practitioner of the *Lotus Sutra* appears, all those gods, such as the sun god and the moon god, who heard the teaching of the *Lotus Sutra* in the three assemblies at two locations will hurry to his aid just as a lodestone attracts pieces of iron and the moon reflects itself on the water. They will bear his difficulties and carry out the vows they made before the Buddha at those assemblies. Nevertheless, they have not come to rescue me, Nichiren. Is it because I am not a practitioner of the *Lotus Sutra*? I must reconsider the sutras in the light of my own background in order to see whether or not I am wrong.

179. Question: By what eye of wisdom do you know that the Nembutsu school and the Zen school today are enemies of the *Lotus Sutra* and evil friends to all sentient beings?

Answer: I will not answer in my own words. Instead, I would show them the ugly faces of slanderers of the True Dharma reflected in the mirror of the sutras and commentaries, although I can't help those who were born blind.

180. In the "Beholding the Stupa of Treasures" chapter of the fourth fascicle of the *Lotus Sutra* it says:

> Thereupon Many Treasures Buddha in the stupa of treasures offered half of his seat to Shakyamuni Buddha … The great assembly, having seen the two tathagatas sitting cross-legged on the lion seat in the stupa of the seven treasures … Shakyamuni Buddha … said to the four assemblies with a loud voice, "Who will expound the *Sutra of the Lotus Flower of the Wonderful Dharma* in this Saha world? Now is the time to do this. I shall enter into nirvana before long. I wish to transmit this *Sutra of the Lotus Flower of the Wonderful Dharma* to someone so that this sutra may be preserved."

This was the first proclamation of the Buddha.

181. It also says:

Thereupon the World Honored One, wishing to repeat what he had said, sang in gathas:

The Saintly Master, the World Honored One,
Who had passed away a long time ago,
Came riding in the stupa of treasures

To hear the Dharma [direct from me].
Could anyone who sees him
Not make efforts to hear the Dharma?

...

The emanation-body buddhas
As innumerable as there are sands in the Ganges River
Also came here
From their wonderful worlds,
Parting from their disciples,
And giving up the offerings made to them
By gods, humans, and dragons,
In order to hear the Dharma ...
And to have the Dharma preserved forever.

...

Wonderful fragrance is set
Forth from the bodies of those buddhas
To the worlds of the ten directions.
The sentient beings of those worlds
Smell the fragrance joyfully,
Just as the branches of a tree bend before a strong wind.
Those buddhas employ these skillful means
In order to have the Dharma preserved forever."

[The Buddha said to the great assembly,]
"Who will protect
And keep, this sutra,
And read and recite it
After my extinction?
Make a vow before me to do this!"

This was his second proclamation.

182. [Shakyamuni Buddha continued:]

Many Treasures Tathagata and I
And the emanation-body buddhas,
Who have assembled here,
Wish to know who will do [all this].

...

Good men! Think this over clearly!
It is difficult
[To expound this sutra].
Make a great vow to do this!
It is not difficult
To expound all the other sutras
As many as there are sands
In the Ganges River.
It is not difficult
To grasp Mt. Sumeru
And hurl it to a distance
Of countless Buddha-worlds.

...

It is difficult
To expound this sutra
In the evil world
After my cessation.

...

It is not difficult
To shoulder a load of hay
And stay unburned in the fire
At the end of the kalpa [of dissolution].
It is difficult
To keep this sutra
And expound it to even one person
After my cessation.

...

Good men!
Who will receive and keep this sutra,
And read and recite it
After my cessation?
Make a vow before me
[To do all this]!

This was the third proclamation. The fourth and fifth exhortations, which appear in the "Devadatta" chapter, will be considered later.

183. The meaning of the words from these passages from the sutra is as clear as the great sun shining in the blue sky or a mole on a white face. Nevertheless, those who were born blind, those who are squint-eyed or one-eyed, those who believe that only their own teachers are wise men, or those who are stuck to extreme views will not be able to see this. Despite all these difficulties, however, I will try to explain what it all means for those who aspire to awakening.

184. [It is more difficult to have the chance to hear the *Lotus Sutra*,] than it is to see the peach flowers in the orchard of the Queen Mother of the West or the udumbara flowers that foretell the coming of a wheel-turning noble king, [both of which only bloom once every three millennia]. You should know that even the eight-year war between the Governor of Pei and Xiang Yu for the control of China, the seven-year war in Japan between Yoritomo and Munemori, the struggle for power between the asuras and Shakra, or the battle between the golden-winged birds and the dragon king at Lake Anavatapta, do not exceed in importance and intensity [the war between the *Lotus Sutra* and all other sutras].

185. The truth has been revealed in Japan twice, once in the past by the Great Master Dengyo and now at this time by me, Nichiren. Blind persons will not believe this. It can't be helped. The above sutra passages are an assessment of all the sutras that exist in Japan, China, India, the Dragon Palace, the heavens, and all the worlds of the ten directions by Shakyamuni, Many Treasures, and the buddhas of the ten directions.

186. Question: Are those sutras such as the *Flower Garland Sutra*, Vaipulya sutras, Prajna sutras, *Revealing the Profound Secrets Sutra*, *Lankavatara Sutra*, *Mahavairochana Sutra*, and *Nirvana Sutra* among what the *Lotus Sutra* calls the nine easier ones or the six difficult ones to spread after the cessation of Shakyamuni Buddha?

Answer: Those tripitaka masters and great masters of the three baskets of the Flower Garland school such as Dushun, Zhiyan, Fazang, and Chengguan say that both the *Flower Garland Sutra* and the *Lotus Sutra* are among the six difficult ones because in name they are separate sutras, but their teachings are one in principle. [Tiantai expresses this perspective in his *Great Calming and Contemplation* as follows,] "They are distinct in the way they contemplate the four gates or teachings, but are the same in their perception of the real truth."

187. Tripitaka Master Xuanzang, Great Master Ci'en and other Dharma Characteristics school teachers maintain, "Both the *Revealing the Profound Secrets Sutra* and the *Lotus Sutra* are among the six difficult ones because they both teach the consciousness-only doctrine expounded as the last of the three periods of teaching."

Jizang of the Three Treatises school said, "The Prajna sutras and *Lotus Sutra* are different in name but identical in essence because they expound the same Dharma."

Tripitaka masters Shubhakarasimha, Vajrabodhi, Amoghavajra, and other teachers of the Mantra school in India and China said, "The *Mahavairochana Sutra* and the *Lotus Sutra* are equal in principle; they both are among the six difficult ones." However, Great Master Kobo in Japan stated, "The *Mahavairochana Sutra* is not among the sutras expounded by Shakyamuni; it was taught by the Dharma-body of Mahavairochana Buddha."

Some say, "As the *Flower Garland Sutra* was taught by the reward-body of the Buddha, it does not belong to either the six difficult ones nor the nine easier ones."

Founders and teachers of these four schools maintain this; several thousand later students repeat it.

188. It is regrettable to say that if I, Nichiren, spoke up against them without reservation, people today would not even look at me; they would further heap injustices upon me even to the point of slandering me to the ruler and endangering my life. Nevertheless, in his final instructions given under the twin sal trees, our loving father, [Shakyamuni Buddha,] said, "Rely on the Dharma, not upon the person." Not relying upon the person means that even those in the first, second, third, or fourth ranks of the four reliances, including bodhisattvas of preliminary awakening such as Universal Sage or Manjushri, should not be trusted unless they teach with the sutras in hand.

189. [It also said in the *Nirvana Sutra* that we should] "rely on the sutra of definitive meaning, not upon the sutra of provisional meaning." This means that we must distinguish the sutra of definitive meaning from the sutra of provisional meaning before relying upon it. The *Exegesis on the Ten Grounds Treatise* by Nagarjuna Bodhisattva also says, "We should rely upon the treatises that clarify the sutras and not upon treatises that obscure the sutras." Great Master Tiantai says [in his *Profound Meaning of the Lotus Sutra*], "Adopt whatever agrees with the sutra, and do not believe in that which is not found in the sutra in word or meaning." Great Master Dengyo states [in his *Outstanding Principles of the Lotus Sutra*], "Rely upon the discourses of the Buddha, do not put faith in oral transmissions." Enchin, the Great Master Chisho, states [in his *A Collection of Orally Transmitted Teachings*], "Transmit the teachings only in accord with what is written."

190. Now, as for the assessments of those teachers mentioned above, their judgements seem to conform, more or less, to the sutras and treatises. However, they all seem to stick to the teachings of their own schools without correcting the errors of their own teachers. Their opinions are based on distorted interpretations and personal feelings. Their teachings are just self-aggrandizement! The wrong views and false Dharmas of Vatsiputra and Vaipulya after the cessation of the Buddha or the non-Buddhist scriptures after the Later Han became stronger and more elaborate than the views of the non-Buddhist teachings before the teaching of the Buddha Dharma or Confucianism in the time of the Three Sovereigns and

Five Emperors. In the same way, the merely human teachers of such schools as the Flower Garland, the Dharma Characteristics, and the Mantra, envious of Tiantai's true teaching, tend to resort to distorted interpretations of the true *Lotus Sutra* in order to fit it into their provisional teachings. Surely, those who aspire to awakening should not be biased, stay away from sectarian quarrels, and not despise other people.

191. In the ["Teacher of the Dharma" chapter of the] *Lotus Sutra*, [the Buddha] says:

> [I] have [expounded many sutras, I] am now [expounding this sutra, and [I also] will [expound many sutras in the future. The total number of sutras will amount to many thousands of billions. This *Sutra of the Lotus Flower of the Wonderful Dharma* is the most difficult to believe and the most difficult to understand.]

Miaole, [in his *Notations on the Words and Phrases of the Lotus Sutra*,] says [in regard to this]:

> Besides the *Lotus Sutra*, some sutras claim to be the king of sutras, but they are not really the first among sutras as they do not claim to be foremost among those which have already been expounded, are now being expounded, and will be expounded.

He also says [in his *Elucidation of the Profound Meaning of the Lotus Sutra*],

> Although [the *Lotus Sutra*] is an incomparable Dharma above all the sutras expounded in the past, present, and future, many are confused about this. ... They will suffer for interminable kalpas due to the transgression of slander of the True Dharma.

192. Surprised by this statement in the *Lotus Sutra* and his commentaries on it, I have read all the sutras and commentaries by later teachers. As a result, all my doubts have melted away. It is not even worth mentioning that ignorant followers of the Mantra school today believe that their school is superior to the *Lotus Sutra* because they have mudras and mantras or simply because Great Master Jikaku said so.

193. The *Mystic Glorification Sutra* says:

> Such sutras as the *Ten Grounds Sutra*, *Flower Garland Sutra*, *Great Tree Kimnara King Sutra*, *Supernatural Powers Sutra* and *Shrimala Sutra* are all begotten from this *Mystic Glorification Sutra*. As such, this sutra is superior to all the other sutras.

194. The *Great Cloud Sutra* says:

This *Great Cloud Sutra* is the wheel-turning noble king among sutras because it expounds the everlasting Dharma treasury that is the true nature, the buddha-nature, of sentient beings.

195. The *Six Paramita Sutra* says:

All the true Dharmas taught by numerous buddhas in the past and all the eighty-four thousand wondrous Dharmas I am expounding in this world can be grouped into five types: 1. sutra, 2. vinaya, 3. abhidharma, 4. prajnaparamita, and 5. dharani. With these five baskets, I shall guide sentient beings. ... If sentient beings are incapable of upholding the sutras, regulations [of the vinaya], abhidharma, and prajnaparamita of the Buddha, or if they have committed such evil deeds as the four or eight extreme transgressions, or five heinous transgressions, or even if they are *icchantika* who have committed extreme transgressions of slandering the Vaipulya sutras, I can still enable them to eliminate their transgressions, swiftly attain liberation and suddenly awaken to nirvana. It is for this reason that I expound the basket of dharanis. These five types of Dharmas are analogous to the flavors of milk, and its four derivatives, the most refined of which is the wondrous flavor of ghee. ... The dharani teaching is like the taste of ghee, which is the most exquisite of the five. It can cure various sicknesses and keep the bodies and minds of sentient beings healthy. Likewise, the dharani teaching among the sutras is of the foremost perfection that absolves heinous transgressions.

196. The *Revealing the Profound Secrets Sutra* says:

Superlative Meaning Arising Bodhisattva again said to the Buddha, "The World Honored One, in the country of Varanasi at Rishipatana in the Deer Park, for those setting out in the voice-hearer vehicle, first turned the wheel of the True Dharma by teaching the four noble truths. This extraordinarily rare turning of the Dharma had never been done before in the whole world by any human or god. Nevertheless, that turning of the wheel of the Dharma was not without room for improvement and criticism. It was not yet the teaching of definitive meaning and was the source of endless controversy.

"The World Honored One, in the time of the second [turning of the wheel of the Dharma], for those who aspired to practice Mahayana Buddhism, taught that all phenomena are without self-nature, non-arising and non-ceasing, originally tranquil, and intrinsically in the state of nirvana. Nevertheless, that turning of the wheel of the True Dharma was still concealing the whole truth. It was even more extraordinarily rare than the one taught in the first period. Nevertheless, that turning of the wheel of the Dharma was not without room for improvement and criticism. It was not yet the teaching of the definitive meaning and was also a source of constant squabbling.

"The World Honored One, in the present third [turning of the wheel of the Dharma], for those who aspire to practice all vehicles, teaches that all phenomena are without self-nature, non-arising and non-ceasing, originally tranquil, intrinsically in the state of nirvana, of the nature of being without a self-nature. This turning of the wheel of the True Dharma clarifies the whole truth. It is the most extraordinarily rare of all teachings. This present turning of the wheel of the Dharma by the World Honored One is the unsurpassed teaching with no room for improvement or criticism. It is the teaching of definitive meaning, which does not cause any controversy."

197. The *Larger Prajna Sutra* says:

By following whatever teaching one listens to, whether mundane or supramundane, as a skillful means, one can grasp the exquisite principle of the perfection of wisdom. All worldly matters and actions can lead to the Dharma-nature by this perfection of wisdom. Nothing exists outside the Dharma-nature.

198. The first fascicle of the *Mahavairochana Sutra* says:

Lord of Mysteries! Practicing the Mahayana means to generate the thought of the unconditioned vehicle and know that phenomena have no self-nature. Why is that? It is because, like practitioners in the past, one observes the storehouse consciousness of the aggregates and realizes that its self-nature is illusory.

It also says:

Lord of Mysteries, thus abandoning the non-self, the mind king being free, one realizes that his own mind is originally non-arising.

It also says:

So-called emptiness is apart from the realm of the [sense] faculties and their objects, is without characteristics or objects, transcends conceptual proliferation and is analogous to space. … [It is] utterly without self-nature.

It also says that Mahavairochana Buddha said to the Lord of Mysteries:

> Lord of Mysteries, what is awakening? It is to know one's mind as it really is.

199. Then it is asserted in the *Flower Garland Sutra*:

> Among all the beings in all the worlds,
> There are few who aspire to the voice-hearer vehicle.
> Even fewer seek the privately-awakened one vehicle.
> Those who seek the Great Vehicle are exceedingly rare.
> Even then, it is easier to seek the Great Vehicle
> Compared to the extreme difficulty of taking faith in this Dharma,
> How much more difficult it is to keep it, remember it correctly,
> Practice as it teaches, and understand it truly!
> To balance a trichiliocosm
> Upon one's head for as long as a kalpa without moving
> Is not as difficult
> As the extreme difficulty of taking faith in this Dharma.
> Offering various comforting necessities for as long as a kalpa
> To sentient beings as numerous as the dust of a trichiliocosm
> Is not more meritorious
> Or as outstanding as taking faith in this Dharma.
> To place ten buddha-lands in one's palm
> And abide in space for as long as a kalpa
> Is not as difficult
> As the extreme difficulty of taking faith in this Dharma.
> Offering various comforting necessities for as long as a kalpa
> To sentient beings as numerous as the dust of ten buddha-lands
> Is not more meritorious
> Or as outstanding as taking faith in this Dharma.
> Making respectful offerings for a kalpa
> To tathagatas as as numerous as the dust of ten lands
> Will not accrue greater merit
> Than being able to keep this chapter.

200. Finally, it is said in the *Nirvana Sutra*:

> Although these Mahayana Vaipulya sutras have immeasurable merits, they cannot even be compared with this sutra by any simile. The latter is a hundred, a thousand, a hundred thousand myriad times, or infinite number of times more meritorious than any simile can express. Good men! It is analogous to a cow producing milk, which in turn produces cream, which in turn produces

curds, which in turn produces fresh butter, which in turn produces the clarified butter called ghee, which is supreme. It cures the many illnesses of all who take it as if it contained all medicines in itself. Good men! The Buddha is also like this. He expounded the twelve kinds of scriptures which in turn produced the [Agama] sutras, which in turn produced the Vaipulya sutras, from which stemmed the Prajnaparamita [sutras], from which was produced the final nirvana, which is like the flavor of ghee. Here, the ghee is a simile for [this teaching concerning] buddha-nature.

201. Each of the sutras cited above thus claims to be the supreme one. However, when compared to the references in the *Lotus Sutra* to "have, am now, and will" or the six difficult and nine easier actions, those statements are like stars [being outshined by] the moon [or how, in comparing the world's nine mountain ranges, [all other mountains are overshadowed by] Mt. Sumeru.

202. Nevertheless, even such master teachers as Chengguan of the Flower Garland school, Ci'en of the Dharma Characteristics school, Jiaxiang of the Three Treatises school, and Kobo of the Mantra school, who appeared to have the buddha eye, were confused by those sutras. How much more confused are those blind present-day scholars! How can they see the comparative merits of those sutras? They are unable to perceive even a clear distinction between black and white or Mt. Sumeru and a mustard seed, not to speak of a principle as abstract as space. Since they do not know the depth of the teaching, none of them knows the depth of the principle expounded in the teaching. As the citations from those sutras above are in separate fascicles and are out of sequence, it may be difficult for the ignorant to differentiate the doctrine contained in them. Therefore, let me explain them in order to help foolish people.

203. In considering kings, we must know the difference between the great ones and the minor ones. In considering "all" we must know the difference between all of a portion and all of a total. In considering the five flavors, we must know whether they are applicable to all of Buddhism or only a portion of Buddhism. [For example,] the *Six Paramita Sutra* cited above talks of the buddhahood attained by those with buddha-nature but not by those without buddha-nature. However, it does not reveal the buddhahood attained in the remotest past! The doctrine of the five flavors in this sutra cannot even compare to that of the *Nirvana Sutra,* much less with the Trace Gate and the Original Gate of the *Lotus Sutra*. Confused by this sutra, however, Great Master Kobo of Japan classified the *Lotus Sutra* as the fourth [or the second from the top] among the five flavors. Even the fifth and most refined flavor of ghee of the dharani teaching cannot equal that of the *Nirvana Sutra*. How can it face up to that of the *Lotus Sutra*, which is superior to the *Nirvana Sutra*? What happened to Great Master Kobo? Nevertheless, he called Great Master

Tiantai and other teachers thieves when he claimed [in his *Distinguishing the Two Teaching of the Exoteric and Esoteric Treatise*], "Chinese teachers competed against one another to steal this ghee." Praising his own school, he further stated, "It is regrettable that wise men in the past had not been able to taste this ghee. "

204. Leaving aside this question, I will write this for my followers. Others will not take faith and will form a reverse relationship [with my teaching about the *Lotus Sutra* that will in turn cause them to attain buddhahood eventually]. It is possible to know the saltiness of the ocean by tasting one drop of water, and the advent of spring by seeing a single flower bloom. In the same way, without sailing a vast distance to Song China, without spending as long as three years [as Faxian did] to visit Mt. Sacred Eagle, without entering the Dragon Palace as Nagarjuna did, without visiting Maitreya Bodhisattva as Asanga did, or without attending the three assemblies at two locations [of the *Lotus Sutra*] you will be able to perceive the relative merits of all the sutras expounded by the Buddha during his lifetime by reading this writing of mine. Since snakes are relatives of dragons, they can foretell a flood seven days in advance. Since crows had been diviners in past lives, they can foretell the year's fortunes. Birds are superior to humans in their ability to fly. In knowing the comparative merits of the sutras, I, Nichiren, am superior to Chengguan of the Flower Garland school, Jiaxiang of the Three Treatises school, Ci'en of the Dharma Characteristics school, and Kobo of the Mantra school. It is because I follow the tradition of Tiantai and Dengyo; how could those others avoid committing slander of the True Dharma?

205. It is I, Nichiren, who is the richest person in Japan today, because I sacrifice my life for the sake of the *Lotus Sutra* and leave my name for posterity. Gods of rivers take orders from the master of a great ocean, and gods of mountains follow the king of Mt. Sumeru. Likewise, when one knows the meaning of the six difficult and nine easier actions of the *Lotus Sutra*, one will automatically know the comparative merits of all the sutras without reading them.

206. Besides the three proclamations made in the "Beholding the Stupa of Treasures" chapter mentioned above, there are two exhortations in the following "Devadatta" chapter. Devadatta had been regarded as an *icchantika*. He, nevertheless, was assured of becoming Heavenly King Tathagata in the future. The forty-fascicled *Nirvana Sutra* teaches [the existence of the buddha-nature in all], but the actual proof is in this chapter. Numerous transgressors such as Sunakshatra and Ajatashatru committed the five heinous transgressions or slander of the True Dharma. Since the worst of them, [Devadatta,] was assured of becoming a buddha in the future, all others would naturally be assured just as people follow their leader and twigs and leaves are all parts of a tree. That is to say the example of Devadatta assured of being the future Heavenly King Tathagata had made it un-

mistakable that all transgressors of the five or seven heinous transgressions, slanderers of the True Dharma, and *icchantika* would all attain buddhahood someday. This is somewhat like deadly poison turning into amrita, the best of all flavors.

207. Also, the example of the dragon girl attaining buddhahood does not mean only her. It means the attainment of buddhahood by all women. In the hinayana sutras expounded before the *Lotus Sutra*, women are not thought capable of attaining buddhahood. Various Mahayana sutras appear to recognize women attaining buddhahood or being reborn in a pure land, but only after they transform themselves. This is not the [immediate] attainment of buddhahood in this world, which can only be possible through the three thousand realms in a single thought-moment doctrine. Therefore, that previous teaching about attaining buddhahood or being reborn in the pure land is in name only. On the other hand, the attainment of buddhahood by a dragon girl is the precedent that opens the way for women of the Latter Age to attain buddhahood or be reborn in the pure land.

208. Filial devotion taught in Confucianism is limited to this life. Confucian sages and wise men exist in name only because they cannot help their parents in their future lives. Non-Buddhist teachings [in India] know of the past as well as the future, but they do not know how to help parents. Only Buddhism is worthy of being the way of sages and wise men, as it helps parents in future lives. However, both the Mahayana and hinayana sutras expounded before the *Lotus Sutra* expound buddhahood in name only, without substance. Therefore, the practitioners of such sutras cannot even attain the way themselves, let alone help their parents. Now, coming to the *Lotus Sutra*, when the attainment of buddhahood by women was revealed, the buddhahood of our compassionate mothers was realized; and when a man as wicked as Devadatta could attain buddhahood, the buddhahood of our loving fathers was realized. These two exhortations are the reason why this sutra is the sutra of the filial way within the Buddhist canon.

209. Surprised by the five proclamations [of the Buddha, the bodhisattvas of the Trace Gate] swore to live up to his expectations in the "Encouragement for Keeping this Sutra" chapter. Holding up these sutra passages as a mirror reflecting the truth, I will show how leaders of the Zen, Discipline, and Nembutsu schools and their followers today commit slander of the True Dharma.

210. A man called Nichiren was beheaded at the time of the rat and ox during the night of the twelfth day in the ninth month last year. His spirit has come to Sado Province and is writing this amid the snow in the second month of the following year to be sent to his closely related disciples. As such, this writing of mine may sound frightening to you, but it should not. How fearful others will be when they read this writing! This is the bright mirror in which Shakyamuni, Many Treasures, and the buddhas of the ten directions reflect the future state of Japan, namely the conditions of Japan today. Consider this as my memento in case I die.

211. [The bodhisattvas in the] "Encouragement for Keeping this Sutra" chapter said [to the Buddha]:

> Do not worry!
> We will expound this sutra
> In the dreadful, evil world
> After the Buddha's cessation.
>
> Ignorant people will speak ill of us,
> Abuse us, and threaten us
> With swords and staves.
> But we will endure all this.
>
> Some monks in the evil world will be cunning.
> They will be ready to flatter others.
> Thinking that they have obtained what they have not,
> Their minds will be filled with arrogance.
>
> Some monks will live in *aranyas* or retired places,
> And wear patched pieces of cloth.
> Thinking that they are practicing the true way,
> They will despise others.
>
> Being attached to worldly profits,
> They will expound the Dharma to men in white robes.
> They will be respected by the people of the world
> As the arhats who have the six supernatural powers.
>
> They will have evil thoughts.
> They will always think of worldly things.
> Even when they live in *aranyas*,
> They will take pleasure in saying that we have faults.
>
> …
>
> In the midst of the great assembly
> In order to speak ill of us, in order to slander us
> They will say to kings, ministers of state,
> To brahmins and also to householders,
>
> And to other assemblies of monks,
> "They have wrong views.
> They are expounding

The teaching of non-Buddhists."

…

There will be many dreadful things
In the evil world of the kalpa of defilements.
Devils will enter the bodies [of those monks]
And cause them to abuse and insult us.

…

Evil monks in the defiled world will not know
The teaching that you have expounded with skillful means
According to the capacities of all sentient beings

They will speak ill of us,
Or frown at us,
Or drive us out of our monasteries
From time to time.

212. The *Notations* [*on the Words and Phrases of the Lotus Sutra*] says:

This citation [describes] three [presumptuous groups]. The first quatrain [about them] refers to wicked people as a whole, that is, the [presumptuous] lay followers. The next quatrain refers to presumptuous clergy, while the following seven quatrains refer to the presumptuous sages. Of the three, persecution by the first group is endurable. That of the second group is harder to endure, while that of the third group is the most difficult to endure. This is because the second and third groups are more cunning and less likely to reveal their faults.

213. The *Dongchun* by Dharma Master Zhidu says:

First, in the five quatrains starting with "ignorant people" in the "Encouragement for Keeping this Sutra" chapter, the first quatrain refers to enduring the three kinds of evil actions committed by non-Buddhists and evil people. The next quatrain beginning with "monks in the evil world" refers to presumptuous home-leavers. Third, the three quatrains beginning with "Some monks will live in *aranyas*" refers to the acts of home-leavers who are leaders of all the evil people.

He also says:

The two quatrains beginning with "In the midst of the great assembly" refer to reporting to the authorities in order to slander the True Dharma and those who spread it.

214. Fascicle nine of the *Nirvana Sutra* says,

> Good sons! Suppose an *icchantika* pretending to be an arhat stays in a secluded place, slandering the Vaipulya sutras of the Mahayana. Ordinary people who see him may think he is an arhat or a great bodhisattva.

The sutra also says:

> At the time this *Nirvana Sutra* spreads all over Jambudvipa, evil monks will steal it and forcibly divide it into many parts, thereby destroying the excellent color, fragrance, and taste of the True Dharma. Although these evil monks may recite such sutras, they will miss the true teaching of the Buddha, replacing it with meaningless words of flowery rhetoric. They will rearrange the sutra taking the beginning part of the sutra and putting it at the end or vice versa, or they will move the beginning and ending parts to the mid-section, or the mid-part to the beginning or ending part. You must know that such evil monks are Mara's companions.

The *Six-Fascicle Nirvana Sutra* says:

> There will be *icchantikas* who act like arhats but commit evil acts; and there will be arhats who act like *icchantikas* but have compassion. The *icchantikas* who seem to be arhats refer to sentient beings who slander the Vaipulya sutras. The arhats who seem like *icchantikas* refer to sentient beings who censure voice-hearers and widely expound the Vaipulya sutras. They will say to sentient beings, "You and I are both bodhisattvas. Why is this? It is because we all have the nature of the tathagata." Nevertheless, those sentient beings will consider them *icchantikas*.

[The *Nirvana Sutra*] also says:

> After the cessation of the Buddha, and after the Age of the True Dharma is over, monks in the Age of the Semblance Dharma will no longer be sages. On the surface, they will appear to keep the precepts and to read and recite the sutras a little, but they will devour rich food and enjoy a prosperous life … Although they will wear *kesas* they will act for selfish gain just like hunters stalking game with narrow eyes, or cats stalking a rat. They will

always say, "I have attained arhatship." ... They will appear to be wise and virtuous people, but in their hearts they will harbor greed and jealousy just like brahmins practicing the exercise of keeping silence. They will appear to be shramanas but actually are not. With their rampant wrong views they will commit slander of the True Dharma.

215. Now in the light of the *Lotus Sutra* expounded on Mt. Sacred Eagle and the *Nirvana Sutra* expounded under the twin sal trees, that are as bright as the sun and moon, and the commentaries by [Miaole of] Pitan and [Zhidu of] Dongchun that are as brilliant as a clear mirror, the sectarian schools today and the ugly faces of the Zen, Discipline, and Nembutsu followers in all of Japan are seen without a trace of obscurity.

216. It is said in the *Sutra of the Lotus Flower of the Wonderful Dharma* that it would be spread "in the dreadful, evil world after the Buddha's cessation." In the "Peaceful Practices" chapter it speaks of "in the evil world after [my cessation]," "in the latter days," and "in the age of the decline of the Dharma after my cessation"; "The Variety of Merits" chapter speaks of "in the evil world in the age of the decline of my Dharma"; and "The Previous Life of Medicine King Bodhisattva" chapter speaks of "in the later five hundred years after my cessation." Likewise, it is said in the "Encouragement to Expound the Dharma" chapter of the *Flowering of the True Dharma Sutra* that the sutra would be spread "in the latter days" and "in the coming latter days." The *Supplemented Lotus Sutra* says the same.

217. Tiantai says, "The three southern and seven northern [schools of Buddhism in China] during the Age of the Semblance Dharma have become the enemies of the *Lotus Sutra*." Dengyo said, "Toward the end of the Age of the Semblance Dharma, scholars of the six schools of Nara Buddhism were the enemies of the *Lotus Sutra*." During the time of these two great masters, however, the enemies of the *Lotus Sutra* had not yet become apparent.

218. Nevertheless, statements cited above from the *Lotus Sutra* were made in the presence of Shakyamuni the World Honored One and Many Treasure Buddha sitting side by side in the stupa of treasures like the sun and moon, as well as the emanation buddhas of the ten directions sitting under the trees like stars in the sky. Innumerable bodhisattvas, eighty *kotis* of *nayutas* in number, consulted one another and discerned that there would be three kinds of enemies of the *Lotus Sutra* at the beginning of the Latter Age of Degeneration after the one thousand-year Age of the True Dharma and the one thousand-year Age of the Semblance Dharma after the Buddha's cessation. How could this be false?

219. It has been some two thousand and two hundred years since the Tathagata's cessation. Even if a finger pointing to the earth misses it, or flowers fail

to bloom in the spring, the three kinds of enemies of the *Lotus Sutra* are bound to appear in Japan. If so, who will be among the three kinds of enemies? Or, who will be considered to be a practitioner of the *Lotus Sutra*? We are not sure. Are we among the so-called three kinds of powerful enemies? Or are we among the practitioners of the *Lotus Sutra*? We are not sure.

220. It was during the night of the eighth day of the fourth month in the twenty-fourth year of King Zhao, the fourth sovereign of the Zhou dynasty in ancient China, that rays of light in five colors flashed in the sky from north to south, brightening it as though it were daytime. The earth trembled six ways; rivers, ponds, and wells rose without rain, and all the grasses and trees bloomed and bore fruit. It was miraculous! Greatly alarmed, King Zhao consulted historian Su You about this and was told that this was an omen of the birth of a sage in the land to the west. The historian continued, "Nothing will happen for now, but in a millennia the teaching of that sage, who was just born in the western land, will come to this land to benefit sentient beings." Su You was a scholar of non-Buddhist scriptures who had not yet eliminated even a single hair of the delusions of views and attitudes. Yet he was able to foretell events a millennia in advance. As he predicted, the Buddha Dharma was introduced to China one thousand and fifteen years after the cessation of the Buddha, in the tenth year of the Yongping era (67 CE) during the reign of Emperor Ming, the second emperor of the Later Han dynasty.

221. This prediction [of the *Lotus Sutra*] is incomparably superior [to that of Su You], as it was presented by bodhisattvas in the presence of Shakyamuni, Many Treasures, and the emanation buddhas of the ten directions. As such, how could there not be three kinds of enemies of the *Lotus Sutra* in Japan today? Shakyamuni Buddha had predicted in the *Transmission of the Dharma Treasury Sutra*, "During the millennia of the Age of the True Dharma after my cessation, twenty-four successors will come to spread the True Dharma." Besides such direct disciples as Mahakashyapa and Ananda, a century later the monk Parshva appeared, after six centuries Ashvaghosha appeared, and after seven centuries Nagarjuna Bodhisattva appeared. Why is it that only this prediction of three kinds of enemies of the *Lotus Sutra* has not come true? If this prediction has not come true, the whole teaching of the *Lotus Sutra* will be false, and the assurance that Shariputra and Mahakashyapa will be the future Flower Light Tathagata and Light Tathagata respectively would come to naught. This would mean that the prior sutras would in turn become true and final with the result that the voice-hearers would never attain buddhahood. It would mean that we should not offer any alms to such voice-hearers as Ananda, even if we should do so to dogs and foxes. What should we do then? What should we do?

222. The first enemy are the "ignorant people," who are great supporters of the second and third enemies referred to as "monks in the evil world" and "monks

wearing patched pieces of cloth" in the sutra. Therefore, Great Master Miaole, [in his *Notations on the Words and Phrases of the Lotus Sutra*,] referred to the first kind of enemy as "presumptuous lay followers," while the *Dongchun* said that they would "raise false charges to the authorities."

223. As for the second kind of enemy of the *Lotus Sutra*, the sutra says, "Some monks in the evil world will be cunning. They will be ready to flatter others. Thinking that they have obtained what they have not, their minds will be filled with arrogance."

224. The *Nirvana Sutra* says, "At the time … these evil monks may recite such sutras, they will miss the true teaching of the Buddha…"

225. The *Great Calming and Contemplation* says, "Those without faith consider sagehood to be so elevated that it could not possibly become part of their own knowledge. Those without knowledge become presumptuous and consider themselves equal to the Buddha."

226. Meditation Master Daochuo stated [in his *Collection of Passages on the Land of Peace and Bliss*] that the second reason [why the holy way gate should be given up] was that its teachings are too exquisitely profound [for ordinary people] to understand deeply. Likewise, Honen states [in his *A Collection of Passages on the Nembutsu Chosen in the Original Vow*], "The various practices [except for the nembutsu] do not suit the capacity of the people nor the time."

227. Fascicle ten of the *Notations on the Words and Phrases of the Lotus Sutra* says, "Those who would misunderstand [the *Lotus Sutra*] perhaps do not know how meritorious the beginner's mind can be. They give credit to those of high rank and take lightly those with a beginner's mind. For this reason, I will show that even the shallow practice of those with a beginner's mind has profound efficacy through the strength of the [*Lotus*] *Sutra*."

228. The Great Master Dengyo says, [in his *Essay on the Protection of the Nation*], "The True and Semblance ages are about to pass with the Latter Age of Degeneration just around the corner. It is exactly the time now for the One Vehicle teaching of the *Lotus Sutra*. How do I know it? It is said in the "Peaceful Practices" chapter that the sutra will spread in the Latter Age when the Dharma is about to disappear." Eshin says [in his *Essentials of the One Vehicle Teaching*], "The whole of Japan has the capacity for the perfect teaching."

229. Whom should we believe, Daochuo and Honen or Dengyo and Eshin? The former do not have any proof text from any of the sutras, while the latter base their assertions firmly on the *Lotus Sutra*. Moreover, to all Buddhist monks in Japan, Great Master Dengyo of Mt. Hiei is their preceptor. How could they lean toward Honen, who is haunted by a heavenly devil, and abandon the preceptor who shaved their heads?

230. If Honen were a knowledgeable person, why did he not mention in his *A Collection of Passages on the Nembutsu Chosen in the Original Vow* those interpretations of Dengyo and Eshin to compare with his own? Since he did not do so, he is to be blamed for having concealed them. It is Honen and other monks without any precepts and with wrong views that [the *Lotus Sutra*] points to as "some monks in the evil world," the second of the three kinds of enemies.

231. The *Nirvana Sutra* says, "Before listening to the *Nirvana Sutra*, we had all been of wrong views." Miaole says [of this in his *Elucidation of the Profound Meaning of the Lotus Sutra*], "They themselves called the prior three doctrinal teachings wrong views." The *Great Calming and Contemplation* says, "In the *Nirvana Sutra* they called themselves wrong. Isn't wrong the same as evil?" The *Supplemental Amplifications on the Great Calming and Contemplation* [of Miaole] says:

> "Wrong" means "evil." Therefore we must know that only the perfect teaching is good. But this has two meanings. First, it means that following the perfect teaching is to do good while rejecting it is evil. This is a viewpoint of relative [subtlety]. [Secondly,] it means that attachment [to even the perfect teaching] is considered evil while transcending it is good. The perspectives of both relative subtlety and absolute subtlety are that we have to stay away from evil. It is evil to attach ourselves even to the perfect teaching. How much worse it is to attach ourselves to the other [three doctrinal teachings].

232. Compared to the hinayana sutras, all the non-Buddhist teachings are in error about good and evil and are an evil way. Compared to the *Lotus Sutra*, the good way of the hinayana, and the four flavors and three teachings, are all wrong and evil. The *Lotus Sutra* alone is true and good. The perfect teaching of the prior sutras is so only from the viewpoint of relative subtlety, but from the viewpoint of absolute subtlety it is still evil. Also, [the perfect teaching of the prior sutras] is still the evil way because it does not go beyond the first three doctrinal teachings. Therefore, we are still treading the evil way even if we practice the ultimate teaching of the prior sutras. How much worse to depend on the inferior teaching of sutras like the *Contemplation of the Buddha of Infinite Life Sutra*, that cannot even compare to the *Flower Garland* and Prajna sutras, and claim that it is the fundamental Dharma? Isn't saying that the *Contemplation of the Buddha of Infinite Life Sutra* includes the *Lotus Sutra* and urging nembutsu believers to abandon, close, set aside, and cast away [all other sutras including the *Lotus* Sutra,] as Honen and his disciples and supporters have done, to commit slander of the True Dharma? Shakyamuni, Many Treasures, and the buddhas of the ten directions came to this world "in order to have the Dharma preserved forever." Honen and the nembutsu practitioners in Japan claim that the *Lotus Sutra* in the Latter Age of Degeneration

will perish before the nembutsu. Aren't they the enemies of [Shakyamuni, Many Treasures, and the buddhas of the ten directions who are] the three sages?

233. As for the third kind of enemy, the *Lotus Sutra* says:

> Some monks will live in *aranyas* or retired places and wear patched pieces of cloth. … They will expound the Dharma to men in white robes. They will be respected by the people of the world as the arhats who have the six supernatural powers.

234. The *Six-Fascicle Nirvana Sutra* says:

> There will be *icchantikas* who act like arhats but commit evil acts; and there will be arhats who act like *icchantikas* but have compassion. The *icchantikas* who seem to be arhats refer to sentient beings who slander the Vaipulya sutras. The arhats who seem like *icchantikas* refer to sentient beings who censure voice-hearers and widely expound the Vaipulya sutras. They will say to sentient beings, "You and I are both bodhisattvas. Why is this? It is because we all have the nature of the tathagata." Nevertheless, those sentient beings will consider them *icchantikas*.

235. The *Nirvana Sutra* says:

> After the cessation of the Buddha, and after the Age of the True Dharma is over, monks in the Age of the Semblance Dharma will no longer be sages. On the surface, they will appear to keep the precepts and to read and recite the sutras a little, but they will devour rich food and enjoy a prosperous life … Although they will wear *kesas* they will act for selfish gain just like hunters stalking game with narrow eyes, or cats stalking a rat. They will always say, "I have attained arhatship." … They will appear to be wise and virtuous people, but in their hearts they will harbor greed and jealousy just like brahmins practicing the exercise of keeping silence. They will appear to be shramanas but actually are not. With their rampant wrong views they will commit slander of the True Dharma.

236. Miaole says [in his *Notations on the Words and Phrases of the Lotus Sutra*], "…the third group is the most difficult to endure. This is because the second and third groups are more cunning and less likely to reveal their faults."

237. The *Dongchun* says, "Third, the three quatrains beginning with "Some monks will live in *aranyas*" refer to the acts of home-leavers who are leaders of all the evil people."

238. Where are those the *Dongchun* calls "home-leavers who are leaders of all the evil people" in Japan today? Are they on Mt. Hiei, in the Onjoji Temple, Toji Temple, temples in Nara, Kenninji Temple, Jufukuji Temple, or in the Kenchoji Temple? We must find them. Are they the home-leavers of Enryakuji Temple who put on helmets and armor? Or, are they those monks of the Onjoji Temple who don armor and brandish staves in order to protect their fivefold Dharma-bodies? However, they do not look like those referred to in the sutra who "live in *aranyas* or retired places and wear patched pieces of cloth." People do not suppose that they are "respected by the people of the world as the arhats who have the six supernatural powers." Or, should I say that they are those who are "more cunning and less likely to reveal their faults." Thus, it seems that the third kind of enemy refers to such monks as Shoichi of Kyoto and Ryokan of Kamakura. Do not blame me for saying this. If you have eyes, look at yourselves in the light of the sutras.

239. The first fascicle the *Great Calming and Contemplation* says, "The brightness and tranquility of calming and contemplation was unheard of in previous ages."

240. The first fascicle of the *Supplemental Amplifications on the Great Calming and Contemplation* says, "Ever since the Later Han Emperor Ming introduced Buddhism into China, after he had dreamed of a golden man, till the Chen dynasty … many have learned the Zen teachings and received the transmission of its robe and bowl."

241. The *Additional Annotations to the Three Major Works of Tiantai* says, "The one who transmitted the robe and bowl [of Zen to China] was Bodhidharma."

242. The fifth fascicle of the *Great Calming and Contemplation* says, "Again there are Zen people… both teachers and their students are blind and lame."

243. The seventh fascicle of the *Great Calming and Contemplation* says:

> Except for translation, in nine out of the ten [means of adaptation to the Buddha Dharma], I am vastly different from those Dharma masters in the world who only study the writings or those meditation masters who are only concerned with phenomenal practice. Some meditation masters only practice contemplation of the mind, but their practice is either shallow or false. They practice none of the remaining nine [except for contemplation]. This is not idle talk. Wise men in the future who have eyes should consider this seriously.

244. The seventh fascicle of the *Supplemental Amplifications on the Great Calming and Contemplation* says:

> Dharma masters who only study the writings refer to those who are only concerned with the external appearance of the Dharma

without inwardly cultivating contemplative understanding; while meditation masters who are only concerned with phenomenal practice refer to those who only practice calming the mind by focusing exclusively on [the breath going in and out of] their nostrils without cultivating the tranquil knowledge of objects. ... Theirs is the kind of meditative absorption that is still fundamentally contaminated by outflows. The statement that some meditation masters concentrate only on meditation is only to take their part for the sake of argument. Strictly speaking, they lack contemplative understanding. Those meditators in the world today consider only the contemplation of principle important but are not fully versed in the teachings. Their contemplative interpretations negate the sutras when they say that the eight errors and the eight winds make the sixteen-foot Buddha, or that the five aggregates and three poisons are called the eight errors. They confuse the six sense entrances with the six supernatural powers, or confuse the four primary elements with the four noble truths. That such an understanding of the sutras are the worst of all is beyond question, an absurdity not worthy of discussion.

245. The seventh fascicle of the *Great Calming and Contemplation* says:

Once there lived a meditation master in Ye and Luo, whose fame spread throughout the land. Wherever he stayed, people gathered like clouds from the four directions to gaze up at him. Whenever he left, people thronged the roads to bid him farewell. Of what benefit was all this roaring and rumbling? They all regretted it on their deathbeds.

246. The seventh fascicle of the *Supplemental Amplifications on the Great Calming and Contemplation* says:

Regarding the meditation master of Ye and Luo, Ye is in Xiang Province. It was the capital of the [Northern] Qi and [Northern] Wei dynasties. The Buddha Dharma greatly flourished there. The first ancestor of the Zen school converted the king to Buddhism. Names will not be given out of deference to the people of that time. Luo refers to Luoyang.

247. The *Six-Fascicle Nirvana Sutra* says, "Without seeing the ultimate end, one cannot see how evil the actions of the *icchantika* really are."

248. Miaole says [in his *Notations on the Words and Phrases of the Lotus Sutra*], "...the third group is the most difficult to endure. [This is because the second and third groups are] more cunning and less likely to reveal their faults."

249. Those who are blind or one-eyed, or those who have wrong views may not see the "three kinds of enemies" at the beginning of the Latter Age of Degeneration, but those who have a portion of the buddha eye should be able to see this. [The *Lotus Sutra* says] "In order to speak ill of us, in order to slander us they will say to kings, ministers of state, to brahmins and also to householders..." The *Dongchun* explains [that this passage means], "...reporting to the authorities in order to slander the True Dharma and those who spread it." So in the past toward the end of the Age of the Semblance Dharma, such monks as Gomyo and Shuen petitioned the imperial court, slandering the Great Master Dengyo. Now at the beginning of the Latter Age, such monks as Ryokan and Nen'a have written letters full of falsehoods to the shogunate. How can they not be of the three kinds of enemies?

250. Today, Nembutsu practitioners also say to the king, his ministers, brahmins and householders, who are followers of the Tiantai Lotus school, that the *Lotus Sutra* is too exquisitely profound for us to understand or that its doctrines are too profound for our shallow capacities. Isn't this like those who, "...consider sagehood to be so elevated that it could not possibly become part of their own knowledge."

251. The Zen school maintains:

> The *Lotus Sutra* is a finger pointing to the moon while the Zen school is the moon itself. After grasping the moon there is no need for the finger to point at it. Zen is the heart of the Buddha while the *Lotus Sutra* is merely his words. Having finished expounding all the sutras, including the *Lotus Sutra*, the Buddha picked up a flower and gave it to Mahakashyapa because he alone understood what the Buddha meant. As proof the Buddha entrusted him with his *kesa*, which has been handed down through twenty-eight Indian ancestors of Buddhism [in India] and to six Chinese ancestors.

It has been a long time since such nonsense as this fooled and confused the people of Japan.

252. Eminent monks of the Tiantai and Mantra schools enjoy high reputation within their respective schools without knowing what their own schools are about. Being greedy and afraid of courtiers and warriors, they approve and even praise what the Nembutsu and Zen schools claim. In the past, Many Treasures and the emanation buddhas of the ten directions attested to the truth of the *Lotus Sutra* "in order to have the Dharma preserved forever." Now the eminent monks of the Tiantai school seem to agree with the false claims of the Zen and Pure Land schools that the *Lotus Sutra* is "too exquisitely profound for ordinary people to understand." As a result, the *Lotus Sutra* exists in name only in Japan, without

anyone attaining the way. Now whom should we consider a practitioner of the *Lotus Sutra*? Numerous monks were exiled for burning temples and stupas. Many eminent monks are frowned at for catering to the whims of courtiers and warriors in power. Should we call them practitioners of the *Lotus Sutra*?

253. Exactly as the Buddha predicted, the three kinds of enemies fill the land. Nevertheless, we don't see any practitioners of the *Lotus Sutra*. Does this mean that the golden words of the Buddha are untrue? Could this be? After all, who has been abused and despised by the laity? Which monk has been attacked with swords and staves? Which monk has been brought to the attention of courtiers and warriors because of the *Lotus Sutra*? Which monk has been driven out of monasteries from time to time? No such man exists in Japan, except for Nichiren. However, as Nichiren has been abandoned by the gods, he probably is not a practitioner of the *Lotus Sutra*. Then, who would be a practitioner of the *Lotus Sutra* who can validate the Buddha's prediction?

254. The Buddha and Devadatta remained together, life after life, just as a shadow follows a body. Prince Shotoku and Moriya were always together just as the flowers and fruits of the lotus appear at the same time. By the same token, when there is a practitioner of the *Lotus Sutra*, there must be the three kinds of enemies. As the three kinds of enemies already exist, who is a practitioner of the *Lotus Sutra*? Shouldn't we seek him out to make him our teacher? To meet such a man is as rare an occasion as a one-eyed turtle finding a piece of wood with the right size hollow floating in the ocean.

255. Some say:

> Although there seem to be three kinds of enemies in the world today, practitioners of the *Lotus Sutra* are not found anywhere. It is difficult for us to call you a practitioner of the *Lotus Sutra* because there is a great deal of discrepancy. The sutra says, "Celestial pages will serve him. He will not be struck with swords or staves. He will not be poisoned." It also says, "If anyone speaks ill of him, the speaker's mouth will be shut." It also says, "[Having heard these teachings,] they became peaceful in their present lives. In their future lives, they will have rebirths in good places…" It also says, "[Anyone who does not keep our spells, but troubles the expounder of the Dharma] shall have his head split into seven pieces just as the branches of the arjaka-tree [are split]…" It also says, "He will be able to obtain the rewards of his merits in his present life." It also says, "Those who, upon seeing the keeper of this sutra, blame him justly or unjustly, will suffer from white leprosy in their present life."

256. Answer: They have good reason to doubt me. So I will clear away their doubts. In the "Never Despising Bodhisattva" chapter [of the *Lotus Sutra*] it speaks of [Anyone who] "speaks ill of or abuses" [those who keep the *Lotus Sutra*.] It also speaks of [people who] "would strike [Never Despising Bodhisattva] with a stave, a piece of wood, a piece of tile, or a stone." The *Nirvana Sutra* speaks [of the corrupt monks who would attack the pure monks], "…perhaps even injuring them or even killing them." The *Lotus Sutra* states, "Many people hate [this sutra] with jealousy even in my lifetime."

257. The Buddha himself encountered nine great difficulties during his lifetime, such as having his toe injured by Devadatta. Wasn't he a practitioner of the *Lotus Sutra*? Can't we call Never Despising Bodhisattva a practitioner of the One Vehicle teaching? Maudgalyayana was beaten to death with bamboo staves. This occurred after he received the assurance [of future buddhahood] in the *Lotus Sutra*. Aryadeva Bodhisattva and Aryasimha, the fourteenth and twenty-fifth successors [of the Dharma] were both murdered. Were they not practitioners of the *Lotus Sutra*? Daosheng was banished to a mountain in Suzhou. Fadao was branded on the face with a hot iron rod and exiled to the south of the [Yangtze] River. Were these monks not practitioners of the *Lotus Sutra*? Kitano Tenjin and Bai Juyi were also banished. Were they not worthy of being practitioners of the One Vehicle?

258. I wonder why these men were persecuted? If someone does not commit the transgression of slandering the *Lotus Sutra* in a previous life, they will be able to uphold the *Lotus Sutra* in their present life. Whoever accuses him of a trivial worldly transgression, or for no offense at all, will immediately receive punishment. The asuras who attacked Shakra were immediately repulsed and the golden-winged birds who invaded Lake Anavatapta [to devour the dragon king] were killed on the spot. Tiantai says [in fascicle six of his *Profound Meaning of the Lotus Sutra*], "Our troubles and sufferings in this world are all due to our transgressions in our past lives, and recompense for our meritorious acts in this life will be received in our future lives." It is said in the *Contemplation on the Mind-Ground Sutra*, "If you want to know what causes were made in the past, then look at the effects experienced in the present; if you want to know what the effects will be in the future, then look at the causes made in the present," The "Never Despising Bodhisattva" chapter [of the *Lotus Sutra*] states, "Thus he expiated his transgressions." It seems that the Never Despising Bodhisattva was attacked with rocks and tiles because of his past transgression of slandering the *Lotus Sutra*.

259. It seems also that those who are destined for hell in the next life do not receive punishment even for heinous transgressions in this life. The *icchantika* are like this. The *Nirvana Sutra* says, "Kashyapa Bodhisattva addressed the Buddha, saying, 'World Honored One! The Buddhas explained that the light of this great nirvana enters into the pores of all sentient beings.'" And also, "Kashyapa

Bodhisattva addressed the Buddha, saying, 'World Honored One! if a person is not yet generating the thought of awakening, how can they attain the cause for awakening?'" The Buddha answered this question by saying:

> The Buddha replied to Kashyapa, "Suppose there is a person who, after listening to the *Nirvana Sutra*, does not generate the thought of awakening and slanders the True Dharma instead. Such a person will soon have a nightmare in which they will see a rakshasa. The rakshasa will say, 'Hey! Good man! If you do not generate the thought of awakening I will end your life.' Suppose he, frightened, awoke, and began to generate the thought of awakening. ... It should be understood that this person will become a great bodhisattva."

Thus, except for the extremely wicked, when people slander the True Dharma, they will immediately have a nightmare like this and aspire to awakening.

260. [The *Nirvana Sutra*] also says [that *icchantika* will never generate the thought of awakening just as "…rain that pours down from a great cloud covering the sky, bringing water to the earth,] dried trees, rocky cliffs, [high plains, and earthen mounds. The water does not remain where it falls but flows downward…"] It also says, "…like a charred seed. Even if exposed to sweet rain [for a billion kalpas, in the end that seed will not germinate]." It also says, "[…this situation is also analogous to] a *mani* jewel. [If placed in murky water, its radiant power would make the water clear but if thrown into] mud [it would not have the same effect.]" It also says, "…consider someone who has injured his hand. If he applies strong, poisonous medicine, [such as scorpion's tail, the poison will penetrate into him. But if he had no wound, the poison could not seep into him]." It also says, "…it is like a great rain that, after falling, no longer remains in the sky." A number of these similes are cited in the sutra to show that *icchantika* are not punished in this world, because it is certain that they will go to the Hell of Incessant Suffering in the next life. It is just like the notorious reigns of King Jie of Xia and King Zhou Xin of Yin in ancient China. Natural calamities did not occur during their reigns as their rule was to be destroyed for their great transgressions.

261. It could also be that the True Dharma has been slandered and guardian deities have abandoned this land of Japan. As a result, slanderers of the True Dharma are not punished while those upholding it are left without divine assistance and are subjected to great difficulties. What is said in the *Supreme Golden Light Sutra*, "The number of those who cultivate wholesome practices become fewer day by day," refers to this evil country and evil age. I have explained this in detail in my *Treatise On Spreading Peace Throughout the Country by Establishing the True Dharma*.

262. In the final analysis, even if I am abandoned by the gods and no matter how many difficulties I encounter, I will uphold the *Lotus Sutra* at the cost of my own life. Shariputra had practiced the way of the bodhisattvas for as long as sixty kalpas but fell away because he could not endure the difficulty presented by a brahmin who asked him for one of his eyes. Those who had [received the seed of buddhahood] from the Eternal Shakyamuni Buddha or Great Universal Wisdom Excellence Buddha as long as five hundred or three thousand dust-particle kalpas ago [could not attain buddhahood] because they had been misled by evil friends. Whether for good or bad reasons, abandoning the *Lotus Sutra* will cause us to be plunged into hell.

263. I will make this my original vow. Even if someone says that he would make me the ruler of Japan on the condition that I give up the *Lotus Sutra* and rely upon the *Contemplation of the Buddha of Infinite Life Sutra* for my salvation in the next life, or even if someone threatens me saying that he will execute my parents if I do not chant the nembutsu, and no matter how many great difficulties fall upon me, I will not submit to them until a wise person defeats me by reason. Other difficulties are like dust in the wind. I will never break my vow to become the pillar of Japan, to become the eyes of Japan, and to become a great vessel for Japan.

264. Question: "How do you know that your banishment and death sentence are the result of transgressions in your previous lives?"

Answer: Copper mirrors reflect only colors and shapes, and the mirror the first emperor of the Qin dynasty used to test his subjects showed only present transgressions, but the mirror of the Buddha Dharma shows the karmic activity of past lives. Therefore, the *Six-Fascicle Nirvana Sutra* says:

> Good men! Since you have committed numerous transgressions and accumulated evil karma, you have to suffer the recompense for those transgressions. ... You may be slighted, may look ugly, may suffer from lack of clothing or from insufficient food and drink, unable to make a fortune, born to a poor family or to a family with wrong views, or suffer from royal persecutions, and many other difficulties. The reason you receive relatively light punishment like these in this world is due to your merit of upholding the Dharma. Otherwise you might have been punished much more severely.

265. This passage from the sutra matches me, Nichiren, as perfectly as two halves of a tally. It explains why I have been persecuted, and all of my numerous doubts have faded away. Let us tally this sutra, phrase by phrase against me. As for "being slighted," which is phrased in the *Lotus Sutra* as "They will hate him, look at him with jealousy..." I have been despised for more than twenty years. "Being ugly-looking," "suffering from lack of clothing," "insufficient food and

drink," "unable to make a fortune," "being born to a poor family," and "suffering from royal persecution" and other passages from the sutra all apply to me. Who can doubt it?

266. The *Lotus Sutra* says, "[They will] … drive us out of our monasteries from time to time…" This is restated in the [*Six-Fascicle Nirvana Sutra*] in terms of "many other difficulties," and it goes on to say, "The reason you receive relatively light punishment like these in this world is due to your merit of upholding the Dharma. Otherwise you might have been punished much more severely." The fifth fascicle of the *Great Calming and Contemplation* explains as follows: "Trivial acts of non-meditative good deeds is too weak to move [the effects of karmic recompense]. Only when we practice calming and contemplation, whether in illness or in health, can we move the wheel of birth and death." It also warns us: "[If you are diligent in both practice and understanding,] then the three obstacles and four devils will confusedly contend with each other and arise."

267. In the beginningless past, I must have been born as a wicked king and must have deprived practitioners of the *Lotus Sutra* of their food and clothing and their properties on numerous occasions just as some people in Japan today have been destroying temples dedicated to the *Lotus Sutra*. I must have also cut off the heads of numerous practitioners of the *Lotus Sutra*. I may have purged myself of some of these heinous transgressions but not all of them. Even if I have, I am still experiencing the residual effects. In order to be delivered from samsara, I must completely renounce all those heinous transgressions. My merits are shallow while my transgressions are deep. If I had practiced only provisional sutras, heinous transgressions would not have been revealed. It is like forging iron, for instance. Unless you hit it and forge it hard, hidden impurities will not be seen. They appear only when the iron is forged many times on an anvil. It is also analogous to squeezing hemp seeds. Unless squeezed hard, there is little oil. Ever since I, Nichiren, strongly condemned those who slander the True Dharma in Japan, I have been persecuted. It must be that heinous transgressions in my past lives are revealed through my merits in defending the Dharma in this life. It is just as a piece of iron remains black unless heated by fire, and becomes red when placed in fire. Even calm water makes great waves when blocked by a log. A sleeping lion roars loudly when disturbed.

268. The *Nirvana Sutra* says:

> For example, say there is a poor woman who does not have a house to live in nor anyone to support her, who is in poor health, and is hard-pressed by hunger and thirst. She wandered about begging until she stopped at an inn, where she gave birth to a child. The innkeeper chased her out. Carrying the infant born only a short while ago, she tried to go to some other country. On the way, she was overtaken by a bad storm, suffered from hunger and

cold and was attacked by mosquitos, horseflies, bees, and other poisonous insects. Coming to the Ganges River, she tried to wade through it carrying her baby. She was carried away by the flowing river, but she clung to her infant until both of them drowned. Such a woman will be reborn in the Heavens of Brahma due to the merit of her loving-kindness [for her child]. Manjushri! If good men wish to protect the True Dharma ... he must do the same as the poor woman in sacrificing her body and life in the Ganges because of the loving-kindness [she feels for her child]. Good man! Bodhisattvas protecting the Dharma should also be ready to sacrifice their bodies and lives. ... Such people will be able to attain liberation without seeking it, just as the poor woman was reborn in the Heavens of Brahma even though she was not seeking the Heavens of Brahma.

269. [In his *Annotations on the Nirvana Sutra*,] Great Master Zhang'an has commented on this passage in terms of the three obstacles. Observe his interpretation: That she is "poor" refers to the person who does not yet have the treasure of the Dharma, and being a "woman" refers to the person with only a little bit of loving-kindness. "An inn" refers to this impure land. "A child" refers to faith in the *Lotus Sutra*, which is the [buddha-nature of the] completing cause. "The innkeeper chased her out" refers to banishment, and "the infant born only a short while ago" stands for the short period of time since the person took faith. The "bad storm" by which she was overtaken refers to the sentence of banishment, while "bees and horseflies" refers to ignorant people who will speak ill of us and abuse us. The drowning of the mother and her baby refers to the person being beheaded for their unwavering faith in the *Lotus Sutra*. "Reborn in the Heavens of Brahma" refers to the person who is reborn in the realm of the buddhas.

270. Directive karma extends to all the realms including the realm of the buddhas. Even a murderer of ten thousand people in China and Japan, unless they have committed one of the five heinous transgressions or slander of the True Dharma, will not fall into the Hell of Incessant Suffering but into one of the other hells and suffer many years there. It would likewise be impossible to be reborn in the form realm through practicing non-meditative good deeds, such as upholding ten thousand precepts and cultivating ten thousand good practices.

271. To be reborn as Brahma Heavenly King, we have to ascend through the practice of meditative absorption with outflows and in addition give rise to loving-kindness and compassion. The rebirth of this poor woman in the Heavens of Brahma because of her mindfulness for her child does not follow the ordinary nature and characteristics of things. Zhang'an has two interpretations on this, but after all it is nothing but motherly loving-kindness for a child that made the dif-

ference. This kind of single mindedness in regard to a child is similar to contemplation on loving-kindness and compassion. This is probably the reason why the mother was reborn in the Heavens of Brahma although she had not done anything else.

272. Also, many ways are claimed for leading to buddhahood, such as the Flower Garland school's doctrine of the Dharma-realm of mind-only, the Three Treatises school's doctrine of the eight negations, the Dharma Characteristics school's doctrine of consciousness-only, and the Mantra school's contemplation of the five wheels, but none of these seem to fully express the truth. The only way seemingly that leads to buddhahood is the three thousand realms in a single thought-moment doctrine of Tiantai. However, we do not possess even a bit of the wisdom to understand it; nevertheless, among all the holy sutras of the Buddha's lifetime, only the *Lotus Sutra* embodies the gem of the three thousand realms in a single thought-moment doctrine. The principles of the other sutras may look like gems, but in actuality they are merely yellow stones. Just as, no matter how hard you squeeze sand, you will not get oil, or barren women will never have children, even knowledgeable people will not be able to attain buddhahood by means of other sutras. But even foolish people will be able to sow the seed that is the cause of buddhahood with this sutra. [As it says in the *Nirvana Sutra*,] "Such people will be able to attain liberation without seeking it."

273. I and my disciples will reach the realm of the buddhas unfailingly so long as we all hold on to unwavering faith no matter what difficulty confronts us. Do not doubt because of the lack of heavenly protection, nor lament the lack of peace and comfort in this world. This is what I have taught my disciples from morning to evening. I am afraid, however, that they might all have doubts about this and no longer listen to me. It seems only natural that ordinary people, in the face of reality, will forget what they promised. Having pity on their families, my lay followers must lament being separated from wives and children in this world. However, had they ever been truly separated from their beloved families throughout many lifetimes over innumerable kalpas? Had they ever been separated for the sake of the Buddha Way? Theirs must have been the same sad separation. We should continue upholding the *Lotus Sutra* and go to Mt. Sacred Eagle, so that we will be able to return to this world to guide the people.

274. Question: You claim that followers of Nembutsu and the Zen school will fall into the Hell of Incessant Suffering. Being so belligerent, you will therefore fall into the realm of the asuras. Moreover, it is said in the "Peaceful Practices" chapter of the *Lotus Sutra*, "[When he expounds or reads this sutra,] he should not point out the faults of other persons or sutras. He should not despise other teachers of the Dharma." Haven't you been abandoned by the gods because you have gone against this passage of the sutra?

Answer: The *Great Calming and Contemplation* says:

> There are two ways of expounding the Buddha [Dharma]: the first is embracing and the second is subduing. Such peaceful practices as not speaking of the merits or demerits of others or mentioning them by name represents the way of embracing, while such phrases in the *Nirvana Sutra* as "wielding swords or staves" or "cuts off his head" stand for the way of subduing. Even though the former is lenient and the latter is forceful, they both bring benefit.

275. The *Supplemental Amplifications on the Great Calming and Contemplation* says:

> Regarding the two ways of expounding the Buddha [Dharma] … the *Nirvana Sutra* says, "wielding swords or staves," and in the third fascicle also states, "Those who are committed to protecting the True Dharma, regardless of whether or not they themselves have accepted the five precepts or practice the regulations of deportment, [will do whatever it takes to defend those pure monks who do keep the precepts, even wielding knives and swords, bows and arrows, or halberds and lances in their defense]." Further on, the sutra tells the story of King Rishidatta, [who is said to have cut off the life force of those brahmins who slandered the Mahayana sutras]. The sutra also cites as an example, a prohibition issued by a new doctor who found that the milk remedies prescribed by his predecessors were harming the people. It says, "Those who would continue to use them should be beheaded." These are two examples of the way of subduing those who would destroy the Dharma. Nothing in all the sutras and treatises depart from these two ways [of embracing and subduing].

276. *Words and Phrases of the Lotus Sutra* says:

> Question: The *Nirvana Sutra* makes it clear that [those who wish to protect the True Dharma] should approach and entrust themselves to the king, arm themselves with bows and arrows, and break and subdue evil people. This [*Lotus Sutra*], however, says that they should keep distance from those in power, humble themselves, have loving-kindness, and be good to others. The former way is hard but the latter is soft. How can we reconcile the difference between the two?
>
> Answer: Although the *Nirvana Sutra* emphasizes the way of subduing, it also expounds the ground of practice [of bodhisattvas

who have compassion for sentient beings just as a parent would for] an only child. So, it also has the way of embracing. Although this [*Lotus Sutra*] emphasizes the way of embracing, it also says that ["Anyone who… troubles the expounder of the Dharma] shall have his head split into seven pieces." [Thus, this sutra] is not without the way of subduing. In other words, each of them emphasizes one or the other to meet the needs of the time.

277. The *Annotations on the Nirvana Sutra* says:

> Whether home-leaver or householder, those who protect the Dharma should not lose sight of the original mind that rejects the phenomenal and cherishes the principle in order to spread the Mahayana teaching. This is what it means to uphold the True Dharma. Disregarding trivial matters means not practicing the regulations of deportment. … In the past, when the world was at peace and the True Dharma could be spread, it was only necessary for them to observe the precepts and no need to carry staves. Today, however, when the world is full of danger and the Dharma is obscured, they should carry staves and not observe the precepts. If both past and present are dangerous, they should carry staves. If both past and present are at peace, they should observe the precepts. Thus, they should choose according to the needs of the time; it cannot be said to be one way or the other.

278. As for your criticisms, I am afraid that scholars today probably agree with you. Even Nichiren's own disciples cannot get rid of the same doubts as yours and act just like *icchantika* despite my repeated remonstration. So I have cited the interpretations of Tiantai and Miaole above to guard against such criticisms.

279. Now, the two ways of propagation, embracing and subduing, are as incompatible with each other as fire and water. The fire dislikes the water, and the water hates the fire. Those who prefer embracing tend to laugh at those who practice subduing and vice versa. So, when the land is full of evil and ignorant people, embracing should take precedence as expounded in the "Peaceful Practices" chapter of the *Lotus Sutra*. However, when there are many cunning slanderers of the True Dharma, subduing should take precedence as expounded in the "Never Despising Bodhisattva" chapter. It is the same as using cold water when it is hot and fire when it is cold. Plants and trees are followers of the sun, so they suffer under the cold moon. Bodies of water are followers of the moon, so they lose their original nature when it is hot. In this Latter Age of Degeneration, there should be both embracing and subduing, because there are lands of evil people as well as those of people who try to destroy the Dharma. Therefore, we have to know whether Japan today is a land of evil people or that of destroyers of the Dharma.

280. Question: Is it of any benefit to carry out the way of subduing when the time requires embracing or to carry out the way of embracing when the time requires subduing?

Answer: The *Nirvana Sutra* says:

> Kashyapa Bodhisattva addressed the Buddha, saying ... The Tathagata's Dharma-body is as indestructible as a *vajra*, but I do not know the cause. Please explain it. The Buddha said, "Kashyapa! I was able to attain this *vajra*-body because I upheld the True Dharma. Kashyapa! Due to the causality of upholding the True Dharma over the ages, I now have this *vajra*-body that is eternal and indestructible. Good man! Those who are committed to protecting the True Dharma, regardless of whether or not they themselves have accepted the five precepts or practice the regulations of deportment, [will do whatever it takes to defend those pure monks who do keep the precepts,] even wielding knives and swords, bows and arrows, [or halberds and lances in their defense.] ... But though they may be able to expound in various ways, they will be unable to make the lion's roar. ... and they will not be able to subdue evil people who violate the Dharma. Monks like this will not be able to benefit themselves or benefit other sentient beings. You should know these people are indolent and lazy. Even if they observe precepts and guard the purity of their practice, you should know, they will not be able to do anything. ... [Wherever there is a monk who can make the lion's roar, the violators of the Buddhist precepts, hearing him speak, will all become filled with hatred and try to harm that teacher of the Dharma. Even if that expounder of the Dharma's life were to end, he could be called one who observed the precepts and was able to benefit himself and benefit others.

281. [In his *Annotations on the Nirvana Sutra*], Zhang'an says, "Whichever we adopt must be decided according to what is appropriate, and therefore, we cannot always use only one." [In his *Words and Phrases of the Lotus Sutra*], Tiantai says, "It all depends on the time." For instance, we cannot harvest rice by cultivating rice paddies and sowing seeds at the end of autumn.

282. During the Kennin era (1201-1204), two people named Honen and Dainichi emerged to establish the Nembutsu school and the Zen school respectively. Honen declared that in the Latter Age of Degeneration not even one out of a thousand could attain [buddhahood] by means of the *Lotus Sutra*, whereas Dainichi maintained that there is a separate transmission outside the sutras. These two false teachings spread throughout the land. Tiantai and Mantra scholars are afraid of the Nembutsu and Zen supporters and try to cater to their whims just

like a dog wagging its tale in front of its master or mice terrified by a cat. Teaching in front of kings and generals, they themselves create the causes and conditions that will lead to the destruction of the Buddha Dharma and the country. Such Tiantai and Mantra scholars will fall into the realm of hungry ghosts in this life and the Hell of Incessant Suffering in their next life. Even if they reside in mountain forests and contemplate the three thousand realms in a single thought-moment doctrine or stay in secluded places and concentrate on the three mysteries, how can they be delivered from samsara without knowing whether the time calls for subduing or embracing?

283. Question: What benefit is there in accusing those followers of the Nembutsu and the Zen school, making enemies of them?

Answer: The *Nirvana Sutra* says:

> Suppose there is a virtuous monk who sees someone trying to destroy the Dharma, but does not try to punish or purge them. You should know that such a person is an enemy within the Buddha Dharma. If you can purge or punish them, then you will be my disciple and a true voice-hearer.

284. [In his *Annotations on the Nirvana Sutra*, Zhang'an says]:

> Those who destroy the Buddha Dharma are the enemies within the Buddha Dharma. Those heartless people who are their false friends are really their enemies. Those who correct them are Dharma protecting voice-hearers who are my true disciples. To prevent a friend from committing evil is really a friendly act. Therefore, one who is able to correct them is my disciple; and one who does not purge them is an enemy within the Buddha Dharma.

285. Why did Shakyamuni, Many Treasures, and the emanation buddhas of the ten directions gather together in the "Beholding the Stupa of Treasures" chapter of the *Lotus Sutra*? It was to "have the Dharma preserved forever." As we think of the intention of those buddhas who wished to spread the *Lotus Sutra* for the benefit of all the children of the Buddha in the future, their compassion seems greater than that of parents who see their only child faced with great suffering. Having no sympathy with them, however, Honen tightly shut the gate to the *Lotus Sutra* so that no one In the Latter Age of Degeneration could enter it. Like someone fooling an idiotic child into throwing away his treasure, he made them cast away the *Lotus Sutra*. Such a shameless thing to do, indeed!

286. Why shouldn't we warn our parents if we know that someone is trying to kill them? Shouldn't we prevent an evil drunken child from killing his parents? Shouldn't we prevent an evil man from setting temples and pagodas on fire?

Shouldn't we give our only child a moxibustion treatment when he or she has a serious illness? Those who do not discourage the followers of Zen and Nembutsu in Japan are the same as those who do nothing on such occasions. [They are what Zhang'an referred to in his *Annotations on the Nirvana Sutra* when he says,] "Those heartless people who are their false friends are really their enemies." I, Nichiren, am like a compassionate parent of everyone in Japan, whereas everyone in the Tiantai school is their worst enemy. [As Zhang'an says in his *Annotations on the Nirvana Sutra*,] "To prevent a friend from committing evil is really a friendly act."

287. Those who do not have the thought of awakening will never attain it. The Lord Teacher Shakyamuni the World Honored One was abused by all non-Buddhists teachers as an evil man. The Great Master Tiantai was spoken ill of as "a man who destroys the five-foot body [of the Buddha] with his three-inch tongue" by the three southern and seven northern schools and Tokuitsu. Great Master Dengyo was laughed at by many people in Nara, who said, "Saicho did not even see the capital of Tang China." However, these masters had nothing to be ashamed of because they were abused just for the sake of the *Lotus Sutra*. Praise by the ignorant should be regarded as most dishonorable. Perhaps the Dharma teachers of the Tiantai and Mantra schools would be happy to see Nichiren disgraced by the Kamakura shogunate, though it is pitiful and strange of them.

288. Shakyamuni the World Honored One entered the Saha world; Kumarajiva entered Qin China; Great Master Dengyo risked his life in going to China; Aryadeva and Aryasimha gave up their bodies; Medicine King burned his arms [as an offering in a past life]; Prince Shotoku peeled off the skin on his hand [to write in blood the title of the *Brahma's Net Sutra* which he copied]; when Shakyamuni was a bodhisattva in a past life, he sold his own flesh [to make an offering to a buddha]; Gladdened by Dharma used one of his own bones as a writing brush [to write down the true teaching]. As Great Master Tiantai says, [in his *Words and Phrases of the Lotus Sutra*,] we must "meet the needs of the time." Keep in mind that the Buddha Dharma must be spread according to the times. Nichiren's exile is merely a trifle in this present life, which is not lamentable at all. Instead, I feel it is a great joy as I am sure I will be rewarded with great bliss in my future lives.

Abbreviations

AKB1	*Abhidharmakośabhāṣyam* (by volume) (Vasubandhu 1988-1990)
b.	born
BCE	Before Common Era
BD	*Buddha-Dharma* (Numata Center 2003)
C	Chinese
c.	circa
CD	*Connected Discourses of the Buddha* (Bodhi 2000)
CE	Common Era
CSQI	*Clear Serenity and Quiet Insight* (Swanson 2018)
CWL	*Ch'eng Wei-Shih Lun* (Tat 1973)
d.	died
DCOT	*Demonstration of Consciousness Only Treatise* (Cook 1999)
d.u.	dates unknown
EET	*Essentials of the Eight Traditions* (Pruden 1994)
EVT	*Essentials of the Vinaya Tradition* (Pruden 1995)
fl.	flourished
FTP	*Foundations of T'ien-t'ai Philosophy* (Swanson 1989)
FOS	*Flower Ornament Scripture* (Cleary 1993)
GTFT	*Guide to the Tiantai Fourfold Teaching* (Ichishima and Chappell 2013)
J	Japanese
LB	*Life of the Buddha* (Ñāṇamoli 20001)
LD	*Long Discourses of the Buddha* (Walshe 1995)
LS	*Lotus Sutra* (Murano 2012)
MD	*Middle Length Discourses of the Buddha* (Ñāṇamoli and Bodhi 2015)
MS	*The Vairocanābhisaṃbodhi Sutra* (Giebel 2005)
ND	*Numerical Discourses of the Buddha* (Bodhi 2012)
NS1	*Nirvana Sutra Volume I* (Blum 2013)
NS	*Mahayana Mahaparinirvana Sutra* (Page and Yamamoto 2007)
P	Pali
PMLS1	*Profound Meaning of the Lotus Sutra* (by volume) (Shen 2005)
r.	reign
S	Sanskrit
SEUM	*Scripture on the Explication of the Underlying Meaning* (Keenan 2000)

Sn	*Suttanipāta* (Bodhi 2017)
TBD	*Transmission of the Buddha Dharma* (Green and Mun 2018)
Thig	*Therigatha* (Davids and Norman 1989)
TPLS	*Three Pure Land Sutras* (Inagaki and Stewart 2016)
TLS	*Threefold Lotus Sutra* (Shinozaki et al. 2019)
WNS1	*Writings of Nichiren Shonin* (by volume) (Hori 2002-2015)

Notes

Taisho text number 2689 in volume 84 accessed from the SAT Daizōkyō Text Database at:

https://21dzk.l.u-tokyo.ac.jp/SAT/satdb2015.php?lang=en

First Fascicle 208b18

1. Taisho text 2689 in volume 84, lines 208b19-208b21

The three people to be respected are designated by the ideograms: 主師親. The ideogram 主 can be translated as "lord," "ruler," or even "sovereign." The ideogram 師 can be translated as "master" or "teacher." The ideogram 親 can be translated as "parents," "relatives," or even "close friend," or "intimate." Collectively the qualities of ruler, teacher, and parent are called the **three virtues**.

The three matters to be studied are designated by the ideograms: 儒外内. The ideogram 儒 is often translated as "**Confucianism**." The ideograms 外 and 内 refer respectively to the **outer way** and the **inner way**. The outer way is understood to mean the non-Buddhist teachings, particularly those in India such as **Brahmanism** or the teachings of the **six non-Buddhist masters** who were contemporaries of Shakyamuni Buddha. The inner way refers to Buddhism.

2. Taisho text 2689 in volume 84, lines 208b21-208b28

The ideograms 皇 and 帝 can both be translated as "emperor" or "sovereign." The legendary rulers of ancient China referred to by these ideograms 三皇五帝 are often referred to in English as the "**Three Sovereigns and Five Emperors**." The ideogram 王 means "king" or "prince." The ideograms 三王 refer to the founders of the Xia, Shang (or Yin), and Zhou dynasties. In English they are referred to as the "**Three Kings**."

Zhonghua was the given name of the legendary Emperor **Shun**.

The Duke of Pei refers to Emperor Gaozu of Han (256-195 BCE), founder of the Han dynasty.

The Count of the West (J. Seihaku; 西伯) is another title for King **Wen** (1112-1050 BCE), the father of King **Wu** (d. 1043 BCE).

Ding Lan was an orphan in the Later Han dynasty who had carvings made of his parents. It is said that he divorced his wife after she pricked one of them and it began to bleed and cry. One of the sources for his story is the *The Twenty-four Filial Exemplars*, which was written in China during the Yuan dynasty (1260-1368).

3. Taisho text 2689 in volume 84, lines 208b28-208c03

Bi Gan (n.d.; 比干) is well known for his remonstration of King **Zhou** Xin, or King Zhou of Shang. The king had him executed by having his heart torn out so that the king could see if it was true that a **sage**'s heart had seven openings, though Nichiren says that he was beheaded.

See glossary for: **Hong Yan**.

4. Taisho text 2689 in volume 84, lines 208c03-208c13

Yao was the fourth of the five emperors.

Shun was the fifth of the five emperors.

Grand Duke Wang (c. 11th century BCE) is more commonly known as Jiang Ziya. He helped King **Wen** and his son King **Wu** overthrow King **Zhou Xin** and establish the Zhou dynasty.

Laozi (or Lao Tzu using the Wade-Giles transliteration) is the well-known legendary Taoist **sage**.

Confucius is the Latinized form of Kong Fuzi (551-479 BCE).

I have not been able to find any further information on Yin Shou or Wu Cheng other than what Nichiren says about them here.

In this passage the "three mysteries" (三玄) refers to a summary of the teaching of the Xuanxue (玄學) or Dark Learning movement, also called Neo-Taoism, of the Six Dynasties (222-589) period of Chinese history. The "mystery of being" was associated with the *Book of Changes* that teaches the natural laws and principles of existence or being. The *Book of Changes* is sometimes called the *Book of Zhou* because the explanations of the individual changing lines within it are attributed to the Duke of Zhou (r. 1042-1035 BCE), the brother of the aforementioned King Wu. The "mystery of non-being" was associated with the teachings of Laozi, who seemed to emphasize non-being. The "mystery of being and non-being" was associated with the teachings of Zhuangzi (c. 369-286) that were concerned with naturalness or spontaneity, rather than one-sidedly emphasizing being or non-being.

"Mystery and "darkness" are translations of the ideogram 玄, that can be translated as "dark," "deep," "mysterious," "obscure," "occult," "profound," or even "black" or "reddish-black." Nichiren is, of course, playing upon many of these different meanings.

"Primordial **life force**" is a translation of the ideograms 元氣, that can be translated as "energy of primal chaos," "original ether," "original substance," "primal force," or "vitality" or "vital energy." The ideogram 元 can be translated as "primary," "original," or "source"; while 氣 can be translated as "**spirit**" or "breath."

"Naturally" is a translation of the ideograms 自然, that can be translated as "nature," "naturally," "naturalness" or "spontaneity," and refer to things happening without any self-conscious deliberation.

5. Taisho text 2689 in volume 84, lines 208c13-209a02

Benevolence and **righteousness** are two of the **five constant virtues** of **Confucianism**.

See glossary for: **Wu** (King).

Emperor Guangwu of the Han (5 BCE - 57 CE) was the restorer of the Han dynasty in 25 CE, and therefore regarded as the founder of the Later Han dynasty.

6. Taisho text 2689 in volume 84, lines 209a02-209a09

For Confucius see note to 4.

The fourth, "Confucius," chapter of the *Liezi* has a passage wherein Confucius claims that there is a **sage** in the West. However, he does not specifically name anyone.

"**Morality**, **concentration**, and **wisdom**" (J. kai-jō-e; 戒定慧) is a reference to the **threefold training**.

See glossary for: **Buddhist scriptures**.

7. Taisho text 2689 in volume 84, lines 209a09-209a15

The citation from the ***Supplemental Amplifications on the Great Calming and Contemplation*** can found in Taisho text 1912, volume 46, lines 343c15-343c16.

The citation from the *Great Calming and Contemplation* can be found in Taisho text 1911, volume 46, lines 77b01-77b02. This passage was translated in CSQI, p. 1041.

The second citation from the *Great Calming and Contemplation* can be found in Taisho text 1911, volume 46, line 78c06. The passage was translated in CSQI, p. 1053.

The second citation from the *Supplemental Amplifications on the Great Calming and Contemplation* can found in Taisho text 1912, volume 46, lines 343c18-343c20.

See glossary for: **Kashyapa**, ***Practicing the Pure Dharma Sutra***, ***Supreme Golden Light Sutra***, **three sages** and **wholesome**.

8. Taisho text 2689 in volume 84, lines 209a15-209a29

See glossary for: **five regions of India, Great Freedom God, Kapila, Neither Perception Nor Non-Perception, ninety-five non-Buddhist schools, Rishabha, three hermits, two gods, Uluka, Vedas,** and **Vishnu**.

9. Taisho text 2689 in volume 84, lines 209a29-209b14

The theory that effects exist within their causes is attributed to the teachings of the **Samkhya** which was established by **Kapila**. The theory that effects do not exist within their causes is attributed to the teachings of the **Vaisheshika** which was established by **Uluka**. The theory that effects both do and do not exist within their causes is attributed to the teachings of the **Nirgranthas**, today more commonly called Jains, which was established by **Rishabha**.

The five fires refers to a practice whereby an ascetic sits in the midst of four bonfires, one for each of the four cardinal directions, under the heat of the noonday sun.

There are **three kinds of meditative absorption**. The first two have **outflows**. The third is **non-outflow**.

See glossary for: **five precepts, form realm, formless realm, Neither Perception Nor Non-Perception, ten virtuous precepts, three evil destinies, wholesome**.

10. Taisho text 2689 in volume 84, lines 209b14-209b21

See glossary for: **ninety-five non-Buddhist schools, samsara,** and **Shakra**.

11. Taisho text 2689 in volume 84, lines 209b21-209b26

The citation from the *Nirvana Sutra* is actually a passage from Miaole's ***Supplemental Amplifications on the Great Calming and Contemplation*** that purports to be citing the *Nirvana Sutra*, though the first half of the statement is a paraphrase. This passage can be found in Taisho text 1911, volume 46, lines 77a29-77b01. The latter half of the passage is a direct citation from the *Nirvana Sutra*, which can be found in Taisho text 374, volume 12, lines 413a01. This passage was translated in NS1, p. 254.

The citation from the *Lotus Sutra* can be found in Taisho text 262, volume 9, lines 28a19-28a20. This passage was translated in LS, p. 160 and TLS, pp. 192-193.

See glossary for: **inner way, outer way,** and **three poisons**.

12. Taisho text 2689 in volume 84, lines 209b26-209c08

The **World Honored One of Great Enlightenment** is of course Shakyamuni Buddha.

The four sages are the four Chinese sages mentioned in section 4.

See glossary for: **cause and effect, delusions of views and attitudes, fundamental ignorance, ordinary people, three categories of delusions, samsara, six destinies, three hermits, transmigration with change and advance,** and **transmigration with differences and limitations**.

13. Taisho text 2689 in volume 84, lines 209c08-209c18

The first instance of "true word" in this section is a translation of the ideograms 眞言, which can also be translated in other contexts as "mantra." The second instance uses the ideograms 實語 that mean true or reliable words but are not used to translate the word "mantra."

See glossary for: **all the holy teachings of the Buddha's lifetime** and **great man**.

14. Taisho text 2689 in volume 84, lines 209c18-210a01

The first instance of "true words" in this section is a translation of 實語, but the second instance translates 眞言, which can also mean "mantra."

The citation from the ***Infinite Meanings Sutra*** and can be found in Taisho text 276, volume 9, lines 386b01-386b02. This passage was translated in TLS, p. 16.

The first citation from the *Lotus Sutra* can be found in Taisho text 262, volume 9, line 6a23. This passage was translated in LS, p. 28 and TLS, p. 60.

The second citation from the *Lotus Sutra* can be found in Taisho text 262, volume 9, lines 32c01-32c02. This passage was translated in LS, p. 187 and TLS, p. 218.

The passage wherein the emanation-body buddhas touch the Heavens of Brahma with their long, wide tongues can be found in Taisho text 262, volume 9, lines 51c20-51c21. The passage was translated in LS, p. 298 and TLS, p. 328.

For "long, wide, tongue" see **buddha's tongue** in glossary.

See glossary for: **Brahma** (Heavens of), **esoteric Buddhism, exoteric Buddhism, provisional sutra, right view, three times, true sutra,** and **World Honored One of Great Enlightenment**.

15. Taisho text 2689 in volume 84, lines 210a01-210a08

The twenty important doctrines of the *Lotus Sutra* refer to Zhiyi's teaching in his *Profound Meaning of the Lotus Sutra* that there are twenty subtleties taught in the *Lotus Sutra*. These consist of the **ten subtleties of the Trace Gate** and the **ten subtleties of the Original Gate**. Some recensions of the *Kaimoku-shō* say that there are only two important doctrines. In such a case, it may be referring to the attainment of buddhahood by adherents of the two vehicles taught in the Trace Gate and the attainment of buddhahood in the remotest past by the **Eternal Shakyamuni Buddha** in the Original Gate.

See glossary for: **Abhidharma Treasury school, Completion of Reality school, Discipline school, Nagarjuna, Vasubandhu,** and **Zhizhe**.

16. Taisho text 2689 in volume 84, lines 210a08-210a18

It may be that what is meant by the Dharma Characteristics and Three Treatises schools only teaching that there are eight realms is that they do not account for the voice-hearers and privately-awakened ones having any pure land to be reborn into after their last existence in the human realm.

The **Abhidharma Treasury school, Completion of Reality school,** and **Discipline school** do not recognize the existence of any pure lands, and so only teach that there are the **six realms** or destinies and that arhats, privately-awakened ones, and buddhas do not appear in any realm after their last existence in the human realm.

In East Asian Buddhism, all Buddhists would consider themselves Mahayana, even if they study or practice schools that focus on pre-Mahayana teachings.

See glossary for: **four realms, mutual possession of the ten realms,** and **ten realms**.

17. Taisho text 2689 in volume 84, lines 210a18-210a22

18. Taisho text 2689 in volume 84, lines 210a22-210b01

19. Taisho text 2689 in volume 84, lines 210b01-210b04

The citation from the *Great Calming and Contemplation* can be found in Taisho text 1911, volume 46, lines 68b19-68b22. This passage was translated in CSQI, p. 946.

20. Taisho text 2689 in volume 84, lines 210b04-210b11

The citation from the ***Supplemental Amplifications on the Great Calming and Contemplation*** can be found in Taisho text 1912, volume 46, lines 324b24-324c09.

The five thousand words in two volumes teachings of Taoism refers to the *Tao Te Ching*.

See glossary for: **eighty thousand teachings**, **layman**, **twelve kinds of scriptures**, and **Wei Yuansong**.

21. Taisho text 2689 in volume 84, lines 210b11-210b16
See glossary for: **Buddhist scriptures** and **three southern and seven northern schools** and **Zhizhe**.

22. Taisho text 2689 in volume 84, lines 210b16-210b23
See glossary for: **Ci'en** (Great Master), **tripitaka master**, and **Xuanzang**.

23. Taisho text 2689 in volume 84, lines 210b23-210c02

The citation from the *Flower Garland Sutra* can be found in Taisho text 278, volume 9, line 465c26. This passage was translated in FOS, p. 452.

See glossary for: **mudra**, **provisional sutra**, **Shubhakarasimha**, **tripitaka master**, and **Vajrabodhi**.

24. Taisho text 2689 in volume 84, lines 210c02-210c16

See glossary for: **Buddhist scriptures**, **Hiei** (Mount), **Kobo** (Great Master), **six schools of Nara Buddhism**, and **Toji Temple**.

25. Taisho text 2689 in volume 84, lines 210c16-210c29

See glossary for: **Amaterasu Omikami**, **demon**, **guardian deity**, **Hachiman**, **Mountain King**, and **six schools of Nara Buddhism**.

26. Taisho text 2689 in volume 84, lines 210c29-211a05

27. Taisho text 2689 in volume 84, lines 211a05-211a13.

See glossary for: **Ananda, Beautiful Form, Dharma Brightness, Emitting Ten Million Rays of Light, Flower Light, Gladly Seen By All Beings, Jambunada Gold Light, Light, Mahakatyayana, Mahaprajapati, Maudgalyayana, Mountain Sea Wisdom Supernatural Power King, Purna, Rahula, Subhuti,**

Tamalapattracandana Fragrance, **Treasure Form**, **Universal Brightness**, **Walking on Flowers of Seven Treasures**, and **Yashodhara**.

28. Taisho text 2689 in volume 84, lines 211a13-211a26

The passage, "This is the one great purpose for which the buddhas appear in the worlds" can be found in Taisho text 262, volume 9, lines 7a23. This passage was translated in LS, p. 33 and TLS, p. 65.

The passage, "[I] have not yet fully revealed the truth," can be found in Taisho text 276, volume 9, lines 386b01-386b02. This passage was translated in TLS, p. 16.

The passage, "The World Honored Ones expound the true teaching only after a long period," can be found in Taisho text 262, volume 9, line 6a23. This passage was translated in LS, p. 28 and TLS, p. 60.

The passage, "I have laid aside all skillful means," can be found in Taisho text 262, volume 9, line 10a19. This passage was translated in LS, p. 49 and TLS, p. 81.

Many Treasures Buddha's testimony to the truth of Shakyamuni Buddha's teaching can be found in LS, pp. 186-187 and TLS, pp. 217-218.

The emanation-body buddhas stretching forth their long, wide tongues as a supernatural display to testify to the truth of Shakyamuni Buddha's teaching can be found in LS, p. 298 and TLS, p. 328.

For "long, wide tongue" see **buddha's tongue** in glossary.
See glossary for: **Flower Light**, **great man**, and **Light**.

29. Taisho text 2689 in volume 84, lines 211a26-211b02

The citation from the *Great Vaipulya Sutra of the Buddha's Flower Garland* can be found in Taisho text 279, volume 10, lines 272b07-272b09. This passage was translated in FOS, pp. 1001-1002.
See glossary for: **greed**, **unconditioned**, **wholesome root**.

30. Taisho text 2689 in volume 84, lines 211b02-211b13

According to traditional Buddhist cosmology, a **Sumeru world** rests upon three disks. The first is a disk of whirling winds, upon which rests the water disk, upon which rests a disk of gold, atop of which are the mountains, oceans, and continents of the Sumeru world.
See glossary for: **Himalayas**, **Jambudvipa**, and **yojana**.

31. Taisho text 2689 in volume 84, lines 211b13-211b17

The citation from the *Great Assembly Sutra* can be found in Taisho text 397, volume 13, lines 88a23-88a27.

See glossary for: **benefiting oneself and benefiting others, liberation**, and **rebirth**.

32. Taisho text 2689 in volume 84, lines 211b17-211b25

There is a pun at work in this paragraph, in that the ideograms for "filial" (孝), "high" (高), and "deep" (厚) are all pronounced kō in Sino-Japanese.

See glossary for: **four debts of gratitude**.

33. Taisho text 2689 in volume 84, lines 211b25-211c06

The **meditative absorption** called "flavored" (味) is one that is "**defiled**."

See glossary for: **attain enlightenment, benefiting oneself and benefiting others, delusions of views and attitudes, leaving home, liberation, non-outflow, three kinds of meditative absorption, three thousand regulations of deportment, triple world,** and **two hundred and fifty precepts**.

34. Taisho text 2689 in volume 84, lines 211c06-211c13

There are several Chinese translations of the ***Vimalakirti Sutra***. Nichiren's citations in this section are from a translation by Zhi Qian (fl. 220-252), which is Taisho number 474. The English translation by John R. McRae, is based on **Kumarajiva**'s (350-409 or 413) translation, which is Taisho number 475. The English translation by Robert A. F. Thurman is based on a Tibetan text with reference to the translations of Kumarajiva and others.

Vimalakirti's question to **Manjushri**, as well as "He answered," can be found in Taisho text, 474, volume 14, lines 529c01-529c02. An equivalent passage can be found in Taisho text, 475, volume 14, line 549a28. This passage was translated in VS, p. 134 and HTV, p. 65.

"The Dust and trouble [of the **defilement**s] are the seeds of the Tathagata," can be found in Taisho text, 474, volume 14, line 529c13. An equivalent passage can be found in Taisho text, 475, volume 14, line 549b17. This passage was translated in VS, p. 135 and HTV, p. 66. In the Tibetan version and **Kumarajiva**'s translation, this statement was made by Mahakashyapa.

"Even those who have committed the **five heinous transgressions** can generate the thought of awakening," can be found in Taisho text 474, volume 14, lines 529c18-529c19. An equivalent passage can be found in Taisho text, 475, volume 14, line 549b19. This passage was translated in VS, p. 135 and HTV, p. 66.

"For example, Good men, just as the beautiful and fragrant, blue lotus flowers bloom in a muddy field and do not bloom on a dry plateau, [those who have entered the **unconditioned** will not be able to generate the qualities of a buddha]," can be found in Taisho text, 474, volume 14, lines 529c08-529c10. An equivalent passage can be found in Taisho text, 475, volume 14, line 549b06-549b08. This passage was translated in VS, p. 135 and HTV, p. 66.

"Those who have already attained arhatship are unable to generate the thought of awakening and attain the Buddha Dharma. It is just like those who have damaged their sense faculties, and cannot enjoy the five [sensual] pleasures," can be found in Taisho text, 474, volume 14, lines 529c19-529c21. An equivalent passage can be found in Taisho text, 475, volume 14, line 549b20-549b21. This passage was translated in VS, p. 135 and HTV, p. 66.

The six sense faculties are the faculties of the eye, ear, nose, tongue, body, and **mind**. The five sensual pleasures are desirable forms, sounds, odors, tastes, and tangible objects.

35. Taisho text 2689 in volume 84, lines 211c13-211c24

See glossary for: **five heinous transgressions**, **killing one's father**, **seed of buddhahood**, **three poisons**, and *Vimalakirti Sutra*.

36. Taisho text 2689 in volume 84, lines 211c24-211c29

The citation from the *Great Expanded Dharani Sutra* is a paraphrase from Taisho text 1339, volume 21, lines 649c13-649c20.

See glossary for: **Manjushri and scorched seeds**.

37. Taisho text 2689 in volume 84, lines 211c29-212a03

See glossary for: **scorched seeds** and **seed of buddhahood**.

38. Taisho text 2689 in volume 84, lines 212a03-212a06

The citation from the *Larger Prajna Sutra* is a paraphrase from Taisho text 223, volume 8, lines 273b28-273c02.

See glossary for: **samsara**.

39. Taisho text 2689 in volume 84, lines 212a06-212a08.

40. Taisho text 2689 in volume 84, lines 212a08-212a11

The citation from the *Shuramgama Sutra* can be found in Taisho text 1863, volume 45, lines 443c19-443c21, which is not the *Shuramgama Sutra* but a treatise by Hui Zhao (651-714).

See glossary for: **five heinous transgressions, outflow, samadhi, unsurpassed complete and perfect awakening**

41. Taisho text 2689 in volume 84, lines 212a11-212a13

The citation from Kumarajiva's translation of the *Vimalakirti Sutra* can be found in Taisho text 475, volume 14, lines 540c07-540c08. This passage was translated in VS, p. 89; HTV, p. 27.

See glossary for: **three evil destinies**.

42. Taisho text 2689 in volume 84, lines 212a13-212a20

See glossary for: **three evil destinies**.

43. Taisho text 2689 in volume 84, lines 212a20-212b07

See glossary for: **asura, five regions of India, form realm, formless realm, four continents, Saha world, six heavens of the desire realm,** and **triple world**.

44. Taisho text 2689 in volume 84, lines 212b07-212b17

See glossary for: **Buddha's dispensation** and **heavenly devil**.

45. Taisho text 2689 in volume 84, lines 212b17-212c03

See glossary for: **seven treasures, Treasure Purity,** and **yojana**.

46. Taisho text 2689 in volume 84, lines 212c03-212c13

The first *Lotus Sutra* citation can be found in Taisho text 262, volume 9, lines 32b27-32c02. This passage was translated in LS, pp. 186-187 and TLS, pp. 217-218.

The second *Lotus Sutra* citation can be found in Taisho text 262, volume 9, lines 51c21. This passage was translated in LS, p. 298 and TLS, p. 328.

The third *Lotus Sutra* citation can be found in Taisho text 262, volume 9, lines 52c26-52c28. This passage was translated in LS, p. 304 and TLS, p. 334.

Supernatural powers refers to the **six supernatural powers**.

For "long, wide tongue" see **buddha's tongue** in glossary.

See glossary for: **asura, Brahma (Heavens of), emanation buddhas of the ten directions, gandharva, garuda, kimnara, layman, laywoman, mahasattva, mahoraga, Manjushri, Saha world,** and **yaksha**.

47. Taisho text 2689 in volume 84, lines 212c13-212c24

For "long, wide tongue" see **buddha's tongue** in glossary.

See glossary for: ***Amitayus Buddha Sutra***, ***Great Assembly Sutra***, **Great Treasure Chamber**, ***Supreme Golden Light Sutra***, **trichiliocosm** and **World Honored One of Great Enlightenment**.

48. Taisho text 2689 in volume 84, lines 212c24-212c29

See glossary for: ***Amitayus Buddha Sutra***, ***Great Assembly Sutra***, ***Larger Prajna Sutra***, and ***Supreme Golden Light Sutra***.

49. Taisho text 2689 in volume 84, lines 212c29-213a09

For "long, wide tongue" see **buddha's tongue** in glossary.

See glossary for: **trichiliocosm**.

50. Taisho text 2689 in volume 84, lines 213a09-213a15

"Isn't he **Mara** in the form of a Buddha?" can be found in Taisho text 262, volume 9, line 11a21. This passage was translated in LS, p. 55 and TLS, p. 87.

51. Taisho text 2689 in volume 84, lines 213a15-213a29

See glossary for: ***Amitayus Buddha Sutra*** and **Buddha's dispensation**.

52. Taisho text 2689 in volume 84, lines 213a29-213b07

The citation from the *Lotus Sutra* can be found in Taisho text 262, volume 9, lines 34a18-34a23. This passage was translated in LS, pp. 195-196 and TLS, p. 226.

See glossary for: **buddha-land** and **Sumeru** (Mount).

53. Taisho text 2689 in volume 84, lines 213b07-213b12

The citation from the *Nirvana Sutra* is a paraphrase. The original passage can be found in Taisho text 374, volume 12, lines 563a24-563b09. This passage was translated in NS, p. 475.

See glossary for: **bit of soil on a fingernail**.

54. Taisho text 2689 in volume 84, lines 213b12-213b19

55. Taisho text 2689 in volume 84, lines 213b19-213b28

According to the ***Great Perfection of Wisdom Treatise***, attributed to **Nagarjuna** (but possibly written by its ostensible translator **Kumarajiva**), **Siddhartha** left home at the age of nineteen, spent twelve years practicing asceticism, and attained buddhahood at the age of thirty. In the East Asian way of counting, the actual day of one's birth is counted as the first year, and the day of beginning something is counted as the first. This should be understood to mean that Siddhartha left home at eighteen, practiced asceticism for eleven years, and attained buddhahood at the age of twenty-nine. Other traditions say that he left home at twenty-nine and attained buddhahood at age thirty-five after six years of practice.

See glossary for: **interim kalpa, kalpa of abiding, Lotus Treasury World, perfect interfusion, Peaceful Place of Awakening, Shuddhodana, Simhahanu, six characteristics, ten profound gates,** and **True Recompense** (Land of).

56. Taisho text 2689 in volume 84, lines 213b28-213c08

The first citation from the *Flower Garland Sutra* is actually from the **Annotations on the Flower Garland Sutra**. It can be found in Taisho text 1735, volume 35, lines 509c28-509c29.

The second citation from the *Flower Garland Sutra* can be found in Taisho text 278, volume 9, line 465c29. This passage was translated in FOS, p. 452.

See glossary for: **wish-fulfilling gem**.

57. Taisho text 2689 in volume 84, lines 213c08-213c13

See glossary for: **attainment of awakening for the first time** and **Bodhi tree**.

58. Taisho text 2689 in volume 84, lines 213c13-213c21

The phrase "attained enlightenment for the first time" from the Agama sutras can be found in several places, but one example can be found in Taisho text 1, volume 1, lines 16a09-16a10. This passage was translated in LD, p. 92 as "when the Buddha, after his realization of the path…"

The citation from the ***Great Assembly Sutra*** is actually from the ***Elucidation of the Profound Meaning of the Lotus Sutra***. It can be found in Taisho text 1717, volume 33, line 959a21.

The citation from the ***Vimalakirti Sutra*** is actually from the *Great Calming and Contemplation*. It can be found in Taisho text 1911, volume 46, lines 2b23-2b24. This passage was translated in CSQI, p. 110.

The citation from the *Mahavairochana Sutra* is found in other sutras but attributed to the *Mahavairochana Sutra* in later commentaries. One example can be found in Taisho text 2372, volume 74, lines 422c06-422c07.

The citation from the ***Benevolent Kings Sutra*** can be found in Taisho text 245, volume 8, line 825b21.

See glossary for: **Bodhi tree** and **Mara**.

59. Taisho text 2689 in volume 84, lines 213c21-214a01

The first citation from the ***Infinite Meanings Sutra*** can be found in Taisho text 276, volume 9, line 386b02. This passage was translated in TLS, p. 16.

The second citation from the ***Infinite Meanings Sutra*** can be found in Taisho text 276, volume 9, line 386b26. This passage was translated in TLS, p. 18.

The third citation from the ***Infinite Meanings Sutra*** can be found in Taisho text 276, volume 9, lines 386a26-386a28. This passage was translated in TLS, p. 16.

See glossary for: **attainment of awakening for the first time**, **Bodhi tree**, **Dharma-realm**, **mind-only**, **mutual identification**, **Ocean Seal Samadhi**, **provisional sutra**, and **unsurpassed complete and perfect awakening**.

60. Taisho text 2689 in volume 84, lines 214a01-214a07

The first citation from the *Lotus Sutra* can be found in Taisho text 262, volume 9, lines 5c10-5c11. This passage was translated in LS, p. 25 and TLS, p. 58.

The second citation from the *Lotus Sutra* can be found in Taisho text 262, volume 9, line 6a23. This passage was translated in LS, p. 28 and TLS, p. 60.

The third citation from the *Lotus Sutra* can be found in Taisho text 262, volume 9, line 10a19. This passage was translated in LS, p. 49 and TLS, p. 81.

The eight chapters of the Trace Gate refers to the teaching of the One Vehicle by Shakyamuni Buddha in chapters two through nine of the *Lotus Sutra*.

The fourth citation from the *Lotus Sutra* can be found in Taisho text 262, volume 9, line 32c02. This passage was translated in LS, p. 187 and TLS, p. 218.

The fifth citation from the *Lotus Sutra* can be found in Taisho text 262, volume 9, line 9c04. This passage was translated in LS, p. 46 and TLS, p. 79.

See glossary for: **concise opening of the three vehicles to reveal the One Vehicle**, **expanded opening of the three vehicles to reveal the One Vehicle**, and **true reality of all things**.

61. Taisho text 2689 in volume 84, lines 214a07-214a13

The citations from the *Lotus Sutra* can be found in Taisho text 262, volume 9, line 41b25 and 41c04-41c07. These passages were translated in LS, pp. 242-243 and TLS, pp. 271-272.

See glossary for: **"Appearance of Bodhisattvas from Underground"** (The, chapter), **Bodhgaya**, **Shakya**, and **unsurpassed complete and perfect awakening**.

62. Taisho text 2689 in volume 84, lines 214a13-214a20

The citations from the *Lotus Sutra* can be found in Taisho text 262, volume 9, lines 42b09-42b13. These passages were translated in LS, p. 247 and TLS, p. 276.

See glossary for: *asamkhya*, asura, Bodhgaya, *nayuta*, Shakya, and **unsurpassed complete and perfect awakening**.

63. Taisho text 2689 in volume 84, lines 214a20-214a27

The "open the provisional" (開權) is part of the phrase "**opening of the provisional to reveal the true.**"

See glossary for: **all the sutras**.

64. Taisho text 2689 in volume 84, lines 214a27-214b04

See glossary for: "**Expedients**" (chapter) and **outgrowing the traces and revealing the origin**.

65. Taisho text 2689 in volume 84, lines 214b04-214b11

See glossary for: **attainment of awakening for the first time, cause and effect, four doctrinal teachings, mutual possession of the ten realms, one hundred realms and one thousand aspects, original cause and original effect, ten realms,** and **Bodhi tree**.

66. Taisho text 2689 in volume 84, lines 214b11-214b20

The citation from the *Profound Meaning of the Lotus Sutra* can be found in Taisho text 1716, volume 33, line 766b19.

See glossary for: ***Amitayus Buddha Sutra***, and ***Supreme Golden Light Sutra***.

67. Taisho text 2689 in volume 84, lines 214b20-214b26

See glossary for: "**Appearance of Bodhisattvas from Underground**" (The, chapter), **attainment of awakening for the first time**, and **Bodhi tree**.

68. Taisho text 2689 in volume 84, lines 214b26-214c02

See glossary for: **accommodative-body**, "**Appearance of Bodhisattvas from Underground**" (The, chapter), **Dharma-body, reward-body,** and **sal tree**.

69. Taisho text 2689 in volume 84, lines 214c02-214c15

Shiladitya is the name of an Indian king and patron of Buddhism who is mentioned in **Xuanzang**'s *Record of the Western Regions of the Great Tang*. Shiladitya may have been Emperor Harsha (c. 590–647) of the Pushyabhuti dynasty in northern India.

Emperor Taizong of Tang (598-649) was the second emperor of the Tang dynasty.

See glossary for: **all the holy teachings of the Buddha's lifetime**, **Asanga**, **Daci'ensi Temple**, **Dharmapala**, **five regions of India**, **Jiashang**, **Kuiji**, **Nanda**, **Puguang**, **Shenfang**, **Shilabhadra**, **treatise master**, **tripitaka master**, **Vasubandhu**, and **Xuanzang**.

70. Taisho text 2689 in volume 84, lines 214c15-215a06

Emperor Shōmu (701-756) was, as Nichiren says, the forty-fifth emperor of Japan.

See glossary for: **Asanga**, **Ci'en** (Great Master), **determined nature**, **Doji**, **Dosho**, **tripitaka master**, **without the nature**, **Vasubandhu**, **Xuanzang**, and **Yamashina-dera Temple**.

71. Taisho text 2689 in volume 84, lines 215a06-215a22

The citation from the *Flower Garland Sutra* can be found in Taisho text 1736, volume 36, lines 699b10-699b11.

The citation from the *Mahavairochana Sutra* can be found in Taisho text, 848, volume 18, line 22b29. This passage was translated in MS, p. 94.

Silla and Baekje were kingdoms in the southern part of the Korean peninsula from the first to the sixth century. In the north was the kingdom of Goguryeo (later called Goryeo). They were unified as one kingdom by Silla in 668.

See glossary for: **Amoghavajra**, **Dushun**, **Fazang**, **Shubhakarasimha**, **Vajrabodhi**, and **Zhiyan**.

72. Taisho text 2689 in volume 84, lines 215a22-215a27

See glossary for: **treatise master**.

73. Taisho text 2689 in volume 84, lines 215a27-215b09

See glossary for: **dull capacity**, **Madhava**, **provisional teaching**, **true teaching**, **Vaipulya**, **Vatsiputra**, and **Vimalamitra**.

74. Taisho text 2689 in volume 84, lines 215b09-215b12

The citation from the *Nirvana Sutra* is a paraphrase. The original passage can be found in Taisho text 374, volume 12, lines 563a24-563b09. This passage was translated in NS, p. 475.

See glossary for: **bit of soil on a fingernail**.

75. Taisho text 2689 in volume 84, lines 215b12-215b18

The citation from the ***Decline of the Dharma Sutra*** is not in the Taisho.

See glossary for: **bit of soil on a fingernail**,

76. Taisho text 2689 in volume 84, lines 215b18-215b29

See glossary for: **establishing a connection to Great Universal Wisdom Excellence Buddha**, **five hundred dust-particle kalpas**, **non-retrogression**, **ordinary stage**, **ordinary stage of the inner level**, **ordinary stage of the outer level**, **samsara**, **seed of buddhahood**, and **six destinies**

77. Taisho text 2689 in volume 84, lines 215b29-215c09

The citation "too exquisitely profound…" and "there has never been anyone…" are citations from the *Collection of Passages On the Land of Peace and Bliss* that can be found in Taisho text 1958, volume, 47, lines 13c08 and 13c09 respectively.

The citation "not even one…" is a citation from *Verses Praising Rebirth in the Pure Land* that can be found in Taisho text 1980, volume 47, line 439c02.

See glossary for: **capacity**, **Daochuo**, **devil**, **provisional sutra**, **Shandao**, and **true sutra**.

78. Taisho text 2689 in volume 84, lines 215c09-215c17

See glossary for: **Incessant Suffering** and **three obstacles and four devils**.

79. Taisho text 2689 in volume 84, lines 215c17-215c26

See glossary for: **awakening mind**, **"Beholding the Stupa of Treasures" chapter**, **six difficult and nine easier actions**, and **Sumeru** (Mount).

80. Taisho text 2689 in volume 84, lines 215c26-216a04

The four severe persecutions of Nichiren were the **Matsubagayatsu Persecution**, the **Izu Exile**, the **Komatsubara Persecution**, and the **Tatsunokuchi Persecution**.

81. Taisho text 2689 in volume 84, lines 216a04-216a11

The citation from the fourth fascicle of the *Lotus Sutra* can be found in Taisho text 262, volume 9, lines 31b20-31b21. This passage was translated in LS, p. 180 and TLS, p. 212.

The citation from the second fascicle of the *Lotus Sutra* can be found in Taisho text 262, volume 9, lines 15b26-15b27. This passage was translated in LS, p. 83 and TLS, p. 114.

The first citation from the fifth fascicle of the *Lotus Sutra* can be found in Taisho text 262, volume 9, line 39a14. This passage was translated in LS, p. 228 and TLS, p. 256.

The second citation from the fifth fascicle of the *Lotus Sutra* can be found in Taisho text 262, volume 9, line 36b23. This passage was translated in LS, p. 212 and TLS, p. 241.

The third citation from the fifth fascicle of the *Lotus Sutra* can be found in Taisho text 262, volume 9, lines 36c08-36c10. This passage was translated in LS, p. 213 and TLS, p. 242.

The fourth citation from the fifth fascicle of the *Lotus Sutra* can be found in Taisho text 262, volume 9, line 36c22. This passage was translated in LS, p. 214 and TLS, p. 243.

The citation from the seventh fascicle of the *Lotus Sutra* can be found in Taisho text 262, volume 9, lines 50c28-50c29. This passage was translated in LS, p. 293 and TLS, p. 323.

82. Taisho text 2689 in volume 84, lines 216a11-216a16

The citation from the *Nirvana Sutra* can be found in Taisho text 374, volume 12, lines 591c17-591c18, 592a13-592a14, and 592a18-592a20. The passage was translated in NS, p. 550.

See glossary for: **Ajatashatru**, **Gautama**, **Magadha**, **Maudgalyayana**, and **shramana**.

83. Taisho text 2689 in volume 84, lines 216a16-216a18

The citation from the *Words and Phrases of the Lotus Sutra* can be found in Taisho text 1718, volume 34, line 110b12.

The citation from the ***Notations on the Words and Phrases of the Lotus Sutra*** can be found in Taisho text 1719, volume 34, lines 306c08-306c09.

84. Taisho text 2689 in volume 84, lines 216a18-216a21

For "face-covering tongue" see **buddha's tongue** in glossary.
See glossary for: **Tokuitsu** and **three southern and seven northern schools**.

85. Taisho text 2689 in volume 84, lines 216a21-216a28

The citation from the ***Dongchun*** is not in the Taisho.

See glossary for: **five vehicles**, **demon**, and **heavenly devil**.

86. Taisho text 2689 in volume 84, lines 216a29-216b03

The citation from the ***Clarification of the Precepts Treatise*** can be found in Taisho text, 2376, volume 74, lines 623a29623b02 and 623b04-623b05.

See glossary for: **archbishop, Bodhidharma, Demonic Eloquence, Huiguang, shramana**, and **six schools of Nara Buddhism**.

87. Taisho text 2689 in volume 84, lines 216b03-216b06

The citation from the *Outstanding Principles of the Lotus Sutra* is not in the Taisho.

See glossary for: **five degenerations**.

88. Taisho text 2689 in volume 84, lines 216b06-216b11

"Moxa treatment" refers to the practice of moxibustion used in traditional Chinese medicine, wherein dried mugwort is burned at certain key meridian points on a patient's body.

89. Taisho text 2689 in volume 84, lines 216b11-216b18

Emperor Kanmu (735-806) and Emperor Saga (786-842) were the fiftieth and fifty-second emperors of Japan.

See glossary for: **seven major temples in Nara**.

90. Taisho text 2689 in volume 84, lines 216b18-216b22

91. Taisho text 2689 in volume 84, lines 216b22-216c01

See glossary for: **all heavenly benevolent deities**.

92. Taisho text 2689 in volume 84, lines 216c01-216c10

The citation from the *Lotus Sutra* can be found in Taisho text 262, volume 9, lines 36b23 and 32a24. The passage was translated in LS, p. 212 and TLS, p. 241.

See glossary for: **"Encouragement for Keeping this Sutra" chapter**, *koti*, and *nayuta*.

93. Taisho text 2689 in volume 84, lines 216c10-216c14

The citations from the *Lotus Sutra* can be found in Taisho text 262, volume 9, lines 36b25 and 36b29-36a30. The passages were translated in LS, pp. 212 - 213 and TLS, p. 241.

See glossary for: **Discipline school** and **six supernatural powers**.

94. Taisho text 2689 in volume 84, lines 216c14-216c16

The citation from the *Lotus Sutra* can be found in Taisho text 262, volume 9, lines 36c07-36c08. The passage was translated in LS, p. 213 and TLS, p. 242.

95. Taisho text 2689 in volume 84, lines 216c16-216c22

The citations from the *Lotus Sutra* can be found in Taisho text 262, volume 9, lines 36c22 and 36b22. The passages were translated in LS, pp. 213 and 212 and TLS, pp. 243 and 241.

The two ideograms are 數數. When 數 is doubled like this it can be translated as "from time to time."

96. Taisho text 2689 in volume 84, lines 216c22-216c28

The citations in this passage are not in the Taisho.

Ashoka the Great (c. 304-232 BCE) was the famed emperor of the Maurya dynasty in India who became a convert and patron of Buddhism.

See glossary for: **Great Compassion Sutra**, **Madhyantika**, **Maya Sutra**, **Nagarjuna**, and **Transmission of the Dharma Treasury Sutra**.

97. Taisho text 2689 in volume 84, lines 216c28-217a01

The phrase "dreadful, evil world" from the *Lotus Sutra* can be found in Taisho text 262, volume 9, line 36b22. The passage was translated in LS, p. 212 and TLS, p. 241.

The phrase "the future Latter Age" from the *Flowering of the True Dharma Sutra* can be found in Taisho text 263, volume 9, line 106c27.

The other phrases can be found in various places throughout the *Lotus Sutra*.

See glossary for: **fifth five-hundred-year period** and ***Flowering of the True Dharma Sutra***.

98. Taisho text 2689 in volume 84, lines 217a01-217a06

See glossary for: **Discipline school, seven major temples in Nara**, and **three southern and seven northern schools**.

99. Taisho text 2689 in volume 84, lines 217a06-217a15

See glossary for: **karma**.

100. Taisho text 2689 in volume 84, lines 217a15-217a24

101. Taisho text 2689 in volume 84, lines 217a24-217b01

There is no additional information about Wang Shou (J. Ō Ju; 王寿).
See glossary for: **Hong Yan** and **Jizha**.

102. Taisho text 2689 in volume 84, lines 217b01-217b04

See glossary for: **delusions of views and attitudes, Shakra, three thousand regulations of deportment, triple world,** and **two hundred and fifty precepts.**

103. Taisho text 2689 in volume 84, lines 217b04-217b12

See glossary for: **eight phases of a buddha's life** and **scorched seeds.**

104. Taisho text 2689 in volume 84, lines 217b12-217b15

Mao Bao (J. Mō Hō; 毛宝) was a general during the Jin dynasty (266-420) in China who once bought a white turtle from a fisherman so that he could release it back into the Yangzi River. Two decades later, Mao Bao was trapped on the shore of the Yangzi by enemy forces. The turtle he had once rescued showed its gratitude by letting him ride on its back to safety on the other shore.

See glossary for: **animal.**

105. Taisho text 2689 in volume 84, lines 217b15-217b20

See glossary for: **Ananda, Dronodana, Mountain Sea Wisdom Supernatural Power King, Rahula, Shuddhodana,** and **Walking on Flowers of Seven Treasures.**

106. Taisho text 2689 in volume 84, lines 217b20-217b28

See glossary for: **Jie** and **Zhou Xin.**

107. Taisho text 2689 in volume 84, lines 217b28-217c09

See glossary for: **focus of devotion.**

108. Taisho text 2689 in volume 84, lines 217c09-217c23

I have not been able to locate any definitive information about the legendary *hakyō* beast.

See glossary for: **buddha eye, dharma eye, divine eye, physical eye, Saha world,** and **wisdom eye.**

109. Taisho text 2689 in volume 84, lines 217c23-218a03

The four great **voice-hearer**s are: **Subhuti, Mahakatyayana, Mahakashyapa,** and **Maudgalyayana.**

The citation from the *Lotus Sutra* can be found in Taisho text 262, volume 9, lines 18c20-19a02. The passage was translated in LS, pp. 105-106 and TLS, pp. 136-137.

See glossary for: **Mara.**

110. Taisho text 2689 in volume 84, lines 218a03-218a14

The lament of **Mahakashyapa** is from the *Vimalakirti Sutra*. The passage can be found in Taisho text 475 volume 14, lines 547a09-547a10. It was translated in VS, p. 121 and HTV, p. 54.

Subhuti dropping his alms bowl is from the *Vimalakirti Sutra*. The passage can be found in Taisho text 475 volume 14, line 540c13. It was translated in VS, p. 89 and HTV, p. 28.

Shariputra spitting out his food is from the *Great Perfection of Wisdom Treatise*, but I have not been able to locate the passage.

Purna's scolding is from the *Vimalakirti Sutra*. The passage can be found in Taisho text 475 volume 14, line 540c27. It was translated in VS, p. 90 and HTV, p. 28.

See glossary for: **alms bowl, Deer Park, first four of the five flavors, three evil destinies, trichiliocosm, two hundred and fifty precepts,** and **Vimalakirti**.

111. Taisho text 2689 in volume 84, lines 218a14-218a24

According to some stories, Devadatta was said to have competed for **Yashodhara**'s hand in marriage but lost to his cousin **Siddhartha**.

See glossary for: **Ananda, Dronodana, Gautama,** and **great man**.

112. Taisho text 2689 in volume 84, lines 218a24-218b11

See glossary for: **Agnidatta, Ajatashatru, alms bowl, Chinchamanavika, five regions of India, four oceans,** and **nine great difficulties**.

113. Taisho text 2689 in volume 84, lines 218b11-218b15

See glossary for: **Kalodayin, Maudgalyayana, Shakya, Shravasti, Utpalavarna,** and **Virudhaka**.

114. Taisho text 2689 in volume 84, lines 218b15-218b28

The slander of Shakyamuni Buddha by the **six non-Buddhist masters** is based on a passage from the *Nirvana Sutra* that can be found in Taisho text 374, volume 12, lines 591c17-592a20. The passage was translated in NS, p. 550.

See glossary for: **Ajatashatru, Gautama, Maudgalyayana, Prasenajit, seven disasters, Subhuti,** and **three calamities**.

115. Taisho text 2689 in volume 84, lines 218b29-218c04

116. Taisho text 2689 in volume 84, lines 218c04-218c06

The citation from the *Vimalakirti Sutra* can be found in Taisho text 475 volume 14, lines 540c08-540c09. The passage was translated in VS, p. 89 and HTV, p. 27.

See glossary for: **field of merit, seed of buddhahood**, and **three evil destinies**.

117. Taisho text 2689 in volume 84, lines 218c06-218c17

See glossary for: **Amrapali Grove, earth** (goddess of the), **four heavenly kings, moon** (god of the), **Shakra, Subhuti, sun** (god of the), **three evil destinies**, and **triple world**.

118. Taisho text 2689 in volume 84, lines 218c17-218c21

See glossary for: **hungry ghost**.

119. Taisho text 2689 in volume 84, lines 218c21-219a03

The citation from the *Infinite Meanings Sutra* is actually from a preface to its translation that can be found at Taisho text 276. volume 9, line 383b27. The passage in the sutra that corresponds most closely to it can be found in lines 386b01-386b02. The passage was translated in TLS, p. 16.

The citation from the *Lotus Sutra* can be found in Taisho text 262, volume 9, line 6a23. The passage was translated in LS, p. 28 and TLS, p. 60.

See glossary for: **Flower Light Tathagata** and **Light Tathagata**.

120. Taisho text 2689 in volume 84, lines 219a03-219a10

See glossary for: **fifth five-hundred-year period** and **samadhi**.

121. Taisho text 2689 in volume 84, lines 219a10-219a21

The phrase "widely propagated" comes from a passage in the *Lotus Sutra* that can be found in Taisho text 262, volume 9, line 54c22. The passage was translated in LS, p. 313 and TLS, p. 344.
See glossary for: **abandon close set aside and cast away, defiled, separate transmission outside the sutras**, and **Sumeru** (Mount).

122. Taisho text 2689 in volume 84, lines 219a21-219a26

123. Taisho text 2689 in volume 84, lines 219a26-219b11

See glossary for: **attainment of awakening for the first time, Bodhi tree, bodhisattva practice, buddha-land, Chief Wise, Dharma Wisdom, Diamond Banner, Diamond Repository, liberation, Merit Forest, Moon of Liberation, ten abodes, ten dimensions of merit transference, ten grounds**, and **ten kinds of practice**.

124. Taisho text 2689 in volume 84, lines 219b11-219b29

See glossary for: **Dharma Wisdom, distinct teaching, good friend, shared teaching,** and **tripitaka teaching.**

125. Taisho text 2689 in volume 84, lines 219b29-219c10

See glossary for: **emptiness, impermanence, ninety-five non-Buddhist schools, non-self, phenomena, three hermits,** and **two gods.**

126. Taisho text 2689 in volume 84, lines 219c10-219c13

The phrase "did not expound even a single word," appears in several places in the *Larger Prajna Sutra* and is also cited in the *Great Perfection of Wisdom Treatise.*

See glossary for: **Dharma Wisdom, first four of the five flavors,** and **Manjushri**.

127. Taisho text 2689 in volume 84, lines 219c13-219c23

The citation from the *Infinite Meanings Sutra* refers to Taisho text 276. volume 9, lines 386b01-386b02, though the latter half of the citation more closely matches a preface to the sutra that can be found at Taisho text 276. volume 9, line 383b27. The passage was translated in TLS, p. 16.

See glossary for: **Magadha**.

128. Taisho text 2689 in volume 84, lines 219c23-220a06

The citation from the *Lotus Sutra* can be found in Taisho text 262, volume 9, lines 6c03-6c06. The passage was translated in LS, p. 30 and TLS, p. 63.

See glossary for: **concise opening of the three vehicles to reveal the One Vehicle, "Expedients"** (chapter), **four flavors and three teachings,** and **wheel-turning noble king.**

129. Taisho text 2689 in volume 84, lines 220a06-220a13

I have not been able to locate the citation from the *Nirvana Sutra* in the Taisho.

I have not been able to locate the citation from the *Profound Meaning of the Four Mahayana Treatises* in the Taisho.

I have not been able to locate **Jizang**'s comment in the Taisho.

I have not been able to locate the citation from the *Profound Meaning of the Lotus Sutra* in the Taisho.

I have not been able to locate the citation from the *Great Perfection of Wisdom Treatise* in the Taisho.

See glossary for: **Dharma Cloud Unhindered King**, **Nagarjuna**, **twenty-three successors**, and **ten grounds**.

130. Taisho text 2689 in volume 84, lines 220a13-220a20

The *shindoku* version of the mantra is given. A closer English transliteration of the Sanskrit would be:

> *namah samyak sambuddhanam*
> *om a am ah*
> *sarvabuddha jna caksurbhyam*
> *gagana samsva raksani*
> *saddharma-pundarika-sutram*
> *jah hum bam ho vajra raksaman*
> *hum svaha*

A possible translation of this would be:

> Devotion to the universally pervading three-bodied Buddha. When the insight of the buddhas is opened, shown, obtained, and entered, like the crisp-clear sky, one will be delivered from all dust of delusion, accept the teaching of the *Saddharma-pundarika-sutra* and live with joy, firmly upholding the teaching.

See glossary for: **Myoho Renge Kyo**, **Shubhakarasimha**, and **tripitaka master**.

131. Taisho text 2689 in volume 84, lines 220a20-220a26

The two ideograms used to transliterate the Sanskrit word *namas* are 南無, which is pronounced "**Namu**" in the Japanese *shindoku* reading.

The ideograms for "Devotion to the Sutra of the Lotus Flower of the Wonderful Dharma," 南無妙法蓮華経, are pronounced "**Namu Myoho Renge Kyo**" in the Japanese *shindoku* reading.

See glossary for: *Flowering of the True Dharma Sutra*.

132. Taisho text 2689 in volume 84, lines 220a26-220b05

The ideogram for "**wonderful**" is 妙.

The compound for "perfect" is composed of the following ideograms: 具足.

The citation from the *Supplemental Amplifications on the Great Calming and Contemplation* can be found in Taisho text 1912, volume 46, line 289c12.

See glossary for: **eighty minor marks**, **six perfections**, **ten realms**, **fruition**, and **thirty-two marks**.

133. Taisho text 2689 in volume 84, lines 220b05-220b09

The citation from the *Lotus Sutra* can be found in Taisho text 262, volume 9, line 7a24. The passage was translated in LS, p. 33 and TLS, p. 65.

The second citation from the *Lotus Sutra* can be found in Taisho text 262, volume 9, lines 8b04-8b06. The passage was translated in LS, p. 38 and TLS, pp. 71-72.

See glossary for: **"Expedients"** (chapter).

134. Taisho text 2689 in volume 84, lines 220b09-220b18

The citation from the *Lotus Sutra* can be found in Taisho text 262, volume 9, lines 12a22-12a23. The passage was translated in LS, p. 60 and TLS, pp. 92-93.

The citation from the *Essay on the Protection of the Nation* can be found in Taisho text 2362, volume 74, lines 241c14-241c16.

See glossary for: **One Buddha Vehicle** and ***Revealing the Profound Secrets Sutra***.

Second Fascicle 220b21

135. Taisho text 2689 in volume 84, lines 220b22-220c01

The citation from the *Lotus Sutra* can be found in Taisho text 262, volume 9, lines 34a04-34a05. The passage was translated in LS, p. 194 and TLS, pp. 225.

See glossary for: **"Beholding the Stupa of Treasures" chapter**, **four heavenly kings**, **kusha grass**, **moon** (god of the), **Shakra**, and **sun** (god of the).

136. Taisho text 2689 in volume 84, lines 220c01-220c08

137. Taisho text 2689 in volume 84, lines 220c08-220c12

See glossary for: **Dharma Wisdom**, **Lotus Treasury World**, and **reward-body**.

138. Taisho text 2689 in volume 84, lines 220c12-220c20

See glossary for: ***Amitayus Buddha Sutra, Diamond Peak Sutra, Great Assembly Sutra, Larger Prajna Sutra, Supreme Golden Light Sutra***, **three bodies**, and **transformation-body**.

139. Taisho text 2689 in volume 84, lines 220c20-220c28

The citation from the *Profound Meaning of the Lotus Sutra* can be found in Taisho text 1716, volume 33, line 798b23.

See glossary for: **"Beholding the Stupa of Treasures" chapter**.

140. Taisho text 2689 in volume 84, lines 220c28-221a07

See glossary for: **"Beholding the Stupa of Treasures" chapter, Manjushri, Shakra, Universal Sage**, and **Vajrasattva**.

141. Taisho text 2689 in volume 84, lines 221a08-221a19

Grand Duke Wang (c. 11th century BCE) is more commonly known as Jiang Ziya. He helped King **Wen** and his son King **Wu** overthrow King **Zhou Xin** and establish the Zhou dynasty.

The Four Whiteheads of Mt. Shang were four elder statesmen who helped establish the Han dynasty.

See glossary for: ***Diamond Peak Sutra***, **emanation buddhas of the ten directions, good friend, Limitless Practice, Pure Practice, Steadily Established Practice, Superior Practice**, and **Vajrasattva**.

142. Taisho text 2689 in volume 84, lines 221a19-221b03

See the note for 55 concerning the age at which **Siddhartha** attained buddhahood.

See glossary for: **emanation buddhas of the ten directions** and **impure land**.

143. Taisho text 2689 in volume 84, lines 221b03-221b11

The "Buddha's power" can be a reference to **"sustaining power"** which is explained in the glossary.

The questions of Maitreya are composed of citations that can be found in Taisho text 262, volume 9, lines 40b23-40b24, 40c18-40c20, and 40c24-40c28. These passages were translated in LS, pp. 237, 239 and TLS, pp. 266-268.

144. Taisho text 2689 in volume 84, lines 221b11-221b15

The citation from the *Words and Phrases of the Lotus Sutra* can be found in Taisho text 1718, volume 34, lines 125c27-126a02.

See glossary for: **mahasattva** and **Peaceful Place of Awakening**.

145. Taisho text 2689 in volume 84, lines 221b15-221b19

The citation from the *Notations on the Words and Phrases of the Lotus Sutra* can be found in Taisho text 1719, volume 34, line 326b21.

146. Taisho text 2689 in volume 84, lines 221b19-221b25

The Buddha's response from the *Lotus Sutra* can be found in Taisho text 262, volume 9, lines 41a29-41b04 and 41b23-41b28. This passage was translated in LS, pp. 241-243 and TLS, p. 270-271.

See glossary for: **Ajita**, *asamkhya*, **attain enlightenment, Bodhgaya, Bodhi tree, bodhisattvas appearing from underground, mahasattva, non-retrogression, Saha world, turning of the Wheel of the Dharma**, and **unsurpassed complete and perfect awakening**.

147. Taisho text 2689 in volume 84, lines 221b26-221c07

White Heron Lake is located within the grounds of the **Bamboo Grove Monastery**.

See glossary for: **bodhisattvas appearing from underground, Dharma Wisdom, good friend**, and **Great Treasure Chamber**.

148. Taisho text 2689 in volume 84, lines 221c07-221c17

Prince Shotoku (574-622) was the son of Emperor Yomei (540-587) who served as the regent of Japan beginning in 593 under his aunt, Empress Suiko (554-628). He helped establish a centralized government in Japan and was a great patron of Buddhism. He is said to have written Japan's Seventeen-Article Constitution in 604 as well as commentaries on the *Lotus Sutra*, the ***Vimalakirti Sutra***, and the ***Shrimala Sutra***.

Silla and Baekje were kingdoms in the southern part of the Korean peninsula from the first to the sixth century. In the north was the kingdom of Goguryeo (later called Goryeo). They were unified as one kingdom by Silla in 668.

149. Taisho text 2689 in volume 84, lines 221c17-221c21

The citation from the *Lotus Sutra* can be found in Taisho text 262 volume 9, lines 41c04-41c07. This passage was translated in LS, p. 243 and TLS, pp. 271-272.

See glossary for: **Bodhgaya, Shakyas**, and **unsurpassed complete and perfect awakening**.

150. Taisho text 2689 in volume 84, lines 221c21-221c26

See glossary for: **attain enlightenment, Great Adornment,** and *Infinite Meanings Sutra*.

151. Taisho text 2689 in volume 84, lines 221c26-222a03

The citation from the *Contemplation of the Buddha of Infinite Life Sutra* can be found in Taisho text 365, volume 12, lines 341b14-341b16. This passage was translated in TPLS, p. 67.

See glossary for: **Ajatashatru, Bimbisara, causes and conditions, Chandraprabha, Jivaka,** and **Vaidehi**.

152. Taisho text 2689 in volume 84, lines 222a03-222a11

See glossary for: **causes and conditions, demon, Shakra, Vaidehi,** and **wheel-turning noble king**.

153. Taisho text 2689 in volume 84, lines 222a11-222a15

See glossary for: **all the holy teachings of the Buddha's lifetime** and **Kashyapa**.

154. Taisho text 2689 in volume 84, lines 222a15-222a22

The first citation from the *Lotus Sutra* can be found in Taisho text 262, volume 9, lines 42b09-42b11. This passage was translated in LS, p. 247 and TLS, p. 276.

The second citation from the *Lotus Sutra* can be found in Taisho text 262, volume 9, lines 42b12-42b13. This passage was translated in LS, p. 247 and TLS, p. 276.

See glossary for: *asamkhya*, **asura, Bodhgaya,** *nayuta*, **Peaceful Place of Awakening, "Peaceful Practices" chapter, Shakya,** and **unsurpassed complete and perfect awakening**.

155. Taisho text 2689 in volume 84, lines 222a22-222a28

The citation from the *Lotus Sutra* can be found in Taisho text 262, volume 9, line 9c04. This passage was translated in LS, p. 46 and TLS, p. 79.

See glossary for: **attainment of awakening for the first time,** *Benevolent Kings Sutra*, **"Expedients" chapter,** *Great Assembly Sutra, Infinite Meanings Sutra*, and *Vimalakirti Sutra*.

156. Taisho text 2689 in volume 84, lines 222a28-222b04

See glossary for: **focus of devotion**.

157. Taisho text 2689 in volume 84, lines 222b04-222b13

See glossary for: **attain enlightenment, devil king of the sixth heaven, Eternal Buddha, Brahma Heavenly King, impure land, original land** (subtlety of the), **Saha world, spirit,** and **transformation-body**.

158. Taisho text 2689 in volume 84, lines 222b13-222b19

See glossary for: **accommodative-body, Ci'en** (Great Master), **Jiaxiang,** and **Kobo** (Great Master).

159. Taisho text 2689 in volume 84, lines 222b19-222b26

See glossary for: **Eternal Buddha**.

160. Taisho text 2689 in volume 84, lines 222b26-222c02

See glossary for: **distinct teaching, eight phases of a buddha's life, ten abodes,** and **ten grounds**.

161. Taisho text 2689 in volume 84, lines 222c02-222c07

See glossary for: **four heavenly kings, kalpa of abiding, moon** (god of the), **Shakra,** and **sun** (god of the).

162. Taisho text 2689 in volume 84, lines 222c07-222c15

See glossary for: **Amitabha,** *Diamond Peak Sutra*, **Diamond-realm, Great Power Obtainer, kalpa of abiding, mandala, Medicine Master, moon** (god of the), **Moonlight, Sunlight, stars** (god of the), **sun** (god of the), **Womb-realm,** and **World Voice Perceiver**.

163. Taisho text 2689 in volume 84, lines 222c15-223a01

See glossary for: **Abhidharma Treasury school, Amitabha, Completion of Reality school, Discipline school, focus of devotion, Rochana, superior accommodative-body,** and **thirty-four enlightened mental states**.

164. Taisho text 2689 in volume 84, lines 223a01-223a06

I have not been able to locate the citation from the *Five Hundred Questions Treatise* in the Taisho.

See glossary for: **all the holy teachings of the Buddha's lifetime, Eternal Buddha,** and **Three Sovereigns and Five Emperors**.

165. Taisho text 2689 in volume 84, lines 223a06-223a13

See glossary for: **Fazang** and **Shubhakarasimha**.

166. Taisho text 2689 in volume 84, lines 223a13-223a17

I have not been able to locate the citation from the *Outstanding Principles of the Lotus Sutra* in the Taisho.

167. Taisho text 2689 in volume 84, lines 223a17-223a22

Zhao Gao (d. 207 BCE) was an extremely treacherous official who served all three emperors of the Qin dynasty and whose actions led to the downfall of that dynasty.

See glossary for: **attain buddhahood with one's present body, Dokyo, sowing maturing and harvesting,** and **ten grounds**.

168. Taisho text 2689 in volume 84, lines 223a22-223a28

See glossary for: *Lotus Sutra Treatise*, **seed of buddhahood**, and **Vasubandhu**.

169. Taisho text 2689 in volume 84, lines 223a28-223b11

The citation from the *Flower Garland Sutra* can be found in Taisho text 278, volume 9, line 465c26. This passage was translated in FOS, p. 452.

The citation from the *Mahavairochana Sutra* can be found in Taisho text 848, volume 18, line 22b29. This passage was translated in MS, p. 94.

I have not been able to locate the citation from the *Dependence on Tiantai of Other Buddhist Schools* in the Taisho.

See glossary for: **Diamond-realm, equal in principle superior in practice, mandala, mudra, mutual possession of the ten realms, Shubhakarasimha, Womb-realm** and **Yixing**.

170. Taisho text 2689 in volume 84, lines 223b11-223b15

Kakinomoto no Hitomaro (c. 655-710) was a Japanese aristocrat and famous poet, whose poems are included in the *Manyōshū*, an anthology of Japan's oldest *waka* poetry.

171. Taisho text 2689 in volume 84, lines 223b15-223b27

See glossary for: **Amoghavajra, Diamond-realm, Encho, Kobo** (Great Master), **Kojo, Jitsue, Liangxu, mandala, Shinga, Shubhakarasimha, ten stages of mind, Womb-realm,** and **Yama**.

172. Taisho text 2689 in volume 84, lines 223b27-223c01

See glossary for: **bodhisattva vehicle, Jiaxiang,** and *Profundity of the Lotus Sutra Treatise*.

173. Taisho text 2689 in volume 84, lines 223c01-223c06

I have not been able to locate citations for **Ci'en**'s assertions in the Taisho.

The four vehicles are the three vehicles and the One Vehicle if the latter is considered to be distinct from the former, which is clearly not the teaching of the *Lotus Sutra* wherein the Buddha declares, "I also expound various teachings to all living beings only for the purpose of revealing the **One Buddha Vehicle**. There is no other vehicle, not a second or a third." (LS, p. 33 and TLS, p. 66)

See glossary for: *Chapters on the Forest of Meanings of the Dharma Garden of the Mahayana* and *Essential Meaning of Praising the Profundity of the Lotus Sutra*.

174. Taisho text 2689 in volume 84, lines 223c06-223c14

See glossary for: **Kobo** (Great Master).

175. Taisho text 2689 in volume 84, lines 223c14-223c19

The citation from the *Lotus Sutra* can be found in Taisho text 262, volume 9, line 8b06. This passage was translated in LS, p. 38 and TLS, p. 72.

See glossary for: **four great vows**.

176. Taisho text 2689 in volume 84, lines 223c19-223c24

See glossary for: *Contemplation of the Buddha of Infinite Life* and **guardian deity**.

177. Taisho text 2689 in volume 84, 223c24-224a03

The seven schools of Buddhism in Japan at the time of Dengyo other than the Tiantai school were the **six schools of Nara Buddhism** and the Mantra school. The Pure Land school and the Zen school were not established until the Kamakuran era (1185-1333).

See glossary for: **guardian deity** and **ten rakshasi**.

178. Taisho text 2689 in volume 84, 224a03-224a11

See glossary for: **moon** (god of the), **sun** (god of the), and **three assemblies at two locations**.

179. Taisho text 2689 in volume 84, 224a11-224a16

See glossary for: **evil friend**.

180. Taisho text 2689 in volume 84, 224a16-224a23

The citation from the *Lotus Sutra* can be found in Taisho text 262, volume 9, lines 33c05-33c15. This passage was translated in LS, p. 192 and TLS, p. 223.

See glossary for: **"Beholding the Stupa of Treasures"** chapter, **four assemblies**, and **Saha world**.

181. Taisho text 2689 in volume 84, 224a23-224b02

The citation from the *Lotus Sutra* can be found in Taisho text 262, volume 9, lines 33c15-34a05. This passage was translated in LS, pp. 192-194 and TLS, pp. 223-225.

See glossary for: **gatha**.

182. Taisho text 2689 in volume 84, 224b02-224b12

The citation from the *Lotus Sutra* can be found in Taisho text 262, volume 9, lines 34a15-34b14. This passage was translated in LS, pp. 194-198 and TLS, pp. 225-228.

See glossary for: **kalpa of dissolution** and **Sumeru** (Mount).

183. Taisho text 2689 in volume 84, 224b12-224b18

184. Taisho text 2689 in volume 84, 224b18-224b23

The Queen Mother of the West is a Chinese goddess of prosperity and longevity.

The eight year war for the control of China refers to the Chu-Han Contention (206-202 BCE). This was a war between Liu Bang (256-195 BCE), the Governor of Pei, and Xiang Yu (c. 232-202 BCE), the Hegemon-King of Western Chu. Liu Bang was the winner of this struggle and he thereafter established the Han dynasty of Emperor Gaozu of Han.

The seven-year war in Japan refers to the Gempei War between the Taira (or Heike) and Minamoto (or Genji) clans, which could be said to have begun in 1179, when the Taira staged a coup d'état and took over the government in Kyoto, and ended with the naval battle of Dan-no-Ura in 1185 with the total destruction of the Taira. In the Japanese way of counting this was a seven year period. Taira no Munemori (1147-1185) led the Taira clan and was captured at the Battle of Dan-no-ura and executed. Minamoto no Yoritomo (1147-1199) led the Minamoto forces and became the first shogun of the Kamakura shogunate.

See glossary for: **Anavatapta** (Lake), **asura**, **dragon king**, **golden-winged bird**, **Shakra**, **udumbara**, and **wheel-turning noble king**.

185. Taisho text 2689 in volume 84, 224b23-224b28

186. Taisho text 2689 in volume 84, 224b28-224c05

The citation from the *Great Calming and Contemplation* can be found in Taisho text 1911, volume 46, lines 74a11-74a12. This passage was translated in CSQI, pp. 1004-1005.

The four gates in the passage cited refers to four different teachings that are gates to the path of practice that culminates in attaining arhatship. These four correspond to the four alternatives of the **tetralemma** in terms of understanding reality in terms of being, non-being, both, and neither. The first is the gate of realizing the **impermanence** of being. The second is the gate of realizing that non-being is the **emptiness** of all things. The third is the gate of realizing that both being and non-being refer to **provisional existence**. The fourth is the gate of realizing that the Middle Way is neither being nor non-being.

See glossary for: **Dushun, Fazang,** *Lankavatara Sutra***,** *Revealing the Profound Secrets Sutra***, six difficult and nine easier actions, tripitaka master,** and **Zhiyan**.

187. Taisho text 2689 in volume 84, 224c05-224c17

See glossary for: **Amoghavajra, Ci'en** (Great Master), **consciousness-only, Dharma-body, equal in principle superior in practice, Jizang,** *Revealing the Profound Secrets Sutra***, reward-body, Shubhakarasimha, six difficult and nine easier actions, three periods of teaching, tripitaka master, Vajrabodhi,** and **Xuanzang**.

188. Taisho text 2689 in volume 84, 224c17-224c25

The citation from the *Nirvana Sutra* can be found in Taisho text 374, volume 12, line 401b28. This passage was translated in NS1, p. 193.

See glossary for: **four reliances, Manjushri, preliminary awakening, rely on the Dharma not upon the person, sal tree,** and **Universal Sage**.

189. Taisho text 2689 in volume 84, 224c25-225a04

The citation from the *Nirvana Sutra* can be found in Taisho text 374, volume 12, lines 401b28-401b29. This passage was translated in NS1, p. 194.

The citation from the *Profound Meaning of the Lotus Sutra* can be found in Taisho text 1716, volume 33, line 800a23-800a25.

I have not been able to locate the citations from *Exegesis on the Ten Grounds Treatise*, or *Outstanding Principles of the Lotus Sutra*, or the *A Collection of Orally Transmitted Teachings* in the Taisho.

See glossary for: **Chisho** (Great Master), **Nagarjuna, rely on the sutra of definitive meaning not upon the sutra of provisional meaning,** and **sutras of definitive meaning, sutras of provisional meaning**.

190. Taisho text 2689 in volume 84, 225a04-225a15

See glossary for: **Confucianism, provisional teaching, Three Sovereigns and Five Emperors, Vaipulya,** and **Vatsiputra.**

191. Taisho text 2689 in volume 84, 225a15-225a18

The citation from the *Lotus Sutra* can be found in Taisho text 262, volume 9, line 31b17. This passage was translated in LS, p. 180 and TLS, p. 211.

The citation from the ***Notations on the Words and Phrases of the Lotus Sutra*** can be found in Taisho text 1719, volume 34, lines 280b04-280b05.

The citation from the ***Elucidation of the Profound Meaning of the Lotus Sutra*** can be found in Taisho text 1717, volume 33, lines 858a24-858a26.

See glossary for: **have am now and will** and **"Teacher of the Dharma"** (The, chapter).

192. Taisho text 2689 in volume 84, 225a19-225a24

See glossary for: **Jikaku** (Great Master), and **mudra.**

193. Taisho text 2689 in volume 84, 225a24-225a26

I have not been able to locate the citation from the *Mystic Glorification Sutra* in the Taisho.

See glossary for: ***Great Tree Kimnara King Sutra, Shrimala Sutra, Supernatural Powers Sutra,*** and ***Ten Grounds Sutra.***

194. Taisho text 2689 in volume 84, 225a26-225a29

I have not been able to locate the citation from the ***Great Cloud Sutra*** in the Taisho.

See glossary for: **wheel-turning noble king.**

195. Taisho text 2689 in volume 84, 225a29-225b12

The citation from the ***Six Paramita Sutra*** can be found in Taisho text 261, volume 8, lines 868b25-868c18.
See glossary for: **abhidharma, dharani, extreme transgressions, five baskets, five heinous transgressions, flavor of milk, flavor of ghee, liberation, Prajnaparamita sutras,** and **vinaya.**

196. Taisho text 2689 in volume 84, 225b12-225b28

The citation from the ***Revealing the Profound Secrets Sutra*** can be found in Taisho text 676, volume 16, lines 697a23-697b09. This passage was translated in SEUM, p. 49.

See glossary for: **Deer Park, definitive meaning, four noble truths, non-arising, non-ceasing, phenomena, Rishipatana, self-nature, Superlative Meaning Arising, three periods of teaching, three turnings of the wheel of the Dharma, turning of the Wheel of the Dharma, Varanasi,** and **voice-hearer vehicle**.

197. Taisho text 2689 in volume 84, 225b28-225c02

The citation from the ***Larger Prajna Sutra*** can be found in Taisho text 220, volume 7, lines 262a25-262a28.

See glossary for: **Dharma-nature, mundane, perfection of wisdom,** and **supramundane**.

198. Taisho text 2689 in volume 84, 225c02-225c10

The first citation from the *Mahavairochana Sutra* can be found in Taisho text 848, volume 18, lines 3b09-3b11. This passage was translated in MS, p. 13.

The second citation from the *Mahavairochana Sutra* can be found in Taisho text 848, volume 18, lines 3b12-3b13. This passage was translated in MS, p. 13.

The third citation from the *Mahavairochana Sutra* can be found in Taisho text 848, volume 18, lines 3b19-3b22. This passage was translated in MS, p. 14.

The fourth citation from the *Mahavairochana Sutra* can be found in Taisho text 848, volume 18, lines 1c01-1c02. This passage was translated in MS, p. 5.

See glossary for: **aggregate, emptiness, Lord of Mysteries, mind king, non-arising, non-self, phenomena, self-nature, space, storehouse consciousness,** and **unconditioned**.

199. Taisho text 2689 in volume 84, 225c10-225c23

The citation from the *Flower Garland Sutra* can be found in Taisho text 278, volume 9, lines 441a14-441a27. This passage was translated in FOS, p. 367.

See glossary for: **buddha-land, Great Vehicle, privately-awakened one vehicle, trichiliocosm,** and **voice-hearer vehicle**.

200. Taisho text 2689 in volume 84, 225c23-226a04

The citation from the *Nirvana Sutra* can be found in Taisho text 374, volume 12, lines 449a03-449a12. The passage was translated in NS, p. 195.

See glossary for: **final nirvana, flavor of ghee, Prajnaparamita sutras,** and **twelve kinds of scriptures**.

201. Taisho text 2689 in volume 84, 226a04-226a07

See glossary for: **have am now and will, six difficult and nine easier actions**, and **Sumeru** (Mount).

202. Taisho text 2689 in volume 84, 226a07-226a17

See glossary for: **buddha eye, Ci'en, Jiaxiang, Kobo** (Great Master), and **Sumeru** (Mount).

203. Taisho text 2689 in volume 84, 226a17-226a28

The first citation from the ***Distinguishing the Two Teaching of the Exoteric and Esoteric Treatise*** can be found in Taisho text 2427, volume, 77, lines 379a05-379a06. This passage was translated in ST, p. 45.

The second citation from the *Distinguishing the Two Teaching of the Exoteric and Esoteric Treatise* can be found in Taisho text 2427, volume, 77, line 375b15. This passage was translated in ST, p. 21.

See glossary for: **dharani, five flavors, flavor of ghee, Kobo** (Great Master), and ***Six Paramita Sutra***,

204. Taisho text 2689 in volume 84, 226a28-226b15

"Diviners" translates the Japanese term *onmyōji* (陰陽師), which translated literally means "master of yin and yang." An *onmyōji* was a practitioner of the "Way of Yin and Yang" (J. Onmyōdō; 陰陽道), a system of magic and divination established in seventh century Japan that combined Japanese folk magic and beliefs with Chinese systems of cosmology and divination. The *onmyōji* were members of the Japanese bureaucracy from the seventh until the nineteenth century.

See glossary for: **Asanga, Ci'en, Faxian, Jiaxiang, Kobo** (Great Master), **Nagarjuna, reverse relationship**, and **three assemblies at two locations**.

205. Taisho text 2689 in volume 84, 226b15-226b21

See glossary for: **six difficult and nine easier actions** and **Sumeru** (Mount).

206. Taisho text 2689 in volume 84, 226b21-226b29

See glossary for: **Ajatashatru, amrita, changing poison into medicine, "Devadatta" chapter, five heinous transgressions, Heavenly King, seven grave, transgressions, Sunakshatra, three proclamations**, and **two exhortations**.

207. Taisho text 2689 in volume 84, 226b29-226c08

See glossary for: **attainment of buddhahood by a dragon girl, attainment of buddhahood by women**, and **rebirth in the pure land**.

208. Taisho text 2689 in volume 84, 226c08-226c18

See glossary for: **attainment of buddhahood by women** and **Confucianism**,

209. Taisho text 2689 in volume 84, 226c18-226c21

See glossary for: **"Encouragement for Keeping this Sutra" chapter** and **five proclamations**.

210. Taisho text 2689 in volume 84, 226c21-226c28

The hour of the rat corresponds to 11 p.m. to 1 a.m., while the hour of the ox corresponds to 1 a.m. to 3 a.m.

"**Spirit**" in this passage is a translation of the Japanese term *konpaku* from the ideograms 魂魄.

211. Taisho text 2689 in volume 84, 226c28-227a13

The citation from the *Lotus Sutra* can be found in Taisho text 262, volume 9, lines 36b21-36c22. The passage was translated in LS, pp. 212-214 and TLS, pp. 241-243.

See glossary for: *aranya*, **capacity, defilement, devil, "Encouragement for Keeping this Sutra" chapter, six supernatural powers**,

212. Taisho text 2689 in volume 84, 227a13-227a17

The citation from the ***Notations on the Words and Phrases of the Lotus Sutra*** can be found in Taisho text 1719, volume 34, lines 315a05-315a08.

The "three presumptuous groups" refers to the three kinds of enemies.

See glossary for: **presumptuous clergy, presumptuous lay followers**, and **presumptuous sages**.

213. Taisho text 2689 in volume 84, 227a17-227a21

The citation from the ***Dongchun*** is not in the Taisho.

The "three kinds of evil actions" refers to evil thoughts, words, and deeds.

"Presumptuous home-leavers" refers to the **presumptuous clergy**.

See glossary for: *aranya*, **Dharma master, "Encouragement for Keeping this Sutra" chapter**, and **Zhidu**.

214. Taisho text 2689 in volume 84, 227a21-227b14

The first citation from the *Nirvana Sutra* can be found in Taisho text 374, volume 12, lines 419a19-419a21. The passage was translated in NS1, p. 286.

The second citation from the *Nirvana Sutra* can be found in Taisho text 374, volume 12, lines 421c26-422a03. The passage was translated in NS1, p. 300.

The citation from the *Six-Fascicle Nirvana Sutra* can be found in Taisho text 376, volume 12, lines 892c09-892c14.

The third citation from the *Nirvana Sutra* can be found in Taisho text 374, volume 12, lines 386b14-386b22. The passage was translated in NS1, p. 113.

See glossary for: **Jambudvipa**, *kesa*, **Mara**, and **shramana**.

215. Taisho text 2689 in volume 84, 227b14-227b16

See glossary for: **sal tree** and **Zhidu**.

216. Taisho text 2689 in volume 84, 227b16-227b22

The first citation from the *Lotus Sutra* is from the **"Encouragement for Keeping this Sutra" chapter** and can be found in Taisho text 262, volume 9, lines 36b21-36b22. The passage was translated in LS, p. 212 and TLS, p. 241.

The first phrase from the **"Peaceful Practices" chapter** of the *Lotus Sutra* can be found in Taisho text 262, volume 9, lines 37a12-37a14, and 37b19. The passage was translated in LS, pp. 216, 218 and TLS, pp. 244, 246.

The second phrase from the "Peaceful Practices" chapter of the *Lotus Sutra* can be found in Taisho text 262, volume 9, lines 37c29. The passage was translated in LS, p. 222 and TLS, p. 250.

The third phrase from the "Peaceful Practices" chapter of the *Lotus Sutra* can be found in Taisho text 262, volume 9, lines 38b02-38b03 and 38c04-38c05. The passage was translated in LS, pp. 224, 226 and TLS, pp. 252, 254.

The phrase from the "The **Variety of Merits**" chapter of the *Lotus Sutra* can be found in Taisho text 262, volume 9, line 46a13. The passage was translated in LS, p. 266 and TLS, p. 295.

The phrase from the "The **Previous Life of Medicine King Bodhisattva**" chapter of the *Lotus Sutra* can be found in Taisho text 262, volume 9, lines 54b29 and 54c22. The passage was translated in LS, pp. 312-313 and TLS, pp. 342, 344.

The first phrase from the "Encouragement to Expound the Dharma" chapter of the ***Flowering of the True Dharma Sutra*** can be found in Taisho text 263, volume 9, line 106c27.

The second phrase from the "Encouragement to Expound the Dharma" chapter of the *Flowering of the True Dharma Sutra* can be found in Taisho text 263, volume 9, line 107a27.

See glossary for: ***Supplemented Lotus Sutra***.

217. Taisho text 2689 in volume 84, 227b22-227b25

The citations from Tiantai and Dengyo are not in the Taisho and may be Nichiren's paraphrasing of passages from their writings.

See glossary for: **six schools of Nara Buddhism** and **three southern and seven northern schools**.

218. Taisho text 2689 in volume 84, 227b25-227c02

See glossary for: **emanation buddhas of the ten directions**, *koti* and *nayuta*.

219. Taisho text 2689 in volume 84, 227c02-227c10

220. Taisho text 2689 in volume 84, 227c10-227c22

The story concerning the omens of Shakyamuni Buddha's birth during the reign of King Zhao comes from the *Complete Chronicle of the Buddha and the Ancestors* (J. Busso-tōki; 佛祖統紀) written in 1269 by a Tiantai monk named Zhipan (1220-1275; J. Shiban; 志磐).

King Zhao of Zhou (1027-957 BCE) was the fourth king of the Zhou dynasty. His reign, however, was only for twenty years (r. 977-957 BCE).

Emperor Ming of Han (28-75) was the second emperor of the Eastern Han dynasty.

It was widely believed in East Asia since at least the sixth century that Shakyamuni Buddha was born on the eighth day of the fourth month of 1029 BCE and died on the fifteenth day of the second month of 949 BCE. This may be why Zhipan set the date of the story about the Buddha's omens during the reign of King Zhao, near the beginning of the Zhou dynasty.

221. Taisho text 2689 in volume 84, 227c22-228a08

See glossary for: **Ananda, Ashvaghosha, emanation buddhas of the ten directions, Flower Light, Light, Nagarjuna, Parshva,** ***Transmission of the Dharma Treasury Sutra***, and **twenty-four successors**.

222. Taisho text 2689 in volume 84, 228a08-228a12

See glossary for: ***Dongchun, Notations on the Words and Phrases of the Lotus Sutra***, and **presumptuous lay followers**.

223. Taisho text 2689 in volume 84, 228a12-228a14

The citation from the *Lotus Sutra* can be found in Taisho text 262, volume 9, lines 36b25-36b26. The passage was translated in LS, p. 212 and TLS, p. 241.

224. Taisho text 2689 in volume 84, 228a14-228a16

The citation from the *Nirvana Sutra* can be found in Taisho text 374, volume 12, lines 421c27-421c29. The passage was translated in NS1, p. 300.

225. Taisho text 2689 in volume 84, 228a16-228a18

The citation from the *Great Calming and Contemplation* can be found in Taisho text 1911, volume 46, lines 10b10-10b11. This passage was translated in CSQI, p. 231.

See glossary for: **knowledge**.

226. Taisho text 2689 in volume 84, 228a18-228a19

The citation from the ***Collection of Passages on the Land of Peace and Bliss*** can be found in Taisho text 1958, volume 47, line 13c08.

The citation from *A **Collection of Passages on the Nembutsu Chosen in the Original Vow*** can be found in Taisho text 2608, volume 83, line 17a08. This passage was translated in SHNS, p. 117.

See glossary for: **capacity** and **Daochuo**.

227. Taisho text 2689 in volume 84, 228a19-228a22

The citation from the ***Notations on the Words and Phrases of the Lotus Sutra*** can be found in Taisho text 1719, volume 34, lines 344c20-344c22.

228. Taisho text 2689 in volume 84, 228a22-228a25

The citation from the ***Essay on the Protection of the Nation*** can be found in Taisho text 2362, volume 74, lines 177b28-177c01.

The citation from the ***Essentials of the One Vehicle Teaching*** can be found in Taisho text 2370, volume 74, line 351a03.

See glossary for: **capacity, Eshin,** and **"Peaceful Practices" chapter**.

229. Taisho text 2689 in volume 84, 228a25-228b01

See glossary for: **Daochuo, Eshin, heavenly devil, Hiei** (Mount), and **preceptor**.

230. Taisho text 2689 in volume 84, 228b01-228b05

See glossary for: *Collection of Passages on the Nembutsu Chosen in the Original Vow*, and **Eshin**.

231. Taisho text 2689 in volume 84, 228b05-228b12

The citation from the *Nirvana Sutra* can be found in Taisho text 374, volume 12, line 407b07. The passage was translated in NS1, p. 226.

The citation from the *Elucidation of the Profound Meaning of the Lotus Sutra* is not in the Taisho.

The citation from the *Great Calming and Contemplation* can be found in Taisho text 1911, volume 46, lines 17b26-17b28. This passage was translated in CSQI, p. 369.

The citation from the *Supplemental Amplifications on the Great Calming and Contemplation* can be found in Taisho text 1912, volume 46, lines 203b20-203b23.

See glossary for: **absolute subtlety**, **four doctrinal teachings**, and **relative subtlety**.

232. Taisho text 2689 in volume 84, 228b12-228b26

See glossary for: **abandon close set aside and cast away**, **absolute subtlety**, *Contemplation of the Buddha of Infinite Life Sutra*, **four doctrinal teachings**, **four flavors and three teachings**, and **relative subtlety**.

233. Taisho text 2689 in volume 84, 228b26-228b28

The citation from the *Lotus Sutra* can be found in Taisho text 262, volume 9, lines 36b27-36b30. The passage was translated in LS, pp. 212-213 and TLS, p. 241.

See glossary for: *aranya* and **six supernatural powers**.

234. Taisho text 2689 in volume 84, 228b28-228c05

The citation from the *Six-Fascicle Nirvana Sutra* can be found in Taisho text 376, volume 12, lines 892c09-892c14.

235. Taisho text 2689 in volume 84, 228c05-228c11

The citation from the *Nirvana Sutra* can be found in Taisho text 374, volume 12, lines 386b14-386b22. This passage was translated in NS1, p. 113.

See glossary for: *kesa* and **shramana**.

236. Taisho text 2689 in volume 84, 228c11-228c12

The citation from the *Notations on the Words and Phrases of the Lotus Sutra* can be found in Taisho text 1719, volume 34, lines 315a08.

237. Taisho text 2689 in volume 84, 228c12-228c14

The citation from the *Dongchun* is not in the Taisho.

See glossary for: **aranya**.

238. Taisho text 2689 in volume 84, 228c14-228c25

See glossary for: **aranya**, **Dongchun**, **Enryakuji Temple**, **fivefold Dharma-body**, **Hiei** (Mount), **Jufukuji Temple**, **Kenchoji Temple**, **Kenninji Temple**, **Onjoji Temple**, **Ryokan**, **Shoichi**, **six supernatural powers**, and **Toji Temple**.

239. Taisho text 2689 in volume 84, 228c25

The citation from the *Great Calming and Contemplation* can be found in Taisho text 1911, volume 46, line 1a07. This passage was translated in CSQI, p. 74.

See glossary for: **calming** and **contemplation**.

240. Taisho text 2689 in volume 84, 228c26-228c27

The citation from the *Supplemental Amplifications on the Great Calming and Contemplation* can be found in Taisho text 1912, volume 46, lines 142b15-142b17.

Emperor Ming of Han (28-75) was the second emperor of the Eastern Han dynasty.

The Chen or Southern Chen dynasty ruled southern China from 557-589.

241. Taisho text 2689 in volume 84, 228c27-228c28

The citation from the *Additional Annotations to the Three Major Works of Tiantai* is not in the Taisho.

See glossary for: **Bodhidharma**.

242. Taisho text 2689 in volume 84, 228c28-228c29

The citation from the *Great Calming and Contemplation* can be found in Taisho text 1911, volume 46, lines 49a21-49a25. This passage was translated in CSQI, pp. 753-754.

243. Taisho text 2689 in volume 84, 228c29-229a04

The citation from the *Great Calming and Contemplation* can be found in Taisho text 1911, volume 46, line 98a07-98a10. This passage was translated in CSQI, pp. 1248-1249.

See glossary for: **contemplation**, **meditation master**, and **ten means of adaptation to the Buddha Dharma**.

244. Taisho text 2689 in volume 84, 229a04-229a11

The citation from the ***Supplemental Amplifications on the Great Calming and Contemplation*** can be found in Taisho text 1912, volume 46, lines 382a24-382b03.

See glossary for: **calming**, **contemplation**, **Dharma master**, **eight errors**, **eight winds**, **five aggregates**, **four noble truths**, **four primary elements**, **meditation master**, **meditative absorption**, **outflow**, **six sense entrances**, **six supernatural powers**, and **three poisons**.

245. Taisho text 2689 in volume 84, 229a11-229a13

The citation from the *Great Calming and Contemplation* can be found in Taisho text 1911, volume 46, lines 99b15-99b17. This passage was translated in CSQI, p. 1264.

The "meditation master in Ye and Luo" may be a reference to **Bodhidharma**.

246. Taisho text 2689 in volume 84, 229a14-229a16

The citation from the ***Supplemental Amplifications on the Great Calming and Contemplation*** can be found in Taisho text 1912, volume 46, lines 385c17-385c19.

The "meditation master in Ye and Luo" may be a reference to **Bodhidharma**.

247. Taisho text 2689 in volume 84, 229a16-229a18

The citation from the ***Six-Fascicle Nirvana Sutra*** can be found in Taisho text 376, volume 12, lines 892b24-892b25.

248. Taisho text 2689 in volume 84, 229a18-229a19

The citation from the ***Notations on the Words and Phrases of the Lotus Sutra*** can be found in Taisho text 1719, volume 34, line 315a08.

249. Taisho text 2689 in volume 84, 229a19-229a27

The citation from the *Lotus Sutra* can be found in Taisho text 262, volume 9, line 36c08. The passage was translated in LS, p. 213 and TLS, p. 242.

The citation from the ***Dongchun*** is not in the Taisho.

See glossary for: **buddha eye**, **Gomyo**, **Nen'a Ryochu**, **Ryokan**, and **Shuen**.

250. Taisho text 2689 in volume 84, 229a27-229b02

The citation from the *Great Calming and Contemplation* can be found in Taisho text 1911, volume 46, lines 10b10-10b11. This passage was translated in CSQI, p. 231.

See glossary for: **capacity** and **Tiantai Lotus school**.

251. Taisho text 2689 in volume 84, 229b02-229b10

See glossary for: *kesa*, **six Chinese ancestors**, and **twenty-eight Indian ancestors**.

252. Taisho text 2689 in volume 84, 229b10-229b21

See glossary for: **emanation buddhas of the ten directions**.

253. Taisho text 2689 in volume 84, 229b21-229c03

254. Taisho text 2689 in volume 84, 229c03-229c09

For Prince Shotoku, see note for 148.

Mononobe no Moriya (d. 587) was the leader of the Mononobe clan that was opposed to Buddhism. In the year 587, they fought the pro-Buddhist Soga clan over who would be crowned the thirty-second emperor of Japan. One of the leaders on the side of the Soga clan was Prince Shotoku. The Mononobe clan wad defeated and Moriya himself was killed at the Battle of Shigisan near Mt. Shigi in July of 587.

See glossary for: **one-eyed turtle**.

255. Taisho text 2689 in volume 84, 229c09-229c17

The first citation from the *Lotus Sutra* can be found in Taisho text 262, volume 9, lines 39b17-39b18. The passage was translated in LS, p. 230 and TLS, p. 259.

The second citation from the *Lotus Sutra* can be found in Taisho text 262, volume 9, line 39b18. The passage was translated in LS, p. 230 and TLS, p. 259.

The third citation from the *Lotus Sutra* can be found in Taisho text 262, volume 9, lines 19b19-19b20. The passage was translated in LS, p. 109 and TLS, p. 141.

The fourth citation from the *Lotus Sutra* can be found in Taisho text 262, volume 9, line 59b13. The passage was translated in LS, p. 335 and TLS, p. 366.

The fifth citation from the *Lotus Sutra* can be found in Taisho text 262, volume 9, line 62a16. The passage was translated in LS, p. 347 and TLS, p. 380.

The sixth citation from the *Lotus Sutra* can be found in Taisho text 262, volume 9, lines 62a19-62a20. The passage was translated in LS, p. 347 and TLS, p. 380.

See glossary for: **arjaka**.

256. Taisho text 2689 in volume 84, 229c18-229c22

The first citation from the *Lotus Sutra* can be found in Taisho text 262, volume 9, line 50b26. The passage was translated in LS, p. 291 and TLS, p. 321.

The second citation from the *Lotus Sutra* can be found in Taisho text 262, volume 9, lines 50c28-50c29. The passage was translated in LS, p. 293 and TLS, p. 323.

The citation from the *Nirvana Sutra* can be found in Taisho text 374, volume 12, lines 384b04-384b05. This passage was translated in NS1, p. 98.

The third citation from the *Lotus Sutra* can be found in Taisho text 262, volume 9, lines 31b20-31b21. The passage was translated in LS, p. 180 and TLS, p. 212.

See glossary for: **"Never Despising Bodhisattva" chapter**.

257. Taisho text 2689 in volume 84, 229c22-230a03

Though there are **twenty-four successors** traditionally listed, wherein **Aryadeva** is the fifteenth and **Aryasimha** is the twenty-fourth, for some reason they are listed here as the fourteenth and twenty-fifth.

Kitano Tenjin, the Shinto god of learning, is the deification of Suguwara no Michizane (845-903), a famous poet and government official in Japan during the Heian period. In 901 he was demoted and exiled from the imperial court in Kyoto to Dazaifu in Kyushu.

Bai Juyi (772-846) was a famous poet and government official in China during the Tang dynasty. He was exiled from the capital of Chang'an from 814-819.

See glossary for: **Daosheng, Fadao, Maudgalyayana**, and **nine great difficulties**.

258. Taisho text 2689 in volume 84, 230a03-230a13

The citation from the *Profound Meaning of the Lotus Sutra* can be found in Taisho text 1716, volume 33, line 748b27-748b28.

The citation from the ***Contemplation on the Mind-Ground Sutra*** is not in the Taisho.

The citation from the *Lotus Sutra* can be found in Taisho text 262, volume 9, line 51b18. The passage was translated in LS, p. 295 and TLS, p. 326.

See glossary for: **Anavatapta** (Lake), **asura, dragon king, golden-winged bird, "Never Despising Bodhisattva" chapter**, and **Shakra**.

259. Taisho text 2689 in volume 84, 230a14-230a26

The first citation from the *Nirvana Sutra* can be found in Taisho text 374, volume 12, lines 417c01-417c02. This passage was translated in NS1, p. 278.

The second citation from the *Nirvana Sutra* can be found in Taisho text 374, volume 12, lines 417c18-417c19. This passage was translated in NS1, p. 279.

The third citation from the *Nirvana Sutra* can be found in Taisho text 374, volume 12, lines 417c19-417c25. This passage was translated in NS1, pp. 279-280.

See glossary for: **heinous transgression, hell, Kashyapa,** and **rakshasa**.

260. Taisho text 2689 in volume 84, 230a26-230b05

The first citation from the *Nirvana Sutra* can be found in Taisho text 374, volume 12, lines 418a01. This passage was translated in NS1, p. 280.

The second citation from the *Nirvana Sutra* can be found in Taisho text 374, volume 12, lines 418a04-418a05. This passage was translated in NS1, p. 280.

The third citation from the *Nirvana Sutra* can be found in Taisho text 374, volume 12, lines 418a10-418a11. This passage was translated in NS1, pp. 280-281.

The fourth citation from the *Nirvana Sutra* can be found in Taisho text 374, volume 12, line 418b05. This passage was translated in NS1, p. 282.

The fifth citation from the *Nirvana Sutra* can be found in Taisho text 374, volume 12, line 418b21. This passage was translated in NS1, p. 283.

See glossary for: **Incessant Suffering, Jie, *mani*,** and **Zhou Xin**.

261. Taisho text 2689 in volume 84, 230b05-230b11

The citation from the ***Supreme Golden Light Sutra*** can be found in Taisho text 664, volume 16, lines 390c01-390c02.

See glossary for: **guardian deity** and ***Spreading Peace Throughout the Country by Establishing the True Dharma***.

262. Taisho text 2689 in volume 84, 230b11-230b17

See glossary for: **Eternal Shakyamuni Buddha, evil friend, five hundred dust-particle kalpas, Great Universal Wisdom Excellence, hell,** and **three thousand dust-particle kalpas**.

263. Taisho text 2689 in volume 84, 230b17-230b25

See glossary for: ***Contemplation of the Buddha of Infinite Life Sutra*** and **three great vows of Nichiren Shonin**.

264. Taisho text 2689 in volume 84, 230b25-230c04

The citation from the *Six-Fascicle Nirvana Sutra* can be found in Taisho text 376, volume 12, lines 877c17-877c22.

See glossary for: **karma** and **recompense**.

265. Taisho text 2689 in volume 84, 230c04-230c12

The citation from the *Lotus Sutra* can be found in Taisho text 262, volume 9, line 15b27. The passage was translated in LS, p. 83 and TLS, p. 114.

See glossary for: **eight kinds of suffering**(2).

266. Taisho text 2689 in volume 84, 230c12-230c16

The citation from the *Lotus Sutra* can be found in Taisho text 262, volume 9, line 36c22. The passage was translated in LS, p. 214 and TLS, p. 243.

The citation from the *Six-Fascicle Nirvana Sutra* can be found in Taisho text 376, volume 12, line 877c21-877c22.

The first citation from the *Great Calming and Contemplation* can be found in Taisho text 1911, volume 46, lines 49b11-49b12. This passage was translated in CSQI, p. 757.

The second citation from the *Great Calming and Contemplation* can be found in Taisho text 1911, volume 46, lines 49a01. This passage was translated in CSQI, p. 747.

See glossary for: **calming, contemplation, non-meditative good deeds, recompense**, and **three obstacles and four devils**.

267. Taisho text 2689 in volume 84, 230c16-231a06

See glossary for: **heinous transgression** and **samsara**.

268. Taisho text 2689 in volume 84, 231a06-231a18

The citation from the *Nirvana Sutra* can be found in Taisho text 374, volume 12, lines 374a12-374b02. This passage was translated in NS1, p. 42-44.

See glossary for: **Brahma** (Heavens of), **loving-kindness**, and **Manjushri**.

269. Taisho text 2689 in volume 84, 231a18-231a27

See glossary for: *Annotations on the Nirvana Sutra*, **Brahma** (Heavens of), **buddha-nature of the completing cause, impure land, loving-kindness, three obstacles**, and **Zhang'an** (Great Master).

270. Taisho text 2689 in volume 84, 231a28-231b04

See glossary for: **five heinous transgressions, form realm, Incessant Suffering,** and **non-meditative good deeds.**

271. Taisho text 2689 in volume 84, 231b04-231b11

See glossary for: **Brahma** (Heavens of), **Brahma Heavenly King, contemplation of loving-kindness and compassion, mindfulness, outflow, three kinds of meditative absorption,**

272. Taisho text 2689 in volume 84, 231b11-231b21

The citation from the *Nirvana Sutra* can be found in Taisho text 374, volume 12, line 374b01. This passage was translated in NS1, p. 43.

See glossary for: **consciousness-only, contemplation of the five wheels, eight negations, liberation, mind-only,** and **seed of buddhahood.**

273. Taisho text 2689 in volume 84, 231b21-231c04

274. Taisho text 2689 in volume 84, 231c04-231c12

The citation from the *Lotus Sutra* can be found in Taisho text 262, volume 9, lines 38a01-38a02. The passage was translated in LS, p. 222 and TLS, p. 250.

The citation from the *Great Calming and Contemplation* can be found in Taisho text 1911, volume 46, lines 137c25-137c28. This passage was translated in CSQI, p. 1583.

The teaching not to speak of the merits or demerits of others or mention them by name in the *Lotus Sutra* can be found in Taisho text 262, volume 9, line 38a03. The passage was translated in LS, p. 222 and TLS, p. 250.

The phrase "wielding swords or staves" from the *Nirvana Sutra* can be found in Taisho text 375, volume 12, lines 624a16-624a17. An equivalent passage can be found in Taisho text 374, volume 12, line 384a23. This passage was translated in NS1, p. 97.

The phrase "cuts off his head" from the *Nirvana Sutra* can be found in Taisho text 375, volume 12, line 618a20. An equivalent passage can be found in Taisho text 374, volume 12, lines 378b12-387b13. This passage was translated in NS1, p. 64.

See the glossary for: **asura** and **"Peaceful Practices" chapter.**

275. Taisho text 2689 in volume 84, 231c12-231c17

The citation from the ***Supplemental Amplifications on the Great Calming and Contemplation*** can be found in Taisho text 1912, volume 46, lines 444a16-444b04.

The phrase "wielding swords or staves" as above for note 274.

The citation from the third fascicle of the *Nirvana Sutra* can be found in Taisho text 375, volume 12, lines 623b11-623b12. An equivalent passage can be found in Taisho text 374, volume 12, lines 383b22-383b23. This passage was translated in NS1, p. 94.

The line from the *Nirvana Sutra* about King **Rishidatta** cutting off the **life force** of the brahmins who slandered the Mahayana sutras can be found in Taisho text 374, volume 12, line 676b05. An equivalent passage can be found in Taisho text 374, volume 12, line 434c19. This passage was translated in NS, p. 164. To be clear the line is 聞已即時斷其命根. The sentence literally means that King Rishidatta, "having heard," (聞已) the brahmins slandering the Vaipulya sutras, he "immediately" (即時) "cut off" (斷) "their" (其) "lifeblood" (命根). The ideograms 命根 can also be translated as "life faculty" or "root of life." The most obvious meaning of this line in context is that he executed them for slandering the Mahayana sutras. A more metaphorical interpretation would be that King Rishidatta enabled the brahmin's to cut off their own clinging to the life faculty by teaching them the Dharma, in other words they were able to attain nirvana.

The phrase, "Those who would continue to use them should be beheaded" from the *Nirvana Sutra* can be found in Taisho text 375, volume 12, line 618a20. An equivalent passage can be found in Taisho text 374, volume 12, lines 378b12-387b13. This passage was translated in NS1, p. 64. This phrase is from a parable about a doctor who has a king outlaw fraudulent milk remedies on pain of death as a skillful means to discourage people from continuing to rely on them.

See glossary for: **five precepts** and **three thousand regulations of deportment**.

276. Taisho text 2689 in volume 84, 231c17-231c22

The citation from the *Words and Phrases of the Lotus Sutra* can be found in Taisho text 1718, volume 34, lines 118c18-118c22.

The teaching of the ground of practice of bodhisattvas who have compassion for sentient beings just as a parent would for an only child in the *Nirvana Sutra* was translated in NS, pp. 221-222.

The citation from the *Lotus Sutra* can be found in Taisho text 262, volume 9, line 59b13. This passage was translated in LS, p. 335 and TLS, p. 366.

See glossary for: **loving-kindness**.

277. Taisho text 2689 in volume 84, 231c22-231c27

The citation from the ***Annotations on the Nirvana Sutra*** can be found in Taisho text 1767, volume 38, lines 84c14-84c24.

See glossary for: **householder** and **three thousand regulations of deportment**.

278. Taisho text 2689 in volume 84, 231c28-232a03

279. Taisho text 2689 in volume 84, 232a03-232a15

See glossary for: **"Never Despising Bodhisattva" chapter** and **"Peaceful Practices" chapter**.

280. Taisho text 2689 in volume 84, 232a15-232a29

The citation from the *Nirvana Sutra* can be found in Taisho text 374, volume 12, lines 383b15-383c16. This passage was translated in NS1, pp. 93-95.

See glossary for: **benefiting oneself and benefiting others, causality, Dharma-body, five precepts, Kashyapa, three thousand regulations of deportment**, and ***vajra***.

281. Taisho text 2689 in volume 84, 232a29-232b03

The citation from the ***Annotations on the Nirvana Sutra*** can be found in Taisho text 1767, volume 38, lines 84c24.

The citation from the *Words and Phrases of the Lotus Sutra* can be found in Taisho text 1718, volume 34, lines 118c22.

See glossary for: **Zhang'an** (Great Master).

282. Taisho text 2689 in volume 84, 232b03-232b17

See glossary for: **causes and conditions, Dainichi Nonin, hungry ghost, Incessant Suffering, samsara, separate transmission outside the sutras,** and **three mysteries**.

283. Taisho text 2689 in volume 84, 232b17-232b21

The citation from the *Nirvana Sutra* can be found in Taisho text 374, volume 12, lines 381a12-381a14. This passage was translated in NS1, p. 79.

284. Taisho text 2689 in volume 84, 232b22-232b25

The citation from ***Annotations on the Nirvana Sutra*** can be found in Taisho text 1767, volume 38, lines 80b01-80b05.

See glossary for: **Zhang'an** (Great Master).

285. Taisho text 2689 in volume 84, 232b25-232c06

The citation from the *Lotus Sutra* can be found in Taisho text 262, volume 9, lines 33c25. The passage was translated in LS, p. 193 and TLS, p. 224.

See glossary for: **"Beholding the Stupa of Treasures" chapter** and **emanation buddhas of the ten directions**.

286. Taisho text 2689 in volume 84, 232c06-232c15

The first citation from the ***Annotations on the Nirvana Sutra*** can be found in Taisho text 1767, volume 38, line 80b01.

The second citation from the *Annotations on the Nirvana Sutra* can be found in Taisho text 1767, volume 38, line 80b02-80b03.

See glossary for: **Zhang'an** (Great Master).

287. Taisho text 2689 in volume 84, 232c15-232c25

See glossary for: **Saicho**, **Tokuitsu**, and **three southern and seven northern schools**.

288. Taisho text 2689 in volume 84, 232c25-233a03

The citation from the *Words and Phrases of the Lotus Sutra* can be found in Taisho text 1718, volume 34, line 118c22.

See glossary for: **Aryadeva, Aryasimha, *Brahma's Net Sutra*, Gladdened by Dharma, Kumarajiva, Medicine King,** and **Saha world**.

Glossary

Abandon, close, set aside, and cast away: (J. sha, hei, kaku, hō; 捨閉閣抛) The phrase "abandon, close, set aside, and cast away" was coined by **Nichiren Shonin** to represent the doctrine of **Honen**, who insisted that only the **nembutsu** is the appropriate teaching for the people in the **Latter Age of Degeneration**, negating all other doctrines and practices. The four ideograms are taken from Honen's *A Collection of Passages on the Nembutsu Chosen in the Original Vow* advising the people to put aside the **holy way gate** (all teachings other than those of the **Pure Land school**). A prominent example of Nichiren Shonin's use of this phrase can be found in his *Treatise on **Spreading Peace Throughout the Country by Establishing the True Dharma***. (WNS1, pp. 51, 121, 125, 137)

abhidharma: (S.; J. abidatsuma or taihō; 阿毘達磨 or 対法). This Sanskrit term consists of the word "**dharma**" with the prefix "*abhi*," which means "towards" or "higher." It means "approaching the Dharma," "Dharma analysis," or "higher Dharma."

The abhidharma is a collection of works that present a classification and analysis of the teachings found in the **sutra**s and the **vinaya** in order to find the irreducible phenomena that compose existence. It also describes Buddhist cosmology and the workings of **cause and effect**, while also detailing the path to **liberation**. It is considered to comprise the third of the **three baskets**.

Abhidharma Treasury school: (J. Kusha-shū; 倶舎宗) One of the schools of Chinese Buddhism and one of the **six schools of Nara Buddhism** in Japan. The Abhidharma Treasury school was founded on the teaching of the *Treasury of Abhidharma Treatise* by **Vasubandhu** that was translated into Chinese by Paramartha (499-569) between 563 and 567 and again by **Xuanzang** between 651 and 654. The Abhidharma Treasury school was not a separate sect of Buddhism but a scholarly endeavor to learn the principles of the **abhidharma** of mainstream Buddhism in preparation for studying the doctrines of **Mahayana** Buddhism.

The Abhidharma Treasury school, or Kusha Shu, was transmitted together with the **Dharma Characteristics school** to Japan by **Dosho** in 661. By 793, the Kusha Shu was merely a curriculum taught within the Dharma Characteristics school.

Nichiren Shonin classified this school, along with the **Discipline school** and **Completion of Reality school**, as a **hinayana** school (WNS2, pp. 192, 252, 267; WNS3, pp. 19, 123, 249; WNS5, p. 163; WNS6, p. 146).

absolute subtlety: (J. zetsudai-myō; 絶待妙) In the *Profound Meaning of the*

Lotus Sutra, **Zhiyi** interpreted the Chinese ideogram 妙 (meaning "subtle" or "**wonderful**"), in terms of **relative subtlety** and absolute subtlety, both of which reveal the profundity of the *Lotus Sutra*. The teachings of absolute subtlety are incomparable, beyond **conceptual proliferation**, and even subsumes the coarse or relative so that there is nothing apart from what is subtle. Specifically, Zhiyi explains that each of the **four doctrinal teachings** can be opened up to reveal what is subtle, that the **dharma** of all **sentient being**s is subtle because of the absolute subtlety of the **Trace Gate**, that the dharma of the **Buddha** is subtle because of the absolute subtlety of the **Original Gate**, and that the dharma of the **mind** is subtle because of the absolute subtlety of the practice of **contemplation** of the mind. Unlike relative subtlety, absolute subtlety is not used to destroy the coarse but rather to open the coarse and thereby reveal the subtle. (FTP, pp. 199-206; PMLS2, pp. 90-92)

accommodative-body: (S. nirmāṇa-kāya; J. ōjin; 応身) One of the **three bodies** of a **buddha**. Also known as the **transformation-body**. The accommodative-body is the physical body that a **buddha** assumes in a specific time and place in order to lead people to **awakening** through his **compassion**ate actions and teaching. **Shakyamuni** Buddha, viewed as the buddha of history in our world, is an example of a buddha appearing with an accommodative-body. Accommodative-bodies seem to have finite lifespans, because they appear as buddhas who are born as **human** beings, **attain buddhahood**, **turn the Wheel of the Dharma**, and when they are done teaching they enter **final nirvana**.

The **Tiantai school** of Buddhism distinguishes between a **superior accommodative-body** that appears in a **pure land** and an **inferior accommodative-body** that appears in an **impure land**.

According to **Nichiren Shonin**, the accommodative-body is like the reflection of the moon in water, while the **Dharma-body** is like the moon itself, and the **reward-body** is like the moonlight. (WNS6, p. 131) He also taught that while the accommodative-body buddhas of the provisional Mahayana teachings are finite, the accommodative-body that is an aspect of the **Eternal Shakyamuni Buddha** has no beginning or end. (WNS3, p. 250)

acharya: (S. ācārya; J. ajari; 阿闍梨) The Sanskrit term *ācārya* literally means "one who teaches proper conduct," and so can be translated as "master" or "teacher." It is often used in the sense of an "eminent **monk**."

In the **Nichiren school**, an *ajari* is an assistant to the officiant of a service. In Japanese **esoteric Buddhism**, it refers to one who has received the transmission of esoteric teachings and practices and is qualified to transmit it to others.

action: (S. karma; J. gō or kōi; 業 or 行為) The Sanskrit term **karma**, is often understood in Buddhism to specifically mean an intentional action. It can also be understood more generally as any kind of activity, even those performed by the insentient.

activity: (J. sa; 作) In the *Profound Meaning of the Lotus Sutra*, activity as the fifth of the **ten suchnesses** is given the following definition by **Zhiyi**: "That which constructs is called 'activity.'" (FTP, p. 184)

In the *Great Calming and Contemplation*, Zhiyi further explained that the **mind** includes all activity because nothing is activated apart from it. (CSQI, p. 809)

Additional Annotations to the Three Major Works of Tiantai: (J. *Tendai-san-daibu-fuchū*; 天台三大部補註): A treatise written by Congyi (1042-1091) of Song dynasty China in fourteen fascicles. In this work, Congyi tried to explain what had been left unexplained by **Zhiyi** in what came to be known as his **three major works of the Lotus school** and by **Zhanran** in his commentaries on those three major works. Also called the *Additional Annotations to the Three Major Works of the Lotus School* (J. *Hokke-sandaibu-fuchū*; 法華三大部補註).

Agama sutras: (S. Āgama-sūtras; J. Agon-gyō; 阿含経). The **scripture**s of pre-**Mahayana** or mainstream Buddhism containing discourses believed to have been taught by the historical **Shakyamuni Buddha**. There are four groups of Agama sutras from India that were translated into Chinese: the *Long Discourses*, the *Middle Length Discourses*, the *Connected Discourses*, and the *Numerical Discourses*.

According to the **Tiantai school**'s comparative classification of doctrines that divides the Buddha's teachings into **five periods** and **four doctrinal teachings**, the Agama sutras are **hinayana** teachings preached in the second or **Deer Park period**, containing the **tripitaka teachings**.

Age of the Semblance Dharma: (J. zōbō-ji; 像法時) Also called the Middle Age of the Semblance Dharma. The term refers to the third and fourth of the **five five-hundred-year periods** after the passing of **Shakyamuni Buddha**, which are respectively the period of reading and listening to Buddhist teachings and the period of building temples. During the Age of the Semblance Dharma, the teachings are spread though the true spirit has been lost.

Age of the True Dharma: (J. shōbō-ji; 正法時) Also called the Former Age of the True Dharma. The term refers to the first two five-hundred-year periods following the passing of **Shakyamuni Buddha**, which are respectively the period of the firm attainment of **liberation** and the period of the firm cultivation of meditation. During the Age of the True Dharma, the Buddha's teachings were spread correctly by his direct disciples and second generation of disciples and practiced in accord with their true spirit.

aggregate: (S. skandha; J. on or un; 陰 or 蘊) The Sanskrit term *skandha* can also be translated as "heap." Usually this word is used in reference to the **five aggregates**, though there are beings who do not possess all five.

Agnidatta: (J. Agidatta, Agita, or Agitatsu; 阿耆達多 or 阿耆多 or 阿耆達) Also known as King **Ajita**. He was a **brahmin** who invited **Shakyamuni Buddha** and the **Sangha** to his home in Vairanja (S. Vairanjā) in the kingdom of Koshala for the twelfth rainy season retreat after the Buddha's **awakening**. When the Buddha and the Sangha arrived, there was a famine in that region and Agnidatta neglected to provide food. Instead, horse traders provided for the Buddha and the Sangha for the duration of the retreat by giving them the oats (or bran) used for horse fodder. (See LB, pp. 126-127)

Ajatashatru: (S. Ajātashatru; J. Ajase-ō or Mishō'on; 阿闍世王 or 未生怨) The Sanskrit name Ajātashatru means "Unborn Enemy," which is what the ideograms 未生怨 mean. He was a king of **Magadha** in central India, whose capital was Rajagriha when **Shakyamuni Buddha** taught the *Lotus Sutra*.

Ajatashatru was the son of King **Bimbisara** and Queen **Vaidehi**. When King Bimbisara and his wife were unable to conceive a child, a **rishi** told them that there was an ascetic living in the forest who was destined to be their child in his next life. King Bimbisara hoped to speed the process along by having the ascetic murdered. Queen Vaidehi did conceive, but now the rishi informed the king that because of what he had done, the boy would grow up to become his father's killer. Alarmed by this, King Bimbisara dropped the baby from the palace walls after his birth, but the infant survived. King Bimbisara apparently decided that he should not do anything else that might make things worse. This is why the newborn prince was given a name that means "unborn enemy." (BD, pp. 550-551)

Eight years before Shakyamuni Buddha passed away, **Devadatta** used his **supernatural power**s to appear before Prince Ajatashatru in the form of a young boy wreathed in snakes. This apparition terrified the prince, but when he discovered that it was Devadatta he was impressed by the display of magical power. The two plotted for Ajatashatru to usurp the throne from his father, and for Devadatta to take over the **Sangha** from the Buddha. In the meantime, Prince Ajatashatru became Devadatta's royal patron and gave him all that he could want and more than he could use. (LB, pp. 257-258)

Shortly after being denounced by the Sangha, Devadatta persuaded the prince to attempt to assassinate King Bimbisara. The plot was discovered, but in the end

King Bimbisara voluntarily relinquished the throne to his son. Despite his acquiescence, upon taking the throne King Ajatashatru imprisoned his father and had him starved to death. When his mother, Vaidehi, tried to smuggle food to her husband, Ajatashatru almost struck her down with his sword; but two of his ministers, **Chandraprabha** and **Jivaka**, persuaded him not to commit such a heinous act as killing one's mother. Instead, he confined her to an inner chamber in the palace. (LB, pp. 259-260, 271; TPLS, pp. 65-66)

After taking the throne, one of King Ajatashatru's first acts, at the instigation of Devadatta, was to dispatch assassins to kill Shakyamuni Buddha. The assassins failed because none of them could go through with the act of killing the Buddha once they were in his presence. In the end, all the assassins became disciples of the Buddha. (LB, pp. 260-261)

According to the ***Nirvana Sutra***, Ajatashatru was eventually overcome by guilt because of his misdeeds and, as a result, developed life-threatening boils all over his body. He worried that he would fall into hell after death. Even the counsel of the **six non-Buddhist masters** could not help him. Jivaka, the court physician, finally persuaded him to go and ask the Buddha for help. Ajatashatru was impressed by the Buddha's teaching and repented. He took refuge in the **Three Treasures** of Buddha, **Dharma**, and Sangha and became a lay disciple of the Buddha. In this way, he absolved the evil **karma** that brought about the boils and was able to prolong his life. (NS, pp. 253-279; BD, pp. 560-569)

Despite accepting the Buddha's teaching, the reign of King Ajatashatru was not a peaceful one, and he was frequently either scheming against or openly at war with his neighbors. (LB, pp. 271-272) He did, however, build a monument for his share of the Buddha's relics after the **final nirvana** of Shakyamuni Buddha. (LB, pp. 331-332) He also supported the first Buddhist council that compiled the Buddha's teachings.

King Ajatashatru and his attendants appear in the first, "Introductory," chapter of the ***Lotus Sutra***.

To **Nichiren Shonin**, the story of Ajatashatru represents the ability to **attain buddhahood** of even the ***icchantika***, incorrigible disbelievers who are believed to be devoid of the **seed of buddhahood**. The *Nirvana Sutra* taught that even *icchantika* like Ajatashatru, who had committed one of the **five heinous transgressions (killing one's father)**, have **buddha-nature**. In the tenth, "The **Teacher of the Dharma**," chapter of the *Lotus Sutra*, the Buddha states that all who were in the assembly, which would have included Ajatashatru, and even Devadatta, who was not, would all eventually attain buddhahood. Nichiren Shonin, therefore, cited Ajatashatru as an example of the redemption of evildoers by virtue of the *Lotus Sutra*'s teaching in his attempt to convert the people in the **Latter Age of Degeneration**. (WNS1, p. 189; WNS2, p. 90, 188; WNS3, p. 81-82, 204; WNS4, pp. 64-65 120; WNS5, pp. 52-53, 108; WNS6, pp. 34, 37, 47-48, 147, 151; WNS7, pp. 80, 113, 117, 133-134) He also cited Jivaka as an example of a **good friend** who was able to lead King Ajatashatru to the Buddha. (WNS1, p. 58)

Ajita: (S.; J. Aitta; 阿逸多) The Sanskrit name Ajita means "Invincible." It is another name for **Maitreya Bodhisattva**. King **Agnidatta** was also known as King Ajita.

all heavenly benevolent deities: (J. shoten-zenjin; 諸天善神) The **guardian deities** who watch over those who uphold the **Buddha Dharma**. They are equivalent to the **eight kinds of supernatural beings**.

all the holy teachings of the Buddha's lifetime: (J. ichidai shōgyō; 一代聖教) The ideograms 聖教 can also translated as **dispensation**. This refers to all the teachings of **Shakyamuni Buddha** taught to liberate people during his lifetime, i.e. since his attainment of **unsurpassed awakening** under the **Bodhi tree** until his **final nirvana** at the age of eighty.

Systematizing them all in the **five periods** and **four doctrinal teachings**, Zhiyi maintained that the *Lotus Sutra* represented the true intent of Shakyamuni Buddha. Following the **Tiantai school** doctrine, **Nichiren Shonin** insisted on the supremacy of the *Lotus Sutra* over all Buddhist **scripture**s.

all the sutras: (J. issai-kyō; 一切経) This term refers to the East Asian Buddhist canon and includes not just all the **sutra**s (discourses) taught by **Shakyamuni Buddha**, but also the **vinaya** (precepts) given by the Buddha, and the **abhidharma** (treatises) written by later scholars or propagators after the Buddha's passing. The Buddhist canon is also called the **three baskets**.

Nichiren Shonin considered them all as "the Buddha's golden words," and he steadfastly affirmed them as the authentic teachings of Shakyamuni Buddha. Nevertheless, he insisted that the *Lotus Sutra* is the supreme Buddhist scripture, and that it is the only one revealing the true intent of the Buddha.

alms bowl: (S. pātra; J. hachi or hatsu; 鉢) A bowl that Buddhist **monk**s and **nun**s are permitted to have so that they may receive alms food on their morning begging rounds.

Amaterasu Omikami: (J. Amaterasu Ōmikami/Tenshō Daijin; 天照大神) The ideograms 天照大神 can be pronounced as either "Amaterasu Omikami" or "Tensho Daijin" in Japanese. She is the Japanese Sun Goddess, who is worshipped as the chief deity of the Ise Shrine. Originally worshipped as the sun goddess in agricultural communities, she came to be regarded as the supreme deity of Japan because she is held to be the initial matriarch of the imperial family, subordinating other **gods** as either her descendants or subjects.

In 742, when the statue of **Mahavairochana Buddha** was being cast for the Todaiji Temple in Nara, an oracle from the Ise Shrine identified her with Mahavairochana, who is known in Japan as Dainichi (大日), which means "Great Sun."

In the letter *Zemmui Sanzō-shō* (*On Tripitaka Master Shubhakarasimha*), attributed to **Nichiren Shonin**, Amaterasu Omikami and her fellow Japanese deity, **Hachiman**, are both identified as provisional manifestations of **Shakyamuni** Buddha. Nichiren Shonin considered her the founder and protector of Japan as well as a **guardian deity** of Buddhism. He also stated that she and the other guardian deities had left the country because of its slander of the *Lotus Sutra* (e.g. WNS1, pp. 137, 149, 173, 235; WNS2, p. 37) He felt that there was a very significant connection between his home in **Awa Province**, where he first began to propagate his **daimoku**, and an important shrine of Amaterasu Omikami. He expressed this in the letter *Nii-ama Gozen Gohenji* (*A Response to My Lady, the Younger Nun*). (WNS7, pp. 149-150) She and Hachiman were the only two Shinto deities Nichiren included on the **Great Mandala of Invoking the Ten Realms**.

Amitabha: (S. Amitābha; J. Amida or Muryōkō; 阿弥陀 or 無量光). The Sanskrit name Amitābha means "Infinite Light." Amitabha **Buddha** presides over the Pure Land of Utmost Bliss in the western region of the universe and is also known as **Amitayus**, or "Infinite Life." He is considered a **superior accommodative-body** buddha by **Zhiyi**, but the **Pure Land school** considers him a **reward-body** buddha.

According to the *Buddha of Infinite Life Sutra*, this buddha was originally a king in the remote past who became a **monk** under World Freedom King Buddha. As a **bodhisattva** he was called Dharma Treasury. He made forty-eight vows to create the best of all pure lands in the western region of the universe beyond all known worlds wherein all **sentient beings** could attain **awakening**. In fulfilling his vows after eons of **bodhisattva practice** he became Amitabha Buddha. (TPLS, pp. 8-22) The eighteenth **vow** in particular became known in the Pure Land school as the **original vow** that expressed his true intention for all beings. The eighteenth vow states:

> If, when I **attain buddhahood**, sentient beings in the lands of the **ten directions**, who sincerely and joyfully entrust themselves to me, desire to be born in my land, and call my name even ten times should not be born there, may I not attain perfect **enlightenment**. Excluded, however, are those who commit the **five heinous transgressions** and abuse the **True Dharma**. (TPLS, p. 14 adapted)

Alternatively, the part that is usually translated as "call my name" could be translated as "are mindful of my name." The Japanese term "**nembutsu**" that refers to the chanting of the name of Amitabha Buddha could mean either "calling on" or "being mindful of the Buddha."

The exclusionary clause in this vow refers to those who "commit the five heinous transgressions," acts that are so heinous that one who commits them is said to be reborn in hell immediately upon dying. The True Dharma refers to the **Wonderful Dharma**. Abusing the Wonderful Dharma means to disparage, misrepresent, or neglect the true intent of the Buddha's teachings as expressed, for instance, in the *Lotus Sutra*. Pure Land Buddhists sometimes claim that this "exclusionary clause" was just a warning and that Amitabha Buddha in fact excludes no one. **Nichiren Shonin**, however, took this passage at its word and pointed out that those who committed **slander of the True Dharma** would in fact be excluded from **rebirth in the pure land**. (e.g. WNS5, pp. 102, 170-171)

Later on, **Shakyamuni** Buddha, who is relating the story of Amitabha Buddha, states that this teaching will outlast all the others:

> I have expounded this teaching for the sake of sentient beings and enabled you to see Amitayus and all in his land. Strive to do what you should. After I have passed into **nirvana**, do not allow doubt to arise. In the future, the Buddhist scriptures and teachings will perish. But, out of pity and **compassion**, I will especially preserve this sutra and maintain it in the world for a hundred years more. Those beings that encounter it will attain deliverance in accord with their aspiration. (TPLS, p. 61)

The *Contemplation of the Buddha of Infinite Life Sutra* opens with the story of Prince **Ajatashatru**'s palace coup. At the urging of **Devadatta** who had ambitions to take over the **Sangha**, Prince Ajatashatru imprisoned his father, King **Bimbisara**, and tried to starve him to death. Queen **Vaidehi**, however, smuggled food and drink on her person when visiting her husband in the dungeon and thereby kept him alive. When Ajatashatru found out about this he threatened to cut her down himself with his sword but was restrained by two of his ministers, **Chandraprabha** and **Jivaka**. Instead, he had the queen locked away in the palace. Filled with despair, Queen Vaidehi looked to Mt. **Sacred Eagle** and called out for the Buddha to send his disciples to comfort her with the teaching of the Dharma. Miraculously, the Buddha appeared himself along with **Ananda** and **Maudgalyayana**. Queen Vaidehi then asked the Buddha what she had done to deserve such an evil son, and why was it that the Buddha also had such an evil cousin as Devadatta. Apparently these questions were taken as rhetorical because they are not answered in this sutra (though the Buddha does discuss his past **karmic** relations with Devadatta in the *Lotus Sutra*). Queen Vaidehi then asks if there is a land where she can be reborn where she will be free of sorrow and afflictions. (TPLS, pp. 65-67) The rest of the sutra is the Buddha's response as he teaches a total of sixteen contemplations. The first thirteen deal with various aspects of the Pure Land of Utmost Bliss and of Amitabha Buddha and his attendants **World Voice Perceiver** Bodhisattva and **Great Power Obtainer** Bodhisattva. (TPLS, pp. 69-79) The last three deal with contemplations involving those of high, middle, or low spiritual **capacity** and their response to the saving power of Amitabha Buddha.

The power of simply hearing and saying the name of Amitabha Buddha is especially stressed towards the end of this sutra. (TPLS, pp. 79-85)

In the *Amitayus Buddha Sutra* the Buddha expounds on the benefits of calling on the name of Amitabha or Amitayus and the advantages of aspiring to birth in the Pure Land of Utmost Bliss. (TPLS, pp. 91-95)

In the seventh chapter, "The Parable of a Magic City," of the *Lotus Sutra*, the story is told of **Great Universal Wisdom Excellence** Buddha and the sixteen princes who were his sons, born to him before taking up Buddhist practice. When his sixteen sons found that their father reached awakening and had become Great Universal Wisdom Excellence Buddha, they renounced their secular lives to follow him. They then begged him to reveal the teaching of perfect enlightenment. Upon awakening, each of his sixteen sons preached the *Lotus Sutra* in the worlds of the ten directions. One of the sixteen sons became Amitayus Buddha in the West, while others became the other **buddhas of the ten directions** except for the sixteenth who became Shakyamuni Buddha of this, the **Saha world**. (LS, pp. 131-134, 143-147)

According to Nichiren Shonin, among all other buddhas in the worlds of the ten directions, Shakyamuni Buddha is the most closely related to the people of this world. Amitabha Buddha and other buddhas who teach in different worlds are not directly related to us. (e.g. WNS3, pp. 140, p. 248; WNS6, pp. 163-164)

Amitayus: (S. Amitāyus; J. Muryōju; 無量寿) The Sanskrit name Amitāyus means "Infinite Life." This is usually taken to be an alternative name for **Amitabha Buddha**.

In the seventh, "The Parable of a Magic City," chapter of the ***Lotus Sutra***, Amitayus is one of the two buddhas of the west who, in a previous life, was one of the sixteen princes who were the sons of **Great Universal Wisdom** Buddha.

Amitayus Buddha Sutra: (S. *Sukhāvatīvyūha-sūtra;* J. *Amida-kyō;* 阿弥陀経). The Sanskrit name *Sukhāvatīvyūha-sūtra* literally means "*Sutra of Displaying Utmost Bliss*," referring to the Pure Land of Utmost Bliss. The Chinese title 阿弥陀経 means *Sutra of Amitayus*. It is also known as the *Shorter Sukhavativyuha Sutra*. This sutra was translated into Chinese by **Kumarajiva** in the fifth century in one fascicle.

It describes the grandeur of the Pure Land of Utmost Bliss, where **Amitayus Buddha** presides. It describes how numerous buddhas of the six directions appeared to praise the virtue of Amitayus Buddha. It also states that one can be reborn in that pure land by chanting the **nembutsu**. It is one of the **three Pure Land sutras**.

Based on the **Tiantai school** teaching of the **five periods**, **Nichiren Shonin** maintained that the *Amitayus Buddha Sutra* is a **provisional sutra** taught in the third period, or **Expanded period**, and that Amitayus Buddha has nothing to do with and is useless to the people in this **Saha world**. (WNS1, p. 238; WNS3, pp. 239-241, p. 248; WNS6, pp. 163-164)

Amoghavajra: (705-774; S.; J. Fukū; 不空) In Japan, he is considered one of the three patriarchs of **esoteric Buddhism** in China and is considered the sixth patriarch of the **Mantra school**. An alternate list of Mantra school patriarchs lists Amoghavajra as the fourth.

Amoghavajra was the son of a **brahmin** father in northern India and a mother from Samarqand in Central Asia. At the age of thirteen he went to Chang'an, China, to become a **monk** and study esoteric Buddhism. He became a teacher of esotericism under the guidance of **Vajrabodhi**. After his master's death in 741, Amoghavajra went to India and Sri Lanka in search of esoteric **scripture**s, returning to China in 746 with twelve hundred fascicles of **sutra**s and discourses. According to some sources he was able to study with Nagabodhi, his master's master, during his travels. Under the patronage of Emperors Xuanzong of the Tang dynasty and his two successors, who established esoteric Buddhism as the state religion, Amoghavajra translated many esoteric scriptures into Chinese. He transmitted the Mantra teachings to a Chinese monk named Huiguo, the seventh patriarch of the Mantra school. Huiguo in turn transmitted them to the Japanese monk **Kukai**.

Nichiren Shonin pointed out Amoghavajra's mistakes in his translation of the *Awakening Mind Treatise* (WNS1, pp. 210-211) and the fact that his prayers for rain resulted in gales (WNS3, pp. 205, 207), and finally condemned him for his **slander of the True Dharma** (WNS1, p. 251).

Amrapali: (S. Āmrapālī; J. Anbara-nyo; 菴婆羅女) The Sanskrit name Amrapali means "mango guardian." Amrapali was a patron of **Shakyamuni Buddha**. She was a famous and beautiful courtesan in the city of Vaishali, at whose mango grove the Buddha resided during his last visit to Vaishali shortly before his **final nirvana**. Her position was a combination of high-class courtesan and royal concubine. She was the mistress of the Licchavi princes and of the neighboring royalty who would come to Vaishali just to see her. She became quite wealthy as a result and was known for her charity and good counsel.

King **Bimbisara** fell in love with her and they even had a child together named Vimala Kaundinya. When Vimala Kaundinya grew up he became a Buddhist **monk** and attained the state of an **arhat**. When Amrapali heard that her son's teacher, Shakyamuni Buddha, was staying at her mango grove, she took her best carriage and drove out to meet him. When Amrapali arrived, she greeted the Buddha with all proper courtesies and sat down to hear the Buddha's teaching. She was so inspired and uplifted by the Buddha's talk that she invited the Buddha and his **Sangha** to eat their meal at her home the next morning. The next day, the Buddha and the Sangha ate their meal at the home of Amrapali. When the meal was over Amrapali donated her mango grove to the Sangha. (LD 2.14-2.19; pp. 242-244) Sometime later, Amrapali received further instruction in the **Dharma** from her son Vimala Kaundinya. She then retired and became a **nun**. Through contemplating the loss of her beauty in old age, as well as all the fame, wealth, and prestige it had brought, she realized that all **phenomena** bear the three marks of **impermanence**, **suffering**, and **non-self**. In this way she also became an arhat and realized the true happiness of **nirvana**. (See Thig. 252–270)

Amrapali Grove: (S. Āmrapālī-vana; J. Ammora-on or Anra-on; 菴没羅園 or 菴羅園) The grove that **Amrapali** donated to the **Sangha** in the last year of the life of **Shakyamuni Buddha**.

amrita: (S. amṛta; J. kanro; 甘露) The Sanskrit term *amṛta* can be translated as "deathlessness." It is the nectar of the **god**s that is said to confer immortality. It is also called soma.

Ananda: (S. Ānanda; J. Anan or Ananda; 阿難 or 阿難陀) One of the **ten great disciples** of **Shakyamuni Buddha**. He is considered foremost among those who are learned, those with a good memory, those with a quick grasp, those who are resolute, and among personal attendants. As the son of either Amritodana or **Dronodana**, he was a cousin of the Buddha and the younger brother of **Devadatta**. He joined the **Sangha** with a number of other **Shakya** nobles when the Buddha returned to Kapilavastu in the second year following his **awakening**. (LB, pp. 79, 82-83) In the sixth year after the Buddha's awakening, Ananda interceded when the Buddha refused to allow **Mahaprajapati** to form an order of **nun**s, which resulted in the Buddha ultimately consenting to the formation of a nun's order. (LB, pp. 104-107) Ananda became the Buddha's attendant in the twentieth year of the Buddha's teaching. (LB, p. 133) He did not become an **arhat** until after the Buddha's passing and just before the beginning of the first Buddhist council. At that council he was called upon to recite all the teachings of the Buddha that he had heard personally and those which had been reported to him from before the time he became the Buddha's attendant. Because he memorized all the discourses, he was known as the foremost in hearing the **sutra**s. It is Ananda who says, "Thus have I heard..." at the beginning of every sutra. (LB, pp. 1-2, 336-340; LS, p. 1)

In the *Transmission of the Dharma Treasury Sutra*, Ananda is the second of the **twenty-three** or **twenty-four successors** or patriarchs after Shakyamuni Buddha. He received the Dharma from **Mahakashyapa**. His successors were **Madhyantika** and Shanavasa, though in the list of twenty-three successors the former is not counted.

He is one of the arhats listed as present in the first, "Introductory," chapter of the *Lotus Sutra*. In the ninth, "Assurance of Future Buddhahood," chapter, Ananda receives the assurance of future buddhahood. He is told that he will become a buddha named **Mountain Sea Wisdom Supernatural Power King**. (LS, pp. 169-172)

When describing the history of the *Lotus Sutra*, **Nichiren Shonin** considers Ananda and Mahakashyapa as the two pioneer leaders of Buddhism during the **Age of the True Dharma** after the passing of Shakyamuni Buddha. (e.g. WNS1, p. 197)

Anavatapta, Lake: (S.; J. Anabadatta or Anokuchi or Anokudatchi or Munetchi; 阿那婆達多 or 阿耨池 or 阿耨達池 or 無熱池) A lake that is believed to be located north of the **Himalayas** and south of Mt. Perfume. Its name means "Heat Free River." From out of that lake flow the four great rivers: the **Ganges River**, the Sindhu (Indus), the Vakṣu (Amu Darya), and the Śītā (Tarim or Yellow). *Jambu* trees grow by the lake. (AKB2, p. 456) It is the home of the **Dragon King** Anavatapta. It has been identified with Lake Manasarovar.

Nichiren Shonin mentions this lake twice in *On the Opening of the Eyes* as the battleground between the **garuda** and the Dragon King Anavatapta (WNS2, pp. 83, 104)

animal: (S. tiryak; J. chikushō; 畜生) The Sanskrit term *tiryak* or the ideograms 畜生 can also be translated as "beast." **Rebirth** as an animal is one of the **three evil destinies**, the lowest of the **six destinies** and of the **ten realms**.

Aniruddha: (J. Anaritsu or Anuruda; 阿那律 or 阿㝹楼馱) One of the **ten great disciples** of **Shakyamuni Buddha**, foremost of those with the **divine eye** or clairvoyance. As the son of King **Dronodana** of Kapilavastu, he was a cousin of **Shakyamuni Buddha** (though some traditions say Amritodana was his father).

It is said that he was never touched by poverty and his wishes were always fulfilled due to his merit of offering a bowl of barnyard millet rice to a hungry **privately-awakened one** in his previous existence.

He is one of the **arhat**s listed as present in the assembly in the first, "Introductory," chapter of the *Lotus Sutra*. In the eighth, **"Assurance of Future Buddhahood of the Five Hundred Disciples,"** chapter he is among the five hundred arhats who receive the assurance of future buddhahood by Shakyamuni Buddha and told that they will become buddhas named **Universal Brightness**.

Nichiren Shonin wrote about the story of Aniruddha to his donors as an example of the great merit that comes from making donations. (WNS7, pp. 9-10; 12-13, 24-26, 96)

annihilationism: (S. uccheda-dṛṣṭi; J. dan-ken; 断見) The Sanskrit term *ucchedadṛṣṭi* can also be translated as "nihilism." It is one form of extreme views. The view of annihilationism refers to the belief that there is a **self** that can be annihilated upon death or through the attainment of **liberation**. This view would also negate the continuity of **cause and effect** because causes made in one lifetime would be annihilated and never come to **fruition**. Avoiding the two extremes of annihilationism and **eternalism**, **Shakyamuni Buddha** taught the **middle way** of **dependent origination**. (CD 12.15, p. 544)

Annotations on the Flower Garland Sutra: (J. *Kegon-kyō-sho*; 華厳経疏) A sixty-fascicle commentary on the *Flower Garland Sutra* written by **Chengguan**.

Annotations on the Nirvana Sutra: (J. *Nehan-kyō-sho*; 涅槃経疏) A commentary on the southern version of the *Nirvana Sutra* written by **Guanding**, the second patriarch of the **Tiantai school** in China.

It is believed that **Nichiren Shonin** often relied on this work when he read the *Nirvana Sutra*.

appearance: (J. sō; 相) The ideogram 相 may also be used to mean **mark**, characteristic or sign.

In the *Profound Meaning of the Lotus Sutra*, appearance as the first of the **ten suchnesses** is given the following definition by **Zhiyi**: "Appearance has its point of reference externally. What can be distinguished by being seen is called 'appearance.'" (FTP, p. 184) In the *Great Calming and Contemplation*, he further explained that appearance or marks are indications of the inner **nature**, and that the **mind** includes all marks. (CSQI, pp. 804-806)

"Appearance of Bodhisattvas from Underground, The" chapter: (J. *Jujiyūjuppon*; 従地涌出品) The fifteenth chapter of the *Lotus Sutra*. In this chapter the **bodhisattvas** from other worlds request permission to preach in the **Saha world**, but **Shakyamuni Buddha** does not commission the celestial bodhisattvas, who are already present, with the task of spreading the *Lotus Sutra* in the **Latter Age of the Dharma**. Instead, he summons innumerable bodhisattvas who emerge from the space beneath the Saha world with their leaders, the **four great bodhisattvas**: **Superior Practice** Bodhisattva, **Limitless Practice** Bodhisattva, **Pure Practice** Bodhisattva, and **Steadily Established Practice** Bodhisattva. On behalf of the bodhisattvas as numerous as eighty thousand times the sands of the **Ganges River**, **Maitreya** Bodhisattva inquires what kind of training they had gone through.

The Buddha then explains that these **bodhisattvas appearing from underground** have long been his disciples in the Saha world. Thus, the Buddha began to hint at his **attainment of buddhahood in the remotest past**.

Following the Buddha's response, Maitreya Bodhisattva asks how the Buddha could have taught the multitude of bodhisattvas appearing from underground for so long if his **attainment of awakening for the first time** was under the **Bodhi tree** in **Bodhgaya** only forty years prior. The Buddha responds to this question in the sixteenth, "**Duration of the Life of the Tathagata**" chapter.

aranya: (S. araṇya; J. kūgen or arennya or arannya; 空閑 or 阿練若 or 阿蘭若) A forest or place of retirement in the wilderness. Mentioned in the thirteenth, "**Encouragement for Keeping This Sutra**," chapter of the *Lotus Sutra*. (LS, p. 212)

archbishop: (J. sōjō or sōtō; 僧正 or 僧統) The ideograms 僧正 literally mean "Sangha administrator" or "Sangha primate." The position was established by the Later Qin and the Eastern Jin dynasties in China in the early fifth century as the highest rank of Sangha officials so that there would be a government appointed supervisor for the Sangha. It was later established by the government in Japan in 624 and first given to the Korean monk Kwalluk (fl. 624). The position was later divided into three subdivisions: great archbishop, archbishop, and archbishop of lower rank.

arhat: (J. ōgu or arakan or araka; 応供 or 阿羅漢 or 阿羅訶) The Sanskrit term *arhat* can also be translated as "worthy one." It is one of the honorable titles for a **buddha**. It is also the highest **fruition** of those who practice the **voice-hearer vehicle**. The arhat has succeeded in extinguishing the **three poisons** and thereby achieved **liberation** from **samsara** by attaining **nirvana**. The arhat has destroyed the fetters of the view that there is a **self**, doubt, seizing upon rules and rituals, sensual desire, ill-will, desire for **form realm** existence, **formless realm** existence, pride, restlessness, and **ignorance**.

arising: (S. utpāda; J. shōki or shō; 生起 or 生) The Sanskrit term *utpāda* can also be translated as "origination," "production," or "created." The ideogram 生 used to translate it also means "birth." It has the connotation of something with a **self-nature** that arises from **causes and conditions**.

arjaka: (J. ari-ju; 阿梨樹) The Sanskrit term *arjaka* is a name for the common basil that grows throughout India. It is said that its branches split into seven pieces.

In the *Suttanipata*, a **brahmin** is threatened by a curse to have his head split into seven pieces. **Shakyamuni Buddha** set him at ease by telling him that the head to be split is actually "ignorance," and that "head-splitting" is clear knowledge conjoined with **faith**, **mindfulness**, **concentration**, **desire**, and **energy**.

(Sn 1025-1026, p. 327)

In the twenty-sixth, "Dharanis," chapter of the *Lotus Sutra*, the Mother of Demon Children and the **ten rakshasi** who are her daughters, all provide **dharani** for the protection of the **practitioner of the *Lotus Sutra***. They all then sing **gatha**s, in which they claim, "Anyone who does not keep our spells, but troubles the expounder of the **Dharma** shall have his head split into seven pieces just as the branches of the arjaka-tree are split." (LS. p. 335)

In the *Shuju Onfurumai Gosho* (*Reminiscences from Tatsunokuchi to Minobu*), **Nichiren Shonin** interpreted this phrase to mean that people who slander the practitioner of the *Lotus Sutra* will suffer from sickness and death. (WNS5, pp. 44-45)

Aryadeva: (c. 170-270; S. Āryadeva; J. Daiba or Shōdaiba; 提婆 or 聖提婆) Also known as Kanadeva. A disciple of **Nagarjuna**, and teacher of the **Middle Way school**. He wrote the *Four Hundred Verse Treatise*, and the *One Hundred Verse Treatise* is attributed to him. The latter work is one of the three treatises that became the basis of the **Three Treatises school**. **Xuanzang** called him one of the "four brilliant suns illuminating the world" along with **Ashvaghosha**, **Nagarjuna**, and **Kumarata**.

In the *Transmission of the Dharma Treasury Sutra*, Aryadeva was the successor of **Nagarjuna** in the list of **twenty-three** or **twenty-four successors** or patriarchs after **Shakyamuni Buddha**.

Aryasimha: (S. Āryasiṃha or Siṃha; J. Shishi; 師子) According to the ***Transmission of the Dharma Treasury Sutra***, Aryasimha was the successor of Haklenayashas and the last of the **twenty-three** or **twenty-four successors** of **Shakyamuni Buddha**. He was executed in Kashmir at the order of King Mihirakula of Dammira, a persecutor of Buddhism. When he was beheaded, milk flowed from his body instead of blood.

Nichiren Shonin frequently alluded to the martyrdom of Aryasimha as an example of those who were persecuted in the past for teaching the **Dharma**. (WNS2, pp. 103, 114, 185, 217; WNS3, p. 9, 46, 55, 104, 199; WNS4, p. 83; WNS5, p. 23, 84-86, 152; WNS6, p. 29, 116)

asaṃkhya: (S. asaṃkhya; J. asōgi; 阿僧祇) The Sanskrit term *asaṃkhya* can be translated as "incalculable," "infinite," or "innumerable." It has been estimated to be an enormous number such as 10^{51} or 10^{59}. (AKB2, p. 480) An *asaṃkhya* **kalpa** can refer to an incalculable number of **great kalpa**s, or it can refer to each of the **four kalpas** that comprise a great kalpa, so that four *asaṃkhya* **kalpa**s equals a great kalpa. (ND 4.156, pp. 521-522)

Asanga: (c. 320-390; S. Asaṅga; J. Mujaku; 無著) Co-founder of the **Consciousness-Only school** of **Mahayana** Buddhism along with his younger brother **Vasubandhu**, whom he converted to Mahayana. He was a native of northern India and a major exponent of the **consciousness-only** doctrine in the fourth century. Traditionally it is said that he often visited **Maitreya Bodhisattva** in the **Tushita Heaven** to receive the ultimate teachings of the Consciousness-Only school. His teacher may have been someone named **Maitreyanatha**.

Ashoka, Emperor: (c. 268-233 BCE; S. Aśoka J. Aiku Daiō; 阿育大王) The third emperor of the Maurya Dynasty, which controlled most of India for the first time in history. He became a Buddhist (c. 268 BCE) and tried to govern India according to Buddhist **morality** as he understood it, protected Buddhism, convened the third of the Buddhist councils for the third compilation of Buddhist **scripture**s, and built many **stupa**s for the Buddha's relics.

There is a story in the *Transmission of the Dharma Treasury Sutra* that during the lifetime of the Buddha two boys, Virtue Victorious and Invincible, donated rice cakes made of sand to **Shakyamuni Buddha**. The Buddha then predicted that Virtue Victorious would be reborn as the Emperor Ashoka and Invincible would be his consort due to the merit of their donation. **Nichiren Shonin** often cited this story as an example of the fulfillment of a prophecy given by the Buddha (WNS1, p. 149; WNS2, p. 57; WNS6, p. 49; WNS7, p. 3) or to show the great **benefit** of making even a small offering. (WNS4, pp. 125-126; WNS7, p. 67, 82, 91, 144)

Ashvaghosha: (c. second century; S. Aśvaghoṣa; J. Memyō; 馬鳴) A second century **Mahayana** scholar-**monk** and poet from **Shravasti**, though there may have been several persons with the same name. Ashvaghosha was supposed to have been the court poet of King Kanishka. He was the author of the earliest Sanskrit biography of the Buddha, the *Acts of the Buddha*. He is also credited with the *Awakening of Faith in the Mahayana Treatise*. **Xuanzang** called him one of the "four brilliant suns illuminating the world" along with **Aryadeva**, **Nagarjuna**, and **Kumarata**.

In the *Transmission of the Dharma Treasury Sutra*, Ashvaghosha was the successor of Punyayashas in the list of **twenty-three** or **twenty-four successors** or patriarchs after **Shakyamuni Buddha**.

asura: (S. asura; J. ashura; 阿修羅) The Sanskrit word *asura* can also be translated "anti-god" or "non-god." A class of demigods or titans, often called fighting demons. They are the constant rivals of the **gods**, especially **Shakra** and the **four heavenly kings**. Asura are characterized by jealousy, envy, pride, and constant competition. **Rebirth** as an asura is one of the **six destinies** and the **ten realms**.

In Vedic legend, the asuras fought against the gods for sovereignty over the world. They had almost succeeded in their arrogant schemes to rule the world when the gods convinced them to agree to a truce so they could assist them in churning the ocean in order to bring forth the **amrita** or soma, the elixir of immortality. Both sides planned on using guile or force to get all the soma for themselves, but the gods deceived the asura by conjuring the image of a beautiful woman to distract them. While the asuras were preoccupied, the gods were able to deprive them of the soma. In this way, the quick-witted gods overcame the lustful and power-hungry asuras in their bid for dominance.

The asura are said to live beneath the ocean and on the mountain ranges immediately surrounding Mount **Sumeru**, where they continue to plot and scheme to someday assail the heavens, drive out or kill the gods, and rule the world as tyrannical overlords. In one discourse, an asura king named Paharada (P. Pahārāda) describes the delight the asuras take in the great ocean to **Shakyamuni Buddha**. (ND 8.19 pp. 1142-1143)

While asuras are generally considered evil and fearsome spirits fond of fighting, they can also be good spirits and protectors of Buddhism and so are considered one of the **eight kinds of supernatural beings** who protect Buddhism.

Four asura kings were listed as being present in the first, "Introductory," chapter of the *Lotus Sutra*.

attain buddhahood: (J. jōbutsu; 成仏) To attain buddhahood is the fundamental purpose of practicing **Mahayana** Buddhism. This is also called attaining **unsurpassed, complete, and perfect awakening**.

According to the *Lotus Sutra*, **Shakyamuni Buddha** taught the **three vehicles** as a **skillful means** to prepare his disciples for the teaching of the **One Vehicle** whereby all could attain buddhahood. The **prior teachings** of the **provisional sutra**s did not present attaining buddhahood as a realistic goal but instead taught that practitioners should only aim to become **arhat**s, or they taught that one could only attain buddhahood after three innumerable **kalpa**s and a hundred **great kalpa**s of practice, or they did not allow for the **attainment of buddhahood by adherents of the two vehicles**, the **attainment of buddhahood by women**, or the attainment of buddhahood by such incorrigible people as the *icchantika*s. The *Lotus Sutra*, however, does allow for the practitioners of the two vehicles, women, and *icchantika*s to attain buddhahood.

Nichiren Shonin, on the basis of the **Tiantai school** doctrines of the **three thousand realms in a single thought-moment** and the Buddha's **attainment of buddhahood in the remotest past**, taught that a practitioner can attain buddhahood in the present lifetime by upholding and chanting the **daimoku**.

attain buddhahood with one's present body: (J. sokushin jōbutsu; 即身成仏) The teaching that an **ordinary person** can **attain buddhahood** with his present body is a doctrine taught in Japan by the **Tendai school** and the **Mantra school**.

This contrasts with the doctrine of **rebirth in the pure land**, where people must practice Buddhism in the next life in order to attain buddhahood.

Nichiren Shonin taught that buddhahood is attainable in the present lifetime for one who upholds and chants the **daimoku**. He criticized the Shingon school for claiming that only through their teachings could this be done and pointed out that only with the **attainment of buddhahood by a dragon girl** in the twelfth, "**Devadatta," chapter** of the *Lotus Sutra* is there any actual proof of anyone attaining buddhahood with their present body. (WNS1, pp. 179,188, 210; WNS3, p. 151, 228; WNS4, pp. 30, 63, 93, 142, 147; WNS6, p. 132)

attaining buddhahood with one's present body: See **attain buddhahood with one's present body**.

attain enlightenment: (J. tokudo or jōdō; 得度 or 成道) The ideogram 得 means "attain." The ideogram 度 means "to cross over," as in the phrase "crossing over to the other shore," which is a metaphor for achieving **liberation** from **samsara** (this shore) and realizing **nirvana** (the other shore). Together, the ideograms 得度 are taken to mean "attain **enlightenment**" or "attain **awakening**." The ideograms 得度 can also refer to the "**lower ordination**" of a **novice**, which is called the "ceremony for bestowing the precepts for **leaving home** and attaining enlightenment" or more simply "bestowing the precepts for attaining enlightenment."

The ideogram 成 can mean "to accomplish." The ideogram 道 can means "the way." Together they literally mean "to accomplish the way," in reference to the way of the **Buddha** or the way to enlightenment. Therefore, they also mean "attain enlightenment."

attainment of awakening for the first time: (J. shijō shōgaku; 始成正覚) The ideograms 始成正覚 literally mean "first attaining true awakening" and refer to **Shakyamuni Buddha**'s attainment of **unsurpassed, complete, and perfect awakening** under the **Bodhi tree** in **Bodhgaya**, India. Contrary to this, the sixteenth, "The **Duration of the Life of the Tathagata," chapter** of the *Lotus Sutra* declares: "To tell the truth, good men, it is many hundreds of thousands of billions of *nayutas* of kalpas since I became the Buddha." (LS, p. 247) Thus, the **attainment of buddhahood in the remotest past** of **five hundred dust-particle kalpas** ago was revealed.

attainment of buddhahood by a dragon girl: (J. ryūnyo jōbutsu; 竜女成仏) In the twelfth, "**Devadatta**," **chapter** of the *Lotus Sutra*, an eight-year-old **dragon girl** transforms into a **buddha**, although it had long been a Buddhist tradition that females cannot become kings or buddhas because of their inherent **five obstacles**.

Considering the attainment of buddhahood by a dragon girl as the precedent for the **attainment of buddhahood by women** and also as actual proof of being able to **attain buddhahood with one's present body**, **Nichiren Shonin** stressed the great compassion of the Buddha embracing all beings without discrimination enabling them to attain buddhahood. (WNS1, pp. 189, 210; WNS4, pp. 63-64, 147, 165-170; WNS6, p. 132)

attainment of buddhahood by adherents of the two vehicles: (J. nijō sabutsu; 二乗作仏) The central theme of the **Trace Gate** of the *Lotus Sutra*. This doctrine maintains that even the two groups of **hinayana** sages following the **two vehicles**, called **voice-hearers** and **privately-awakened ones**, who are declared incapable of becoming **buddhas** in such **Mahayana** sutras as the *Flower Garland Sutra* and the *Vimalakirti Sutra*, can **attain buddhahood** through the **One Vehicle** teaching of the *Lotus Sutra*. It shows that **awakening** through the *Lotus Sutra* is available to all.

Along with the **attainment of buddhahood in the remotest past** doctrine it provided **Nichiren Shonin** with a doctrinal foundation for claiming the superiority of the *Lotus Sutra* over all the teachings taught by **Shakyamuni** Buddha.

attainment of buddhahood by women: (J. nyonin jōbutsu; 女人成仏) Attainment of buddhahood by women had long been denied in Buddhism in Japan, India, and China because of the **five obstacles**. However, the twelfth, "**Devadatta**," **chapter** of the *Lotus Sutra* teaches that women, who had been regarded as incapable of becoming kings or buddhas, can **attain buddhahood**. The chapter tells the story of the **attainment of buddhahood by a dragon girl**.

Stressing the importance of the attainment of buddhahood by the dragon girl, **Nichiren Shonin** said, "The example of the dragon girl becoming a buddha does not mean only her." (WNS2, pp. 90-91; WNS4, pp. 32-34, 54-56, 63, 147; WNS7, pp. 125, 145, 186)

attainment of buddhahood in the remotest past: (J. kuon jitsujō; 久遠実成) The central theme of the **Original Gate**, especially of the sixteenth, "The **Duration of the Life of the Tathagata**," chapter of the *Lotus Sutra*. In that chapter, **Shakyamuni Buddha** states that he did not attain **unsurpassed, complete, and perfect awakening** at Bodhgaya in India for the first time but that he has been awakened since the remotest past. The **attainment of buddhahood** by Shakyamuni Buddha at Bodhgaya was merely a temporal appearance of the **Eternal Shakyamuni Buddha** who has been guiding and saving all **sentient beings** since the remotest past.

The attainment of buddhahood is intimated in the first half of the fifteenth,

"The **Appearance of Bodhisattvas from Underground," chapter** of the *Lotus Sutra*. It is explicitly and fully taught in the latter half of chapter fifteen and in the subsequent chapters up to and including the twenty-second, "Transmission," chapter.

Nichiren Shonin's claim that the *Lotus Sutra* is the ultimate true teaching of the Buddha is based on the two doctrines of the "attainment of buddhahood in the remotest past" and the "**attainment of buddhahood by adherents of the two vehicles**."

attendants, subtlety of: (J. kenzoku-myō; 眷属妙) The ninth of the **ten subtleties of the Trace Gate**. It refers to the subtle nature of the **Buddha**'s attendants with their own activities, **supernatural powers**, **vow**s, responses, and teachings. The attendants of the Buddha are compared to the clouds that hide the moon or the retinue that accompany an emperor. (FTP, p. 208; PMLS2, pp. 94, 289-299)

average capacity: (S. madhyendriya; J. chūkon; 中根) This refers to practitioners of average intelligence, ability to overcome **defilement**s, and aspiration.

awakening: (S. bodhi; J. bodai or kaku/satori; 菩提 or 覚) This refers to the awakening that leads to **liberation** from **suffering** in Buddhism. It may be the awakening of a **buddha**, an **arhat**, or a **privately-awakened one**. In the case of a buddha it is elaborated as **unsurpassed, complete, and perfect awakening**.

awakening mind: (S. bodhicitta; J. bodaishin or hosshin; 菩提心 or 発心) Also known as the "aspiration for **awakening**." This refers to the **bodhisattva**'s initial aspiration, motivated by great compassion, to **attain buddhahood** for the **liberation** of all **sentient being**s.

Bamboo Grove Monastery: (S. Veṇuvana-vihāra; J. Chikurin-shōja; 竹林精舎) A monastery just outside Rajagriha. It was donated to the **Sangha** by King **Bimbisara** during **Shakyamuni Buddha**'s first visit to Rajagriha after he was able to **attain buddhahood**. (LB, pp. 68-69)

Beautiful Form: (S. Śaśiketu; J. Myōsō; 名相) The name of the **buddha** that **Subhuti** will become, according to the sixth, "Assurance of Future Buddhahood," chapter of the *Lotus Sutra*.

beginning and end ultimately equal: (J. honmatsu-kukyō-tō; 本末究竟等) In the *Profound Meaning of the Lotus Sutra*, the phrase "beginning and end ultimately equal" as the tenth of the **ten suchnesses** is given the following definition by **Zhiyi**: "The initial '**appearance**' is called the 'beginning,' the later '**recompense**' is called the 'end,' and the place to which they belong is ultimately equal." (FTP, p. 184)

In the *Great Calming and Contemplation*, Zhiyi further explained that from the beginning to the end the first nine suchnesses all arise from **condition**s and therefore all are equally **empty**; that all are equally nominal designations and relative to one another and therefore all equally have **provisional existence**; and that, even if the **tetralemma** were applied to them, all the possibilities of their existence or non-existence would still be included within the limit of reality and therefore all are equally the **middle way**. (CSQI, p. 810)

"Beholding the Stupa of Treasures" chapter: (J. *Ken-hōtō-hon*; 見宝塔品) The eleventh chapter of the *Lotus Sutra*. In this chapter, a **stupa of treasures** decorated with **seven treasures**(2) springs up from the earth and hangs in the sky before **Shakyamuni Buddha**. A loud voice is heard from within the stupa verifying the truth of Shakyamuni Buddha's teaching: "Excellent, excellent! You, Shakyamuni Buddha, the **World Honored One**, have expounded to this great multitude the *Sutra of the Lotus Flower of the Wonderful Dharma*, the Great Wisdom of Equality, the Dharma for **Bodhisattva**s, the Dharma Upheld by the Buddhas. So it is, so it is. What you, Shakyamuni Buddha, the World Honored One, have expounded is all true." (LS, p. 187 adapted)

On behalf of the four assemblies, Great Eloquence Bodhisattva asks Shakyamuni Buddha about the stupa and the voice within it. The Buddha tells the assembly that inside the stupa is enshrined the perfect body of **Many Treasures** Buddha who made a **vow** that even after his **final nirvana** he would appear to testify to the truth of the *Lotus Sutra* if anyone should teach it after his passing.

Great Eloquence Bodhisattva then asks to see Many Treasures Buddha. Since Many Treasures Buddha had also made a vow that he would allow his stupa to be opened to reveal his body if the buddha who teaches the *Lotus Sutra* recalls all his **emanation buddhas of the ten directions**, Shakyamuni Buddha proceeds to do this. He purifies the **Saha world**, recalls all his emanations, ascends into the sky, and opens the stupa of treasures. Then, at the invitation of Many Treasures Buddha, Shakyamuni Buddha enters the stupa himself. Shakyamuni Buddha then uses his **supernatural power** to raise the entire assembly into the sky as well. This is the beginning of the Assembly in Space.

Shakyamuni Buddha then makes **three proclamations**, urging those in the four assemblies to expound the *Lotus Sutra* in the Saha world. As part of the third proclamation, the Buddha explains the comparative difficulty of teaching the *Lotus Sutra* after his final nirvana in terms of the **six difficult and nine easier actions**. He concludes:

> "It is difficult to keep this sutra. I shall be glad to see anyone keeping it even for a moment. So will all the other buddhas. He will be praised by all the buddhas. He will be a man of valor, a man of endeavor. He should be

considered to have already observed the **precept**s, and practiced the ascetic practices allowed by the Buddha called the *dhuta*. He will quickly attain the unsurpassed **enlightenment** of the Buddha. Anyone who reads and recites this sutra in the future is a true son of mine. He shall be considered to live on the stage of purity and good. Anyone, after my extinction, who understands the meaning of this sutra, will be the eye of the worlds of **god**s and **human**s. Anyone who expounds this sutra even for a moment in this dreadful world, should be honored with offerings by all gods and humans." (LS, pp. 198-199 adapted)

Nichiren Shonin paid particular attention to the twelve chapters, beginning with this chapter to the twenty-second chapter, "Transmission," as the teaching of the Assembly in Space.

benefit: (J. ri or riyaku or yaku; 利 or 利益 or 益) The ideogram 利 can also be translated as "profit." It is synonymous with **merit**.

Zhiyi taught that "merit" (功德) pertains to benefits enjoyed by oneself, while "benefit" (利益) pertains to benefits enjoyed by others. (PMLS2, p. 300)

benefiting oneself and benefiting others: (J. jiri-rinin or jiri-rita or jiyaku-yakuta; 自利利人 or 自利利他 or 自益益他) The principle that **bodhisattva**s, being motivated by great compassion, practice for the sake of the **liberation** from **suffering** of all **sentient being**s, and not just their own **awakening** or liberation.

benevolence: (J. jin or nin; 仁) The first of the **five constant virtues** of Confucianism. In the *Great Calming and Contemplation*, Zhiyi wrote, "Treating people with benevolent humanness and nurturing others without bringing them harm corresponds to the first **precept** to abstain from killing." (CSQI, p. 1042 modified)

Benevolent Kings Sutra. (J. *Ninnō-kyō* or *Ninnō-hannya-kyō*; 仁王経 or 仁王般若経) A discourse of **Shakyamuni Buddha** to King Prasenajit of Koshala regarding the way to protect the nation. It has been revered in China and Japan as one of the three state-protecting **sutra**s. There are two Chinese versions, one by **Kumarajiva** and the other by **Amoghavajra**, both in two fascicles. The **Mantra school** uses the Amoghavajra version.

The **sutra** states that it was taught in the twenty-ninth year since the Buddha began teaching the **Prajna sutras**. The **Tiantai school** understood this to mean that it was taught in the forty-second year of the Buddha's **dispensation** as the last sutra of the **Prajna period** just before the **Lotus-Nirvana period**.

Nichiren Shonin cites from the Kumarajiva version in explaining the **three**

calamities and **seven disasters** and other matters in the *Treatise on **Spreading Peace Throughout the Country by Establishing the True Dharma***. (WNS1, pp. 111, 114, 131, 139)

Bimbisara: (r. c. 465-413 BCE; S. Bimbisāra; J. Bimbashara-ō; 頻婆娑羅王) The fifth king of the Shaishnaga (S. Śaiśnāga) dynasty in **Magadha** and a devout follower of **Shakyamuni Buddha**. He donated the **Bamboo Grove Monastery** to the **Sangha** and became a great patron of Buddhism. In his later years, however, he was imprisoned by his own son, Crown Prince **Ajatashatru**, who had been incited by **Devadatta**. He died in prison. (LB, pp. 259-260, 271; TPLS, pp. 65-66)

bit of soil on a fingernail: (J. sōjō no do/sōjō no tsuchi; 爪上の土) A phrase taken from the *Nirvana Sutra* as a way of referring to something as relatively small as the amount of soil on a fingernail compared to the vast amount of sand on the banks of the **Ganges River**. It is likened to the slight chance of being born in the **human** world compared to the greater likelihood of being born in another one of the **six destinies**, particularly the lower ones. Another passage likens it to the rarity of those who put their **faith** in the *Nirvana Sutra* compared to the great number of those who do not take faith but become *icchantika*.

Nichiren Shonin cited this phrase from the *Nirvana Sutra* to refer to the comparative rarity of people who put **faith** in the **True Dharma** of the *Lotus Sutra* compared to the vast amount of people who take faith in the **prior teachings**. (WNS1, pp. 3, 53-55, 66; WNS3, pp. 34-35, 101, 111, 209; WNS2, pp. 45, 52, 122-123, 174, 112-217, 239; WNS5, p. 60)

Bodhgaya: (S. Buddhagayā; J. Buddagaya; 仏陀伽耶) Also called Gaya (S. Gayā; J. Gaya-jō; 伽耶城). The place where the historical **Shakyamuni Buddha** attained his **unsurpassed, complete, and perfect awakening** under the **Bodhi tree** near Rajagriha, the capital of **Magadha** (now the state of Bihar in northeastern India).

Bodhi tree: (S. Bodhi-druma; J. Bodai-ju or Dō-ju; 菩提樹 or 道樹) The pipal or sacred fig tree (*Ficus religiosa*) in **Bodhgaya** under which **Shakyamuni Buddha** was sitting when he attained **unsurpassed, complete, and perfect awakening**.

Bodhidharma: (c. late-fourth to early-fifth centuries; J. Bodaidaruma; 菩提達磨) The legendary first patriarch of the **Zen school** in China. According to the stories told by the tenth century, he was the third son of a king in southern India who became the disciple of Prajnatara, the alleged twenty-seventh of the **twenty-eight**

Indian ancestors. Bodhidharma was given the transmission of the "treasury of the eye of the True Dharma" by Prajnatara and thus became the twenty-eighth patriarch in India. At his master's urging, Bodhidharma sailed to China in 527 and met with Emperor Wu (r. 502-549) of the Liang dynasty (502-557). In that meeting, Bodhidharma answered the emperor's questions in accord with the **emptiness** teachings of the **Prajna sutras**, leaving the emperor nonplussed. Bodhidharma then left for Mount Song, where he sat in meditation for nine years in a cave near the Shaolin Temple and was called the "Wall Gazing **Brahmin**." In addition to the meditation method called "wall gazing," he is credited with teaching Indian martial arts to the Shaolin monks. It was during this time that Bodhidharma met Huike, the **monk** who would become his successor. Bodhidharma is credited with promulgating the *Lankavatara Sutra* and many centuries after his death some attributed to him the following verse describing Zen: "A **separate transmission outside the sutras**/not founded upon words and letters/a direct pointing to the human mind/seeing the true nature and attaining buddhahood." (See Dumoulin 1994, p. 85)

bodhisattva: (S.; J. bosatsu; 菩薩) The Sanskrit term *bodhisattva* means, "**awakening** being." A being dedicated to attaining buddhahood or **unsurpassed, complete, and perfect awakening** for the sake of all **sentient being**s who take up the practice for "**benefiting oneself and benefiting others**." Like the **lotus flower** in a muddy pond flowering gracefully, bodhisattvas stay in the **Saha world**, helping others achieve **liberation** from **suffering** without thinking of their own happiness. The state of being a bodhisattva is one of the four highest among the **ten realms**.

In mainstream Buddhism only two bodhisattvas are recognized: **Siddhartha Gautama** and his innumerable past lives before his **attainment of awakening for the first time** under the **Bodhi tree** at the age of thirty (or thirty-five) and who became known thereafter as **Shakyamuni Buddha**, and **Maitreya** Bodhisattva who resides in the Heaven of **Tushita** for five hundred and seventy-six million years before he will be reborn to become the next buddha of the Saha world and once more set in motion the **turning of the Wheel of the Dharma**. Mainstream Buddhism leaves open the possibility that there might be other bodhisattvas, but none are named.

In **Mahayana** Buddhism, bodhisattvas are the primary exemplars of Buddhist practice who cultivate the **six perfections** of **generosity, morality, patience**$_{(1)}$, **energy, meditative absorption**, and **wisdom**. These bodhisattvas assist not only Shakyamuni Buddha but also many other buddhas such as **Amitabha** Buddha, **Mahavairochana** Buddha, and **Medicine Master** Buddha. Among the well-known bodhisattvas are **Great Power Obtainer, Manjushri, Medicine King, Universal Sage**, and **World Voice Perceiver**.

bodhisattva practice: (S. bodhisattva-caryā; J. bosatsu-gyō; 菩薩行) In order to

attain buddhahood, one must take up the practice of a **bodhisattva**. This involves the practice of the **six perfections**. According to some schemes, it progresses over **fifty-two stages of bodhisattva practice**, which take three innumerable **kalpa**s and a hundred **great kalpa**s to complete.

bodhisattva vehicle: (S. bodhisattva-yāna; J. bosatsu-jō; 菩薩乗) In the parable of the burning house told in the third, "A Parable," chapter of the *Lotus Sutra*, the teachings and practices taught to the **Buddha**'s disciples are compared to **three vehicles**. The teachings or vehicle for **bodhisattva**s, such as the **six perfections**, are represented in the parable by an ox-cart (or bullock-cart).

bodhisattvas appearing from underground: (J. jiyū no bosatsu; 地涌の菩薩) The **bodhisattva**s and the **four great bodhisattvas**, who are their leaders, appeared from the **space** beneath the ground of the **Saha world** in the fifteenth, "**Appearance of Bodhisattvas from Underground**," chapter of the *Lotus Sutra*.

In chapter fifteen, **Shakyamuni** Buddha did not commission the **bodhisattvas of the trace teaching**, who were already present, with the task of spreading the *Lotus Sutra* in the **Latter Age of Degeneration**. Instead, he summoned innumerable bodhisattvas who emerged from the space beneath the Saha world, along with their leaders, the four great bodhisattvas: **Superior Practice** Bodhisattva, **Limitless Practice** Bodhisattva, **Pure Practice** Bodhisattva, and **Steadily Established Practice** Bodhisattva. The bodhisattvas appearing from underground all have the **thirty-two marks** of greatness and are incomparably greater in stature and power than even the celestial bodhisattvas of the provisional Mahayana teachings. In the sixteenth chapter, "**Duration of the Lifespan of the Tathagata**," the Buddha, now revealed as the **Eternal Shakyamuni Buddha**, states that he has been teaching them since the remotest past. In the twenty-first chapter, "Supernatural Powers of the Tathagata," they are given the specific transmission of the *Sutra of the Lotus Flower of the Wonderful Dharma* consisting of the teachings, the **supernatural power**s, the treasury, and the achievements of the Buddha. Therefore, they are responsible for expounding the *Lotus Sutra* in the Latter Age of Degeneration.

According to **Nichiren Shonin**, anyone who upholds the **daimoku** in this age is said to be one of these bodhisattvas or, more humbly, one of their followers. Realizing himself to be an appearance of Superior Practice Bodhisattva, Nichiren Shonin strove to spread the *Lotus Sutra*. (e.g., WNS4, p. 74-80)

bodhisattvas of the trace teaching: (J. shakke no bosatsu; 迹化の菩薩) These **bodhisattva**s consist of two groups: those who had been in this **Saha world** and those who came from the **pure land**s throughout universe as the attendants of the **emanation buddhas of the ten directions**. The bodhisattvas of the trace teaching were taught and guided by the **prior teachings** and the first half, or **Trace Gate**, of the *Lotus Sutra*. They represent those who cultivate the **six perfections** of **generosity**, **morality**, **patience**(1), **energy**, **meditative absorption**, and **wisdom** in order to **attain buddhahood**.

These bodhisattvas assume that **Shakyamuni Buddha's attainment of awakening for the first time** was only forty some years before under the **Bodhi tree**, and that his attainment was the result of eons of practice. The events of the *Lotus Sutra*, however, challenge this view. In chapter twelve, "**Devadatta**," there is the **attainment of buddhahood by a dragon girl** showing that it is possible to **attain buddhahood with one's present body**, whereas in chapter sixteen, "The **Duration of the Life of the Tathagata**," Shakyamuni Buddha reveals his **attainment of buddhahood in the remotest past**. This can be understood to mean that his gradual cultivation in his present and past lives was a display of **skillful means** to teach others. In the context of the *Lotus Sutra*, these bodhisattvas represent those who follow the **provisional teaching** that it takes over three innumerable kalpas and a hundred great kalpas of bodhisattva practice to attain buddhahood.

In chapters thirteen through fifteen, these bodhisattvas request that they be allowed to expound the *Lotus Sutra* after the Buddha's **final nirvana**. In chapter fifteen, "**Appearance of Bodhisattvas from Underground**," Shakyamuni Buddha denies their request and instead summons the **bodhisattvas appearing from underground** to expound it. In the twenty-first chapter, "Supernatural Powers of the Tathagata," he gives the bodhisattvas who appeared from underground the specific transmission of the ***Sutra of the Lotus Flower of the Wonderful Dharma***. Only in chapter twenty-two, "Transmission," does the Buddha give all the other bodhisattvas the general transmission of the *Lotus Sutra*.

Nichiren Shonin maintained that the bodhisattvas of the trace teaching's mission was to propagate the Dharma in the Buddha's lifetime, the **Age of the True Dharma**, and the **Age of the Semblance of the Dharma**, whereas it was the mission of the disciples of the original teaching to spread the teaching of the **Eternal Shakyamuni Buddha** in the **Latter Age of Degeneration**. He believed himself to have been an appearance of **Superior Practice** Bodhisattva and strived to spread the message of the *Lotus Sutra*. (e.g., WNS4, p. 74-80)

Brahma: (S. Brahmā; J. Bonten; 梵天) Also Great Brahma. The term for the highest class of **gods** residing in the **Heavens** of **Brahma** above Mt. **Sumeru**. According to **Brahmanism**, **Brahma Heavenly King** is the eternal, omniscient, omnipotent, and morally perfect creator of the world who resides in the Heaven of the Great Brahma of the **form realm**. He is the lord of this world, the **Saha world**. In later developments of the Vedic tradition he became a member of the *trimūrti* which represents the three phases of material nature: Brahma the creator, **Vishnu** the preserver, and Shiva (S. Śiva) the destroyer (called the **Great Freedom God** in Buddhism). In the **sutra**s he says of himself, "I am Brahma, Great Brahma, the Conqueror, the Unconquered, the All-Seeing, the All-Powerful, the Lord, the Maker and Creator, Ruler, Appointer, and Orderer, Father of All That Have Been and Shall Be." (LD 1.2.5, p. 76) Other beings believe Brahma's self-testimony or have vague recollections of a past life in the Heavens of Brahma and therefore seek unity with him or at least **rebirth** in his presence.

Union with Brahma or rebirth in the Heavens of Brahma of the form realm (or any of the heavens) is treated by **Shakyamuni Buddha** as a legitimate though lesser goal for those unable to overcome theistic assumptions about the goal of the religious life. It is a lesser goal because it is still within the **six destinies**. Furthermore, even as the first being to arise in this universe, Brahma is still subject to rebirth in accordance with **causes and conditions**. He simply does not remember that, due to causes and conditions, he came into being in the palace of Brahma at the beginning of the unfolding of the world. He believes that he is the sole cause for the creation of the world and its many beings, but once again he has overlooked the many other causes and conditions involved. According to the Buddha, Brahma's self-testimony is nothing more than self-**delusion** and egotism. Despite his pretensions, as a being among beings caught up in **samsara**, Brahma must also be considered in need of the Buddha's instruction.

The Buddha was sharply critical of the **brahmins** who claimed to teach the way to union with Brahma. He pointed out that theistic teachings are based on hearsay and are not able to give direct knowledge of Brahma. As a **skillful means**, the Buddha taught that one may be united with Brahma at death by emulating his good qualities. The Buddha, however, realized that even life in the heavens were temporary and subject to the same shortcomings as other forms of rebirth. So, while life with Brahma (or even rebirth as Brahma) in the heavens is a worthy and attainable goal, it is not the final goal. Only **nirvana** can provide true peace according to the Buddha. The Buddha, however, did say that in his past lives as a **bodhisattva** he too had been Brahma.

According to a story in the *Connected Discourses*, Brahma served another important function in Buddhism. The story says that when he attained **unsurpassed, complete, and perfect awakening**, Shakyamuni Buddha was not sure whether he should trouble himself to teach others the **Buddha Dharma**. Brahma himself came and convinced the Buddha that he should teach, since there were those who would be able to understand. (CD 6.1, pp. 231-233) This story is recounted in the second, "**Expedients**," **chapter** of the *Lotus Sutra* where Brahma appears in the company of **Shakra**, the **four heavenly kings**, and many other gods. Brahma is also one of the deities who periodically makes an offering of music and showers the assembly with heavenly garments and **lotus flower**s. In the seventh, "Parable of a Magic City," chapter Brahma Heavenly Kings from hundreds of billions of worlds all gather to present offerings to **Great Universal Wisdom Excellence Tathagata** and request that he **turn the Wheel of the Dharma**. In the eighteenth, "Merits of a Person Who Rejoices at Hearing the Sutra," chapter the Buddha teaches that anyone who persuades others to sit and hear the *Lotus Sutra* will obtain the seat of Brahma, revealing that one method of being reborn as Brahma is sharing the sutra with others. In the nineteenth, "Merits of the Teacher of the Dharma," chapter the Buddha asserts that Brahma will come to hear anyone who teaches the *Lotus Sutra*. In the twenty-third and twenty-fourth chapters, "Wonderful Voice Bodhisattva" and "Universal Gate of World Voice Perceiver Bodhisattva," it is stated that both the eponymous bodhisattvas of those chapters can transform themselves into Brahma (among other forms) in order to expound the **Dharma** and save **sentient being**s. Based upon this testimony from the *Lotus Sutra*, Great Heavenly King Brahma is a devotee of the sutra and may, in fact, be an appearance of one of the celestial bodhisattvas who are upholders of the sutra.

In the first, "Introductory," chapter of the *Lotus Sutra*, three different Brahmas are present in the assembly on Mt. Sacred Eagle: Brahma Heavenly King, Great Brahma Shikhin, and Great Brahma Light. It is the first of these three who is usually referred to as the one the brahmins believed to be the supreme god and creator of the Saha world.

Nichiren Shonin included Brahma as one of the deities of Brahmanism who appears on the **Great Mandala of Invoking the Ten Realms**.

Brahma Heavenly King: (S. Brahmā; J. Bontennō; 梵天王) Also called Great Brahma Heavenly King (S. Mahābrahmā; J. Daibontennō; 大梵天王). Brahma Heavenly King is usually referred to as the one the **brahmins** believed to be the supreme **god** and creator of the **Saha world**.

One of the three Brahma gods listed as present in the first, "Introductory," chapter of the *Lotus Sutra*.

Brahma, Heavens of: (S. Brahmaloka; J. Bonten or Bonkai; 梵天 or 梵界) The first three of the **heaven**s of the **form realm**.

Brahma's Net Sutra. (J. *Bommō-kyō* or *Bonmō-kyō*; 梵網経) A **sutra** allegedly translated by **Kumarajiva** in 406 but believed to be an apocryphal work produced in China in the middle of the fifth century. According to the *Brahma's Net Sutra*, **Vairochana Buddha** presented a set of ten major precepts and forty-eight minor precepts for **bodhisattva**s. They were not originally intended to replace or provide an alternative to the monastic rules for **monk**s and **nun**s. These bodhisattva precepts were, and continue to be, bestowed upon both lay followers and monastics to provide a code of conduct for aspiring bodhisattvas in many schools of East Asian Buddhism. The ten major precepts for bodhisattvas are in fact a slight variation on the **ten virtuous precepts**. This sutra is also one of the sources for the doctrine of the **three categories of pure precepts** taught in the **Discipline school**. The precepts of this sutra came to be called the **perfect and sudden precepts** of the *Brahma's Net Sutra*.

Brahmanism: (J. Baramon-kyō or Bonkyō; バラモン教 or 梵教) The mainstream religion of the **brahmin** priests in India based upon the **Vedas** at the time of **Shakyamuni Buddha**. It later developed into what is today known as Hinduism.

Nichiren Shonin considered Brahmanism, the **non-Buddhist teachings** of the "**two gods** and **three hermits**," of India as an expedient teaching that prepared the way for Buddhism.

brahmin: (S. brāhmaṇa J. baramon or bonji; 婆羅門 or 梵志) Also anglicized as "brahman" though that leads to confusing the term with "Brahman," the impersonal absolute from which all else in the world springs. A brahmin is a priest of **Brahmanism**. They are priests, scholars, and teachers among the four classes spoken of in the **Vedas**. The other three classes were the *kshatriyas* (warriors and administrators), the *vaishyas* (farmers, merchants, and artisans), and the *shudras* (laborers and servants). During the time of **Shakyamuni Buddha**, the brahmins argued that they were superior to the other classes.

buddha: (S.; J. butsu or kakusha; 仏 or 覚者) The Sanskrit term *buddha* means "awakened one." Someone who has attained **unsurpassed, complete, and perfect awakening** to the **true reality of all things** and is therefore able to teach the **Buddha Dharma** and free all **sentient being**s from **suffering**. The state of being a buddha is the highest of the **ten realms**.

Shakyamuni Buddha taught that it is not possible for more than one buddha to arise at the same time in the same world system. (e.g. ND 1.277, p. 114) This is so that there are no overlapping **dispensation**s of the Dharma by multiple buddhas. The *Treasury of Abhidharma Treatise* recounts arguments about whether this means a single **Sumeru world** or a **trichiliocosm** and seems to favor the idea that only a single Sumeru world is meant, so that there can be multiple buddhas in different Sumeru worlds at the same time. There cannot be more than one buddha per world system for four reasons: 1) It would make one of the buddhas superfluous, 2) the buddhas **vow** to appear in worlds where they do not already have a protector (i.e. a buddha), 3) there is more reverence for a single buddha, and 4) the rare appearance of a single buddha will keep people from taking him for granted. (AKB2, pp. 484-486) The *Lotus Sutra* is either breaking this rule during the Assembly in Space or taking it to mean that no two active buddhas can appear in the same world at the same time, since **Many Treasures** Buddha is a buddha of the past who has already had his **final nirvana** and is no longer active and the **emanation buddhas of the ten directions** are not separate buddhas but the recalled emanations of Shakyamuni Buddha.

Buddha Dharma: (S.; J. buppō; 仏法) The **true reality of all things**; also, the

Dharma or teachings of a **buddha**.

buddha eye: (S. buddha-cakṣus; J. butsu-gen; 仏眼) One of the **five kinds of eyes**. The **buddha** eye is that which can see through the past, present, and future, and which also includes the other four kinds of eyes.

Buddha of Infinite Life Sutra: (S. *Sukhāvatīvyūha-sūtra*; J. *Muryōju-kyō*; 無量寿経) The Sanskrit name *Sukhāvatīvyūha-sūtra* literally means "*Sutra of Displaying Utmost Bliss*," referring to the Pure Land of Utmost Bliss. The Chinese title 無量寿経 means *Sutra of Infinite Life*. It is one of the **three Pure Land sutras**. It originated in India and was first translated into Chinese in the second century.

In this sutra, **Shakyamuni Buddha** describes how the **bodhisattva** Dharma Treasury made fulfilled forty-eight vows, created the Pure Land of Utmost Bliss, and became **Amitabha** Buddha. The eighteenth of those vows is called the **original vow** in the **Pure Land school**. Shakyamuni Buddha also declares that this sutra will outlast the others by a hundred years.

Nichiren Shonin classified this sutra as a **provisional sutra** among the **prior teachings**.

buddha-land: (S. buddha-kṣetra; J. bussetsu or bukkokudo or butsudo; 仏刹 or 仏国土 or 仏土) Another name for a **pure land**.

buddha-nature: (S. buddha-dhātu; J. busshō; 仏性) A term that appears prominently in the *Nirvana Sutra* and other influential **Mahayana sutra**s and treatises that have contributed to the widespread conviction within Mahayana Buddhism that all **sentient beings** have the inborn **nature** of a **buddha** or potential to **attain buddhahood**.

Another term for buddha-nature is "tathagatagarbha." The tathagatagarbha is buddhahood in the state of potential realization. It is what the **Dharma-body** or reality-body of the Buddha is called when still obscured by **defilements**. Defilements cause us to experience life as the passing play of conditioned **phenomena** but when we are free of their influence we awaken to the **true reality of all things** that is **unconditioned** and therefore has the four virtues of **eternity**, bliss, **self**, and **purity**.

There are many controversies related to the notion of buddha-nature and many ambiguities as to its exact meaning. Some have argued that while all beings have buddha-nature this does not mean they will all come to realize its potential, as is taught by the **Dharma Characteristics school**. Some have argued that it only applies to sentient beings, while others, such as **Zhanran**, have argued for the attainment of buddhahood by plants, because even insentient phenomena, like grass, trees, and rocks, have and express the buddha-nature.

Zhanran also taught that it is the power of the buddha-nature in our **mind**s that awakens us, therefore this wonderful power of the buddha-nature is our teacher and protector. (WNS1, p. 60)

It is a term that does not actually appear in the *Lotus Sutra*, nor did **Nichiren Shonin** say much about it, preferring to emphasize other **Tiantai school** teachings such as the **mutual possession of the ten realms**. However, **Zhiyi** and Nichiren Shonin both regarded the *Nirvana Sutra* as a restatement of the *Lotus Sutra*. Therefore, the teachings regarding buddha-nature appearing in that sutra are used to explain the teaching of the *Lotus Sutra*. While Nichiren Shonin did not emphasize the concept of buddha-nature, he did expound the **threefold buddha-nature** taught by Zhiyi. Nichiren Shonin insisted that the *Lotus Sutra* alone teaches that all sentient beings are endowed with the threefold buddha-nature. (WNS2, pp. 16-17, 246)

buddha-nature of the completing cause: (J. ryōin-busshō; 了因仏性) The **wisdom** to realize the inborn **buddha-nature**. One part of the **threefold buddha-nature**.

buddha-nature of the conditional causes: (J. en'in-busshō; 縁因仏性) The **mer**itorious deeds which make **wisdom** grow. One part of the **threefold buddha-nature**.

buddha-nature of the direct cause: (J. shōin-busshō; 正因仏性) The inborn nature to **attain buddhahood**. One part of the **threefold buddha-nature**.

Buddha's dispensation: (S. buddha-śāsana; J. Bukkyō or Butsu-shōgyō; 仏教 or 仏聖教) In Buddhism, the **dispensation** is the amount of time that the **Buddha Dharma** taught by a **buddha** will remain available and efficacious to **sentient beings** within a particular **Sumeru world**. Over time, the true spirit of the Dharma is lost. It becomes increasingly misunderstood and neglected, and there are fewer beings with the **capacity** to put it into practice. In the end, the Dharma is forgotten until a new buddha appears to begin a new dispensation for that world. The dispensation of a buddha can be divided into **three ages of the Dharma**.

buddha's tongue: (hotoke no shita; 仏の舌) Among the **thirty-two marks** of a **buddha** is the face-covering tongue (J. fumen-zetsu; 覆面舌) that is a long, wide tongue (J. kōchō-zetsu or chōzetsu; 広長舌 or 長舌), that is thin, soft, and wide enough to cover a **buddha's** entire face. It means that his utterance is flexible, smooth, and without lies. A buddha's tongue can extend far enough to reach the **heaven**s, thereby signifying the attestation to, or admiration, of truth.

In the twenty-first, "The Supernatural Powers of the Tathagata," chapter of the *Lotus Sutra*, various **emanation buddhas of the ten directions** extended their tongues to attest to the truth of the *Lotus Sutra*.

buddhas of the ten directions: (J. jippō no shobutsu; 十方の諸佛) Refers to the **emanation buddhas of the ten directions**, who are the **emanation-bodies** of the **Eternal Shakyamuni Buddha** who teach in the worlds throughout the universe.

Buddhist scriptures: (J. naiten/naiden; 内典) The ideograms 内典 literally mean "inner scriptures." They are used as an antonym for **non-Buddhist scriptures**, which are the "outer scriptures." In these terms, "inner" refers to that which is within the way of the **Buddha**, while "outer" refers to those scriptures which are considered "outside" the way of the Buddha.

calming: (S. śamatha; J. shi; 止) The Sanskrit term *śamatha* can also be translated as "**concentration**" or "tranquility." It is one of the two major components of Buddhist practice, the other being **contemplation**. Through the practice of calming, a practitioner can achieve a state of concentration that will lead to **meditative absorption**.

capacity: (J. kikon or ki; 機根 or 機) Refers to the mental and spiritual capacity of people to understand and accept the **Buddha Dharma**.

causality: (S. hetu-pratyaya; J. innen; 因縁) The Sanskrit term *hetupratyaya* can also mean "causal condition" or "**causes and conditions**." Causality refers to the activity of **conditioned phenomena** that are the **cause**s that directly contribute to an **effect**.

cause: (S. hetu; J. in; 因) According to the teaching of **dependent origination**, all **phenomena** depend upon causes in order to appear. According to the Buddhism, there is no phenomena that comes from a single cause such as a **god**.

In the *Profound Meaning of the Lotus Sutra*, cause as the sixth of the **ten suchnesses** is given the following definition by **Zhiyi**: "**homogeneous cause**s are called 'causes.'" (FTP, p. 184)

In the *Great Calming and Contemplation*, Zhiyi further explained that the causes or **karmic action**s of the **ten realms** come from the **mind** and are all included in mental activity. (CSQI, pp. 809-810)

cause and effect: (J. inga; 因果) The ideogram 因 means "**cause**" and the ideogram 果 means "**effect**." The "law of cause and effect" encompasses the functioning of various kinds of causes and effects in every area of **conditioned** life.

causes and conditions: (S. hetu-pratyaya; J. innen; 因縁) The Sanskrit term *hetupratyaya* can also be translated as "causal condition," or "**causality**." It can simply mean the **cause**s and secondary or supporting causes, called **condition**s, that bring about the arising of **phenomena**.

cessation: (S. nirodha; J. metsu; 滅) A synonym for **nirvana**. It is the cessation of the **defilement**s that are the **cause**s of suffering.

cessation of suffering, the truth of the: (S. nirodha-satya; J. mettai; 滅諦) The third of the **four noble truths**. The **cessation** of **suffering** is described by **Shakyamuni Buddha** as the remainderless fading away and cessation of the craving that is the **origin of suffering**. (LD 22.20, pp. 347-348; CD 56.11, p. 1844)

Chandraprabha: (d.u.; S. Candraprabha; J. Gakkō-daijin; 月光大臣) One of the ministers of King **Ajatashatru**. Along with **Jivaka**, he dissuaded the king from killing his own mother, Queen **Vaidehi**. (LB, pp. 258-260; TPLS, pp. 65-66)

changing poison into medicine: (J. hendoku-iyaku; 変毒為薬) A passage from the hundredth fascicle of the *Great Perfection of Wisdom Treatise*, attributed to **Nagarjuna**, states that **sutra**s such as the *Lotus Sutra* promise that even **voice-hearer**s who have become **arhat**s can **attain buddhahood**. It goes on to say that only great **bodhisattva**s can teach such a sutra, just as only an excellent physician can change poison into medicine. (WNS1, p. 44)

Zhiyi also referred to this principle in his *Profound Meaning of the Lotus Sutra*, wherein he says that while practitioners of the **two vehicles** have to extirpate the poisons of the **defilement**s, with the advent of the **awakening** taught by the *Lotus Sutra* even those poisons can be changed into medicine. (WNS2, p. 249)

Nichiren Shonin frequently referred to these and other passages to show that Nagarjuna and Zhiyi interpreted the ideogram 妙 or "**wonderful**" to mean that the *Lotus Sutra* alone had the power to change poison into medicine.

Chapters on the Forest of Meanings of the Dharma Garden of the

Mahayana: (J. *Daijō-hō'on-girin-jō*; 大乗法苑義林章) A work in seven (or twelve) fascicles by **Kuiji** summarizing the teachings of the **Dharma Characteristics school**. In it he asserts that **Shakyamuni Buddha**'s teaching of the **three vehicles** is the **true teaching**, while the teaching of the **One Vehicle** is only a **provisional teaching**.

Nichiren Shonin criticized Kuiji for teaching that the One Vehicle is only a **skillful means** in *On the Opening of the Eyes*. (WNS2, pp. 79-80)

Chengguan: (738-839; J. Chōkan; 澄観) Fourth patriarch of the **Flower Garland school** in China who is credited for the revival of the Flower Garland teachings. Chengguan studied various **Mahayana** schools of Buddhism, including **Tiantai** meditation under **Zhanran**. He later concentrated on the study of the *Flower Garland Sutra*, producing many books such as the *Annotations on the Flower Garland Sutra* in sixty fascicles.

Nichiren Shonin harshly criticized Chengguan for claiming the superiority of the *Flower Garland Sutra* over the ***Lotus Sutra*** (WNS1, p. 179; WNS3, pp. 3-5, 7-8, 80, 100, 121, 131-133, 165; WNS5, p. 101; WNS6, p. 75) and for plagiarizing the "**three thousand realms in a single thought-moment**" doctrine of **Zhiyi**. (WNS2, pp. 19, 34-37, 78-80, 85; WNS3, pp. 231-232; WNS4, p. 92; WNS5, pp. 79, 159-160)

Chief Wise: (J. Genju; 賢首) A **bodhisattva** featured in an eponymous chapter of the *Flower Garland Sutra*. He speaks to **Manjushri** Bodhisattva about the benefits of **faith** and the arousal of the **awakening mind**.

Chinchamanavika: (S. Ciñcāmāṇavikā; J. Sensha or Sensha-nyo; 旃遮 or 旃遮女) A **brahmin** woman in **Shravasti** who was a follower of the **non-Buddhist teachings**. Because so many people were leaving the non-Buddhist teachers to become followers of **Shakyamuni Buddha**, she confronted the Buddha at the Jeta Grove Monastery to discredit him by claiming that she was his mistress and was pregnant with his child. Her ruse was discovered when a rat ate through her sash and the wooden bowl she was using to make her belly appear swollen fell out. She ran away but the ground opened beneath her and she fell into **hell**. Her slander is counted among the **nine great difficulties** the Buddha faced. (BD, pp. 129-130)

Chisho, Great Master: (J. Chishō Daishi; 智証 大師) See **Enchin**.

Ci'en, Great Master: (J. Jion Daishi; 慈恩大師) See **Kuiji**.

Ci'ensi Temple: (J. *Jionji*; 慈恩寺) Also called **Daci'ensi Temple**. A temple in Chang'an established in 648 where **Xuanzang** worked on translating the **sutra**s and treatises he had brought back from India until 658. After that, Xuanzang's disciple **Kuiji** continued to reside there and so became known as the **Great Master Ci'en**.

Clarification of the Precepts Treatise: (J. *Kenkai-ron*; 顕戒論) A treatise written in 819 by **Saicho**, who wanted to establish a Mahayana precept platform for ordinations on Mt. **Hiei**. His petition to the imperial court to permit him to do so submitted in the previous year (in 818) was strongly opposed by the **six schools of Nara Buddhism**. Saicho wrote *Clarification of the Precepts* to rebuff their arguments and to explain the Mahayana **perfect and sudden precepts**.

Collection of Orally Transmitted Teachings, A: (J. *Juketsu-shū*; 授決集) A work by **Enchin** consisting of oral teachings he received in China, wherein he taught that the ***Flower Garland Sutra***, the ***Lotus Sutra***, and the ***Nirvana Sutra*** are superior to the teachings of the **Mantra school** and the **Zen school**. (WNS3, p. 24; WNS5, p. 157)

Collection of Passages on the Land of Peace and Bliss: (J. *Anraku-shū*; 安楽集) An important work of the **Pure Land school** in China by **Daochuo**. In this work, the teachings of **Shakyamuni Buddha** are divided into the **holy way gate** and the **Pure Land gate**. (WNS1, p. 28)

Collection of Passages on the Nembutsu Chosen in the Original Vow, A: (J. *Senjaku hongan nembutsu-shū* or *Senjaku-shū*; 選択本願念仏集 or 選択集) A work by **Honen**, founder of the **Pure Land school** in Japan. Citing from **Shandao**'s interpretation of the Pure Land **sutra**s, Honen advocated the Pure Land doctrine of solely relying upon the **nembutsu** for **rebirth in the pure land**. At the beginning, he also cites the ***Collection of Passages on the Land of Peace and Bliss***, proclaiming the establishment of the Pure Land school in Japan by dividing the holy teaching of **Shakyamuni Buddha** into the **holy way gate** and the **Pure Land gate**, insisting that only the Pure Land gate was efficacious in the **Latter Age of Degeneration**.

In *Treatise on* **Spreading Peace Throughout the Country by Establishing the True Dharma**, *Treatise on Protecting the Nation*, and other works, **Nichiren Shonin** harshly criticized Honen and esp. *A Collection of Passages on the Nembutsu Chosen in the Original Vow* for teaching the exclusive practice of nembutsu.

compassion: (S. karuṇā; J. hi or jihi; 悲 or 慈悲) In Buddhism, compassion means to have empathy and to wish that other **sentient being**s be free of **suffering** and the **cause**s of suffering.

Completion of Reality school: (J. Jōjitsu-shū; 成実宗) One of the schools of Chinese Buddhism and one of the **six schools of Nara Buddhism** in Japan. The Completion of Reality school focused on the study of the *Completion of Reality Treatise* by Harivarman that was translated by **Kumarajiva** between 411 and 412. Its teachings were propagated during the Liang and Chen dynasties, especially in conjunction with the teachings of the **Three Treatises school**. In the mid-Tang dynasty, however, the Completion of Reality school was overshadowed by the popularity of the **Dharma Characteristics school**.

The Korean monk Kwalluk brought the Completion of Reality school, or Jojitsu Shu, to Japan in 602, but it was another Korean monk, Hyegwan, who is credited with establishing the Jojitsu Shu in 625. By 806 it had become no more than a curriculum taught within the Three Treatises school.

Nichiren Shonin classifies this school, along with the **Abhidharma Treasury school** and **Discipline school**, as a **hinayana** school (WNS2, pp. 192, 252, 267; WNS3, pp. 19, 123, 249; WNS5, p. 163; WNS6, p. 146).

concentrated and scattered: (J. jōsan; 定散) The ideograms 定散 refer to **meditative good deeds** and **non-meditative good deeds** or more literally "scatter-brained" good deeds. The former means the contemplation of **Amitabha Buddha** and his Pure Land of Utmost Bliss while the latter designates the acts of **merit** one practices in one's daily life. **Shandao** divided the sixteen contemplations for **rebirth in the pure land** taught in the *Contemplation of the Buddha of Infinite Life Sutra* into these two categories of good acts maintaining that the Buddha's real intent was the rightly established act of **nembutsu** for rebirth in the pure land.

Nichiren Shonin argued that according to the teachings of **Zhiyi** and **Zhanran**, the practice of the *Lotus Sutra* can be done with a scattered mind and bring about the same or even more merit than any other practice. Even an **ordinary person** in the **Latter Age of Degeneration** can recite just the **daimoku** during their daily activities, and in doing so will be an upholder of the *Lotus Sutra* at all times. This also refers to those who have a single moment of understanding by faith, or who have a single moment of rejoicing, or are like the fiftieth person in succession who rejoices at hearing a verse or phrase of the *Lotus Sutra* even for a moment and attains incalculable merits. (WNS1, pp. 39-40)

concentration: (S. samādhi; J. sanmai/sammai or sanmaji or jō or tōji; 三昧 or 三摩地 or 定 or 等持) Concentration is the one-pointedness of **mind** on a chosen object in an uninterrupted series of moments without distraction. The practice to reach this state may also be called **samadhi**, meditation, or yoga. As a prerequisite of attaining **awakening**, many kinds of mental concentration are expounded in various **sutra**s.

conceptual proliferation: (S. prapañca; J. keron; 戯論) The Sanskrit term *prapañca* can also mean "diffusion," "elaboration," "expansion," or "superimposition." It is the projection of deluded and egocentric interpretations upon what is experienced.

concise opening of the three vehicles to reveal the One Vehicle: (J. ryaku-kaisan-ken'itsu; 略開三顕一) Refers to the summarization of the doctrine that the **three vehicle** teachings for **voice-hearer**s, **privately-awakened one**s, and **bodhisattva**s are **skillful means** while the **One Vehicle** path to **awakening** is the **True Dharma**. This is found in the first prose section of the second "**Expedients**" **chapter** of the *Lotus Sutra*. What follows it is the **expanded opening of the three vehicles to reveal the One Vehicle**. (LS, pp. 24-32)

condition: (S. pratyaya; J. en; 縁) According to the teaching of dependent origination, all **phenomena** originate from multiple **causes and conditions** and not from a single cause. A condition can be considered a secondary or supporting cause.
In the *Profound Meaning of the Lotus Sutra*, conditions as the seventh of the **ten suchnesses** is given the following definition by **Zhiyi**: "Auxiliary causes are called 'conditions.'" (FTP, p. 184)
In the *Great Calming and Contemplation*, Zhiyi further explained that **karmic** conditions are comprised of **ignorance**, craving, and other such mental qualities and activity. (CSQI, p. 810)

conditioned: (S. saṃskṛta; J. ui; 有為) The Sanskrit term *saṃskṛta* is a passive form of *saṃskāra*. If *saṃskāra* refers to "conditioning factors" or formations that do the conditioning (translated in different contexts as conditioned formations, **mental formation**s, or volitional formations), then *saṃskṛta* are those **phenomena** which are conditioned by those formations. Of course, the phenomena that **condition** other phenomena are themselves conditioned, and what is conditioned then conditions what will follow, and so on. Those phenomena which are conditioned encompass the **five aggregates**. Conditioned phenomena are all the impermanent products of multiple **cause**s momentarily coming together and combining. (AKB1, pp. 60-61).

Confucianism: (J. Ju or Ju-kyō or Ju-ka; 儒 or 儒教 or 儒家) The ideogram 儒 means "scholar." The ideograms 儒教 literally mean "Scholarly Teachings," while the ideograms 儒家 mean "Scholarly Household" or "House of Scholarship." All these are often translated as "Confucianism," though more literally they refer to "scholasticism." In keeping with the Pinyin transliteration of 儒, Confucianism is now more accurately called Ruism. Ruism is often understood to mean the study, dissemination, and practice of the teachings of Confucius (551-479 BCE) and his school of thought.

Nichiren Shonin and his contemporaries, however, used it in a way that was inclusive of Taoist thinkers such as Laozi and Zhuangzi (369-286 BCE), and Neo-Taoists of the Dark Learning movement such as Wang Bi (226-249) and Guo Xian (d. 312).

consciousness: (S. vijñāna; J. shiki; 識) The Sanskrit terms *vijñāna*, *citta* and *manas* all indicate the **mind**, but *vijñāna* is usually translated as "consciousness." *Citta* has the connotation of the mind as that which generates and accumulates **wholesome** and **unwholesome** activity, *manas* has the connotation of the mind as that which cognizes an object, while *vijñāna* has the connotation of discerning the nature of the object. (AKB1, p. 205)

As the fifth of the **five aggregates**, it is the bare impression or general awareness of **form**s, sounds, odors, tastes, tangibles, and mental phenomenon.

consciousness-only: (S. vijñaptimātratā; J. yuishiki; 唯識) The Sanskrit term *vijñaptimātratā* can also be translated as "mere-designation" or "mere-representation." This is the teaching of the **Consciousness-Only school** that all **phenomena** are just the manifestations of **consciousness**.

Consciousness-Only school: (S. Vijñānavāda; J. Yuishiki-shū or Yuishiki-ha; 唯識宗 or 唯識派) The **Mahayana** school founded by **Vasubandhu**, **Asanga**, and **Maitreyanatha** that taught the doctrine of **consciousness-only**, which emphasizes the role of consciousness in shaping our experience of reality. The ideograms 唯識 are used to translate the Sanskrit term *vijñaptimātratā*, that can also be translated as "mere-designation" or "mere-representation." This school is also called Mind-Only or the Yoga Practitioners due to its emphasis on meditation practice.

container world: (S. bhājana-loka; J. kiseken; 器世間) The Sanskrit term *bhājana-loka* can also be translated as "receptacle world." It is the insentient **environment** which is the container or receptacle for the world of **sentient beings**. Together the container world and the world of sentient beings comprises the **triple world**. The container world is brought about by the collective **karma** of sentient beings that live there.

contemplation: (S. vipaśyanā; J. kan; 観) The Sanskrit term *vipaśyanā* can also be translated as "insight." It is one of the two major components of Buddhist practice, the other being **calming**. Through the practice of contemplation, a practitioner can achieve the insight necessary for **liberation** or to **attain buddhahood**.

contemplation of loving-kindness and compassion: (S. maitrīsmṛti; J. jihi-kan; 慈悲観) The practice of the **contemplation** of **loving-kindness** and **compassion** in order to overcome anger. The second of the **five contemplations for settling the mind**.

Contemplation of the Buddha of Infinite Life Sutra: (S.*Amitāyurdhyāna-sūtra*; J. *Kan-muryōju-kyō*; 観無量寿経) A **sutra** allegedly translated into Chinese in the fifth century, though many now believe it was composed in Central Asia or China. It is one of the **three Pure Land sutras**, which are the basic scriptures of the **Pure Land school**.

According to its content, **Shakyamuni Buddha** expounded teachings regarding **Amitabha** Buddha and his Pure Land of Utmost Bliss, including a set of sixteen contemplations, for the imprisoned **Vaidehi** at Rajagriha in **Magadha**.

Inspired by this sutra, **Shandao** of Tang China wrote the *Annotations on the Contemplation of the Buddha of Infinite Life Sutra*, wherein he claimed that the **nembutsu** is the only way to salvation. This writing in turn inspired **Honen** to establish the Pure Land school in Japan.

Based on **Zhiyi**'s **five periods**, **Nichiren Shonin** classified the *Contemplation of the Buddha of Infinite Life Sutra* as a **provisional sutra** of the **Expanded period**.

contemplation of the five wheels: (J. gorin-kan; 五輪観) A method of **contemplation** used in **esoteric Buddhism** to contemplate the five wheels which represent the **five primary elements**.

Contemplation of the Universal Sage Bodhisattva Sutra: (J. *Kan-Fugen-gyō*; 観普賢経) A one-fascicle **sutra** translated into Chinese by Dharmamitra in 442. Its full title would be *Procedures for the Contemplation of Universal Sage Sutra*. It is set shortly before **Shakyamuni Buddha** passed away. The sutra declares that the Buddha will enter **final nirvana** in three months and teaches how to repent of the evils resulting from activity of the five physical senses and the **mind**.

Since this sutra is a continuation of the last chapter of the *Lotus Sutra*, **Zhiyi** considered it as the conclusion of the *Threefold Lotus Sutra*.

Contemplation on the Mind-Ground Sutra: (J. *Shinjikan-gyō* or *Daijō-hon-shō-shinjikan-gyō*; 心地観経 or 大乗本生心地観経) The full title of this **sutra** would be the *Mahayana Sutra of the Contemplation on the Mind-Ground of the Buddha's Life*. It was said to have been translated by Prajna. The sutra teaches that one should become a monastic and take up the practice of contemplation of the mind. It also teaches about the **four debts of gratitude** (which is given as indebtedness to one's parents; indebtedness to one's fellow **sentient being**s; indebtedness to one's ruler; and indebtedness to the **Three Treasures**); the **three bodies**, the doctrine that there are innate **seed**s of **awakening**, and the **three mysteries**. (WNS1, p. 21)

Daci'ensi Temple: (J. Daijionji; 大慈恩寺) See **Ci'ensi Temple**.

daimoku: (J.; 題目) The ideograms 題目 mean "title." Also called Odaimoku (J.; お題目 or 御題目) or "August Title." The daimoku or "title" refers to the practice of chanting the title of the *Lotus Sutra* in the form of **Namu Myoho Renge Kyo**. As one of the **Three Great Secret Dharmas** it is called the **Sacred Title of the Original Gate**.

Nichiren Shonin cited several passages from the *Lotus Sutra* to indicate the great **merit** of simply hearing and accepting the daimoku or "sacred title," an act that implied the acceptance of the sutra itself or any of part of it. (WNS1, p. 65) Nichiren Shonin also cited passages to the effect that it is due to meritorious acts in previous lives that enable even **ordinary people** to hear the daimoku of the *Lotus Sutra* and have **faith** in it.

Dainichi Nonin: (fl. c. twelfth century; J. Dainichi Nōnin; 大日能忍) A self-educated **monk** of the **Zen school** in the early Kamakura period. He founded the Samboji Temple (J. Sambōji) in Settsu Province (Hyōgo Prefecture) and spread Zen Buddhism of the Southern Song tradition (which he named the Nihon Daruma Shū), insisting that the essence of Buddhism is transmitted by non-literary and non-verbal means.

Nichiren Shonin was critical of Dainichi Nonin for relying on the *Lankavatara*

Sutra, which is a **provisional sutra** expounded in the third period of the **five periods**, and for insisting on "a **separate transmission outside the sutras**," which Nichiren Shonin saw as "an act of **heavenly devil**s."

Daochuo: (562-645; C.; J. Dōshaku; 道綽) The second patriarch of the **Pure Land school** in China. He was ordained at the age of fourteen. Daochuo was originally a teacher of the *Nirvana Sutra*, but at age forty-eight, inspired by Tanluan's teachings and the *Contemplation of the Buddha of Infinite Life Sutra*, he became a fervent practitioner and popularizer of Pure Land Buddhism. He wrote the two-fascicled *Collection of Passages on the Land of Peace and Bliss*, a work that established the division between the **holy way gate** and the **Pure Land gate**. He also taught that the **Latter Age of Degeneration** had already begun (according to his calculations, wherein the **Age of the True Dharma** only lasted five hundred years) so the difficult-to-practice way of the holy way gate was no longer viable and people should turn instead to the easy-to-practice way of the Pure Land gate. One of his disciples was **Shandao**.

Honen considered him one of the five patriarchs of the Pure Land school of Buddhism, along with Tanluan, Shandao, Huaigan, and Shaokang.

Nichiren Shonin criticized the Pure Land masters for disregarding the relative profundity of doctrines and the differences between the **true teaching** and the **provisional teaching**. (WNS1, pp. 4, 23, 27-28)

Daosheng: (355-434; C.; J. Dōshō or Jiku-dōshō; 道生 or 竺道生) One of the four great disciples of **Kumarajiva**. He is known for having made the controversial claim that even *icchantika* can **attain buddhahood**, even though the translation of the *Six-Fascicle Nirvana Sutra* completed by Faxiang and Buddhabadra's in 418 said that they could not. He was vindicated when Dharmakshema's forty fascicle translation of the *Nirvana Sutra* was completed between 421 and 430, wherein were statements that the *icchantika* could attain buddhahood.

Decline of the Dharma Sutra: (J. *Hōmetsujin-kyō*; 法滅尽経) A one-fascicle sutra explaining the extinction of the **Buddha Dharma** after the **final nirvana** of **Shakyamuni Buddha**. The translator of the Chinese version is unknown, and it is suspected to be a fabrication. As its content are somewhat similar to such **Mahayana** sutras like the *Nirvana Sutra* and the *Great Assembly Sutra*, it is believed to have been written in the fourth century. It is a short sutra reflecting the decadence of the world as the Buddha Dharma is forgotten.

Deer Park: (S. Mṛgadāva or Mṛgadāya; J. Rokuon; 鹿苑) Also called **Rishipatana**, the "place where the **rishi**s gather." It was the location of **Shakyamuni Buddha**'s initial **turning of the wheel of the Dharma** in Varanasi.

Deer Park period: (J. Rokuon-ji; 鹿苑時) The second of the **five periods**. Also called the Agama period (J. Agon-ji; 阿含時). This period lasted twelve years beginning with the initial **turning of the wheel of the Dharma** at the **Deer Park** in Varanasi. During this period, **Shakyamuni Buddha** began the gradual teaching and solely taught the **tripitaka teaching** for the **voice-hearer**s, so this period is considered to only contain the coarse teaching. At this stage, the Buddha taught the **four noble truths** and **dependent origination** in order to free people from worldly attachments and to overcome self-centeredness. This period is compared to the **flavor of cream** derived from milk.

defiled: (S. saṃkleśa; J. zen or zōzen; 染 or 雜染) The Sanskrit term *saṃkleśa* can also be translated as "**defilement**," "impurity," or "pollution." It refers to impure or defiled **dharma**s.

defilement: (S. kleśa; J. bonnō; 煩悩) The Sanskrit term *kleśa* can also be translated as "afflictions." There are many different enumerations of different kinds of defilements, but they all derive from the **three poisons** of **greed**, **hatred**, and **delusion**.

defilements are innumerable; I vow to resolve them all: (J. bonnō-muhen-seigandan; 煩悩無辺誓願断) The second of the **four great vows** of a **bodhisattva**. It is a vow to free all **sentient being**s from all **defilement**s and **delusion**s.

definitive meaning: (S. nītārtha; J. ryōgi; 了義) A teaching of definitive meaning does not need to be further interpreted and can be taken literally as the final or definitive meaning of the **Buddha Dharma**, in contrast to teachings that are only of **provisional meaning**.

deluded attitudes: (J. shi-waku; 思惑) These are innate **delusion**s that are eliminated on the path of cultivation of Buddhist practice, such as the ten defilements of perception: 1) attachment, 2) aversion, 3) **ignorance**, 4) pride, 5) doubt, 6) view that there is a **self**, 7) extreme views, 8) **wrong views**, 9) seizing upon views, and 10) seizing upon rules and rituals.

deluded views: (J. ken-waku; 見惑) These are the **delusion**s produced by false discrimination that leads to self-grasping that are eliminated upon having a direct and penetrating understanding of the **four noble truths**.

delusion: (S. moha; J. chi or guchi or mumyō; 痴 or 愚痴 or 無明) The Sanskrit term *moha* can also be translated as "error" or "confusion." The ideograms 愚痴 are also used to translate *mūḍha*, or foolishness. The ideograms 無明 are also used to translate *avidyā*, or **ignorance**, which is synonymous with *moha*. Delusion is also understood to be lack of **knowledge** and clarity. (AKB1, p. 193)

delusion of fundamental ignorance: (J. mumyō-waku; 無明惑) One of the **three categories of delusions** in which the **Tiantai school** doctrine divides all delusions and harmful attitudes or emotions. This delusion hinders the **knowledge** of the **middle way**. It is counteracted by the correct contemplation of the middle way.

delusions as innumerable as grains of sand: (J. jinja-waku; 塵沙惑) One of the **three categories of delusions** in which the **Tiantai school** doctrine divides all delusions and harmful attitudes or emotions. This delusion hinders the **knowledge** of **skillful means**. It is counteracted by the contemplation that enters provisionality from emptiness.

delusions of views and attitudes: (J. kenji-waku; 見思惑) One of the **three categories of delusions**, comprising **deluded attitudes** and **deluded views**, in which the **Tiantai school** divides all delusions and harmful attitudes or emotions. This delusion hinders the **knowledge** of **emptiness**. It is counteracted by the contemplation that enters emptiness from provisionality.

demon: (J. akki or ki; 悪鬼 or 鬼) An evil spirit, such as the **rakshasa**s. Demons are a metaphor for any forces that drain vitality or distracts one from Buddhist practice.

Demonic Eloquence, the brahmin: (J. Kiben-baramon; 鬼弁婆羅門) A demon-worshipping **brahmin** who used to teach paradoxical theories from behind a curtain until he was defeated in debate by **Ashvaghosha**, who tore the curtain down and exposed him.

Demonstration of Consciousness-Only Treatise: (S. *Vijñapti-mātratā-siddhi*; J. *Jō-yuishiki-ron*; 成唯識論) A composition by **Xuanzang** that includes a Chinese translation of the *Thirty Verses on Consciousness-Only* along with a commentary focusing on the teachings of **Dharmapala**, but also including those of Sthiramati and eight others, altogether known as the ten great treatise masters of the Consciousness-Only school. Altogether, it is a primary source for the teachings of the **Dharma Characteristics school**, which propagated the teachings of the **Consciousness-Only school** of **Mahayana** Buddhism.

Dengyo, Great Master: (J. Dengyō Daishi; 伝教 大師) See **Saicho**.

Dependence on Tiantai of Other Buddhist Schools: (J. *Ehyō-tendai-shū / Ebyō-tendai-shū*; 依憑天台集) An essay by **Saicho** written in 813 with a preface written in 816 that explains how the **six schools of Nara Buddhism** and the **Mantra school** were all indebted and subordinate to the **Tiantai school**.

Nichiren Shonin frequently cited or referred to this work in making his case that the founders of the six schools of Nara Buddhism and the Mantra school had all acknowledged the superiority of the teachings of the Tiantai school, though the Mantra school and the **Flower Garland school** had tried to hide their appropriation of Tiantai doctrine.

dependent origination: (S. pratītya-samutpāda; J. innen or engi; 因縁 or 縁起) **Shakyamuni Buddha**'s general teaching of dependent origination is as follows: "When this exists, that comes to be; with the **arising** of this, that arises. When this does not exist, that does not come to be; with the **cessation** of this, that ceases." (CD 12: 37, p. 575)

desire: (S. chanda; J. yoku; 欲) The Sanskrit term *chanda* can also be translated as "will" or "zeal."

desire realm: (S. *kāma-dhātu*; J. yokkai/yoku-kai; 欲界) The first part of the **triple world**, consisting of the realms of the **hell-dwellers**, **hungry ghost**s, **animal**s, **asura**s, **human**s, and the **six heavens of the desire realm**, wherein live those **sentient being**s with sensual desire and other appetites.

determined nature: (J. ketsujō-shō or jō-shō; 決定性) This term refers to those whose **nature** is determined or fixed to become **voice-hearer**s, **privately-awakened one**s, or **buddha**s according to the **Dharma Characteristics school**'s doctrine of the **five natures**. The first two of these three are believed to have no chance to **attain buddhahood** according to the Dharma Characteristics school but it is guaranteed in the *Lotus Sutra* that those of the **two vehicles** will be buddhas in the future.

Devadatta: (S.; J. Daibadatta or Daiba or Chōdatsu/Jōdatsu; 提婆達多 or 提婆 or 調達) As the son of either Amritodana or **Dronodana**, he was a cousin of **Shakyamuni Buddha** and also the older brother of **Ananda**. He joined the **Sangha** along with his brother and other **Shakya** nobles. He was extremely intelligent and is said to have memorized all the eighty thousand teachings of Buddhism. Nevertheless, attached to worldly gain and fame, he tried to take over the leadership of the Sangha, and even tried to kill the Buddha. He is said to have fallen into the Hell of **Incessant Suffering** while yet alive for committing three of the **five heinous transgressions**.

Some versions of the Buddha's life portray Devadatta as a rival from childhood. In one story he shoots a swan that falls to earth near Prince **Siddhartha**. Siddhartha takes out the arrow and nurses the swan back to health, but Devadatta insists that the swan belongs to him since he shot it. The two boys took the case to the court where the king's counselors argue over the merits of each case. In the end, a wise man declares that the swan belongs to the one who saved its life rather than the one who tried to take it away. Devadatta was also said to have competed for **Yashodhara**'s hand in marriage but lost to his cousin Siddhartha.

Devadatta joined the Sangha along with his brother Ananda and other Shakya nobles not long after the Buddha's first visit to **Kapilavastu** in the second year following his **awakening**. (LB, pp. 79, 82-83) For a long time, Devadatta was a respected member of the Sangha and developed the **supernatural power**s that can be acquired through **meditative absorption**. His hidden jealousy and envy, however, prevented him from attaining any genuine insight or **liberation**.

Eight years before Shakyamuni Buddha's **final nirvana**, Devadatta magically appeared before Prince **Ajatashatru** in the form of a young boy wreathed in snakes. Though terrified by the apparition, when Ajatashatru found out it was actually Devadatta he was very impressed by this supernatural display. From that time on, Prince Ajatashatru became Devadatta's patron, giving him more than he could ever use. Devadatta soon after lost his supernatural powers due to the debilitating mental effects of his **greed** and ambition.

Devadatta made a bid to take over the Sangha by arguing that the Buddha should retire and trust it to his care. The Buddha firmly rejected this offer. When Devadatta persisted, the Buddha said, "I would not hand over the Sangha of **monk**s even to **Shariputra** or **Maudgalyayana**. How should I do to such a wastrel, a clot of spittle, as you?" (LB, p. 258) Finally, Shakyamuni Buddha had Devadatta publicly denounced by the Sangha. From that point on, the Sangha was no longer responsible for his behavior; only Devadatta could be held accountable for his actions.

Shortly thereafter, Devadatta talked Ajatashatru into usurping the throne from his father, King **Bimbisara**. One of King Ajatashatru's first acts after taking the throne was to dispatch assassins on behalf of Devadatta to kill Shakyamuni Buddha. The assassins found that they could not bring themselves to kill the Buddha once they were in his presence, and instead they became his disciples.

Deciding that he would have to kill the Buddha himself, Devadatta rolled a boulder down on him from Mt. **Sacred Eagle**, but the boulder split so that both halves missed the Buddha, though a shard injured his foot.

Another time, Devadatta used his influence at court to get the stable hands to set loose the maddened elephant Nalagiri so that it would trample the Buddha to death. The Buddha stopped its rampage through the streets of Rajagriha by emanating feelings of **loving-kindness** so that it calmed down and was tamed. After that, Devadatta's reputation became so bad that King Ajatashatru was forced to withdraw his patronage.

Devadatta later succeeded in instigating a schism within the Sangha by proposing that the Buddha make five ascetic practices mandatory: 1) monks should become forest-dwellers and no longer live in villages or towns, 2) monks should only beg for food and no longer accept invitations to meals, 3) monks should only use rags from rubbish heaps and should no longer accept donated robes, 4) monks should only sleep under trees and not in buildings, and 5) monks should no longer accept any offerings of meat or fish. The Buddha refused to make these practices mandatory. Devadatta then convinced five hundred younger members of the Sangha to join him because his practices were more rigorous than the Buddha's.

Shariputra and Maudgalyayana, however, visited the schismatic group. Devadatta arrogantly assumed that they had come to join him, even though they had not said so. Filled with overconfidence and wishing to rest, he left the teaching of his schismatic group to them. While Devadatta slept, the Buddha's two chief disciples convinced the five hundred to return to the true Sangha of the Buddha.

After Devadatta's attempt to create a rival Sangha failed, it is said that the ground opened and he fell into the Hell of Incessant Suffering. Other sources say that on his deathbed he tried to repent, but was only able to say, "**Namu** Buddha," before dying, which was too little too late.

Devadatta is not present in the *Lotus Sutra*, but King Ajatashatru is present. So, the assembly on Mt. Sacred Eagle must have taken place after Devadatta's death and King Ajatashatru's meeting with the Buddha and repentance. In the twelfth, "**Devadatta**," **chapter** of the *Lotus Sutra*, Shakyamuni Buddha revealed that in a previous life he had been a king (known in Japan as Suzudan) who had renounced his throne and become the servant of Devadatta. In that previous life, Devadatta was a **rishi** named Asita. The Buddha stated that he was able to **attain buddhahood** because Devadatta had been his teacher in that lifetime. The Buddha then made the astonishing prediction that in the future Devadatta would become a buddha named **Heavenly King**.

Devadatta represents the quintessential *icchantika* and **hell-dweller**, but he is also a primary example of the universality of the teaching of the *Lotus Sutra* that even someone as evil as Devadatta will eventually attain buddhahood. Devadatta also shows that even the worst of people can be considered our teachers and may have made contributions that we are unable to recognize without the insight of the

Buddha.

Based on the "Devadatta" chapter of the *Lotus Sutra*, in which Devadatta is given the **assurance of future buddhahood**, **Nichiren Shonin** maintained that all evil-doers, even one who commits **slander of the True Dharma**, can be saved by the *Lotus Sutra*.

"Devadatta," chapter: (J. Daibadatta-hon; 提婆達多品) The twelfth chapter of the *Lotus Sutra*. In the first half of the chapter, **Shakyamuni Buddha** reveals that in a previous life he had been a king (known in Japan as Suzudan) who had renounced his throne and become the servant of **Devadatta**. In that previous life, Devadatta was a **rishi** named Asita. The Buddha states that he was able to **attain buddhahood** because Devadatta had been his teacher in that lifetime. Astonishingly, the Buddha then gave the **assurance of future buddhahood** to Devadatta, stating that he will become a buddha named **Heavenly King**.

In the second half of the chapter, Accumulated Wisdom **Bodhisattva** requests of **Many Treasures** Buddha that they return to their home world, but Shakyamuni Buddha asks them to wait and speak to **Manjushri** Bodhisattva, who is about to appear. Manjushri then appears from the palace of the **Dragon King** Sagara under the sea where he had been teaching the *Lotus Sutra*. The innumerable bodhisattvas whom he had been teaching then appear. Accumulated Wisdom asks Manjushri if there is any whom he had taught who is able to attain buddhahood quickly. Manjushri tells him that the eight-year-old **dragon girl**, Sagara's daughter, is such a one. Accumulated Wisdom and Shariputra doubt that she is able to become a buddha quickly or at all due to the **five obstacles** that prevent a woman from attaining buddhahood. The dragon girl responds by offering Shakyamuni Buddha a priceless gem. The Buddha receives the gem immediately. The girl asks both Accumulated Wisdom and Shariputra whether the Buddha received her gift quickly or not. Both answer that he did it quickly. She says that she will become a Buddha more quickly. Thereupon she magically appears to become a male, goes to the Spotless world in the south, and becomes a buddha, thereby showing that she was indeed capable of attaining buddhahood in just a moment. Accumulated Wisdom and Shariputra silently accept this with faith.

Based on the "Devadatta" chapter of the *Lotus Sutra*, **Nichiren Shonin** maintained that all evil-doers, even one who, like Devadatta, had committed **slander of the True Dharma**, can be saved by the *Lotus Sutra*. He also considered the **attainment of buddhahood by a dragon girl** as evidence for the **attainment of buddhahood by women** and as an example of being able to **attain buddhahood with one's present body**.

devil: (S. māra; J. ma; 魔) The Sanskrit term *māra* literally means "maker of death." It can also be translated as "**demon**." The **Mahayana sutra**s sometimes refer to **four devils**, a group consisting of the **devil of the aggregates**, the **devil of**

the **defilements**, the **devil of death**, and **Mara**, the **devil king of the sixth heaven**.

Zhiyi explains that a devil is a murderer "…because it robs the practitioner of his treasure of **merit** and kills the life of **wisdom**. As the role of the **Buddha** is, through his powers of virtue and **wisdom**, to lead beings to **liberation** and enter **nirvana**, so the role of devilish forces is to constantly destroy the good roots of all beings and cause them to drift forever in **samsara**." (CSQI, p. 1735 adapted)

devil king of the sixth heaven: (S. devaputra-māra; J. tenshima or jizaitenma or dairokuten-no-ma-ō or ma-ō; 天子魔 or 自在天魔 or 第六天の魔王 or 魔王) One of the **four devils**. Also called **King Mara of the Sixth Heaven**. The ideograms 自在天 are an abbreviation for 他化自在天, the Chinese translation of the name of the sixth heaven of the **desire realm**, the Heaven of Controlling the Creations of Others.

The devil king of the sixth heaven is explained by **Zhiyi** in the context of "supernatural devils" encompassing the following three kinds: "form-shifting devils" who appear as animals at different times of the day or night, "nerve-racking" devils that cause various distracting bodily sensations or noises, and finally Mara himself, who tries to tempt or intimidate the practitioner. (CSQI, pp. 771, 1390-1396, 1735-1737)

devil of death: (S. mṛtya-māra; J. shi-ma; 死魔) One of the **four devils**. **Zhiyi** identified disease with the devil of death, as it is the cause of death. (CSQI, p. 771)

devil of the aggregates: (S. skandha-māra; J. on-ma or un-ma; 陰魔 or 蘊魔) One of the **four devils**. **Zhiyi** identified the devil of the aggregates with such things as the **five aggregates**, the **fruition**s of past **karma**, attachment to **meditative absorption**, attachment to the **two vehicles**, and attachment to **bodhisattva**hood. (CSQI, p. 771)

devil of the defilements: (S. kleśa-māra; J. bonnō-ma; 煩悩魔) One of the **four devils**. **Zhiyi** identified the devil of the defilements with such things as the **defilement**s, mistaken views, and self-conceit. (CSQI, p. 771)

dharani: (S. dhāraṇī; J. darani or sōji; 陀羅尼 or 総持) The Sanskrit term *dhāraṇī* can be translated as "code" or "mnemonic device." Dharani are also called mystic sacred spells. In **esoteric Buddhism** they are protective spells like **mantra**s but are generally longer.

Dharma: (S.; J. hō; 法) A Sankrit term meaning Truth, Law, Reality, or the teachings and methods of practice taught by the **Buddha**. Sometimes the lower-case form of *dharma* is used in English when the word refers to a "**phenomena**," "reality," "entity," "element, "factor," or "event." In Sanskrit there is no capitalization, so the sense of the word must be inferred from context. The equivalent Pali term is "Dhamma. "

In **abhidharma** thought, a dharma is a mental or physical constituent of reality that bears a unique characteristic and is not merely an abstraction. By engaging in analysis, a practitioner of abhidharma can discern which dharmas are **defiled** and which are undefiled, as well as what is only a nominal designation, such as a "**self**" or a "person," and what are actual dharmas that are the seemingly irreducible elements of existence. Such actual dharmas might include such things as the **four primary elements**, **feeling**, **perception**, **desire**, **concentration**, **mind**, and many other **conditioned** physical or mental phenomena. **Unconditioned** phenomena such as **space**, **cessation** occurring through natural processes, and cessation occurring as the result of analysis were also considered dharmas.

In the **Mahayana** teachings of the **Middle Way school**, all dharmas are considered to be **empty** of **self-nature** because they are all nothing but **causes and conditions**, and therefore are **non-arising** and **non-ceasing** in any kind of substantial way. According to the teachings of the **Consciousness-Only school**, all dharmas are just the transmutations of **consciousness**.

Dharma Brightness: (J. Hōmyō; 法明) The name of the **buddha** that **Purna** will become, according to the eighth, "Assurance of Future Buddhahood of the Five Hundred Disciples," chapter of the *Lotus Sutra*.

Dharma Characteristics school: (J. Hossō-shū; 法相宗) One of the schools of Chinese Buddhism and one of the **six schools of Nara Buddhism** in Japan. The Dharma Characteristics school is primarily based on the *Demonstration of Consciousness-Only Treatise*, which itself cites various **sutra**s and treatises such as the *Flower Garland Sutra*, the *Lankavatara Sutra*, the *Revealing the Profound Secrets Sutra*, and the *Stages of Yoga Practice Treatise*. The teachings of this school were transmitted to China by **Xuanzang** during the Tang dynasty. Xuanzang's disciple **Kuiji** established the school in China and is known as its first patriarch.

The Dharma Characteristics school, or Hosso Shu, was first brought to Japan by the Japanese **monk Dosho** who had traveled to China in 653 to study with Xuanzang and then returned in 661. The Hosso Shu became one of the most popular of the six schools of Nara Buddhism.

This school analyzes and studies the reality of all things from the perspective of the **Consciousness-Only school**, particularly the teachings translated by Xuanzang in the *Demonstration of Consciousness-Only Treatise.*

This school's comparative classification of doctrines divides **Shakyamuni**

Buddha's teachings into **three turnings of the wheel of the Dharma** as taught in the *Revealing the Profound Secrets Sutra*: the first turning it identifies as the **hinayana** teaching of the selflessness of persons but the existence of **dharma**s, the second turning is the teaching of **emptiness** or the selflessness of phenomena, while the third is the teaching of the **middle way** of neither existence nor emptiness. Among sutras it includes in the third turning are the *Revealing the Profound Secrets Sutra*, the *Flower Garland Sutra*, the *Supreme Golden Light Sutra*, the *Lotus Sutra*, and the *Nirvana Sutra*. (Keenan 2000, p. 49; EET, pp. 59-60)

This school also teaches that **sentient being**s have one of **five natures**: some have the **determined nature** to become a **bodhisattva** and **attain buddhahood**, some have the determined nature to become **voice-hearer**s and become **arhat**s, some have the determined nature to become **privately-awakened one**s, some have the **indeterminate nature of the three vehicles** who can attain any of the goals of the three vehicles, and some are sentient beings **without the nature** who can at best accrue **merit** for **rebirth** as a **human** or in the **heaven**s. This school teaches that the three vehicles are the **definitive meaning** of Shakyamuni Buddha's teaching, and that the **One Vehicle** is just the **provisional meaning**, taught only to encourage those of the indeterminate nature to aspire to attain buddhahood. (EET, pp. 61-62) This means that this school considers the *Revealing the Profound Secrets Sutra* superior to the other sutras included in the third turning. (WNS1, p. 17) This teaching put it at odds with the One Vehicle doctrine of the **Tiantai** and **Three Treatises** schools. In Japan, the issue was debated between **Tokuitsu** of the Hosso Shu and **Saicho** of the Tendai Shu (the **Tiantai school** in Japan) in the ninth century.

Nichiren Shonin classifies this school as a provisional Mahayana teaching that is hinayana or like an inferior medicine in comparison with *Lotus Sutra* and the Tiantai school because it relies upon the **prior teachings** (WNS2, pp. 192, 252, 267; WNS3, pp. 19, 80, 124, 153, 240; WNS6, p. 146). Nichiren Shonin in particular insisted that the teachings concerning the three turnings of the wheel of the Dharma (which put the *Lotus Sutra* on a par with the *Revealing the Profound Secrets Sutra*) and the five natures of the Dharma Characteristics school (which denied the One Vehicle) had already been refuted by the Tiantai school. (WNS1, pp. 17, 216, 227; WNS2, pp. 140-141; WNS3, pp. 14, 152, 116-117, 165-166; WNS4, pp. 157-159; WNS5, pp. 6, 14; WNS6, p. 115; WNS7, p. 67)

Dharma Cloud Unhindered King: (J. Hōunjizai; 法雲自在王) According to **Nichiren Shonin**, the "original state" of **Nagarjuna** is Dharma Cloud Unhindered King **Buddha**. (WNS3, p. 238)

dharma eye: (S. dharma-cakṣus; J. *hō-gen*; 法眼) One of the **five kinds of eyes**. The **dharma** eye of **bodhisattva**s is able to penetrate all dharmas.

Dharma gates are inexhaustible; I vow to know them all: (J. hōmon-mujin-seiganchi; 法門無尽誓願知) The third of the **four great vows** of a **bodhisattva**. It is a vow to learn, practice, and understand all the teachings of the **Buddha Dharma**.

Dharma master: (J. hosshi; 法師) One who learns and teaches the **Dharma**. In **Nichiren Shu** it is a title given to novices.

Dharma Wisdom: (J. Hō'e; 法慧) One of the four main **bodhisattva**s who expounds the **Dharma** in the *Flower Garland Sutra*. He teaches about the **ten abodes**.

Dharma-body: (S. Dharma-kāya; J. hosshin; 法身) Also known as the **fivefold Dharma-body**. It is also one of the **three bodies** of a **buddha**, which can also be viewed as three aspects of the Dharma-body itself. It is not produced but realized as the **unconditioned** true nature by all buddhas. As the omnipresent universal body of a buddha, it is the ineffable ultimate reality itself, the suchness of things that is **non-arising** and **non-ceasing**. The Dharma-body is also ornamented with all the sublime qualities of buddhahood. Therefore, it is called a "body" because it is the accumulation (as in a "body of work") of these qualities.

According to **Nichiren Shonin**, the Dharma-body is like the moon itself, while the **accommodative-body** is like the shadow or reflection of the moon in water, and the **reward-body** is like the moonlight. (WNS6, p. 131)

Dharma-nature: (S. dharmatā; J. hosshō; 法性) The Sanskrit term *dharmatā* can also be translates as "**nature** of **phenomena**," "nature of reality," "nature of things," or "true reality."

Dharma-realm: (S. Dharma-dhatu; J. hokkai; 法界) Reality as experienced by a **buddha**. The Dharma-realm is **pure** because all **outflows** are forever extinguished, so it is naturally pure, and perfectly bright. It is a realm that stores boundless virtuous qualities. It is also **inconceivable**, **wholesome**, and eternal. It can also be called the **Dharma-body**.

Dharma-wheel: (S. Dharmacakra; J. hōrin; 法輪) An eight spoked wheel that represents the **Buddha Dharma** because it is always in motion and crushes all evil in its path.

Dharmapala: (530-561; S. Dharmapāla; J. Gohō; 護法) A **monk** from southern India who studied under Dignaga and became a teacher of **Consciousness-Only**

school doctrines at Nalanda. **Shilabhadra** was his disciple. Dharmapala's commentary on the *Thirty Verses on Consciousness-Only* of **Vasubandhu** was incorporated into **Xuanzang**'s ***Demonstration of Consciousness-Only Treatise.***

Diamond Banner: (J. Kongōdō; 金剛幢) One of the four main **bodhisattva**s who expound the **Dharma** in the *Flower Garland Sutra*. He teaches about the **ten dimensions of merit transference**.

Diamond Peak Sutra: (S. *Vajraśekhara-sūtra* or *Sarvatathāgata-tattvasaṃgraha*; J. *Kongōchō-kyō* or *Issainyorai shinjitsushō daijōgenshōzanmai daikyōōgyō*; 金剛頂経 or 一切如来真実摂大乗現証三昧大教王経) One of the two basic scriptures of **esoteric Buddhism** in East Asia together with the *Mahavairochana Sutra*. It came into existence in the latter half of the seventh century of the common era as a type of yoga tantra. Two Chinese versions of this **sutra** exist: a translation by **Amoghavajra** in three fascicles around 754 and a translation by **Vajrabodhi** in six fascicles between 723 and 724. While the *Mahavairochana Sutra* reveals the **Womb-realm**, this sutra expounds the teaching of the **Diamond-realm**, on which the Diamond-realm **mandala** is based.

According to **Zhiyi**'s doctrine of the **five periods**, **Nichiren Shonin** relegates this sutra to the status of a **provisional sutra** taught during the third or **Expanded period**.

Diamond Repository: (S. Vajragarbha; J. Kongōzō; 金剛蔵) One of the four main **bodhisattva**s who expound the **Dharma** in the *Flower Garland Sutra*. He teaches about the **ten grounds**.

Diamond-realm: (S. Vajra-dhātu; J. Kongō-kai; 金剛界) The realm described in the *Diamond Peak Sutra* that represents the **wisdom** of **Mahavairochana Buddha**.

Discipline school: (J. Ritsu-shū; 律宗) One of the schools of Chinese Buddhism and one of the **six schools of Nara Buddhism** in Japan. The Discipline school was founded when the discipline or **vinaya** of the Dharmaguptaka school was established in China based on the *Four-part Discipline* translated by Buddhayashas and Zhu Fonian between 410 and 412. From that time on, **Mahayana monks** and **nuns** in China, Korea, and Vietnam have all been ordained in the Dharmaguptaka precept lineage.

The Discipline school was brought to Nara, the capital of Japan, by Jianzhen in 754, where it was called the Ritsu Shu. Jianzhen then established a **precept platform** to confer the Dharmaguptaka precepts upon monks and nuns at Todaiji Temple in Nara. Two more precept platforms were established in 761 at Yakushiji Temple (in present day Tochigi Prefecture) and Kanzeonji Temple (in present day Fukuoka Prefecture), so that in Japan there were three precept platforms for bestowing the complete precepts of the *Four-part Discipline*. The Discipline school's popularity declined in Japan after the eighth century. During the Kamakura period, **Eison** revived the school in conjunction with **esoteric Buddhism**, thereby establishing the **Mantra-Discipline school** (J. Shingon Risshū; 真言律宗).

The Discipline school's teaching encompassed both **hinayana** and **Mahayana precept**s in terms of the **three categories of pure precepts**. The first of these three, the precepts for maintaining restraint, includes all the various kinds of hinayana **training rules** and precepts for **bodhisattva**s such as found in the *Brahma's Net Sutra*. This school's interpretation of practicing the precepts was in accordance with the teachings of the **Consciousness-Only school**, and therefore saw the hinayana precepts as being a part of Mahayana practice to **attain buddhahood**.

Nichiren Shonin classifies this school, along with the **Abhidharma Treasury** and **Completion of Reality** schools, as a hinayana school (WNS2, pp. 192, 252, 267; WNS3, pp. 19, 123, 249; WNS5, p. 163; WNS6, p. 146). He was especially critical of the Discipline school masters Eison and **Ryokan**, his contemporaries, and he insisted that in the **Latter Age of Degeneration** the observance of the hinayana precepts is useless and that upholding the *Lotus Sutra* is the true observance of the precepts.

dispensation: (S. śāsana; J. shōgyō; 聖教) The Sanskrit term *śāsana* can also be translated as "**scripture**" or "teaching." See **Buddha's dispensation**.

distinct teaching: (J. bekkyō; 別教) The third of the **four doctrinal teachings**. This teaching can primarily be found in the *Flower Garland Sutra* and is intended for advanced **bodhisattva**s, so it is distinct from the teachings for **voice-hearer**s. In this teaching, it is understood that a one-sided realization of **emptiness** can obscure the appreciation for the particulars of contingent **phenomena** that is needed to counteract specific **delusion**s so that the **suffering** arising from them can be eliminated. In the distinct teaching, the truth of provisionality is cultivated to enable adequate responses to each and every circumstance. While continuing to recognize that all things are empty, the bodhisattvas also see that this emptiness is not a blank void or nothingness. Rather, the lack of a fixed or independent **self-nature** is what allows all things to flow and move, change and grow, and ultimately interrelate so thoroughly that all things affect all other things like a web that quivers all at once when any one strand is touched. All things, all beings, are provisional manifestations of this interpenetrating dynamic process. Realizing this, bodhisattvas negate the negation of emptiness. They are free to reengage the world and appreciate all things without clinging or attachment. Gradually they realize the truth of the middle that integrates peaceful detachment with compassionate involvement. **Zhiyi** stated that the truths of emptiness, provisionality, and the middle are all aspects of the threefold truth. In this teaching they are approached dialectically as the differentiated threefold truth. Emptiness is the thesis, provisionality is the antithesis, and the synthesis is the middle. The distinct teaching is found in the **Flower Garland**, **Expanded**, and **Prajna period**s of the **five periods** of **Shakyamuni Buddha**'s teachings.

The distinct teaching is representative of the **bodhisattva vehicle** and is followed by bodhisattvas with a **sharp capacity**. The truth of the middle is viewed as a negation of the extremes of emptiness and existence, so there is not a full integration with the other two truths. Because bodhisattvas of this teaching do not see the middle as unifying and fully embracing all dharmas their approach to practice is step-by-step and gradual (PMLS2, p. 144)

Distinguishing the Two Teaching of the Exoteric and Esoteric Treatise: (J. *Ben-kemmitsu nikyō-ron*; 弁顕密二教論) Sometimes abbreviated as *Two Teachings Treatise*. It is a treatise by **Kukai**, in which he argues that the **provisional teaching**s of **exoteric Buddhism** were a **skillful means** taught by the **buddha**s of the **accommodative-body** and the **other-enjoyment-body**, while the **true teaching** of **esoteric Buddhism** that expounds the **three mysteries** were taught by the buddhas of the **self-enjoyment-body** and the **self-nature-body**.

divine eye: (S. divya-cakṣus; J. tengen-chishōtsū; 天眼智証通) The fifth of the **six supernatural powers**. It is also one of the **five kinds of eyes**. The practitioner with this power has sight which is purified and surpasses the **human**, being able to see the death and **rebirth** of other **sentient beings**, inferior and superior, beautiful and ugly, fortunate and unfortunate, and understand their destinations in accordance with their **karma**.

Doji: (d. 744; J. Dōji; 道慈) A Japanese **monk** who was a disciple of Chizo, from whom he received the teachings of the **Three Treatises school**. Doji went to China to further his studies in 701, returning to Japan in 718. He relocated Daianji Temple from the old capital to Nara, modeling it upon the Ximingsi Temple in China. From there he primarily taught the Three Treatises school, but also the teachings of the **Dharma Characteristics school** and the **Mantra school** teachings that he had studied with **Shubhakarasimha** in China. He is credited with the third transmission of the Three Treatises school to Japan. (TBD, pp. 121-122)

Dokyo: (d. 772; J. Dōkyō; 道鏡) A **monk** of the **Dharma Characteristics school** who resided at Todaiji Temple. His prayers were held responsible for the recovery from illness of Retired Emperess Koken (J. Kōken) in 761. When she became Empress Shotoku (J. Shōtoku) in 764, she made Dokyo her advisor. He gained so much power that it was feared he was plotting to usurp the throne. After the death of Empress Shotoku, he was exiled to Yakushiji Temple.

Dongchun: (C.; J. Tōjun/Tōshun; 東春) A work by **Zhidu** named after the place where he lived. Its full title is *A Supplement to the Meanings of the Commentaries on the Lotus Sutra*.

Dosho: (629-700; J. Dōshō; 道昭) The Japanese **monk** who is credited with transmitting the teachings of the **Abhidharma Treasury school** and the first transmission of the **Dharma Characteristics school** to Japan. He went to China in 653 and studied with **Xuanzang**. He returned to Japan in 660 and resided at Gangoji Temple. (TBD, pp. 125-126) He also studied and passed on the teachings of the **Zen school**, establishing a hall for Zen practice at Gangoji. (Matsunaga I, p. 112)

dragon: (S. nāga; J. ryū; 竜) The dragons of **Brahmanism** dwell beneath the oceans, control the tides, the flow of rivers, and the rain. Though intelligent and extremely powerful, they are classified as **animals** among the **six destinies**. They are one of the **eight kinds of supernatural beings**.
The **eight great dragon kings** were present to hear the *Lotus Sutra*.

dragon girl: (S. nāgakanyā; J. ryūnyo; 竜女) In the twelfth, "**Devadatta**," chapter of the *Lotus Sutra*, **Manjushri Bodhisattva** returns from the palace of the **Dragon King** Sagara in the ocean where he had been teaching the *Lotus Sutra*. He then introduced all the innumerable bodhisattas that he had taught, including the eight-year-old daughter of the dragon king. The dragon king's daughter then demonstrated how to **attain buddhahood with one's present body** by offering the Buddha a priceless gem, and then just as swiftly as the offering had been made transforming herself into a buddha. This occurred despite the belief that because of the **five obstacles** a woman could not attain buddhahood.
Considering the **attainment of buddhahood by a dragon girl** as evidence for the **attainment of buddhahood by women**, **Nichiren Shonin** stressed the great compassion of the Buddha covering all people without discrimination.

dragon king: (S. nāga-rāja; J. ryū'ō; 竜王) See **eight great dragon kings**.

Dronodana: (S. Droṇodana; J. Kokubonnō; 斛飯王) The younger brother of King **Shuddhodana**. According to the sixth chapter of the *Great Perfection of Wisdom Treatise*, he was the father of **Ananda** and **Devadatta**.

Nichiren Shonin sometimes refers to him as the father of the former pair (WNS2, pp. 59, 61; WNS4, pp. 43, 64; WNS6, p. 43), but on other occasions refers to him as the father of **Aniruddha** as well (WNS7, pp. 9-10, 24, 96).

dull capacity: (S. mṛdvindriya; J. donkon; 鈍根) This refers to practitioners of dull intelligence, who are all but overcome by **defilement**s and have low aspirations.

"Duration of the Life of the Tathagata, The" chapter: (J. Nyorai-juryō-hon; 如来寿量品) The sixteenth chapter of the *Lotus Sutra*. In this chapter, **Shakyamuni Buddha** responds to **Maitreya Bodhisattva**'s question from the previous chapter about how he could have taught the **bodhisattvas appearing from underground** if his **attainment of awakening for the first time** was under the **Bodhi Tree** in **Bodhgaya** only forty years prior. Three times the Buddha said to Maitreya Bodhisattva and the rest of the assembly, "Good men! Understand my sincere and infallible words by **faith**!" Four times they replied, "Tell us! We will receive your words by faith!" (LS, p. 247) After those exchanges, the Buddha revealed to them his **attainment of buddhahood in the remotest past**. He explained the length of time since he attained buddhahood in terms of a practically unquantifiable span of time referred to in abbreviated form as the **five hundred dust-particle kalpas**. Since then, he has been teaching through the **six occasions of showing the deeds and figures of buddhas**.

Shakyamuni Buddha also reveals in this chapter that though he will appear to enter **final nirvana**, in fact his remaining lifespan is twice as long as the span of time that has already passed since attaining buddhahood. He is thereby revealed to be the **Eternal Shakyamuni Buddha** who always abides in this **Saha world** where we live, which is actually his **pure land**. Borrowing the term used in the *Contemplation of the Universal Sage Bodhisattva Sutra*, this pure land is called the Pure Land of Eternally Tranquil Light by **Zhiyi**. In order to explain why he uses the **skillful means** of saying that he will enter final nirvana, when in fact he will remain on Mt. **Sacred Eagle** teaching the **Dharma**, he tells the assembly the parable of the excellent physician and his children.

The chapter ends with verses that recapitulate what was stated in the prose portion. These verses are considered to be the heart of the *Lotus Sutra*.

Nichiren Shonin made the doctrine of the Eternal Shakyamuni Buddha, who controls all other buddhas and their pure lands, central to his teaching and practice. He also taught that hidden with the lines of chapter sixteen were the **Three Great Secret Dharmas**.

Dushun: (557-640; J. Tojun; 杜順) Also known as Fashun (C.; J. Hōjun; 法順). The first patriarch of the Chinese **Flower Garland school**; also known as the Meditation Master Dushun or the Venerable Fashun. He took ordination as a **monk** at seventeen and practiced meditation under Weichen of the Yinshengsi Temple. He lived on Mt. Zhongnan, expounding Flower Garland Buddhism. He is said to have worked miracles and was worshipped as an appearance of **Manjushri Bodhisattva**. He died at eighty-four and was succeeded by his disciple **Zhiyan**.

earth, goddess of the: (S. Dṛḍhayā Pṛthivī; J. Kenrō Jijin; 堅牢地神) The name Dṛḍhā means Steady One, while the ideograms 堅牢 mean "strong" or "robust." Pṛthivī literally means "Vast One" and is also the Sanskrit name for the element earth, while the ideograms 地神 can be translated as "earth spirit" or "earth goddess." She is the Vedic **god**dess of the earth who was adopted into Buddhism as a **guardian deity**.

There is a story that when **Siddhartha** sat beneath the **Bodhi tree**, **Mara** challenged him by asking him to produce a witness who could attest that he had accrued enough **merit** to **attain buddhahood**. Siddhartha the touched the earth and the goddess appeared to testify that there was nowhere on earth where he had not given up his life for the sake of other **sentient being**s over his many lifetimes of **bodhisattva practice**.

effect: (S. phala; J. ka; 果) The Sanskrit term *phala* can also be translated as "**fruition**" or "result."

In the *Profound Meaning of the Lotus Sutra*, effect as the eighth of the **ten suchnesses** is given the following definition by **Zhiyi**: "**Repetitive effect**s are called 'effects.'" (FTP, p. 184)

In the *Great Calming and Contemplation*, Zhiyi further explained that the **homogeneous cause**s are sown repeatedly and then the repetitive effects are harvested. (CSQI, p. 810)

eight errors: (J. hachi-ja; 八邪) the eight erroneous ways of living that are in opposition to the **eightfold noble path**. For example, **wrong views** as opposed to **right view**.

eight great dragon kings: (J. hachidai-ryū'ō; 八大竜王) The eight are: Nanda, Upananda, Sagara, Vasuki, Takshaka, Anavatapta, Manasvin, and Utpalaka. These eight are listed as present in the first, "Introductory," chapter of the *Lotus Sutra*.

eight kinds of acceptance: (J. hachi-nin; 八忍 or 八認) Eight mental states that are part of the **thirty-four enlightened mental states**. The eight kinds of acceptance (see **patience**(1)) consist of the acceptance of each of the **four noble truths** and the acceptance of having realized each of the four noble truths. Together with the **eight kinds of knowledge** they are needed to sever **deluded views** according to the **tripitaka teaching**.

eight kinds of knowledge: (J. hachi-chi; 八智) Eight mental states that are part of the **thirty-four enlightened mental states**. The eight kinds of **knowledge** consist of the knowledge of each of the **four noble truths** and knowledge of having realized each of the four noble truths. Together with the **eight kinds of acceptance** they are needed to sever **deluded views** according to the **tripitaka teaching**.

eight kinds of suffering: (1) (S. aṣṭa-duḥkha; J. hakku; 八苦) **Shakyamuni Buddha** enumerated eight kinds of **suffering** in his explanation of the truth of suffering. They are the sufferings of birth, aging, illness, death, encountering what is disliked, separation from what is loved, not getting what is desired, and the **five aggregates** subject to clinging. (CD 56.11, p. 1844)

(2) (J. hasshu-no-dainan; 八種の大難) The eight kinds of suffering enumerated in the *Six-Fascicle Nirvana Sutra* are: 1) to be slighted, 2) to look ugly, 3) to be poorly clad, 4) to lack clothing and food, 5) to be unable to make a fortune, 6) to be born into a poor family, 7) to be born into a family that follows **non-Buddhist teachings**, and 8) to be persecuted by the ruler.

Nichiren Shonin cited these eight and stated that they applied to him in his writing *On the Opening of the Eyes*. (WNS2, p. 106)

eight kinds of supernatural beings: (S. aṣṭa-senā; J. hachibu-shū; 八部衆) These eight are supernatural beings who are traditional recipients and protectors of the **Dharma**. They all appear, for instance, in the first, "Introductory," chapter of the *Lotus Sutra* as present in the assembly. The eight are: 1) **god**s, 2) **dragon**s, 3) **yaksha**s, 4) **gandharva**s, 5) **asura**s, 6) **garuda**s, 7) **kimnara**s, and 8) **mahoraga**s.

eight negations: (S. aṣṭānta; J. happu; 八不) These eight appear in the dedicatory verse that opens the *Root Verses on the Middle Way*. They are: 1) no **cessation** (see **non-ceasing**), 2) no arising (see **non-arising**), 3) no annihilation (see **annihilationism**), 4) no permanence (see **eternalism**); 5) no coming, 6) no going, 7) no difference, and 8) no sameness. This verse declares that, since **Shakyamuni Buddha** taught **dependent origination**, it can be understood that none of the items negated apply to any **phenomena**. This understanding can bring about an end to conceptual proliferation. (Siderits & Katsura, p. 13; Garfield, p. 100)

eight phases of a buddha's life: (S. aṣṭa-buddha-kārya; J. hassō or hassō-jōdō or hassō-sabutsu; 八相 or 八相成道 or 八相作仏) The eight phases of the life of a **buddha** are: 1) descending into the world from the **Tushita** Heaven, 2) entering the womb, 3) emerging from the womb, 4) **leaving home**, 5) overcoming **Mara**, 6) attaining the way (i.e. **attaining buddhahood**), 7) **turning of the Wheel of the Dharma**, and 8) entering **final nirvana**. There are variations.

eight winds: (J. happū; 八風) Eight things that cause disturbance, such as attachment and aversion, among people in the world, the way winds raise waves in a body of water. The eight are: 1) gain, 2) loss, 3) fame, 4) infamy, 5) praise, 6) blame, 7) pleasure, and 8) pain. (ND 8.5, p. 1116)

eightfold noble path: (S. āryāṣṭāṅga-mārga; J. hasshō-dō; 八正道 or 八聖道) **Shakyamuni Buddha** described the truth of the **way leading to the cessation of suffering**, which is also the **middle way**, in terms of eight components: 1) **right view**, 2) **right intention**, 3) **right speech**, 4) **right action**, 5) **right livelihood**, 6) **right effort**, 7) **right mindfulness**, and 8) **right concentration**. (LD 22.21, pp. 348-349)

The eightfold noble path can be divided into three categories as the **threefold training**.

eighty minor marks: (S. anuvyañjana; J. hachijisshugō; 八十種好) The minor marks of a "great man" that are possessed by a **buddha**, an advanced **bodhisattva**, major **god**s, or a **wheel-turning king**.

eighty thousand teachings: (J. hachiman-hōmon or hachiman-hōzō; 八万法門 or 八万法蔵) A way of referring to all the teachings of **Shakyamuni Buddha**.

Eison: (1201-1290; J. alt. Eizon; 叡尊) A **monk** of the **Mantra school** in Japan who became the founder of the Mantra-Discipline school (J. Shingon Risshū; 真言律宗). In 1235, Eison studied the **vinaya** at Saidaiji Temple, but at that time the complete monastic precepts were no longer being followed in Japan. In 1236, Eison and three other monks conferred upon themselves the higher ordination at Todaiji Temple. He traveled around Japan to propagate the precepts among both the clergy and the laity, and later settled at Saidaiji Temple. In 1274 and 1281 he conducted rites of **esoteric Buddhism** to ward off the Mongol invasions. **Ryokan**,

Nichiren Shonin's arch-rival in Kamakura, was a disciple of Eison.

Elucidation of the Profound Meaning of the Lotus Sutra: (J. *Hokke-gengi-shakusen*; 法華玄義釈籤) A commentary by **Zhanran** on **Zhiyi**'s *Profound Meaning of the Lotus Sutra*.

emanation-bodies: See **emanation-body**.

emanation-body: (J. funjin; 分身) The ideograms 分身 literally mean "divided-body." The term refers to the emanations of a **buddha** or **bodhisattva** that appear in various forms as a means of guiding **sentient being**s in the worlds all over the universe so that they may attain **liberation** from **suffering**. In the eleventh, "**Beholding the Stupa of Treasures,**" **chapter** of the *Lotus Sutra*, the **emanation buddhas of the ten directions** who had all been produced by **Shakyamuni** Buddha gathered to listen to the *Lotus Sutra* assembly in front of the **stupa of treasures**; and in the twenty-first, "**Supernatural Powers of the Tathagatas,**" **chapter**, they testified to the truth of Shakyamuni Buddha's teaching by touching the **Brahma Heaven** with their **long, wide tongue**s.

emanation-bodies: See **emanation-body**.

emanation buddhas of the ten directions: (J. jippō-funjin-no-shobutsu; 十方分身の諸佛) See **emanation-body**.

embracing: (J. shōju; 摂受) The ideograms 摂受 literally mean "to accept and receive." The method of embracing refers to the means of propagating the **Buddha Dharma** by embracing the **provisional teaching**s or **wholesome view**s that others already have and then using gentle persuasion to lead them to the **True Dharma**.

Emitting Ten Million Rays of Light: (S. Raśmi-śata-sahasra-paripūrṇa-dhvaja; J. Gusoku-semmankōsō; 具足千万光相) The name of the **buddha** that **Yashodhara** will become, according to the thirteenth, "**Encouragement for Keeping This Sutra,**" **chapter** of the *Lotus Sutra*.

emptiness: (S. śūnyatā; J. kū; 空) The lack of a static, independent **self** or **self-nature** in any entity or **phenomena**. What is empty is also **non-arising** and **non-ceasing**, and in that way like **nirvana**.

empty: See **emptiness**.

Enchin: (814-891; J.; 円珍) Also called the **Great Master Chisho**. A **monk** of the **Tiantai school** in Japan who was ordained when he was fifteen by **Gishin**. He later became the fifth head abbot of **Enryakuji Temple**. He studied the teachings of the **Tiantai school** and Tendai Esotericism with Gishin, **Encho**, **Kojo**, and **Ennin**, and studied the teachings of Eastern Temple Esotericism at the **Toji Temple**. He furthered his studies of **esoteric Buddhism** in China from 853 to 858. Upon his return to Japan he restored the **Onjoji Temple** at Mii, from where he had a great impact on the development of Tendai Esotericism. Thus, he is regarded as the founder of the Temple school faction (J. Jimon-ha; 寺門派) within the Japanese Tiantai school.

In his *Guide to the Mahavairochana Sutra*, he ranked the *Mahavairochana Sutra* first and the *Lotus Sutra* second among teachings of **Shakyamuni Buddha**. In his *A Collection of Orally Transmitted Teachings*, he taught that the *Flower Garland Sutra*, the *Lotus Sutra*, and the *Nirvana Sutra* are superior to the teachings of the **Mantra school** and the **Zen school**. In his *Notations on the Universal Sage Sutra* and *Notations on the Lotus Sutra Treatise* he states that the *Mahavairochana Sutra* and the *Lotus Sutra* are the same. (WNS3, p. 24)

Nichiren Shonin severely criticized him for betraying the Tendai founder **Saicho** just as Ennin had done, committing **slander of the True Dharma** by converting the principal center for the practice of the *Lotus Sutra*, Enryakuji Temple, to a center of esotericism.

Encho: (772-837; J. Enchō; 円澄) Also known as the **Great Master** Jakko (J. Jakkō Daishi; 寂光 大師). The second head abbot of **Enryakuji Temple**. Born in Musashi Province, he was ordained as a **monk** at the age of eighteen as a disciple of Dochu (J. Dōchū) and named himself Hokyo (J. Hōkyō). He received the **perfect and sudden precepts** of the *Brahma's Net Sutra* from **Saicho** at the age of twenty-seven. He studied the teachings of the **Tiantai school** from Saicho while at the same time studying the **Mantra school** teachings with **Kukai**. He was requested to become the head abbot of Enryakuji on Mt. **Hiei** in Saicho's will.

Nichiren Shonin, criticized him as being half a disciple of Saicho and half a disciple of Kukai. Nevertheless, he also stated that Mt. Hiei remained a center for the teaching and practice of the *Lotus Sutra* up through the time of the Head Abbot Encho.

"Encouragement for Keeping This Sutra," chapter: (J. Kanji-hon; 勧持品) The thirteenth chapter of the *Lotus Sutra*. **Shakyamuni Buddha** had made **three proclamations** urging those among the **four assemblies** to propagate the *Lotus Sutra* after his passing in the eleventh, **"Beholding the Stupa of Treasures," chapter**. In this chapter, **Medicine King Bodhisattva**, Great Eloquence Bodhisattva, their twenty-thousand attendants, and the **voice-hearer**s respond by **vow**ing that they will propagate it in the **Saha world** after the Buddha's **final nirvana**. Then five hundred **arhat**s and eight thousand voice-hearers vow that they will spread the *Lotus Sutra* in other worlds.

The Buddha next gives the assurance of future buddhahood to **Mahaprajapati**, who will become the buddha named **Gladly Seen by All Beings**$_{(1)}$, and to **Yashodhara**, who will become the buddha named **Emitting Ten Million Rays of Light**.

The chapter concludes with eighty billion *nayuta* of bodhisattvas making a vow to spread the teaching at the risk of their lives. In the twenty-line verse wherein these bodhisattvas reiterate their vow, they state that propagators will encounter **three kinds of enemies**: 1) **presumptuous lay followers** who support the following two kinds, 2) **presumptuous clergy** who mislead suffering people, and 3) **presumptuous sages** who are highly respected Buddhist leaders who consider themselves to be living buddhas and look down on all others even though they are still strongly attached to worldly matters.

Nichiren Shonin regarded the twenty-line verse of this chapter as a prediction by Shakyamuni Buddha. As his experiences matched this forecast of the Buddha, it strengthened his belief that he was the real **practitioner of the *Lotus Sutra***.

energy: (S. vīrya; J. gon or shōjin or biriya; 勤 or 精進 or 毘梨耶) The Sanskrit term *vīrya* can also be translated as "diligence," "effort" or "vigor." Energy is a continual effort to do what is **wholesome**.

In **Mahayana** Buddhism, energy is the fourth of the **six perfections** of a **bodhisattva**. As a **bodhisattva practice**, energy includes "donning the armor" of aspiration, embracing the wholesome, and bringing **benefit** and happiness to others.

enjoyment-body: (S. saṃbhoga-kāya; J. jijuyū-jin; 受用身) One of the **three bodies** of a **buddha**. It can also be viewed as one of the three aspects of the **Dharma-body**. Also called the **reward-body**. It is an idealized **form-body** attained as the reward for a buddha's accrued **merit** from previous **bodhisattva practice**.

According to the *Demonstration of Consciousness-Only Treatise*, there are two kinds of enjoyment-body: the **self-enjoyment-body** and the **other-enjoyment-body**. (DCOT, pp. 360-361; CWL, p. 793)

enlightenment: (J. satori; 悟/覚) A common translation for *bodhi*, or "**awakening**," though the latter is a better translation of the Sanskrit term.

Ennin: (794-864; 円仁) Also called the **Great Master Jikaku**. The third head abbot of **Enryakuji Temple**. At the age of fifteen he was ordained by Kochi but then became a disciple of **Saicho** on Mt. **Hiei**. In 838 he went to China, where he further studied the doctrine of the **Tiantai school** at Mt. **Wutai**, and the teachings of the **Mantra school** in Chang'an. There he was also able to receive the teachings of the *Act of Perfection Sutra* that had not previously been transmitted to Japan. He then had to flee the persecution of Buddhism by Emperor Wuzong. He was able to return to Japan in 847. The record of his travels to China is the *Pilgrimage to China in Search of the Dharma*.

He shaped the original form of the Japanese Tiantai school's Pure Land teaching by introducing the slow-chanting **nembutsu** as a form of the "ceaseless practice **samadhi**," which is another name for the constantly-walking samadhi. He also established the original base of Tendai Esotericism at Sōji-in Temple. He wrote many works including the *Annotations on the Diamond Peak Sutra* and the *Annotations on the Act of Perfection Sutra*.

Nichiren Shonin harshly criticized Ennin for maintaining that **esoteric Buddhism** can be characterized as **"equal in principle, superior in practice"** in comparison to the ***Lotus Sutra*** and for saying that the *Lotus Sutra* is like the moon while the Mantra teachings were like the sun. (WNS1, pp. 170-171) He branded him a parasite in the belly of Saicho who had insisted on the supremacy of the *Lotus Sutra*.

Enryakuji Temple: (延暦寺) The head temple of the Japanese **Tiantai school**. It had its beginnings as a small straw hut built by **Saicho** on Mt. **Hiei** as a hermitage in 785. In 788 he built the main hall, that was later called Konpon chūdō. In 806, the temple complex was proclaimed a temple that would protect the new capital of Kyoto from **demon**s that were said to threaten it from the northeast. In 822, soon after the death of Saicho, the imperial court granted permission to establish a Mahayana precept platform there for the conferral of the **perfect and sudden precepts** of the *Brahma's Net Sutra*. The platform was completed in 827. In 823, the temple complex was given the name Enryakuji.

entity: (S. vastu; J. tai; 体) The Sanskrit term *vastu* can also be translated as "bases," "body," "embodiment," "essence," "real entity," or "substance." It is often understood to refer to the entity which produces a function.

In the ***Profound Meaning of the Lotus Sutra***, entity as the third of the **ten suchnesses** is given the following definition by **Zhiyi**: "That which is the central quality [of something] is called its 'essence.'" (FTP, p. 184)

In the ***Great Calming and Contemplation***, Zhiyi further explained that the function of the name and form of the **aggregate**s in the **ten realms** is their entity. (CSQI, p. 809)

environment: (J. kokudo; 国土) As the third of the **three categories of existence**, the environment or **container world** for **sentient beings** is a component of the **three thousand realms in a single thought-moment**. (CSQI, p. 815)

equal in principle, superior in practice: (J. ridō-jishō; 理同事勝) Tendai Esotericism claimed that the *Lotus Sutra* and the *Mahavairochana Sutra* were equal in doctrinal principle, but that the latter was superior in ritual practice because it taught the use of **mudra**s and **mantra**s. This doctrine was initiated by **Ennin** based on the *Annotations on the Mahavairocana Sutra* by **Yixing** and was transmitted to **Enchin** and others.

Ranking the *Lotus Sutra* below the *Mahavairochana Sutra*, the doctrine of "equal in principle, superior in practice" clearly shows the shift of the Japanese Tiantai school's doctrine towards **esoteric Buddhism**. **Nichiren Shonin** vehemently criticized this trend as in opposition to the true intent of **Shakyamuni Buddha**. Nichiren Shonin protested the disappearance of the orthodox teaching established by **Zhiyi** and **Saicho**, saying that the pure *Lotus Sutra* based Buddhism, with its doctrine of **three thousand realms in a single thought-moment**, is the **true teaching** completely equipped with both doctrine and practice.

Eshin: (942-1017; J.; 惠心) Also known as Genshin (J.; 源信) or the Venerable of Yokawa. A **monk** of the Japanese **Tiantai school** who studied on Mt. **Hiei** the teachings of both **exoteric Buddhism** and **esoteric Buddhism** under Ryogen, eighteenth head abbot of **Enryakuji Temple**. He was from Yamato Province (Nara Prefecture today) and is the founder of the Eshin faction. He wrote the *Essential Collection Concerning Rebirth in the Pure Land*, which exerted a tremendous influence on the **Pure Land school** in Japan. Eshin later wrote the ***Essentials of the One Vehicle Teaching***, stressing the universal existence of the **buddha-nature** and the **One Vehicle** teaching of the *Lotus Sutra* as opposed to the **Dharma Characteristics school**'s doctrine of the **five natures**. (WNS1, p. 29)

Nichiren Shonin at first considered Eshin an outstanding monk of the Japanese Tiantai school, but later criticized him harshly as a parasite within the **Tiantai Lotus school**. (WNS1, pp. 27, 29-30, 35-41)

esoteric Buddhism: (J. mikkyō; 密教) The ideograms 密教 mean "esoteric teaching" but it is understood to refer to esoteric Buddhism. In East Asia these are secret teachings and practices given by **Mahavairocana Buddha** that are held to be beyond the understanding of **ordinary people**. The **Mantra school** maintains that **exoteric Buddhism** was taught by **Shakyamuni** Buddha, the **accommodative-body** of the Buddha, and is therefore inferior to esoteric Buddhism taught by Mahavairocana Buddha, the **Dharma-body** of the Buddha.

Nichiren Shonin insisted that esoteric sutras, which taught neither the **attainment of buddhahood by adherents of the two vehicles**, nor the **attainment of buddhahood in the remotest past** by Shakyamuni Buddha, are inferior to the *Lotus Sutra*, which is the true esoteric teaching.

Essay on the Protection of the Nation: (J. *Shugo-kokkai-shō*; 守護国界章) An essay written by **Saicho** in 818 to refute **Tokuitsu**.

Essential Meaning of Praising the Profundity of the Lotus Sutra: (J. *Hokke-genzan-yōshū*; 法華玄賛要集) A writing by a disciple of **Kuiji** in which it is asserted that Kuiji taught that the **One Vehicle** teaching of the *Lotus Sutra* is the true teaching.

Essentials of the One Vehicle Teaching: (J. *Ichijō-yōketsu*; 一乗要決) A treatise written by **Eshin** in 1006 based on the **One Vehicle** teaching of the *Lotus Sutra*. It asserts the possession of the **buddha-nature** by all people, contradicting the doctrine of the **five natures** of the **Dharma Characteristics school**.

In this work, Eshin also stated that Japan was a country whose people believed solely in the **perfect teaching** of the One Vehicle. (WNS1, p. 67)

Regarding Eshin's purpose in writing the *Essential Collection Concerning Rebirth in the Pure Land* and *Essentials of the One Vehicle Teaching*, **Nichiren Shonin** maintained that Eshin's true intent was to publish the *Essential of the One Vehicle Teaching* later, thereby following the example of **Shakyamuni Buddha**'s expounding the **provisional teaching** first in order to reveal the **True Dharma** in the end. (WNS1, p. 38)

establishing a connection to Great Universal Wisdom Excellence Buddha: (J. daitsū-kechien; 大通結縁) According to the seventh, "The Parable of a Magic City," chapter of the *Lotus Sutra*, **three thousand dust-particle kalpas** ago, there was a king who became a **buddha** called **Great Universal Wisdom Excellence**. The sixteen princes who were his sons renounced the world and became **bodhisattva**s. After teaching the *Lotus Sutra*, Great Universal Wisdom Excellence Buddha entered into **samadhi**. The sixteen bodhisattva sons thereupon each sat on a seat of the **Dharma** to expound the *Lotus Sutra* as transmitted from their father, the Buddha of that time and place. Thus, they planted the **seed of buddhahood** in peoples' **mind**s by teaching the *Lotus Sutra*. This is defined as establishing a connection by sowing the seed of buddhahood through the *Lotus Sutra* in the remotest past.

The third of the three standards of doctrinal comparison established by **Zhiyi** is based on "The Parable of a Magic City" chapter of the *Lotus Sutra*: the length of the relationship between teacher and disciple, recognizing the connection established by the Great Universal Wisdom Excellence Buddha in this chapter as the beginning of the process of awakening the people by the Buddha.

Nichiren Shonin, however, discerned the Buddha's true intention in the **Original Gate** of the *Lotus Sutra*, so he instead found the meaning of establishing connection in the sixteenth chapter, "The **Duration of the Life of the Tathagata**." He thus maintained that all people have had an established connection with the **Eternal Shakyamuni Buddha** since the remotest past.

Eternal Buddha: (J. Butsu Kuon; 仏久遠) See **Eternal Shakyamuni Buddha**.

Eternal Shakyamuni Buddha: (J. Kuon Jitsujō Honshi Shakamuni Butsu; 久遠 実成 本師 釈迦牟尼仏) The ideograms literally mean "**Shakyamuni Buddha**, the original teacher, who attained in the remotest past." Also called the **Original Buddha**.

In **prior teachings** as well as in the **Trace Gate** (first fourteen chapters) of the *Lotus Sutra*, the Buddha is the historical **Siddhartha Gautama**, who left home and accomplished the **attainment of awakening for the first time** under the **Bodhi tree** at the age of thirty (or thirty-five). He taught others the way to **liberation** for approximately fifty years in northeastern India, and at the time of teaching the *Lotus Sutra* his **final nirvana** seemed imminent.

This view is challenged in the eleventh, "**Beholding the Stupa of Treasures**," chapter of the *Lotus Sutra*. In that chapter, **Many Treasures** Buddha appears in his stupa of treasures and testifies to the truth and excellence of the **One Buddha Vehicle** that Shakyamuni Buddha taught in the first ten chapters of the sutra. The assembly then asks to see Many Treasures Buddha, but to open the stupa of treasures Shakyamuni Buddha must recall his **emanation buddhas of the ten directions**. Shakyamuni Buddha purifies the world three times and then recalls the emanations. In doing this, he is no longer merely the historical Buddha but is revealed as the source of all the ideal buddhas of the **pure land**s throughout the universe. He opens the stupa of treasures, joins Many Treasures Buddha in the stupa floating in the sky, and uses his **supernatural power** to lift the entire assembly into the air with them. This is the beginning of the Assembly in Space.

In the fifteenth, "The **Appearance of Bodhisattvas from Underground**," chapter, Shakyamuni Buddha summons forth the **bodhisattvas appearing from underground**, who emerge from the **space** beneath the ground and reveal that they are the Buddha's original disciples from the remote past. The assembly wonders how the Buddha could have taught these innumerable bodhisattvas from the remote past when he had only been teaching for the past forty years.

In chapter sixteen, "The **Duration of the Life of the Tathagata**," **chapter** the Buddha responds to their questions by revealing that he did not first attain awakening beneath the Bodhi tree some forty years before the events in the *Lotus Sutra*. Rather, he had accomplished his **attainment of buddhahood in the remotest past**. The time frame he gives is in the form of an analogy referred to as the **five hundred dust-particle kalpas**. It is at this point in chapter sixteen that Shakyamuni Buddha reveals himself as the Original Buddha or Eternal Buddha and not simply the historical Buddha or even merely the source of the emanated buddhas of the present. This view of Shakyamuni Buddha, specifically in the sixteenth chapter of the *Lotus Sutra*, is the key to the true nature of buddhahood according to the **Nichiren school** of Buddhism.

The Eternal Shakyamuni Buddha represents the unity of the **three bodies** of a Buddha. (Stone 1999, p. 26): the universal **Dharma-body**, the idealized **reward-body**, and the historical **accommodative-body**. The Eternal Shakyamuni Buddha is distinguished from the historical Shakyamuni Buddha by the presence of the **four great bodhisattvas**, the leaders of the bodhisattvas appearing from underground, whereas the historical Shakyamuni Buddha is only accompanied by the **voice-hearer** disciples, such as **Ananda** and **Mahakashyapa**, and only represents the accommodative-body. The more exalted Shakyamuni Buddha of the provisional Mahayana teachings is accompanied by such bodhisattvas as **Manjushri** and **Universal Sage**, but only represents the reward-body perceived by advanced bodhisattvas who have reached the **ten grounds** of the path of cultivation. Only the Eternal Shakyamuni Buddha accompanied by the four leaders of the bodhisattvas appearing from underground represents all three bodies at once, the unity of the universal, ideal, and historical aspects of buddhahood. All the other buddhas are merely his emanations or aspects. For this reason, the Eternal Shakyamuni Buddha is considered to be the **Focus of Devotion of the Original Gate**.

The Eternal Shakyamuni Buddha also displays the **three virtues** of ruler, teacher, and parent of all who live in the **Saha world**. This means that the Eternal Shakyamuni Buddha nourishes, teaches, and protects humanity through the power of the **Wonderful Dharma**. This is because those who have **faith** in the *Lotus Sutra* mature their **wisdom**, open their eyes to the truth, and are freed from **suffering**.

The **pure land** of the Eternal Shakyamuni Buddha is the true reality of this world where the Original Buddha is always present expounding the Wonderful Dharma. As such it is sometimes called the Pure Land of Mount Sacred Eagle. In the *Contemplation of the Universal Sage Bodhisattva Sutra* this pure land is called the Pure Land of Eternally Tranquil Light.

eternalism: (S. śāśvata-dṛṣṭi; J. jō-ken; 常見) One form of extreme views. The view of eternalism is that there is a **self** or other **phenomena** that are not affected by **impermanence**. This view would also negate law of **cause and effect** because something that is unchanging does not have any **causality**. Avoiding the two extremes of **annihilationism** and eternalism, **Shakyamuni Buddha** taught the **middle way** of **dependent origination**. (CD 12.15, p. 544)

eternity: (S. nitya; J. jō; 常) The Sanskrit term *nitya* and the ideogram 常 can also be translated as "constancy," or "permanence." The eternity of the **Dharma-realm** is due to the absence of **arising** and **cessation**, and its unchanging **nature**.

evil destinies: (S. durgati or apāya; J. akudō or akushu; 悪道 or 悪趣) The **three**

evil destinies that lead to the realms of the **hell-dwellers**, **hungry ghosts**, **animals**. Sometimes the destiny of **asuras** in included as well, so that there are four evil destinies.

evil friend: (S. pāpamitra; J. aku-chishiki; 悪知識) The Sanskrit term *pāpamitra* can be translated literally as "bad knowledge." The ideograms 悪知識 refers to an evil friend or teacher who teaches false views that lead people astray and block them from the right way to **attain buddhahood**. The third "A Parable," chapter of the *Lotus Sutra* uses it as an antonym of "**good friend**."

Nichiren Shonin uses the term to mean an "evil teacher" like **Honen** who destroys the virtuous **mind**s of people while leading them to commit **slander of the True Dharma**. (WNS1, p. 66)

Exegesis on the Ten Grounds Treatise: (S. *Daśabhūmika-vibhāṣā*; J. *Jūjū-bibasha-ron*; 十住毘婆沙論) A commentary on the "**Ten Grounds**" chapter of the *Flower Garland Sutra* attributed to **Nagarjuna** and translated into Chinese by **Kumarajiva** in 405. Only the Chinese translation is extant. This treatise explains the **provisional teaching**s of the *Flower Garland Sutra*, the **Vaipulya sutras**, and the **Prajna sutras**. It also divides the teachings of **Shakyamuni Buddha** into the difficult-to-practice way of being able to **attain buddhahood** through self-**cultivation** and the easy-to-practice way of attaining **rebirth in the pure land** by thinking of and calling upon the names of the **buddhas of the ten directions**. Devotion to **Amitabha** Buddha is particularly recommended. (WNS1, pp. 27-28) This treatise also teaches that practitioners of the **two-vehicles** will be unable to attain buddhahood. (WNS1, p. 43)

Nichiren Shonin points out that this treatise does not name the *Lotus Sutra*, the *Nirvana Sutra*, or the three Mantra sutras as among the difficult-practice-way, and that **Honen**'s interpretation which does include those sutras among the difficult-to-practice way is unwarranted. (WNS1, pp. 28, 32-33, 42-43, 58)

exoteric Buddhism: (J. kengyō; 顕教) Teachings taught clearly in words and writings according to the **capacity** of the listeners, in contrast to **esoteric Buddhism**.

expanded discourse: See **Vaipulya sutras**.

expanded opening of the three vehicles to reveal the One Vehicle: (J. kō-kai-san-ken'itsu; 広開三顕一) The fuller exposition of the doctrine that the **three vehicle** teachings for **voice-hearers**, **privately-awakened ones**, and **bodhisattvas** are **skillful means** while the **One Vehicle** path to **awakening** is the **True Dharma**

and that the true intent of **Shakyamuni Buddha** is to enable all people to **attain buddhahood**. This part of the *Lotus Sutra* begins in the second, **"Expedient,"** chapter of the *Lotus Sutra* following the **concise opening of the three vehicles to reveal the One Vehicle** when the Buddha responds to **Shariputra**'s three requests to teach the **Dharma** by expounding the one great purpose for which the buddhas appear in the world and continues until the end of the ninth, "The Assurance of Future Buddhahood of the Shravakas Who Have Something More to Learn and the Shravakas Who Have Nothing More to Learn," chapter. (LS, pp. 32-175)

Expanded period: (J. Hōdō-ji; 方等時) The third of the **five periods**. This period lasted eight years, during which **Shakyamuni Buddha** taught provisional Mahayana teachings in order to castigate the **voice-hearer**s for their complacency and to inspire the novice **bodhisattva**s by teaching the **six perfections**, the **emptiness** of all **phenomena**, and the existence of the buddhas in the **pure land**s of the ten directions. The ***Vimalakirti Sutra***, the **three Pure Land sutras**, those sutras that inspired the **Consciousness-Only school**, and later the teachings of **esoteric Buddhism** are all lumped into this catch-all category that contains and contrasts all **four doctrinal teachings** depending on how they correspond to the needs of the listeners at any given time and place. This period is compared to the **flavor of curds**.

"Expedients," chapter: (J. Hōben-pon; 方便品) The second chapter of the *Lotus Sutra*. At the beginning of this chapter, **Shakyamuni Buddha** rises from **samadhi** and says to **Shariputra** that only buddhas together with buddhas (J. yui butsu yo butsu; 唯仏与仏 / 唯佛與佛) can realize the **true reality of all things**. Shariputra then asks the Buddha three times to explain why only buddhas can understand it. This section is called the **concise opening of the three vehicles to reveal the One Vehicle**. (LS. pp. 24-32) The rest of the chapter up to and including the ninth chapter is called the **expanded opening of the three vehicles to reveal the One Vehicle**. (LS, pp. 32-175)

In response to Shariputra's repeated requests, and after five thousand arrogant members from among the **four assemblies** left, the Buddha expounded the one great purpose for which the buddhas appear in the world, which is to let all people attain the buddha's **wisdom**. He explains that because people were of **dull capacity** and little wisdom, he used **skillful means** to teach them but now reveals that the three vehicles are expedient, but the One Vehicle is the truth. In this chapter the Buddha also explains that even small gestures of **faith** will enable people to **attain buddhahood**.

expounding the Dharma, subtlety of: (J. seppō-myō; 説法妙) The eighth of the **ten subtleties of the Trace Gate**. It refers to the **Buddha**'s subtle expounding of the Dharma in the form of the **twelve kinds of scriptures**, both **Mahayana** and **hinayana**, and inclusive of the teaching according to the minds of others and the **perfect teaching** of the teaching according to one's own mind that is subtle in both manner of teaching and underlying doctrine. (FTP, p. 208; PMLS2, pp. 94, 278-289)

extreme transgressions: (S. pārājika; J. jūzai or harai or henzai; 重罪 or 波羅夷 or 辺罪) The Sanskrit term *pārājika* can be translated as "defeats." These are the first and most serious division of the binding rules in the **vinaya**. Having committed any of these transgressions a monastic is permanently expelled from the monastic **Sangha**.

The four for **monk**s are: 1) incontinence, 2) theft, 3) killing of a human being, and 4) lying about one's higher spiritual achievements. (EET, p. 42)

The eight for **nun**s are: 1) incontinence, 2) theft, 3) killing of a human being, 4) lying about one's higher spiritual achievements, 5) to lustfully make physical contact with a lustful male between the collarbone and the knee, 6) to lustfully flirt with a lustful man, 7) concealing the extreme transgression of another nun, and 8) even after having been admonished up to three times, to continue following a monk who is on probation. (Kabilsingh, pp. 222-225)

faculties: See **faculty**.

faculty: (S. indriya; J. kon; 根) The Sanskrit term *indriya* can also be translated as "dominant," or "predominant factor." The ideogram 根 can also mean "basis," "root," "origin," or "source." The faculties include such things as the five physical senses and the mental faculty, or the five faculties of spiritual practice: **faith, energy, mindfulness, concentration, and wisdom**.

Fadao: (1086-1147; C.; J. Hōdō; 法道) A Chinese **monk** who remonstrated with Emperor Huizong (1082-1135) when the emperor tried to replace Buddhist terms with Taoist ones. He was branded on the face and exiled to the south.

faith: (S. śraddhā; J. shin; 信) The Sanskrit term *śraddhā* can also be translated as "confidence" or "trust." It has also been translated as "belief," though *śraddhā* does not have the connotations of "blind belief."

faithfulness: (J. shin; 信) The fifth of the **five constant virtues** of **Confucianism**. In the *Great Calming and Contemplation*, Zhiyi wrote, "To keep tokens of trust, to record things truthfully, and to act sincerely without taking advantage of others corresponds to the fourth precept to abstain from lying." (CSQI, p. 1042 adapted)

Faxian: (c. 340-420; C.; J. Hokken; 法顯) A Chinese **monk** who left Chang'an in 399 to travel to Central Asia, India, Sri Lanka, and Java. He returned in 413 bearing many Buddhist texts, such as the *Five-part Discipline*. He collaborated with Buddhabhadra on Chinese translations of the *Great Canon of Monastic Discipline* between 416 and 418 and the ***Six-Fascicle Nirvana Sutra*** in 418. He also wrote a travelogue called the *Record of Buddhist Kingdoms*.

Fazang: (643-712; C.; J. Hōzō; 法蔵) Also known as the **Great Master** Xianshou (J. Genju Daishi; 賢首 大師). The third patriarch of the Chinese **Flower Garland school** who is considered the systematizer of the Flower Garland doctrines. After studying Buddhism on Mt. Tai-po, he became a disciple of **Zhiyan**. After the death of his master, Fazang became a **monk**, writing many books and spreading the Flower Garland teachings. Empress Wu Zetian became his patron and he was given the title of Great Master Xianshou.

feeling: (S. vedanā; J. ju; 受) The Sanskrit term *vedanā* can also be translated as "sensation," however *vedanā* is not just about physical sensations but the affect or feeling that arises in regard to any object, including mental objects.

As the second of the **five aggregates**, it can be divided into three or five different kinds. The three kinds of feeling are pleasure, displeasure, and indifference. The five kinds of feeling are the pleasure and displeasure that arise respectively in regard to pleasant and unpleasant physical objects, the feelings of satisfaction and dissatisfaction that arise respectively in regard to pleasant and unpleasant mental objects, and the indifference that arises in regard to physical and mental objects that are neither pleasant nor unpleasant. (See CD 36.22, p. 1280; CD 48.38, p. 1682; AKB1, pp. 72, 160-162, 189)

field of merit: (S. puṇya-kṣetra; J. fuku-den; 福田) A simile for **buddha**s and the monastic **Sangha**. It means that just as a fertile farmland produces a good harvest when one works on it, one can gain great **merit** by making offerings to buddhas and the Sangha.

fifth five-hundred-year period: (J. go-gohyaku-sai; 後五百歳) Also called the "age of fighting and remonstration." See the **five five-hundred-year periods**.

fifty-two stages of bodhisattva practice: (J. gojūni-i; 五十二位) The ideograms 五十二位 mean "fifty-two stages" but it is understood that they refer to the stages of **bodhisattva practice** as enumerated in various **sutras**. **Zhiyi** chose to use the fifty-two stages listed in the *Bodhisattva Practice Jeweled Necklace Sutra*, to explain the stages of practice for bodhisattvas in the **distinct teaching** and the **perfect teaching**. His explanations were also based upon the teachings of other sutras such as the *Flower Garland Sutra* (wherein are found all but the first group of ten), the *Larger Prajna Sutra*, and the *Nirvana Sutra*. The fifty-two stages are: 1) **ten degrees of faith**, 2) **ten abodes**, 3) **ten kinds of practice**, 4) **ten dimensions of merit transference**, 5) **ten grounds**, 6) **preliminary awakening**, and 7) **supreme subtle awakening**. The first category corresponds to the **ordinary stage of the outer level**, the second through fourth correspond to the **ordinary stage of the inner level**, and the fifth through seventh correspond to the sagehood stage.

final nirvana: (S. parinirvāṇa; J. hatsu-nehan or nehan or dai-nehan; 般涅槃 or 涅槃 or 大涅槃) The "final **nirvana**" or "complete nirvana" that is the complete extinguishing of all **defilement**s and even physical needs and vulnerabilities upon the death of the physical **body**. Also called the great final nirvana. It is also equivalent to nirvana without remainder, which is the term for the passing away of an **arhat**, **privately-awakened one**, or a **buddha**.

first four of the five flavors: (J. zen-shimi; 前四味) The first four of the **five flavors** which corresponds to various **sutras** other than the *Lotus Sutra* and *Nirvana Sutra*. (WNS1, p. 70)

five aggregates: (S. pañca-skandha; J. go-on or go-un; 五陰 or 五蘊) The components of a **sentient being**. Buddhist philosophy considers all physical and mental things and **phenomena** in this world to consist of five aggregates: 1) **form**, 2) **feeling**, 3) **perception**, 4) **mental formation**, and 5) **consciousness**.
As the first of the **three categories of existence** they are a component of the **three thousand realms in a single thought-moment**. (CSQI, p. 815)

five baskets: (S. pañca-piṭaka; J. go-zō; 五蔵) According to the *Six Paramita Sutra* there are five parts to the Buddhist canon, consisting of the **three baskets** as well as the basket of **Prajna sutras** and the basket of **dharani**. This division of the canon is used by the **Mantra school**.

five constant virtues: (J. go-jō; 五常) The ideograms 五常 literally mean "five constants." The five most essential and universal virtues taught by **Confucianism**

according to the scholastic tradition of the Han dynasty are: 1) **benevolence**, 2) **righteousness**, 3) **propriety**, 4) **knowledge**, and 5) **faithfulness**.

five contemplations for settling the mind: (J. go-jōshin-kan; 五停心観) They are the: 1) contemplation of impurity for those who need to overcome **greed**, 2) **contemplation of loving-kindness and compassion** for those who need to overcome **hatred**, 3) contemplation of the breath for those who need to overcome distraction, 4) contemplation of causes and conditions for those who need to overcome **ignorance**, and 5) contemplation of the Buddha for those who have many obstructions such as sleepiness.

five degenerations: (S. pañca-kaṣāyāḥ; J. go-joku; 五濁) The degenerations that appear towards the end of the first nineteen **interim kalpa**s of the **kalpa of abiding**. They are the degenerations of age, views, **defilements**, **sentient being**s, and lifespan. (AKB2, p. 482) In Japanese literature the term "the evil world with the five degenerations" means corruption and pollution of the world.

five five-hundred-year periods: (J. go-gohyaku-sai; 五五百歳) According to the *Great Assembly Sutra*, the history of Buddhism after the passing of **Shakyamuni Buddha** is divided into five five-hundred-year periods, each with a characteristic feature: 1) the period of the firm attainment of liberation, 2) the period of the firm practice of meditation, 3) the period of reading and listening to Buddhist teachings, 4) the period of building temples, and 5) the period or age of fighting and remonstration. Applying these five periods to the theory of the gradual decline of Buddhism over three periods, the **Age of the True Dharma** comprises the first two periods, the **Age of the Semblance Dharma** comprises the next two periods, and the beginning of the **Latter Age of Degeneration** (sometimes said to last for ten thousand years) corresponds to the last or **fifth five-hundred-year period**.

In his major writing, *On the Selection of the Time*, **Nichiren Shonin** regarded the fifth five-hundred-year period as the time for the spread of the *Lotus Sutra*.

five flavors: (J. go-mi; 五味) The *Nirvana Sutra* likens the teachings of **Shakyamuni Buddha** to the five flavors of milk and milk products, claiming itself to be the supreme **flavor of ghee** or clarified butter.

Zhiyi applied these five flavors to the **five periods** of the teaching of the Buddha during his lifetime, assigning the flavor of ghee to the **Lotus-Nirvana period**. The other correspondences are as follows: the **flavor of milk** corresponds to the **Flower Garland period**, the **flavor of cream** to the **Deer Park period**, the **flavor of curds** to the **Expanded period**, and the **flavor of fresh butter** to the **Prajna period**.

five heinous transgressions: (S. pañca-ānantaryam-karman; J. go-gyaku, go-gyakuzai, go-juzai, go-mukenzai, or go-mukengō; 五逆, 五逆罪, 五重罪, 五無間罪 or 五無間業) The Sanskrit term *pañca-ānantaryam-karman* literally means "five acts that bring immediate recompense" or "five inexpiable **transgression**s."(AKB2, p. 680) The ideograms 五逆 or 五逆罪 literally mean "five rebellious transgressions," while the ideograms 重罪 literally mean "five crimes." The ideograms 五無間罪 or 五無間業 are more straightforward translations of the Sanskrit term; however, since the ideograms 無間 are also used to translate *avīci*, or "incessant," 五無間罪 or 五無間業 can also be understood to mean five transgressions or **karmic action**s that lead to the **Hell** of **Incessant Suffering**.

Those who committed any of the five heinous transgressions are said to fall into the Hell of Incessant Suffering after death. The following crimes are not just acts of violence, but a rejection of the very basis of **morality** and **liberation** from suffering: killing one's mother, **killing one's father**, killing an arhat, injuring the Buddha, and causing a schism in the Sangha. The order of these varies, sometimes "killing one's father is first," and sometimes "injuring the Buddha" is last. (ND 5.129, pp. 743-744; also see ND 6.87 and 6.94 on pp. 978, 980-981)

Nichiren Shonin explains that in the **Latter Age of Degeneration** the five heinous transgressions cannot occur because there are no longer any arhats nor is the Buddha physically present. He also stated that in the Latter Age of Degeneration, **slander of the True Dharma** is a transgression more serious than the five heinous transgressions, insisting that only the *Lotus Sutra* can save those who have committed the transgressions of slander of the True Dharma and the five heinous transgressions.

five hundred dust-particle kalpas: (J. gohyaku-jindengō; 五百塵点劫) An abbreviation for an inconceivably long period of time that has elapsed since **Shakyamuni Buddha**'s **attainment of buddhahood in the remotest past** that is described in the sixteenth, "The **Duration of the Life of the Tathagata," chapter** of the *Lotus Sutra*. In the passage, the Buddha says, "Suppose someone smashed into dust five hundred thousand billion ***nayuta asamkhya*** worlds, which were each composed of one thousand million **Sumeru world**s and went to the east [carrying the dust with him]. When he reached a world at a distance of five hundred thousand billion nayuta asamkhya worlds [from this world], he put a particle of dust on that world. Then he went on again to the east, and repeated the putting of a particle of the dust [on the world at every distance of five hundred thousand billion nayuta asamkhya worlds] until the particles of the dust were exhausted… Suppose those worlds, whether they were marked with the particles of dust or not, were smashed into dust. The number of the **kalpa**s which have elapsed since I became the Buddha is one hundred thousand billion nayuta asamkhyas larger than the number of the particles of the dust thus produced. All this time I have been living in this Saha world, and teaching [the **sentient being**s of this world] by expounding the **Dharma** to them. I have also been leading and **benefit**ing the sentient beings of one hundred thousand billion nayuta asamkhya worlds outside this world." (LS, pp. 247-248)

Nichiren Shonin highly esteemed the doctrine that Shakyamuni Buddha had attained buddhahood so long ago, together with the doctrine of the "**three thousand dust particle kalpas**" described in the seventh chapter, as proof of the superiority of the *Lotus Sutra*.

Five Hundred Questions Treatise: (J. *Gohyaku-mon-ron*; 五百問論) A treatise by **Zhanran** refuting *Praising the Profundity of the Lotus Sutra* by **Kuiji** in the form of a series of questions and answers.

five kinds of eyes: (S. pañca-cakṣūṃṣi; J. *go-gen*; 五眼): They are: 1) the **physical eye**; 2) the **divine eye**, like that of the **gods**, that can see beyond physical limitations; 3) the **wisdom eye** of **voice-hearers** and **privately-awakened ones** that can perceive the principle of **emptiness**; 4) the **dharma eye** of **bodhisattva**s penetrating all **dharma**s; and 5) the **buddha eye** which can see through the past, present, and future, and which also includes the other four kinds of eye. (CSQI, pp. 475-476, 1282-1283)

five natures: (S. pañca-gotrāṇi; J. go-shō; 五性) Also called the "five mutually distinct natures." The **Dharma Characteristics school** doctrine dividing **sentient being**s into five groups by their spiritual capabilities. These five natures are: 1) the **determined nature** of a **bodhisattva**, 2) the **determined nature** of a **privately-awakened one**, 3) the **determined nature** of a **voice-hearer**, 4) the **indeterminate nature of the three vehicles**, 5) those **sentient being**s **without the nature** for **awakening**.

This is a doctrine taught in the *Lankavatara Sutra* and the *Revealing the Profound Secrets Sutra*. This doctrine holds that these natures are innate and cannot be changed or acquired in the course of a lifetime, and that therefore, those of categories 2), 3), and 5) will not be able to **attain buddhahood**. (WNS1, p. 21) The **Dharma Characteristics school** emphasizes this doctrine in opposition to the **Tiantai school** doctrine that all can **attain buddhahood** in accordance with the teaching of the **One Vehicle** in the *Lotus Sutra*. (e.g. WNS3, p. 117)

five obstacles: (J. go-shō; 五障) Refers in general to a belief in Buddhism that women are inferior in **capacity**, and thus ineligible to become **Brahma**, **Indra**,

Mara, a **wheel-turning king**, or a **buddha**.

five periods: (J. go-ji; 五時) During the lifetime of **Shakyamuni Buddha**, a great number of **sutra**s were taught. **Zhiyi** divided them into five categories according to the period in which they were taught: 1) the **Flower Garland period** spanning the first three weeks after his **unsurpassed, complete, and perfect awakening** wherein the *Flower Garland Sutra* was taught, 2) the **Deer Park period** or Agama period spanning the twelve years wherein the **Agama sutras** were taught, 3) the **Expanded period** spanning the eight years wherein the initial **Mahayana** sutras were taught, 4) the **Prajna period** spanning the twenty-two years wherein the **Prajna sutras** were taught, and 5) the **Lotus-Nirvana period** spanning the last eight years before the Buddha's **final nirvana** wherein the *Lotus Sutra* and *Nirvana Sutra* were taught.

Zhiyi also systematized what was taught during these five periods by the Buddha in the **four doctrinal teachings**. The Buddha's ultimate intent was expressed in the *Lotus Sutra*.

Following this comparative classification of doctrines of the **Tiantai school**, **Nichiren Shonin** emphasized the supremacy of the Lotus teaching. (e.g. WNS1, pp. 5-10)

five precepts: (S. pañca-śīla; J. go-kai; 五戒) The Sanskrit term *śīla* is best translated into English as **morality**, but the ideogram 戒 is usually translated as "**precept**." In many schools of Buddhism, the five precepts are given as **training rule**s to a **layman** or **laywoman** along with the **threefold refuge**. The five are to: 1) abstain from killing, 2) abstain from taking what is not given, 3) abstain from sexual misconduct, 4) abstain from lying, and 5) abstain from consuming intoxicants.

five primary elements: (S. pañca-mahābhūtani; J. go-dai or go-daishu; 五大 or 五大種) The five material elements which compose the world. They are earth, water, fire, air, and **space**.

five proclamations: (J. goka-no-hōsho; 五箇の鳳詔) Refers to the **three proclamations** from chapter eleven, "**Beholding the Stupa of Treasures**," and the **two exhortations** from the twelfth, "**Devadatta**," **chapter** of the *Lotus Sutra*. (WNS2, pp. 81-83, 90-91)

five regions of India: (J. go-tenjiku or go-ten; 五天竺 or 五天) The five regions of India are the northern, southern, eastern, western, and central regions. According to some accounts, of the sixteen major countries that existed during the lifetime of **Shakyamuni Buddha**, all but Gandhara and Kamboja were part of the central region. Gandhara and Kamboja were in the northern region. (Law 2014)

five vehicles: (J. go-jō; 五乗) The **three vehicles** as well as the **human vehicle** and the **heavenly vehicle**.

fivefold Dharma-body: (S. pañca-dharma-kāya or asamasama-pañca-skandha; J. gobun-hosshin; 五分法身) The five **non-outflow aggregates** that comprise the virtuous qualities of the **arhat**s, **privately-awakened one**s, and **buddha**s. It consists of the bodies or aggregates of 1) **morality**, 2) **concentration**, 3) **wisdom**, 4) **liberation**, and 5) knowledge of liberation. (ND 5.251-253, pp. 838-839)

flavor of curds: (J. shōso-mi; 生酥味) One of the **five flavors**. It refers to the **Expanded period** of **Shakyamuni Buddha**'s teachings.

flavor of cream: (J. raku-mi; 酪味) One of the **five flavors**. It refers to the **Deer Park period** of **Shakyamuni Buddha**'s teachings.

flavor of fresh butter: (J. jukuso-mi; 熟酥味) One of the **five flavors**. It refers to the **Prajna period** of **Shakyamuni Buddha**'s teachings.

flavor of ghee: (J. daigo-mi; 醍醐味) One of the **five flavors**. It refers to the **Lotus-Nirvana period** of **Shakyamuni Buddha**'s teachings. Ghee represents the most excellent taste of the five flavors. The *Lotus Sutra* is called the "taste of ghee exceeding the eight teachings," meaning that the sutra has the most excellent taste of all the Buddha's teachings.

flavor of milk: (J. nyū-mi; 乳味) One of the **five flavors**. It refers to the **Flower Garland period** of **Shakyamuni Buddha**'s teachings.

Flower Garland period: (J. Kegon-ji; 華厳時) The first of the **five periods**. This period encompassed the first three weeks after **Shakyamuni Buddha**'s **awakening** when the *Flower Garland Sutra* was expounded. It was only perceived by the **god**s and advanced **bodhisattva**s. This period is the sudden teaching that combines the **perfect teaching** with the **distinct teaching**, so its teaching is one part subtle and one part coarse. This means that while the *Flower Garland Sutra* presents the final goal of Buddhism, many parts are aimed only at the bodhisattvas and so exclude those who do not share their aspirations or insight. This period is compared to the **flavor of milk** before it undergoes any further refinement.

Flower Garland school: (J. Kegon-shū; 華厳宗) One of the schools of Chinese Buddhism and one of the **six schools of Nara Buddhism** in Japan. This school was founded on the teaching of the *Flower Garland Sutra* that was translated by Buddhabhadra between 418 and 421 and again by Shikshananda between 695 and 704. A third translation of just the final chapter was done by Prajna between 795 and 798. This school sometimes considers **Ashvaghosha** and **Nagarjuna** to be its first and second patriarchs. However, **Dushun** is considered the first patriarch in China, and his disciple **Zhiyan** the second patriarch. The third patriarch, **Fazang**, systematized the teachings. The fourth patriarch was **Chengguan**. Zongmi was the fifth patriarch. The Chinese monk Daoxuan introduced the Flower Garland teachings to Japan in 736, but its establishment as a school is credited to the Korean monk Simsang, a student of Fazang who gave a lecture to the emperor on the Flower Garland teachings in 740 at Todaiji Temple. Ryoben, the first head abbot of Todaiji Temple is considered to be the second patriarch of the school in Japan after Simsang.

This school's comparative classification insists upon the superiority of the *Flower Garland Sutra*.

This school teaches that all things in the **Dharma-realm** come into existence through **dependent origination** and that all phenomenal things are mutually unhindered and in a state of **perfect interfusion**. This is illustrated by such doctrines as the **ten profound gates**, the **six characteristics**, and the non-obstruction of actualities.

Nichiren Shonin classifies this school, though it is superior to the other **Mahayana** schools, as a **provisional Mahayana teaching** that is **hinayana** or like an inferior medicine in comparison with *Lotus Sutra* and the **Tiantai school** because it relies upon the **prior teachings**.

Nichiren Shonin frequently criticized the Flower Garland school, and in particular Chengguan, for plagiarizing the "**three-thousand realms in a single thought-moment**" doctrine of **Zhiyi** and putting it into the doctrine of his own school while criticizing the Tiantai school. (WNS2, pp. 19, 34-37, 78-80, 85; WNS3, pp. 231-232; WNS4, p. 92; WNS5, pp. 79, 159-160)

Flower Garland Sutra: (S. *Avataṃsaka-sūtra*; J. *Kegon-kyō*; 華厳経) The full Sanskrit title, *Buddha-avataṃsaka-mahā-vaipulya-sūtra*, in English means "The **Mahayana** Expanded **Sutra** of Adorning **Awakening** with Garlands." Buddhabhadra translated this sutra into Chinese in sixty fascicles and thirty-four chapters between 418 and 421. Shikshananda translated it again between 695 and 704 with the help of Yijing and Bodhiruchi. This second translation was eighty fascicles and thirty-nine chapters long. A third translation of just the *Gaṇḍavyuhā-sūtra*, considered the final chapter of the *Flower Garland Sutra*, was done by Prajna between 795 and 798 in forty-fascicles.

The *Flower Garland Sutra* is said to have been taught by **Shakyamuni Buddha** upon attaining awakening under the **Bodhi tree** in **Bodhgaya**. Saying that the whole world is a manifestation of **Vairochana** Buddha, the sutra maintains that one is the whole and the whole is one, insisting that a particle of dust contains the whole world and a moment includes eternity. In the sutra, upon the request of **Moon of Liberation Bodhisattva**, four bodhisattvas expound forty of the **fifty-two stages of bodhisattva practice**: **Dharma Wisdom (ten abodes)**, **Merit Forest (ten kinds of practice)**, **Diamond Banner (ten dimensions of merit transference)**, and **Diamond Repository (ten grounds)**.

Based on the comparative classification of doctrines of the **Tiantai school**, **Nichiren Shonin** insisted that the *Flower Garland Sutra* is inferior to the *Lotus Sutra* because it teaches neither the **attainment of buddhahood by adherents of the two vehicles** nor the **attainment of buddhahood in the remotest past** by Shakyamuni Buddha. (WNS1, p. 18)

Flower Light: (S. Padmaprabha; J. Kekō; 華光) The name of the **buddha** that **Shariputra** will become, according to the third, "A Parable," chapter of the *Lotus Sutra*.

Flowering of the True Dharma Sutra: (J. *Shō-hoke-kyō*; 正法華経) A translation of the *Lotus Sutra* made by Dharmaraksha in 286. In this version, the eleventh and twelfth chapters are a single chapter, so that there are in total only twenty-seven chapters. This translation puts the "Transmission," chapter at the end. (WNS1, p. 21)

focus of devotion: (J. honzon or gohonzon; 本尊 or 御本尊) The ideogram 本 can mean "basis," "foundation," "fundamental," "origin," "root," or "source." The ideogram 尊 can mean that which is "honored," "respected," or "revered." The compound 本尊 has also been translated as "main revered," "most venerable one" or "object of worship," though these terms have anthropomorphic or even idolatrous connotations that are not necessarily intended in many uses of this term. The prefix 御 is an honorific. A *honzon* or *gohonzon* is the main focus of devotion whose image, whether in the form of a statue, a set of statues, a painting, calligraphy, or a **mandala**, is enshrined in a temple.

Such symbols as footprints of **Shakyamuni Buddha** and the **Dharma-wheel** were regarded as foci of devotion in Buddhism in early Buddhism, but later images of Shakyamuni Buddha began to appear in the late first century. Many images of the various buddhas, **bodhisattva**s, and disciples of the Buddha were made in East Asia and Tibet, but in Southeast Asia it is Shakyamuni Buddha who is usually regarded as the focus of devotion.

In the **Nichiren school**, the focus of devotion is a depiction of the scene during the Assembly in Space in the **Original Gate** of the *Lotus Sutra* wherein the **Eternal Shakyamuni Buddha** transmits the **Wonderful Dharma** to all **sentient being**s, especially the **bodhisattvas appearing from underground**. This is often, but not always, depicted in the form of the **Great Mandala of Invoking the Ten Realms**, which is a calligraphic mandala.

Focus of Devotion of the Original Gate: (J. hommon-no-honzon; 本門の本尊) In the **Nichiren school**, the **focus of devotion** is a depiction of the scene during the Assembly in Space in the **Original Gate** of the *Lotus Sutra* wherein the **Eternal Shakyamuni Buddha** transmits the **Wonderful Dharma** to all **sentient being**s, especially the **bodhisattvas appearing from underground**. This focus of devotion has three characteristics: 1) command of fundamental reverence, 2) being the most revered since the eternal past, and 3) possession of a constant character since the eternal past. It rests on the "**three thousand realms in a single thought-moment**" doctrine, and represents the symbolic world wherein Shakyamuni Buddha in the Original Gate of the *Lotus Sutra* saved, is saving, and will be saving all sentient beings without discrimination. It is one of the **Three Great Secret Dharmas**.

There are several ways to show this focus of devotion in concrete form: 1) as the **daimoku** of the *Lotus Sutra* (i.e. **Namu Myoho Renge Kyo**) written in Chinese ideograms (WNS2, p. 259); 2) as a statue of the Eternal Shakyamuni Buddha (WNS1, p. 184); 3) as the **Great Mandala of Invoking the Ten Realms** (WNS2, p. 149); 4) as the daimoku accompanied by Shakyamuni Buddha and **Many Treasures** Buddha (WNS2, p. 149; WNS3, p. 57); or 5) as Shakyamuni Buddha accompanied by the four leaders of the bodhisattvas appearing from underground (WNS2, p. 149; WNS3, p. 57). In essence, however, these are one. They are all representing the transmission of the Wonderful Dharma by the Eternal Shakyamuni Buddha, as revealed in the Original Gate of the *Lotus Sutra*.

form: (S. rūpa; J. shiki; 色) The Sanskrit term *rūpa* can also be translated as "matter." It can also be translated in a more limited sense as "outward appearance," "shape," or "color," therefore the ideogram 色 meaning "color" is used. Form is that which can be localized, impact or be impacted, and is resistant or even impenetrable to other forms.

As the first of the **five aggregates** it encompasses all but that which pertains to the **mind**. The aggregate of form or matter is composed of the **four primary elements**.

form realm: (S. rūpa-dhātu; J. shiki-kai; 色界) The second part of the **triple world**, consisting of the eighteen heavens of the **form realm**, wherein the inhabitants have material form but are not overcome by sensual desire.

form-body: (S. rūpa-kāya; J. shiki-shin; 色身) The **form** or material body of a **buddha** as distinct from the **Dharma-body**. In **Mahayana** Buddhism it can be subdivided into the **reward-body** (or **enjoyment-body**) and the **accommodative-body** (or **transformation-body**), which are two of the **three bodies** of a **buddha**.

formless realm: (S. ārūpya-dhātu or arūpa-dhātu; J. mushiki-kai; 無色界) The third part of the **triple world**, consisting of the four formless heavens of Boundless Space, Boundless Consciousness, Nothingness, and Neither Perception nor Non-Perception, wherein the inhabitants are free from sensual desire and the restrictions of material **form**.

forty years or so: (J. shijū yonen; 四十余年) The "Expounding the Dharma" chapter of the *Infinite Meanings Sutra* states, "The truth has not been revealed during the forty years or so," and it says in "The **Appearance of Bodhisattvas from Underground**," chapter of the *Lotus Sutra*, "It is only forty years or so since then." (LS, p. 243 adapted) These passages mean that the *Lotus Sutra* which reveals the true intent of **Shakyamuni Buddha** was expounded during the last eight years of his **dispensation** after he expounded **provisional sutra**s in the **Flower Garland period**, **Agama period**, and **Prajna period**. The phrase, "forty years or so," is used to divide the **provisional teaching**s from the **true teaching** in the Buddha's dispensation.

four assemblies: (S. catasraḥ parṣadaḥ; J. shi-shu; 四衆) The assemblies gathered to hear the **Buddha Dharma** comprise four types of followers: **monk**s, **nun**s, a **laymen**, and **laywomen**.

four continents: (J. shi-shū; 四洲) In the great outer ocean of a **Sumeru world** there are four continents in the four cardinal directions around Mt. **Sumeru**. They are: Puravavideha to the east, **Jambudvipa** to the south, Aparagodaniya to the west, and Uttarakuru to the north. Two large islands or intermediate continents surround each of these continents. (AKB2, p. 455)

four debts of gratitude: (J. shi-on; 四恩) There are various lists of what comprises the four debts of gratitude. According to the *Contemplation on the Mind-Ground Sutra*, the four debts of gratitude are: indebtedness to one's parents; indebtedness to one's fellow **sentient being**s; indebtedness to one's ruler; and indebtedness to the **Three Treasures**.
    Nichiren Shonin frequently mentioned gratitude as the basic motivation for practicing Buddhism and enabling others to **attain buddhahood**.

four devils: (S. catur-māra; J. shi-ma; 四魔) The four devils are things which distract or scare us away from **awakening**. They are the **devil of the defilements**, our self-centered desires; the **devil of the aggregates**, our mental and physical needs; the **devil of death**, our fear of death; and the **devil king of the sixth heaven**, a personification of all the various distractions, fears, and temptations that can disrupt or hinder practice. (CSQI, pp. 771, 1387-1390)

According to **Zhiyi**, "The first three types are all constantly part of this world, and people give rise to them within their own **mind**s; therefore, you should correctly remove and chase them away in your own mind." (CSQI, p. 1735) The fourth type he defines as "supernatural devils" encompassing the following three kinds: "form-shifting devils" who appear as animals at different times of the day or night, "nerve-racking" devils that cause various distracting bodily sensations or noises, and finally **Mara** himself, who tries to tempt or intimidate the practitioner. (CSQI, pp. 771, 1390-1396, 1735-1737)

four doctrinal teachings: (J. shikyō or kehō no shikyō; 四教 or 化法の四教) **Zhiyi** classified **Shakyamuni Buddha**'s fifty-years of teaching from the time of teaching the *Flower Garland Sutra* to the time of teaching the *Lotus Sutra* and *Nirvana Sutra* into **five periods** according to the order of teaching. They are further categorized into four doctrinal teachings: 1) the **tripitaka teaching** that is regarded as **hinayana**, 2) the **shared teaching** for **voice-hearer**s, **privately-awakened one**s, and **bodhisattva**s, 3) the **distinct teaching** for advanced bodhisattvas, and 4) the **perfect teaching** that is complete and well-rounded without taking sides.

four flavors and three teachings: (J. shimi-sankyō; 四味三教) Refers to the **first four of the five flavors** and the first three of the **four doctrinal teachings**.

four foundations of mindfulness: (S. catvāri-smṛtyupasthāna; J. shi-nenjo or shi-nenjū; 四念処 or 四念住) The four foundations of **mindfulness** are **Shakyamuni Buddha**'s explanation of **right mindfulness** among the **eightfold noble path**. They are: 1) mindfulness of the body, 2) mindfulness of **feeling**s, 3) mindfulness of mental states, and 4) mindfulness of **phenomena** (**dharma**s). (LD 22, pp. 335-350)

four fruitions: (S. catur-phala; J. shi-ka; 四果): To attain the state of a **stream-enterer**, a **once-returner**, a **non-returner**, or an **arhat** are the four **fruition**s of mainstream Buddhist practice.

four great bodhisattvas: (J. shidai-bosatsu; 四大菩薩) These four are **Superior Practice Bodhisattva**, **Limitless Practice Bodhisattva**, **Pure Practice Bodhisattva**, and **Steadily Established Practice Bodhisattva**. They are the four leaders of the **bodhisattvas appearing from underground** in the fifteenth, "Appearance of Bodhisattvas from Underground," chapter of the *Lotus Sutra*.

four great vows: (J. shigu-seigan; 四弘誓願) Also called "four universal **vows**" of a **bodhisattva**. The four great vows can be traced back to an apocryphal Chinese **sutra** of the fifth century called the *Bodhisattva Practice Jeweled Necklace Sutra*. They were popularized by **Zhiyi**. (Donner and Stevenson, p. 26 and GTFT, p. 183) The four great vows are as follows:
Sentient beings are infinite; I vow to liberate them all,
Defilements are innumerable; I vow to resolve them all,
Dharma gates are inexhaustible; I vow to know them all,
The **Way of the Buddha is unsurpassed; I vow to become it.**

four heavenly kings: (S. Catur-mahārājika or Catur-lokapāla; J. shi-tennō or shidai-tennō; 四天王 or 四大天王) The four heavenly kings are **guardian deities** who watch over the world. As they vowed to protect the world and the **Buddha Dharma**, they are given the title, "Four Heavenly Kings Who Protect the World." They reside in the **Heaven** of the Four Heavenly Kings, the lowest of the **six heavens of the desire realm**, located midway up Mt. **Sumeru**. Each heavenly king is responsible for one of the four cardinal directions. As generals serving under **Shakra**, they lead an army drawn from the eight kinds of supernatural beings to fight the **asura**s. The four are: Nation Upholding in the east, Growth Increasing in the south, Observing Everything in the west, and Hearing Everything in the north.

The four heavenly kings were said to have offered the Buddha four **alms bowl**s which he merged into one. They were also present during his **final nirvana**.

The four heavenly kings along with ten thousand attendants are present in the assembly in the first, "Introductory," chapter of the *Lotus Sutra*. According to the second chapter, "**Expedients**," the four heavenly kings accompanied **Brahma** and Shakra go to see **Shakyamuni Buddha** right after his **awakening**. Together they all requested that he **turn the Wheel of the Dharma**. In the twenty-third and twenty-fourth chapters, "Wonderful Voice Bodhisattva" and "Universal Gate of World Voice Perceiver Bodhisattva," it is stated that both the eponymous **bodhisattva**s of those chapters can transform themselves into the four heavenly kings, Hearing Everything in particular, in order to expound the Dharma and save **sentient being**s. In chapter twenty-six, "Dharanis," two of the four, Hearing Everything and Nation Upholding (or Observing Everything according to a Sanskrit manuscript of the *Lotus Sutra*), utter **dharani** for the protection of those who uphold the *Lotus Sutra* by keeping it and teaching it to others. Based upon this testimony from the *Lotus Sutra*, the four heavenly kings are devotees of the sutra and may, in fact, be an appearance of one of the celestial bodhisattvas who are upholders of the sutra.

According to the **Zhiyi** in his *Words and Phrases of the Lotus Sutra*, Observing Everything, Nation Upholding, Hearing Everything, and Growth Increasing respectively represent true **self**, **eternity**, purity, and bliss of the four virtues of **nirvana** or buddhahood as taught in the *Nirvana Sutra*.

Nichiren Shonin highly esteemed the four heavenly kings as protectors of the *Lotus Sutra*, inscribing their names in large ideograms at the four corners of the **Great Mandala of Invoking the Ten Realms**.

four kalpas: (S. catur-kalpa; J. shi-kō; 四劫) According to Buddhist cosmology, a **great kalpa** consists of the **kalpa of formation**, the **kalpa of abiding**, the **kalpa of dissolution**, and the **kalpa of nothingness**. These four kalpas are sometimes called the four *asamkhya* kalpas. (ND 4.156, pp. 521-522)

four noble truths: (S. catvāry āryasatyāni; J. shi-tai or shi-shōtai; 四諦 or 四聖諦) In the first **turning of the wheel of the Dharma** at the **Deer Park** in Varanasi, **Shakyamuni Buddha** taught the four noble truths to his five former companions in asceticism. These are the truths of: **suffering**, which is to be understood; the **origin of suffering**, which is to be abandoned; the **cessation of suffering**, which is to be realized; and the **way leading to the cessation of suffering**, which is to be cultivated. (CD 56.11, pp. 1843-1847)

Suffering is the result of the origins. Cessation is the result of practicing the way. The causal relationship between suffering and its origin pertain to **samsara**, and that between cessation and the path pertain to the realization of **nirvana**.

four oceans: (J. shi-kai; 四海) Refers to the four great oceans or seas which surround the mythical Mount **Sumeru** and separate the **four continents** of a **Sumeru world**. They lie between the outermost of the seven golden mountains and the Encircling Iron Mountains. They are three hundred and twenty-two thousand **yojana**s wide. (AKB2, p. 456)

four primary elements: (S. mahābhūtani; J. daishu or shi-dai; 大種 or 四大) The Sansrit term *mahābhūtani* can also be translated as "great elements." They are the four material elements, earth, water, fire, and air that compose the world. All other **form dharma**s are said to derive from them. (AKB1, pp. 99-101; AS, pp. 4-5)

four realms: (J. shi-kai; 四界) Also called the **four noble states** (J. shi-shō/shi-sei; 四聖). In dividing all living beings into **ten realms** of existence, the lower six are called the **six destinies** wherein **sentient being**s undergo **rebirth** according to their **karma**, while the top four stages of increasing degrees of **awakening** are the realms of the four noble ones. These four are: **voice-hearers**, **privately-awakened ones**, **bodhisattvas**, and **buddhas**.

four reliances: (S. catuḥ-pratisaraṇa; J. shi-e; 四依) (1) Four standards that Buddhists can rely upon according to the ***Nirvana Sutra*** and the ***Vimalakirti Sutra***: **rely on the Dharma, not upon the person; rely on the meaning, not upon the words; rely on wisdom, not upon discriminative consciousness;** and **rely on the sutra of definitive meaning, not upon the sutra of provisional meaning.** (NS1, pp. 193-199)

(2) Four kinds of people described in the *Nirvana Sutra* that can be relied upon after the passing of **Shakyamuni Buddha** to protect, promote, and keep the **True Dharma**. The first are **ordinary people** who nevertheless still uphold the **precept**s and the True Dharma. The second are **stream-enterer**s and **once-returner**s. The third are **non-returner**s. The fourth are **arhat**s. Though these four are described in terms of the **four fruitions** of mainstream Buddhism, they are also identified as **bodhisattva**s who will receive the assurance of future buddhahood because they all uphold the True Dharma. (NS1, pp. 169-171)

Nichiren Shonin claimed that the Dharma on which people should rely is the ***Lotus Sutra.*** He identified the four reliances as the teachers of the **hinayana**, **Mahayana**, the **Trace Gate**, and the **Original Gate** during the **Age of the True Dharma** and the **Age of the Semblance Dharma**, while claiming that those whom people in the **Latter Age of Degeneration** should depend on are the **bodhisattvas appearing from underground** and that he himself was the leader of those bodhisattvas. (WNS1, pp. 3, 20, 27; WNS2, pp. 84, 156-157, 161-162, 171, 185, 230-231)

four wholesome roots: (S. catuṣ-kuśala-mūla; J. shi-zenkon; 四善根) They are: 1) **heat**, 2) the **summit**, 3) **patience**₍₂₎, and 4) **highest mundane dharma**.

fruition: (S. phala; J. ka; 果) The Sanskrit term *phala* can also be translated as "effect" or "result." This refers to an effect generally. Those effects that pertain to moral causation are usually called **ripening**.

fundamental ignorance: (S. mūla-avidyā; J. gampon-mumyō or konpon-mumyō; 元品無明 or 根本無明) The root source of all forms of **ignorance**. It is the most fundamental of all **delusion**s and **defilement**s innate in ignorant **ordinary people**. It is extremely difficult to eliminate this darkness of **mind** as **Nichiren Shonin** teaches that one cannot become a **buddha** unless one cuts it off with the sharp sword of the Buddha's secret divine powers.

Fuxi: (J. Fukki; 伏羲) In Chinese myth and legend, Fuxi and his sister Nuwa were the grandchildren of the creator **god** and the first married couple. They became the progenitors of all **human**kind and they are credited with teaching hunting, fishing, divination, and writing. Fuxi was the first sovereign of the **Three Sovereigns and Five Emperors**.

gandharva: (S.; J. kendatsuba; 乾闥婆) The gandharvas are celestial musicians who can fly through the air and are sometimes depicted with wings, and they are the husbands of the celestial nymphs called the apsaras. Another name for a gandharva is "**god** of fragrance." They are classified as gods among the **six destinies** and they are one of the **eight kinds of supernatural beings**. Gandharvas are also included among the army and attendants of Nation Upholding, one of the **four heavenly kings**.

Ganges River: (S. Gaṅgā; J. Gōga; 恒河) Refers to the River Ganges in India. It is widely believed that by bathing in this river one can wash off one's **transgression**s. Frequently the "sands of the Ganges river" is a phrase used to indicate a vast practically unquantifiable number.

garuda: (S. garuḍa; J. karura; 迦楼羅) They are depicted as giant **golden-winged bird**s who prey upon the **dragon**s. **Vishnu** has a garuda as a mount. Though intelligent and extremely powerful, they are classified as **animal**s among the **six destinies**. They are one of the **eight kinds of supernatural beings**.

gatha: (S. gāthā; J. ge or kada; 偈 or 伽陀) A set of verses found in Buddhist **scripture**s in which the contents of the preceding prose are not repeated. It is one of the **twelve kinds of scriptures**.

Gautama: (S.; J. Kudon; 瞿曇) In Sanskrit *gautama* means "excellent cow." The name of the family or clan of the **Shakya** tribe into which Prince **Siddhartha**, who became the historical **Shakyamuni Buddha**, was born

general characteristic: (S. sāmānya-lakṣaṇa; J. gū-sō; 共相) The Sanskrit term *sāmānyalakṣaṇa* can also be translated as "generic **mark**" or "shared mark."
In terms of the **four foundations of mindfulness**, body, **feeling**s, mental states, and **phenomena** (**dharma**s) are all generally characterized by impurity, **suffering**, **impermanence**, and **non-self**.

generating the thought of awakening: (S. bodhicittotpāda; J. hotsu-bodaishin or hotsu-dōi or hotsu-dōshin; 発菩提心 or 発道意 or 発道心) The ideogram 発 can mean to "generate." The ideograms 菩提心 are used to translate the Sanskrit term *bodhicitta*, which means "**awakening mind**." The ideograms 道意, and 道心 are also used to translate *bodhicitta*, though respectively they literally mean "thought of the way" and "mind of the way." Generating the thought of awakening is to give rise to the awakening mind, which means to resolve to attain the **unsurpassed, complete, and perfect awakening** of a **buddha**.

generosity: (S. *dāna*; J. *fuse*; 布施) The Sanskrit term *dāna* can also be translated as "charity" or "giving."

In **Mahayana** Buddhism, generosity is the first of the **six perfections** of a **bodhisattva**. Generosity includes the giving of material goods for the support of the **Sangha** or those in need, the giving of fearlessness, and the giving of the **Dharma**.

Gishin: (781-833; 義真) The first head abbot of the **Enryakuji Temple** on **Mt. Hiei**. Well versed in Chinese, Gishin accompanied **Saicho** to Tang China in 804 as his interpreter. According to the will of Saicho, he succeeded the **Great Master** as the head of the **Tiantai school** in Japan and established the Mahayana precept platform on Mt. Hiei, performing ordination ceremonies.

Nichiren Shonin maintained that the **Tiantai Lotus school** established by Saicho in Japan based on the *Lotus Sutra* disappeared upon the passing of the Head Abbot Gishin. (WNS3, p. 29)

Gladdened by Dharma: (J. Gyōbō; 楽法) According to the *Great Perfection of Wisdom Treatise*, **Shakyamuni Buddha**, in his previous life, was named Gladdened by Dharma. Gladdened by Dharma was seeking the **Buddha Dharma** so earnestly that he did not hesitate to peel off his own skin to use as paper, or to use his own bone as a pen and his own blood as ink to write down a verse of the Dharma.

Gladly Seen by All Beings: (S. Sarva-sattva-priyadarśana; J. Issai-shujō-kiken or Kiken; 一切衆生喜見 or 喜見) (1) The name of the **buddha** that **Mahaprajapati** will become, according to the thirteenth, "**Encouragement for Keeping This Sutra**," **chapter** of the *Lotus Sutra*.

(2) The name of **Medicine King Bodhisattva** in a previous life according to the twenty-third, "The **Previous Life of Medicine King Bodhisattva**," chapter of the *Lotus Sutra*.

god: (S. *deva*; J. *ten*; 天) The Sanskrit term *deva*, that can also be translated as "radiant one" or "shining one," has been accepted into the English language, but the devas are commonly referred to as gods or deities. The devas are originally the deities of the sacred **scripture**s of **Brahmanism** called the **Veda**s. They personify and preside over the powers of nature and principles of life. **Rebirth** as a god in the various **heaven**s is the highest and most pleasant of the **six destinies** among the **ten realms**. The ranks of the gods include the **four heavenly kings**, **Shakra**, **Brahma**, and the **Great Freedom God**, as well as various kinds of supernatural beings, such as the **gandharva**s and their wives the apsaras.

Those who dwell in the heavens exist in a state of heedless bliss, for they have at least temporarily achieved their goals. However, this is also a state of complacency and self-satisfaction. The gods tend to be preoccupied with their own pleasure and success. Though the heavens seem to be free of **suffering**, in the fullness of time the **merit** that is the condition for existence there runs its course. When this happens, they begin to show the signs of decay. The other deities begin to avoid them and before long they vanish from the heavens and are plunged back into rebirth in one of the lower destinies.

Not all the gods are heedless or self-satisfied. The **sutra**s say that some may in fact be **bodhisattva**s. Brahma, Indra, and the four heavenly kings are all noted in the sutras for their service to the **Three Treasures** and for the encouragement and assistance they lend to Buddhist practitioners as **guardian deities**. In any case, the gods are by far the wisest, most benevolent, and most powerful of **all heavenly benevolent deities**, which includes the **eight kinds of supernatural beings**, who protect and revere the **Dharma**.

Nichiren Shonin taught that all the gods had promised to protect those who uphold the *Lotus Sutra*. He frequently invoked the Vedic deities and the Shinto kami as his protectors and frequently addressed prayers to the gods and encouraged his followers to do so, but always in the context of overarching **faith** in the *Lotus Sutra*. He also taught that the gods would abandon and punish those who committed **slander of the True Dharma**.

golden-winged bird: (S. garuda; J. konji-chō; 金翅鳥) See **garuda**.

Gomyo: (750-834; J. Gomyō; 護命) A Japanese **monk** of the **Dharma Characteristics school** who opposed the Mahayana precept platform advocated by **Saicho**. He also lost to Saicho in a competition to ceremonially produce rain.

good friend: (S. kalyāṇamitra; J. zenchishiki; 善知識) The Sanskrit term *kalyāṇamitra* literally means "good knowledge," the term refers to a reliable friend or teacher who leads one to arouse the **awakening mind**. The twenty-third, "**The Previous Life of Medicine King Bodhisattva,"** chapter of the *Lotus Sutra* uses the term to refer to one who causes people to arouse the awakening mind.

Nichiren Shonin taught that in the **Latter Age of Degeneration** we must take the *Lotus Sutra* and the *Nirvana Sutra* as our "good friends" because there are no longer any worthy human teachers and so the **sutra**s must become our teachers. (WNS1, pp. 58-61) When Nichiren called Hōjō Tokimune, the shogunal regent who persecuted him, a "good friend," he meant that Tokimune gave him a chance to prove himself to be a **practitioner of the** *Lotus Sutra*.

gratitude: See **four debts of gratitude**.

Great Adornment: (J. Daishōgon; 大荘厳) A **bodhisattva** in the *Infinite Meanings Sutra*.

Great Assembly Sutra: (S. *Mahāsaṃnipāta*; J. *Daijik-kyō* or *Daishū-kyō*; 大集経) Or *Sutra of the Great Assembly*. A **sutra** that was translated into Chinese by Dharmakshema, Narendrayashas, and others separately and finally compiled into sixty fascicles in 586 by a **monk** named Senjiu (C.; 僧就). In the sutra, **Shakyamuni Buddha** describes the **three ages of the Dharma** in terms of **five five-hundred-year periods** to Moon Storehouse **Bodhisattva**.

Nichiren Shonin's conception of the **Latter Age of Degeneration** stems from the descriptions in this and other sutras about the causes of calamities and the gradual decline of Buddhism culminating in the **fifth five-hundred-year period**. Nichiren insisted that the Latter Age of Degeneration, when the *Great Assembly Sutra* predicts the disappearance of the **True Dharma**, is the very period when the virtuous teaching of the *Lotus Sutra* would widely spread. (WNS1, p. 22)

Great Calming and Contemplation: (J. *Maka-shikan* or *Shikan*; 摩訶止観 or 止観) Consisting of ten fascicles, The *Great Calming and Contemplation* is a series of lectures given by **Zhiyi** recorded by his disciple **Guanding**. It teaches the practice of the perfect and sudden **calming** and **contemplation** (J. endon-shikan; 円頓止観) to attain the truth of the *Lotus Sutra* expounded in Zihyi's *Profound Meaning of the Lotus Sutra* and *Words and Phrases of the Lotus Sutra*. Together with the latter works, the *Great Calming and Contemplation* is considered as one the **three major works of the Lotus school**.

Nichiren Shonin considered the doctrine of **three thousand realms in a single thought-moment** taught in the seventh chapter on "Right Meditation" the ultimate essence of the **Tiantai school** and the fundamental truth of the *Lotus Sutra*. Considering the practice of meditation on the three thousand realms in a single thought-moment not fully appropriate for the **Latter Age of Degeneration**, Nichiren Shonin maintained that upholding the five or seven characters of the **daimoku** is the actuality of the three thousand realms in a single thought-moment and chanting the daimoku the suitable practice in the Latter Age of Degeneration.

(WNS2, pp. 4, 161, 257)

Great Cloud Sutra: (S. *Mahāmegha-sūtra*; J. *Daiun-kyō* or *Dai-hōdō-musō-kyō*; 大雲経 or 大方等無想經) A **sutra** doctrinally related to the ***Nirvana Sutra*** that expounds the teaching of the four virtues of **eternity,** bliss, **self,** and purity. It was translated by Dharmakshema between 414 and 421.

Nichiren Shonin refused to accept its claim to be supreme among Buddhist sutras, though it might be regarded in some respects as having teachings of **definitive meaning** compared to other sutras teaching the **provisional meaning** regarding certain topics or issues. (WS1, p. 11)

Great Compassion Sutra: (S. *Mahākaruṇā-puṇḍarīka-sūtra*; J. *Daihi-kyō*; 大悲経) A **Mahayana sutra** translated in 558 by Narendrayashas.

Great Freedom God: (S. Maheśvara; J. Daijizai-ten or Makeishura-ten; 大自在天 or 摩醯首羅天) An alternate name of Shiva (S. Śiva), who lives in the Akanishtha Heaven in **Brahmanism**. Buddhism accepts him as a **guardian deity**.

In later developments of the Vedic tradition, Shiva (S. Śiva) is a member of the *trimūrti* representing the three phases of material nature: **Brahma** the creator, **Vishnu** the preserver, and Shiva the destroyer. Among the Shaivites, he is the supreme deity.

One of the **god**s listed as present in the assembly in the first, "Introductory," chapter of the *Lotus Sutra*.

great kalpa: (S. mahākalpa; J. dai-kō; 大劫) The time it takes for the formation, abiding, and dissolution of a **container world**, as well as a period of nothingness following its dissolution. A great kalpa can be divided into **four kalpas** (the **kalpa of formation**, the **kalpa of abiding,** the **kalpa of dissolution**, and the **kalpa of nothingness**). (ND 4.156, pp. 521-522)

Shakyumuni Buddha gave two analogies for the length of a great kalpa in the *Connected Discourses*. In the first he describes it as the time it would take to wear away a stone cube a **yojana** in length, width, and height by stroking it with a soft cloth once a century. (CD 15.5, p. 654) In the second he describes it as the time it would take to deplete a pile of densely packed mustard seeds a yojana in length, width, and height by taking away a single seed once a century. (CD, 15.6, pp. 654-655)

great man: (S. mahāpuruṣa; J. dainin; 大人) See the **thirty-two marks** and **eighty minor marks**.

Great Mandala of Invoking the Ten Realms: (J. Jikkai Kanjo no Daimandara; 十界勧請の大曼荼羅) The proper title of the calligraphic **mandala** form of the **Focus of Devotion of the Original Gate** inscribed by **Nichiren Shonin**.

great master: (J. daishi; 大師) An honorific title given posthumously to Buddhist priests by the Japanese emperor. **Dengyo** and **Jikaku** were the first to be granted such titles in 856.

Great Expanded Dharani Sutra: (S. *Mahā-vaipulya-dhāraṇī-sūtra*; J. *Dai-hōdō-darani-kyō*; 大方等陀羅尼経) The basis of the Expanded Samadhi, included by **Zhiyi** as one type of both-walking-and-sitting samadhi practice in his *Great Calming and Contemplation*.

Great Perfection of Wisdom Treatise: (S. **Mahāprajñāpāramitā-śāstra*; J. *Daichido-ron*; 大智度論) A commentary on the *Larger Prajna Sutra* in one hundred fascicles, attributed to **Nagarjuna**. Some scholars today doubt Nagarjuna's authorship and argue that it may have been written by **Kumarajiva**, who allegedly translated it from Sanskrit into Chinese between 402 and 406. No text in Sanskrit or Tibetan is extant. The commentary not only annotates each sentence of the sutra, but also discusses numerous theories on various doctrines, especially concerning those of the *Lotus Sutra* and the *Flower Garland Sutra*, such as the teachings of **emptiness**, the **middle way**, and ultimate reality. This treatise also teaches in some passages that practitioners of the **two-vehicles** will be unable to **attain buddhahood** but in other passages that they will be able to do so based on the teaching of the *Lotus Sutra*. (WNS1, pp. 43-44)

According to **Nichiren Shonin**, this treatise distinguishes between the *Lotus Sutra* and the **Prajna sutras**, claiming the former to be the true **Mahayana** teaching. (WNS1, p. 28)

Great Power Obtainer: (S. Mahāsthāmaprāpta; J. Seishi or Tokudaisei; 勢至 or 得大勢) In the *Contemplation of the Buddha of Infinite Life Sutra* he is one of the two attendants of **Amitabha** Buddha and represents **wisdom**, while **World Voice Perceiver** represents **compassion**.

Great Power Obtainer appears among the eighty thousand bodhisattvas present in the assembly in the first, "Introductory," chapter of the *Lotus Sutra*, and the Buddha taught the twentieth chapter of the *Lotus Sutra* to him.

Great Treasure Chamber: (J. Daihō-bō; 大宝坊) The place where **Shakyamuni**

Buddha taught the *Great Assembly Sutra*.

Great Tree Kimnara King Sutra: (J. *Daiju-kinnara-ō-kyō*; 大樹緊那羅王経) A Mahayana sutra. (WNS2, p. 86)

Great Universal Wisdom Excellence: (S. Mahābhijñā-jñānābhibhū; J. Daitsūchishō or Daitsū; 大通智勝 or 大通) The story of this **buddha** who appeared **three thousand dust-particle kalpas** ago is told in the seventh, "The Parable of a Magic City," chapter of the ***Lotus Sutra***. He sat in meditation for ten kalpa before he attained **unsurpassed, complete, and perfect awakening**. At that time there were sixteen princes who were the sons that Great Universal Wisdom Excellence Buddha had prior to his leaving the home life. The sixteen princes went to see their father after his awakening and begged him to **turn the Wheel of the Dharma**. Then the **Brahma**s of the **ten directions** also came to request that he turn the Wheel of the Dharma. Great Universal Wisdom Excellence Buddha agreed and taught the **four noble truths** and **dependent origination**. The sixteen princes then became novices and requested that the Buddha teach the unsurpassed awakening. Again, the Buddha agreed, and after twenty thousand kalpas he taught the *Lotus Sutra* for a period of eight thousand kalpas. The Buddha then sat in meditation for eighty-four thousand kalpas. During that time the sixteen princes expounded the *Lotus Sutra* in the worlds of the ten directions. They subsequently became the **buddhas of the ten directions**. The sixteenth son became **Shakyamuni** Buddha who taught the *Lotus Sutra* in this **Saha world** to save those who received the **seed of buddhahood** by having previously listened to Great Universal Wisdom Excellence Buddha.

Based on this story, **Zhiyi** divided the process of **attaining buddhahood** into three stages: **sowing, maturing, and harvesting**. According to this teaching, those who currently embrace the *Lotus Sutra* had the opportunity to listen to the sutra in the distant past. Also, based on this story of **establishing a connection to Great Universal Wisdom Excellence Buddha**, Zhiyi also taught the principle of the beginning and ending of the path of guidance and the principle of the length of the relationship between teacher and disciple, the second and third of the three standards of doctrinal comparison.

Great Vaipulya Sutra of the Buddha's Flower Garland: (S. *Mahāvaipulya-Buddhāvataṃsaka-sūtra*; J. *Dai-hōkō-butsu-kegon-kyō/Dai-hōdō-butsu-kegon-kyō*; 大方広佛華厳経) See *Flower Garland Sutra*.

Great Vehicle: See **Mahayana**.

greed: (S. rāga or lobha; J. ton, ton'yoku, or ai; 貪, 貪欲, or 愛) One of the **three poisons**. The ideogram 貪 can also mean attachment.

Guanding: (561-632; Kanjō; 潅頂) Also known as the Great Master Zhang'an (J. Shōan Daishi; 章安 大師). He became a disciple of **Zhiyi** and learned from him the doctrine and meditation of the **Tiantai school**. He recorded and compiled the master's lectures including the **three major works of the Lotus school** in more than one hundred fascicles. His relationship to Zhiyi was analogous to that of **Ananda** to **Shakyamuni Buddha**. He himself wrote the *Profound Meaning of the Nirvana Sutra* and the *Annotations on the Nirvana Sutra*, two works that **Nichiren Shonin** often cited.

guardian deities: See **guardian deity**.

guardian deity: (J. shugojin; 守護神) Any of the beings who protect the **Dharma**, including the **eight kinds of supernatural beings** and **bodhisattva**s.

Guide to the Tiantai Fourfold Teachings, A: (J. *Tendai shikyōgi*; 天台四教儀) An outline of the **Tiantai school**'s doctrine by the Korean **monk** Chegwan.

Hachiman: (J.; 八幡) The Shinto kami who presides over archery, war, agriculture, and other important parts of historic Japanese life. His name means "Eight Flags." Originally a Shinto **god** of agriculture worshipped by the Usa clan of Kyushu in southern Japan, Hachiman in association with Buddhism began to be worshipped in the capital region during the Nara period in the eighth century.

In the early Heian period (894-1185) oracles proclaimed him the protector of Todaiji Temple. This led to the imperial court granting Hachiman the title of "Great **Bodhisattva**" in 781, the first Shinto kami to be so honored. In 860, the monk Gyoko (J. Gyōkō) invoked the Shinto god Hachiman at the Iwashimizu section of Kyoto and worshipped him as the protector of the imperial capital. It was around this time that Hachiman began to be regarded to have been Emperor Ojin (J. Ōjin), the legendary fifteenth emperor of the third century, in his previous life. Subsequently the Hachiman Shrine at Iwashimizu was greatly venerated by the imperial court as the holiest of shrines second only to the Ise Shrine for the goddess **Amaterasu**. In the late twelfth century, Minamoto Yoritomo, the first of the Kamakuran shoguns, regarded Hachiman as the tutelary deity of the Minamoto clan and founded the Tsurugaoka Shrine in Kamakura to honor him. With the spread of the military government, the worship of Hachiman became nationwide as the **guardian deity** of local communities.

Hachiman and Amaterasu were the two Shinto kami Nichiren included on the **Great Mandala of Invoking the Ten Realms**.

hatred: (S. dveṣa; J. shinni or shin; 瞋恚 or 瞋) The Sanskrit term *dveṣa* can also be translated as "aversion," or "ill-will."

have, am now, and will: (J. i-kon-tō; 已今当) A reference to the **three expoundings** of all the **sutra**s by **Shakyamuni Buddha**, with the exception of the *Lotus Sutra*.

heat: (S. ūṣman or ūṣmagata; J. nan or nan-i or nampō; 煖 or 煖位 or 煖法) The first stage of the **four wholesome roots**. It arises from the cultivation of the **four foundations of mindfulness**. It is called "heat" because it anticipates the fire of the **eightfold noble path** which consumes the **defilement**s. This **contemplation** of the four foundations of mindfulness also involves different aspects of the **four noble truths**. This stage progresses from weak to medium to strong states and leads into the stage of the **summit**. At this stage the practitioner's appreciation for the four noble truths is relatively weak, so they can still fall away from further progression.

heaven: (S. deva-loka or svarga; J. ten or tenjō; 天 or 天上) The abodes of the **god**s and other beings who are their retainers. The heavens of Buddhist cosmology are not permanent, though the varying lifespans within each of the particular heavens are of astronomical length.

heavenly devil: (J. temma; 天魔) Another term for **King Mara of the Sixth Heaven**.

Heavenly King: (S. Devarāja; J. Tennō; 天王) The name of the **buddha** that **Devadatta** will become, according to the twelfth, "**Devadatta**," **chapter** of the *Lotus Sutra*.

heavenly vehicle: (ten-jō; 天乗) The practice of the **ten virtuous precepts** in order to create the **causes and conditions** for rebirth in the **heavens** as a **god**.

heinous transgression: One of the **five heinous transgressions** or **seven heinous transgressions**.

hell: (S. naraka; J. jigoku or naraka; 地獄 or 那洛迦) **Rebirth** in one of the hells, the abodes of the **hell-dwellers**, is one of the **three evil destinies**, the lowest of the **six destinies** and of the **ten realms**. The worst is the Hell of **Incessant Suffering** The hells of Buddhist cosmology are not permanent, though the varying lifespans within each of the particular hells are of astronomical length.

hell-dweller: (S. nāraka; J. jigoku; 地獄) A **sentient being** who is being punished in one of the **hell**s.

highest mundane dharma: (S. laukikāgradharma; J. sedai-ippō-i; 世第一法位) The fourth stage of the **four wholesome roots**. It arises from the stage of **patience**₍₂₎. It lasts only a moment and considers **suffering** within the **form realm**. This is the last moment at which a practitioner is still an **ordinary person**, which is why it is called the "highest mundane dharma." This moment is followed by direct insight wherein the practitioner becomes a **stream-enterer**.

Hiei, Mount: (Hiei-zan; 比叡山) Mt. Hiei has become synonymous with the **Enryakuji Temple**, the head temple of the Japanese **Tiantai school** located at the northern end of the Higashiyama Range at Sakamoto-sho in Ōtsu-shi, Shiga Prefecture. Mt. Hiei has been revered as the sacred mountain for the protection of the imperial capital, as it is situated to the northeast of Kyoto, a direction believed to be vulnerable to the incursion of **demon**s. It was founded by **Saicho** in the seventh year of the Enryaku era (788). Many founders of the new Buddhist schools in the Kamakura period studied at this temple. It is believed that **Nichiren Shonin** spent most of his study period in the Kyoto area at Enryakuji Temple. Nichiren Shonin later regarded this temple as a center of **esoteric Buddhism** that had abandoned the *Lotus Sutra* since the time of the head abbot **Ennin**.

Himalayas: (S. Himālaya or Himavat; J. Sessen; 雪山) The Himalaya mountain range in a **Sumeru world** is in the northern reaches of **Jambudvipa**.

hinayana: (S. hīnayāna; J. shōjō; 小乗) Literally, "**lesser vehicle**" or "small vehicle." A **Mahayana** term for those who only wish to attain **liberation** for themselves and do not try to **benefit** others by striving to **attain buddhahood**.

holy way gate: (J. shōdō-mon; 聖道門) According to the **Pure Land school**, the holy way gate is the teaching of such Buddhist schools as the **Dharma Characteristics**, **Three Treatises**, **Tiantai**, and **Mantra** that advocate practicing Buddhism in this **Saha world** in order to **attain buddhahood**. It is contrasted to the **Pure Land gate**, which teaches that one can be saved by **rebirth in the pure land**, specifically the Pure Land of Utmost Bliss of **Amitabha Buddha**, instead of the continuing practice of the **threefold training** (**morality**, **concentration**, and **wisdom**) over many lifetimes in this Saha world. The holy way gate is also identified with the difficult-to-practice way.

Pure Land Buddhism maintains that even transgressors and **ordinary people** with **defilement**s can be reborn in the pure land by practicing the **nembutsu**, which is easy for people of **inferior capacity** in the **Latter Age of Degeneration** to practice. On the contrary, they insist, the holy way gate teaching is too difficult for **ignorant** people in the Latter Age to practice, and therefore should be cast away.

The Pure Land gate, in contrast to the holy way gate, was first established in the ***Collection of Passages on the Land of Peace and Bliss*** by the Chinese **monk**, **Daochuo**. and it provided the basic doctrine for **Honen** to establish the Pure Land school in Japan. (WNS1, pp. 4, 28)

homogeneous cause: (S. sabhāga-hetu; J. shū-in or dōrui-in; 習因 or 同類因) The Sanskrit word *sabhāgahetu* can also be translated as "parallel **cause**," "repetitive cause," or "similar cause." A homogeneous cause results in an **effect** similar to itself in terms of its moral quality within the **triple world**. (AKB1, pp. 263-271, 289-290)

Honen: (1133-1212; J. Hōnen; 法然) Also known as Genku (J. Genkū; 源空). Founder of the **Pure Land school** in Japan. At the age of thirteen, he went to Mt. **Hiei** to become a **monk**. At the age of forty-three, he was converted to Pure Land Buddhism after he read **Shandao**'s *Annotations on the Contemplation of the Buddha of Infinite Life Sutra*. Soon thereafter he left Mt. Hiei to preach the teaching of the exclusive **nembutsu**. As the teaching of the nembutsu spread, monks on Mt. Hiei and in Nara appealed to the authorities for its suppression with the result that Honen was banished to Tosa Province.

Nichiren Shonin harshly criticized the exclusive nembutsu practice and called Honen one who had committed **slander of the True Dharma** because he insisted in A ***Collection of Passages on the Nembutsu Chosen in the Original Vow*** that everyone should "**abandon, close, set aside, and cast away**" all the **holy way gate** sutras including the ***Lotus Sutra***.

Hong Yan: (d. 660 BCE; J. Kō En; 弘演) The retainer of Duke Yi (J. I-kō; 懿公) of the state of Wei (J. Ei; 衛 from 衞) Upon returning from a political mission he found that northern barbarians had killed Duke Yi and eaten all but his liver, which was left on the road. To save the honor of his lord, Hong Yan cut open his own stomach to insert the liver and then died.

householder: (S. gṛhapati; J. koji or chōja or zaike; 居士 or 長者 or 在家) One of the four stages of life according to **Brahmanism**. Also, in Buddhism, lay followers who have not renounced home-life.

Huiguang: (486-537; C.; J. Ekō; 慧光) A Chinese **monk** associated with the third northern school of the **three southern and seven northern schools**. He is credited as the founder of the Fourfold Discipline school.

human: (S. manuṣya; J. nin; 人) **Rebirth** as a human is one of the three good destinies, the highest of the **six destinies** among the **ten realms**. Humans are the inhabitants of the **four continents** and their flanking islands (except for the island of Camaras where **rakshasa**s live) of a **Sumeru world**. They have different heights and lifespans depending on which continent they reside, and the lifespans of those in **Jambudvipa** fluctuate.

human teachers: (J. ninshi; 人師) **Nichiren Shonin** used this term to mean Buddhist **monk**s in China and Japan who spread Buddhism guided by commentators and translators. (WNS1, pp. 3, 28)

human vehicle: (nin-jō; 人乗) The practice of the **five precepts** to create the **causes and conditions** for **rebirth** as a **human**.

hungry ghost: (S. preta; J. gaki or heirei or heireita; 餓鬼 or 薜荔 or 薜荔多) **Rebirth** as a spirit which suffers from hunger in the realm of hungry ghosts is one of the **three evil destinies**, the lowest of the **six destinies** and of the **ten realms**. There are many kinds of hungry ghosts and some of them are as powerful as **god**s. Hungry ghosts are also included among the army and attendants of Growth Increasing, one of the **four heavenly kings**.

icchantika: (S.; J. issendai; 一闡提) The Sanskrit term *icchantika* can be translated as "incorrigible one." An *icchantika* is inherently unreceptive to the teaching of the **True Dharma** and therefore, can never **attain buddhahood**. The *Lotus Sutra* and *Nirvana Sutra*, however, teach that *icchantika*, too, can attain buddhahood.
 Nichiren Shonin taught that even those *icchantika* who commit **slander of the True Dharma** can attain buddhahood due to the **great compassion** of the **Eternal Shakyamuni Buddha**. He thus stresses the great power of the *Lotus Sutra* as the savior of all beings.

ignorance: (S. avidyā; J. mumyō; 無明) The ideograms 無明 are also used to translate the Sanskrit term *moha*, or **delusion**, which is synonymous with *avidyā*.

The deepest-rooted kind of ignorance is called **fundamental ignorance** or beginningless ignorance.

ignorant: See **ignorance**.

impermanence: (S. anitya or anityatā; J. metsu or mujō; 滅 or 無常) The Sanskrit terms *anitya* or *anityatā* can also be translated as "ceasing" or "termination." Impermanence is the characteristic of all **conditioned phenomena** to be transitory.

impure land: (J. edo; 穢土) This **Saha world** where we live is the impure land. Unlike the Pure Land of Utmost Bliss to the west, this world is conceived as being polluted by the **three poisons** where people must endure **suffering**.

It is taught in the sixteenth, "**The Duration of the Life of the Tathagata**," chapter of the *Lotus Sutra* that this Saha world is actually the pure land where **Shakyamuni Buddha** always resides.

Nichiren Shonin insisted that the true pure land, the Land of Eternally Tranquil Light, is nowhere other than this Saha world.

Incessant Suffering, Hell of: (S. avīci; J. abi-jigoku or abi-goku or muken-jigoku; 阿鼻地獄 or 阿鼻獄 or 無間地獄). The Sanskrit term *avīci* means "incessant." It is the lowest and worst of the **hell**s that are said to exist under the ground of **Jambudvipa**. This is a hell where **hell-dweller**s suffer continuously without any respite. This hell is reserved for those who deliberately and cold-bloodedly commit one or more of the **five heinous transgressions**. It is also for those who commit **slander of the True Dharma**. The tortures here are so great and the flames so hot that the other hells seem like **heaven**s in comparison. This hell is often described as a gargantuan red-hot iron cube with two doors. One door opens to entice the evildoers to run across the cube in a desperate race to get out, but it always shuts just as they arrive. Then the other door opens. This process repeats itself without interruption. Those who are in this hell constantly cry out for help from their incessant anguish, so it is called the Incessant Crying Hell. This hell is also called Incessant Castle because the area is so vast that no one can find their way out easily.

Nichiren Shonin said that all the people in Japan were walking on the path to the Hell of Incessant Suffering and characterized the **daimoku** as the surest way to stop one's descent to this hell.

indeterminate: (S. avyākṛta; J. muki; 無記) The Sanskrit term *avyākṛta* can also be translated as "unascertainable." It refers to that which is morally neutral, or to questions that cannot be answered.

indeterminate nature of the three vehicles: (J. sanjō-fujō-shō; 三乗 不定性) One of the **five natures** taught by the **Dharma Characteristics school**. Those with this nature may enter any of the **three vehicles**. According to the Dharma Characteristics school, the **One Vehicle** was taught for those with an indeterminate nature so that they would aspire to **attain buddhahood**.

inferior accommodative-body: (J. retsu-ōjin; 劣応身) In the **Tiantai school** of Buddhism the accommodative-body of a **buddha** is further divided into an inferior and a superior form. The inferior accommodative-body is the one that appears to **ordinary people** and other beings in the lower portion of the Land of the Coexistence of Sages and Ordinary People that is considered the **impure land**. It is the body accommodated to **bodhisattva**s who have not yet reached the **ten grounds**. To most beings the inferior accommodative-body would appear to be an ordinary human being, though it is also said to be as tall as sixteen feet.

According to **Nichiren Shonin**, **Shakyamuni** Buddha as the **focus of devotion** for the **Discipline**, **Abhidharma Treasury**, and **Completion of Reality** schools of Buddhism is an inferior accommodative-body.

inferior capacity: (S. mṛdu; J. gekon or gebon; 下根 or 下品) See **dull capacity**.

Infinite Meanings Sutra: (J. *Muryōgi-kyō*; 無量義経) Also called *Innumerable Meanings Sutra*. Translated into Chinese by Dharmagatayashas in 481, it consists of three chapters: "Virtuous Practices," "Dharma Discourse," and "Ten Blessings." From its content, the **sutra** is regarded as an introductory teaching to the *Lotus Sutra*. It is also the opening sutra of the *Threefold Lotus Sutra*.

Nichiren Shonin claimed that all the **prior sutras** are **provisional sutra**s and considered the *Lotus Sutra* as the **True Dharma** based on the statement in the "Dharma Discourse" chapter, "The truth has not been revealed for forty years or so," that he took to mean the differentiation of the *Lotus Sutra* from all the sutras taught before it. Nevertheless, this sutra itself is considered a provisional sutra in comparison to the *Lotus Sutra*. WNS1, pp. 11-12)

inner way: (J. naidō; 内道) The inner way refers to Buddhism as the "inside track" to **liberation** and **awakening**, in contrast to the **outer way**, which refers to **non-Buddhist teachings**.

interim kalpa: (S. antara-kalpa; J. chū-kō; 中劫) The Sanskrit term *antarakalpa* can also be translated as "intermediate kalpa." It is also sometimes referred to as a "small kalpa." Within each of the **four kalpas** that comprise a **great kalpa**, there are twenty interim kalpas. (AKB2, pp. 475-479)

The first interim kalpa of the **kalpa of abiding** is called the **kalpa of decrease**, because it is during that period that the longevity of **human**s in **Jambudvipa** gradually decreases by a year every century from a practically infinite length until it is only ten years. During each of the next eighteen interim kalpas the lifespan increases by a year every century until it reaches eighty thousand years and then decreases again at the same rate until it is back to only ten years. The twentieth and last interim kalpa of this period is the **kalpa of increase**, wherein there is only a gradual increase of the lifespan until the age of eighty thousand years is reached. (AKB2, pp. 478-479)

Izu Exile: (J. Izu-ruzai; 伊豆流罪) On May 12, 1261, **Nichiren Shonin** was arrested by the Kamakura shogunate and sent into exile on a small rocky peninsula in Izu Province. His enemies hoped that he would die of exposure to the elements, but he survived with the assistance of a local fisherman and his wife. Later, the local steward also befriended him after overcoming a serious illness with the help of Nichiren Shonin's prayers. Far from feeling defeated, Nichiren Shonin felt that being exiled had enabled him to live the ***Lotus Sutra*** with his whole being in every moment of his life. On February 22, 1263, he was finally pardoned and allowed to return to Kamakura. This was the second of the four major persecutions.

Jambudvipa: (S. Jambudvīpa; J. Nan-embudai, Embudai/Enbudai, or Sembu-shū; 南閻浮提, 閻浮提 or 贍部洲) *Jambu* is the name of a tree, and *dvīpa* stands for a continent. According to traditional Buddhist cosmology **four continents** exist on four sides of Mt. **Sumeru**, and the one to the south is called Jambudvipa because it is abundant with *jambu* trees. Its shape is trapezoidal, as its southern tip is three and a half **yojana**s long and the other three sides two thousand yojanas long, so it looks like a chariot seen from overhead. The diamond seat where the **bodhisattva**s **attain buddhahood** is only located in the center of Jambudvipa. North of that are three sets of three small black mountains called the Ant Mountains, and beyond those are the **Himalayas**. On the other side of the Himalayas is Lake **Anavatapta**. From out of that lake flow four rivers: the **Ganges River**, the Sindhu, the Vakṣu, and the Sītā. *Jambu* trees grow by the lake. North of the lake is Mt. Perfume (S. Gandhamādana). Located on either side of Jambudvipa are two smaller continents with the same shape called Camaras (S. Cāmaras) and Avaracamaras (S. Avarac-āmaras). The island of Camaras is where **rakshasa**s live. (AKB2, pp. 455-456)

The **human** inhabitants of Jambudvipa are basically the people of Earth, as Jambudvipa represented the known world to the ancient Indians. Buddhist cosmology, however, believes that the lifespan of human beings can range from as little as ten years at the end of the **kalpa of decrease** to as great as eighty thousand years at the end of the **kalpa of increase**, and even to a practically incalculable length that cannot be measured in the thousands by the end of the **kalpa of formation**. (ABK2, pp. 469-470, 478-479)

Jambunada Gold Light: (S. Jāmbūnada-prabhāsa; J. Embunadai-konkō; 閻浮那提金光) The **buddha** that **Mahakatyayana** will become according to the sixth, "Assurance of Future Buddhahood," chapter of the *Lotus Sutra*.

Jiashang: (J. Kashō; 嘉尚) A disciple of **Xuanzang**.

Jiaxiang, Great Master: (C.; J. Kajō Daishi; 嘉祥 大師) See **Jizang**.

Jie, King: (d. 1675 BCE; J. Ketsu-ō; 桀王) The last ruler of the of the Xia dynasty who was overthrown by King **Tang**. King Jie is the first of the **Three Kings**(2).

Jikaku, Great Master: (J. Jikaku Daishi; 慈覚 大師) See **Ennin**.

Jitsue: (786-847; 実慧) A disciple of **Kukai**.

Jivaka: (S. Jīvaka; J. Giba; 耆婆) A great physician in India during the lifetime of **Shakyamuni Buddha**. While serving King **Ajatashatru** of **Magadha** in central India, he prevented the king from killing his mother, **Vaidehi**, and later urged the king, who had become increasingly anxious about falling into **hell** for the transgression of **killing one's father**, to see the Buddha and embrace Buddhism.
Nichiren Shonin cited Jivaka as an example of a **good friend** who was able to lead King Ajatashatru to the Buddha.

Jizang: (549–623; C.; J. Kichizō; 吉蔵) The **monk** who systematized the **Three Treatise school** in Sui China. He is called the **Great Master Jiaxiang** after the temple where he lived. He lectured on not only the *Three Treatises* but also the *Lotus Sutra* and *Flower Garland Sutra*, and wrote such commentaries as the *Profound Meaning of the Three Treatises*, the *Annotations on the Meaning of the Lotus Sutra*, and the *Profundity of the Lotus Sutra Treatise*.
Nichiren Shonin maintained that Jizang misinterpreted the *Lotus Sutra* but later repented, becoming a disciple of **Zhiyi**. Jizang is said to have been impressed by Zhiyi so deeply that he offered himself as a stepladder whenever Zhiyi mounted the preaching platform. (WNS2, p. 79)

Jizha: (c. 561–515 BCE; C.; J. Kisatsu; 季札) A son of Shoumeng, the king of Wu in the Spring and Autumn period in ancient China. On the way to a diplomatic mission he met the lord of Xu, who deeply admired Jizha's treasured sword. Jizha wanted to give it to the lord on his way back from the mission; however, when he tried to see him again on the way back, the lord was already dead. Jizha, therefore, presented the sword to the lord at his grave and prayed for the repose of the lord's spirit. This story is told in the *Records of the Grand Historian* by the Han dynasty official Sima Qian (145-86 BCE).

Jufukuji Temple: (寿福寺) A temple belonging to the Rinzai school of **Zen Buddhism**. It is located at the Ōgigayatsu section in Kamakura, Kanagawa Prefecture. It is one of the "five major temples in Kamakura." It was burnt down but rebuilt in the first year of Kōan (1278).

Nichiren Shonin regarded this temple along with **Kenchoji Temple** as a stronghold of those who commit **slander of the True Dharma**.

Kalodayin: (S. Kālodāyin; J. Karudai or Karu; 迦留陀夷 or 迦盧) Also known as Udayin (S. Udāyin; J. Udai; 優陀夷). One of **Shakyamuni Buddha**'s disciples during his lifetime, who is said to have been the foremost in popularity among lay men and women. A **brahmin** in origin, he was a teacher of Prince **Siddhartha**. According to the *Ten Recitations Discipline*, he was beheaded by the jealous husband of a woman who had given him offerings and his head was buried in horse manure. (WNS1, p. 62)

In the eighth, "Assurance of Future Buddhahood of the Five Hundred Disciples," chapter of the ***Lotus Sutra***, he is among the five hundred **arhat**s who receive the assurance of future buddhahood by Shakyamuni Buddha and told that they will become buddhas named **Universal Brightness**.

kalpa: (J. *kō*; 劫) The Sanskrit term *kalpa* can also be translated as "age" or "eon." There are kalpas of varying time spans though all of them are of astronomical length. The largest is the **great kalpa**. A great kalpa can be divided into the **four kalpas** of formation, abiding, dissolution, and nothingness. (ND 4.156, pp. 521-522) Each of these four kalpas can itself be subdivided into twenty **interim kalpas**. (AKB2, pp. 475-479)

kalpa of abiding: (S. vivartasthāyikalpa; J. jū-kō; 住劫) This is the time when the **container world** is fully operational. The first of the twenty **interim kalpa**s of this period of abiding is the **kalpa of decrease**, during which the longevity of **humans** in **Jambudvipa** gradually decreases from a practically infinite length until it is only ten years. During each of the next eighteen interim kalpas the lifespan increases by a year every century until it reaches eighty thousand years and then decreases again until it is back to only ten years. The twentieth and last interim kalpa of this period is the **kalpa of increase**, wherein there is only a gradual increase to the lifespan until the age of eighty thousand years is reached. (AKB2, pp. 478-479)

kalpa of decrease: (S. apakarśa-kalpa; J. gen-kō; 減劫) The first of the twenty **interim kalpa**s of the **kalpa of abiding**, during which the longevity of **humans** in **Jambudvipa** gradually decreases by a year every century from a practically infinite length until it is only ten years. (AKB2, pp. 478-479)

kalpa of dissolution: (S. saṃvartakalpa; J. e-kō; 壊劫) The period from the time when **sentient beings** cease to be reborn in the **hell** of that particular **container world** until the moment when that world is destroyed by one of the **three major calamities** of fire, water, or wind due to the exhaustion of the collective **karma** of the **sentient beings** that caused that world to arise. As the different regions are emptying out, the sentient beings are either born into a higher region that is not yet emptying or will not be destroyed at the end of the kalpa or they are reborn in another container world where the conditions they require for the **ripening** of their **karma** are ongoing. (AKB2, pp. 475-477) The disappearance of the world of sentient beings occurs during all but the last of the **interim kalpa**s of the kalpa of dissolution. In the last interim kalpa the container world itself is destroyed. (AKB2, p. 479)

kalpa of formation: (S. vivartakalpa; J. jō-kō; 成劫) The period from the time when, due to the collective **karma** of **sentient being**s, the primordial winds begin to create the wind disk for a new **container world** until the time when that world has been populated from the **heaven**s down to the **hell**s. (AKB2, pp. 477-478) The formation of the container world occurs during the first **interim kalpa** of the kalpa of formation, and the repopulation of the world of sentient beings, beginning with the appearance of **Brahma** and continuing downwards until the appearance of the **hell-dwellers** occurs during the following nineteen interim kalpas. (AKB2, p. 479)

kalpa of increase: (S. utkarśa-kalpa; J. zō-kō; 増劫) The twentieth and last **interim kalpa** of the **kalpa of abiding**, wherein there is a gradual increase to the lifespan of **humans** in **Jambudvipa** by a year every century until it reaches eighty thousand years. (AKB2, pp. 478-479)

kalpa of nothingness: (S. saṃvartasthāyikalpa; J. kū-kō; 空劫) During this period there is nothing in the **space** where there was once a **container world** and where there will once more arise a new container world. (AKB2, pp. 477)

Kapila: (J. Kabira; 迦毘羅) One of the **three hermits** in India, who are upheld as the legendary **rishi**s who revealed the **Vedas** and were the founders of ancient Indian philosophy and religion. Kapila was the legendary founder of the **Samkhya** who may have lived as early as the seventh century BCE.

karma: (S.; J. gō; 業) The Sanskrit term *karma* means an intentional **action** or deed which is either **wholesome, unwholesome,** or **indeterminate**. The uninflected *karman* can also be translated as "proceedings" or the "object" of an action. Sometimes it is used to refer to the consequences of past actions, though that is technically incorrect as the Sanskrit terms, *phala* and *vipāka*, are the correct terms for the **fruition** and **ripening** of past actions. Karmic acts are often likened to **seed**s. These acts are said to be sown like seeds in the **storehouse consciousness** and/or to **perfume** the seeds that are already there. The simplest statement about karma is expressed by **Shakyamuni Buddha** in the following verse: "Whatever sort of seed is sown,/That is the sort of fruit one reaps:/The doer of good reaps good;/The doer of evil reaps evil./By you, dear, has the seed been sown;/Thus you will experience the fruit."(CD 11.10.903, p. 328)

In answer to the question as to what are the **causes and conditions** that differentiate the fortunes and characteristics of **human** beings, Shakyamuni Buddha answered, "Student, beings are owners of their actions, heirs of their actions; they originate from their actions, are bound to their actions, have their actions as their refuge. It is action that distinguishes beings as inferior and superior." (MD 135.4, p. 1053)

The Buddha also taught that not everything that happens is the result of karma. He explained that some feelings arise from bile disorders, phlegm disorders, wind disorders, an imbalance all three, or they are produced by changes in climate, careless behavior, or caused by assault, or produced as the result of karma. He said that while it might be true for a person to say that some feelings were produced by karma if they knew that was the case, it was overstating things to say that everything a person experiences is caused by what was done in the past. The Buddha declared that this overstatement of the role of karma was wrong. (CD 36.21, pp. 1278-1279)

Among the three kinds of activities (physical, verbal, and mental) the Buddha clearly stated, "Of these three kinds of action, Tapassi, thus analyzed and distinguished, I describe mental action as the most reprehensible for the performance of evil action, for the perpetration of evil action, and not so much bodily action and verbal action." (MD, 56.4, pp. 478-479) This is because, in the Buddha's teaching, karma is not just any act but specifically an act that involves volition. In other words, it must be an intentional act. The underlying motivation therefore determines whether a given act is wholesome or unwholesome. The origin or root motivations for unwholesome actions are the **three poisons** of **greed**, **hatred**, and **delusion**, while the root motivations for wholesome actions are the three wholesome roots of non-greed, non-hatred, and non-delusion. (ND 3.34, pp. 230-232)

The Buddha differentiated karma into dark actions with dark results that lead to the **evil destinies**, particularly **hell**; bright actions with bright results that lead to good destinies, particularly **heaven**; dark-and-bright actions with dark-and-bright results that can lead to any of the **six destinies** with the possible exception of some of the worst hells and some of the highest heavens which are the destinies of those who only commit dark or bright deeds respectively; and actions that are neither dark nor bright that lead to the destruction of karma by abandoning the three above types of actions, thereby leading to the end of **samsara** and the attainment of **nirvana**. (MD 57.7-11, pp. 495-496) Dark or unwholesome actions are equivalent to the ten evil acts, while bright or wholesome actions are equivalent to the **ten virtuous precepts**. Acts that are neither dark nor bright would be the cultivation of the **eightfold noble path**.

The Buddha also pointed out that the results of karma do not immediately follow but can ripen in another lifetime. Therefore, someone who commits wholesome actions may soon meet with or be reborn in unfortunate circumstances, while someone who commits unwholesome actions may soon meet with or be reborn in fortunate circumstances, but this is only because some other previous karmic seeds they had are ripening and the karma for the wholesome or unwholesome actions in question will take more time until causes and conditions bring about their ripening. (MD 136, pp. 1058-1065) Another complication when it comes to discerning karma and its ripening is that a trifling act can have great consequences or be barely noticeable depending on the circumstances. For instance, someone who has committed a trifling evil but who has no good to counterbalance it may be reborn in hell because of it, while another person who has committed a trifling evil may otherwise have done much good and so they briefly experience the ripening of that evil in the present life. The Buddha compares this to the way putting salt into a cup of water can make a big difference while putting salt into the **Ganges River** will not make it salty. (ND 3.100, pp. 331-335)

An especially important consideration concerning karma is that the Buddha warned people that it is one of the "four inconceivables" that will bring madness and frustration to anyone who speculates about them. These four are the nature of the buddhas, the experience of **meditative absorption**, the precise workings of karma, and metaphysical speculations about the world. (ND 4.77, p. 463) Presumably, only buddhas can fathom the workings of karma.

karmic: That which pertains to the workings of **karma**.

Kashyapa: (S. Kāśyapa; J. Kashō-bosatsu; 迦葉菩薩) A **bodhisattva** who was a young **brahmin** who became a Buddhist **monk**. He is the main interlocutor in the *Nirvana Sutra*.

Nichiren Shonin stated that Kashyapa Bodhisattva and his followers were not able to **attain buddhahood** by hearing the *Lotus Sutra* because they were continuing to hold **false view**s. When they heard the *Nirvana Sutra*, they were finally able to relinquish those false views and attain buddhahood. However, this has nothing to do with the comparative superiority between those two sutras. (WNS1, p. 13)

Kenchoji Temple: (J. Kenchōji; 建長寺) Located in Kamakura of Kanagawa Prefecture, Kenchoji Temple is the head temple of the Kenchoji branch within the Rinzai school of the **Zen school of Buddhism.** It is one of the "five major temples in Kamakura."

Nichiren Shonin regarded this temple along with **Jufukuji Temple** as a stronghold of those who commit **slander of the True Dharma**.

Kenninji Temple: (建仁寺) Located in Kyoto, the Kenninji is the head temple of the Kenninji branch within the Rinzai school of **Zen Buddhism**.

kesa: (S. kāṣāya or kaṣāya; J.; 袈裟) The patchwork robe of a Buddhist **monk** or **nun**. It is traditionally dyed saffron or ochre.

killing one's father: (S. pitṛ-ghāta; J. gai-fu or satsu-fu; 害父 or 殺父) One of the **five heinous transgressions**. This is a particularly grave transgression because it is to kill the benefactor who at the very least gave one life. (AKB2, p. 685)

To kill a **bodhisattva** who has received an assurance of future buddhahood is considered a similar transgression but may not immediately lead to **hell**. (AKB2, p. 689)

kimnara: (S. kiṃnara; J. kinnara; 緊那羅) Kimnaras are celestial musicians and dancers who have the bodies of birds with human heads and torsos. Though intelligent and extremely powerful, they are classified as **animal**s among the **six destinies**. They are one of the **eight kinds of supernatural beings**. Kimnaras are also included among the army and attendants of Hearing Everything, one of the **four heavenly kings**.

King Mara of the Sixth Heaven: (S. Māra; J. Dairokuten-no-Māo; 第六天の魔王) King Mara is said to live in the Heaven of Controlling the Creations of Others, the sixth heaven in the **desire realm**. He is said to cause obstacles to the followers of Buddhism and, as the **devil king of the sixth heaven**, is the last of the so-called "**three obstacles** and **four devils**."

knowledge: (S. jñāna; J. chi; 智 or 知) The Sanskrit term *jñāna* can also be translated as "awareness," "gnosis," "understanding," or "**wisdom**."

In **Mahayana** Buddhism, knowledge includes the knowledge of the bliss of the **Dharma** and the knowledge that enables a **bodhisattva** to unfold their wisdom in a way that will lead **sentient beings** to full maturity.

It is also the fourth of the **five constant virtues** of **Confucianism**. In the *Great Calming and Contemplation*, **Zhiyi** wrote, "To have clear and sharp knowledge like a mirror, to be straightforward in your actions, and to act in accordance with the principles of the path, corresponds to the fifth precept to abstain from consuming intoxicants." (CSQI, p. 1042 adapted)

knowledges, subtlety of: (J. chi-myō; 智妙) The second of the **ten subtleties of the Trace Gate** described in the *Profound Meaning of the Lotus Sutra*. It refers to the various deepening kinds of **knowledge** that are as subtle as their objects and ultimately beyond **conceptual proliferation**. (FTP, p. 207; PMLS2, p. 93, 132-169)

Kobo, Great Master: (J. Kōbō Daishi; 弘法 大師) See **Kukai**.

Kofukuji Temple: (J. Kōfukuji; 興福寺) Originally known as **Yamashina-dera Temple**. One of the **seven major temples in Nara**. A major temple of the **Dharma Characteristics school**.

Kojo: (779-858; J. Kōjō; 光定) A **monk** of the Japanese **Tiantai school** in the early Heian period known also as **Great Master** Betto (J. Bettō Daishi; 別当 大師). At the age of twenty, he became a disciple of **Saicho**, studying the teachings of the Tiantai school, but he also studied Eastern Temple Esotericism from **Kukai**. Following the wish of Saicho, Kojo worked hard to establish the Mahayana Precept Platform on Mt. **Hiei**, for which an imperial permission was granted seven days after Saicho's death.

He is referred to in **Nichiren Shonin**'s writings as having received esoteric teachings from Kukai and transmitting it to **Enchin**. Nichiren Shonin, however, is mute about Kojo's effort for the establishment of the Mahayana Precept Platform.

Komatsubara Persecution: (J. Komatsubara-no-hōnan; 小松原の法難) On November 11, 1264, **Nichiren Shonin** and his disciples were invited to the home of Kudo Yoshitaka, the steward of Amatsu. On the way, they were ambushed by Tojo Kagenobu and his men in a place called Komatsubara, or the Pine Forest. Hearing of the ambush, Kudo Yoshitaka rushed to the rescue with his own forces. In the ensuing skirmish, both Kudo Yoshitaka and Tojo Kagenobu received mortal wounds. Another one of Nichiren Shonin's disciples was also killed, and two more were seriously wounded. Nichiren Shonin himself barely escaped with his life, having received a blow to the head. This was the third of the four major persecutions. (WNS3, p. 145; WNS5, p. 118)

koti: (S. koṭi; J. kutei; 倶胝) The Sanskrit term *koṭi* refers to the end or limit of a large number, such as a crore, or ten million.

Ku: (J. Koku; 嚳) A legendary emperor who is sometimes said to have been the great-grandson of the Yellow Emperor, a grandson of **Shaohao**, and a cousin of **Zhuanxu**. Ku was the third emperor of the **Three Sovereigns and Five Emperors**.

Kuiji: (632-682; J. Kiki; 窺基) Also known as the **Great Master Ci'en**, he founded the **Dharma Characteristics school** in China and is considered its first patriarch. He was one of the disciples of **Xuanzang**, with whom he translated Buddhist **sutra**s and treatises including the ***Demonstration of Consciousness-Only Treatise***. He also wrote commentaries such as the *Praising the Profundity of the Lotus Sutra*, *Praising the Profundity of the Heart Sutra*, and the ***Chapters on the Forest of Meanings of the Dharma Garden of the Mahayana***.

Nichiren Shonin criticized him for admiring the *Lotus Sutra* while continuing to insist that the **One Vehicle** teaching was only a **skillful means**. Nichiren Shonin also said that Kuiji inwardly subjected himself to **Zhiyi** but not externally or publicly.

Kukai: (774-835; J. Kūkai; 空海) Founder of the **Mantra school**, which is known as the Shingon Shu in Japan, he is also known as the **Great Master Kobo**. He is considered the eighth patriarch of the Shingon Shu.

Kukai was born into Japanese nobility in Sanuki Province on Shikoku. At the age of eighteen he entered the imperial university to study **Confucianism** to prepare for a career as a government official. However, he soon dropped out and become a self-ordained **monk**. He retreated into the mountains to practice a ritual for acquiring good memory that involved the recitation of the **mantra** of Space Repository **Bodhisattva** that he was taught by Gonso. It was this practice that apparently whetted the appetite of the young Kukai for esoteric Buddhism. He was ordained as a monk by Gonso in 793 and was able to receive the higher ordination at Todaiji Temple the following year. In 804, he was able to get officially ordained and assigned to travel to Tang China as part of an official delegation. One of the other members of that delegation was **Saicho**. In the capital, Chang'an, he met Huiguo and became his disciple. Huiguo was apparently very impressed by Kukai and gave him initiation and transmission of the practices relating to both the

Womb-realm mandala and the **Diamond-realm** mandala. Though Huiguo died in the twelfth month of 805, Kukai was able to study with other teachers of esoteric Buddhism in China, such as Prajna, and collect many texts and ritual implements. He returned to Japan in 806 as an **acharya** of the Mantra school to begin propagating its teachings and practices. Kukai received the patronage and friendship of Emperor Saga (r. 809-823). His base of operations was Takaosanji Temple in the suburbs of Kyoto where he stayed until 823. From 810-813 he was also appointed the administrative head of the prestigious Todaiji Temple in Nara. In 816 he was given permission by the imperial court to establish a temple on Mt. Koya, this became Kongobuji Temple. In 823, **Toji Temple** was given to Kukai by Emperor Saga in 823 as a practice center of the Mantra school.

Saicho and Kukai may have first met when they were traveling to China together in 804, but they may have only met after their return to Japan in 809 or 810. For many years Saicho and Kukai were friends. When he had returned to Japan, Saicho had even performed esoteric initiations at the request of the imperial court in 805 and he was eager to learn more about esoteric Buddhism. In 809, Kukai had gone to Mt. **Hiei** to learn about the teachings of the **Tiantai school** from Saicho. In turn, Saicho borrowed texts from Kukai and even received esoteric initiations from him into the practices of the Womb-realm mandala and Diamond-realm mandala in 812 at the Takaosanji Temple. Unfortunately, their relationship soured in later years, as one of Saicho's disciples defected to the Mantra school and Kukai refused to lend texts he had requested and insisted that Saicho become his disciple if he wished to study Mantra teachings. They also had fundamental disagreements over the relative importance of the *Lotus Sutra* and esoteric Buddhism. Not surprisingly, Kukai compared the *Lotus Sutra* and Tiantai teachings unfavorably with the Mantra sutras, teachings, and practices. By 816, the two monks were no longer corresponding with each other.

The esoteric initiations performed by Kukai at Takaosanji in 812 for Saicho and almost two hundred leading monks and nobles of Nara established Kukai as the master of esoteric Buddhism in Japan. In 816, Kukai requested and was granted permission to establish a training center on Mt. Koya. Actual construction did not begin until 819 and it would not be completed until after Kukai's death. In 823, Kukai was appointed the head of Toji Temple in the new imperial capital of Kyoto that was still under construction. Up until that time, the temples in the capital did not belong to a single school of Buddhism, but the Toji became the headquarters of Mantra Buddhism during Kukai's lifetime, and in later times the Shingon Shu version of esotericism would be called Eastern Temple Esotericism in reference to the Toji Temple. When Emperor Saga retired, Kukai continued to receive the patronage of the two subsequent emperors. Unlike Saicho, Kukai also became popular among the monks of the other schools of Nara Buddhism and he rose high in the ranks of the state-controlled Buddhist bureaucracy. In 834 he was given permission to establish a chapel in the imperial palace where esoteric rites for the peace and security of the nation were held for a week in the beginning of each year following a week of Shinto rites. In 835 the Mantra school was officially recognized as a state sponsored school of Buddhism alongside the **six schools of Nara Buddhism** and the Japanese Tiantai school. Two months later, Kukai passed away on Mt. Koya, though the Mantra school maintains that he has actually entered a state of **samadhi** and that he still lives on Mt. Koya.

Kukai wrote such treatises as *Ten Abiding States of Mind Treatise*, **Distinguishing the Two Teaching of the Exoteric and Esoteric Treatise**, and the *Precious Key to the Secret Treasury* that advocated the superiority of the Mantra teachings for **attaining buddhahood with one's present body**. He also wrote *Secret Key to the Heart Sutra* and the *Annotations on the Peacock Sutra*.

Nichiren Shonin harshly criticized Kukai for ignoring the golden words of **Shakyamuni Buddha** in the ***Lotus Sutra*** by ranking the *Lotus Sutra* below the ***Mahavairochana Sutra***.

Kumarajiva: (344-413; S. Kumārajīva; J. Kumarajū or Rajū; 鳩摩羅什 or 羅什) The famed scholar and translator of Buddhist **sutra**s and treatises in China. He was given the title "**tripitaka master**." He was the son of a princess and a minister named Kumarayana in the city state named Kucha, which was located at an oasis in the northern periphery of the Tarim Basin, far west of China. When he was seven years old, his mother became a **nun** and he became a novice. When he was nine, his mother took him to Kashmir so he could study the **Agama sutras**. When he was twelve, they returned to Kucha and on the way stayed for a year in Kashgar where he studied the six feet of the main treatise of the Sarvastivada with Buddhayashas. Back in Kucha, he is said to have studied the ***Lotus Sutra***, the ***Larger Prajna Sutra***, and the teachings of **Nagarjuna** and **Aryadeva** from Shuryasoma. At the age of twenty he became a **monk**, according to the rule of the *Ten Recitations Discipline*, the **vinaya** of the Sarvastivada.

In 383, General Lü Guang (337-400) conquered Kucha for Emperor Fu Jian (337-385) of the Former Qin dynasty. He was returning with Kumarajiva as a prize of war for the emperor when the Former Qin dynasty began to collapse in 384. By 386, General Lü Guang had taken over Liang Province and declared the establishment of the Later Liang dynasty. During his time as a captive in Liang Province, Kumarajiva learned Chinese. Yaoxing (366-416), the emperor of the Later Qin dynasty that had replaced the Former Qin, sent an army to Liang Province in 401 and was able to retrieve Kumarajiva and bring him back to Chang'an.

In Chang'an, Kumarajiva translated into Chinese seventy-four sutras and commentaries into three hundred and eighty-four fascicles, including *Heart Sutra* around 400, the *Diamond Sutra* and *All Dharmas as Indeterminable Sutra* in 401, the *Questions of Brahma Excellent Thought Sutra* in 402, the **Great Perfection of Wisdom Treatise** between 402 and 406, the *Larger Prajna Sutra* in 404, the *One Hundred Verse Treatise* in 404, the **Exegesis on the Ten Grounds Treatise** and the *Buddha Repository Sutra* in 405, the *Lotus Sutra* and the **Vimalakirti Sutra** in 406, the *Smaller Prajna Sutra* in 408, and the *Middle Way Treatise* and the *Twelve Gates Treatise* in 409. The excellence of his translation of the *Lotus Sutra* is especially recognized. Between 404 and 409 he collaborated with Punyatara and Dharmaruchi to translate the *Ten Recitations Discipline*. Between 411 and 412 he translated the *Completion of Reality Treatise*. He also translated the **Amitayus Buddha Sutra**. His disciples are said to have numbered more than three thousand.

Nichiren Shonin thought of him very highly and respected him for laying the foundation of the **Tiantai Lotus school** of Buddhism.

Kumarata: (c. third century; S. Kumārata or Kumāralāta or Kumāralabdha; J. Kumarada or Kumarata; 鳩摩羅馱 or 鳩摩邏多) A **monk** from Takshashila who is alleged to have established the Sautrantika school and to have been the teacher of Harivarman. **Xuanzang** called him one of the "four brilliant suns illuminating the world" along with **Ashvaghosha**, **Aryadeva**, and **Nagarjuna**.

In the *Transmission of the Dharma Treasury Sutra*, Kumarata was the successor of Samghayashas in the list of **twenty-three** or **twenty-four successors** or patriarchs after **Shakyamuni Buddha**.

kundoku: (J.; 訓読) The Japanese term *kundoku* means "understandable chanting." This is the way of chanting the *Lotus Sutra* in the vernacular, as opposed to the Sino-Japanese or *shindoku* reading. The word, however, particularly connotes chanting the sutra in the written style of Meiji period Japanese. This was begun by Udana Nichiki.

kusha grass: (S. kuśa; J. kichijō-sō; 吉祥草) A type of grass in India that was woven into mats that could be sat on for meditation practice.

Lankavatara Sutra: (S. *Laṅkāvatāra-sūtra*; *Nyū-ryōga-kyō* or *Ryōga-kyō*; 入楞伽経 or 楞伽経) A later **Mahayana sutra** written around the fourth century. It was translated by Gundabhadra in 443. It teaches about the **storehouse consciousness** and **buddha-nature**. **Bodhidharma**, the first patriarch of the **Zen school** of Buddhism in China, is credited with having brought it to China, despite the claim of Zen that the truth is not transmitted through words or language.

Larger Prajna Sutra: (S. *Pañcaviṃśatisāhasrikā-prajñāpāramitā-sūtra*; J. *Daibon-hannya-kyō*; 大品般若経) The Sanskrit *Pañcaviṃśatisāhasrikā-prajñāpāramitā-sūtra* can be translated as the *Sutra of the Perfection of Wisdom in Twenty-five Thousand Lines*. It can also be called the *Mahaprajna Paramita Sutra*. This sutra teaches the **Mahayana** doctrines of **emptiness** and the practice of the **bodhisattva vehicle**. It was translated into Chinese in ninety chapters by **Kumarajiva** in 404.

The *Great Perfection of Wisdom Treatise* is a commentary on this sutra attributed to **Nagarjuna**.

Latter Age of Degeneration: (J. mappō-ji or masse or matsudai; 末法時 or 末世 or 末代) Or Latter Age of the **Dharma**. One of the **three ages of the Dharma** after the passing of **Shakyamuni Buddha**. This is the period of degeneration which starts two thousand years after the Buddha's passing (or the **fifth five-hundred-year period**). During this period, nobody can achieve **awakening**, no matter how hard they study and practice, because the true spirit of the Dharma is completely lost and all that is left is sectarianism and bickering. The idea of the "latter age" appeared around the sixth century in India; in China, it occurred during the Sui and Tang dynasties (589-907); and in Japan, during the Heian and Kamakuran periods (793-1333). **Honen** and **Nichiren Shonin** were both influenced by it. Nichiren Shonin tried to save people in the Latter Age by putting **faith** in the *Lotus Sutra* and chanting the **daimoku** of **Namu Myoho Renge Kyo**.

layman: (S. upāsaka; J. ubasoku; 優婆塞) A Buddhist layman is a male who has taken the **threefold refuge** and, in many schools of Buddhism, also undergone the "ceremony of bestowing the precepts," wherein they receive the **five precepts** as **training rule**s.

laywoman: (S. upāsikā; J. ubai; 優婆夷) A Buddhist laywoman is a female who has taken the **threefold refuge** and, in many schools of Buddhism, also undergone the "ceremony of bestowing the precepts," wherein they receive the **five precepts** as **training rule**s.

leaving home: (S. pravrajita or pravajyā; J. shukke; 出家) The Sanskrit term *pravrajita* literally means "going forth," and is part of a longer phrase that means "going forth from the household life." The ideograms 出家 simply mean "leaving home." This term refers to one of the **eight phases of a buddha's life**, when the **bodhisattva** leaves home to become a **shramana** in order to practice asceticism and achieve **liberation** from **suffering**. The term "leaving home" is also used to refer to the "lower ordination" of a novice. The novice ordination is also called the "ceremony for bestowing the precepts for leaving home to **attain enlightenment**."

Liangxu: (c. ninth century; C.; J. Ryōjo; 良諝) A Chinese **monk** of the **Tiantai school** who was the teacher of **Enchin**.

liberation: (S. mokṣa or vimokṣa or vimukti; J. gedatsu; 解脱) The Sanskrit terms *mokṣa, vimokṣa,* and *vimukti* can all also be translated as "deliverance," "emancipation," or "freedom." They are synonyms for attaining **nirvana**, and they all refer to liberation from bondage to **samsara**.

life force: (S. jīvitendriya; J. myō-kon; 命根) The Sanskrit term *jīvitendriya* can also be translated as "life faculty." It is the support of warmth and **consciousness**. Its duration is affected by the **action**s of previous lives.

Light: (S. Raśmiprabhāsa; J. Kōmyō; 光明) The name of the **buddha** that **Mahakashyapa** will become, according to the sixth, "Assurance of Future Buddhahood," chapter of the *Lotus Sutra*.

Limitless Practice: (S. Anantacāritra; J. Muhengyō; 無辺行) One of the **four great bodhisattvas** who are the four leaders of the **bodhisattvas appearing from underground** described in the fifteenth, "The **Appearance of Bodhisattvas from Underground**," **chapter** of the *Lotus Sutra* who were guided by the **Original Buddha** since the remotest past and entrusted with the task of spreading the *Lotus Sutra* in the **Latter Age of Degeneration**.

This bodhisattva represents the **eternity** that is the unborn and deathless **nature** of **nirvana**.

lion seat: (S. siṃhāsana; J. shishi-za; 師子座 or 獅子座) A term for the seat or preaching platform of a **buddha**.

Lord of Mysteries: (S. Guhyakādhipatiḥ; J. Himitsushu; 祕密主) See **Vajrasattva**.

lotus flower: (S. puṇḍarīka; renge; 蓮華) The lotus flower as a symbol of the **Wonderful Dharma** that encompasses the **true teaching** and **provisional teaching** is explained in the *Profound Meaning of the Lotus Sutra*. (PMLS2, pp. 380-386)

Lotus Sutra: (S. *Saddharma-puṇḍarīka-sūtra*; J. *Myōhō-renge-kyō* or *Hoke-kyō*; 妙法蓮華経 or 法華経) It's full title in English would be *Sutra of the Lotus Flower of the Wonderful Dharma*. It was translated by **Kumarajiva** in eight fascicles (originally seven) in 406. There exist two other Chinese translations of the sutra: the *Flowering of the True Dharma Sutra* translated by Dharmaraksha in ten fascicles in 286 and the *Supplemented Lotus Sutra* translated by Dharmagupta in seven fascicles in 601. Lost Chinese translations include the *Saddharma Pundarika Sutra* and the *Lotus Samadhi Sutra*.

According to **Zhiyi**, the first half of Kumarajiva's version of the *Lotus Sutra* is called the **Trace Gate** with the second, **"Expedients,"** **chapter** at its core, teaching that the three vehicles are expedient, but the One Vehicle is the truth. The latter half of the sutra is called the **Original Gate**, with the sixteenth, "The **Duration of the Life of the Tathagata," chapter** as its core, teaching **Shakyamuni Buddha**'s **attainment of buddhahood in the remotest past**. It reveals that this **Saha world** is the eternal, imperishable **pure land** (or the Pure Land of Eternally Tranquil Light) wherein the **Eternal Shakyamuni Buddha** is always trying to enable all **sentient being**s to **attain buddhahood**.

While Zhiyi formulated his doctrine based on the Trace Gate, **Nichiren Shonin** formulated his doctrine and faith based on the Original Gate and promulgated the **daimoku** of **Namu Myoho Renge Kyo**.

Lotus Sutra Treatise: (S. *Saddharma-puṇḍarīka-upadeśa; J. Hokke-ron or Hokekyō-ron; 法華論 or 法華経論) A commentary on the *Lotus Sutra* attributed to **Vasubandhu**. Its full title would be the *Sutra of the Lotus Flower of the Wonderful Dharma Treatise*. It was translated by Bodhiruchi and Tanlin (d.u.) and by Ratnamati and Senglang.

Nichiren Shonin states that there were discrepancies between this treatise and **Kumarajiva**'s translation of the *Lotus Sutra*. (WNS1, p. 21, p. 71) He also believed that Bodhiruchi's translation was not trustworthy. (WNS1, p. 71)

Lotus Treasury World: (J. Rengezō-sekai or Kezō-sekai; 蓮華蔵世界 or 華蔵世界) The **pure land** of **Vairochana Buddha**.

Lotus-Nirvana period: (J. Hokke-nehan-ji; 法華涅槃時) The fifth of the **five periods**. This period encompassed the last eight years of the life of **Shakyamuni Buddha**. During this period, he taught only the unadulterated **perfect teaching** in the *Lotus Sutra* and reiterated it in the *Nirvana Sutra*, so this period only has the subtle teaching. This period is a return to the Buddha's own understanding, but now all those who heard the sudden and gradual teachings are also able to understand and **attain buddhahood** through the **One Vehicle teaching**. This period is compared to the **flavor of ghee**.

Nichiren Shonin argued that the teachings of this period would persist for immeasurable centuries even during the **Latter Age of Degeneration**. (WNS1, p. 27)

loving-kindness: (S. maitrī; J. ji; 慈) In Buddhism, loving-kindness means to have empathy and to wish that other **sentient being**s be well and happy.

Madhava: (S. Mādhava; J. Matōba; 摩沓婆) An adherent of **non-Buddhist teachings**. A story is told in **Xuanzang**'s *Record of the Western Regions of the Great Tang* about the **monk** Gunamati (c. sixth century; S. Guṇamati; J. Tokue; 徳慧) of the **Consciounsess-Only school** who bested Madhava in debate and thereby converted the king of **Magadha** to Buddhism.

Nichiren Shonin compared his own refutation of the **Pure Land school** to Gunamati's refutation of Madhva. (WNS5, p. 61)

Madhyantika: (S. Madhyāntika; J. Madendai or Madenji; 末田提 or 末田地) In the *Transmission of the Dharma Treasury Sutra*, Madhyantika and Shanavasa were the successors of **Ananda** in the list of **twenty-four successors** or patriarchs after **Shakyamuni Buddha**. Madhyantika is not counted in the list of twenty-three successors.

Magadha: (J. Makada-koku; 摩掲陀国 / 摩訶陀国) One of the sixteen major countries in India at the time of **Shakyamuni Buddha**, located in the southern part of Bihar state today. The Buddha attained **unsurpassed, complete, and perfect awakening** under the **Bodhi tree** by the Nairanjana River in this kingdom, the capital of which, Rajagriha, was the center of the Buddha's missionary activities. Mount **Sacred Eagle**, where the *Lotus Sutra* was taught, is located northeast of Rajagriha. It became the location of Nalanda, which was a very influential Buddhist monastic university.

Mahakashyapa: (S. Mahākāśyapa; J. Makakashō or Daikashō or Kashō; 摩訶迦葉 or 大迦葉 or 迦葉) One of the **ten great disciples** of **Shakyamuni Buddha**, Mahakashyapa was known as the foremost practitioner of those forms of asceticism allowed by the Buddha called the *dhuta*.

Mahakashyapa grew up in a **brahmin** family near Rajagriha, the capital of the kingdom of **Magadha** in central India. His father was very wealthy and owned a large estate encompassing sixteen villages. Despite growing up in luxury - or perhaps because of it - Mahakashyapa wished to renounce the world and live a simple life in search of **liberation** from **suffering**. His parents insisted that he marry, so he reluctantly agreed. However, he commissioned an artist to cast a golden statue based on his idea of what a perfectly beautiful woman should look like. He demanded his parents choose a wife for him who looked exactly like the statue. Of course, he never imagined they would find a woman to match the statue, but to his dismay they succeeded.

The woman they found, Bhadra Kapilani, also wished to leave the home life. In fact, she and Mahakashyapa had deep **karmic** affinities for each other due to having spent many past lives together perfecting virtue and seeking **liberation**.

They ended up being a good match for each other due to their shared aspiration. Not long after Mahakashyapa's parents passed away and he inherited their estate, the couple agreed that the time had finally come when they could both leave the home life and take to the road as **shramana**, homeless wanderers striving for liberation. To prevent a scandal, they agreed to part company and take different roads.

Bhadra Kapilani ended up going to **Shravasti**, the capital of Koshala. There she stayed with an order of non-Buddhist **nun**s near the Jeta Grove Monastery. When the Buddha agreed to create an order of nuns at the urging of **Ananda** on behalf of **Yashodhara**, the Buddha's former wife, and **Mahaprajapati**, the Buddha's aunt and foster mother, Bhadra Kapilani became a Buddhist nun. Soon thereafter, Bhadra Kapilani became an **arhat**. She became known as the foremost among the nuns for recalling past lives, many of which were spent as the wife of Mahakashyapa as noted above. Bhadra Kapilani was also known for her **patience**[1] and **compassion** and was a popular teacher of the **Dharma**.

Mahakashyapa ended up meeting the Buddha on the road. The Buddha was sitting beneath a banyan tree emitting rays of light. Mahakashyapa saw this and recognized the **thirty-two marks** of a **great man**. He immediately went up to him and declared that he would be his disciple. The Buddha responded by saying that any unawakened person who presumed to explain **awakening** in the presence of someone as perceptive and sincere as Mahakashyapa would have their head split into seven pieces. The Buddha then gave him a brief teaching and accepted him as a disciple. Mahakashyapa then folded his outer robe and gave it to the Buddha to use as a seat. The Buddha remarked upon the softness of the robe and Mahakashyapa promptly asked the Buddha to keep it. In return, Shakyamuni Buddha offered his own ragged robe that had come from a cremation ground. Mahakashyapa received it joyfully. This was the only time that Shakyamuni Buddha ever exchanged robes with a disciple.

From that time on Mahakashyapa took up the *dhuta*, the various ascetic disciplines sanctioned by the Buddha for those who wished to strengthen their self-discipline and live as simply as possible. These disciplines included wearing only cast-off rags instead of donated robes, eating only by begging door-to-door instead of accepting invitations to dinner, eating only once a day, sleeping only outdoors, and other such practices that were austere but not harmful in sub-tropical India. Mahakashyapa was declared by the Buddha to be the foremost practitioner of the *dhuta*.

Mahakashyapa was traveling to Kushinagara with many other **monk**s when the Buddha passed away. Mahakashyapa and the other arhats were not upset, but many of the unawakened monks were overcome with grief. One monk, however, was actually happy because he assumed that they would now be able to do as they pleased. Mahakashyapa and the monks continued to Kushinagara where they paid homage to the Buddha one last time. After Mahakashyapa finished paying homage, the funeral pyre spontaneously burst into flames.

After the funeral, Mahakashyapa thought of the monk who had hoped to cast off all restraint after the Buddha's death. Mindful that others might have similar reactions, Mahakashyapa gathered and presided over the first of the Buddhist Councils in order to preserve the **Buddha Dharma** by memorizing the Buddha's discourses (the **sutra**s) and discipline for the monastics (the **vinaya**).

In the *Transmission of the Dharma Treasury Sutra*, Mahakashyapa is the first of the **twenty-three** or **twenty-four successors** or patriarchs after Shakyamuni Buddha. His successor was **Ananda**. Eventually the story arose that Shakyamuni Buddha transmitted the Buddha Dharma to Mahakashyapa when the former twirled a flower before an assembly and only Mahakashyapa smiled in understanding, whereupon the Buddha said, "I have the treasury of the eye of the True Dharma, the wonderful mind of **nirvana**, which I entrust Mahakashyapa. Propagate it throughout the future, never letting it be cut off." This story is related as the sixth case of the koan collection called *The Gateless Gate*.

He is one of the arhats listed as present in the assembly in the first, "Introductory," chapter of the *Lotus Sutra*. Mahakashyapa, along with **Subhuti**, **Mahakatyayana**, and **Maudgalyayana** all express their joy at hearing the teaching of the **One Vehicle** in chapter four, "Understanding by Faith." These four disciples then tell the parable of the wealthy man and his poor son. In chapter five, "The Simile of Herbs," the Buddha addresses the parable of the three kinds of medicinal herbs and two kinds of trees to these four disciples. In chapter six, "Assurance of Future Buddhahood," the Buddha gives the assurance of future buddhahood to these four beginning with Mahakashyapa, who he announces will become a buddha named **Light** in the world of Light Virtue.

Nichiren Shonin pointed to Mahakashyapa's future buddhahood as an example of **attainment of buddhahood by adherents of the two vehicles**, stressing the superiority of the *Lotus Sutra* over all other sutras.

Mahakatyayana: (S. Mahākātyāyana or Kātyāyana; J. Makakasennen or Daikasennen or Kasennen; 摩訶迦旃延 or 大迦旃延 or 迦旃延) Also known simply as Katyayana. One of the **ten great disciples** of **Shakyamuni Buddha**.

He is one of the **arhat**s listed as present in the assembly in the first, "Introductory," chapter of the *Lotus Sutra*. Mahakatyayana, along with **Mahakashyapa**, **Subhuti**, and **Maudgalyayana** all express their joy at hearing the teaching of the One Vehicle in the fourth, "Understanding by Faith," chapter. These four disciples then tell the parable of the wealthy man and his poor son. In chapter five, "The Simile of Herbs," the Buddha addresses the parable of the three kinds of medicinal herbs and two kinds of trees to these four disciples. In chapter six, "Assurance of Future Buddhahood," the Buddha gives the assurance of future buddhahood to these four, at which time he announces that Mahakatyayana will become a buddha named Jambunada Gold Light.

Mahaprajapati: (S. Mahāprajāpatī; J. Makahajahadai; 摩訶波闍波提) Aunt and foster mother of **Shakyamuni Buddha**. She was also called Gautami or the Lady of the **Gautama** family.

When Shakyamuni's mother, Maya, passed away seven days after giving birth to him, her younger sister Mahaprajapati, married his father, King **Shuddhodana** of Kapilavastu, and raised him.

After the passing of King Shuddhodana, Mahaprajapati together with **Yashodara** (mother of **Rahula**) entered the Buddhist **Sangha**, becoming the first **nun**s.

She is one of the nuns listed as present in the assembly in the first, "Introductory," chapter of the *Lotus Sutra*. In the thirteenth chapter, **"Encouragement for Keeping This Sutra,"** she receives the assurance of future buddhahood by Shakyamuni Buddha and told that she will become a buddha named **Gladly Seen by All Beings**[1]. That buddha will in turn give the assurance of future buddhahood to the six thousand nuns who were her attendants.

mahasattva: (S. mahāsattva; J. makasatsu or daishi; 摩訶薩 or 大士) The Sanskrit term *mahāsattva* means "great being." This term is sometimes applied to the **bodhisattva**s, especially to the "celestial" or extremely advanced bodhisattvas.

Mahavairochana: (S. Mahāvairocana; J. Dainichi; 大日) The Sanskrit name Mahāvairocana means "Great Illuminator" or "Greatly Resplendent," though the ideograms 大日 literally mean "Great Sun." This **buddha** is an indispensable focus of devotion in **esoteric Buddhism**. He is defined as the **Dharma-body**, in which the truth of the whole universe is contained. It is claimed in esoteric Buddhism that this buddha is the fundamental buddha from which all other buddhas emerge.

In Tendai Esotericism the buddhas Mahavairochana and **Shakyamuni** are identical, while in Eastern Temple Esotericism of the **Mantra school** they are regarded as different buddhas, Mahavairochana of the Dharma-body being superior to Shakyamuni Buddha of the **accommodative-body**.

In the Mantra school, Mahavairochana Buddha is considered the first patriarch, who transmitted the teachings of esoteric Buddhism to the second patriarch **Vajrasattva**.

In the *Lotus Sutra Rite* translated by **Amoghavajra**, **Many Treasures** Buddha is attended by the Mahavairochana Buddha of the **Diamond-realm mandala** and the Mahavairochana Buddha of the **Womb-realm** mandala. (WNS3, pp. 28-29; WNS4, pp. 52-53)

Nichiren Shonin, from the viewpoint of the supremacy of the *Lotus Sutra*, regarded Mahavairochana Buddha as subordinate to the Original and **Eternal Shakyamuni Buddha** revealed in the sixteenth, "The **Duration of the Life of the Tathagata**," chapter of the *Lotus Sutra*. He also pointed out the unhistorical nature of Mahavairochana Buddha and criticized the Mantra school for claiming that he appeared beside Shakyamuni Buddha to expound the esoteric **sutra**s.

Mahavairochana Sutra: (S. *Mahāvairocana-sūtra* or *Vairocanābhisaṃbodhi-sūtra;* J. *Dainichi-kyō* or *Daibirushana-jōbutsu-jinben-kajikyō* ; 大日経 or 大毘盧遮那成仏神変変加持経) An influential **sutra** of **esoteric Buddhism** in East Asia that came into existence in the early seventh century of the common era as a type of *caryā* tantra. Together with the ***Diamond Peak Sutra*** and the *Act of Perfection Sutra*, this sutra is regarded as one of the three Mantra sutras taught by **Mahavairochana Buddha**, not by **Shakyamuni** Buddha. The esoteric teachings that had been spread in the form of fragmentary spells were organized in this sutra so that a practitioner can **attain buddhahood**, exerting a strong influence upon the development of esotericism in China and Japan. It was translated by **Shubhakarasimha** and his disciple **Yixing** into Chinese between 724 and 725 in seven fascicles.

In the sutra, Mahavairochana Buddha is the **Dharma-body** teaching **Vajrasattva** the doctrine of **attaining buddhahood with one's present body** through coordinated practices of the **three mysteries** of body, mouth, and mind using **mudra**s, **mantra**s, and **mandala**s.

According to **Zhiyi**'s doctrine of the **five periods**, **Nichiren Shonin** relegates this sutra to the status of a **provisional sutra** taught during the third or **Expanded period**.

Mahayana: (S. Mahāyāna; J. Daijō; 大乗) The Sanskrit term *mahāyāna* can be translated as "great vehicle," in contrast to the **hinayana** or "lesser vehicle." It is one of the two major streams of Buddhism. Doctrines leading people to **awakening** were likened to vehicles. A Great vehicle is a large and superior means of transportation in which not only the practitioners themselves, but also many others, are carried to the "other shore" of **liberation**; while a small vehicle is inferior because it only allows a single person to attain the "other shore" of self-liberation.

Nichiren Shonin, following the comparative classification of doctrines of the **Tiantai school**, regarded the **Agama sutras** of the **Deer Park period** of the **five periods** as hinayana and sutras taught during the **Flower Garland**, **Expanded**, **Prajna**, and **Lotus-Nirvana period**s as Mahayana. He also declared that the true Mahayana teaching is the **Original Gate** section of the ***Lotus Sutra*** alone, considering all the **prior teachings** as hinayana. (WNS1, pp. 13-14)

mahoraga: (S. mahorāga; J. magoraga; 摩睺羅伽) The mahoragas are large serpents that dwell beneath the earth whose movements cause earthquakes. Though intelligent and extremely powerful, they are classified as **animal**s among the **six destinies**. They are one of the **eight kinds of supernatural beings**.

Maitreya: (J. Miroku; 弥勒) Also called **Ajita** or the Loving One. A **bodhisattva** who is said to be the next **buddha** in the future, long after the disappearance of the **dispensation** of the historical **Shakyamuni** Buddha. It is believed that he resides in the Heaven of **Tushita** for five hundred and seventy-six million years before being reborn in the **Saha world** to save those who had not been saved by Shakyamuni Buddha. (See Sadakata, fn. 11, pp. 201-204)

Maitreya Bodhisattva is the only bodhisattva who is revered in both mainstream Buddhism and **Mahayana** Buddhism aside from **Siddhartha Gautama** and his past lives before becoming Shakyamuni Buddha. His advent is predicted in the Pali canon (e.g. LD 26.25, pp. 403-404) as well as in the Mahayana **sutra**s. From as early as the first century, Indian Buddhists began to aspire to be reborn in the Tushita Heaven in the presence of Maitreya Bodhisattva with the hope that they could be reborn as his disciples when he became Maitreya Buddha. The cult of Maitreya spread throughout East Asia and later into Tibet.

There is a Mahayana legend that when the first Buddhist council was compiling the **three baskets** of the **hinayana** teachings, Maitreya and others were compiling the Mahayana sutras in the Encircling Iron Mountains. (EET. Pruden, p. 9)

Until his advent as the next buddha, it is believed that Maitreya Bodhisattva makes his appearance in this world to help **suffering sentient being**s and to propagate the **Buddha Dharma**. For instance, **Asanga**, the fourth century co-founder of the **Consciousness-Only** school of Mahayana Buddhism, was allegedly taught by a **monk** named **Maitreyanatha** who was allegedly an appearance of Maitreya Bodhisattva.

A particularly popular manifestation of Maitreya Bodhisattva is the jovial monk often shown with a hemp sack full of goodies for children, known as the "Fat Buddha" or the "Laughing Buddha." This image was inspired by a legendary tenth century monk named Budai, who came to be viewed as an appearance of Maitreya Bodhisattva.

Maitreya Bodhisattva appears among the eighty thousand bodhisattvas present in the assembly in the first, "Introductory," chapter of the ***Lotus Sutra***. In that chapter, he inquires of **Manjushri** Bodhisattva the reason for the ray of light emitted by Shakyamuni Buddha. Manjushri Bodhisattva says that, based on his experiences in previous lives with other buddhas, he surmises that Shakyamuni Buddha is also about to teach the *Lotus Sutra*.

Maitreya Bodhisattva has an important role in the Assembly in Space as well. In chapter fifteen, "The **Appearance of Bodhisattvas from Underground**," he inquires as to the origin of the **bodhisattvas appearing from underground**. He also asks how Shakyamuni Buddha could be the teacher of these primordial bodhisattvas when his **attainment of awakening for the first time** was little more than forty years ago. This second question prompts the revelation of the **attainment of buddhahood in the remotest past** in chapter sixteen, "The **Duration of the Life of the Tathagata**." In that chapter, Maitreya Bodhisattva heads the assembly in declaring that they will faithfully receive the Buddha's answer. In chapters seventeen and eighteen, the Buddha addresses Maitreya Bodhisattva when explaining the boundless **merit**s of those who accept the teaching of the Buddha's unborn and deathless **nature** with **faith**.

The closing chapter of the *Lotus Sutra*, "Encouragement of Universal Sage Bodhisattva," refers to Maitreya Bodhisattva in a more favorable light than the first chapter. In that chapter, **Universal Sage** Bodhisattva states that those who read and understand the *Lotus Sutra* will be reborn in the Tushita Heaven with Maitreya Bodhisattva who already bears all the **thirty-two marks** of a buddha.

Nichiren Shonin's **Great Mandala of Invoking the Ten Realms** includes the name of Maitreya Bodhisattva to represent the **bodhisattvas of the trace teaching**.

Maitreyanatha: (c. 270-350; S. Maitreyanātha; J. Jison or Miroku; 慈尊 or 弥勒) The Sanskrit name Maitreyanātha means "Protector **Maitreya**" or "Protected by Maitreya." Maitreyanatha was **Asanga**'s teacher and supposedly an appearance of Maitreya **Bodhisattva**. He is credited with the authorship of the following five major treatises: *The Ornament of Clear Realization, Ornament for the Mahayana Sutras Treatise, Analysis of the Lineage of the Three Treasures, Differentiation of the Middle Way and the Extremes,* and *Differentiation of Dharmas and Dharma-nature*.

mandala: (S. maṇḍala; J. mandara; 曼荼羅) The Sanskrit term *maṇḍala* can also be translated as "circle." A mandala is therefore understood to be a "circle of blessings." A mandala is a diagram or painting used to focus the **mind** and express the ultimate truth. Originally the mandalas were platforms into which the initiate and the initiator would enter. In China, such platforms were not used, and the mandala became a painting instead, though the practitioner is still supposed to enter into them through contemplative union with the **buddha**s, **bodhisattva**s, and **guardian deities** represented in them.

The **concentration** of the mind on an esoteric object such as a mandala is one of the **three mysteries** (of body, mouth, and mind) by which **attaining buddhahood with one's present body** can be accomplished. The **Womb-realm** and **Diamond-realm** mandalas used in the **Mantra school** represent the realm of **Mahavairochana Buddha** and the five knowledge-tathagatas, bodhisattvas, and guardian deities who are his **emanation-bodies** and personifications of his **wisdom** and **merit**.

mani: (S. maṇi; J. mani or shu; 摩尼 or 珠) A magical jewel that can avert misfortune, cure disease, and make muddy waters clear. Also called the **wish-fulfilling gem**.

Manjushri: (S. Mañjuśrī; J. Monjushiri or Monju; 文殊師利 or 文殊) The name

Mañjuśrī can be translated as "Gentle Glory." He is also called "Gentle Voice." This **bodhisattva** represents the **wisdom** and **awakening** of the **Buddha**. He is especially associated with the **Prajna sutras** that he is often shown carrying, along with the sword of wisdom that cuts through **delusion**. Since the teaching of the **Buddha Dharma** is said to be like the lion's roar that nothing can withstand, Manjushri Bodhisattva is frequently shown as the left-hand attendant of **Shakyamuni** Buddha mounted on a lion. He and **Universal Sage** Bodhisattva are the bodhisattva attendants most often associated with Shakyamuni Buddha. He is also supposed to have been the disciple of Akshobhya Buddha.

Manjushri Bodhisattva appears in **Mahayana** sutras such as the *Vimalakirti Sutra*, the *Flower Garland Sutra*, and many others. Manjushri Bodhisattva is considered to be near equal to the Buddha. At times, he is even said to have already realized buddhahood, but he is still voluntarily acting in the capacity of a bodhisattva. Some sutras even call him the teacher of all the buddhas, which is the role he takes in the *Lotus Sutra*.

Manjushri Bodhisattva appears among the eighty thousand bodhisattvas present in the assembly in the first, "Introductory," chapter of the *Lotus Sutra*. In that chapter, he answers **Maitreya** Bodhisattva's questions about the ray of light emitted by Shakyamuni Buddha. He reveals that in a past life, when he was known as Wonderful Light Bodhisattva, he witnessed Sun Moon Light Buddha produce a ray of light just before teaching the *Lotus Sutra*, so he surmises that Shakyamuni Buddha is also about to teach the *Lotus Sutra*.

Manjushri Bodhisattva reappears in the middle of the twelfth, **"Devadatta" chapter**, from the palace of the **Dragon King** Sagara in the ocean where he had been teaching the *Lotus Sutra*. He introduces all the innumerable bodhisattvas that he taught, including the eight-year-old **dragon girl**. The dragon king's daughter then proceeds to demonstrate how to **attain buddhahood with one's present body**.

In the fourteenth, **"Peaceful Practices," chapter**, Manjushri Bodhisattva asks the Buddha how ordinary bodhisattvas should expound the *Lotus Sutra* in the evil world after the Buddha's **final nirvana**.

Finally, in the twenty-fourth, "Wonderful Voice Bodhisattva," chapter, it is Manjushri Bodhisattva who asks about the jeweled **lotus flower**s that float down from the sky to herald the arrival of Wonderful Voice Bodhisattva. He also asks the Buddha about the bodhisattva and asks to see him.

Based on a passage in the Chinese translation of the *Flower Garland Sutra*, Manjushri Bodhisattva is believed to have his earthly home on Mt. Wutai in China.

Nichiren Shonin's **Great Mandala of Invoking the Ten Realms** includes the name of Manjushri Bodhisattva to represent the **bodhisattvas of the trace teaching**.

mantra: (S.; J. shingon; 真言) The Sanskrit term *mantra* can also be translated as "charm," "invocation," "magic formula," or "spell." Mantras are used to invoke protective powers and the ultimate truth. They are believed to contain the **sustaining power** and **merit** of the **buddha, bodhisattva**, or **guardian deity** that they are associated with. Mantras contain Sanskrit **seed**-syllables that are the concentrated essence of the being they refer to. To recite a mantra and form **mudra** is to invoke the actual presence of a buddha, bodhisattva, or deity. It is also a form of **contemplation** of and identification with the buddha, bodhisattva, or deity. Mantras are one of the **three mysteries** (of body, mouth, and mind) by which **attaining buddhahood with one's present body** can be accomplished. In the **Mantra school**, mantras correspond to **Mahavairochana Buddha**'s words.

Mantra school: (J. Shingon-shū; 真言宗) One of the schools of Chinese Buddhism. According to the beliefs of the Mantra school, the transmission of **esoteric Buddhism** began when **Nagarjuna** opened an iron tower in India and encountered **Vajrasattva**, who transmitted to him the teachings of **Mahavairochana Buddha**. Nagarjuna then transmitted the teachings to his disciple Nagabodhi, who in turn transmitted them to **Shubhakarasimha** and **Vajrabodhi**. It was introduced to China when Shubhakarasimha came to China and translated the *Mahavairochana Sutra* with his disciple **Yixing** in 725. At some point they also translated the *Act of Perfection Sutra*. In 720, two more Indian masters of esoteric Buddhism came to China, Vajrabodhi and his disciple **Amoghavajra**. Amoghavajra translated the *Diamond Peak Sutra* in 746 and transmitted the Mantra teachings to Huiguo who in turn transmitted them to the Japanese monk **Kukai**.

Kukai had gone to China in 804 and returned to Japan in 806 whereupon he founded the Japanese Shingon Shu. He propagated its teachings at the Kongobuji Temple on Mt. Koya and the **Toji Temple** in Kyoto. The esoteric teachings and practices of the Shingon Shu are known in Japan as Eastern Temple Esotericism, in reference to the Toji Temple where it was propagated.

Shingon Shu's comparative classification of doctrines divides **Shakyamuni Buddha**'s teachings into the **ten stages of mind** to show the superiority of the practice of **esoteric Buddhism** over **exoteric Buddhism**.

This school teaches that Mahavairochana Buddha is the **awakened** nature of the **mind**s of **sentient being**s, and all the various deities are his attendant mental states. The active functions of buddhahood are the **three mysteries** of body, word, and thought: the gestures called **mudra**s, the recitation of **mantra**s, and the **concentration** of the mind. Mahavairochana Buddha is identical to the elements that encompass all **dharma**s and is the union of principle, represented by the **Womb-realm mandala**, and **wisdom**, represented by the **Diamond-realm mandala**. (EET, pp. 114-115) Through the practice of the three mysteries it is possible to **attain buddhahood with one's present body**.

Nichiren Shonin classifies this school, though it is superior to the other **Mahayana** schools, as a provisional Mahayana teaching that is **hinayana** or like an inferior medicine in comparison with *Lotus Sutra* and the **Tiantai school** because it relies upon the **prior teachings**. (WNS2, pp. 192, 252, 268; WNS3, pp. 19-21, 124,

153, 240-241; WNS5, p. 158; WNS6, p. 146)

Nichiren Shonin called both the Eastern Temple Esotericism and Tendai esotericism the Shingon Shu, or Mantra school. He frequently criticized the Mantra school, and in particular Yixing, Shubhakarasimha, Vajrabodhi, and Amoghavajra for plagiarizing the "**three-thousand realms in a single thought-moment**" doctrine of **Zhiyi** and putting it into the doctrine of his own school while criticizing the **Tiantai school**. (WNS2, pp. 19-21, 34-37, 78-79, 85; WNS4, p. 92; WNS5, pp. 79, 160)

From the viewpoint of the *Lotus Sutra* as the **True Dharma**, Nichiren Shonin severely criticized the Mantra school, which insisted on the superiority of the Mantra teachings and practices over the *Lotus Sutra* according to its doctrines of the "ten stages of mind" and the "superiority of esotericism over exotericism."

Many Treasures: (S. Prabhūtaratna; J. Tahō; 多宝) This **buddha** appears in the eleventh, "**Beholding the Stupa of Treasures**," **chapter** of the *Lotus Sutra* when he emerges from beneath the earth inside the **stupa of treasures** that ascends into the sky above Mt. **Sacred Eagle**. In that chapter, he testifies to the truth of what **Shakyamuni Buddha** had been expounding about the **One Buddha Vehicle**. Shakyamuni Buddha then tells the assembly that Many Treasures Buddha taught in the world **Treasure Purity** many ages ago. He made a **vow** that even after his **final nirvana** he would appear to testify to the truth of the *Lotus Sutra* if anyone should teach it after his passing.

Many Treasures Buddha also made a vow that he would allow his stupa to be opened to reveal his body if the buddha who teaches the *Lotus Sutra* recalls all his **emanation buddhas of the ten directions**. Shakyamuni Buddha proceeds to do this. He purifies the **Saha world**, recalls all his emanations, ascends into the sky, and opens the stupa of treasures. Then, at the invitation of Many Treasures Buddha, Shakyamuni Buddha enters the stupa himself. Shakyamuni Buddha uses his **supernatural power** to raise the entire assembly into the sky as well. This is the beginning of the Assembly in Space.

At first, Shakyamuni Buddha is the guest within the stupa of treasures, but after he reveals his true status as the **Eternal Shakyamuni Buddha** in the sixteenth chapter, "The **Duration of the Life of the Tathagata**," he becomes the host and Many Treasures Buddha becomes the guest.

Many Treasures Buddha and the stupa of treasures return to their place of origin after the general transmission of the *Lotus Sutra* in the twenty-second, "Transmission," chapter though **World Voice Perceiver Bodhisattva** makes an offering to him and the stupa in the twenty-fifth, "Universal Gate of World Voice Perceiver Bodhisattva," chapter.

Many Treasures Buddha represents many things. On one level, he represents all the buddhas of the past, and his testimony shows that Shakyamuni Buddha's teachings are in accord with the universal truth, valid in all ages and on all worlds. On another level, when Shakyamuni Buddha and Many Treasure Buddha share the seat within the stupa of treasures, they are demonstrating the perfect unity of reality and wisdom in that Shakyamuni Buddha personifies subjective wisdom while Many Treasures Buddha personifies objective reality. The emergence of the stupa of treasures itself and the testimony of Many Treasures Buddha from within it could also indicate the emergence of buddhahood from within the lives of **sentient being**s and each being's inner recognition and response to the truth when they hear it.

Nichiren Shonin took Many Treasures Buddha's testimony as evidence that the *Lotus Sutra* should be considered supreme among all Buddhist sutras. He also taught that Many Treasures Buddha was attended by the **Mahavairochana** Buddha of the **Diamond-realm mandala** and the Mahavairochana Buddha of the **Womb-realm** mandala. (WNS3, pp. 28-29)

Mara: (S. māra; J. ma; 魔) The name *māra* literally means "maker of death." It can also be translated as "**devil**" or "**demon**." **King Mara of the Sixth Heaven** is also the name of the **heavenly devil** or **devil king of the sixth heaven** who presides over the Heaven of Controlling the Creations of Others.

Though a personification of **delusion** and all that is **unwholesome**, he is vastly different from the devil in other religious traditions. To begin with, he is not the leader of the **asura** (or fighting demons) who are the enemies of the **god**s, nor does he dwell in **hell**. Rather, he lives in the highest heaven of the **six heavens of the desire realm**, from whence he is able to manipulate, exploit, and trick all the other **sentient being**s in that realm - including other deities in the lower heavens.

His primary purpose is ensuring that no one escapes **samsara**. In some ways he is like a jail warden who is trying to ensure that none of his prisoners can escape. In other ways, he is like the owner of a casino who employs all kinds of entertainments and even occasional payouts in order to keep the gamblers at the roulette wheels and card tables. In the end, the gamblers always lose, but Mara does his best to keep them fooled into thinking that somehow they can hit the jackpot and find ultimate bliss within the desire realm.

In the **sutra**s, Mara sends his daughters to seduce **Siddhartha** on the eve of his **unsurpassed, complete, and perfect awakening**. When Siddhartha sees through their beauty and reduces them to aged crones, Mara sends an army of devils to scare him into abandoning his goal. This also fails. Siddhartha sits unmoved as the arrows and spears of the devils turn into flowers before they can hit him. Finally, Mara asks Siddhartha what entitles him to attain buddhahood. Siddhartha touches the ground and calls upon the earth itself to witness to the countless **merit**s that he had accumulated over innumerable past lives of **bodhisattva practice**.

After **Shakyamuni Buddha**'s awakening, Mara tried to convince him that it would be impossible to teach anyone else the **Dharma** and that he should immediately enter **final nirvana**, but **Brahma** appeared and convinced the Buddha that it would be possible to teach others. Mara also appeared later in the Buddha's life and unsuccessfully attempted to convince him to pass into final nirvana prematurely, before the Dharma and the **Sangha** could be firmly established. The Buddha also saw through these attempts and dismissed Mara, telling him that he would not enter final nirvana before his followers were fully trained and able to practice the Dharma, explain it to others, and correct errors.

According to **Zhiyi**, "Mara is also called 'the plunderer,' because the destroying of **contemplation** is called 'plundering life' and the destroying of **calming** is called 'plundering the body.' Mara is also called 'deceitful grinder,' because he grinds down contemplation and deceitfully leads to darkness and grinds down attempts to practice calming and deceitfully leads to distraction and licentiousness." (CSQI, p. 771 adapted)

Mara is also called the Lord of Desires, Flower Arrows, or Five Arrows. This is because he is said to have a floral arrow that he can shoot at each of the five physical senses to destroy the mind. Some of the arrows are "soft" and represent temptations, others are "hard" and represent things the practitioner fears, while others are "flat" and arouse neither desire nor fear but nevertheless hinder practice (perhaps through lethargy or boredom). Mara can also work through the people around the practitioner, such as their supporters, teachers, fellow practitioners, and students. Mara can also try to trick practitioners into complacence or even into regressing into lesser paths (a bodhisattva falling into the practice of the **two vehicles**) or the **outer way** (**non-Buddhist teachings**). (CSQI, pp. 1393-1396)

Zhiyi includes Mara as the fourth of the **four devils**.

mark: (S. lakṣaṇa; J. sō; 相) The Sanskrit term *lakṣaṇa* can also be translated as "**appearance**," "attribute," "characteristic," or "sign."

Matsubagayatsu Persecution: (J. Matsubagayatsu-no-hōnan; 松葉ケ谷の法難) **Nichiren Shonin**'s efforts to promote the ***Lotus Sutra*** and condemn **slander of the True Dharma** aroused the resentment of the Buddhist establishment and the Kamakura shogunate. On the night of August 27, 1260, an angry mob burned down Nichiren Shonin's hut at the district of the city called Matsubagayatsu. Fortunately, he had been alerted to the threat and was able to escape into the hills behind his residence. This was the first of the four major persecutions.

Maudgalyayana: (S. Maudgalyāyana; J. Mokuren or Mokkenren; 目連 or 目犍連) Also called Mahamaudgalyayana. One of **Shakyamuni Buddha**'s **ten great disciples**. He is said to have been foremost in mastering **supernatural power**s. He became a disciple of the Buddha together with **Shariputra**, mastering this power and becoming an **arhat**. In the ***Lotus Sutra*** he was assured of becoming a buddha in the future, He was beaten to death by jealous **brahmin** ascetics during the Buddha's lifetime.

He is one of the **arhat**s listed as present in the assembly in the first, "Introductory," chapter of the *Lotus Sutra*. Maudgalyayana, along with **Mahakashyapa**, **Subhuti**, and **Mahakatyayana** all express their joy at hearing the teaching of the **One Vehicle** in the fourth, "Understanding by Faith," chapter. These four disciples then tell the parable of the wealthy man and his poor son. In the fifth, "The Simile of Herbs," chapter the Buddha addresses the parable of the three kinds of medicinal herbs and two kinds of trees to these four disciples. In the sixth, "Assurance of Future Buddhahood," chapter the Buddha gives the assurance of future buddhahood to these four, at which time he announces that Maudgalyayana will become a buddha named **Tamalapattracandana Fragrance**.

Nichiren Shonin cites his death as an example of persecution against Buddhism during the Buddha's lifetime in contrast to the difficulties encountered by those who spread the Dharma after the passing of Shakyamuni Buddha. Nichiren also states that Maudgalyayana, in order to save his late mother from her **suffering** in the realm of **hungry ghost**s held the *Ullambana* service according to the teaching of the Buddha. According to Nichiren Shonin, it was the teaching of the *Lotus Sutra* that saved Maudgalyayana's mother from the realm of the hungry ghosts.

Maya Sutra: (S. *Mahāmāyā-sūtra*; J. *Maya-kyō*; 摩耶経) The first half of this **sutra** relates how **Shakyamuni Buddha** ascends to the Heaven of the Thirty-three Gods where he expounded his teachings for three months to his mother Maya, who had died seven days after giving birth to him. The latter half describes the teaching of Shakyamuni Buddha and **Ananda** to Lady Maya who had descended from the Heaven of the Thirty-three Gods to this world to see the Buddha off as he entered **final nirvana**.

Medicine King: (S. Bhaiṣajyaraja; Yakuō; 薬王) This **bodhisattva** represents the healing **power** of the **Buddha**. He and his brother Medicine Superior figure prominently in the ***Lotus Sutra***.

According to the *Medicine King and Superior Medicine Sutra* (sometimes called the *Two Bodhisattvas Sutra*), many **kalpa** ago, in the **Age of the Semblance Dharma** of a buddha named Lapis Lazuli Brightness, there was a **monk** named Sun Store and a rich man named Constellation Light. When Constellation Light heard the magnificent teaching of the monk Sun Store he rejoiced and offered good medicine from the **Himalayas** to him and many other people. He dedicated the **merit** from this act to the realization of **unsurpassed awakening**. He also **vow**ed that he would cure anyone hearing his name from the three illnesses of **greed**, **hatred**, and **delusion**. Because of this, people praised him and called him Medicine King. The sutra predicts that in the future he will become a buddha named Pure Eyes Tathagata. Medicine King had a younger brother named Lightning Glow who also offered medicine and made vows to help those who heard his name; he came to be called Superior Medicine. In the future he will become a buddha named Pure Store

Tathagata.

Medicine King Bodhisattva appears among the eighty thousand bodhisattvas present in the assembly in the first, "Introductory," chapter of the *Lotus Sutra*. In the tenth, "The **Teacher of the Dharma**" **chapter**, **Shakyamuni** Buddha directs his teaching to Medicine King Bodhisattva. In the thirteenth, **"Encouragement for Keeping This Sutra" chapter**, he and Great Eloquence Bodhisattva, along with their twenty thousand attendants, vow to the Buddha to expound the *Lotus Sutra* after his passing.

Chapter twenty-three, "The **Previous Life of Medicine King Bodhisattva**," describes his past life as **Gladly Seen by All Beings**$_{(2)}$ Bodhisattva. In this past life, he sets his own body on fire for one thousand and two hundred years as an offering to Sun Moon Pure Bright Virtue Buddha who had taught him the *Lotus Sutra*. In his very next life, he again became a disciple of Sun Moon Pure Bright Virtue Buddha. After that buddha passed away he made eighty-four thousand **stupa**s to enshrine that buddha's **relic**s and then set his arms on fire for seventy-two thousand years as an offering to the stupas. In the end, he miraculously restored his arms by the power of his merits, virtues, and **wisdom**. In this story, the bodhisattva's offering of his body and arms is a metaphorical way of showing his burning zeal to offer all of his deeds (his arms) and even his very life (his body) for the sake of the Buddha.

Medicine King Bodhisattva offers **dharani**s, or spells, in the twenty-sixth chapter, **"Dharanis,"** for the protection of the teachers of the *Lotus Sutra*.

Another past life of Medicine King Bodhisattva is given in the twenty-seventh chapter, "King Wonderful Adornment as the Previous Life of a Bodhisattva." In the time of Cloud Thunderpeal Star King Flower Wisdom Buddha, Medicine King Bodhisattva and Medicine Superior Bodhisattva were the sons of King Wonderful Adornment, named Pure Store and Pure Eyes. The Buddha was expounding the *Lotus Sutra*, and the two sons asked their mother, Queen Pure Virtue, to come with them to make offerings to the Buddha. Their mother, however, asked them to first receive permission from King Wonderful Adornment who was attached to the teachings of the **brahmin**s. The two sons then performed various miracles for their father who was so impressed that he took faith in the **Dharma**. He not only gave them permission but also accompanied them; together they all became disciples of the Buddha. King Wonderful Adornment then praised his two sons, declaring that they were his teachers who had done the work of the Buddha by causing him to convert.

Medicine King Bodhisattva and Medicine Superior Bodhisattva are sometimes depicted as the attendants of Amoghasiddhi Buddha. Medicine King Bodhisattva in that case is considered one of the forms of **World Voice Perceiver** Bodhisattva.

Nichiren Shonin regarded the bodhisattva's burning himself as an exemplary act of upholding the **True Dharma**. Nichiren also considered both Medicine King Bodhisattva and **Zhiyi** (regarded as an appearance of Medicine King Bodhisattva) as foretelling the appearance of **bodhisattvas appearing from underground** (disciples of the **Eternal Shakyamuni Buddha**). Nichiren Shonin's **Great Mandala of Invoking the Ten Realms** includes the name of Maitreya Bodhisattva to represent the **bodhisattvas of the trace teaching**.

Medicine Master: (S. Bhaiṣajyaguru or Bhaiṣajya-guru-vaiḍūrya-prabhā-rāja; J. Yakushi; 薬師) The **buddha** presiding over the **pure land** called Pure Emerald World who is described in the *Medicine Master Sutra*.

meditation master: (J. zenji; 禅師) An honorific title for a teacher of meditation, regardless of what school of Buddhism they are affiliated with. In the **Zen school**, the title **"zen master"** is used to refer to their lineage holders.

meditative absorption: (S. dhyāna; J. zenjō or zenna or zen or jōryo; 禅定 or 禅那 or 禅 or 靜慮) Through the practice of **calming**, a practitioner can achieve a state of meditative absorption that temporarily suppresses the **defilement**s that bind them to the **desire realm**. From this state of **concentration**, the practitioner can go on to cultivate either the four formless meditative absorptions, the five supernatural powers, or the kind of **contemplation** that leads to **awakening**.

In **Mahayana** Buddhism, meditative absorption is the fifth of the **six perfections** of a **bodhisattva**. As a **bodhisattva practice**, meditative absorption is for peaceful abiding, inducing the **six supernatural powers**, and for accomplishing great deeds.

meditative good deeds: (J. jōzen; 定善) **Wholesome** deeds done when in a state of **meditative absorption**. See **concentrated and scattered**.

mental formation: (S. saṃskāra; P. saṅkhāra; J. gyō; 行) When the Sanskrit term *saṃskāra* is used to refer to the fourth of the **five aggregates** it is best translated as "mental formations," though in other contexts the word is translated as "the **conditioned**," or "conditioned formation," or "volitional formation." Mental formations form and construct the **mind** by directing it towards **wholesome**, **unwholesome**, and **indeterminate** activity. Mental formations comprise a collection of cognitive processes and affects that are classified and enumerated in different ways by different systems of **abhidharma**.

merit: (S. puṇya; J. fuku or kudoku or fukutoku; 福 or 功徳 or 福徳) The Sanskrit term *puṇya* can also be translated as "blessing" or "**benefit**" depending on context. **Zhiyi** taught that "merit" (功徳) pertains to benefits enjoyed by oneself, while "benefit" (利益) pertains to benefits enjoyed by others. (PMLS2, p. 300)

Merit Forest: (J. Kudokurin; 功徳林) One of the four main **bodhisattva**s who expound the **Dharma** in the *Flower Garland Sutra*. He teaches about the **ten kinds of practice**.

merits and benefits, subtlety of: (J. kudoku-riyaku-myō; 功徳利益妙) The tenth of the **ten subtleties of the Trace Gate**. Also simply called the "subtlety of **benefit**s." It refers to the **merit**s and benefits of **cause and effect**, the **Buddha**'s transformations, and in particular the benefits bestowed by the Buddha, the *Lotus Sutra*, and the practice of contemplation of the mind. (FTP, p. 208; PMLS2, pp. 94, 299-312)

Miaole, Great Master: (J. Myōraku Daishi; 妙楽 大師) See **Zhanran**.

middle way: (S. madhyamā-pratipad; J. chū-dō; 中道) In the first **turning of the Wheel of the Dharma**, **Shakyamuni Buddha** describes the **eightfold noble path** as the middle way. (CD 56.11, p. 1844)
The middle way can refer to the selflessness that avoids self-indulgence and self-denial. It also refers to the **right view** that avoids the **extreme views** of **eternalism** or **annihilationism**. It is the principle of ultimate reality beyond existence and non-existence. In the teachings of the **Tiantai school** it is the "truth of the middle," i.e. the **true reality of all things** which cannot be explained in either negative or affirmative terms.

Middle Way school: (S. Madhyamaka; J. Chūgon-ha; 中観派) The school of **Mahayana** Buddhism founded by **Nagarjuna**. This school emphasizes the dialectics of **emptiness** and a system of logical analysis that shows the unsoundness of any metaphysical **view** that presupposes any kind of **self-nature**. A follower of the school is called a "Madhyamika." In China, the Middle Way school was initially represented by the **Three Treatises school**, though its teachings were found or assimilated by all other schools of East Asian Buddhism.

middling capacity: (S. udāsīna-pakṣa; J. chūkon or chūbon; 中根 or 中品) See **average capacity**.

mind: (S. citta or manas; J. shin or i; 心 or 意) The synonymous Sanskrit terms *citta* and *manas* both mean mind, and can also be translated as "mental states," "mentality," "mentation," or "thought." These two words are also synonymous with the Sanskrit term *vijñāna*, or **consciousness**. (ABK1, p. 205) *Citta* has the connotation of the mind as that which generates and accumulates **wholesome** and **unwholesome** activity, *manas* has the connotation of the mind as that which cognizes an object and is the support of the moment of mind which follows it, while *vijñāna* has the connotation of discerning the nature of the object and of grasping the support of an object and a sense faculty. (AKB1, p. 205)

mind king: (S. citta-rājan; J. shin-ō; 心王) the basic essence of **mind**.

mind-only: (S. citta-mātra; J. yui-shin; 唯心) See **consciousness-only**.

mindfulness: (S. smṛti; J. nen or oku; 念 or 憶) The Sanskrit term *smṛti* can also be translated as "memory," "recall," or "remembrance."

monk: (S. bhikṣu; J. biku; 比丘) A Buddhist monk or male mendicant. A man who has taken the higher ordination and therefore lives in accord with the **vinaya**.

Moon of Liberation: (S. Vimukticandra; J. Gedatsugatsu; 解脱月) A **bodhisattva** mentioned in the *Ten Grounds Sutra* that is also a chapter of the *Flower Garland Sutra*. Representing the mass of people, this bodhisattva requests **Diamond Repository** Bodhisattva to teach the ten grounds doctrine. **Liberation** represents the highest of the ten grounds and the waxing moon stands for a bodhisattva progressing in practice and traversing the ten grounds.

moon, god of the: (S. Candra; J. Gatsu or Gatten or Gattenji; 月 or 月天 or 月天子) The Vedic **god** of the moon who was adopted into Buddhism as a **guardian deity**.
In **esoteric Buddhism**, the god of the moon represents the purity of **buddha-nature** that cools the passions and removes the **three poisons**.
Together with the gods of the **sun** and **stars**, the god of the moon is one of the three heavenly gods of light, whom **Nichiren Shonin** considered protectors of the **practitioner of the *Lotus Sutra***.

Moonlight: (S. Candraprabha) In the *Medicine Master Sutra* he is one of the two attendants of **Medicine Master Buddha**.

morality: (S. śīla; J. jikai or kai; 持戒 or 戒) The Sanskrit term *śīla* can also be translated as "virtue." The ideogram 戒 can be translated as **precept**.

In mainstream Buddhism, morality can be practiced in terms of the precepts for maintaining restraint, of which there are different sets of precepts for different kinds of practitioners. There are the **five precepts** for a **layman** or **laywoman**, the ten precepts for novices, the six precepts for postulants, and the **two hundred and fifty precepts** for **monk**s and **nun**s.

In **Mahayana** Buddhism morality is one of the key **bodhisattva practice**s. It is the second of the **six perfections**. Morality encompasses the **three categories of pure precepts** (the aforementioned precepts for maintaining restraint, the precepts that encompass all good deeds, and the precepts for benefiting sentient beings). Morality has the nature of the three kinds of activities (physical, verbal, and mental) learned at the time of taking up the bodhisattva precepts. (DCOT, pp. 316-317; CWL, pp. 711-713) The cultivation of morality by bodhisattvas is also expressed in terms of bodhisattva precepts such as the ten major precepts and forty-eight minor precepts of the *Brahma's Net Sutra*.

Mountain King: (J. Sannō Gongen; 山王権現) The ideograms 山王 mean "mountain king," while 権現 is a title used to refer to a **buddha** or **bodhisattva** manifesting as a Shinto deity, or kami. The Mountain King is the tutelary deity of Mt. **Hiei** and the Japanese **Tiantai school**.

Nichiren Shonin considered Mountain King the third most powerful kami after **Amaterasu Omikami** and **Hachiman**. (WNS1, p. 173)

Mountain Sea Wisdom Supernatural Power King: (S. Sāgara-varadhara-buddhi-vikrīḍitābhijña; J. Sengaie-jizaitsū-ō; 山海慧自在通王) The name of the **buddha** that **Ananda** will become according to the ninth, "The Assurance of Future Buddhahood of the Shravakas Who Have Something More to Learn and the Shravakas Who Have Nothing More to Learn" chapter of the *Lotus Sutra*. (LS, p. 169)

mudra: (S. mudrā; J. in, ingei, inzō, geiin, shuin, or mitsuin; 印, 印契, 印相, 契印, 手印, or 密印) The Sanskrit term *mudrā* can also be translated as "**mark**," "seal," or "sign." In **esoteric Buddhism** it usually refers to certain ritual gestures or handseals of which there are many. Each mudra communicates or embodies a different principle or activity of a **buddha**, **bodhisattva**, or **guardian deity**. In these gestures, the left hand represents **concentration** and the right hand represents **wisdom**; each finger represents one of the **five primary elements** (earth, water, fire, air, and **space**). Mudras are one of the **three mysteries** (of body, mouth, and mind), by which **attaining buddhahood with one's present body** can be accomplished. In the **Mantra school**, all mudras ultimately correspond to **Mahavairochana Buddha**'s actions.

mundane: (S. laukika; J. seken; 世間) In terms of Buddhist practice, mundane **action**s that are **wholesome** are still **defiled** by **ignorance** but can lead to **rebirth** as an **asura**, **human** or **god**.

mutual identification: (J. sōsoku; 相即) The mutual identification between **phenomena** in the context of the **perfect interfusion** of all things that arise from **dependent origination** (e.g., waves can be identified as water, and water can be identified as waves).

mutual possession of the ten realms: (J. jikkai-gogu; 十界互具) According to **Zhiyi**, the world consists of the **ten realms** of **hell-dwellers**, **hungry ghosts**, **animal**s, **asura**s, **human**s, **god**s, **voice-hearer**s, **privately-awakened one**s, **bodhisattva**s, and **buddha**s. Each of these realms mutually contain characteristics of the nine others in and of itself. This means that, for instance, human beings have characteristics of the nine other realms from beings in hell up to buddhas; asuras have those of the rest of the ten realms; buddhas also have characteristics of the nine other realms. This idea was set up by Zhiyi based on passages in the *Lotus Sutra* such as "The buddhas appear in the worlds in order to cause all living beings to open the insight of the buddha." It meant to him that those beings in the nine realms other than the realm of buddhas also possessed the characteristics of buddhas. The idea of "mutual possession" provided the basis for another important **Tiantai school** doctrine, the "**three thousand realms in a single thought-moment.**"

Nichiren Shonin established and spread the practice of chanting **Namu Myoho Renge Kyo** on the foundation of the three thousand realms in a single thought-moment and the mutual possession of the ten realms as the ultimate means of **attaining buddhahood** by an **ordinary person**.

Myoho Renge Kyo: (J. *Myōhō-renge-kyō*; 妙法蓮華経) The *shindoku* pronunciation of the full Chinese title of the *Lotus Sutra*.

Mystic Glorification Sutra: (S. *Ghanavyūha-sūtra*; J. *Mitsugon-gyō*; 密厳経) Also known as the *Mystic Glorification of the Mahayana Sutra* (J. *Daijō-mitsugon-kyō*; 大乗密厳経). This sutra is one of the basic canons of the **Dharma Characteristics school** as it teaches the **consciousness-only** doctrine. There are two translations into Chinese, one by Divakara and one by **Amoghavajra**.

Nichiren Shonin refused to accept its claim to be supreme among Buddhist sutras, though it might be regarded in some respects as having teachings of **defin-**

itive meaning compared to other sutras teaching the **provisional meaning** in regard to certain topics or issues. (WS1, p. 11; WNS2, pp. 85-86)

Nagarjuna: (c. 150-250; S. Nāgārjuna; J. Ryūju or Ryūmyō; 竜樹 or 竜猛) A great exponent of early **Mahayana** Buddhism. He was supposedly born into a **brahmin** family in southern India. After completely mastering **Brahmanism**, he moved to northern India, studying mainstream Buddhism and the Mahayana. Some sources say that he studied, and later taught, at Nalanda. He systematized the doctrine of **emptiness** and was the founder of the **Middle Way school**. He is also said to have recovered the Mahayana **sutra**s, specifically the **Prajna sutras**, from the dragons under the ocean. **Xuanzang** called him one of the "four brilliant suns illuminating the world" along with **Ashvaghosha**, **Aryadeva**, and **Kumarata**.

In the *Transmission of the Dharma Treasury Sutra*, Nagarjuna was the successor of Kapimala in the list of **twenty-three** or **twenty-four successors** or patriarchs after **Shakyamuni Buddha**. Nagarjuna's successor was **Aryadeva**. He is also regarded as the honorary patriarch of eight Buddhist schools in China and Japan: the **six schools of Nara Buddhism**, the **Mantra school** and the **Tiantai school**. In the Mantra school he is considered the third patriarch who received initiation into the teachings of **esoteric Buddhism** from **Vajrasattva**. An alternate list of Mantra school patriarchs lists Nagarjuna as the first. In the Tiantai school he is sometimes considered the first patriarch.

His most important work is the *Root Verses on the Middle Way*. This is the main basis of the Middle Way school's teachings. The *Great Perfection of Wisdom Treatise* was attributed to him by **Kumarajiva**, its ostensible translator, and was also an important basis for Zhiyi's teachings. The *Twelve Gates Treatise* and *Exegesis on the Ten Grounds Treatise* were also attributed to him.

namu: (S. namas; J.; 南無) The ideograms 南無 are a Chinese transliteration of the Sanskrit term *namas* that means "devotion to," "homage to," "putting absolute faith in," or "taking refuge in."

Namu Myoho Renge Kyo: (J. Namu-myōhō-renge-kyō; 南無妙法蓮華経) The ideograms 南無妙法蓮華経 mean "**Namu**" or "Devotion to" the "*Sutra of the Lotus Flower of the Wonderful Dharma*." This is the "**Daimoku** of the **Original Gate**," one of the **Three Great Secret Dharmas** of **Nichiren Shonin**. According to Nichiren Shonin, the daimoku of the *Lotus Sutra* is not a mere title of a sutra but it is charged with all the **merit**s of the *Lotus Sutra* taught by **Shakyamuni Buddha**. Therefore, those who put their **faith** in and chant the daimoku we will be given all the merits of the sutra. Thus, he considered chanting the daimoku the basis of practicing the *Lotus Sutra* and the only way to **attain buddhahood** in the **Latter Age of Degeneration**.

Nanda: (J. Nanda; 難陀) A **monk** of the **Consciousness-Only school** in the sixth century. Nanda's commentary was incorporated into the *Demonstration of Consciousness-Only Treatise*.

nature: (J. shō; 性) Nature may also be understood to mean **self-nature**.

In the *Profound Meaning of the Lotus Sutra*, nature as the second of the **ten suchnesses** is given the following definition by **Zhiyi**: "Nature has its point of reference internally. That which intrinsically belongs to one's **self** and does not change is called 'nature.'" (FTP, p. 184) In the *Great Calming and Contemplation*, Zhiyi further explained that nature can refer to the unmoving nature that does not change, which corresponds to the truth of **emptiness**; to the distinctive nature of an individual that is unchanging (at least for a time), which corresponds to the truth of provisionality; and to the true nature or **buddha-nature**, which corresponds to the truth of the middle. (CSQI, pp. 806-809)

nayuta: (J. nayuta; 那由多) The Sanskrit term *nayuta* means "hundred thousand million."

Neither Perception nor Non-Perception, Heaven/Sphere of: (S. Naivasamjñānāsamjñāyatana; J. Hisō-hihisō-jo-ten; 非想非非想処天) Also referred to as the highest heaven or the summit of existence. The fourth of the four formless meditative absorptions and the fourth of the four formless heavens. It is referred to throughout **Shakyamuni Buddha**'s teachings. (e.g., LD 33.1.11(7), p. 489; MD 77.22, p. 639; CD 36.19, p. 1277-1278; ND 4.190, p. 561) It is attained when the practitioner completely surmounts the perception of nothingness and enters and dwells in the sphere of neither perception nor non-perception.

This was the state attained by Udraka Ramaputra, one of the two great masters of yogic meditation that **Siddhartha Gautama** practiced with before he became Shakyamuni Buddha. (LB, p. 14; MD 36:16, pp. 258-259)

nembutsu: (S. buddhānusmṛti; J. nembutsu; 念仏) The Sanskrit word *buddhānusmṛti* means "thinking of **buddha**," as do the ideograms 念仏. The practice of chanting the name of a buddha, though in the **Pure Land school** this is exclusively understood to refer to the name of **Amitabha Buddha** in the form of "Namu Amida Butsu."

Nembutsu school: (J. Nembutsu-shū; 念仏宗) See **Pure Land school**.

Nen'a Ryochu: (1199-1287; J. Nen'a Ryōchū or Nen-amidabutsu Ryōchū; 然阿良忠 or 然阿弥陀仏 良忠) The third patriarch of the Chinzei faction of the Japanese **Pure Land school**. He systematized the Pure Land doctrine and founded many temples in the Kantō (eastern Japan).

Nichiren Shonin considered him and Dō Amidabutu the two pillars of the Pure Land school in Kamakura.

Never Despising: (S. Sadāparibhūta; J. Fukyō or Jōfukyō; 不軽 or 常不軽) The Sanskrit name Sadāparibhūta can be parsed as *sadā-aparibhūta* to mean "Never Despising, or as *sadā-paribhūta* to mean "Always Despised." The ideograms 常不軽 mean "Never Despising." As described in the twentieth, **"Never Despising Bodhisattva" chapter** of the *Lotus Sutra*, this bodhisattva lived in the **Age of the Semblance Dharma** following the **final nirvana** of Powerful Voice King Buddha. Whenever he saw people who belonged to the **four assemblies**, he would say to them, "'I respect you deeply. I do not despise you. Why is that? It is because you will be able to practice the way of bodhisattvas and become buddhas." Some people became angry because they thought he was ridiculing them with a false assurance of future buddhahood. They beat him with sticks and threw stones and other debris at him. He dodged their attacks but never stopped bowing and uttering those words to them. He subsequently heard a voice in the sky which taught him the *Lotus Sutra*. He was then able to purify his six senses, prolong his life, and to teach the *Lotus Sutra* to those who had formerly abused him but in time took **faith** in him and became his followers. After the end of that lifetime, in other lifetimes, he met two hundred thousand million buddhas named Sun Moon Light, and two hundred thousand million buddhas named Cloud Freedom Light King. He eventually became **Shakyamuni** Buddha.

Nichiren Shonin exerted himself to follow the example of this bodhisattva as the **practitioner of the *Lotus Sutra*** in the **Latter Age of Degeneration**. He interpreted the **subduing** method of propagation practiced by this bodhisattva as well as by himself as the way to sow the **seed** of the *Lotus Sutra* in the hearts of those who persecuted them. He even equated the five or seven characters of the **daimoku** with the twenty-four character *Lotus Sutra* which was the greeting of Never Despising Bodhisattva. Nichiren Shonin also taught that, like this bodhisattva, we should cultivate **patience**(1) in the face of persecution. In the *Sushun Tennō Gosho* (*The "Emperor Sushun" Letter*) he wrote, "The essence of Buddhism is the *Lotus Sutra*, and the gist of practicing the *Lotus Sutra* is shown in the "Never Despising Bodhisattva," chapter. Contemplate why the Never Despising Bodhisattva stood on the street to bow to passerby. The true purpose of Shakyamuni Buddha appearing in this world was to teach us how to behave ourselves on a daily basis. Consider this well. The wise are called **human** beings while the foolish are beasts."

(WNS4, p. 124)

"Never Despising Bodhisattva" chapter: (J. Jōfukyō-bosatsu-hon; 常不軽菩薩品) The twentieth chapter of the *Lotus Sutra*. In this chapter, **Shakyamuni Buddha** taught **Great Power Obtainer Bodhisattva** the story of **Never Despising** Bodhisattva, who bowed in respect to all. **Shakyamuni** Buddha revealed that the story of this bodhisattva was a jataka tale about the previous life of the Buddha as a practitioner of the bodhisattva way. The chapter also stated that those who persecuted him had to endure the **suffering** in the Hell of **Incessant Suffering** but, upon attending Shakyamuni Buddha's discourse of the *Lotus* Sutra, they were given the assurance of future buddhahood.

Nichiren: (1222-1282; J.; 日蓮) A **monk**, originally ordained and educated in the Tendai Shu (The Japanese branch of the **Tiantai school**), who is regarded as the founder of the **Nichiren school** when he began to publicly declare and teach the practice of **daimoku**, the chanting of "**Namu Myoho Renge Kyo**," on April 28, 1253, after many years of study and contemplation.

Nichiren **Shonin**'s strongly worded critiques of Buddhists he considered to have committed **slander of the True Dharma** by neglecting or misrepresenting the *Lotus Sutra* earned him the enmity of both the Buddhist establishment and the Kamakura shogunate that patronized that establishment. He suffered four major persecutions and several minor ones at their hands, but Nichiren Shonin never relented. He knew that the *Lotus Sutra* could **awaken** people to the possibility that all people can **attain buddhahood** and of seeing this **Saha world** as the Pure Land of Eternally Tranquil Light of the **Eternal Shakyamuni Buddha**.

Nichiren school: (J. Nichiren-shū; 日蓮宗) This school was established by **Nichiren Shonin** (1222–1282) on April 28, 1253, when he first proclaimed the chanting of **daimoku** (the "sacred title") which is **Namu Myoho Renge Kyo**. Nichiren Shonin started off as a **monk** of the Japanese **Tiantai school** who wished to return to the teachings of **Zhiyi** and what he felt was the true intention of **Shakyamuni Buddha** hidden within the depths of the *Lotus Sutra*.

Nichiren Shonin vociferously denounced those forms of Buddhism that he felt were leading away from the true teaching of Shakyamuni Buddha found in the *Lotus Sutra*. He condemned the **Pure Land school** for discarding all other buddhas and sutras including the *Lotus Sutra* and for teaching that people are incapable of attaining **awakening** in this life and must only hope for **rebirth in the pure land**. He condemned the **Zen school** because its rhetoric also led people away from the *Lotus Sutra* and instead led people towards depending upon the subjective opinions and practice of **Zen Masters**, whom Nichiren Shonin felt were corrupt, ill-informed about Buddhism, and arrogant. He condemned the esoteric teachings of both Eastern Temple Esotericism and Tendai Esotericism for claiming that esotericism was more important than the simple **faith** in the *Lotus Sutra* that was accessible to all people and could also enable all people to sow the **seed of buddhahood** or even **attain buddhahood with one's present body**. He condemned the **Discipline school** for trying to get people to depend for their awakening on following what he considered to be **hinayana precept**s.

Nichiren Shonin especially emphasized Zhiyi's teaching of the **three thousand realms in a single thought-moment**, because it meant that the buddha embraces all beings and all beings contains the world of buddhahood within.

Nichiren Shonin eventually broke with classical Tiantai school teaching by claiming that while there was an external transmission of the **Dharma** from Shakyamuni Buddha to Zhiyi, to **Saicho**, and then to Nichiren Shonin, there was also an inner transmission from the **Eternal Shakyamuni Buddha** of the *Lotus Sutra* to **Superior Practice Bodhisattva** (this occurs in chapter twenty-one of the sutra) and he believed that he himself was that bodhisattva appearing in the **Latter Age of Degeneration** to spread the daimoku. Nichiren Shonin also taught that hidden in the depths of chapter sixteen of the *Lotus Sutra* were **Three Great Secret Dharmas**: the Eternal Shakyamuni Buddha as the **Focus of Devotion of the Original Gate**, the **Sacred Title of the Original Gate** (i.e. the chanting of Namu Myoho Renge Kyo to encounter, praise, assimilate, and share the Wonderful Dharma), and the **Precept Platform of the Original Gate** (i.e. the place of practice occurs wherever and whenever someone upholds the practice of daimoku, thereby taking faith in the *Lotus Sutra*). In a way, Nichiren Buddhism is a streamlined form of Tendai practice for the masses, but in another way it was intended by Nichiren Shonin as the direct practice of the inner essence of the *Lotus Sutra* which he believed had not previously been revealed by the classical Tiantai/Tendai school but could only be transmitted in the Latter Age by Superior Practice Bodhisattva at the behest of the Eternal Shakyamuni Buddha.

nine great difficulties: (J. kuō-no-dainan; 九横の大難) The nine major hardships that **Shakyamuni Buddha** encountered during his lifetime as described in the *Great Perfection of Wisdom Treatise*.

1) A beautiful but evil woman named Sundari spread rumors that she was having an affair with Shakyamuni Buddha.
2) A maid servant gave the Buddha an offering of stinking rice gruel in a **brahmin** village.
3) The Buddha was forced by King **Agnidatta** to feed himself and five hundred disciples nothing but horse fodder for three months.
4) Many of the members of the **Shakya** clan were slaughtered by King **Virudhaka** of Koshala.
5) Shakyamuni Buddha was unable to receive alms in a brahmin village.
6) A brahmin woman named **Chinchamanavika** claimed that she was made pregnant by the Buddha.

7) **Devadatta** injured the Buddha's foot when attempting to murder him.
8) Once the Buddha suffered from an icy wind that continued to blow for eight days.
9) Shakyamuni Buddha endured six years of ascetic practices before **attaining buddhahood**.

The term "nine great difficulties" was coined by **Nichiren Shonin**, stressing the difficulty of spreading the teaching of the *Lotus Sutra* during the **Latter Age of Degeneration**, which he claimed to be harder than the nine ordeals Shakyamuni Buddha had to endure during his lifetime.

nine liberations: (J. ku-gedatsu; 九解脱) Nine mental attitudes that are part of the **thirty-four enlightened mental states**. The nine liberations are needed to break through the nine degrees of **delusion**, which are the **deluded attitudes** divided into the categories of mild, moderate, and severe and each of those categories subdivided into mild, moderate, and severe. Together with the **nine non-obstructions** they are needed to sever deluded attitudes on the path of cultivation according to the **tripitaka teaching**.

nine non-obstructions: (J. ku-muge; 九無礙) Nine mental attitudes that are part of the **thirty-four enlightened mental states**. The nine non-obstructions are needed to break through the nine degrees of **delusion**, which are the **deluded attitudes** divided into the categories of mild, moderate, and severe and each of those categories subdivided into mild, moderate, and severe. Together with the **nine liberations** they are needed to sever deluded attitudes on the path of cultivation according to the **tripitaka teaching**.

ninety-five non-Buddhist schools: (J. kujūgoshu-no-gedō; 九十五種の外道) A theoretical enumeration of all the possible false views held by non-Buddhists. Sometimes the number is given as ninety-six non-Buddhist schools.

Nirgrantha Jnatiputra: (599-527 BCE; S. Nirgrantha Jñātīputra; J. Nikenda Nyakudaishi; 尼揵陀 若提子) One of the **six non-Buddhist masters**. Though **Rishabha** is considered by the Jains to be the first teacher of Jainism in the present era of the world, Nirgrantha Jnatiputra was the teacher of Jainism in the time of **Shakyamuni Buddha**. His followers are called the **Nirgranthas** in early Buddhist writings. He taught that **action**s bind **sentient being**s to **suffering** regardless of intentions and that only complete inaction and non-violence can lead to **liberation**.

Nirgranthas: (S.; J. Nikenshi; 尼揵子) The followers of **Nirgrantha Jnatiputra**. Today the teachings and practices of Nirgrantha Jnatiputra is known as Jainism.

nirvana: (S. nirvāṇa; J. nehan; 涅槃) The Sanskrit term *nirvāṇa* means "extinction" The ultimate goal of Buddhist practice, **awakening**, or buddhahood, in which the **defilements** are all extinguished; the state of **mind** completely free from the **three poisons** (**greed**, **hatred**, and **delusion**).

Nirvana Sutra: (J. *Daihatsu-nehan-gyō* or *Dainehan-gyō* or *Nehan-gyō*; 大般涅槃経 or 大涅槃経 or 涅槃経) The full title would be the *Great Nirvana Sutra*. Two versions of the Chinese translation of this **sutra** exist: (1) the northern version translated by Dharmkshema in forty fascicles between 421 and 430; and (2) the southern version called the ***Six-Fascicle Nirvana Sutra*** translated by **Faxian** and Buddhabadra in 418. The Dharmakshema version was revised and re-organized by Huiguan, Huiyan, and Xie Lingyun in thirty-six fascicles between 433 and 452.

The sutra focuses on the passing of **Shakyamuni Buddha** as a **skillful means** and teaches that the Buddha's life is unborn and deathless. (NS1, pp. 91-93) It teaches also the "existence of the **buddha-nature** in all **sentient being**s." (NS1, p. 180)

The **Tiantai school** regarded this sutra, together with the *Lotus Sutra*, as part of the **Lotus-Nirvana period**, and therefore it is supreme among all the sutras taught by the Buddha during the **five periods** of his teaching. Unlike the *Lotus Sutra*, that only contains the unadulterated **perfect teaching**, the *Nirvana Sutra* also has the "additional teaching" that draws upon all **four doctrinal teachings** and the "further elimination of **wrong views**" that again presents the perfect teaching in contrast to the other three teachings.

Nichiren Shonin considered it to be the teaching of the gleaning for those who did not **attain buddhahood** by hearing the *Lotus Sutra* from the Buddha. (NS1, pp. 291-292) Nichiren Shonin also placed great importance on such doctrines taught in the *Nirvana Sutra* as "**rely on the Dharma, not upon the person**" (NS1, pp. 193-199) and that "those of the **four assemblies** should redouble their efforts to defend the **True Dharma**." (NS1, p. 97) The *Nirvana Sutra* inspired Nichiren Shonin to devote himself to the *Lotus Sutra*, to proclaim a new Buddhist tradition, and to propagate the *Lotus Sutra*. He also used the sutra to support his journey through a difficult life as a **practitioner of the *Lotus Sutra***. Nevertheless, this sutra itself is considered a **provisional sutra** in comparison to the *Lotus Sutra*. (WNS1, pp. 12-13, 69-72)

non-arising: (S. anutpāda; J. mushō or fushō; 無生 or 不生) The Sanksrit term *anutpāda* can also be translated as "non-origination," "non-production," or "uncreated." The ideograms 不生 can also mean "unborn."

non-Buddhist scriptures: (J. geten; 外典) The ideograms 外典 literally mean "outside scriptures." The terms refer to scriptures of non-Buddhist teachings in India, but more inclusively non-Buddhist writings in general such as those of **Confucianism** and Taoism. See **Buddhist scriptures**.

non-Buddhist teachings: (S. tīrthika; J. gedō; 外道) The Sanskrit term *tīrthika* means "ford-maker," and it is a reference to non-Buddhist teachers of **shramana**s who were claiming that their teachings and practices would lead to the other shore of **liberation** from **suffering**. The ideograms 外道 literally mean "**outer way**," meaning any non-Buddhist religion or philosophy. It is used in contrast to the "**inner way**" meaning Buddhism. It is sometimes used as a derogatory term to mean **wrong views** or false views. The **six non-Buddhist masters** who were contemporaries of **Shakyamuni Buddha** are often referred to as prime examples of teachers of the outer way.

Nichiren Shonin considered such non-Buddhist teachings of the "**two gods** and **three hermits**" of India as initial steps leading to Buddhism.

non-ceasing: (S. aniruddha; J. fumetsu; 不滅) The ideograms 不滅 can also mean "deathless."

non-meditative good deeds: (J. sanzen; 散善) The ideograms 散善 can also be translated as "scatterbrained good deeds." Non-meditative good deeds are **wholesome** deeds done when not in a meditative state. See **concentrated and scattered**.

non-outflow: (S. anāsrava; J. mu-ro; 無漏) The Sanskrit term *anāsrava* can also be translated as "uncontaminated," "untainted," or "without outflow." It is synonymous with **pure**.

non-retrogression: (S. avaivartika or avivartika or avinivartanīy; J. abibatchi/abeibatchi or futaiten or futai or ayui-otchi; 阿毘跋致/阿鞞跋致 or 不退転 or 不退 or 阿惟越致) Also translated as "irreversible" or "irrevocable." It is the mental state in which the practitioners of Buddhism proceed to the highest **awakening** without falling back into lower spiritual stages. This is the state wherein one is assured of **attaining buddhahood**.

The name for the seventh of the **ten abodes**.

non-returner: (S. anāgāmin; J. fugen or furai or anagon; 不還 or 不来 or 阿那含) The third of the **four fruitions** of those who practice the **voice-hearer vehicle**

and thereby extinguish the **three poisons** and achieve **liberation** from **samsara** by attaining **nirvana**. The non-returner has destroyed the fetters of the view that there is a **self**, doubt, seizing upon rules and rituals, sensual desire, and ill-will and will never return to the **desire realm**, but is susceptible to **rebirth** in the pure abodes, the five highest heavens of the **form realm**, wherein they will attain nirvana.

non-self: (S. anātman; J. muga or higa; 無我 or 非我) **Shakyamuni Buddha** denied that there is a permanent, unchanging, indivisible, and independent **self** (or Self) and instead taught the doctrine of non-self to the five ascetics right after teaching the first **turning of the wheel of the Dharma** at the **Deer Park** in **Varanasi**. In his second discourse, he pointed out that none of the **five aggregates** are totally under one's control, and that they are all impermanent, therefore they are unsatisfactory, and therefore they do not qualify as the self. (CD 22.59, pp. 901-903) In later discourses the Buddha clarified that, in the case of each of the aggregates, they are not the self, nor does the self possess them, nor are they in the self, nor is the self in them. (e.g. CD 22.82, p. 926) In another discourse, in reference to himself, the Buddha made it clear that he was not any of the aggregates, nor in any of them, nor apart from any of them, nor was he all of them together, nor was he without any of them. (CD 22.86, p. 937) From this it is evident that even with the Buddha, there is not a self apart from the aggregates.

Notations on the Words and Phrases of the Lotus Sutra: (J. *Hokke mongu-ki*; 法華文句記) A commentary by **Zhanran**, sometimes abbreviated by **Nichiren Shonin** simply as the *Ki*. Claiming the supremacy of the ***Lotus Sutra***, Nichiren Shonin often cited both **Zhiyi**'s *Words and Phrases of the Lotus Sūtra* and Zhanran's *Notations* to strengthen his points.

nun: (S. bhikṣuṇī; J. bikuni; 比丘尼) A Buddhist nun or female mendicant. A woman who has taken the higher ordination and therefore lives in accord with the **vinaya**.

objects, subtlety of: (J. kyō-myō; 境妙) The first of the **ten subtleties of the Trace Gate** described in the ***Profound Meaning of the Lotus Sutra***. It refers to the subtle objects of **contemplation**, such as the **ten suchnesses**, **dependent origination**, the **four noble truths**, and the one true reality, that are all praised as the "teachers of all **buddha**s." (FTP, p. 207; PMLS2, pp. 92-93)

Ocean Seal Samadhi: (J. kaiin-zammai; 海印三昧) A form of **concentration** wherein all truths appear within the **Buddha**'s **wisdom**, just as all **phenomena** are reflected in the waters of the ocean when it is quiet and calm.

once-returner: (S. sakṛdāgāmin; J. ichirai/ichidai or shidagon; 一来 or 斯陀含) The second of the **four fruitions** of those who practice the **voice-hearer vehicle** and thereby extinguish the **three poisons** and achieve **liberation** from **samsara** by attaining **nirvana**. The once-returner has destroyed the fetters of the view that there is a **self**, doubt, and seizing upon rules and rituals) and diminished the fetters of sensual desire, ill-will, and **ignorance**. They are still susceptible to **rebirth** in the **desire realm**, but at most only once more as a **human** or **god**.

One Buddha Vehicle: (J. ichi-butsujō; 一仏乗) See **One Vehicle**.

one hundred realms and one thousand aspects: (J. hyakkai-sennyo; 百界千如) According to the teaching of **Zhiyi** in the *Profound Meaning of the Lotus Sutra*, an individual **mind** has **ten realms** (from the realm of the **hell-dweller**s up to and including the **buddha**-realm), each of which includes in itself characteristics of the other nine realms, as per the teaching of the **mutual possession of the ten realms**, making one hundred realms. Each of these one hundred realms has **ten suchnesses**, so there are one thousand aspects of existence. (FTP, p. 182; PMLS2, p. 74) In the *Great Calming and Contemplation*, Zhiyi further taught that as these one thousand aspects have **three categories of existence**, there are t**hree thousand realms in a single thought-moment**. (CSQI, pp. 815-816)

One Vehicle: (S. ekayāna; J. ichijō; 一乗) Also called the "**One Buddha Vehicle**" and represented by the great white ox-cart. The One Vehicle refers to the teaching that enables all **sentient beings** to **attain buddhahood**. All other Buddhist teachings, particularly those associated with the **three vehicles**, are therefore **skillful means** of expressing the One Vehicle.

The One Vehicle is stressed in the *Lotus Sutra*, in which **Shakyamuni Buddha** states, "I also expound various teachings to all living beings only for the purpose of revealing the One Buddha Vehicle. There is no other vehicle, not a second or a third." (LS, p. 33) The One Vehicle also means unification: unification of the teaching as well as the practitioners. Thus, the *Lotus Sutra* teaches the **attainment of buddhahood by adherents of the two vehicles**.

While the **Tiantai school** doctrine stressed unification with the term **opening of the three vehicles to reveal the One Vehicle**, **Nichiren Shonin** maintained that the One Vehicle doctrine shows the superiority of the *Lotus Sutra* over other sutras.

one-eyed turtle: (J. ichigen-no-kame; 一眼の亀) The story of the one-eyed turtle is an analogy for how rare and difficult it is to encounter a **buddha**. According to the story, at the bottom of the ocean there lives a one-eyed turtle whose belly is too hot and upper shell is too cold. Every hundred (or a thousand years) the turtle rises to the surface in the hope that it will happen to find a floating sandalwood log with a hollow in it that is just the right size for it to fit into so it can simultaneously cool its belly and have its shell warmed by the sun. A version of this analogy is found in the *Connected Discourses* (CD 56.48, p. 1872) and is referred to in the *Lotus Sutra*, and the *Nirvana Sutra*. (LS, p. 339; NS1, p. 36)

Onjoji Temple: (J. Onjōji; 園城寺) Also called Mii-dera after the name of the area where it is located. The head temple of the Temple school faction of the Japanese **Tiantai school** located in Onjōji-machi, Ōtsu-shi, Shiga Prefecture today, which was formerly called Ōmi Province. The name Temple school is used in contrast to the **Enryakuji Temple** faction of the Tendai Shu, which is called the Mountain school. Onjoji was founded by Otomoyota-ō in 668. It was restored by **Enchin** in 858 and called Mii-dera, thus he is regarded as the founder of the Temple school faction within the Tendai Shu.

Nichiren Shonin is believed to have visited it while studying in Kyoto and Nara.

opening of the provisional to reveal the true: (J. kaigon-kenjitsu; 開権顕実) A reference to the statement in the tenth, "The **Teacher of the Dharma**," chapter of the *Lotus Sutra* that "This sutra opens the gate of expedients and reveals the seal of the truth." (LS, p. 182) This means that the *Lotus Sutra* as the **true sutra** reveals or opens up the implicit meaning or final intent of the **provisional sutra**s, or more specifically it relates to the **opening of the three vehicles to reveal the One Vehicle**.

opening of the three vehicles to reveal the One Vehicle: (J. kaisan ken'itsu/kaisan-kenichi; 開三顕一) The opening of the **three vehicles** for **voice-hearers**, **privately-awakened ones**, and **bodhisattvas** and revealing the **One Vehicle** to attain **buddhahood** is the central theme taught in the **Trace Gate** of the *Lotus Sutra*.

ordinary people: See **ordinary person**.

ordinary person: (S. pṛthagjana; J. bombu/bonbu; 凡夫) An unawakened person still bound to **samsara**, as opposed to a noble person who has attained one of the **four fruitions**. **Nichiren Shonin** considered all the people in the **Latter Age of Degeneration** to be **ignorant** and guilty of committing **slander of the True Dharma**, so he stressed the great compassion of the **Eternal Shakyamuni Buddha** to save the ordinary people in the Latter Age.

ordinary stage: (J. bon-i; 凡位) The initial portion of the stages of **voice-hearer** practice in the **tripitaka teaching**. It consists of the **ordinary stage of the outer level** and the **ordinary stage of the inner level**. (PMLS2, pp. 200-202)

ordinary stage of the inner level: (J. nai-bon; 内凡) The latter stage of the **ordinary stage** of the stages of **voice-hearer** practice in the **tripitaka teaching**. There are four sub-stages to the stage of the inner level which are equivalent to the **four wholesome roots**: 1) **heat**, 2) the **summit**, 3) **patience**₍₂₎, and 4) **highest mundane dharma**.

ordinary stage of the outer level: (J. ge-bon; 外凡) The initial stage of the **ordinary stage** of the stages of **voice-hearer** practice in the **tripitaka teaching**. There are three sub-stages to the stage of the outer level: 1) the stage of practice of the **five contemplations for settling the mind**; 2) the stage of contemplating the **particular characteristics** of the **four foundations of mindfulness**; and 3) the stage of contemplating the **general characteristics** of the four foundations of mindfulness. In this way, the practitioner can overcome the four inverted views of believing that **conditioned** phenomena can be characterized by purity, bliss, **eternity**, or **self**hood.

origin of suffering, the truth of the: (S. samudaya-satya; J. jittai or jūttai; 集諦) The second of the **four noble truths**. The origin of **suffering** is described by **Shakyamuni Buddha** as craving for pleasure which leads to **rebirth**. He further specifies that it is craving for sensual pleasure, for existence, and for non-existence. (LD 22.19, p. 346; CD 56.11, p. 1844)

Original Buddha: (J. honbutsu/hommbutsu; 本仏) Also called the **Eternal Shakyamuni Buddha**. The Original Buddha is Shakyamuni Buddha as he appears in chapter sixteen, "The **Duration of the Life of the Tathagata**," chapter of the *Lotus Sutra*.

original attendants, subtlety of the: (J. hon-kenzoku-myō; 本眷属妙) The seventh of the **ten subtleties of the Original Gate**. It refers to the **bodhisattvas appearing from underground** who were the **Eternal Shakyamuni Buddha**'s disciples at the time of origin, or **attainment of buddhahood in the remotest past**. The Buddha speaks of it, in "The **Appearance of Bodhisattvas from Underground**," chapter of the *Lotus Sutra*, when he says, "Ajita, know this, these great bodhisattvas have studied and practiced the **wisdom** of the Buddha for the past innumerable **kalpa**s. They are my sons because I taught them and caused them to aspire for great **awakening**. They have been living in this world [for the past innumerable kalpas]." (LS, p. 242 adapted) The subtlety of the original attendants contains the subtlety of attendants of the **ten subtleties of the Trace Gate**. (PMLS2, pp. 320-325)

original benefits, subtlety of the: (J. hon-riyaku-myō; 本利益妙) The tenth of the **ten subtleties of the Original Gate**. This refers to the **Eternal Shakyamuni Buddha**'s constant bestowal of **benefits** upon **sentient beings** since the time of origin, or **attainment of buddhahood in the remotest past**. The Buddha speaks of it, in "The **Duration of the Life of the Tathagata" chapter** of the *Lotus Sutra*, when he says, "I expounded the **Wonderful Dharma** with these various expedients, and caused the living beings to rejoice," (LS, p. 248) and in the "The **Variety of Merits" chapter** when he says, "Thereupon the innumerable, *asamkhya* living beings in the great congregation, who had heard from the Buddha that the duration of his life was so many **kalpa**s as previously stated, obtained great benefits." (LS, p. 256) The subtlety of the original benefits contains the subtlety of **merits and benefits** of the **ten subtleties of the Trace Gate**. (PMLS2, pp. 320-326)

original cause and original effect: (J. hon'in-honga; 本因本果) The original cause is the causal conduct of the **Eternal Shakyamuni Buddha** revealed in the **Original Gate** of the *Lotus Sutra*. The original effect is his resulting virtue. That is to say, the original cause and original effect means the great **merit** of Shakyamuni Buddha's practice since the eternal past and the great virtue he gained as a result of his great conduct.

Original **cause** and original **effect** are the first two of the **ten subtleties of the Original Gate**. They also refer to the **mutual possession of the ten realms**. This is because the realm of **buddhahood**, the effect aimed for in Buddhist practice, includes the other nine realms that are the causes of buddhahood's unfolding. Conversely, the realm of buddhahood is nascent within each of the nine realms. (WNS2, p. 48)

original cause, subtlety of the: (J. hon-in-myō; 本因妙) The first of the **ten subtleties of the Original Gate**. It refers to the initial cultivation of **bodhisattva practice** in the remote past by the **Eternal Shakyamuni Buddha**. The Buddha speaks of it, in "The **Duration of the Life of the Tathagata" chapter** of the *Lotus Sutra*, when he says, "The duration of my life, which I obtained by the practice of the way of bodhisattvas, has not yet expired." (LS, p. 249) The subtlety of the original **cause** contains the subtleties of **objects**, **knowledges**, **practices**, and **stages** of the **ten subtleties of the Trace Gate**. (PMLS2, pp. 320-324)

original effect, subtlety of the: (J. hon-ka-myō; 本果妙) The second of the **ten subtleties of the Original Gate**. It refers to the **attainment of buddhahood in the remotest past** by the **Eternal Shakyamuni Buddha**. The Buddha speaks of it, in

"The **Duration of the Life of the Tathagata" chapter** of the *Lotus Sutra*, when he says, "To tell the truth, good men, it is many hundreds of thousands of billions of *nayuta*s of **kalpa**s since I became the Buddha," (LS, p. 247) and also, when he says, "In reality I became the Buddha in the remotest past as I previously stated. I told them this as an expedient to teach them, to lead them into the Way to Buddhahood." (LS, p. 249) The subtlety of the original **effect** contains the subtlety of the **threefold Dharma** of the **ten subtleties of the Trace Gate**. (PMLS2, pp. 320-324)

original expounding of the Dharma, subtlety of: (J. hon-seppō-myō; 本説法妙) The sixth of the **ten subtleties of the Original Gate**. It refers to the **Eternal Shakyamuni Buddha expounding the Dharma** at the time of origin, or **attainment of buddhahood in the remotest past**. The Buddha speaks of it in "The **Appearance of Bodhisattvas from Underground," chapter** of the *Lotus Sutra*, when he says, "Then I taught them, and caused them to aspire for **awakening**. Now they are in the stage of **non-retrogression**. They will be able to become buddhas." (adapted LS, pp. 242-243) The subtlety of the original expounding of the Dharma contains the subtlety of the expounding of the Dharma of the **ten subtleties of the Trace Gate**. (PMLS2, pp. 320-325)

Original Gate: (J. hommon or honmon; 本門) The latter fourteen chapters of the *Lotus Sutra* from the fifteenth chapter on "The **Appearance of Bodhisattvas from Underground**" to the last chapter, "The Encouragement of Universal Sage Bodhisattva," is referred to as the Original Gate, meaning the teaching of the **Original Buddha**. The main theme of this section is replacing the teaching of the **attainment of awakening for the first time** by **Shakyamuni Buddha** under the **Bodhi tree** in **Bodhgaya** with the doctrine of the **attainment of buddhahood in the remotest past** by the **Eternal Shakyamuni Buddha**. In the **Trace Gate** the world of the Buddha's awakening is expounded to guide the Buddha's contemporaries, whereas in the Original Gate the Original Buddha was revealed to show that the Buddha's guidance of **sentient being**s continues from the remotest (or eternal) past on into the infinite future.

While **Zhiyi** established his doctrine based on the Trace Gate, **Nichiren Shonin** based his teaching concerning the Eternal Shakyamuni Buddha on the Original Gate as the means of saving **ordinary people** living in the **Latter Age of Degeneration**.

original land, subtlety of the: (J. hon-kokudo-myō; 本国土妙) The third of the **ten subtleties of the Original Gate**. It refers to the Land of Co-existence, where the **Eternal Shakyamuni Buddha** resided at the time of origin, or **attainment of buddhahood in the remotest past**. The Buddha speaks of it, in "The **Duration of**

the Life of the Tathagata" chapter of the *Lotus Sutra*, when he says, "All this time I have been living in this **Saha world**, and teaching [the **sentient being**s of this world] by expounding the **Dharma** to them. I also have been leading and benefiting the sentient beings of one hundred thousand billion *nayuta asamkhya* worlds outside this world." (LS, p. 248 adapted) The other worlds mentioned in the passage indicate the other three of the four lands and all four lands together comprise the subtlety of the original land. (PMLS2, pp. 320-324)

original lifespan, subtlety of the: (J. hon-jumyō-myō; 本寿命妙) The ninth of the **ten subtleties of the Original Gate**. This refers to the **Eternal Shakyamuni Buddha**'s constant display of various lives with different lifespans since the time of origin, or **attainment of buddhahood in the remotest past**. The Buddha speaks of it in "The **Duration of the Life of the Tathagata**" chapter of the *Lotus Sutra* when he says, "Then I named myself differently, and told them of the duration of my life differently, according to their **capacities**." (LS, p. 248) (PMLS2, pp. 320-326)

original nirvana, subtlety of the: (J. hon-nehan-myō; 本涅槃妙) The eighth of the **ten subtleties of the Original Gate**. This refers to the attainment of **nirvana** by the **Eternal Shakyamuni Buddha** at the time of origin, or **attainment of buddhahood in the remotest past**. The Buddha speaks of it in "The **Duration of the Life of the Tathagata**" chapter of the *Lotus Sutra* when he says, "Although I shall never enter into nirvana, I say to men of little virtue, 'I shall pass away.'" (LS, pp. 249-250) According to **Zhiyi**, the **final nirvana** of the perfect teaching is the great final nirvana with the four virtues of **eternity**, bliss, **self**, and purity. (PMLS2, pp. 320-326)

original receptivity and response, subtlety of the: (J. hon-kannō-myō; 本感応妙) The fourth of the **ten subtleties of the Original Gate**. It refers to the **Eternal Shakyamuni Buddha** being able to perceive the **capacities** of all **sentient beings** and respond to them out of **loving-kindness** and **compassion** at the time of origin, or **attainment of buddhahood in the remotest past**. The Buddha speaks of it in "The **Duration of the Life of the Tathagata**" chapter of the *Lotus Sutra* when he says, "When some people came to me, I saw the strength of the power of their **faith** and of the other **faculties** of theirs with the **buddha eye**." (LS, p. 248 adapted) The subtlety of the original **receptivity and response** contains the subtlety of the receptivity and response of the **ten subtleties of the Trace Gate**. (PMLS2, pp. 320-324)

original supernatural powers, subtlety of the: (J. hon-jinzū-myō; 本神通妙)

The fifth of the **ten subtleties of the Original Gate**. It refers to the **Eternal Shakyamuni Buddha**'s use of **supernatural powers** at the time of origin, or **attainment of buddhahood in the remotest past**. The Buddha speaks of it in "The **Duration of the Life of the Tathagata**" chapter of the *Lotus Sutra* when he says, "I will tell you about my hidden core and supernatural powers," (LS, p. 247) and when he says, "I showed my replicas [in some sutras,] and my transformations [in other sutras]. I described my deeds [in some sutras,] and the deeds of others [in other sutras]." (LS, p 249) His showing of replicas and transformations refers respectively to the revealing of the **perfect teaching** or the other three of the **four doctrinal teachings**. The subtlety of the original supernatural powers contains the subtlety of supernatural powers of the **ten subtleties of the Trace Gate**. (PMLS2, pp. 320-325)

original vow: (S. pūrva-praṇidhāna; J. hongan; 本願) The Sanskrit term *pūrvapraṇidhāna* can also be translated as "prior vow." The Chinese ideogram 本 means "original" or "initial"; while 願 means "desire" or "wish" and is taken to mean "vow." It refers to the original **vows** of a **bodhisattva** that are made when they are first **generating the thought of awakening**. In the **Pure Land school**, the original vow specifically refers to the eighteenth vow made by Dharma Treasury Bodhisattva before he became **Amitabha Buddha**.

other-enjoyment-body: (S. parasaṃbhoga-kāya; J. tajūyū-shin; 他受用身) One of the two kinds of **enjoyment-body**.

According to the *Demonstration of Consciousness-Only Treatise*, the other-enjoyment-bodies are bodies of subtle, **pure** qualities that abide in completely **pure lands** manifested by **tathagatas** by means of their equality knowledge. For all the **bodhisattvas** on the **ten grounds**, they manifest great **supernatural powers**, turn the true **Wheel of the Dharma**, and rend the net of doubts, enabling the bodhisattvas to enjoy the bliss of the **Mahayana Dharma**. (DCOT, p. 361; CWL, p. 793)

The treatise also says that an other-enjoyment-body is devoid of real **mind** and **form** but is an apparition manifested in order to teach others and bring them **benefit** and happiness. (DCOT, pp. 361-367; CWL, pp. 795-805)

outer way: See **non-Buddhist teachings**.

outflow: (S. āsrava or āśrava; J. ro; 漏) The Sanskrit term *āsrava* can also be translated as "canker," "contaminant," "effluent," "flux," "leaking," or "taint." It is a contaminated outflow of the tendencies that **causes suffering** through the leaking or flowing away of the **mind** into objects. The outflows are connected with sensuality, becoming, and **ignorance**. (CD 45.163, pp. 1560-1561; AKB3, pp. 829, 834-835) Views are sometimes added to this list. (MD 2.5-11, pp. 91-93)

outgrowing the traces and revealing the origin: (J. hosshaku-kempon; 発迹顕本) Refers to teachings that outgrow the perspective of the **Trace Gate** of the *Lotus Sutra* and reveal the concept of the **Eternal Shakyamuni Buddha** in the **Original Gate**. According to the Trace Gate, Shakyamuni Buddha attained **awakening three thousand dust-particle kalpas** ago, but in the Original Gate it is expounded that his **attainment of awakening for the first time** happened in the remote past of **five hundred dust-particle kalpas** ago (despite the phrase this is actually a countless number of kalpa). This means that because the Trace Gate of the *Lotus Sutra* does not reveal the eternity of the Buddha, actual buddhahood is not available. In the Original Gate, in which the **attainment of buddhahood in the remotest past** is taught, the **mutual possession of the ten realms** and the three thousand realms in a single thought-moment doctrines are truly established, through which all beings attain buddhahood.

Outstanding Principles of the Lotus Sutra: (J. *Hokke-shūku*; 法華秀句) An essay in ten chapters written by **Saicho** in order to refute the argument of **Tokuitsu**, a **monk** of the **Dharma Characteristics school** and prove the superiority of the *Lotus Sutra*.

Parshva: (c. second century; S. Pārśva; J. Barishiba or Kyō-biku or Kyō-sonja; 波栗濕縛 / 婆栗濕婆 or 脇比丘 or 脇尊者 / 脅尊者) In the *Transmission of the Dharma Treasury Sutra*, Parshva was the successor of Buddhamitra in the list of **twenty-three** or **twenty-four successors** or patriarchs after **Shakyamuni Buddha**.

particular characteristic: (S. sva-lakṣaṇa; J. ji-sō; 自相) The Sanskrit term *sva-lakṣaṇa* can also be translated as "own **mark**" or "specific mark." It is sometimes considered synonymous with **self-nature**.

In terms of the **four foundations of mindfulness**, body is particularly characterized by impurity, **feeling**s are particularly characterized by **suffering**, mental states are particularly characterized by **impermanence**, and **phenomena** (**dharma**s) are particularly characterized by **non-self**.

patience: (1) (S. kṣānti; J. nin or ninniku; 忍 or 忍辱) The Sanskrit term *kṣānti* can also be translated as "endurance," "forbearance," and "steadfastness." It can also be translated as "acquiescence," "acceptance" or "receptivity" in relation to a practitioner's assimilation of the **four noble truths** and/or the teaching of **emptiness**.

In **Mahayana** Buddhism, patience is the third of the **six perfections** of a **bodhisattva**. As a **bodhisattva practice**, patience includes patience with resentment and violence shown by others, patience to endure **suffering** generally, and the patience to investigate the **Dharma** (or the **non-arising** of dharmas).

(2) (J. nin-i or nin-pō; 忍位 or 忍法) is the name of the third stage of the **four wholesome roots**. According to the *Treasury of Abhidharma Treatise*, it arises from the stage of the **summit**, and continues the **contemplation** of the **four foundations of mindfulness**. It is called *kṣānti* here in the sense of "acquiescence," "acceptance" or "receptivity" because at this stage the practitioner's appreciation for the **four noble truths** is strong and there is no longer any danger of falling away from further progress. In its weak state, it continues to develop **mindfulness** of **phenomena**. In the final two moments of the medium state the focus is restricted to the **impermanence** and **suffering** of the **form realm**. The strong state of this stage last only for a moment as the practitioner considers only the impermanence of the form realm. (AKB3, pp. 931-933)

Peaceful Place of Awakening: (S. upaśama-bodhimaṇḍa; J. jakumetsu-dōjō; 寂滅道場) Refer to the place at the foot of the **Bodhi tree** to the south of **Bodhgaya** where **Shakyamuni Buddha** attained **unsurpassed, complete, and perfect awakening** located in the vicinity of the Nairanjana River in **Magadha**, India. This was also the place where Shakyamuni Buddha is supposed to have taught the *Flower Garland Sutra*.

"Peaceful Practices," chapter: (J. *Anraku-gyō-hon*; 安楽行品) The fourteenth chapter of the *Lotus Sutra*. In this chapter, in response to **Manjushri Bodhisattva**'s question about how bodhisattvas in the initial stages of practice should spread the sutra in the evil age after the passing of **Shakyamuni Buddha**, the Buddha taught the four peaceful practices of peaceful deeds, peaceful words, peaceful thoughts, and peaceful vows. The chapter also contains the parable of the brilliant gem in the topknot showing how difficult it is to encounter and listen to the *Lotus Sutra*.

perception: (S. saṃjñā; J. sō 想) The Sanskrit term *saṃjñā* can also be translated as "conception," "discrimination," or "ideation." The ideogram 想 can also be translated as "thought." Perception is that which apprehends the characteristics of an object, labels it with a name or concept, and recognize what it is based upon previous labeling.

It is the third of the **five aggregates**.

perfect and sudden precepts: (J. endon-kai; 円頓戒) **Saicho** hoped to establish the **precept platform** of the perfect and sudden **Mahayana precepts** on Mt. **Hiei**. Saicho's plan on this was approved by the imperial government seven days after his death in 822, and the first Mahayana precept platform in Japan was completed in 827 at **Enryakuji Temple**. **Nichiren Shonin** highly esteemed the establishment of the first Mahayana precept platform in Japan but was dissatisfied with it, saying that it was based on the teaching of the **Trace Gate** whereas what is needed in the **Latter Age of Degeneration** is the one based on the **Original Gate** of the *Lotus Sutra*.

perfect interfusion: (J. ennyū; 円融) The teaching that because all **phenomena** are **empty** of **self-nature** and arise through **dependent origination**, they are all perfectly interfused, interpenetrating, and mutually containing, yet able to maintain their distinct **characteristic**s.

In the **Tiantai school**, perfect interfusion is part of the teaching of the **three thousand realms in a single thought-moment**, and the **mutual possession of the ten realms**.

In the **Flower Garland school**, perfect interfusion is illustrated by such doctrines as the **ten profound gates** or the **six characteristics**.

perfect teaching: (J. en-gyō; 円教) The fourth of the **four doctrinal teachings**. This teaching can primarily be found in the *Lotus Sutra* and the *Nirvana Sutra*. It is considered complete and well-rounded without taking sides (the ideogram 円 used for this teaching can be translated as "perfect," "complete," or "round") because it presents the integration of all three of the threefold truth - the truths of emptiness, provisionality, and the middle - into a seamless whole as the perfectly interfused threefold truth. Each of the three terms, if properly understood, immediately leads to an understanding of the other two in this teaching. Also, the affirmative aspects of the earlier negations are made explicit. Negative and limiting aspects are emptied, while the positive and boundless **phenomena** of the **buddha-nature** are provisionally affirmed, and all phenomena manifests the **liberation** of the middle. The perfect teaching is found in the **Flower Garland**, **Expanded**, **Prajna period**s, and the **Lotus-Nirvana period**s of the **five periods** of **Shakyamuni Buddha**'s teachings.

The perfect teaching represents the **One Buddha Vehicle** for **bodhisattva**s with a supreme **capacity**. The truth of the middle is viewed as embracing the other two truths which also manifest the middle way. Because the bodhisattvas of this teaching see the middle as unifying and fully embracing all **dharma**s, their approach is perfect and sudden because one practice fulfills all practices. (PMLS2, pp. 144, 245)

perfection of wisdom: (S. prajñāpāramitā; J. hannya-haramitsu; 般若波羅蜜) The perfection of wisdom is the sixth of the **six perfections.** It guides and informs the others and is their culmination. The **Prajnaparamita sutras** are named for this perfection because their major theme is its cultivation by **bodhisattva**s to **attain**

buddhahood.

perfume: See **perfuming**.

perfuming: (S. vāsanā; J. kunjū or jikke; 薫習 or 習氣) Perfuming refers to the way **karmic** activity either sows **seed**s in the **storehouse consciousness** or nourishes and strengthens those that are already there. These seeds perpetuate themselves until the right **condition**s are met, whereupon they come to **fruition** as active experienceable **dharma**s.

phenomena: See **Dharma** or **actuality**.

physical eye: (S. māṃsa-cakṣus; J. niku-gen; 肉眼) One of the **five kinds of eyes**. It is the physical "eye" or vision of ordinary **sentient being**s.

place of awakening: (S. bodhimaṇḍa; J. dōjō; 道場) The Sanskrit term *bodhimaṇḍa* means "seat of **awakening**." The ideogram 道 means "way," while the ideogram 場 means "place," so that together they literally mean "place of the way."

power: (S. bala; J. riki; 力) The Sanskrit term *bala* can also be translated as "strength."
In the *Profound Meaning of the Lotus Sutra*, power as the fourth of the **ten suchnesses** is given the following definition by **Zhiyi**: "The ability to influence is called 'power.'" (FTP, p. 184)
In the *Great Calming and Contemplation*, Zhiyi further explained that power is the enduring potential to function, like a champion with many skills who may be too sick to use them but who recovers them when his illness is overcome. Likewise, the **mind** includes all powers, though **defilement**s may prevent them from being active. (CSQI, p. 809)

practices, subtlety of: (J. gyō-myō; 行妙) The third of the **ten subtleties of the Trace Gate**. It refers to various practices that are subtle because the **knowledge** that guides them is subtle. In that respect, knowledge is compared to the eyes and practice to the feet that together can bring one to the cool pond of the **perfection of wisdom**. (FTP, p. 207; PMLS2, pp. 93, 169-196)

Practicing the Pure Dharma Sutra: (J. *Shōjō-hōgyō-kyō*; 清浄法行経) The text of this one fascicle **sutra**, which has been cited as the source of the contention that three Chinese sages (Laozi, Confucius, and Yan Hui) were dispatched by **Shakyamuni Buddha**, has never been found. Scholars consider it to be an apocryphal Chinese sutra.

practitioner of the *Lotus Sutra*: (J. Hokekyō-no-gyōja; 法華経の行者) One who practices the teaching of the ***Lotus Sutra***. As it is taught in the *Lotus Sutra* that those who practice the sutra after the passing of **Shakyamuni Buddha** will encounter great difficulties, **Nichiren Shonin** believed that he was a practitioner of the *Lotus Sutra* because he experienced the various persecutions and difficulties that were predicted.

Prajna period: (J. Hannya-ji; 般若時) The fourth of the **five periods**. This period lasted twenty-two years, during which **Shakyamuni Buddha** taught the **Prajna sutras** that include the **shared**, **distinct**, and **perfect teachings**, so its teaching has two coarse parts and one subtle part. In this period, the sudden and gradual teachings were shown to be complimentary to one another. This period emphasized the **emptiness** of all **phenomena** and negated all the distinctions and dichotomies set up in the previous teachings so the way would be clear for the Buddha's ultimate teaching in the following period. This period is compared to the **flavor of fresh butter**; or the time in the parable of the wealthy man and his poor son when the father entrusts the son with his storehouses of gold, silver, and other treasures; or the sun late in the morning. (FTP, pp. 224, 232; PMLS2, pp. 20, 105)

Prajna sutras: (S. Prajñā-sūtras; J. Hannya-kyō; 般若経) Abbreviation of the **Prajnaparamita sutras**, a general term covering various sutras which claim to have the power of leading upholders to **awakening** though the power of the **perfection of wisdom**. There are many Chinese translations of the Prajna sutras including those by **Kumarajiva** and **Xuanzang**. The list of Prajna sutras includes the *Smaller Prajna Sutra*, the ***Larger Prajna Sutra***, the *Diamond Sutra*, the *Heart Sutra*, and the ***Benevolent Kings Sutra***.

According to **Zhiyi**'s comparative classification of doctrines, **Nichiren Shonin** criticized the Prajna sutras as **provisional sutras**, stressing the supremacy of the *Lotus Sutra* over all Buddhist scriptures.

Prajnaparamita sutras: (S. Prajñāpāramitā-sūtras; J. Hannya-haramitsu-kyō; 般若波羅蜜経) See **Prajna sutras**.

Prasenajit, King: (J. Hashinoku-ō; 波斯匿王) The king of Koshala during the first forty or more years when **Shakyamuni Buddha** was teaching. His palace was in the capital of **Shravasti**. He and his wife Mallika became devout followers of the Buddha. Shortly after usurping the throne of **Magadha**, **Ajatashatru** invaded Koshala. King Prasenajit won the second battle of that brief war and captured Ajatashatru, but he freed him because Ajatashatru was his nephew. In the last year of the Buddha's life, Prasenajit's wife Mallika passed away and he was disconsolate. Due to a palace intrigue, he was deposed by his son, Crown Prince **Virudhaka**. He died of illness with only one lay-in-waiting at a common rest house outside the gates of Rajagriha, where he had gone to seek help from Ajatashatru. (LB, pp. 280-285)

precept: (J. kai; 戒) The ideogram 戒 can also be translated as "**morality**." There are many different sets of precepts in Buddhism. There are the **five precepts** for a **layman** or **laywoman**, the ten precepts for novices, the six precepts for postulants, and the **two hundred and fifty precepts** for **monk**s and **nun**s. In **Mahayana** Buddhism, **bodhisattva practice** includes the **three categories of pure precepts** (the precepts for maintaining restraint, the precepts that encompass all good deeds, and the precepts for benefiting **sentient being**s). In East Asian Mahayana Buddhism, one especially influential set of precepts for bodhisattvas are the ten major precepts and forty-eight minor precepts of the *Brahma's Net Sutra*.

Nichiren Shonin taught that, in the **Latter Age of Degeneration**, upholding the *Lotus Sutra* single-mindedly may be called observing the precepts and the ascetic practices called the *dhuta*. (WNS1, p. 15) This is based on a passage from the eleventh, **"Beholding the Stupa of Treasures" chapter** of the *Lotus Sutra* that says, "It is difficult to keep this sutra. I shall be glad to see anyone keeping it even for a moment. So will all the other **buddha**s. He will be praised by all the buddhas. He will be a man of valor, a man of endeavor. He should be considered to have already observed the precepts and practiced the *dhuta*. He will quickly attain the **unsurpassed awakening** of the Buddha." (LS, p. 198 adapted)

Nichiren Shonin also cited the *Nirvana Sutra* as further evidence that the true spirit of observing the precepts is to uphold the **True Dharma**. (WNS1, p. 15; NS1, pp. 97, 185)

precept platform: (J. kaidan; 戒壇) Originally, an officially sanctioned place for the ceremony of bestowing the precepts, especially the ceremony for bestowing the complete precepts that is the higher ordination for a **monk** or **nun**.

In the **Nichiren school**, the **Precept Platform of the Original Gate** refers to anywhere that one upholds the **daimoku**.

Precept Platform of the Original Gate: (J. homon-no-kaidan; 本門の戒壇) Refers to the place where one upholds the **daimoku**, even if only for a single moment, and puts it into practice. It is one of the **Three Great Secret Dharmas**.

According to **Nichiren Shonin**'s *Sandai Hihō Honjō-ji* (*The Transmission of the Three Great Secret Dharmas*), the Precept Platform of the Original Gate should be established at a place resembling the Pure Land of Mount Sacred Eagle with the blessing of an imperial edict and a shogunal directive in a time when the worldly law and the **Buddha Dharma** are in accord and both the rulers and the people believe in the Three Great Secret Dharmas revealed in the **Original Gate** of the *Lotus Sutra*. This precept platform will supersede the Mahayana precept platform at Mt. **Hiei** that is based on the **Trace Gate** teachings. The Precept Platform of the Original Gate will be a place where all the people of the world can repent of their **transgression**s. (WNS2, p. 290)

preceptor: (S. upādhyāya; J. kaishi or kai-wajō or kashō/oshō/wajō/washō; 戒師 or 戒和尚 or 和尚) The ideograms 和尚 were originally a Chinese transliteration of the Khotanese translation of the Sanskrit term for a preceptor, *upādhyaya*. In mainstream Buddhism a preceptor is a monastic who has been in good standing for at least ten years and is thereby qualified to confer the lower ordination or higher ordination upon those who wish to become monastic members of the **Sangha**.

preliminary awakening: (J. tōgaku; 等覚) According to **Zhiyi**, preliminary **awakening** is the sixth of the seven categories of the **fifty-two stages of bodhisattva practice**. (PMLS2, p. 213; GTFT, p. 193)

According to both the *Profound Meaning of the Lotus Sutra*, in this stage the bodhisattvas sever recurring **defilement**s as they realize the **perfection of wisdom**. According to *A Guide to the Tiantai Fourfold Teachings*, even more of the **delusion of fundamental ignorance** is eliminated at this stage. (PMLS2, p. 213-214; GTFT, pp. 159, 193)

presumptuous clergy: (J. dōmon-zōjōman; 道門増上慢) The second of the **three kinds of enemies**. Presumptuous clergy are Buddhist leaders who mislead **suffering** people, especially the **presumptuous lay followers**.

presumptuous lay followers: (J. zokushū-zōjōman; 俗衆増上慢) The first of the **three kinds of enemies**. Presumptuous lay followers are those who support the **presumptuous clergy** and the **presumptuous sages**.

presumptuous sages: (J. senshō-zōjōman; 僭聖増上慢 or 僣聖増上慢) The third of the **three kinds of enemies**. Presumptuous ages are highly respected Buddhist leaders who consider themselves to be living **buddha**s and look down on all others even though they are still strongly attached to worldly matters.

"Previous Life of Medicine King Bodhisattva, The" chapter: (J. Yakuō-bosatsu-honji-hon; 薬王菩薩本事品) The twenty-third chapter of the *Lotus Sutra*. In this chapter, Star King Flower **Bodhisattva** asks **Shakyamuni Buddha** about **Medicine King** Bodhisattva. The Buddha explains that in the past, there was a buddha named Sun Moon Pure Bright Virtue who taught the *Lotus Sutra* to **Gladly Seen by All Beings**(2) Bodhisattva. Out of gratitude, Gladly Seen by All Beings Bodhisattva offered his own body as incense, which burned for twelve hundred years until it was totally consumed. He was then reborn as the son of King Pure Virtue and he again became a follower of Sun Moon Pure Bright Virtue Buddha. That Buddha then transmitted his teachings to Gladly Seen by All Beings Bodhisattva and entered his **final nirvana**. After that, Gladly Seen by All Beings Bodhisattva burned his arms as an offering to the relics of the Buddha for seventy-two thousand years. After that he miraculously restored his arms. After relating this story, Shakyamuni Buddha states that Gladly Seen by All Beings Bodhisattva is now Medicine King Bodhisattva. He also states that the **merit** of upholding even a single **gatha** of the *Lotus Sutra* is far superior to burning a finger or toe as an offering.

prior sutras: (J. nizen-kyō; 爾前経) This term is used by **Nichiren Shonin** to mean the **sutras** taught by **Shakyamuni Buddha** before the *Lotus Sutra* was expounded. According to **Zhiyi**'s **five periods** classification, sutras taught before the *Lotus Sutra* are **provisional sutras** and therefore contain only expedient teachings. Following Zhiyi's idea, Nichiren maintains that **attaining buddahood** or even **rebirth in the pure land** is not possible through the teachings of the prior sutras. (WNS1, p. 25)

prior teachings: See **prior sutras**.

privately-awakened one: (S. pratyekabuddha; J. dokukaku/dokkaku or byakushibutsu/hyakushibutsu; 独覚 or 辟支仏) The Sanskrit term *pratyekabuddha* means "privately-awakened one," though sometimes the term *pratyayabuddha* or "one awakened to conditions" has been used. The ideograms 独覚 mean "self-awakened." The ideograms 辟支仏 are a transliteration of *pratyekabuddha*. This type of practitioner has a **sharp capacity** and, unlike a **voice-hearer** who strictly follows and listens to a **buddha**, attains **liberation** without a teacher's guidance by contemplating **dependent origination**. The state of being a privately-awakened one is one of the four highest of the **ten realms**.

Mahayana Buddhism considers **voice-hearers** and privately-awakened ones the practitioners of the **two vehicles** who are barred from being able to **attain**

buddhahood because they seek only their own liberation from **samsara**. In East Asian Mahayana Buddhism, the **final nirvana** sought by the **arhat**s and privately-awakened ones is pejoratively looked upon as a lowly aspiration to reduce the body to ashes and annihilate consciousness.

privately-awakened one vehicle: (S. pratyekabuddha-yāna; J. engaku-jō or byakushi-butsu-jō; 縁覚乗 or 辟支仏乗) In the parable of the burning house told in the third, "A Parable," chapter of the *Lotus Sutra*, the teachings and practices taught to the **Buddha**'s disciples are compared to **three vehicles**. The teachings or vehicle for **privately-awakened one**s are represented in the parable by a **deer-cart**.

Profound Meaning of the Four Mahayana Treatises: (J. *Daijō-shiron-gengi*; 大乗四論玄義) A commentary on the *One Hundred Verse Treatise*, the *Middle Way Treatise*, the *Twelve Gates Treatise*, and the *Great Perfection of Wisdom Treatise* by Huijun, a Tang dynasty **monk** of the **Three Treatises school**.

Profound Meaning of the Lotus Sutra: (J. *Hokke-gengi*; 法華玄義) A commentary on the *Lotus Sutra* in Chinese consisting of ten fascicles. **Zhiyi**'s lectures on the title of the *Lotus Sutra* was recorded and compiled by his disciple **Guanding**. It explains the title in detail and all the profound doctrines of Buddhism in terms of the *Lotus Sutra*.

Profundity of the Lotus Sutra Treatise: (J. *Hokke-genron*; 法華玄論) A commentary on the *Lotus Sutra* by **Jizang**.

Zhanran said of it, "As the commentary contains slander within the very words of admiration, it is not really praising the sutra." (WNS3, pp. 35-36)

Nichiren Shonin said that this treatise does not slander the *Lotus Sutra* very much, but it does fundamentally slander it by teaching that the *Lotus Sutra* only differs in its depth of teaching but does not differ in spirit from the other sutras. (WNS3, p. 37)

propriety: (J. rai/rei; 礼) The third of the **five constant virtues** of **Confucianism**. In the *Great Calming and Contemplation*, **Zhiyi** wrote, "Keeping propriety and behaving according to social custom, such as binding up your hair in preparation for marriage, corresponds to the third precept to abstain from sexual misconduct." (CSQI, p. 1042 adapted)

provisional existence: (S. prajñapti; J. ke or kemyō; 仮 or 仮名) The Sanskrit term *prajñapti* can also be translated as "convention," "designation," "imputation," or "nominal" or even "conceptual imputation" or "nominal designation." It indicates the provisional nature of contingent **phenomena** which are **empty** of static, independent existence or **self-nature**.

provisional meaning: (S. neyārtha; J. furyōgi; 不了義) A teaching of provisional meaning uses **skillful means** that require further interpretation and cannot be taken literally as the final or **definitive meaning** of the **Buddha Dharma**.

provisional sutra: (J. gon-kyō; 権経) The ideogram 権 means "provisional," in contrast to the ideogram 実, which means "true." **Provisional teaching**s taught in the provisional sutras were used by **Shakyamuni Buddha** and his assistants as the most effective means of accommodating the circumstances of the time and the **capacity** of the people to understand, until such time as the **true sutra** could be taught.

Nichiren Shonin considered all Buddhist teachings, except the *Lotus Sutra*, to be provisional and that **attaining buddhahood** or even **rebirth in the pure land** is not possible through them. (WNS1, pp. 3-5, 25) Other sutras claimed to be supreme, but Nichiren Shonin regarded such claims as pertaining to only a relative superiority, in that a sutra might be regarded as superior in some respects due to expressing teachings of **definitive meaning** compared to **provisional meaning** in regard to certain limited topics or issues. (WS1, pp. 10-13)

provisional teaching: (J. gon-kyō; 権教) See **provisional sutra**.

Puguang: (fl. 645-664; J. Fukō; 普光) A close disciple of **Xuanzang**.

pure: (S. śubha or śuddha; J. jō; 浄) The Sanskrit terms *śubha* or *śuddha* can also be translated as "beautiful."

According to the *Demonstration of Consciousness-Only Treatise*, the **Dharma-realm** is pure because all **outflow**s are forever extinguished, so that no outflow or tendency can ever grow again, and it is naturally pure and perfectly bright. This purity also includes the **aggregate**s of the **Dharma-body** which are all without outflows. (DCOT, pp. 355-358; CWL, pp. 783-789)

pure land: (J. jōdo; 浄土) The land where a **buddha** or advanced **bodhisattva** reside, where the **condition**s are optimal for attaining **nirvana** or even **attaining buddhahood**.

Based on the teaching of the **Original Gate** of the *Lotus Sutra*, Nichiren Shonin taught that the true pure land is this **Saha world** where the **practitioner of** the *Lotus Sutra* resides, negating the Pure Land of Utmost Bliss as taught in the **Pure Land school**. Furthermore, the *Lotus Sutra* uses the names of the other pure lands to indicate this true pure land. (WNS1, pp. 67-69)

Pure Land gate: (J. Jōdo-mon; 浄土門) According to the **Pure Land school**, the Pure Land gate is the teaching that one can be saved by **rebirth in the pure land**, specifically the Pure Land of Utmost Bliss of **Amitabha Buddha**, instead of through cultivation of the **threefold training** of **morality**, **concentration**, and **wisdom** over many lifetimes in this **Saha world**. It is contrasted to the **holy way gate** which advocates practicing Buddhism in this Saha world to **attain buddhahood**. The Pure Land gate is also identified with the easy-to-practice way.

Pure Land Buddhism maintains that even transgressors and **ordinary people** with **defilement**s can be reborn in the pure land by practicing the **nembutsu**, which is easy for people of **inferior capacity** in the **Latter Age of Degeneration** to practice. On the contrary, they insist, the holy way gate teaching is too difficult for **ignorant** people in the Latter Age to practice, and therefore should be cast away.

The Pure Land gate, in contrast to the holy way gate, was first established in the *Collection of Passages on the Land of Peace and Bliss* by the Chinese **monk**, **Daochuo**, and it provided the basic doctrine for **Honen** to establish the Pure Land school in Japan. (WNS1, pp. 4)

Pure Land school: (J. Jōdo-shū or Jōdo-mon or Jōdo-kyō; 浄土宗 or 浄土門 or 浄土教) Also called the **Nembutsu school**. It is one of the schools of Chinese Buddhism. Pure Land devotions were known and practiced by members of all schools of East Asian Buddhism going back at least to the time of the monk Huiyuan (334-416) and his White Lotus Society that was dedicated to the practice of visualizing **Amitabha Buddha** and his Pure Land of Utmost Bliss, as well as chanting "Namu Amida Butsu." The practice of nembutsu, understood as both visualizing a buddha and chanting the name of the buddha being visualized, was also one of the methods utilized for **calming** and **contemplation** meditation by **Zhiyi**. After the persecution of Buddhism by the Emperor Wu in 845, only the Pure Land school and the **Zen school** continued to flourish in China. The Zen school initially held itself aloof from, and even criticized, Pure Land Buddhism. Eventually however, the Zen school assimilated nembutsu practice.

The Pure Land Buddhism which survived the persecution of 845 and later attained mass appeal throughout East Asia was not the same as that championed by Huiyuan or Zhiyi. Rather, it was a form of Pure Land Buddhism inspired by the **three Pure Land sutras**. This form of Pure Land Buddhism deemphasized the visualization of Amitabha Buddha and the Pure Land of Utmost Bliss and reinterpreted the practice of nembutsu as simply chanting of the name of Amitabha Buddha, even to the virtual exclusion of all other practices, in order attain **rebirth in the pure land** after death in accordance with Amitabha Buddha's eighteenth vow, also called the **Original Vow**. Three teachers in particular spread this kind of Pure Land Buddhism in China: Tanluan (476-542), **Daochuo** (562-645), and **Shandao** (613-681). (WNS1, pp. 4)

In Japan, the practice of the exclusive **nembutsu** was advocated by **Honen** (1133-1212) beginning in 1175. Based on the teachings of his predecessors, Honen divided all the teachings of **Shakyamuni** Buddha into the **holy way gate** and the **Pure Land gate**. According to this classification, this school negates all other buddhas and sutras insisting on the exclusive nembutsu. By the Kamakura era, Honen's version of Pure Land Buddhism had become immensely popular, though it was considered a movement within the Japanese **Tiantai school** and was not recognized as a separate school until the early fifteenth century. In Japan, the Pure Land lineages associated with Honen are known as the Jodo Shu. (WNS1, pp. 4)

Nichiren Shonin harshly criticized this school for committing **slander of the True Dharma** because they neglected the Original and **Eternal Shakyamuni Buddha**, and the true teaching of Shakyamuni Buddha, the *Lotus Sutra*, in favor of **provisional sutras** and thereby going against the Buddha's true intent. He said the followers of the Pure Land school would all fall into the Hell of **Incessant Suffering**.

Pure Practice: (S. Viśuddhacāritra; Jōgyō; 浄行) One of the **four great bodhisattvas** who are the four leaders of the **bodhisattvas appearing from underground** described in the fifteenth, "Appearance of Bodhisattvas from Underground," **chapter** of the *Lotus Sutra* who were guided by the **Original Buddha** since the remotest past and entrusted with the task of spreading the *Lotus Sutra* in the **Latter Age of Degeneration**.

This bodhisattva represents the **purity** that is **nirvana**'s freedom from all that is impure.

Purna: (S. Pūrṇa; J. Furuna; 富楼那) One of **Shakyamuni Buddha's ten great disciples**, noted as the foremost in teaching the **Dharma**. Originally a follower of **non-Buddhist teachings**, Purna was converted to Buddhism and thereafter actively assisted the Buddha in propagating the Dharma. He was also called Maitrayaniputra (S. Maitrāyaṇiputra) because his mother was Maitrayani.

He is one of the **arhat**s listed as present in the assembly in the first, "Introductory," chapter of the *Lotus Sutra*. In the eighth, "Assurance of Future Buddhahood of the Five Hundred Disciples," chapter of the *Lotus Sutra* he is revealed to have been a **bodhisattva** all along who had only been appearing as a **voice-hearer** as a **skillful means**. The Buddha gives him the assurance of future buddhahood and he is told that he will become a buddha named **Dharma Brightness**.

Rahula: (S. Rāhula; J. Ragora; 羅睺羅) Son of **Siddhartha Gotama** and Princess

Yashodhara before Siddhartha left his family. Rahula later became one of **Shakyamuni Buddha**'s **ten great disciples**, respected as the foremost in the inconspicuous observance of the **precept**s.

He is one of the **arhat**s listed as present in the assembly in the first, "Introductory," chapter of the *Lotus Sutra*. In the ninth chapter, "Assurance of Future Buddhahood," of the *Lotus Sutra*, Rahula receives the assurance of future buddhahood. He is told that he will become a buddha named **Walking on Flowers of Seven Treasures**. (LS, pp. 172-173)

rakshasa: (S. rākṣasa; J. rasetsu; 羅刹) A flesh-eating, blood-drinking, or spirit-draining malevolent spirit. The tamer ones are known as **yaksha**s. They are considered a powerful type of **hungry ghost**.

rakshasi: (S. rākṣasī; J. rasetsu-nyo; 羅刹女) A female **rakshasa**.

rebirth: (S. punar-janman; J. saishō; 再生) Other Sanskrit terms that are often translated as "rebirth" in English are *punarbhava* and *punarmṛtyu* which literally mean "re-becoming" and "re-death" respectively. This term has been translated as "reincarnation," but in Buddhism there is no **self** or even a "soul" or "**spirit**" with a **self-nature** that "incarnates" or takes on a series of physical bodies while remaining essentially unchanged.

rebirth in the pure land: (J. ōjō; 往生) The ideograms 往生 literally mean "next life" or just "**rebirth**." Upon death in the **Saha world**, a **sentient being** with sufficient **merit** or who has received assistance from the Other-power of an advanced **bodhisattva** or **buddha** can be reborn in a **pure land** such as the Heaven of **Tushita**, the Heaven of the Thirty-three Gods, or pure land of an advanced bodhisattva or buddha. In the **Pure Land school**, the term specifically refers to rebirth in the Pure Land of Utmost Bliss.

The aspiration to attain rebirth in the pure land was expressed in writings by or attributed to past Buddhist teachers such as **Vasubandhu**, **Nagarjuna**, **Zhiyi**, and **Zhanran**. (WNS1, p. 24)

Based on the teaching of the **Original Gate** of the *Lotus Sutra*, **Nichiren Shonin** taught that the true pure land is this Saha world where the **practitioner of the *Lotus Sutra*** resides, negating the rebirth in the Pure Land of Utmost Bliss taught by **Honen** and his followers. Furthermore, the *Lotus Sutra* uses the names of the other pure lands to indicate this true pure land. (WNS1, pp. 67-69)

receptivity and response: (J. kannō or kannō-dōkō; 感応 or 感応道交) The ideograms 感応 can also be translated as "sympathetic resonance" or "stimulus and response" or "resonance and response." The correspondence between the **capacity** or receptivity of **sentient beings** and a **buddha** or advanced **bodhisattva**'s response.

receptivity and response, subtlety of: (J. kannō-myō; 感応妙) The sixth of the **ten subtleties of the Trace Gate**. It refers to the subtlety of the **Buddha**'s **wholesome** influence and assistance given in response to the needs of **sentient beings** in accord with their **capacity** or receptivity to his teachings. The receptivity of sentient beings is like a pond that can reflect the moon above, while the Buddha's response is like the moon reflecting in the pond below, even though neither pond nor moon actually move. (FTP, pp. 207-208; PMLS2, pp. 93-94, 265-275)

recompense: (S. vipāka; J. hō; 報) The Sanskrit term *vipāka* can also be translated as "**fruition**," "maturation," "result," "ripening," or "retribution."
In the *Profound Meaning of the Lotus Sutra*, recompense as the ninth of the **ten suchnesses** is given the following definition by **Zhiyi**: "The **recompensive effect** is called 'recompense.'" (FTP, p. 184)
In the *Great Calming and Contemplation*, Zhiyi further explained that **homogeneous causes** and **repetitive effects** are together the **causes** for recompense in the future, and that recompense is the requital for those causes. (CSQI, p. 810)

recompensive effect: (S. vipāka-phala; J. hō-ka or ijuku-ka; 報果 or 異熟果) In Sanskrit the term *vipākaphala* can also be translated as "ripened fruit." It has also been translated as "retribution" or "retributive **effect**," but *vipākaphala* refers to the effects of both **wholesome** and **unwholesome causes**, whereas "retribution" only seems appropriate for the ripening or **fruition** of unwholesome **karma**.

relative subtlety: (J. sōdai-myō; 相待妙) In the *Profound Meaning of the Lotus Sūtra*, Zhiyi interpreted the ideogram 妙, or "subtle" (usually translated as "**wonderful**"), in terms of relative subtlety and **absolute subtlety**, both of which reveal the profundity of the *Sutra of the Lotus Flower of the Wonderful Dharma*. The teachings of relative subtlety are subtle in comparison to teachings that are coarse. Referring to an analogy from the *Nirvana Sutra*, the teachings of relative subtlety are like a complete word in comparison with a single letter or phoneme which is only a partial word, likewise the teaching of the *Lotus Sutra* is complete and subtle in comparison to the teachings of the **Deer Park period** which is incomplete and coarse. Zhiyi further explained that while the complete teachings are found in all the **Mahayana sutra**s, only the *Lotus Sutra* is direct and has no admixture of **skillful means**, therefore relative to the other Mahayana sutras only the *Lotus Sutra* is truly subtle. Finally, relative subtlety is used to destroy the coarse and reveal the subtle teaching. (FTP, pp. 199-206; PMLS2, pp. 90-92)

rely on the Dharma, not upon the person: (S. dharmapratisaraṇena bhavitavyaṃ na pudgalapratisaraṇena; J. e-hō-fue-nin; 依法不依人) One of the **four reliances**(1) taught in the *Nirvana Sutra* and the *Vimalakirti Sutra* that Buddhists should follow. In the *Nirvana Sutra*, **Shakyamuni Buddha** instructed his followers to rely on what the Buddha Dharma expounded in the **sutra**s rather than the opinions of the Buddhist masters in China and Japan.

Nichiren Shonin considered this instruction fundamental if people were to understand the true intent of the Buddha's lifetime teachings correctly, and he quoted it often in his writings. Firmly upholding this standard as the Buddha's golden words, Nichiren Shonin came to the conclusion that when one honestly believes and accepts the words of the Buddha as stated in the sutras, then it will be clear that the ***Lotus Sutra*** is the **True Dharma**. Thus, according to Nichiren Shonin, "rely on the Dharma" means "rely on the *Lotus Sutra*." He insisted that we should rely on the *Lotus Sutra*, rather than the opinions of the various masters of the various schools of Buddhism.

rely on the meaning, not upon the words: (S. arthapratisaraṇena bhavitavyaṃ na vyañjanapratisaraṇena; J. e-gi-fue-go; 依義不依語) One of the **four reliances**(1) taught in the *Nirvana Sutra* and the *Vimalakirti Sutra* that Buddhists should follow.

rely on the sutra of definitive meaning, not upon the sutra of provisional meaning: (S. nītārthasūtrapratisaraṇena bhavitavyaṃ na neyārthasūtrapratisaraṇena; J. e-ryōgi-kyō-fue-furyōgi-kyō; 依了義経不依不了義経) One of the **four reliances**(1) taught in the *Nirvana Sutra* and the *Vimalakirti Sutra* that Buddhists should follow.

rely on wisdom, not upon discriminative consciousness: (S. jñānapratisaraṇena bhavitavyaṃ na vijñānapratisaraṇena; J. e-chi-fue-shiki; 依智不依識) One of the **four reliances**(1) taught in the *Nirvana Sutra* and the *Vimalakirti Sutra* that Buddhists should follow.

repetitive effect: (S. niṣyanda-phala; J. shū-ka or tōru-ka; 習果 or 等流果) The Sanskrit term *niṣyandaphala* can also be translated as "correlative **effect**," "habitual effect," "outflowing effect," or "uniform-emanation effect." Repetitive effects are those **dharma**s that immediately follow and are similar to their **cause**s. They are the effect of all-pervasive causes and **homogeneous cause**s. (AKB1, pp. 287, 289-290)

Revealing the Profound Secrets Sutra: (J. *Gejimmitsu-kyō* or *Jimmitsu-kyō*; 解深密経 or 深密経) This five-fascicled **sutra** translated into Chinese by **Xuanzang** is the basic canon of the **Dharma Characteristics school**. It is regarded as the first Buddhist sutra to teach the **Consciousness-Only school** doctrine that insists that all phenomena represent the **mind**. It also teaches that there were **three turnings of the wheel of the Dharma**.

According to the **Tiantai school** doctrine of the **five periods**, **Nichiren Shonin** considered it to be a **provisional sutra** taught in the third or **Expanded period**.

reverse relationship: (J. gyaku-en; 逆縁) A negative **karmic** relationship that at least establishes a relationship that will ultimately bring about **liberation**. An example of this would be the poison-drum relationship, an analogy from the *Nirvana Sutra* in which a drum smeared with a certain poison is believed to have a fatal effect upon anyone who hears it beaten, even if he has no desire to hear. Likewise, the sutra teaches, as all beings possess **buddha-nature**, anyone who hears the teaching of the *Nirvana Sutra* will get rid of their **defilement**s.

reward-body: (S. saṃbhoga-kāya; J. hōjin/hōsshin; 報身) One of the **three bodies** of a **buddha**. Also known as the **enjoyment-body**. It is an idealized **form-body** that resides in a **pure land** that is attained as the reward for a buddha's accrued **merit** from previous **bodhisattva practice**. **Amitabha** Buddha or **Rochana** Buddha are examples of reward-body buddhas. Their lifespans are so long that they can be are measured in **kalpa**s.

According to **Nichiren Shonin**, the reward-body is like the moonlight, while the **Dharma-body** is like the moon itself, and the **accommodative-body** is like the shadow or reflection of the moon in water. (WNS6, p. 131) He also taught that while the reward-body buddhas of the provisional Mahayana teachings have a beginning (when a bodhisattva is able to **attain buddhahood**) but no ending (because they do not necessarily enter **final nirvana**), the reward-body that is an aspect of the **Eternal Shakyamuni** Buddha has no beginning or end. (WNS3, p. 250)

right action: (S. samyak-karmānta; J. shōgō; 正業) The fourth part of the **eightfold noble path**. Shakyamuni Buddha defined it as to abstain from killing, abstain from taking what is not given, and abstain from sexual misconduct. (LD 22.21, p. 348)

right concentration: (S. samyak-samādhi; J. shōjō; 正定) The eighth part of the **eightfold noble path**. **Shakyamuni Buddha** defined it in terms of the four meditative absorptions that lead to a rarified state purified by equanimity and **mindfulness**. (LD 22.21, p. 349)

right effort: (S. samyag-vyāyāma; J. shōshōjin; 正精進) The sixth part of the **eightfold noble path**. **Shakyamuni Buddha** defined it in terms of the four right efforts to prevent **unwholesome** states that have not yet arisen; overcome unwholesome states that have already arisen; generate **wholesome** states that have not yet arisen; and maintain wholesome states that have already arisen. (LD 22.21, p. 348)

right intention: (S. samyak-saṃkalpa; J. shōshi; 正思) The second part of the **eightfold noble path**. **Shakyamuni Buddha** defined it as renunciation, non-ill-will, and non-violence. (LD 22.21, p. 348)

right livelihood: (S. samyag-ājīva; J. shōmyō; 正命) The fifth part of the **eightfold noble path**. **Shakyamuni Buddha** defined it as the giving up of wrong livelihood. (LD 22.21, p. 348) Wrong livelihood for monastics is to get alms by "…scheming, talking, hinting belittling, pursuing gain with gain…" (MD 117.29, p. 938) Wrong livelihood for lay followers is to traffic in weapons, **sentient being**s, meat, intoxicants, and poisons. (ND 5.177, p. 790)

right mindfulness: (S. samyak-smṛti; J. shōnen; 正念) The seventh part of the **eightfold noble path**. **Shakyamuni Buddha** defined it in terms of the **four foundations of mindfulness**, which encompasses mindfulness of the body, **feeling**s, mental states, and **phenomena**. (LD 22.21, pp. 348-349)

right speech: (S. samyag-vāc; J. shōgo; 正語) The third part of the **eightfold noble path**. **Shakyamuni Buddha** defined it as to abstain from lying, abstain from malicious speech, abstain from harsh speech, and abstain from idle chatter. (LD 22.21, p. 348)

right view: (S. samyag-dṛṣṭi; J. shōken; 正見) The first part of the **eightfold noble path**. **Shakyamuni Buddha** defined it as **knowledge** of each of the **four noble truths**. (LD 22.21, p. 348)

righteousness: (J. gi; 義) The second of the **five constant virtues** of **Confucianism**. In the *Great Calming and Contemplation*, **Zhiyi** wrote, "Yielding to what is dutiful and honest, and sacrificing yourself to favor others, corresponds to the precept to abstain from taking what is not given." (CSQI, p. 1042 adapted)

ripening: (S. vipāka; J. kahō or ijuku; 果報 or 異熟) The Sanskrit term *vipāka* can also be translated as "**fruition**," "maturation," "**recompense**," "result," or "retribution." It is the moral subset of **fruition**.

Rishabha: (S. Rṣabha; J. Rokushaba; 勒沙婆) One of the **three hermits** in India, who are upheld as the legendary **rishi**s who revealed the **Vedas** and were the founders of ancient Indian philosophy and religion. Rishabha is considered by the Jains to have been the first of twenty-four teachers of Jainism in the present era of the world.

rishi: (S. ṛṣi; J. sen or rishi; 仙 or 梨師) The Sanskrit term *ṛṣi* was also used to refer to the sages or seers of ancient India who revealed the **Vedas**. The rishis of **Brahmanism** were believed to have **supernatural power**s. The ideogram 仙 can be translated as "**sage**" or "hermit" and can refer to Taoist immortals or reclusive wizards.

Rishidatta, King: (S. Ṛṣidatta; J. Senyo Koku-ō or Senyo-ō; 仙予国王 or 仙予王) The name of **Shakyamuni Buddha** in a previous life taught in the seventh, "Holy Behavior," chapter of the *Nirvana Sutra*. When Shakyamuni Buddha was undertaking **bodhisattva practice** as King Rishidatta in a previous life, he had five hundred **brahmin**s who slandered **Mahayana** Buddhism put to death. Because of this act of protecting Mahayana Buddhism, the sutra says that he was never in danger of falling into **hell** in all his subsequent **rebirths**.

Further on in the sutra the Buddha explains to **Kashyapa** Bodhisattva that his killing of the brahmins does not really count as killing because he did it out of **compassion** so that the brahmins would be cast into hell wherein they would realize their error and then be reborn from there into the **pure land** of a Buddha and gain a life of ten **kalpa**s. Therefore, the Buddha was actually giving them a life of ten kalpas. The Buddha explains that sometimes he must take harsh measures to help people.

Nichiren Shonin esteemed King Rishidatta for upholding the **True Dharma**. Citing the act of King Rishidatta, Nichiren Shonin insisted that those who commit **slander of the True Dharma** should be dealt with strictly according to the method of teaching the **Buddha Dharma** called "**subduing**." (WNS1, pp. 52, 130-131, 159)

Rishipatana: (S. Ṛṣipatana; J. Sennin-dasho; 仙人堕処) The Sanskrit name Ṛṣipatana means "place where **rishi**s gather." It is another name for the **Deer Park** in **Varanasi**.

Rochana: (J. Rushana; 盧舎那/盧遮那) An abbreviated form of **Vairochana Buddha**. **Zhiyi**, however, associated Rochana with the **reward-body** and Vairochana with the **Dharma-body**.

Ryokan: (1217-1303; J. Ryōkan; 良観) Also known as Ryokan-bo Ninsho (J. Ryōkan-bō Ninshō; 良観房忍性). A **monk** from Yamato Province (Nara Prefecture) who was ordained by **Eison** of the Saijdaiji Temple in Nara. He was invited to Kamakura to propagate the Mantra-Discipline school (J. Shingon Risshū; 真言律宗) teaching by Hojo Nagatoki. He founded such temples as Gokurakuji Temple in Kamakura under the patronage of Hojo Tokiyori and Nagatoki and undertook several social welfare projects such as building hospitals and roads.

He was one of those who despised, slandered, and persecuted **Nichiren Shonin**, who was harshly critical of him and the Mantra-Discipline school for misleading the people. Nichiren Shonin believed that both **hinayana** and **Mahayana precept**s were evil teachings that confused people, leading them to evil realms. He also disparagingly referred to Ryokan as Ryoka or "Two Fires" (J. Ryōka-bō; 両火房) in reference to the fire that burned down Gokurakuji Temple and the shogun's palace in March of 1275.

Sacred Eagle, Mount: (S. Gṛdhrakūṭa-parvata; J. Ryōju-sen, Gishakussen/Gishakutsu-sen, or Ryō-zen; 霊鷲山 or 耆闍崛山 or 霊山) The Sanskrit name Gṛdhrakūṭaparvata means "Vulture Peak." However, the ideogram 鷲 can mean "eagle" or "vulture," so that 霊鷲山 can mean "Sacred Eagle Peak" or "Sacred Vulture Peak." It is a hill located to the northeast of Rajagriha in **Magadha**, India. The top of this peak is shaped like an eagle or vulture. It is said that **Shakyamuni** Buddha had expounded the *Lotus Sutra* on this hill for the last eight years of his life.

Nichiren Shonin regarded this peak as the most important of all **pure land**s. He later he likened it to Mount Minobu, considering them both the sacred mountains of the Lotus school.

Sacred Title of the Original Gate: (J. hommon-no-daimoku; 本門の題目) Refers to the **daimoku** of the *Lotus Sutra*. It is one of the **Three Great Secret Dharmas.**

sage: (S. muni; J. seija or shōnin or muni; 聖者 or 聖人 or 牟尼) The Sanskrit term *muni* refers to those who attain **liberation** through silent meditation. The name **Shakyamuni**, therefore, means "Silent **Sage** of the **Shakya** clan." The ideograms 聖者 can also be translated as "holy person" or "saint."

Saha world: (S. Sahā-loka; J. Shaba-sekai or nindo or nin-kai or kannin-sekai; 娑婆世界 or 忍土 or 忍界 or 堪忍世界) The Sanskrit term *sahāloka* literally means the "world of endurance." It is the name of this world in which we live. Unlike the Pure Land of Utmost Bliss to the west, this world is conceived of as being polluted by the **three poisons** and the people in it must endure many kinds of **suffering**.
Based on the sixteenth, "The **Duration of the Life of the Tathagata**," chapter of the *Lotus Sutra*, **Nichiren Shonin** insists that this Saha world is the Pure Land of Eternally Tranquil Light, where the **Eternal Shakyamuni Buddha** resides, and that we should uphold the **daimoku** in order to purify this world that is polluted with **defilement**s in the present **Latter Age of Degeneration**. (WNS1, pp. 3)

Saicho: (767-822; J. Saichō; 最澄) The founder of the Japanese **Tiantai school**. He is also known posthumously as the **Great Master Dengyo**.
At age eleven, Saicho began his studies with Gyohyo. He was ordained at Todaiji Temple at the age of nineteen in 785. He immediately went into retreat on Mt. **Hiei**, where he stayed in a small hermitage that would eventually become **Enryakuji Temple**. There he spent his time meditating, reciting, and copying **sutra**s, and studying the teachings of **Zhiyi**, the founder of the **Tiantai school** in China, that had been brought to Japan by Jianzhen.
In 802, Saicho was invited to a lecture retreat at Takaosanji Temple. His lectures on the **three major works of the Lotus school** are said to have greatly impressed the other fourteen participants who came from the **seven major temples in Nara**. (Groner, pp. 34-37)
In 804, the imperial court sent him to Tang China along with his disciple and translator **Gishin**. There, he was able to spend nine months studying Tiantai Buddhism with Daosui and Xingman. Some of that time was spent on Mt. **Tiantai** itself. Saicho also received the **bodhisattva precept**s of the *Brahma's Net Sutra* from Daosui, some limited training in **esoteric Buddhism** from Shunxiao, and a transmission in the Ox Head school of **Zen** Buddhism.
He returned to Japan in 805 and set up two study programs on Mt. Hiei: one

for the practice of esoteric Buddhism and one for the meditation practice of **calming** and **contemplation**. The former study program attracted the attention of **Kukai**, the founder of the **Mantra school** in Japan. From 809 until 816, Saicho and Kukai exchanged teachings and assistance. The relationship broke down when Kukai demanded that Saicho become his disciple if he wanted to continue to study esoteric Buddhism with him, and also because one of Saicho's disciples refused to return to Mt. Hiei, preferring to study esoteric Buddhism under Kukai at Mt. Koya.

Saicho is also renowned for conducting a heated debate, via letters and treatises, with **Tokuitsu**, a monk of the **Dharma Characteristics school**, beginning in 817. Saicho argued for the universality of the **buddha-nature** against the doctrine of the **five natures**, that held that some people are not able to **attain buddhahood**. The debate ended only when Saicho died.

Starting in 818, Saicho began lobbying the imperial court for the establishment of a Mahayana precept platform on Mt. Hiei based upon the bodhisattva precepts of the *Brahma's Net Sutra*. Permission was finally granted a week after his death in 822.

Gishin became his successor and the second patriarch of the Japanese Tendai Shu. In 823, Emperor Saga renamed the temple on Mt. Hiei "Enryakuji Temple." In 866, Emperor Seiwa bestowed upon Saicho the title "Great Master" and the posthumous name "Dengyo." This was the first time an emperor awarded the title "Great Master."

Saicho's major works include An ***Essay on the Protection of the Nation***, ***Outstanding Principles of the Lotus Sutra***, ***Clarification of the Precepts Treatise***, and ***Dependence on Tiantai of Other Buddhist Schools***.

Nichiren Shonin regarded Saicho as a **practitioner of the *Lotus Sutra*** who was an indispensable transmitter of the teaching of the *Lotus Sutra*. Probably based on traditional Tendai Shu accounts, he characterized the 802 Takaosanji Temple lecture retreat as a debate wherein Saicho refuted the teachings of the **six schools of Nara Buddhism**, whose scholars were censured so that they had to submit a letter of apology to the emperor. (WNS1, pp. 48, 264)

sal tree: (J. śāla; J. shara-ju; 沙羅樹) The *shorea robusta*, a tree native to the Indian subcontinent. When Queen Maya, Prince **Siddhartha's** mother, gave birth to him, she was standing up and holding onto the branch of a sal tree. At the **final nirvana**, **Shakyamuni Buddha** was lying down between twin sal trees.

samadhi: See **concentration**.

Samkhya: (S. Sāṃkhya; J. Sōkiya or Suron or Shuron-ha; 僧企耶 or 数論 or 数論派) A system of analysis established in India by **Kapila** whose purpose is to show how the spiritual person (S. *puruṣa*) is separate from material nature (*prakṛti*). The spiritual person is much like the Vedic atman or **self** except that there may be a plurality of them. Material nature is composed of three qualities: 1) tranquility (S. *sattva*), 2) passion (S. *rajas*), and 3) inertia (S. *tamas*). When the spiritual person and material nature interact, the material nature that was in a state of unmanifest equilibrium evolves into **mind** (S. manas), ego (S. ahaṅkāra), and intellect (S. buddhi) as well as all the five sense organs; their corresponding objects; the physical organs of speaking, grasping, walking, excreting, and procreating; and the five elements of earth, air, fire, water, and **space**. The practice of yoga can be undertaken so that the spiritual nature can achieve **liberation** from its false identification with the evolutions of material nature.

samsara: (S. saṃsāra; J. rinne or or shōji or shōji-rinne; 輪廻 or shōji or 生死 or 生死輪廻) The Sanskrit term *saṃsāra* means "wandering on" or "flowing." The ideograms 生死輪廻 mean the "wandering or flowing on of birth and death." Samsara refers to the wanderings of **sentient being**s within the cycle of birth and death (i.e. **rebirth**) among the **six destinies**. **Shakyamuni Buddha** taught that samsara has no discoverable beginning (CD 15.1, p. 651) and presumably has no discernible end unless a sentient being attains **nirvana**.

Sangha: (S. saṃgha; J. sōgya; 僧伽) The Sanskrit term *saṃgha* can be translated as "assembly," "community," or "order." It is the community of those who uphold the **Buddha Dharma**. Specifically, **Shakyamuni Buddha** taught that the noble Sangha refers to those who have attained or are about to attain one of the **four fruitions** of **stream-enterer**, **once-returner**, **non-returner**, or **arhat**. (ND 11.11.8; p. 1566) However, the term Sangha is often taken to mean the monastic practitioners, who may or may not have attained one of the four fruitions. In broader sense, Sangha refers to the four categories of Buddhists: monks and nuns, laymen and laywomen.

scorched seeds: (J. shōshu; 焦種) **Seed**s that are no longer capable of germinating.

scripture: (S. āgama or pravacana or śāsana or sūtra; J. shōgyō-ryo/seikyō-ryō or shōgon-ryō; 聖教量 or 聖言量) The Sanskrit terms agama and **sutra** can be translated as "scripture." The Sanskrit term *śāsana* can also be translated as "**dispensation**" or "teaching."

seed: (S. bīja; J. shuji/shūji; 種子) In **esoteric Buddhism**, a Sanskrit seed-syllable or **mantra** represents a **god** or a specific thing or concept.
A "seed" can also refer to **karmic** seeds sown in the **storehouse consciousness**.

These seeds undergo **perfuming** by **action**s which perpetuate them and cause them to come to **fruition** as **dharma**s which are experienced.

seed of buddhahood: (J. busshu; 仏種) In some sutras, there is a question as to whether all **sentient beings** have or retain the **seed**s of **buddhahood**. The **Dharma Characteristics school** doctrine of the **five natures** derived from the *Lankavatara Sutra* and the *Revealing the Profound Secrets Sutra* is that not all beings have the seed of buddhahood. Sutras such as the *Great Expanded Dharani Sutra* and the *Vimalakirti Sutra* teach that even the **defilement**s might eventually lead a person to buddhahood and therefore can be considered seeds of buddhahood. The seeds of buddhahood of the practitioners of the **two vehicles** are like **scorched seeds** because they can no longer undertake **rebirth**. (WNS1, p. 274; WNS2, pp. 40-41; WNS4, pp. 58-60) There are also teachings that claim that women's seeds are scorched. (WNS7, p.121; WNS4, pp. 44-46)

In the *Lotus Sutra*, **Shakyamuni Buddha** says, "The seed of buddhahood comes from **dependent origination**." (LS, p. 44) He also warns, "Those who do not believe this sutra but slander it, will destroy the seeds of buddhahood of all living beings in the world." (LS, p. 82)

Nichiren Shonin emphasized the process of **sowing, maturing, and harvesting** of the seeds of buddhahood. He claimed that through his own practice of the *Lotus Sutra* he had been able to plant the seed of buddhahood in the bottom of his heart. (WNS1, p. 242) He also stated that practices based on other sutras, such as the **nembutsu**, were not the seeds of buddhahood. (WNS4, p. 148) He taught that it was the characters of **Namu Myoho Renge Kyo** alone that are the seeds of buddhahood. (WNS4, p. 153) Furthermore, he taught that the chanting of the **daimoku** will transform evil **karma** into the seeds of buddhahood. (WNS4, p. 142) Nichiren Shonin insisted that the present **Latter Age of Degeneration** is the time for the Buddhism of sowing. This means that the daimoku of the *Lotus Sutra* should be sown in the **mind**s of all people, even if they initially reject it, because they have either not had the seed sown in their minds before or they have committed **slander of the True Dharma** thereby forgotten the seeds that they had previously received. (WNS1, p. 42; WNS2, p. 197-199; WNS3, pp. 98, 144-145, 151, 162; WNS4 163; WNS6, p. 12; WNS7, p. 33)

self: (S. ātman; J. ga; 我) The Sanskrit term *ātman* literally means "breath." *Ātman* is a reflexive pronoun that can mean a living body or the spiritual essence of a person or just "oneself." **Shakyamuni Buddha**, however, denied that there is such a self (or Self) and instead taught the doctrine of **non-self**. (e.g. CD 22.59, pp. 901-903; 22.82, p. 926; 22.86, p. 937) However, there were at least one occasion when the Buddha refused to say whether there was a self or not, so that he would not be misinterpreted as espousing **eternalism** if he said there was a self, or **annihilationism** if he denied that there was a self. (CD 44.10, pp. 1393-1394)

self-enjoyment-body: (S. svasaṃbhoga-kāya; J. jijuyū-shin; 自受用身) One of the two kinds of **enjoyment-body** of a **buddha**.

According to the *Demonstration of Consciousness-Only Treatise*, the self-enjoyment body consists of the boundless real qualities generated by the innumerable **merit**s and **wisdom** accumulated by **tathagatas** over the course of three innumerable kalpas of cultivation, along with a perfect, **pure**, eternal, and omnipresent **form-body**. It continues, placid, to the end of time, and always enjoys for itself the great **bliss** of the **Dharma**. (DCOT, pp. 360-361; CWL, p. 793)

The treatise also says that the self-enjoyment-body is in effect identical with its **pure land**. Each buddha has a particular self-enjoyment-body and pure land, but they are all limitless without obstructing one another. (DCOT, pp. 361-367; CWL, pp. 795-805)

self-nature: (S. svabhāva; J. jishō or shō; 自性 or 性) The Sanskrit term *svabhāva* can also be translated as "essence," "inherent existence," "intrinsic existence," or "**nature**."

self-nature-body: (S. svabhāva-kāya; J. jishō-shin; 自性身) Another name for the **Dharma-body** but can also be viewed as one of the aspects of that body.

According to the *Demonstration of Consciousness-Only Treatise*, the self-nature-body is the **tathagata**'s true and **pure Dharma-realm**, the immutable equal support for the **enjoyment-body** and the **transformation-body**, free of **mark**s, quiescent, the severance of all **conceptual proliferation**, endowed with boundless real and eternal qualities, and the unchanging **true reality of all things**. The self-nature-body is in particular the support for the dharmas of great quality, so it is also called the Dharma-body. (DCOT, p. 360; CWL, p. 793)

sentient being: (S. sattva; J. ujō or shujō; 有情 or 衆生) The Sanskrit term *sattva* can also be translated as "living being." It refers to those beings with a **mind** who undergo **rebirth** among the **six destinies**.

As the second of the **three categories of existence**, sentient beings are a component of the **three thousand realms in a single thought-moment**. (CSQI, p. 815)

sentient beings are infinite; I vow to liberate them all: (J. shujō-muhen-seigando; 衆生無辺誓願度) The first of the **four great vows** of a **bodhisattva**. It is a vow to lead all **sentient being**s throughout the vast ocean of **suffering** to the other shore of **nirvana**.

separate transmission outside the sutras: (J. kyōge-betsuden; 教外別伝) The first line of a verse that maintains that the essence of Buddhism, according to the **Zen school**, is not transmitted by literary or verbal means but from **mind**-to-mind, and that it is a **way** of directly pointing to the true nature that can be found through contemplation of the mind. The four lines of the verse are: "A separate transmission outside the sutras/not founded upon words and letters/a direct pointing to the human mind/seeing the true nature and attaining buddhahood." (See Dumoulin 1994, p. 85) The verse was attributed to **Bodhidharma**, but the earliest appearance of these four phrases put together as a verse in any extant writing is in the *Garden of Matters from the Patriarch's Hall* (C. *Zuting shiyuan*) compiled in 1108 (See Foulk 1999, p. 265).

Nichiren Shonin considered the *Lotus Sutra* as the king of **all the sutras**, so this claim of the Zen school was unacceptable since it slights the sutras, especially the *Lotus Sutra*.

seven disasters: (J. shichi-nan; 七難) Refers to seven misfortunes caused by **slander of the True Dharma**, but the **sutras** do not agree on what constitutes them. According to the ***Benevolent Kings Sutra***, they are irregularity in the movement of the sun and moon, extraordinary phenomena in the heavenly bodies, frequent fires, floods, typhoons, droughts, and bandits. According to the *Medicine Master Sutra*, misfortunes of epidemics, foreign invasion, internal revolt, extraordinary phenomena in the heavenly bodies, irregular movement of the sun and moon, unseasonable winds and rains, and droughts. The twenty-fifth, "The Universal Gate of World Voice Perceiver Bodhisattva," chapter of the *Lotus Sutra* says that the seven disasters are: fire, floods, **devil**s, kings, **demon**s, being locked up in chains, and bandits.

Nichiren Shonin warned in his *Treatise on **Spreading Peace Throughout the Country by Establishing the True Dharma*** that of these seven, the disaster of foreign invasion and the disaster of internal revolt were bound to occur unless the government leaders stopped slandering the True Dharma and put **faith** in the *Lotus Sutra*.

seven heinous transgressions: (J. shichi-gyaku; 七逆) The **five heinous transgressions** plus killing one's **preceptor** and killing an **acharya**.

seven major temples in Nara: (J. *shichi-daiji*; 七大寺) The ideograms 七大寺 literally mean "seven major temples" or "seven great temples." These seven are the base temples of the **Three Treatises, Completion of Reality, Dharma Characteristics, Abhidharma Treasury, Flower Garland**, and **Discipline school**s of the **six schools of Nara Buddhism**. They are: Todaiji Temple (Flower Garland), **Kofukuji Temple** (Dharma Characteristics), Gangoji Temple (Three Treatises), Daianji Temple (Three Treatises), Yakushiji Temple (Dharma Characteristics), Saidaiji Temple (Discipline), and Horyuji Temple (Dharma Characteristics). Occasionally they include Toshodaiji Temple (Discipline) instead of Horyuji.

seven treasures: (S. sapta-ratna; J. shichi-hō/shippō; 七宝) (1) The seven treasures of a **wheel-turning king** are the wheel or war-quoit that may be gold, silver, copper, or iron, the **wish-fulfilling gem** that can turn day into night and fulfill any wish, the perfect queen, the able treasurer, the divine flying white elephant, the invincible general, and the milk-white horse that is swift as thought.

(2) The seven treasures may also refer to seven kinds of gems or precious stones, of which there are different lists. The first chapter of the *Lotus Sutra* has a list that includes gold, silver, pearl, *mani*, shell, agate, and diamond; the second chapter has a list that includes gold, silver, crystal, shell, agate, ruby, and lapis lazuli; the **stupa of treasures** in chapter eleven has a list that includes gold, silver, lapis lazuli, shell, agate, pearl, and ruby; and chapter fourteen has a list that includes gold, silver, lapis lazuli, shell, agate, coral and amber.

Shakra: (S. Śakra; J. Taishaku; 帝釈) See **Shakra Devanam Indra**.

Shakra Devanam Indra: (S. Śakra-devānām-indraḥ or Śakro-devānām-indraḥ; J. Shakudai-kan'in; 釈提桓因) The Sanskrit name Śakra-devānām-indraḥ means "The Mighty One, who is the lord and chief of the **god**s." The name **Shakra** means "mighty," while "Devanam" means "chief of the gods," and "Indra" (S. ; J. Indara; 因陀羅) means "lord." Shakra is sometimes called Vajrapani, which means "Vajra Wielder," because the thunderbolt that he wields is called the "*vajra*."

Indra is the Vedic god of thunder and lightning, the bringer of rain, the most powerful of the gods in the **desire realm**. He lives in a palace called Joyful to Behold in the Heaven of the Thirty-three Gods atop Mt. **Sumeru**. Indra is also the commander of the **four heavenly kings** and the other thirty-two gods of Mt. Sumeru in their battles against the **asura**s. Unlike the distant and serene **Brahma**, who sees himself as the aloof but omnipotent creator, Indra sees himself as the almighty lord who oversees the world and leads the heavenly hosts into battle. Indra is also a follower of the **Buddha** as well as one of the two main **guardian deities** along with Brahma. Indra's Net is also well-known as a symbol of universal interdependence and the mutual containment of all **phenomena** taught by the Buddha.

Indra often appears to test the resolve, **patience**$_{(1)}$, **generosity**, and **compassion** of the **bodhisattva**s, including the bodhisattva who would become **Shakyamuni** Buddha. For example, the *Nirvana Sutra* tells the story of Shakyamuni Buddha's past life as the Young Ascetic of the Himalayas. The Young Ascetic saw Indra in the form of a ferocious **rakshasa** who was reciting the first half of a verse, "All is changeable, nothing is constant./This is the law of **samsara**." The boy insisted on hearing the rest of the verse, but the rakshasa demanded that the boy offer himself as food after hearing it. The boy agreed, so the demon recited "Extinguishing samsara/one enters the joy of nirvana." The boy inscribed the complete verse on all the surrounding rocks and trees and then leaped into the monster's maw, but at the last moment Indra changed back into himself and caught the boy in his arms. In other past lives, while still practicing as a bodhisattva, the Buddha himself was reborn as Indra. The other bodhisattvas are also reborn, at times, as Indra.

He is one of the gods listed as present in the assembly in the first, "Introductory," chapter of the ***Lotus Sutra***. In the second chapter, "**Expedients**," of the *Lotus Sutra*, Indra is one of the deities accompanying Brahma when he convinces the Buddha to teach the **Dharma**. Indra is also one of the deities who offer the assembly heavenly garments, **lotus flowers**, and music. In chapter eighteen, "The Merits of a Person Who Rejoices at Hearing This Sutra," the Buddha says that anyone who persuades others to sit and hear the *Lotus Sutra* will obtain the seat of Indra, so one of the **cause**s by which one can be reborn as Indra is to share the *Lotus Sutra* with others. In chapter nineteen, "The Merits of the Teacher of the Dharma," the Buddha asserts that Indra will come to hear anyone who teaches the *Lotus Sutra*. In the twenty-third and twenty-fourth chapters, "Wonderful Voice Bodhisattva" and "Universal Gate of World Voice Perceiver Bodhisattva," it is stated that both the eponymous bodhisattvas of those chapters can transform themselves into Indra (among other forms) in order to expound the Dharma and save **sentient beings**. Based upon this testimony from the *Lotus Sutra*, Indra is a devotee of the sutra and may, in fact, be an appearance of one of the celestial bodhisattvas who are upholders of the sutra.

Shakya: (S. Śākya; J. Shaka or Shaka-zoku; 釈迦 or 釈迦族) The clan or more properly tribe into which was born **Siddhartha Gautama**, who became the historical **Shakyamuni Buddha**. This tribe lived in the southern foothills of the **Himalayas**, around the border of modern-day India and Nepal. Their capital was Kapilavastu.

Shakyamuni: (S. Śākyamuni; J. Shakamuni or Shakuson; 釈迦牟尼 or 釈尊) Founder of Buddhism. The Sanskrit name Śākyamuni literally means "**Sage of the Shakya**s." The ideograms 釈尊 are a contraction of 釈迦牟尼, Shakyamuni, and 世尊, **World Honored One**."

His father was **Shuddhodana**, the king of the Shakya clan whose capital was Kapilavastu. His mother was Maya. The name of his family or clan was **Gautama**, and his given personal name was **Siddhartha**.

On her way to her parents' home, Queen Maya gave birth to Siddhartha at the Lumbini Park. It is said upon birth the infant Siddhartha declared, "Above and under **heaven**. I alone am revered." Seven days after his birth, Maya died, and he was brought up by **Mahaprajapati**, the younger sister of his mother and the second wife of his father.

When Siddhartha grew up, the king sought a wife for his son. A message was sent to Suprabuddha of Koli asking for his daughter, **Yashodhara**. The answer came that daughters of the family were given only to those who excelled in various arts and martial exercises. Siddhartha proved himself the superior of all. Among the defeated Shakyas were two cousins of his, **Ananda** and **Devadatta**. He married Yashodhara and became the father of **Rahula**.

Determined to find a solution to life's **suffering**, Siddhartha abandoned his family at the age of nineteen (another version says twenty-nine) to seek the way of **liberation** through asceticism. When he renounced the world, five of his attendants also became the five ascetics and followed him by the order of the king. The five ascetics were Ajnata Kaundinya, Ashvajit, Bhadrika, Vashpa (according to some sources it was Dashabala Kashyapa), and Mahanaman. Siddhartha and the five ascetics went to the village of Uruvilva near the city of **Bodhgaya** in the kingdom of **Magadha**. In this village they practiced asceticism under three fire-worshippers. The fire-worshippers were the brothers Uruvilva Kashyapa, Gaya Kashyapa, and Nadi Kashyapa. After six years Siddhartha gave up asceticism. The five ascetics left him, and he went to **Varanasi** the capital of Kashi.

After giving up ascetic practice, he sat in **meditative absorption** under the **Bodhi tree**, and finally gained **unsurpassed, complete, and perfect awakening** at dawn on the eighth day of the twelfth month. He became the **Buddha** (Awakened One) at the age of thirty (or thirty-five). After seven weeks he went to the **Deer Park** in Varanasi to find the five ascetics so he could begin **turning of the Wheel of the Dharma**. The five ascetics heard the Dharma and became the first **monk**s, the first **arhat**s, and the first members of the **Sangha**. In this way the **Three Treasures** were established, and the **dispensation** of Shakyamuni Buddha was initiated in the **Saha world**.

After that the Buddha went back to Uruvilva and expounded the Dharma to the three Kashyapa brothers. They and their one thousand followers became disciples of the Buddha.

Then he went to Rajagriha, the capital of Magadha. He expounded the Dharma on Mt. **Sacred Eagle** outside the city and other places in the city itself. King **Bimbisara** and Queen **Vaidehi** and their court physician **Jivaka** became his lay followers and royal patrons. **Shariputra** and **Maudgalyayana**, who were prominent ascetic disciples of Sanjaya Vairatiputra living near Rajagriha, also became followers of the Buddha along with two hundred and fifty other disciples of Sanjaya. During that first visit, the ascetic **Mahakashyapa** (who became known as the first patriarch after the Buddha's **final nirvana**) encountered the Buddha on the road outside the city and became a follower.

Hearing stories about his son's travels and following, King Shuddhodana sent his minister **Kalodayin** to invite the Buddha back to Kapilavastu. Kalodayin also became a follower of the Buddha. Upon the Buddha's return to Kapilavastu, or soon after, his son Rahula, his cousins Ananda (who became the Buddha's attendant in the twentieth year of the Buddha's teaching), Sundarananda, Devadatta, and **Aniruddha**, as well as their barber **Upali** and many others joined the Sangha. Mahaprajapati and Yashodhara became the first **nun**s sometime after the fifth year of the Buddha's teaching.

After the third year of the Buddha's teaching, monasteries began to be established such as the **Bamboo Grove Monastery** in Rajagriha, the Great Forest Monastery in Vaishali, and the Jeta Grove Monastery in **Shravasti** donated by the wealthy merchant Anathapindada and Prince Jeta where the Buddha spent all the rainy season retreats starting in the twentieth year of his teaching. The last monastery donated was the **Amrapali Grove** donated by **Amrapali** in the last year of the Buddha's life.

Other disciples numbered among the **ten great disciples** who joined the Sangha after the establishment of the monasteries were Anathapindada's nephew **Subhuti**, **Mahakatyayana**, and **Purna**.

For fifty long years, the Buddha traversed northern India expounding both the **hinayana** and **Mahayana** teachings. The Buddha's teachings during his fifty year missionary life were collected and compiled by disciples after his passing as the **three baskets** consisting of the **sutra**s (Buddha's discourses), the **vinaya** (monastic rules, regulations, and procedures), and the **abhidharma** (systematized and technical commentaries on the discourses). These teachings were organized by **Zhiyi**, the founder of the **Tiantai school**, into the **five periods and eight teachings**. According to this system, **Nichiren Shonin** regarded the *Lotus Sutra* to be the conclusion of Shakyamuni Buddha's lifetime teachings.

During his fifty years of teaching, Shakyamuni Buddha had to face **nine great difficulties**. The worst of these were the attempts of his cousin Devadatta to take over the Sangha. At one point, Devadatta caused a schism in the Sangha but those who joined him were quickly brought back to the Buddha's Sangha by Shariputra and Maudgalyayana. Devadatta then urged Prince **Ajatashatru** to overthrow his father, King Bimbisara. With the help of Ajatashatru, Devadatta sent assassins and then a rampaging elephant to kill the Buddha. When those attempts failed, he tried to kill the Buddha by rolling a boulder down on him. This also failed, although the Buddha's foot was injured. Devadatta died soon after, though in the *Lotus Sutra* the Buddha predicted that even he would someday **attain buddhahood**. After Devadatta's death, Jivaka convinced Ajatashatru to see the Buddha and repent. The *Lotus Sutra* even lists Ajatashatru as present during the opening assembly of the sutra. Nichiren Shonin saw these persecutions as incredibly significant. Feeling that he had experienced similar persecutions, Nichiren Shonin taught that a **practitioner of the *Lotus Sutra*** in the **Latter Age of Degeneration** could attain buddhahood due to the great compassion of the **Eternal Shakyamuni Buddha**.

Around 485 BCE (other sources say 386 or 383 BCE) Shakyamuni Buddha passed away under the twin **sal tree**s in Kushinagara at the age of eighty.

A tradition arose that there are always **eight phases of a buddha's life**, and each of these events were modeled on the life of Shakyamuni Buddha.

In the seventh, "The Parable of a Magic City," chapter of the *Lotus Sutra*, Shakyamuni Buddha is the buddha of the Saha world who, in a previous life, was one of the sixteen princes who were the sons of **Great Universal Wisdom** Buddha.

In the sixteenth, "The **Duration of the Life of the Tathagata," chapter** of the *Lotus Sutra*, Shakyamuni Buddha reveals his **attainment of buddhahood in the remotest past** and true identity as the Eternal Shakyamuni Buddha.

Shakyamuni the World Honored One: (J. Shakuson; 釈尊) The ideograms 釈尊 are a contraction of 釈迦牟尼 for **Shakyamuni**, and 世尊 for **World Honored One**.

Shandao: (613-681; J. Zendō; 善導) Third of the five patriarchs of the **Pure Land school** in China. He was popularly known as the Master of Guangmingsi after the temple where he lived and was also called the Great Master Zhongnan. He learned Pure Land Buddhism from **Daochuo** and wrote such works as the *Annotations on the Contemplation of the Buddha of Infinite Life Sutra* and the ***Verses Praising Rebirth in the Pure Land***, establishing the doctrinal foundation of Pure Land Buddhism.

Shandao divided all Buddhist practice into those practices that were based upon the **three Pure Land sutras** and all those that were not. Shandao then selected the practice of **nembutsu**, specifically chanting the name of **Amitabha Buddha**, as the rightly established act that would assure **rebirth in the pure land**. Shandao also expounded the three kinds of mind discussed in the ***Contemplation of the Buddha of Infinite Life Sutra*** as essential for rebirth: the mind of sincerity, the mind of profundity, and the mind that vows to transfer merits towards rebirth in the pure land. Finally, Shandao provided a very graphic depiction of the way of Pure Land Buddhism in terms of his famous parable of the two rivers and the white path.

Honen, the founder of the Pure Land school in Japan, especially revered Shandao and depended on him. He considered him one of the five patriarchs of the Pure Land school of Buddhism, along with Tanluan, **Daochuo**, Huaigan, and Shaokang.

Nichiren Shonin criticized Shandao for not knowing the relative profundities of the Buddha's teachings. A story was circulated, which Nichiren Shonin believed, that he committed suicide by jumping from a willow tree at the Guangmingsi Temple. (WNS5, p. 35) He further said that Shandao fell into hell alive for committing **slander of the True Dharma** by saying that "not even one out of one thousand" can **attain buddhahood** by the teaching of the *Lotus Sutra*. (WNS1, pp. 4, 23, 27, 32, 45, 69)

Shaohao: (C.; J. Shōgō; 少昊) A legendary emperor who is sometimes said to have been the son of the **Yellow Emperor**. Shahao was the first emperor of the **Three Sovereigns and Five Emperors**.

shared teaching: (J. tsū-gyō; 通教) The second of the **four doctrinal teachings**. This teaching can primarily be found in the **Prajna sutra**s as the teaching given to the more advanced **voice-hearer**s and those just starting out on the **bodhisattva** path. Because these teachings are directed at both voice-hearers and bodhisattvas it is called the teaching they share in common. This level of discourse approaches **emptiness** more immediately or intuitively because it does not involve analysis. Instead, the practitioner can enter into an understanding of emptiness by realizing the entity of phenomena just as they are. It is also more thoroughgoing in its application of emptiness in that it applies it not just to the realization of selflessness of persons but also the selflessness of phenomena. The shared teaching is found in the **Expanded** and **Prajna period**s of the **five periods** of **Shakyamuni Buddha**'s teachings.

Though representative of the **privately-awakened one vehicle**, practitioners of all **three vehicles** can follow the shared teaching. Practitioners of the **two vehicles** use it for their own liberation, but the practitioners of the **bodhisattva vehicle** also realize non-emptiness so they can temporarily stay in the world and liberate others as well. (PMLS2, p. 143)

Shariputra: (S. Śāriputra; J. Sharihotsu; 舍利弗) One of **Shakyamuni** Buddha's **ten great disciples**. He is known as foremost in **wisdom**.

Shariputra and his lifelong friend **Maudgalyayana** were born into **brahmin** families in neighboring villages near Rajagriha, the capital of the kingdom of **Magadha** in central India. As young men they were both disillusioned with worldly life. Together they left home to become **shramana**s in order to find **liberation** from **suffering** and eventually became the leading disciples of the skeptical philosopher Sanjaya Vairatiputra. This teaching did not satisfy them for long, however, so they both set out again to find the truth. The two friends made an agreement that whoever discovered it first would find and tell the other.

Shariputra traveled to Rajagriha. There he encountered Ashvajit, one of the five ascetics who were the recipients of **Shakyamuni Buddha**'s initial **turning of the Wheel of the Dharma** at the **Deer Park** in **Varanasi**. Ashvajit's calm demeanor so impressed Shariputra that he asked him who his teacher was and what teaching he had received. Ashvajit told Shariputra about Shakyamuni Buddha and gave him a summary of the **Buddha Dharma** as he understood it in the following verse: "Of those things that arise from a **cause**,/ The **Tathagata** has told the cause,/ And also what their **cessation** is:/ This is the doctrine of the Great Recluse." (BD, p. 38) Upon hearing these words, Shariputra's quick mind realized the profound implications of this seemingly simple verse and he became a **stream-enterer**. At that moment, he knew that Shakyamuni Buddha was the teacher he and his friend had been looking for.

Shariputra quickly found Maudgalyayana and shared Ashvajit's verse with him. Maudgalyayana also became a stream-enterer and together the two shramans agreed to see Shakyamuni Buddha. But first, Shariputra insisted that they go to their former teacher Sanjaya and try to convince him to join them. Sanjaya, however, was not willing to relinquish his position as a teacher to become the disciple of another. He even tried to convince Shariputra and Maudgalyayana to stay, offering them positions as co-leaders of his own movement. The two friends were not interested in mere leadership. They were determined to attain liberation under a true teacher, so they both left, taking half of Sanjaya's five hundred disciples with them.

When Shakyamuni Buddha saw the two friends coming to meet him, he announced to the **Sangha** that they would become his chief disciples. The Buddha ordained the two as **monk**s right away. After a week of intensive practice, Maudgalyayana became an **arhat**. After another week had passed, Shariputra also became an arhat while listening to the Buddha's teaching to Dighanaka, Shariputra's nephew. It is said that Shariputra took two weeks to attain **awakening** because he needed to think through and examine all the implications and permutations of the Buddha Dharma. Because he did this, he was second only to the Buddha in explaining the Dharma, and several **sutra**s are taught by Shariputra with the full approval of the Buddha.

Shariputra was known for having the clearest understanding of the Dharma in terms of analysis and systemization. According to some traditions, the Buddha taught the Dharma in detail to his mother Queen Maya in the Heaven of the Thirty-three Gods over a period of three months. Each day, the Buddha would explain to Shariputra what he had taught here there. This transmission became the basis for the **abhidharma**, the systematic explanation of the Buddha's teachings.

Because **Mahayana** doctrine is based on **emptiness** rather than the systematic analysis of abhidharma, Shariputra is often the focus of criticism and ridicule in many Mahayana sutras. The point is that an analytical understanding of the Dharma, represented by Shariputra, is inferior to the **bodhisattva**'s intuitive insight into the empty nature of all phenomena. However, as one can see from the story of Shariputra's introduction to the Dharma, this may not be entirely fair to the actual Shariputra of history as revealed by the earlier teachings. He seems to have been a very intuitive person, not a dry intellectual. Nevertheless, in the Mahayana canon he came to represent a certain type: a humorless, narrow-minded monk whose understanding of the Dharma was too literal and naive. He is portrayed as someone who took himself and his status as a monk too seriously. He is often represented as a male chauvinist and is used to epitomize those whose spiritual concern is limited to their own liberation.

The picture that emerges from the Pali canon is very different. There, Shariputra is the Buddha's principal teaching assistant up to the very end of his life. He is even known as the "regent of the Dharma." He is compassionate, helpful, and solicitous of the welfare of the other disciples. He is also given responsibility for the administration and material well-being of the Sangha. He has great facility in reaching the highest stages of **meditative absorption**, including the ability to "abide in emptiness." Contrary to his depiction in the Mahayana sutras, Shariputra at times seems to be the prototype of the **zen master**: a master of meditation, a compassionate teacher, and one who can abide in emptiness at will. In the Pali canon, the Buddha himself holds up Shariputra and Maudgalyayana as models for all his disciples.

One of the most critical events in the life of the early Sangha was **Devadatta**'s instigation of a schism. Devadatta convinced five hundred newly ordained monks to follow him instead of Shakyamuni Buddha. Out of **compassion** for those five hundred monks, the Buddha sent Shariputra and Maudgalyayana to visit them. Devadatta was eager to have these two revered disciples of the Buddha join his group, so he invited them to join him and even to preach to the monks while he rested. Devadatta's overconfidence was his undoing, however, for Shariputra and Maudgalyayana taught the **True Dharma** which the monks had not heard before. They were thereby convinced to return to the Sangha of Shakyamuni Buddha. Devadatta awakened to discover that all his followers had left him.

In the last year of the Buddha's life, Shariputra returned to his home in the village of Nalaka. He made this trip because his mother had not yet taken the **threefold refuge**, though he knew that she had the potential to become a stream-enterer. So, he returned home to try one last time to awaken this potential. Upon his return, he fell gravely ill with dysentery. All the **god**s visited him on his deathbed. When she saw this, his mother realized that the gods she worshipped paid their respects to her son because he had attained liberation. She asked Shariputra to tell her about the Buddha and to explain the Dharma to her. Finally, she was able to open her mind and become a stream-enterer by taking refuge in the **Three Treasures**.

Shortly after that, Shariputra summoned the monks who had accompanied him and asked forgiveness for anything he might have done to upset them. He then entered the highest stages of meditative attainment and passed away.

In the *Kyōdai-shō* (*A Letter to the Ikegami Brothers*), **Nichiren Shonin** related the story that in the age of a past Buddha Shariputra had begun cultivating **bodhisattva practice**. When Shariputra had only forty more **kalpa**s of practice left until he would **attain buddhahood**, **Mara**, the **devil king of the sixth heaven**, transformed himself into a brahmin and begged for Shariputra's eye. When Shariputra took out his eye and gave it to the brahmin, who then threw it away. This caused Shariputra to regret his **generosity** and lose the **awakening mind** that aspired to buddhahood. Because of that he fell into the Hell of **Incessant Suffering**. (WNS6, p. 76)

Shariputra is one of the arhats listed as present in the assembly in the first, "Introductory," chapter of the ***Lotus Sutra***. The Buddha addresses Shariputra first when he emerges from the **samadhi** of "infinite meanings" at the beginning of chapter two, "**Expedients**." He tells Shariputra that the wisdom of the buddhas is profound, immeasurable, and beyond the capabilities of the **voice-hearer**s, of whom Shariputra was the chief representative. Three times Shariputra enthusiastically requests the Buddha to teach this greater wisdom. Finally, the Buddha teaches the one great purpose for which the buddhas appear in the world. The Buddha teaches the **One Vehicle**, in which he reveals that he only teaches bodhisattvas; therefore, by implication, Shariputra and all the other disciples are actually bodhisattvas who will be able to attain buddhahood.

In chapter three, "A Parable," Shariputra is the first to understand the import of the **opening of the three vehicles to reveal the One Vehicle** doctrine and says that he felt like dancing for joy. Shariputra explains that he had wanted to be a bodhisattva all along and is now very happy to learn that he too will attain buddhahood. Shakyamuni Buddha then explains that Shariputra had aspired to awakening in a previous existence but had forgotten. Now, upon hearing the *Lotus Sutra*, he was able to return to that **original vow**. So, in a sense, Shariputra had been a bodhisattva all along without realizing it. Shakyamuni Buddha then gives Shariputra an assurance of future buddhahood, announcing that in the future he will become a buddha named **Flower Light**. He also explains that even someone as wise as Shariputra can only understand the *Lotus Sutra* through faith.

Shariputra then recedes into the background until reappearing in the latter half of chapter twelve, "**Devadatta**." In that chapter, Shariputra appears once more as a male chauvinist monk who cannot believe that an eight-year-old **dragon girl** can attain buddhahood. Shariputra is proved wrong. Unlike his earlier joyful reception of the Dharma, the sutra states that he "received the Dharma faithfully and in silence." (LS, p. 208)

Nichiren Shonin took Shariputra as an example of **attainment of buddhahood by adherents of the two vehicles** and put his name on his **Great Mandala of Invoking the Ten Realms** as the representative of the practitioners of the **two vehicles**.

sharp capacity: (S. tīkṣṇendriya; J. rikon; 利根) This refers to practitioners of sharp intelligence, who have all but overcome **defilement**s, and have high aspiration.

Shenfang: (J. Jimbō; 神肪) A disciple of **Xuanzang**.

Shennong: (C.; J. Shinnō; 神農) The ideograms 神農 mean "Divine Farmer." Shennong is credited with teaching agriculture, medicine, and trade. Shennong was the second of the **Three Sovereigns and Five Emperors**.

Shilabhadra: (529-645; S. Śīlabhadra; J. Kaigen; 戒賢) A disciple of **Dharmapala** and a teacher of **Xuanzang** at Nalanda Monastery.

shindoku: (J.; 真読) "proper chanting." It means to chant the Chinese translation of the **sutra**s using the Japanese approximation of the pronunciations used by the Wu dynasty (222-280) in China. It also means to chant the sutra from the beginning to the end. A vernacular reading of the sutras is called *kundoku*.

Shinga: (801-879; J. Shinga; 真雅) **Kukai**'s younger brother and one of his ten great disciples.

Shoichi: (1202-1280; J. Shōichi; 聖一) A **monk** of the **Zen school** in the Kamakura period, who was also known as Ben'en, Enni, and Enni-bo. After studying the doctrine of the **Tiantai school**, he studied Zen from Masters Eichō and Shin'yū before going over to Song China in 1235 for further study. Having studied the teachings and practices of the Linji school of Zen Buddhism from Master Wuzhun, he returned to Japan and established the Shōtenji Temple at Hakata. He was posthumously given the title of State Master Shoichi by Emperor Hanazono in 1311. He is the first Zen monk in Japan to have received this honor.

shonin: (J. shōnin; 聖人) See **sage**.

shramana: (S. śramaṇa; J. shamon; 沙門) The Sanskrit term means "striver" and refers to an ascetic, recluse or mendicant. At the time of **Shakyamuni Buddha**, a large movement of people known as shramanas renounced the householder life to become mendicants and practice asceticism in order to attain **liberation** from the cycle of birth and death. They did not recognize the **Vedas** as authoritative, and their ranks included both the Buddha and his followers and the **six non-Buddhist masters** and their followers.

Shravasti: (S. Śrāvastī; J. Shae-jō or Shae-koku; 舎衛城 or 舎衛国) The capital of Koshala. It was the location of the Jeta Grove Monastery.

Shrimala Sutra: (S. Śrīmālādevī-siṃhanāda-sūtra; J. *Shōman-gyō*; 勝鬘経) A one-fascicled **sutra**, whose full title is *The Lion's Roar of Queen Shrimala Sutra*. The sutra is in the form of a dialogue between **Shakyamuni Buddha** and Queen Shrimala. It expounds the doctrines of the **One Vehicle** and the innate existence of the **buddha-nature** in all **sentient being**s. It was translated into Chinese by Gunabhadra in 436.

Shubhakarasimha: (637-735; S. Śubhakarasiṃha; J. Zemmui; 善無畏) In Japan, he is considered one of the three patriarchs of **esoteric Buddhism** in China. One list of **Mantra school** patriarchs lists him as the fifth patriarch.

He was a prince from Udyana who became a **monk** at the age of thirteen and studied at Nalanda. There he studied **exoteric Buddhism** with a teacher named Dharmagupta and earned the title of **tripitaka master**. He then studied esoteric Buddhism from Nagabodhi and earned the title of **acharya**. In 716, under the patronage of Emperor Xuanzang of the Tang dynasty, he came to Chang'an, the capital of China. In 724 he moved to Luoyang, the "Eastern Capital." There he translated the *Mahavairochana Sutra* with the help of his disciple **Yixing** between 724 and 725, the *Act of Perfection Sutra* in 726, and wrote discourses, thereby laying the foundations for the Mantra school in China.

There were legends that Shubhakarasimha came to Japan in 728 and stayed in a hermitage on the grounds of Todaiji Temple, later moving to a hut in a cave at Kumeji Temple. (TBD, pp. 122-123)

Nichiren Shonin pointed out that according to the *Annotations on the Mahavairochana Sutra*, Shubhakarasimha had a near-death experience during which fell into hell due to his **slander of the True Dharma** and was only able to escape by reciting passages from the *Lotus Sutra*. (WNS1, pp. 179-181; WNS2, p. 79; WNS5, p. 57)

Shuddhodana: (S. Śuddhodana; J. Jōbonnō; 浄飯王) The father of Prince **Siddhartha** and grandfather of **Rahula**. He was married to Maya, the mother of Siddhartha, and her sister **Mahaprajapati**.

Shuen: (771-835; J. Shūen; 修円) A Japanese **monk** of the **Dharma Characteristics school** who opposed the Mahayana precept platform advocated by **Saicho**. **Tokuitsu** was his disciple.

Shun: (J. Shun; 舜) His given name was Zhonghua (J. Chōka; 重華). A legendary **sage** emperor who had married the two daughters of Emperor **Yao** and was made successor to the throne when his father-in-law abdicated. Emperor Shun, in turn, appointed **Yu the Great** as his successor. Shun was the fifth of the **Three Sovereigns and Five Emperors**.

Shuramgama Samadhi: (S. śūraṃgama-samādhi; J. shuryōgon-zammai; 首楞厳三昧) The "Heroic March Concentration" explained in the *Shuramgama Samadhi Sutra* and the apocryphal *Shuramgama Sutra*.

Shuramgama Samadhi Sutra: (S. Śūraṃgama-samādhi-sūtra; J. Shuryōgon-

zammai-kyō or *Shuryōgon-kyō*; 首楞厳三昧経 or 首楞厳経) One of the early **Mahayana sutra**s which is referred to in the *Flower Garland Sutra* and often cited in the *Great Perfection of Wisdom Treatise*. In response to questions put forth by Free Will **Bodhisattva** about what kind of meditation would enable him to quickly **attain buddhahood**, **Shakyamuni Buddha** taught him to practice the **Shuramgama Samadhi** or "Heroic March Concentration" and explained it. He also explained that the **compassion** of Mahayana teachings would embrace all, including impure **sentient being**s in their future lives.

Shuramgama Sutra: (S. **Śūraṃgama-sūtra*; J. *Daibutsuchō-shuryōgon-kyō* or *Shuryōgon-kyō* or *Daibutsuchō-nyorai-mitsuin-shushō-ryōgi-sho-bosatsu-shuryōgon-kyō*; 大仏頂首楞厳経 or 首楞厳経 or 大仏頂如来密因修証了義諸菩薩萬行首楞厳経) A translation of the full title of this **sutra** would be the *Sutra of the Heroic March at the Great Crown of the Buddha's Top Concerning the Tathagata's Secret Cause of All Bodhisattva Practices that Verify the Definitive Meaning*. An apocryphal sutra that was allegedly translated into Chinese in 705. The sutra recounts how **Ananda** was almost seduced by a prostitute, but **Shakyamuni Buddha** sent **Manjushri** to him to save him with the **Shuramgama Samadhi**. The sutra contains teachings concerning the **consciousness-only** teachings, **buddha-nature**, and **esoteric Buddhism**.

Despite containing "**definitive meaning**" in its title, **Nichiren Shonin** considered it to be one of the **sutras of provisional meaning**. (WNS1, p. 17)

Siddhartha: (S. Siddhārtha; J. Shidatta/Shittata; 悉達多) The Sanskrit name Siddhārtha literally means "He Who Has Achieved His Aim." The given name of the historical **Shakyamuni Buddha**.

Simhahanu: (S. Siṃhahanu; J. Shishikyō-ō; 師子頬王) A king of the **Shakya** clan whose capital was Kapilavastu, father of **Shuddhodana** and grandfather of **Shakyamuni Buddha**.

single thought-moment: (J. ichinen-; 一念) The ideograms 一念 can be translated as either "single thought" or "single moment" but always connotes both because a single moment is the time it takes for a being to have a single thought. This is often taken to mean the time it would take to make a single invocation, such as of the **nembutsu** or the **daimoku**. In Japanese, can also mean to have firm determination to accomplish something.

six characteristics: (J. roku-sō; 六相) The teaching of **Fazang** of the **Flower Garland school** that any **phenomena** can be considered in terms of six characteristics.

Using a statue of a golden lion to provide examples, the six are explained as follows:
1) the generic characteristic, which is the totality of all the parts sharing in the general character of being a statue of a golden lion,
2) the constituent characteristic, which is the distinct limbs and features that constitute the statue of a golden lion each having their own character,
3) the identity characteristic, which is that all the golden limbs and other parts all share in their identity of being parts of the golden lion statue,
4) the differentiated characteristic, which is that the golden limbs each have their own differentiated character to contribute to the whole,
5) the integrated characteristic, which is that the parts of the golden lion are integrated into the single character of a golden lion statue, and
6) the disintegration characteristic, which is that integrated whole that is the statue of the golden will inevitably disintegrate back into its various components.

six Chinese ancestors: (J. chūgoku-rokuso; 中国六祖) The ideograms 中国 refer to China. The ideogram 祖 means "ancestor" though it has been translated as "patriarch." In the **Zen school**, the list of successors to **Shakyamuni Buddha** in China are: 1) **Bodhidharma**, 2) Huike, 3) Sengcan, 4) Daoxin, 5) Hongren, and 6) Huineng.

six destinies: (S. ṣaḍ-gati; J. roku-shu or roku-dō; 六趣 or 六道) Also called the **six realms**, or six lower realms, or six worlds of illusion. The six are the destinies or paths of: 1) **hell-dwellers**, 2) **hungry ghosts**, 3) **animals**, 4) **asuras**, 5) **humans**, and 6) **gods**.

These are sometimes further divided into the four evil destinies (consisting of the first four), and the realms of humans and gods, or into **three evil destinies** (the first three) and the three good destinies (the last three).

six difficult and nine easier actions: (J. rokunan-kui; 六難九易) The eleventh, **"Beholding the Stupa of Treasures," chapter** of the *Lotus Sutra* mentioned nine things considered relatively easy compared to six difficult things relating to the work of spreading the *Lotus Sutra* after the passing of **Shakayamuni Buddha**. Each of the nine "easy" things seems impossible to do, but it means that they are easier than: 1) expounding, 2) copying, 3) reading, 4) upholding, 5) listening to, and 6) revering the *Lotus Sutra*. The nine easy actions are: 1) expounding sutras other than the *Lotus Sutra*, 2) grasping Mt. **Sumeru** and hurling it to other buddha-worlds, 3) hurling the whole universe with the tip of one's toe, 4) expounding sutras in the Highest Heaven, 5) grasping the sky and walking around with it, 6) putting the earth on one's toenail and going up the Heavens of **Brahma**, 7) shouldering a load of hay and staying unburned in the fire at the end of the age, 8) expounding eighty-four thousand teachings and enabling people to attain the **six supernatural powers**, and 9) expounding the **Dharma** and enabling people to become **arhat**s and attain the six supernatural powers.

six heavens of the desire realm: (S. Kāmadhātu-deva; J. Roku-yoku-ten; 六欲天) In the **triple world** where **sentient being**s live there are six **heaven**s comprising the **desire realm**: Heaven of the **Four Heavenly Kings**, Heaven of the Thirty-three Gods, Heaven of Yama, Heaven of **Tushita**, Heaven of Delight in Creation, and the Heaven of Controlling the Creations of Others.

six non-Buddhist masters: (J. rokushi-gedō; 六師外道) The ideograms 六師外 literally mean the "six teachers of the **outer way**." These were six influential thinkers in central India during **Shakyamuni Buddha**'s lifetime who openly challenged **Brahmanism**. These were: **Nirgrantha Jnatiputra**, the founder of Jainism; Purana Kashyapa, who advocated amorality; Kakuda Katyayana, who advocated hedonism; Maskarin Goshaliputra, who condoned *ajivaka* or making a living in immoral ways; Ajita Keshakambala, who taught Lokayata or materialism; and Sanjaya Vairatiputra, who advocated skepticism. They are considered teachers of the outer way as contrasted to the **inner way** of Buddhism.

six occasions of showing the deeds and figures of buddhas: (J. roku-waku-shi-gen; 六或示現) In the sixteenth, "**The Duration of the Life of the Tathagata**" **chapter** of the *Lotus Sutra*, **Shakyamuni Buddha** said, "I told the stories of my previous lives in some sutras, and the stories of the previous lives of other buddhas in other **sutra**s. I showed my **emanation-bodies** in some sutras, and my **transformation-bodies** in other sutras. I described my deeds in some sutras, and the deeds of others in other sutras." (LS, p. 249 adapted) These are the six occasions of showing the deeds and figures of buddhas.

Six Paramita Sutra: (J. Rokuharamitsu-kyō/Ropparamitsu-kyō; 六波羅蜜経) A **sutra** that was translated by Prajna in 788. The sutra describes the **six perfections** and divides the Buddhist canon into **five baskets** by adding the basket of **Prajna sutras** and the basket of **dharani**. It identifies the basket of dharani with the **flavor of ghee**, insisting that it is superior to the rest.

six perfections: (S. ṣaṭ-pāramitā; J. roku-haramitsu/ropparamitsu or rokudo; 六波羅蜜 or 六度) The six **bodhisattva practice**s consisting of: **generosity, morality, patience**(1), **energy, meditative absorption**, and **wisdom**.

six realms: (J. roku-kai/rokkai; 六界) See **six destinies**.

six schools of Nara Buddhism: (J. Nanto-rokushū; 南都六宗) The ideograms 南都六宗 mean "six schools of Nara" but it is understood that this refers to Buddhist schools. Refers to the three **hinayana** and three **Mahayana** schools of Nara Buddhism. The three hinayana schools include the **Abhidharma Treasury school** (J. Kusha Shu), **Completion of Reality school** (J. Jojitsu Shu), and the **Discipline school** (J. Ritsu Shu). The three Mahayana schools include the **Dharma Characteristics school** (J. Hosso Shu), **Three Treatises school** (J. Sanron Shu), and the **Flower Garland school** (J. Kegon Shu).

six sense bases: (S. ṣaḍ-āyatana; J. roku-sho; 六処) The *Treasury of Abhidharma Treatise* defines the Sanskrit term *āyatana* as "gate of entry" (AKB1, pp. 77-78) Therefore, the ideogram 入, sometimes used to translate *āyatana*, literally means "entrance." Because of this, the six sense bases are sometimes translated into English as the "**six sense entrances**." Also called the six sense faculties.

six sense entrances: (S. ṣaḍ-āyatana; J. roku-nyū; 六入) See **six sense bases**.

six supernatural powers: (S. ṣaḍ-abhijñā; J. roku-jinzū or roku-tsū; 六神通 or 六通) The Sanskrit term *abhijñā* can also be translated as "direct **knowledge**" or "superknowledge." The ideograms 神通 used to translate this term means "**supernatural power**." They are referred to throughout **Shakyamuni Buddha**'s teachings. (e.g., LD 2.87-98, p. 105-108; MD 77.31-36, pp. 643-647; CD 16.9, pp. 673-674; CD 51.11, pp. 1727-1728; ND 5.23, pp. 641-643) The six supernatural powers are: 1) the supernatural power of unimpeded bodily action, 2) the divine ear, 3) mind-reading, 4) past life recall, 5) the **divine eye**, and 6) knowledge of the extinction of the outflows.

The first five supernatural powers are **mundane** but the sixth is **supramundane** and only possessed by an **arhat**, **privately-awakened one**, or a buddha.

Six-Fascicle Nirvana Sutra: (J. Daihatsu-naion-gyō or Hatsu-naion-gyō; 大般泥洹経 or 般泥洹経) Refers to the *Nirvana Sutra* translated into Chinese by **Faxian** in six fascicles, which correspond to the first ten of the forty fascicles of the sutra translated into Chinese by Dharmakshema.

skillful means: (S. upāya or upāya-kauśalya; J. hōben or hōben-zengyō; 方便 or 方便善巧) The Sanskrit term *upāyakauśalya* can also be translated as "expedients," or "expedient means" or "skillful methods." These refer to the skillful means that **buddha**s and **bodhisattva**s use to teach **sentient being**s and lead them to **awakening**.

slander of the True Dharma: (S. saddharma-pratikṣepa; J. hōbō or hihō-shōbō/hibō-shōbō; 謗法 or 誹謗正法) In general, the Sanskrit term *pratikṣepa* means "opposing" or "repudiating," while the term *saddharma* can be translated as "**True Dharma**" or "**Wonderful Dharma**." The ideograms 謗 or 誹謗 mean "to slander," while the ideograms 正法 means "True Dharma."

Nichiren Shonin specifically stated that abusing or denigrating the *Lotus Sutra*, the true teaching of **Shakyamuni Buddha**, was an act of slander, the most serious **transgression** of all. (WNS1, pp. 30-31) He insisted that those who knew the true intent of Shakyamuni Buddha and did not try to spread it were committing the transgression of slander. Nichiren Shonin tried to secure the tranquility of the country by stopping people from slandering the True Dharma or providing patronage and support to those who were doing so. For this purpose, he tried to spread the teaching of the *Lotus Sutra* throughout his lifetime at the risk of his own life.

sowing, maturing, and harvesting: (J. shu-juku-datsu; 種熟脱) The three phases of the process by which **Shakyamuni Buddha** leads **sentient being**s to **buddhahood**. In the first stage, the Buddha plants the **seed of buddhahood** in the **mind**s of the people in the way seeds are sown in the soil. This is called "sowing." In the second stage, the Buddha nurtures the seed he has planted by helping the people cultivate the **Buddha Dharma** and gradually approach buddhahood. This stage is compared to the sprouting and growth of a plant called "maturing." In the third and final stage, the Buddha leads the people to **awakening**. This is like a plant coming to complete **fruition** and is called "harvesting." Based on the "Parable of a Magic City," chapter seven of the *Lotus Sutra*, **Zhiyi** maintains that it is only in the *Lotus Sutra* that this process is made clear. The seed was planted by the teaching of the *Lotus Sutra* by the sixteen princes in the **three thousand dust-particle kalpas** in the past, it was nurtured over innumerable subsequent *kalpa* by the teaching of the **prior sutras**, and it was finally brought to full maturity (complete awakening) in the *Lotus Sutra*. From the standpoint of the **Original Gate** of the *Lotus Sutra*, the **Eternal Shakyamuni Buddha** began to sow the seeds in the remotest past of **five hundred dust-particle kalpas** ago, nurtured it since then by teaching various prior sutras as well as the **Trace Gate** of the *Lotus Sutra*, until in the end full awakening is granted in the Original Gate. Contrary to this, **Nichiren**

Shonin embodied the whole process of sowing, maturing, and harvesting in the form of chanting the **daimoku** for the people in the **Latter Age of Degeneration**. In other words, daimoku chanting contains the **merit** of the whole process of the Buddha's sowing, maturing, and harvesting in the Latter Age of Degeneration.

space: (S. ākāśa; J. kokū or kū; 虚空 or 空) The Sanskrit term *ākāśa* can also be translated as "sky," or "ether." As an **unconditioned dharma**, space is considered to have the nature of neither hindering nor being hindered by matter. (AKB1, p. 59) It is therefore immaterial, invisible, and **non-outflow**.

spirit: (J. tamashii or kijin or konjin or konpaku or reikon; 魂 or 鬼神 or 魂神 or 魂魄 or 霊魂) All of these various ideograms have been translated as "soul" or "spirit" into English, though they are not Buddhist terms and they refer to spiritual entities which are very different from popular ideas about a soul or spirit in English speaking cultures.

In Buddhism there is no **self**, in the sense of an uncompounded, independent, eternal, and unchanging real entity, that takes **rebirth**. Rather, there is a mental continuum that either immediately contributes to the **causes and conditions** for rebirth or becomes what is called a **gandharva** that traverses an intermediate existence before rebirth.

In popular Buddhist writing, when speaking of the being to be reborn in the intermediate existence, there are various terms used such as the Japanese *tamashii* (魂), which in Chinese culture refers to the *hun*, a yang spirit (or literally "cloud soul" or "cloud sprit") that represents a person's more rational faculties and which ascends into **heaven** upon death. A related term is what the Chinese call the *po* (魄), a yin spirit (or literally "white soul" or "white spirit") that represents the more instinctual faculties and which descends into the earth with the body at death. Some even believe that there are three types of yang spirit and seven types of yin spirit for a total of ten. Another word that could be translated as "soul," "spirit," or "psyche" combines both ideograms 魂魄 to refer to the composite spirit as a whole. The other terms above are similarly drawn from non-Buddhist concepts and are sometimes used in popular Buddhist writing to refer to the gandharva or a being in the intermediate existence.

Whether speaking of a gandharva or a *tamashii*, or using the rough English equivalents "spirit" or "soul," it is important to note that these words do not imply a real entity or self that is reborn, and they are all in reference to the mental continuum or activity of the **aggregate** of **consciousness**.

Spreading Peace Throughout the Country by Establishing the True Dharma,

Treatise on: (J. *Risshō Ankoku-ron*; 立正安国論) A one-fascicled essay of remonstration written by **Nichiren Shonin** on the sixteenth day of the seventh month of 1260 and submitted to Hōjō Tokiyori, former shogunal regent of the Kamakura shogunate. Motivated by successive calamities that had been overtaking Japan for several years, Nichiren Shonin claimed that heavenly calamities and disasters on earth resulted from **slander of the True Dharma** and the spread of evil teachings, and that unless the rulers of the land established the True Dharma, Japan soon would be troubled by the disaster of internal revolt and the disaster of foreign invasion. This is the central principle underlying the religious activities of Nichiren Shonin throughout his life.

stages, subtlety of: (J. i-gyō; 位妙) The fourth of the **ten subtleties of the Trace Gate**. It refers to the various stages of practice that are subtle because the practices that lead to them are subtle. (FTP, p. 207; PMLS2, p. 93, 196-238)

stars, god of the: (J. Myōjō-ten; 明星天) The name Myōjō-ten literally means the Bright Star **God**. He is also called the god (or more literally "son of the gods") Heavenly Bright Star. This Vedic god of the stars was adopted into Buddhism as a **guardian deity**.

Together with the gods of the **sun** and **moon**, the god of the stars is one of the three heavenly gods of light, whom **Nichiren Shonin** considered protectors of the **practitioner of the *Lotus Sutra***.

Steadily Established Practice: (S. Anryūgyō; J. Anryūgyō; 安立行) One of the **four great bodhisattvas** who are the four leaders of the **bodhisattvas appearing from underground** described in the fifteenth, "**Appearance of Bodhisattvas from Underground**," chapter of the *Lotus Sutra* who were guided by the **Original Buddha** since the remotest past and entrusted with the task of spreading the *Lotus Sutra* in the **Latter Age of Degeneration**.

This bodhisattva represents the bliss of **nirvana**'s **liberation** from **suffering**.

stream-enterer: (S. srota-āpanna; J. yoru or shudaon; 預流 or 須陀洹) The first of the **four fruitions** of those who practice the **voice-hearer vehicle** and thereby extinguish the **three poisons** and achieve **liberation** from **samsara** by attaining **nirvana**. The stream-enterer has destroyed the three fetters of the view that there is a **self**, doubt, and seizing upon rules and rituals. They are still susceptible to **rebirth** in the **desire realm**, but at most only seven times as a **human** or **god**.

storehouse consciousness: (S. ālaya-vijñāna; J. araya-shiki or zō-shiki; 阿賴耶

識 or 蔵識) The *Demonstration of Consciousness-Only Treatise* explains that the eighth **consciousness** is called the "storehouse consciousness" because it actively stores all **karmic seed**s until they come to **fruition**. Seeds are stored and developed in this consciousness when it is subject to **perfuming** by impurity. It is also mistaken for a **self** by the seventh or defiled consciousness. (DCOT, pp. 13, 47-48, 81; CWL, pp. 21, 105, 185)

stupa: (S. stūpa; J. sotoba or tōba; 率塔婆 or 塔婆) A Buddhist memorial monument or reliquary used to store sacred relics.

stupa of treasures: (J. hōtō; 宝塔) The enormous **stupa** (five hundred **yojana**s high and two hundred and fifty yojanas wide and deep) with many canopies adorned with streamers and made of the **seven treasures**₍₂₎ (gold, silver, lapis lazuli, shell, agate, pearl, and ruby) that springs up from underground and hangs in the sky in the eleventh, **"Beholding the Stupa of Treasures," chapter** of the *Lotus Sutra*. The stupa of treasures is a mausoleum enshrining the perfect body of **Many Treasures Buddha**.

subduing: (J. shakubuku; 折伏) The ideograms 折伏 literally mean "to break and subdue." The method of subduing refers to the means of propagating the **Buddha Dharma** by subduing the false views of others through harsh criticism and/or directly exposing them to the **True Dharma**.
Nichiren Shonin considered the beginning of the **Latter Age of Degeneration** to be filled with those who committed **slander of the True Dharma** and therefore as the time to use the method of subduing. He practiced the method of subduing in order to sow the **seed of buddhahood** in the hearts of slanderers.

Subhuti: (S. Subhūti; J. Shubodai; 須菩提) One of the **ten great disciples of the Buddha**. Originally a merchant in **Shravasti**, the capital of the kingdom of Koshala, Subhuti was converted by **Shakyamuni** Buddha when he heard him speak at the dedication of the Jetavana Monastery. Gentle in nature, he did not quarrel even against non-Buddhists who attacked and persecuted him so that he was respected by many and received a great number of offerings. Thus, he is known as the foremost in receiving alms among the Buddha's disciples.
He is one of the **arhat**s listed as present in the assembly in the first, "Introductory," chapter of the *Lotus Sutra*. Subhuti, along with **Mahakashyapa**, **Mahakatyayana**, and **Maudgalyayana** all express their joy at hearing the teaching of the **One Vehicle** in the fourth, "Understanding by Faith," chapter. These four disciples then tell the parable of the wealthy man and his poor son. In chapter five,

"The Simile of Herbs," the Buddha addresses the parable of the three kinds of medicinal herbs and two kinds of trees to these four disciples. In chapter six, "Assurance of Future Buddhahood," the Buddha gives the assurance of future buddhahood to these four, at which time he announces that Subhuti will become a buddha named **Beautiful Form**.

suffering: (S. duḥkha; J. ku; 苦) The Sanskrit term *duḥkha* can also be translated as "displeasure," "pain," or "unsatisfactoriness."

There are various enumerations of suffering such as the **eight kinds of suffering**(1).

suffering, the truth of: (S. duḥkha-satya; J. ku-tai; 苦諦) The first of the **four noble truths**. The truth of **suffering** is described by **Shakyamuni Buddha** in terms of the **eight kinds of suffering**(1). (LD 22.18, pp. 344-346; CD 56.11, p. 1844)

Sumeru world: (J. Shumisen-sekai; 須弥山世界) A Sumeru world is a kind of world system, of which there are many in the **container world**. Its foundation is a disk of whirling winds sixteen thousand **yojana**s (80,000 miles) deep and of immeasurable circumference. Resting upon the whirling winds is a disk of water eight hundred thousand yojanas (4,000,000 miles) deep and resting upon the disk of water is a disk of gold three hundred and twenty thousand yojanas (1,600,000 miles) deep. Both have a diameter of twelve hundred three thousand four hundred and fifty yojanas (6,017,250 miles). At the center of the summit of the gold disk is Mt. **Sumeru**. Seven golden mountains (a cluster of mountain ranges) surround Mt. Sumeru. In the intervals between Mt. Sumeru and each of these seven inner mountain ranges are seven freshwater oceans. Outside of the seventh mountain range are the **four oceans** that separate **four continents** located in the four cardinal directions. Each of these continents is flanked by two smaller continents or large islands. The four oceans and the four continents are enclosed by the Encircling Iron Mountains. (AKB2, pp. 451-455) The sun, moon, and stars revolve around Mt. Sumeru at an altitude equal to half the mountain's elevation. (AKB2, p. 460)

The **six destinies** can all be found within the container world. Twenty thousand yojanas (100,000 miles) below the southern continent of **Jambudvipa** are the eight hot **hell**s and eight cold hells as well as many other subsidiary hells. The principal realm of the **hungry ghost**s is also beneath Jambudvipa, at a depth of five hundred yojanas (2,500 miles). The **animal**s are found throughout the land, water, and air. **Human**s live on the four continents. Along the slopes of Mt. Sumeru and above it is located the **six heavens of the desire realm**. The eighteen heavens of the **form realm** are above that and the four formless heavens of the **formless realm** are above those.

Sumeru, Mount: (J. Shumi-sen or Myōkō-sen; 須弥山 or 妙高山 or 妙光山) Also called Mt. Meru. The mountain at the center of a **container world** according to Buddhist cosmology. Its north face is gold, its eastern face is silver, its southern face is lapis, and its western face is crystal. It stands eighty thousand **yojana** above sea level and is eighty thousand yojana wide. (AKB2, pp. 452-454) **Nichiren Shonin** likens the *Lotus Sutra* to this mountain as preeminent over all other sutras.

summit: (S. mūrdhan; J. chō or chō-i or chō-hō; 頂 or 頂位 or 頂法) The Sanskrit term *mūrdhan* can also be translated as "climax," "head" or "peak." The second stage of the **four wholesome roots**. It arises from the stage of **heat** and continues the contemplation of the **four foundations of mindfulness** and thereby the **four noble truths**. It is called "summit" because it is the highest point that can be reached wherein there is still the possibility of falling away. It progresses from weak to medium to strong states, it then leads into the stage of **patience**$_{(2)}$. At this stage, the practitioner's appreciation for the four noble truths is of medium strength, so they can still fall away from further progression.

sun, god of the: (S. Sūrya; J. Nitten; 日天) The Vedic god of the sun who was adopted into Buddhism as a **guardian deity**.

In **esoteric Buddhism**, the god of the sun represents the **awakening mind** that aspires to attain awakening for the sake of all **sentient beings**.

Together with the gods of the **moon** and **stars**, the god of the sun is one of the three heavenly gods of light, whom **Nichiren Shonin** considered protectors of the **practitioner of the *Lotus Sutra***.

Sunakshatra: (S. Sunakṣatra; J. Zenshō; 善星比丘) The *Nirvana Sutra* states that Sunakshatra was a child of Prince **Siddhartha** before he left the palace, and he later became one of **Shakyamuni Buddha**'s disciples. He was regarded as an **arhat** who kept all of the binding rules for a Buddhist **monk** and was able to memorize **all the sutras**. However, he later was induced by **evil friend**s, such as Painfully Acquired, to put his **faith** in **non-Buddhist teachings** and gained the evil notion that there is no **buddha**, no **Dharma**, and no **nirvana**, with the result that he fell into the **Hell** of **Incessant Suffering**. (NS, pp. 469-474; WNS1, p. 52, 56-57)

Sunlight: (S. Sūryāprabha; J. Nikkō; 日光) In the *Medicine Master Sutra* he is one of the two attendants of **Medicine Master Buddha**.

superior accommodative-body: (J. shō-ōjin; 勝応身) In the teachings of the **Tiantai school** the **accommodative-body** of a **buddha** is further divided into an inferior and a superior form. The superior accommodative-body is the one that appears to **sages** in the higher portion of the Land of the Co-existence of Sages and Ordinary People that is considered the **pure land**. More specifically, it is the body accommodated to **bodhisattva**s who have reached at least the first of the **ten grounds**. The superior accommodative-body is a more exalted form of a historical buddha. It is said to be able to appear as large or as small as needed.

According to **Nichiren Shonin**, **Shakyamuni** Buddha as the **focus of devotion** for the **Dharma Characteristics** and **Three Treatises** schools of Buddhism is a superior accommodative-body, while **Amitabha** Buddha as the focus of devotion in the Tiantai school is also a superior accommodative-body.

superior capacity: (S. adhimātra; J. jōkon or jōbon; 上根 or 上品) See **sharp capacity**.

Superior Practice: (S. Viśiṣṭacāritra; J. Jōgyō; 上行) One of the **four great bodhisattvas** who are the four leaders of the **bodhisattvas appearing from underground** described in the fifteenth, "**Appearance of Bodhisattvas from Underground**," chapter of the *Lotus Sutra* who were guided by the **Original Buddha** since the remotest past and entrusted with the task of spreading the *Lotus Sutra* in the **Latter Age of Degeneration**.

This bodhisattva represents the true **self** that is the selflessness of **nirvana**.

After being exiled to Sado, **Nichiren Shonin** was firmly convinced that he was fulfilling the mission of Superior Practice Bodhisattva. The **Nichiren school** considers Nichiren Shonin to be the appearance of this bodhisattva because he alone fulfilled this bodhisattva's mission by being the first person to spread the **daimoku** as the essential practice of the *Lotus Sutra* in the Latter Age of Degeneration. (WNS5, p. 110 adapted)

Superlative Meaning Arising: (S. Paramārthasamudgata; J. Shōgishō; 勝義生) A **bodhisattva** who is one of the main interlocutors in the *Revealing the Profound Secrets Sutra*. (WNS1, p. 73; WNS2, p. 86)

supernatural power: See **six supernatural powers**.

Supernatural Powers Sutra: (J. *Jinzū-kyō*; 神通経) A **Mahayana** sutra. (WNS2, p. 86)

supernatural powers, subtlety of: (J. jinzū-myō; 神通妙) The seventh of the **ten subtleties of the Trace Gate**. It refers to the subtle activities of the **Buddha** to assist **sentient beings** using his **six supernatural powers**. The supernatural powers attained through the **perfect teaching** are said to be inconceivably superior to that derived from other sources. (FTP, p. 208; PMLS2, p. 94, 275-277)

Supplemental Amplifications on the Great Calming and Contemplation: (J. *Maka-shikan bugyōden guketsu*; 摩訶止観輔行伝弘決) Abbreviated as "*Guketsu*" or "*Gu*" in **Nichiren Shonin**'s writings. In this writing, **Zhanran** annotated **Zhiyi**'s ***Great Calming and Contemplation*** in ten fascicles, revealing the profound practices expounded by Zhiyi and refuting misunderstandings which arose after his death. Along with the *Great Calming and Contemplation*, this writing of Zhanran had a great influence on the doctrine of Nichiren Shonin, who often cites from them to prove his points.

Supplement to the Meanings of the Commentaries on the Lotus Sutra: (J. *Hokekyō-shogisan*; 法華経疏義纘) Also called the ***Dongchun***. A work by **Zhidu**, a Tang dynasty **monk** of the **Tiantai school**.

Supplemented Lotus Sutra: (J. Tembon-hoke-kyō; 添品法華経) A translation of the ***Lotus Sutra*** done by Jnanagupta and Dharmagupta that was completed in 601. This translation differs from **Kumarajiva**'s version in that the "**Devadatta**," **chapter** is made part of the "**Beholding the Stupa of Treasures**," **chapter** so that there are only twenty-seven chapters, the "Transmission" chapter is placed as the last chapter, and the "Dharanis" chapter is made the twenty-first chapter.

supramundane: (S. lokottara; J. shusse; 出世) In the Buddhism, the supramundane encompasses those stages of practice wherein the practitioner successively attains the **four fruitions**.

Supreme Golden Light Sutra: (S. *Suvarṇaprabhāsottama-sūtra*; J. *Konkōmyō-saishō'ō-kyō* or *Konkōmyō-kyō* or *Saishō'ō-kyō*; 金光明最勝王経 or 金光明経 or 最勝王経) Two Chinese translations of this **sutra** exist, one by Dharmakshema in four fascicles and one by Yijing in ten fascicles in 703. Together with the ***Lotus Sutra*** and the ***Benevolent Kings Sutra***, it has been revered as one of the three state-protecting sutras. Yijing's version has been recited and taught in Japan in state-temples and in the imperial court since the Nara period.

Nichiren Shonin cited the "Shitennō Gokoku-bon" chapter of the sutra translated by Yijing when he talked about the calamities and disasters in the **Latter Age of Degeneration**. However, he refused to accept its claim to be supreme among Buddhist sutras, though it might be regarded in some respects as having teachings of **definitive meaning** compared to other sutras teaching the **provisional meaning** in regard to certain topics or issues. (WS1, p. 11)

supreme subtle awakening: (J. myōgaku; 妙覚) According to **Zhiyi**, supreme subtle **awakening** is the seventh of the seven categories of the **fifty-two stages of bodhisattva practice**. (PMLS2, p. 213; GTFT, p. 193)

According to the *Profound Meaning of the Lotus Sutra*, in this stage the bodhisattvas completely eliminate recurring **defilement**s and **attain buddhahood**. According to *A Guide to the Tiantai Fourfold Teachings*, at this stage a bodhisattva of the **distinct teaching** attains buddhahood, manifests the **reward-body**, and can then **turn the Wheel of the Dharma** for the bodhisattvas of **dull capacity**. (PMLS2, p. 213-214; GTFT, pp. 159, 193-194)

sustaining power: (S. adhiṣṭhāna; J. kaji; 加持) The Sanskrit term *adhiṣṭhāna* can also be translated as "decisive resolution," "determination," or "empowerment." It refers to the **supernatural power** of the **buddha**s and advanced **bodhisattva**s to provide sustaining power to other practitioners. It can also refer to the determination or resolve to remain in a state of **meditative absorption**, or to develop and utilize supernatural powers.

sutra: (S. sūtra; J. shūtara or sotaran or kyō; 修多羅 or 素呾纜 or 経) The Sanskrit term *sūtra* literally means a "thread." In Buddhism it means a "thread of discourse" of the Buddha, and later a written Buddhist **scripture**. The ideogram 経 also means a "warp" or "thread running lengthwise." It can be translated as "scripture" or "classic," and is the same character used for Confucian and Taoist "classics." It is one of the **twelve kinds of scriptures**.

Sutra of the Lotus Flower of the Wonderful Dharma: See *Lotus Sutra*.

sutras of definitive meaning: (J. ryōgi-kyō; 了義経) Used in the *Nirvana Sutra*, the term refers to **true sutra**s in which the **definitive meaning** is thoroughly revealed, in contrast to the **sutras of provisional meaning**.

Nichiren Shonin taught that relative to each other some sutras are of definitive meaning and some of provisional meaning, but ultimately the *Lotus Sutra* is the sole sutra of definitive meaning. (WNS1, p. 17)

sutras of provisional meaning: (J. furyōgi-kyō; 不了義経) Used in the *Nirvana Sutra*, the term refers to **provisional sutra**s in which only the **provisional meaning** is taught and the **definitive meaning** is not thoroughly revealed, in contrast to the **sutras of definitive meaning**.

Nichiren Shonin taught relative to each other, some sutras are of definitive meaning and some of provisional meaning, but ultimately the *Lotus Sutra* is the sole sutra of definitive meaning. (WNS1, p. 17)

Tamalapattracandana Fragrance: (S. Tamālapattra-candana-gandha; J. Tamarabatsu-sendankō/Tamaraba-sendankō; 多摩羅跋栴檀香) The name of the **buddha** that **Maudgalyayana** will become, according to the sixth, "Assurance of Future Buddhahood," chapter of the *Lotus Sutra*.

Tang, King: (d. 1646; J. Tō-ō; 湯王) Tang overthrew King **Jie** of the Xia dynasty to become the first ruler of the dynasty known as Shang or Yin. King Tang is the second of the **Three Kings**(1).

tathagata: (S. tathāgata; J. nyorai or tada-akado; 如来 or 多陀阿伽度) The title *tathāgata* is composed of the Sanskrit words *tathā*, which means "suchness" or "thusness," and either *gata*, which means "gone," or *āgata*, which means "come." Therefore, the compound word *tathāgata* can mean either "one thus come" or "one thus gone." The ideograms 如來 mean "thus come one." It is one of the honorable titles for a **buddha**.

Tatsunokuchi Persecution: (J. Tatsunokuchi-no-hōnan; 竜の口の法難) On September 12, 1271, **Nichiren Shonin** was arrested by Hei no Saemon-no-jo Yoritsuna, deputy commander of the board of retainers, as part of the Kamakura shogunate's efforts to quell dissidents and present a united front against threat of Mongol invasion. At midnight, the deputy commander had Nichiren Shonin taken to the execution grounds on Tatsunokuchi beach, a section of the beach near Kamakura located at Fujisawa City, Kanagawa Prefecture, today. Nichiren Shonin was saved from beheading when the executioner and the other samurai were frightened by a mysterious ball of light which flew through the sky. A messenger from the regent arrived soon after with orders that Nichiren Shonin was not to be executed in any case but exiled to Sado Island. This attempted execution is known as the Tatsunokuchi Persecution, the fourth and severest of all the persecutions Nichiren Shonin encountered during his lifetime. To commemorate that event, Ryukoji Temple (J. Ryūkōji) was later built at this former execution ground.

"Teacher of the Dharma, The" chapter: (J. Hosshi-hon; 法師品) The tenth chapter of the *Lotus Sutra*. In this chapter, **Shakyamuni Buddha** tells **Medicine Master Bodhisattva** and eighty thousand other bodhisattvas that anyone who has even a single moment of rejoicing upon hearing just a **gatha** or phrase of the *Lotus Sutra*, whether in his presence or after his **final nirvana**, can be considered to have received the assurance of future buddhahood from him. He goes on to state the person who teaches the *Lotus Sutra* to others should be considered a messenger of the Tathagata and should be praised as such. He also says that only those bodhisattvas who hear and accept the *Lotus Sutra* are close to **unsurpassed, complete, and perfect awakening**.

The Buddha also states, "If a teacher of the Dharma expounds this sutra after my extinction, I will manifest the **four assemblies**: **monk**s, **nun**s, and men and women of pure **faith**, and dispatch them to him so that they may make offerings to him, and that they may lead many **sentient being**s, collecting them to hear the Dharma from him. If he is hated and threatened with swords, sticks, tiles, or stones, I will manifest men and dispatch them to him in order to protect him." (LS, p. 184 adapted)

ten abodes: (J. jū-jū; 十住) According to **Zhiyi** the ten abodes are the second of the seven categories of the **fifty-two stages of bodhisattva practice**. They are called: 1) **awakening mind**, 2) groundwork, 3) practice, 4) noble rebirth, 5) perfection of **skillful means**, 6) rectification of the **mind**, 7) **non-retrogression**, 8) childlike simplicity, 9) **Dharma** prince, and 10) coronation. (PMLS2, p. 212; GTFT, pp. 191-192)

ten degrees of faith: (J. jū-shin; 十信) According to **Zhiyi** the ten degrees of faith are the first of the seven categories of the **fifty-two stages of bodhisattva practice**. They are called: 1) **faith**, 2) **mindfulness**, 3) **energy**, 4) **wisdom**, 5) **concentration**, 6) **non-retrogression**, 7) **merit** transference, 8) dharmapala, 9) **morality**, and 10) **vow**s. (PMLS2, p. 212; GTFT, p. 191)

ten dimensions of merit transference: (J. jū-ekō; 十廻向) According to **Zhiyi** the ten dimensions of merit transference are the fourth of the seven categories of the **fifty-two stages of bodhisattva practice**. They are called: 1) free of the **mark** of **sentient being**s, but still rescuing all sentient beings, 2) not destroying [phenomenal distinctions while realizing the **emptiness** of all distinctions], 3) equality with all the **buddha**s, 4) reaching every corner of the universe [to pay homage to all the buddhas], 5) a treasury of inexhaustible **merit** [accumulated from the above practices to be used for the salvation of others], 6) entering into the "**wholesome** root" of non-differentiation, 7) treating all sentient beings as equally deserving, 8) the mark of suchness [seen underlying all **phenomena**], 9) being liberated without restraints or attachments [though realizing that all things are one], and 10) penetrating into the infinitude of every single phenomenon. (PMLS2, p. 213; GTFT, p. 192)

ten directions: (J. jippō; 十方) The ten are the four cardinal directions (east, south, west, and north), the four intercardinal directions (northeast, southeast, southwest, and northwest), the zenith, and the nadir.

ten great disciples: (J. jūdai-deshi; 十大弟子) Also called "ten principal" or "ten major" disciples of **Shakyamuni Buddha**. These are ten especially exceptional disciples of the Buddha. In the "Foremost" chapter of the "Book of the Ones" in the *Numerical Discourses*, each of these disciples is listed as foremost in one or more qualities. (ND 1.188-1.234, pp. 109-111)

In the *Vimalakirti Sutra*, they are successively asked by the Buddha to visit the wealthy layman **Vimalakirti**, but they each decline because they had all been upbraided by him in the past. (McRae, pp. 85-96)

Below is a listing of the ten in the order given in the *Vimalakirti Sutra*, along with those qualities or characteristics of which they were considered foremost:

1) **Shariputra**, foremost among those with great **wisdom**.
2) **Maudgalyayana**, foremost among those with **supernatural power**.
3) **Mahakashyapa**, foremost of those who expound and cultivate the *dhuta* or ascetic practices.
4) **Subhuti**, foremost among those who dwell without conflict, those worthy of gifts, and those who understand **emptiness**.
5) **Purna**, foremost among those who teach the **Dharma**.
6) **Mahakatyayana**, foremost among those who explain brief teachings in detail.
7) **Aniruddha**, foremost of those with clairvoyance or the **divine eye**.
8) **Upali**, foremost among those who uphold the **vinaya**.
9) **Rahula**, foremost among those who **desire** training, and those who practice inconspicuously.
10) **Ananda**, foremost among those who are learned, those with a good memory, those with a quick grasp, those who are resolute, and among personal attendants.

ten grounds: (S. daśa-bhūmi; J. jū-ji; 十地) According to **Zhiyi** the ten grounds are the fifth of the seven categories of the **fifty-two stages of bodhisattva practice**. They are called: 1) joyful, 2) free from taint, 3) light giving, 4) brilliant **wisdom**, 5) difficult to conquer, 6) facing true reality, 7) thoroughgoing practice, 8) immovable, 9) wonderfully **wise**, and 10) **Dharma** cloud. (PMLS2, p. 213; GTFT, p. 193)

Ten Grounds Sutra. (S. *Daśabhūmika-sūtra*; J. *Jūji-kyō*; 十地経) A **sutra** that expounds the **ten grounds** that are considered part of the **fifty-two stages of bodhisattva practice**. This sutra was incorporated into the ***Flower Garland Sutra*** as its twenty-sixth chapter. A commentary on it called the *Ten Grounds Sutra Treatise* was attributed to Vasubandhu, and this later became the basis of the Ten Grounds school in China.

ten kinds of practice: (J. jū-gyō; 十行) According to **Zhiyi** the ten kinds of practice are the third of the seven categories of the **fifty-two stages of bodhisattva practice**. They are called: 1) joyful, 2) beneficial, 3) unobstructed, 4) unwavering, 5) unconfused, 6) attractive, 7) unattached, 8) hard-won (or honored), 9) exemplary, and 10) true. (PMLS2, p. 213; GTFT, p. 192)

ten means of adaptation to the Buddha Dharma: (J. jū-i-yūzū-buppō; 十意融通佛法) **Zhiyi**, in his *Great Calming and Contemplation*, set out ten things that Buddhist teachers should keep in mind when teaching and practicing the **Buddha Dharma**. Roughly these ten are to: 1) Clarify that the principle of the path is the quiescent and inconceivable true nature of reality. 2) Establish the structure and framework of the **sutra**s, 3) Reconcile seeming contradictions with the four aims of practice, 4) Eliminate **wrong views** and **deluded attitudes**. 5) Practice in a way that is appropriate to one's ability and without pride. 6) Deeply understand the meaning of the teachings both broadly and deeply. 7) Unfold the meaning of the sutras gradually with attention to context and in coordination with the meanings in other sutras. 8) Gradually settle the interpretation of the sutras in agreement with what they actually say. 9) Make sure to match meanings and connotations when translating sutras. 10) Fully assimilate the meaning of the sutras through **contemplation**.

ten profound gates: (J. jū-genmon/jū-gemmon; 十玄門) Ten gates or teachings concerning the profound implications of the **dependent origination** of the **Dharma-realm** according to the **Flower Garland school**. The ten are: 1) the gate of simultaneous complete mutual correspondence, 2) the gate of the broad and narrow being free and unhindered, 3) gate of the mutual inclusion and differentiation of the one and many, 4) gate of the mutual identification and freedom of all dharmas, 5) gate of the mutual establishment of concealment and disclosure, 6) gate of the peaceful establishment of the infinitesimal's mutual inclusivity with the whole, 7) gate of the Dharma-realm of Indra's net, 8) gate of the creation of understanding by revealing the Dharma through actualities, 9) gate of the differentiation of the ten time periods, and 10) gate of the perfectly clear endowed qualities of master and attendant.

ten rakshasi: (J. jū-rasetsu-nyo; 十羅刹女) In the twenty-sixth chapter, "**Dharanis**," of the *Lotus Sutra*, the ten daughters of the Mother of Demon Children swore before **Shakyamuni Buddha** that they will protect the **practitioner of the *Lotus Sutra*** and also offered **dharani** spells for their protection. They are often portrayed as beautiful women (though sometimes they have fangs) dressed in courtly attire and bearing various weapons or other symbolic objects. Their names are: Lamba,

Vilamba, Crooked Teeth, Flower Teeth, Black Teeth, Many Hairs, Insatiable, Necklace Holding, Kunti, and Plunderer of Energy of All Beings.

ten realms: (S. daśa-dhātu; J. jikkai; 十界) The combination of the **six destinies** and the four noble states. The realms of the: 1) **hell-dwellers**, 2) **hungry ghosts**, 3) **animals**, 4) **asuras**, 5) **humans**, 6) **gods**, 7) **voice-hearers**, 8) **privately-awakened ones**, 9) **bodhisattvas**, and 10) **buddhas**.

ten stages of mind: (J. jū-jūshin; 十住心) **Kukai**'s own system of comparative classification of doctrines in terms of ten stages of the maturation of the **mind**. The ten are as follows:
1) The mind of the **ordinary person**, like a ram: this is the mind of ordinary people who follow their impulses without any self-restraint, hold false views, commit the ten evil acts, and transmigrate in the six worlds of illusion, especially the **three evil destinies**. (Giebel 2004, pp. 135-136, 139, 141-144)
2) The mind of the foolish child, observing abstinence: this is the mind of the followers of **Confucianism** who take up self-discipline, **generosity**, and practice the **five constant virtues** (which are equivalent to the **five precepts**) and the **ten virtuous precepts**, and are thereby able to make the **causes** to be born in favorable circumstances in the **human** realm. (Giebel 2004, pp. 136, 139, 144-148)
3) The mind of the young child, without fear: this is the mind of the followers of the **Vedas** and other **non-Buddhist teachings** who take up the practice of the **four meditative absorptions** and the four formless meditative absorptions that lead to the temporary respite of the **heavens**. (Giebel 2004, pp. 136, 139, 148-155)
4) The mind of **aggregates**-only and **non-self**: this is the mind of the **voice-hearers** who contemplate the **five aggregates** and realize non-self in order to attain the eight liberations and **six supernatural powers**, thereby escaping the **six destinies** of **rebirth**. This stage is associated with the teaching of the **four noble truths** and the practice of the thirty-seven requisites of awakening. The teaching for this stage of mind only speaks of six consciousnesses. The goal of practice is to reduce the body to ashes and annihilate consciousness. (Giebel 2004, pp. 136, 140, 156-176)
5) The mind that has eradicated the causes and **seeds** of **karma**: this is the mind of the **privately-awakened ones** who contemplate **dependent origination** in order break the bonds of **karma** and escape the six destinies of rebirth. They have no teachers, follow spontaneous precepts, and **awaken** to **impermanence** when they see flowers scatter or leaves fall to the ground. (Giebel 2004, pp. 136, 140, 176-182)
6) The mind of the **Mahayana** concerned for others: this is the mind of the **bodhisattvas** who arouse the aspiration to **attain buddhahood** for the sake of

all **sentient beings** and take up the practice of the **six perfections**. This mind is equated with the teachings of the **Consciousness-Only school**, such as the doctrine of the **five natures**. At this stage the practitioner transforms deluded forms of consciousness into direct knowledge, thereby perfecting the **three bodies** of the buddhas and realizing **buddhahood**. (Giebel 2004, pp. 136-137, 140, 182-186)

7) The mind awakened to the **non-arising** of the mind: this is the mind of the bodhisattvas who realize the truth of **emptiness**. It is equated with the teachings of the **Middle Way school**, such as the doctrine of the **eight negations**. (Giebel 2004, pp. 137, 140, 186-191)

8) The mind of the one path or knowing the mind as it really is: this is the mind that realizes the **One Vehicle**. This is the teachings of the *Lotus Sutra* and the **Tiantai school**. (Giebel 2004, pp. 137, 140, 191-196)

9) The mind of ultimate own-naturelessness: this is the mind that realizes that nothing has its own nature apart from the mutual interpenetration of all **phenomena**. This is the teachings of the *Flower Garland Sutra* and the **Flower Garland school**. (Giebel 2004, pp. 137, 140-141, 197-204)

10) The mind of secret adornment: this is the mind that realizes the true nature of **Mahavairochana Buddha** through the practice the **three mysteries** of the **Mantra school**. This practice includes the **contemplation** of **mandala**s in order to attain the direct knowledge. (Giebel 2004, p. 137, 141, 205-215)

The first three stages of mind represent worldly views and attitudes, the next six are different types of **exoteric Buddhism**, while the tenth stage represents the practice of **esoteric Buddhism**. (EET, p. 113) Kukai insisted that the first nine do not represent the ultimate fruit of buddhahood and that the teaching of each stage of mind "when viewed in light of the subsequent [vehicles], it becomes a frivolous assertion." (Giebel 2004, p. 214)

ten subtleties of the Original Gate: (J. honmon jūmyō; 本門十妙) A part of the explanation of "subtle" or "wonderful" as part of the explanation of the name of the *Lotus Sutra* in the *Profound Meaning of the Lotus Sutra*. This could also be translated as "ten wonders of the Original Gate." The ten subtleties consist of: 1) the **original cause**, 2) the **original effect**, 3) the **original land**, 4) the **original receptivity and response**, 5) the **original supernatural powers**, 6) the **original expounding of the Dharma**, 7) the **original attendants**, 8) the **original nirvana**, 9) the **original lifespan**, and 10) the **original benefits**. (PMLS2, pp. 320-331, 401)

ten subtleties of the Trace Gate: (J. shakumon jūmyō; 迹門十妙) A part of the explanation of "subtle" or "wonderful" as part of the explanation of the name of the *Lotus Sutra* in the *Profound Meaning of the Lotus Sutra*. This could also be translated as "ten wonders of the Trace Gate." The ten subtleties consist of: 1) **ob-**

jects, 2) **knowledges**, 3) **practices**, 4) **stages**, 5) the **threefold Dharma**, 6) **receptivity and response**, 7) **supernatural powers**, 8) **expounding the Dharma**, 9) **attendants**, and 10) **merits and benefits**. (FTP, pp. 206-207; PMLS2, p. 92) The first four deal with the **cause** and the fifth with the **effect** of one's own practice to **attain buddhahood**, while the latter five deal with the power of the Buddha to enable one to attain buddhahood. In addition, these ten are provisional or coarse when taught in terms of the first three of the **four doctrinal teachings**, but they are subtle or true when they are taught in terms of the **perfect teaching**. The coarse version exists to manifest the subtle, and when the subtle is revealed the coarse also becomes subtle. (FTP, p. 211; PMLS2, pp. 95, 312-317, 401)

ten suchnesses: (J. jū-nyoze; 十如是) The **true reality of all things** or **dharmas** are spoken of in the second, **"Expedients,"** chapter of the *Lotus Sutra* in terms of ten suchnesses: 1) **appearance**, 2) **nature**, 3) **entity**, 4) **power**, 5) **activity**, 6) **cause**, 7) **condition**, 8) **effect**, 9) **recompense**, and 10) **beginning and end ultimately equal**.

ten virtuous precepts: (S. daśa-kuśala-karmapatha; J. jū-zen-kai; 十善戒) The Sanskrit term *daśakuśalakarmapatha* can also be translated as "ten courses of wholesome conduct" or the "ten good acts" (J. jū-zen-gō; 十善業). They are to refrain or abstain from committing the ten evil acts. The ten good acts lead to **rebirth** in good destinies, particularly in the **heavens**, and are descriptive of the ethical dimension of the **eightfold path**. They consist of three good bodily actions: 1) abstain from killing, 2) abstain from taking what is not given, and 3) abstain from sexual misconduct; four good verbal actions: 4) abstain from lying, 5) abstain from malicious speech, 6) abstain from harsh speech, and 7) abstain from idle chatter; and three good mental actions: 8) abstain from covetousness, 9) abstain from ill-will, and 10) abstain from wrong views. An explanation of these can be found in various discourses where they are said to lead to rebirth as wealthy **human**s, or even in **heaven**. (e.g. MD 41.7-11-14, pp. 382-383) Due to the ideograms chosen to translate the Sanskrit terms, the last three of the ten good acts are sometimes given as abstaining from **greed**, **hatred**, and **delusion**.

tetralemma: (S. catuḥ-koṭi or catuṣkoṭika; J. shi-ku; 四句) The four alternatives are: there is x (J. u; 有), there is not x (J. mu; 無), there is both x and not-x (J. yaku-u yaku-mu; 亦有亦無), and there is neither x nor non-x (J. hi-u hi-mu; 非有非無) The tetralemma is often used in Buddhism to show that all the various ways of affirming or denying whether something is the case will lead to contradictions, particularly if the **phenomena** in question is assumed to have a **self-nature**.

thirty-four enlightened mental states: (J. sanjūshi-shin; 三十四心) The mental states achieved by one who is able to **attain buddhahood** according to the **tripitaka teaching** that include sixteen mental states consisting of **eight kinds of acceptance** and **eight kinds of knowledge** that sever **deluded views** on the path of seeing and eighteen attitudes consisting of **nine non-obstructions** and **nine liberations** that sever the **deluded attitudes** that constitute the obstacle to knowledge on the path of cultivation. (CSQI, pp. 490-491)

thirty-two marks: (S. dvātriṃśadvara-lakṣaṇa; J. sanjūni-sō; 三十二相) The major **marks** of a "great man" that are possessed by a **buddha**, an advanced **bodhisattva**, major **god**s, or a **wheel-turning king**.

three ages of the Dharma: (J. san-ji; 三時) The three ages after **Shakyamuni Buddha**'s **final nirvana** are: 1) the Former **Age of the True Dharma**, lasting one thousand years (or five hundred depending on the source) during which the **Buddha Dharma** is properly practiced and practitioners can **attain buddhahood**; 2) the Middle **Age of the Semblance of the Dharma** lasting one thousand years (or five hundred depending on the source) during which the teaching is practiced but buddhahood is no longer attainable; and 3) the **Latter Age of Degeneration** lasting ten thousand years, in which only the teaching exists.

Accepting the theory that the **Ages of the True and Semblance Dharmas** each lasted for a thousand years, **Nichiren Shonin** held that the Latter Age began two thousand years after the death of the Buddha. Because the *Record of Wonders in the Book of Zhou* stated that the Buddha was born on the eighth day of the fourth month of 1029 BCE and died on the fifteenth day of the second month of 949 BCE, Nichiren Shonin and many other Buddhists of East Asia believed that the Latter Age began in 1052 CE.

three assemblies at two locations: (J. nisho-san'e; 二処三会) The places where **Shakyamuni** Buddha taught the *Lotus Sutra* can be divided into three assemblies at two locations. The assembly that takes place at the first location is called the former Assembly on Mount Sacred Eagle, which takes place from the beginning of the sutra until the middle of chapter eleven. The assembly at the second location is called the Assembly in Space, which takes place from the middle of chapter eleven until the end of chapter twenty-two. The third assembly returns to the first location and is called the latter assembly on Mount Sacred Eagle, which takes place in chapters twenty-three to twenty-eight.

three baskets: (S. tripiṭaka; J. san-zō; 三蔵) The Sanskrit term *tripiṭaka* means "three baskets." The **tripitaka** or three part canon of Buddhism consists of 1) the sutras, or discourses of the **Buddha**; 2) the prohibitive binding rules of monastic discipline, their analysis, and the collection of rules governing monastic procedures that together comprise the **vinaya**; and 3) the systemization and technical commentaries on the discourses called the **abhidharma**.

three bodies: (S. tri-kāya; J. san-shin or san-jin; 三身) A **buddha** is supposed to have three bodies: the **Dharma-body** representing the ultimate truth to which a buddha is **awakened**; the **reward-body**, also called the **enjoyment-body**, which is the embodiment of the accumulated **merit** of a buddha and is both enjoyed by the buddha and by the advanced **bodhisattva**s who are able to perceive it, and the **accommodative-body** which appears to lead unawakened **sentient being**s to liberation from **suffering**. (PMLS2, pp. 262-263)

The **Eternal Shakyamuni Buddha** revealed in the sixteenth, "The **Duration of the Life of the Tathagata**," chapter of the *Lotus Sutra* is equipped with all three bodies according to the teaching of the **Tiantai school**. (Stone, p. 26)

Nichiren Shonin taught that in the provisional Mahayana teachings the three bodies are considered to be separate, with the accommodative-bodies having a beginning and end, the reward-bodies having a beginning but no end, and the Dharma-body having no beginning or end. However, in the **Original Gate** of the *Lotus Sutra*, the Eternal Shakyamuni Buddha is revealed to possess all three bodies and that all three are without beginning or end. (WNS2, p. 18; WNS3, p.250)

three calamities: (J. sansai; 三災) According to Buddhist cosmology, the world endlessly goes through **four kalpas**: the **kalpa of formation**, the **kalpa of abiding**, the **kalpa of dissolution**, and the **kalpa of nothingness**. The three calamities of warfare, epidemics, and famine that occur in the kalpa of abiding are called the **three minor calamities**, while fires, floods, and severe winds in the kalpa of dissolution constitute the **three major calamities**.

three categories of delusions: (J. san-waku; 三惑) (1) The **three poisons** of **greed, hatred**, and **delusion**.

(2) In **Tiantai school** doctrine the term refers to the three delusions into which all delusions and **defilements** are classified: (1) **delusions of views and attitudes** that hinder the **knowledge** of **emptiness**, (2) **delusions as innumerable as grains of sand** that hinder the **knowledge** of **skillful means**, and (3) **delusion of fundamental ignorance** that hinder **knowledge** of the **middle way**.

three categories of existence: (J. sanshu-seken or san-seken; 三種世間 *or* 三世間) The three categories into which the world can be divided according to the *Great Perfection of Wisdom Treatise* are: (1) the **five aggregates**, (2) of **sentient**

beings, and (3) their **environment**s. (CSQI, p. 801, 2093)

Zhiyi utilized them as a component of the **three thousand realms in a single thought-moment**. (CSQI, p. 815)

three categories of pure precepts: (S. trividhāni śīlāni or śīla-traya; J. sanju-jō-kai; 三聚浄戒) Three kinds of **precept**s that encompass both **hinayana** precepts and **Mahayana** precepts that are integral to **bodhisattva practice**.

The three categories are: 1) prohibitive precepts for maintaining restraint and not committing what is **unwholesome**, 2) injunctive precepts that encompass all good deeds for cultivating what is **wholesome**, and 3) precepts for benefiting sentient beings. According to the **Discipline school**, there is a separate reception of the precepts for maintaining restraint from the other two categories by hinayana practitioners, and there is a general reception of all three categories of pure precepts by bodhisattvas. (EVT, p. 53) In principle, however, any precept from the **training rule**s or from the various sets of Mahayana precepts embraces all three categories of pure precepts. (EVT, p. 52)

three expoundings: (J. san-setsu; 三説) The three expoundings are set forth in the tenth, "The **Teacher of the Dharma**," **chapter** of the *Lotus Sutra*, wherein **Shakyamuni Buddha** states, "I have expounded many **sutra**s. I am now expounding this sutra. I also will expound many sutras in the future. The total number of the sutras will amount to many thousands of billions. This *Sutra of the Lotus Flower of the Wonderful Dharma* is the most difficult to believe and the most difficult to understand." (LS, p. 180)

Zhiyi states in his *Words and Phrases of the Lotus Sutra* that "have expounded" refers to the **prior teachings** expounded in some forty years before the *Lotus Sutra*; "am now expounding" refers to the *Infinite Meanings Sutra*, which is an introduction to the *Lotus Sutra*; "will expound" refers to the *Nirvana Sutra*, and that the *Lotus Sutra* is superior to all these sutras. The shorthand of the above statement, "**have, am now, and will**", is understood to refer to the Buddha's expounding of any sutra aside from the *Lotus Sutra*.

According to **Nichiren Shonin**, these three categories of sutras are easy to believe and comprehend because they were **provisional sutra**s taught according to the **capacity** of the people while the *Lotus Sutra* is difficult to believe and comprehend because it is the **true teaching** expounding the true intent of the Buddha without compromise. Thus the phrase "have, am now, and will" is often used by Nichiren Shonin to prove the superiority of the *Lotus Sutra*, in the same way that he quotes "The truth has not been revealed during the prior period of forty years or so" from the *Infinite Meanings Sutra* and the **Many Treasures** Buddha testifying to the veracity of Shakyamuni Buddha's words in the eleventh, "**Beholding the Stupa of Stupa of Treasures**," **chapter** of the *Lotus Sutra*.

three evil destinies: (S. tri-durgati; J. san-akudō or san-akushu or san-zu; 三悪道 or 三悪趣 or 三途) The three lowest of the **six destinies** (**hell-dwellers**, **hungry ghosts**, and **animals**) of the **ten realms** wherein **sentient beings** undergo **rebirth** due to the **transgressions** they have committed. If the realm of the **asuras** are included they are called the four evil destinies.

According to **Nichiren Shonin**, people fall into these three evil destinies due to transgressions committed for the sake of family and relatives, for killing and other brutal acts, for the transgression of neglecting the sorrows of the people if one is a ruler, for taking refuge in depraved teachings, or for listening to the encouragement of wicked teachers. (WNS1, pp. 3)

Three Great Secret Dharmas: (J. sandai-hihō; 三大秘法) The three important doctrines **Nichiren Shonin** established as the basis for practice for the people living in the **Latter Age of Degeneration**: the **Focus of Devotion of the Original Gate**, the **Precept Platform of the Original Gate**, and the **Sacred Title of the Original Gate**. (WNS2, pp. 214, 286-291; WNS3, pp. 57-58)

Ever since proclaiming the establishment of his own teaching and practice on April 28, 1253, (which is considered the establishment of the **Nichiren school**) Nichiren Shonin claimed that he was a **practitioner of the *Lotus Sutra*** who was tasked with conveying **Shakyamuni Buddha**'s predictions in the sutra to the people living in the **Latter Age of Degeneration**. Nichiren Shonin's narrow escape from death during the **Tatsunokuchi Persecution** marked the turning point of his religious life. Realizing that he was the appearance of **Superior Practice Bodhisattva**, Nichiren Shonin taught the Three Great Secret Dharmas as the model for practicing Buddhism in the Latter Age of Degeneration, fulfilling the duty of messenger of the Tathagata.

three great vows of Nichiren Shonin: (J. Nichiren Shōnin-no-sandai-seigan; 日蓮の三大誓願) Toward the end of *On the Opening of the Eyes*, **Nichiren Shonin** declared that he would never break his **vows** to become a pillar of Japan, the eyes of Japan, and a great vessel for Japan. (WNS2, pp. 105-106) They are referred to as the "three great vows of Nichiren," which lay at the base of his religious activities ever since his proclamation of Nichiren Buddhism for the purpose of saving all the people in Japan.

three hermits: (J. san-sen; 三仙) The three hermits are **Kapila**, **Uluka**, and **Rishabha**, who are upheld as the legendary **rishis** who revealed the **Vedas** and were the founders of ancient Indian philosophy and religion. (WNS2, p. 32)

three kinds of enemies: (J. sanrui-no-tekijin; 三類の強敵) The ideograms 三類

の強敵 can also be translated as "three kinds of powerful enemies" or "three formidable enemies." The thirteenth, "**Encouragement for Keeping This Sutra**," **chapter** of the *Lotus Sutra* predicts that after the passing of **Shakyamuni Buddha** its propagators will be persecuted by three kinds of people with "self-conceit" or presumption: 1) **presumptuous lay followers** who support the second and third groups, 2) **presumptuous clergy** who mislead suffering people, and 3) **presumptuous sages** who are highly respected Buddhist leaders who consider themselves to be living buddhas and look down on all others even though they are still strongly attached to worldly matters. (LS, pp. 212-215)

Nichiren Shonin considered the third group as the worst of the three kinds of enemies of the *Lotus Sutra*. Encountering all these enemies as predicted in chapter thirteen, Nichiren Shonin strengthened his belief that he was the **practitioner of the *Lotus Sutra*.** (WNS2, pp. 91-104)

three kinds of meditative absorption: (J. san-tōji, san-jō, or san-jōryo; 三等至 or 三定 or 三静慮) According to the *Treasury of Abhidharma Treatise*, the four meditative absorptions and the first three of the four formless meditative absorptions (on **space**, **consciousness**, nothing, and neither perception nor non-perception) can either be 1) **defiled**, 2) **pure**, or 3) **non-outflow**. The pure meditative absorptions and formless meditative absorptions are **wholesome** in a **mundane** sense. They can be succeeded by defiled meditative absorptions that enjoy the taste or "flavor" of the previous moment of pure meditative absorption and are therefore tainted by craving. Non-outflow meditative absorptions are free of such craving and cannot become the objects of such craving. The formless attainment of Neither Perception nor non-Perception does not have a non-outflow meditative absorption. (AKB4, pp. 1227-1228)

Three Kings: (J. sannō; 三王) (1) Three **sage** kings of ancient China: 1) King **Yu the Great** who established the Xia dynasty, 2) King **Tang** of the Shang dynasty or Yin dynasty, and 3) either King **Wen** or King **Wu** of the Zhou dynasty.

(2) Three evil rulers who lost their kingdoms in ancient China: 1) King **Jie** of the Xia dynasty, 2) King **Zhou Xin** of the Shang or Yin dynasty, and 3) King **You** of the Zhou dynasty. According to **Nichiren Shonin**, these three lost their kingdoms because they violated the **five constant virtues**, which are equivalent to the **five precepts**.

three major calamities: (J. dai-no-sansai; 大の三災) According to the *Treasury of Abhidharma Treatise*, the three major calamities are the fires, floods, and severe winds that bring an end to the **container world** and even some **heaven**s of the

form realm in the last **interim kalpa** of the **kalpa of dissolution** due to the exhaustion of the collective **karma** of the **sentient beings** that caused that world to arise. For seven **great kalpas** the destruction is caused by fire when seven suns appear and burn everything up to and including the Heavens of **Brahma**, since those heavens are imperfect because those in them still have thought and examination which burn the mind. In the eighth great kalpa, the destruction is caused by rains which basically wash away everything up to and including the three heavens of the second **meditative absorption**, since those heavens are imperfect because those in them still have rapture which "rends the body soft and flabby: it is similar to water." When that cycle of seven destructions by fire and one by water has happened seven times there is a final cycle of seven destructions by fire followed by destruction caused by powerful winds that blow everything away up to and including the three heavens of the third meditative absorption, since those heavens are imperfect because those in them continue to inhale and exhale, which is still a slight distraction for them. Altogether, in a cycle of sixty-four great kalpas, there are fifty-six destructions caused by fire, seven by water, and one by wind. The heavens of the fourth meditative absorption are beyond such agitation but neither are they permanent. They arise and cease along with their residents. (AKB2, pp. 477, 479, 490-491, 494-495)

three major works of the Lotus school: (J. *Hokke-sandai-bu*; 法華三大部) Also called three major works of the Tiantai school. These are the *Words and Phrases of the Lotus Sutra*, the *Profound Meaning of the Lotus Sutra*, and the *Great Calming and Contemplation*. All three were compiled from notes **Guanding** took on his master **Zhiyi**'s lectures. Together they record the core of Zhiyi's doctrine.

three minor calamities: (J. shō-no-sansai; 小の三災) According to the *Treasury of Abhidharma Treatise*, the three calamities of warfare, epidemics, and famine that occur in **Jambudvipa** at the end of each of the first nineteen **interim kalpas** of the **kalpa of abiding**. As those interim kalpas end, and lifespans decrease to only ten years, people become full of **greed** and **hatred**, and espouse false views. This leads to seven days of warfare; followed by seven months and seven days of epidemics; and finally, seven years, seven months, and seven days of famine. Purvavideha and Aparagodaniya are not directly affected but during this time they also become wicked, lose their color, and become physically weak, and are subject to hunger and thirst. (AKB2, pp. 489-490)

three mysteries: (S. tri-guhya; J. san-mitsu; 三密) The Sanskrit term *triguhya* can also be translated as "three secrets." In **esoteric Buddhism**, the three mysteries are the physical, verbal, and mental activities of **Mahavairochana Buddha** that are communicated through the practice of **mudra**s, **mantra**s, and **mandala**s so that one can **attain buddhahood with one's present body**. Various mudras, mantras, and mandalas are associated with different buddhas, **bodhisattva**s, and **guardian deities** but ultimately all of them are expressions of Mahavairochana Buddha.

three obstacles: (S. tri-āvaraṇa; J. san-shō; 三障) The Sanskrit term *āvaraṇa* can also be translated as "hindrance" or "obstruction." According to the *Treasury of Abhidharma Treatise*, the three obstacles to the **way leading to the cessation of suffering** are: the obstacle of karma, the obstacle of defilement, and the obstacle of recompense. Among the three the gravest is the obstacle of defilement because the defilements produce karma, and the obstacle of karma is heavier than the obstacle of recompense because karma produces recompense. (AKB2, pp. 678-680) This is, of course, a vicious circle because the defilements then arise from the **five aggregates** which are the recompense of past karma.

three obstacles and four devils: (S. tri-āvaraṇa catur-māra; J. sanshō-shima; 三障四魔) **Zhiyi** states in his *Great Calming and Contemplation*:

> "If you are diligent in both practice and understanding, then the **three obstacles** and **four devils** [that hinder **contemplation**] will confusedly contend with each other and arise [in your thoughts]; this will multiply your darkness and magnify your distractions, thus shading and disturbing the light of your **concentration**. You should not follow after, nor be afraid [of these phenomena]. If you follow after them, they will lead you to **evil destinies**; if you fear them, they will hinder your cultivation of the correct **Dharma** practice. You should utilize [the practice of] contemplation to contemplate the darkness, and thus brighten the darkness. You should utilize [the practice of] **calming** to stop the distractions, and thus the distractions will be quiescent." (CSQI pp. 747-748 adapted)

Following Zhiyi's concept of the three obstacles and four devils, **Nichiren Shonin** maintains that those who spread the teaching of the *Lotus Sutra* in the **Latter Age of Degeneration** are bound to be persecuted by the three obstacles and four devils and that only those who endured the difficulty could claim to be a **practitioner of the *Lotus Sutra*.**

three periods of teaching: (J. sanji-kyō; 三時教) Classification of the Buddhist **sutra**s into three periods or **three turnings of the wheel of the Dharma**.

According to the **Dharma Characteristics school** the three periods are: 1) the teaching of existence taught first in the **Agama sutras**, 2) the teaching of **emptiness** taught next in the **Prajna sutras**, and finally 3) the teaching of the **middle way** taught last in sutras such as the *Flower Garland Sutra*, the *Lotus Sutra*, the *Nirvana Sutra*, and the *Revealing the Profound Secrets Sutra*. The teaching of the middle way insists that reality lies beyond existence and non-existence and is considered supreme. (WNS3, p. 124)

According to the **Three Treatises school** the three periods are: 1) the teaching of existence, 2) the teaching of **consciousness-only**, and 3) the teaching of emptiness. (WNS3, p. 124)

Nichiren Shonin points out that the *Revealing the Profound Secrets Sutra* does not clearly state that sutras such as the *Lotus Sutra* are to be included among those that teach merely the middle way. (WNS1, p. 18)

three poisons: (S. tri-viṣa; J. san-doku; 三毒) The three major **defilement**s of **greed**, **hatred**, and **delusion** that spoil wholesome roots are referred to as the three poisons.

three proclamations: (J. sanka-no-chokusen or sanka-no-hōshō; 三箇の勅宣 or 三箇の鳳詔) In the eleventh chapter, "**Beholding the Stupa of Treasures**," of the *Lotus Sutra*, **Shakyamuni Buddha** three times urged those among the **four assemblies** to propagate the *Lotus Sutra* after his passing. The first exhortation was accompanied by his **desire** to transmit the sutra; at the next exhortation he expressed his desire to perpetuate the **Dharma**; and finally, he taught how difficult it will be to spread the Dharma after his passing. These three proclamations together with the **two exhortations** from the twelfth, "**Devadatta**," **chapter** comprise the **five proclamations**. (WNS2, pp. 81-83)

three Pure Land sutras: (J. Jōdo-sambu-kyō; 浄土三部経) Refers to the three canonical **sutra**s of the **Pure land school** that teach **rebirth in the pure land**, specifically in the Pure Land of Utmost Bliss of **Amitabha Buddha**: 1) the *Buddha of Infinite Life Sutra*, 2) the *Contemplation of the Buddha of Infinite Life Sutra*, and 3) the *Amitayus Buddha Sutra*.

three sages: (J. san-sei; 三聖) The three sage rulers of ancient China, usually listed as **Yao**, **Shun**, and **Yu**.

Nichiren Shonin, however, considered the three sages to be Laozi, Confucius, and Yan Hui, based on statements made by **Zhiyi** and **Zhanran**, who in turn were basing their idea upon what was taught in the *Practicing the Pure Dharma Sutra*. (WNS2, p. 32)

three southern and seven northern schools: (J. nansan-hokushichi; 南三北七) The term used in the *Profound Meaning of the Lotus Sutra* by **Zhiyi** to refer to the different Buddhist schools of thought in China during the Northern and Southern dynasties centered in the south of the Yangtze River and north of the Yellow River. These were not distinct institutions but rather different systems of comparative classification of doctrines held by various Buddhist teachers. They generally held that the *Flower Garland Sutra* was supreme among **all the sutras**, followed by the *Nirvana Sutra* and then the *Lotus Sutra*. (WNS2, pp. 14-15)

The three southern schools all divided **Shakyamuni Buddha**'s teachings into the sudden teaching associated with the *Flower Garland Sutra*, the gradual teaching associated with the **Agama sutras** and the **Prajna sutras**, and the indeterminate teaching associated with the *Vimalakirti Sutra* and the *Supreme Golden Light Sutra*. The differences between them have to do with how they subdivided the gradual teaching. The first school is associated with Jishi (岌師) of Mt. Huqiu (虎丘). This school taught that the gradual teaching consists of the doctrine with **mark**s found in the Agama sutras, the doctrine without marks found in the Prajna sutras, and the doctrine of **eternity** as found in the *Nirvana Sutra*. The second school is associated with Zongai (宗愛). This schools added the doctrine of common convergence of the **three vehicles** into the **One Vehicle** as found in the *Lotus Sutra* before the doctrine of eternity. The third school is associated with Sengrou, Huici (the teacher of Fayun), and Huiguan. This school added the doctrine of depreciation of **hinayana** and valuation of **Mahayana** as found in the *Vimalakirti Sutra* and the *Questions of Brahma Excellent Thought Sutra*.

The first northern school is similar to the second southern school except that it added the doctrine of the **human vehicle** and the **heavenly vehicle** as found in the *Trapusa and Bhallika Sutra* before the other doctrines. The second northern school is associated with Bodhiruchi. This school divided the Buddha's teachings into that of the partial word and that of the complete word. The third northern school is associated with **Huiguang**. This school divided the Buddha's teachings into the doctrine of **causality** as found in the *Treasury of Abhidharma Treatise*, the doctrine of **provisional existence** as found in the *Completion of Reality Treatise*, the doctrine of illusory appearance as found in the Prajna sutras and the teachings of the **Three Treatises school**, and the doctrine of eternity as found in the *Nirvana Sutra* and the *Flower Garland Sutra*. The fourth school divided the Buddha's teachings as the third, except that the *Flower Garland Sutra* forms its own category called the doctrine of the **Dharma-realm**. The fifth school divided the Buddha's teachings the same as the third, except that it added the doctrine of the ultimate truth as found in the *Lotus Sutra* and the doctrine of the **perfect teaching** as found in the *Great Assembly Sutra*. The sixth school divided the Buddha's teachings into two Mahayana doctrines, those with marks and those without marks. The seventh school said that the Buddha taught with one voice, by which they meant that he taught only the One Vehicle but was understood by his listeners in terms of the three vehicles. (PMLS1, pp. 73-76)

Zhiyi rearranged and integrated these earlier systems of comparative classification of doctrines into his own system of the **five periods** and eight teachings (consisting of the **four doctrinal teachings** and the four methods of teaching: sudden, gradual, secret, and indeterminate), thereby asserting the supremacy of the *Lotus Sutra*. (PMLS1, pp. 76-84 and PMLS2, p. 454)

Nichiren Shonin praised Zhiyi in the highest terms for completely refuting the false doctrines of the three southern and seven northern masters and establishing the new comparative classification of doctrines centering on the *Lotus Sutra* for the first time in the history of Buddhism. He also pointed out that the southern and northern masters did not know of the doctrine of the **mutual possession of the ten realms**. (WNS1, pp. 179, 182, 199, 203, 213, 219, 247; WNS2, pp. 54, 57-58, 94-95, 140, 171, 196; WNS3, pp. 5, 10-15, 28-29, 55-56, 124, 126, 166, 168, 213; WNS6, pp. 65, 82)

Three Sovereigns and Five Emperors: (J. sankō-gotei; 三皇五帝) The **sage** rulers of ancient China. The Three Sovereigns were three legendary rulers of ancient China who are credited with creating Chinese civilization: **Fuxi**, who taught divination and fishing, invented the writing system, and instituted marriage; **Shennong**, who taught agriculture, medicine, and trade; and the **Yellow Emperor**, inventor of clothing, boats, carts, and archery. The Five Emperors were five model rulers of ancient China who are credited with developing Chinese civilization and its system of government: **Shaohao, Zhuanxu, Ku, Yao,** and **Shun**.

According to **Nichiren Shonin**, these sages ruled their kingdoms in accord with the **five constant virtues**. (WNS1, p. 101) He also pointed out that the early Chinese chronicles about the Three Sovereigns and Five Emperors teach only the morals of the present life. Compared to Buddhism, which is the teaching of the past, the present, and the future, their focus is limited. (WNS2, pp. 30-31)

three thousand dust-particle kalpas: (J. sanzen-jintengō/sanzen-jindengō; 三千塵点劫) An analogy mentioned in the seventh, "Parable of a Magic City," chapter of the *Lotus Sutra* to indicate how much time has passed since **Great Universal Wisdom Excellence Buddha** had appeared in the world: "Suppose someone smashed all the earth-particles of one thousand million **Sumeru world**s into ink-powder. Then he went to the east [carrying the ink-powder with him]. He inked a dot as large as a particle of dust [with that ink-powder] on the world at a distance of one thousand worlds from his world. Then he went again and repeated the inking of a dot on the world at every distance of one thousand worlds until the ink-powder was exhausted. Suppose he puts all the worlds he passed together and smashes them into dust, the number of dust particles equals the number of **kalpa**s that have passed since the time of the Great Universal Wisdom Excellence Buddha." (LS, pp. 129-130 adapted)

The Great Universal Wisdom Excellence Buddha had sixteen sons. These sixteen princes became **bodhisattva**s and taught the **Buddha Dharma** in their respective worlds. The sixteenth bodhisattva is said to have taught the *Lotus Sutra* in the **Saha world, attaining buddhahood** as **Shakyamuni** Buddha. Based on all of this, **Nichiren Shonin** insisted that all sentient beings in the Saha world had received the **seed of buddhahood** through the *Lotus Sutra* from Shakyamuni Buddha three thousand dust-particle kalpas in the past, and all those who do not believe in the *Lotus Sutra* commit the **transgression** of contradicting Shakyamuni Buddha to whom they are deeply indebted.

three thousand realms in a single thought-moment: (J. ichinen sanzen; 一念三千) The **Tiantai school** doctrine taught in the *Great Calming and Contemplation* by **Zhiyi** maintaining that three thousand realms of existence are contained in every **single thought-moment** of an ordinary **sentient being** at any given moment. It is based on the teaching of the **ten suchnesses** of all **phenomena** taught in the second, "**Expedients**," **chapter** of the *Lotus Sutra*. The three thousand realms (conditions under which all things exist and phenomena take place) is arrived at by squaring the **ten realms**, because of the **mutual possession of the ten realms**, multiplying the resulting one hundred realms by the ten suchnesses, and then multiplying the resulting one thousand realms by the **three categories of existence** (**five aggregates**, sentient beings, and their **environment**s). As it is shown that three thousand realms are included in an individual's every thought-moment and therefore at least potentially accessible, it follows that practitioners of the **two vehicles**, who have been denied the possibility that they can **attain buddhahood** in the **prior teachings**, as well as **ordinary people**, can enter the world of buddhahood attained by the Buddha.

Nichiren Shonin advocated that chanting the **daimoku** of "**Namu Myoho Renge Kyo**" is the only practical way for ordinary people in the **Latter Age of Degeneration** to attain buddhahood.

three thousand regulations of deportment: (J. sanzen-igi; 三千威儀) The number of monastic regulations for deportment that are arrived at by multiplying the **two hundred and fifty precepts** by the four postures of standing, sitting, walking, and lying down and then multiplying the product by either the **three times** of past, present, and future or by the **three categories of pure precepts**.

three times: (S. tri-kāla; J. san-ze; 三世) Or three existences. Refers to past, present, and future lives. In Buddhism, **phenomena** are not conceived of as static but are observed to be always changing throughout the past, present, and future. These three are, however, never in separation; rather, like an array of mirrors facing one another, they are always mutually reflecting one another from their own unique perspectives. When referring to all the buddhas throughout time and space, the phrase "the **buddhas of the ten directions** throughout the three times" is often used. Also, the sixteenth, "The **Duration of the Life of the Tathagata**," **chapter** of the *Lotus Sutra* teaches that the **Eternal Shakyamuni Buddha** is always expounding various teachings to all **sentient beings** throughout the past, present, and future so that they may quickly **attain buddhahood**.

Three Treasures: (S. Triratna or Ratna-traya; J. Sambō; 三宝) Refers to the **Buddha** (the **awakened** teacher), the **Dharma** (the teaching, the practice, and reality itself), and the **Sangha** (the community of those who uphold the teaching and practice and pass it on) that every Buddhist takes refuge in so they can achieve **liberation** from **suffering**. The Three Treasures are basic elements of **Buddha Dharma**, and putting **faith** in them is the prerequisite for Buddhists. They are the objects of the **threefold refuge**.

Three Treatises school: (J. Sanron-shū; 三論宗) One of the schools of Chinese Buddhism and one of the **six schools of Nara Buddhism** in Japan. It is the East Asian branch of the **Middle Way school** based on the study of three treatises translated by **Kumarajiva**. In 404 Kumarajiva translated the *One Hundred Verse Treatise* attributed to **Nagarjuna**'s disciple **Aryadeva**. In 409 he translated the *Middle Way Treatise* (a translation of Nagarjuna's *Root Verses on the Middle Way* and a commentary by Pingala), and the *Twelve Gates Treatise* attributed to Nagarjuna. This school is sometimes referred to as the Four Treatises school if the ***Great Perfection of Wisdom Treatise*** attributed to Nagarjuna and ostensibly translated by Kumarajiva between 401 and 406 is counted as part of its curriculum. **Jizang** is considered the founder of the Three Treatises school because he was the one who systematized and refined its teachings.

The Korean monk Hyegwan, a disciple of Jizang, brought the Three Treatises school, or Sanron Shu, to Japan in 625, along with the teachings of the **Completion of Reality school**. A second and third transmission of the school to Japan is credited to Chizo and **Doji** respectively. The Sanron Shu died out as an independent school by the mid-twelfth century.

This school emphasizes the teachings of the two truths as taught by Nagarjuna and Aryadeva, wherein the ultimate truth is **emptiness**, and other Middle Way school doctrines such as the **eight negations**. This school's comparative classification of doctrines divides **Shakyamuni Buddha**'s teachings into **two storehouses**: one for the **voice-hearer**s and one for the **bodhisattva**s. It also divides them into **three turnings of the wheel of the Dharma**: the first one it identifies as the fundamental **Dharma-wheel** taught in the *Flower Garland Sutra*, the second is the secondary Dharma-wheel taught in the **Agama sutras** and subsequent **Mahayana** sutras except for the *Lotus Sutra*, while the third is the **One Vehicle** teaching of the *Lotus Sutra*. (EET, pp. 76-82)

Nichiren Shonin classifies this school as a **provisional Mahayana teaching** that is **hinayana** or like an inferior medicine in comparison with *Lotus Sutra* and the **Tiantai school** because it relies upon the **prior teachings**. (WNS2, pp. 192, 252, 267; WNS3, pp. 19, 80, 124, 153, 241-242; WNS6, p. 146).

three turnings of the wheel of the Dharma: (J. san-tembōrin; 三転法輪) According to the *Revealing the Profound Secrets Sutra*, the first **turning of the wheel of the Dharma** by **Shakyamuni Buddha** is identified as the **hinayana** teaching of the selflessness of persons but the existence of dharmas that began with the teaching of the **four noble truths** at the **Deer Park**. The second turning and third turnings both involved the teaching of **emptiness** or the selflessness of phenomena, though the **Consciousness-Only school** interprets the third turning as the teaching of the **middle way** of neither existence nor emptiness. The *Revealing the Profound Secrets Sutra* differentiates the three turnings by identifying the first and second as the teaching of **provisional meaning**, while the third is the teaching of **definitive meaning**. (Keenan 2000, p. 49; EET, pp. 59-60)

The **Three Treatises school** divides the three turnings of the wheel of the Dharma differently: the first one it identifies as the fundamental **Dharma-wheel** taught in the *Flower Garland Sutra*, the second is the secondary Dharma-wheel taught in the **Agama sutras** and subsequent **Mahayana** sutras except for the *Lotus Sutra*, while the third is the **One Vehicle** teaching of the *Lotus Sutra*. (EET, pp. 76-82)

three vehicles: (S. tri-yāna; J. san-jō; 三乗) These are the three kinds of vehicles that lead three categories of people to **awakening**: the goat-cart (or sheep-cart) symbolizing the **voice-hearer vehicle**, the deer-cart symbolizing the **privately-awakened one vehicle**, and the ox-cart (or bullock-cart) symbolizing the **bodhisattva vehicle**. The first two are **hinayana** while the third is **Mahayana**. Voice-hearers are said to attain awakening through the doctrine of the **four noble truths**, privately-awakened ones through that of the **dependent origination**, and bodhisattvas through that of the **six perfections**. In the **prior teachings**, **Shakyamuni Buddha** had taught the three vehicles as a **skillful means** according to the **capacity** of his listeners to understand, but in the *Lotus Sutra* he declared that the three vehicles are expedient, but the **One Vehicle** is the truth.

The **Dharma Characteristics school**'s doctrine of the **five natures** contradicts the *Lotus Sutra* by insisting that the teaching of the One Vehicle is a **provisional teaching** taught to encourage those with the **indeterminate nature of the three vehicles** so that they would aspire to **attain buddhahood**, while the three vehicles teaching is the **true teaching**.

Nichiren Shonin called the Dharma Characteristics school doctrine that the three vehicles is the true teaching a **slander of the True Dharma**. Nichiren Shonin emphasized the doctrine of the **attainment of buddhahood by adherents of the two vehicles** taught in the *Lotus Sutra* as revealing the true intent of the Buddha.

three virtues: (J. san-toku; 三徳) The three virtues of ruler, teacher, and parent possessed by a **buddha**. A buddha is supposed to have all three virtues in that they have the mastery of a ruler over the **suffering**s of the world, they are teachers of the **Dharma**, and they have the **loving-kindness** and **compassion** of a parent for all **sentient being**s.

Nichiren Shonin maintained that **Shakyamuni Buddha**, who has the three virtues of a ruler, teacher, and parent, is the sole savior of the people in the **Latter Age of Degeneration**. The possession of these three virtues by one person is a prerequisite of the savior-buddha, and only the Lord Shakyamuni Buddha has this qualification according to Nichiren Shonin.

three wholesome roots: (S. tri-kuśala-mūla; J. san-zengon; 三善根) The three **root**s that are **wholesome** are: 1) non-greed, 2) non-hatred, and 3) non-delusion. They are called roots because they are predominant in producing what is wholesome and because they are the antidotes for the three unwholesome roots of **greed**, **hatred**, and **delusion**. (DCOT, p. 175; CWL, p. 395)

threefold buddha-nature: (J. san'in busshō; 三因仏性) One of the aspects of the **threefold Dharma**, the fifth of the **ten subtleties of the Trace Gate**. Three kinds of **buddha-nature** that all **sentient being**s are endowed with: 1) the **buddha-nature of the direct cause**, 2) the **buddha-nature of the completing cause**, and 3) the **buddha-nature of the conditional causes**. The buddha-nature of the direct cause corresponds to the innate nature to **attain buddhahood**, the buddha-nature of the completing cause corresponds to the **wisdom** to perceive the true nature, and the buddha-nature of the conditional causes corresponds to the practices that lead to **buddhahood**. (PMLS2, p. 257, 261)

Nichiren Shonin believed that only the *Lotus Sutra* reveals the threefold buddha-nature and only with **faith** in the *Lotus Sutra* can the threefold buddha-nature be actualized. Nichiren Shonin stressed positive and concrete faith and practice, such as receiving the **seed of buddhahood** through acts of faith in the *Lotus Sutra*, rather than just trying to contemplatively discern the buddha-nature originally endowed in people.

threefold Dharma, subtlety of the: (J. sanbō-myō; 三法妙) The fifth of the **ten subtleties of the Trace Gate**. It refers to the three aspects of the **One Buddha Vehicle**: 1) the truth of the supreme meaning, 2) the realization of **emptiness** as the supreme meaning, and 3) the functioning of the **buddha-nature**. These three encompass all the **cause**s and **effect**s of **attaining buddhahood**. (FTP, p. 207; PMLS2, pp. 93, 238-265)

Threefold Lotus Sutra: (J. *Hokke-sambu-kyō*; 法華三部経) The ideograms 法華三部経 literally mean "*Threefold Sutra of the Dharma Flower.*" The *Threefold Lotus Sutra* consists of the ***Infinite Meanings Sutra*** as the opening sutra, the *Lotus Sutra* itself, and the *Contemplation of the Universal Sage Bodhisattva Sutra* as the closing sutra.

threefold refuge: (J. san-ki, san-kie, or san-kikai; 三帰 or 三帰依 or 三帰戒) The threefold refuge is the same as the **Three Treasures** of 1) **Buddha**, 2) **Dharma**, and 3) **Sangha**. In many schools of Buddhism, a **layman** or a **laywoman** will convert to Buddhism by taking the threefold refuge and then receiving the precepts, such as the **five precepts**, as **training rule**s.

threefold training: (S. tri-śikṣā; J. san-gaku; 三學) The **eightfold noble path** divided into three components of Buddhist practice: 1) **morality**, consisting of **right speech**, **right action**, and **right livelihood**; 2) **concentration**, consisting of **right effort**, **right mindfulness**, and **right concentration**, and 3) **wisdom**, consisting of **right view** and **right intention**. (MD 44.11, p. 398)

Tiantai Lotus school: (J. Tendai Hokke-shū; 天台法華宗) Refers to the Tendai Shu in Japan established by **Saicho** on Mt. **Hiei** based on the *Lotus Sutra*. Most leaders of the new Buddhism during the Kamakura period studied and trained in the **Enryakuji Temple** on Mt. Hiei.

Tiantai school: (J. Tendai-shū; 天台宗) One of the schools of Chinese Buddhism. The Tiantai school in China was founded by its first patriarch **Zhiyi** in the sixth century with the *Lotus Sutra* as its basic canon. The Tiantai school reformer **Zhanran**, in his *Interpretations and Precedents of the Calming and Contemplation*, clarified that this school was also guided by the *Great Perfection of Wisdom Treatise*, supported by the *Nirvana Sutra*, and derives its teachings on **calming** and **contemplation** practice from the *Larger Prajna Sutra*. (EET, p. 85) The Tiantai school had its beginnings with the teachings and practices of Huiwen, his disciple Huisi, and his disciple Zhiyi, who lived on Mt. **Tiantai**. Zhiyi's lectures were recorded by his disciple **Guanding**, among them what became known as the **three major works of the Lotus school**: the *Words and Phrases of the Lotus Sutra*, the *Profound Meaning of the Lotus Sutra*, and the *Great Calming and Contemplation*. Zhanran, the sixth patriarch and revitalizer of the Tiantai school, wrote commentaries on Zhiyi's writings, and in particular the following definitive commentaries on each of Zhiyi's three major works: the *Notations on the Words and Phrases of the Lotus Sutra*, the *Elucidation of the Profound Meaning of the Lotus Sutra*, and the *Supplemental Amplifications on the Great Calming and Contemplation*. Among Zhiyi's disciples were Daosui, the school's seventh patriarch, and Xingman. (EET, pp. 85-87) Sometimes the Tiantai school regards **Nagarjuna** as its honorary first patriarch, Huiwen the second, Huisi the third, and Zhiyi as the fourth. In this case, Zhanran is considered the ninth patriarch.

The Tiantai school, or Tendai Shu, was transmitted to Japan by **Saicho**, who went to China in 804, where he was able to study with Daosui and Xingman. He returned to Japan and founded the **Tiantai Lotus school** based at **Enryakuji Temple on** Mt. **Hiei** in 805. As Saicho also transmitted the teachings of **esoteric Buddhism**, **Zen** meditation, and the **perfect and sudden precepts**, the Tiantai school in Japan incorporated these teachings and practices as well. The second head abbot of Enryakuji Temple after Saicho was **Gishin**, who had accompanied Saicho in China. The third and fourth head abbots were **Ennin** and **Enchin**, who both studied esoteric Buddhism in China so that under their leadership the Tendai Shu developed Tendai Esotericism and became an exoteric-esoteric system.

Zhiyi's comparative classification of doctrines divides **Shakyamuni Buddha**'s teachings into **five periods** and **eight teachings** (consisting of the **four doctrinal teachings** and the four methods of teaching: sudden, gradual, secret, and indeterminate). Included in his description of the practice of contemplation is the teaching of the **three thousand realms in a single thought-moment**.

Nichiren Shonin, originally a Tiantai **monk**, through experience as the **practitioner of the *Lotus Sutra***, established his own unique doctrine based on the **Original Gate** of the *Lotus Sutra*. Perceiving himself to be a transmitter of the true teaching of Shakyamuni Buddha, namely the *Lotus Sutra*, Nichiren harshly criticized Ennin, Enchin, and others who made the Tiantai Lotus school strongly esoteric.

Tiantai, Great Master: (J. Tendai Daishi; 天台 大師) See **Zhiyi**.

Tiantai, Mount: (J. Tendai-san; 天台山) Located in Zhejiang Province in China, Mt. Tiantai is where **Zhiyi** (also known as the **Great Master Tiantai**) founded the **Tiantai school** in 575. After the passing of Zhiyi, Sui Emperor Yang Di established the Guoqingsi Temple in 598 on the mountain, and it became the main temple of the Tiantai school in China.

Toji Temple: (J. Tōji; 東寺) Located at Kujō-machi, Minamiku, Kyoto, the Toji Temple refers to Kyo-o Gokokuji Temple, Grand Temple of the Toji group of the **Mantra school** in Japan. Originally built by Emperor Kammu in 796 after the capital had been moved to Kyoto in 794 as a guardian temple of the new capital. Later, in 823, it was given to **Kukai** by Emperor Saga in 823 as a practice center of the Shingon Shu. Kukai renamed it Konkōmyō Shitennō Kyō'ō Gokokuji, and it regained popularity as the representative of all Shingon temples. Together with Kongobuji Temple on Mt. Koya in Wakayama Prefecture, it is one of the two main centers of the Shingon Shu in Japan.

Tokuitsu: (fl. ninth century; 徳一) A **monk** of the **Dharma Characteristics school** in Nara during the Nara period. At the age of thirty-three or thereabouts in 782, he moved to the northern Kantō and northeastern Honshu area building many temples including the Enchiji Temple in Aizu, Fukushima Prefecture, where he died and was buried. Tokuitsu was critical of the doctrine of the **Tiantai school** and engaged in a heated dispute with **Saicho**, arguing that the **three vehicles** are the **definitive meaning** of **Shakyamuni Buddha**'s teaching, and that the **One Vehicle** is just the **provisional meaning**, taught only to encourage those of the **indeterminate nature of the three vehicles** to aspire to **attain buddhahood**. (WNS1, p. 227)

Trace Gate: (J. shakumon; 迹門) The first half or fourteen chapters of the *Lotus Sutra*, from the first **"Introductory" chapter** to the fourteenth **"Peaceful Practices" chapter**s, are called the Trace Gate, meaning the teaching of the traces of the emanated **buddha**s, particularly the historical **Shakyamuni** Buddha. The main theme of this section is the **opening of the three vehicles to reveal the One Vehicle** leading people to buddhahood. **Zhiyi** classified all the Buddha's teachings on the basis of the Trace Gate, but **Nichiren Shonin** reinterpreted them from the standpoint of the **Original Gate** (latter half) of the *Lotus Sutra* in order to save the people in the **Latter Age of Degeneration**.

training rule: (S. śikṣāpada; J. gakusho; 學處) Any of the sets of **precept**s, such as the **five precepts** for lay followers, the eight precepts of abstinence taken by some lay followers on the six days of fasting, the ten precepts for novices, or the **two hundred and fifty precepts** for **monk**s and **nun**s, that are considered training rules for Buddhist practitioners.

transformation-body: (S. nirmāṇa-kāya; J. henge-shin or ke-shin; 変化身 or 化身) Also called **accommodative-body**. According to the *Demonstration of Consciousness-Only Treatise*, those who undergo **transmigration with change and advance** can be said to have transformation-bodies because the **power** of **non-outflow concentration** enables them to change their bodies as if by a magical transformation. (DCOT, p. 277; CWL, p. 611)

The treatise also explains that the transformation-bodies are innumerable bodies abiding in **pure land**s and **impure land**s in accordance with the needs of **sentient being**s that are manifested by **tathagata**s by means of their all performing knowledge. They are manifest for the **bodhisattva**s who have not yet entered the **ten grounds**, for the practitioners of the **two vehicles**, and **ordinary people**. Taking into account the capacities of all these, they display **supernatural power**s, preach the **Dharma**, and cause all beings to gain **benefit** and happiness. (DCOT, p. 361;

CWL, p. 795)

The treatise also says that a transformation-body is devoid of real **mind** and **form** but is an apparition manifested in order to teach others and bring them benefit and happiness. (DCOT, pp. 361-367; CWL, pp. 795-805)

transgression: (S. pāpa; J. aku or zai; 悪 or 罪) The Sanskrit term *pāpa* can also be translated as "offense" or "sin." The opposite of **merit**.

transmigration with change and advance: (S. pariṇāmiki-jarā-maraṇa or acintya-pariṇāmiki-jarā-maraṇa; J. hennyaku-shōji or fushigi-hennyaku-shōji; 変易生死 or 不思議変易生死) The full name for this would be the "transmigration of inconceivable change and advance." The **rebirth**s taken up by the **bodhisattva**s and even the **arhat**s and **privately-awakened one**s (who believe themselves to be exempt from rebirth but in fact find themselves taking up the way of the bodhisattva according to the **One Vehicle** teaching of the *Lotus Sutra*) in order to accumulate the **merit** and **wisdom** needed to **attain buddhahood**.

According to the *Demonstration of Consciousness-Only Treatise*, this type of transmigration consists of especially powerful and subtle **recompensive effect**s that are brought about by **non-outflow** discriminating activity along with the power of the **condition** that is the obstacle to **knowledge**. It is named "change and advance" because due to the power of compassionate **vow**s, the transformations taken up are without limitations. It is called "inconceivable" because its wondrous functioning, directly assisted and motivated by the practice of **concentration** without outflows and **vow**s, is difficult to fathom. The kind of body taken up in this form of transmigration can be called the mind-made body or the **transformation-body**. (DCOT, pp. 276-277; CWL, p. 611)

transmigration with differences and limitations: (S. pariccheda-jarā-maraṇa; J. bundan-shōji; 分段生死) Compulsory **rebirth** within the **six destinies** wherein **sentient being**s are differentiated and limited by the **effect**s of their **wholesome** and **unwholesome karma**.

According to the *Demonstration of Consciousness-Only Treatise*, this type of transmigration consists of the coarse **recompensive effect**s experienced in the **triple world** that are brought about by various wholesome and unwholesome actions possessed of **outflow**s along with the power of the **condition** that is the obstacle of defilement. This kind of transmigration is with "differences and limitations" because the length or shortness of body and lifespan is definitely limited in accordance with the power of **causes and conditions**. (DCOT, p. 276; CWL, pp. 609-611)

Transmission of the Dharma Treasury Sutra: (J. *Fuhōzō-kyō*; 付法蔵経) Also known as the *History of the Transmission of the Dharma Treasury* (J. *Fuhōzō-innenden*; 付法蔵因縁伝), it is a record of the **twenty-four** or **twenty-three successors** of **Shakyamuni Buddha**. The number of successors differs depending on whether **Madhyantika** is counted among them or not. The Chinese "translation" by Kinkara (n.d.; S. Kiṅkara) and Tanyao (fl. 450-490; C.) is in six fascicles and was supposed to have been done in 472. It was allegedly a translation from a Sanskrit original, but this has never been proved. According to it, the first transmitter of Buddhism after the Buddha was **Mahakashyapa**, and the last, **Aryasimha**, was killed by King Dammira.

This list appears in the introduction to the *Great Calming and Contemplation* and was accepted by the **Tiantai school**. A variant of the list became the basis for the legendary **Zen** lineage of **twenty-eight Indian ancestors**, of which **Bodhidharma** was the last.

Nichiren Shonin considered this an actual **sutra**, and therefore as a prediction of **Shakyamuni** Buddha, maintaining that those transmitters of Buddhism appeared exactly as predicted by the Buddha. (WNS6, p. 106)

Treasure Form: (S. Ratnaketurāja; J. Hōsō; 宝相) The name of the **buddha**s that two thousand **voice-hearer**s will become in the ninth, "The Assurance of Future Buddhahood of the Shravakas Who Have Something More to Learn and the Shravakas Who Have Nothing More to Learn," chapter of the *Lotus Sutra*. Two thousand voice-hearers are also listed as present in the assembly in the first, "Introductory," chapter of the *Lotus Sutra*.

Treasure Purity: (S. Ratnaviśuddha; J. Hōjō; 宝浄) The **pure land** of **Many Treasures Buddha**.

treatise master: (J. ron-ji; 論師) A general term for commentators on **sutras**, **abhidharma**, and Buddhist teachings. **Nichiren Shonin** uses it to refer to revered **monk**s in India.

trichiliocosm: (S. trisāhasra-mahāsāhasraloka-dhātu; J. sanzen-daisen-sekai; 三千大千世界) Or "three thousandfold great-thousandfold world system." A set of worlds where one **buddha** guides and saves **sentient beings**. According to Buddhist cosmology, a "world" is a **Sumeru world**. A set of one thousand of these worlds is called the small thousandfold world, one thousand of which make the middle thousandfold world, one thousand of which in turn becomes the great-thousandfold world. The great thousandfold world is called the three thousandfold great-thousandfold world system because this group includes one thousand to the third power (or one billion) worlds. The term is often used in the sense of the whole world or universe.

tripitaka master: (S. trepiṭaka; J. sanzō-hosshi; 三蔵法師) Meaning literally "Dharma teacher of the three baskets," the Sanskrit term *tripiṭaka* refers to the **three baskets** or divisions of the Buddhist scriptures: **sutras**, **vinaya**, and **abhidharma**. It also refers to one who is well-versed in all the three divisions of the Buddhist teachings. Sometimes the word "tripitaka" alone is used as a title for a master of the canon.

tripitaka teaching: (J. zō-kyō; 蔵教) The first of the **four doctrinal teachings**. The teachings of mainstream Buddhism (sometime pejoratively called **hinayana** Buddhism) as found in the Chinese **Agama sutras** or the Pali canon. It is directed to the **voice-hearer**s who strive to become **arhat**s. According to **Zhiyi**, the tripitaka, or **three baskets** teachings, enable a practitioner to enter into an understanding of **emptiness** by analytically breaking down phenomena. In other words, this teaching aims to reveal the emptiness of the **self** by examining the components of existence, which it considers real **dharma**s, such as the **five aggregates**. The tripitaka teaching is found in the **Deer Park** and **Expanded period**s of the **five periods** of **Shakyamuni Buddha**'s teachings.

Though representative of the **voice-hearer vehicle**, practitioners of all **three vehicles** can follow the tripitaka teaching, but they do so in different ways. The voice-hearers focus on the **five contemplations for settling the mind** and the **four foundations of mindfulness** and contemplate the **four noble truths** to attain their own **liberation**. The **privately-awakened ones** contemplate **dependent origination** in order to attain their own liberation. The **bodhisattva**s practice the **six perfections** in order to liberate themselves and others. (PMLS2, pp. 142-143)

triple world: (S. trailokya or traidhātuka or triloka or trilokadhātu; J. san-gai; 三界) The triple world refers to the "three realms" of **samsara**: 1) the **desire realm**, 2) the **form realm**, and 3) the **formless realm**. The unawakened **sentient being**s undergo **rebirth** through these three realms.

The third, "A Parable," chapter of the *Lotus Sutra*, likens the triple world of **delusion** and **suffering** to a house on fire.

The world of desire extends from the **hell**s up to the more concrete **heaven**s. The worlds of form and formlessness include the higher heavens of increasing refinement.

true reality of all things: (S. sarva-dharmāṇāṃ-dharmatā; J. shohō-jissō; 諸法

実相抄) The ideograms 諸法実相 literally mean "true **mark** of all **dharma**s." It is the principle of all **phenomena** being ultimately **unconditioned** because they are all **empty** of any **self-nature** that can be **conditioned**.

True Dharma: See Wonderful Dharma.

True Recompense, Land of: (J. jippō-do; 実報土). Also called the Land of Unobstructed True Recompense (J. jippō-mushō-gedō; 實報無障礙土) or just Land of Recompense. It is the third of the four lands mentioned in the **sutra**s where **buddha**s appear as classified by the **Tiantai school**. The Land of Unobstructed True Recompense is the land inhabited by the **bodhisattva**s of higher stages who are enjoying the rewards of their practice of the bodhisattva way and are contemplating the truth of the **middle way**. This land is associated with the teaching of the four noble truths as immeasurable of the **distinct teaching**, however **suffering** and the **origin of suffering** are not found in such a **pure land** because those dwelling in it no longer suffer or perpetuate the causes of suffering. (CSQI, p. 165)

true sutra: (J. jikkyō; 実経) Refers to the **sutra** in which **Shakyamuni Buddha** revealed his true intent or the **True Dharma** without compromising with the circumstances of the time or **capacity** of the people to understand.

Nichiren Shonin regarded the *Lotus Sutra* alone as the sole true sutra and all others as **provisional sutra**s. (WNS1, pp. 3-5) Other sutras claimed to be supreme, but Nichiren Shonin regarded such claims as pertaining to only a relative superiority, in that a sutra might be regarded as superior in some respects due to expressing teachings of **definitive meaning** compared to **provisional meaning** in regard to certain limited topics or issues. (WS1, p. 10-13) The *Lotus Sutra*, however, is the true sutra because it teaches that all people can **attain buddhahood** through its teaching and practice. (WNS1, pp. 44-45)

true teaching: (J. jikkyō; 実教) See **true sutra**.

turn the Wheel of the Dharma: See **turning of the Wheel of the Dharma**.

turning of the Wheel of the Dharma: (S. Dharmacakra-pravartana; J. tembōrin; 転法輪) The **teaching** of the **Dharma**, which eliminates the **defilement**s of **sentient being**s, is likened to the **wheel-turning noble king**'s wheel treasure which crushes all the evils of sentient beings. The first "turning of the wheel of the Dharma" usually refers to **Shakyamuni Buddha**'s first teaching for the five ascetics (former companions when he practiced austerities) at the **Deer Park** in **Varanasi**.

In **Mahayana** Buddhism, it is taught that there were **three turnings of the wheel of the Dharma**.

Tushita, Heaven of: (S. Tuṣita; J. Tosotsu-ten or Toshita-ten; 兜率天 or 覩史多天) The Sanskrit name Tuṣita can also be translated as "Contentment." The fourth of the **six heavens of the desire realm**. It is the second of the heavens located above Mt. **Sumeru** and is of the same size as the summit of the mountain. (AKB2, pp. 465, 468)

In this heaven the future **buddha** abides during his last life as a **bodhisattva** before coming down to the **Saha world**. It is believed that **Shakyamuni** Buddha riding on a white elephant came down from this heaven to the womb of Queen Maya. At present, **Maitreya** Bodhisattva dwells there until his lifespan in this heaven is complete, whereupon he will descend to earth.

twelve kinds of scriptures: (S. dvādaśāṅga-pravacana; J. jūnibu-kyō; 十二部経) A division of the **Buddhist scriptures** into twelve categories according to the style of exposition:
1) **sutra**, a prose discourse of the **Buddha**, or Buddhist scripture.
2) **gatha**, a verse that does not repeat a prose passage.
3) fable, a story of a previous life of a disciple of the Buddha.
4) jataka, a story of a previous life of the Buddha.
5) marvelous event, a story about an unprecedented marvel or supernatural event during the lifetime of the Buddha.
6) framing story, a story that explains why a sutra was expounded.
7) parable, a story about a past life of a follower of the Buddha and the **fruition** of their past **merit**orious **action**s.
8) *geya*, a verse that repeats the contents of a prose passage.
9) instruction, further instructions or elaborations on a discourse of the Buddha.
10) utterance, an unprompted expounding of the **Dharma.**
11) **expanded discourse**s with more elaborate explanations.
12) assurance of future buddhahood.

twenty subtleties: (J. nijū-myō; 二十妙) The combination of the **ten subtleties of the Trace Gate** and the **ten subtleties of the Original Gate**.

twenty-eight Indian ancestors: (J. Tenjiku-nijūhasso, Saiten-nijūhasso, or nijūhasso; 天竺二十八祖 or 西天二十八祖 or 二十八祖) The ideograms 天竺 and 西天 refer to India. The ideogram 祖 means "ancestor" though it has been translated as "patriarch." In the **Zen school**, the list of successors to **Shakyamuni Buddha** based upon the earlier list of **twenty-four successors** from the *Transmission of the Dharma Treasury Sutra* was expanded to twenty-eight. The Zen list of Indian ancestors is composed of: 1) **Mahakashyapa**, 2) **Ananda**, 3) Shanavasa, 4) Upagupta, 5) Dhritaka, 6) Micchaka, 7) Vasumitra, 8) Buddhananda, 9) Buddhamitra, 10) **Parshva**, 11) Punyayashas, 12) **Ashvaghosha**, 13) Kapimala, 14) **Nagarjuna**, 15) **Aryadeva**, 16) Rahulabhadra, 17) Samghanandi, 18) Samghayashas, 19) **Kumarata**, 20) Jayata, 21) **Vasubandhu**, 22) Manorhita, 23) Haklenayashas, 24) **Aryasimha**, 25) Vasi-Asita, 26) Punyamitra, 27) Prajnatara, and 28) **Bodhidharma**.

twenty-four successors: (J. fuhōzō-no-nijūyo-nin; 付法蔵の二十四人) The ideograms 二十四人 can be translated as "twenty-four persons," while 付法蔵 can be translated as "entrusted with the Dharma Treasury." According to the *Transmission of the Dharma Treasury Sutra* there were twenty-four successors to **Shakyamuni Buddha** after his **final nirvana**. They are listed as: 1) **Mahakashyapa**, 2) **Ananda**, 3) **Madhyantika**, 4) Shanavasa, 5) Upagupta, 6) Dhritaka, 7) Micchaka, 8) Buddhananda, 9) Buddhamitra, 10) **Parshva**, 11) Punyayashas, 12) **Ashvaghosha**, 13) Kapimala, 14) **Nagarjuna**, 15) **Aryadeva**, 16) Rahulabhadra, 17) Samghanandi, 18) Samghayashas, 19) **Kumarata**, 20) Jayata, 21) **Vasubandhu**, 22) Manorhita, 23) Haklenayashas, and 24) **Aryasimha**.

Madhyanitka can be omitted from the list, in which case there are only **twenty-three successors**. This is because Madhyantika, who was a successor to Ananda along with Shanavasa, did not himself leave a successor.

twenty-three successors: (J. fuhōzō-no-nijūsan-nin or nijūsan-so; 付法蔵の二十三人 or 二十三祖) See **twenty-four successors**.

two exhortations: (J. nika-no-kangyō; 二箇の諫暁) The assurance of future buddhahood for **Devadatta** and the **attainment of buddhahood by a dragon girl** in the twelfth, "**Devadatta**," **chapter** of the *Lotus Sutra* are interpreted as the Buddha's exhortation for evil persons and females to spread the sutra. Together with the **three proclamations** from chapter twelve, these two exhortations comprise the **five proclamations**. (WNS2, p. 90-91)

two gods: (J. niten-sansen; 二天) The two **god**s refer to Shiva, or the **Great Freedom God**, and **Vishnu**, two of the most important deities in **Brahmanism** and Hinduism in India. The Great Freedom God is the supreme deity and Vishnu is the caretaker of the whole universe. (WNS, p. 32) Many adherents of what is called Hinduism are devotees of either Shiva or Vishnu.

two hundred and fifty precepts: (J. nihyaku-gojikkai; 二百五十戒) According to the Dharmagupta tradition explained in the *Four-part Discipline* followed in East Asia the binding rules for **monk**s consisted of two hundred and fifty precepts and for **nun**s three hundred forty-eight.

If the two hundred and fifty precepts are applied to the four postures of standing, sitting, walking, and lying down there would be one thousand precepts. If these were multiplied again by the **three times** of past, present, and future or multiplied by the **three categories of pure precepts** then it can be said that there are **three thousand regulations of deportment**.

two vehicles: (J. nijō; 二乗) The **hinayana** teachings for the **voice-hearer**s and **privately-awakened one**s are referred to as the teachings of the two vehicles. Voice-hearers who have become **arhat**s and privately-awakened ones are those who have practiced these teachings and completely gotten rid of **defilement**s, but **Mahayana** Buddhists consider them selfish because they are concerned with self-salvation, forgetting to help others. Most Mahayana **sutra**s regard arhats and pratyekabuddhas as unable to **attain buddhahood**, but the *Lotus Sutra* teaches the possibility of the **attainment of buddhahood by adherents of the two vehicles**.

Nichiren Shonin placed great importance on the doctrine of the attainment of buddhahood by adherents of the two vehicles, considering it one of the two reasons for the superiority of the *Lotus Sutra* over all other sutras.

udumbara: (S.; J. udonge; 優曇華) A type of flower that only blossoms every three thousand years and heralds the advent of a **buddha** or **wheel-turning king**. Mentioned in the twenty-seventh, "King Wonderful Adornment as the Previous Life of a Bodhisattva," chapter of the *Lotus Sutra*.

Uluka: (S. Ulūka; J. Uruka or Urusōgya; 優楼迦 or 漚楼僧佉) Also known as Kanada. One of the **three hermits** in India, who are upheld as the legendary **rishi**s who revealed the **Vedas** and were the founders of ancient Indian philosophy and religion. Uluka was the founder of the **Vaisheshika** school who lived in the third century BCE.

unconditioned: (S. asaṃskṛta; J. mui; 無為) Unconditioned **dharma**s are those which have no activity, are not **cause**d or **conditioned** and do not produce **effect**s. (AKB1, pp. 185, 286) It can be taken as a synonym for **nirvana**.

Universal Brightness: (S. Samantaprabhāsa; J. Fumyō; 普明) The name of the

buddhas that five hundred **arhat**s will become, according to the eighth, "Assurance of Future Buddhahood of the Five Hundred Disciples," chapter of the *Lotus Sutra*. Included among these arhats who received this assurance were Ajnata Kaundinya, Uruvilva Kashyapa, Gaya Kashyapa, Nadi Kashyapa, **Kalodayin**, Udayin, **Aniruddha**, Revata, Kapphina, Bakkula, Chunda, and Svagata.

Universal Sage: (S. Samantabhadra; J. Fugen; 普賢) The name Samantabhadra can also be translated as "Universal Good" or "Universal Worthy." This **bodhisattva** represents the principle, **samadhi**, and practice of all **buddha**s. He leads other bodhisattvas to help the Buddha and is particularly well known in East Asian Buddhism for his ten great vows that appear in chapter forty of the *Flower Garland Sutra*. Universal Sage is frequently shown as the right-hand attendant of **Shakyamuni** Buddha mounted on an elephant. He and **Manjushri** Bodhisattva are the bodhisattva attendants most often associated with **Shakyamuni** Buddha.

Universal Sage Bodhisattva appears in the twenty-eighth chapter, "The Encouragement of Universal Sage Bodhisattva," of the *Lotus Sutra*. He comes from the world of Treasure Power Virtue Superior King Buddha far to the east in order to hear and receive the *Lotus Sutra*. He promises to protect and support those who keep the *Lotus Sutra* in the **Latter Age of Degeneration** and provides them with **dharani** spells. He even declares that the ability to keep the *Lotus Sutra* is made possible through the aid of his **sustaining power**. He goes on to say that those who keep this sutra, read and recite it, memorize it, understand it, and act according to it are doing the same practice as he does. Nevertheless, the Buddha tells Universal Sage Bodhisattva that he should greet a keeper of the *Lotus Sutra* in the same way that he would greet the Buddha himself.

The *Contemplation of the Universal Sage Bodhisattva Sutra*, which is the closing third of the *Threefold Lotus Sutra*, elaborates on the promise of Universal Sage Bodhisattva in the final twenty-eighth chapter of the *Lotus Sutra* to appear on his six-tusked white elephant to those who practice repentance and recite the *Lotus Sutra*. That sutra also explains how the practitioner can visualize Universal Sage Bodhisattva and eventually the entire Assembly in Space.

Universal Sage Bodhisattva is believed by many Chinese Buddhists to reside on Mt. Omei in Western China.

Nichiren Shonin's **Great Mandala of Invoking the Ten Realms** includes the name of Universal Sage Bodhisattva to represent the **bodhisattvas of the trace teaching**.

unsurpassed: (S. anuttara; J. anokutara or mujō; 阿耨多羅 or 無上) The Sanskrit term *anuttara* means "unsurpassed."

unsurpassed awakening: (S. anuttara-saṃbodhi; J. mujō-bodai; 無上菩提) See **unsurpassed, complete, and perfect awakening**.

unsurpassed, complete, and perfect awakening: (S. anuttara-samyak-saṃbodhi; J. mujōshōtōgaku or anokutara-sanmyaku-sambodai; 無上正等覺 or 阿耨多羅三藐三菩提) This refers to the **awakening** of a **buddha**.

unwholesome: (S. akuśala; J. aku or fuzen; 悪 or 不善) The Sanskrit term *akuśala* can also be translated as "inauspicious," or "unvirtuous." Unwholesome **karmic** activity or **cause**s (not **effect**s or **ripening**s) are those that lead to bad consequences and bring about **transgression** in present and future lives. (DCOT, p. 155; CWL, p. 349)

Upali: (S. Upāli; J. Ubari; 優婆離) One of the **ten great disciples**, foremost among those who uphold the **vinaya** or discipline.

Utpalavarna: (S. Utpalavarṇā; J. Rengeshiki or Keshiki; 蓮華色 or 華色) A **nun** and disciple of **Shakyamuni Buddha**, who is said to have attained the state of **arhat**. According to the *Great Perfection of Wisdom Treatise*, she was beaten to death by **Devadatta** when she admonished him for his evil deeds.

Vaidehi: (S. Vaidehī; J. Idaike; 韋提希) The wife of King **Bimbisara** of the **Magadha** kingdom in central India and mother of King **Ajatashatru** who killed his own father and imprisoned his mother.

Vaipulya: (S.; J. Hōkō; 方広) A Buddhist **monk**, or perhaps a faction or school, who takes an extreme view of **emptiness**, understanding it in a way that falls into the error of **annihilationism**. (Ramanan, p. 155)

Vaipulya sutras: (S. vaipulya or or vaidalya or Vaipulya sūtra; J. Hōdō or Hōkō or Hōdō-kyō; 方等 or 方広 or 方等経) The Sandkrit terms *vaipulya* or *vaidalya* can be translated as "extended" or "vast." These are general terms used to refer to **Mahayana sutra**s as a whole. The Vaipulya sutras, or **expanded discourse**s, are among the **twelve kinds of scriptures**.

It is also used to mean the expanded discourses taught during the **Expanded period** according to the **five period** classification of the **Tiantai school**. In the latter use, such sutras as the **three Pure Land sutras** are included in this category. **Nichiren Shonin** used the term in the latter sense. (WNS1, pp. 8)

Vairochana: (S. Vairocana; J. Dainichi or Birushana; 大日 or 毘盧遮那/毘盧舍

那) The Sanskrit name Vairocana can be translated as "Illuminator" or "Resplendent." The ideograms 大日 means "Great Sun" and can indicate Vairochana or **Mahavairochana Buddha**. Vairochana is the name of the Buddha as he appears in the *Flower Garland Sutra*, the *Brahma's Net Sutra*, the *Mahavairochana Sutra*, the *Diamond Peak Sutra*, and the *Contemplation of the Universal Sage Bodhisattva Sutra*.

The **pure land** of Vairochana Buddha is the **Lotus Treasury World** or (in the *Contemplation of the Universal Sage Bodhisattva Sutra*) the Pure Land of Eternally Tranquil Light.

He is the central buddha of the **Diamond-realm mandala** described in the *Diamond Peak Sutra*, symbolizing the essential nature of the **Dharma-realm knowledge** that is the knowledge of the embodied nature of the Dharma-realm.

Zhiyi identified Vairochana as the **Dharma-body**, **Rochana** (an abbreviated version of Vairochana) as the **reward-body**, and **Shakyamuni** as the **accommodative-body** of the Buddha. (PMLS2, p. 265)

Vaisheshika: (S. Vaiśeṣika; J. Bisei or Eiseishi or Katsuron-ha; 毘世 or 衛世師 or 勝論派) A philosophical system of analysis established in India by **Uluka** that teaches that there are six categories (S. padārthas) of things that can be objects of experience: substance, quality, **action**, generality (S. sāmānya), particularity (S. viśeṣa), and inherence (S. samavāya). The Vaisheshika attempts to discern the ultimate realities of life to end **ignorance** and bring about **liberation** from **samsara**. In this school of thought a distinction is made between the individual **self** (S. *jīvātman*) that suffers the cycle of birth and death and the Supreme Self (S. *paramātman*) that is **God**. Vaisheshika became associated with the Nyāya school of Gautama (c. third century BCE) that concerns itself with logic and epistemology.

vajra: (S.; J. kongō or kongō-sho; 金剛 or 金剛杵) The Sanskrit term *vajra* can be translated as "adamantine," "diamond," "diamond pounder," or "thunderbolt." It is a kind of scepter made of an unbreakable material with prongs curling in to form a ball on the ends. It represents a thunderbolt, the weapon of **Shakra**. In **esoteric Buddhism**, it represents the utilization of **skillful means**.

Vajrabodhi: (671-741; J. Kongōchi; 金剛智) Also known as Vajramati. In Japan, he is considered one of the three patriarchs of **esoteric Buddhism** in China and is considered the fifth patriarch of the **Mantra school**. An alternate list of Mantra school patriarchs lists Vajrabodhi as the third.

Vajrabodhi became a **monk** at the age of nine at Nalanda, where he studied **abhidharma**, **vinaya**, and **Mahayana** Buddhism. From 701 to 708 he studied esoteric Buddhism from Nagabodhi, the fourth patriarch of the Mantra school, and thereby became an **acharya** and the fifth patriarch. He then traveled to Sri Lanka and Sumatra. He entered Tang China by sea in 720. At first, he resided in Luoyang, the eastern capital, but by 721 he and his disciple **Amoghavajra** were in Chang'an, the main capital. Between 723 and 724 he translated the *Diamond Peak Sutra*. Vajrabodhi also founded a temple in China under the patronage of Emperor Xuanzong of the Tang dynasty where Buddhist esoteric initiations were performed.

In criticizing the Mantra school, **Nichiren Shonin** pointed out Vajrabodhi's failure in prayers for rain-making.

Vajrasattva: (S.; J. Kongōsatta; 金剛薩埵) Also known as a Vajrapani the **Lord of Mysteries** in the *Mahavairochana Sutra*. As an **emanation-body** of **Mahavairochana Buddha**, Vajrasattva personifies the **awakening mind** within all **sentient being**s who aspire to **attain buddhahood**.

Vajrasattva is sometimes called a **bodhisattva**, but he is more properly a vajradhara or "*vajra*-holder," which is to say a practitioner of **esoteric Buddhism** as distinct from those who simply cultivate the **six perfections**. In fact, he is the leader of the vajradharas.

He is considered the second of the eight patriarchs of the **Mantra school**, who is said to have received the teachings of **esoteric Buddhism** directly from the first patriarch **Mahavairochana Buddha**. These teachings were written down in the form of the *Mahavairochana Sutra* and sealed in an iron tower in southern India. According to the Mantra school, this tower was opened by **Nagarjuna** several centuries later, whereupon Vajrasattva appeared and gave him initiation and the transmission of the esoteric teachings.

Varanasi: (S. Vārāṇasī or Bārāṇasī; J. Harana-koku or Haranai; 波羅奈国 or 波羅奈) The capital of Kashi. The **Deer Park** where **Shakyamuni Buddha** began to **turn the Wheel of the Dharma** was close to Varanasi.

"Variety of Merits, The" chapter: (J. Funbetsu-kudoku-hon; 分別功徳品) The seventeenth chapter of the *Lotus Sutra*. In this chapter, **Shakyamuni Buddha** explains to **Maitreya Bodhisattva** about the great **benefit**s obtained by those in the assembly who heard about the immeasurable duration of his life as stated in chapter sixteen, "**Duration of the Life of the Tathagata**." Maitreya Bodhisattva then repeats the description of these benefits in verse. This first half of the chapter is the last part of the one chapter and two half-chapters that comprise the main discourse of the Original Gate of the *Lotus Sutra*.

The Buddha then explains how those who hear about his immeasurable lifespan and have even a single moment of understanding by faith will obtain innumerable **merit**s a hundred, thousand, ten thousand, and a hundred million times greater than that of practicing the first five of the **six perfections**. The Buddha continues to elaborate the way to have faith in and practice the *Lotus Sutra*'s teaching both during his lifetime and after his **final nirvana**.

Vasubandhu: (fl. c. fourth or fifth centuries; S.; J. Tenjin or Seshin; 天親 or 世親) A scholar-**monk** who is believed to have lived around the fifth century in Gandhara in northern India. At first, he studied **hinayana** Buddhism but was later converted to **Mahayana** by his elder brother **Asanga**, becoming a great promoter of the **Consciousness-Only school** of Mahayana Buddhism. He wrote many works such as the *Treasury of Abhidharma Treatise, Twenty Verses on Consciousness-Only*, and the *Thirty Verses on Consciousness-Only*. He is also credited as the author of commentaries on the *Summary of the Mahayana Treatise*, the *Differentiation of the Middle Way and the Extremes*, the *Differentiation of Dharmas and Dharma-nature*, the *Ornament for the Mahayana Sutras Treatise*, the **Lotus Sutra Treatise**, the *Nirvana Sutra Treatise*, the *Pure Land Treatise*, and the *Ten Grounds Sutra Treatise*.

In the ***Transmission of the Dharma Treasury Sutra***, Vasubandhu was the successor of Jayata in the list of **twenty-three** or **twenty-four successors** or patriarchs after **Shakyamuni Buddha**.

Nichiren Shonin says of him that living in the **Age of the True Dharma**, Vasubandhu spread the provisional Mahayana teachings although he grasped the true meaning of the *Lotus Sutra* in his heart - because he knew that the time and **capacity** of the people to understand were not ripe for the **True Dharma**.

Vatsiputra: (S. Vātsīputra; J. Tokushi; 犢子) The founder of the **Vatsiputriya**.

Vatsiputriya: (S. Vātsīputrīya; J. Tokushi-bu; 犢子部) A school of mainstream Buddhism named for its founder, **Vatsiputra**. By the third century BCE it was counted as one of the eighteen schools of pre-Mahayana or mainstream Buddhism that developed in India. The other schools of mainstream Buddhism and **Mahayana** Buddhism derided the Vatsiputriya and its sub-schools as the "personalists" who contradicted the teaching of **non-self**. This is because the Vatsiputriya taught that there is an "inexpressible person" that is neither the same as nor different from the **five aggregates**.

Vedas: (S.; J. bēda; 吠陀) The foundational **scripture**s of **Brahmanism** consisting of the four Vedas, that preserve the sacred hymns and teachings of the Aryans that were brought into India when they migrated into the sub-continent around 1500 BCE. The Vedas were not a written text at that time, and even today are passed on as an oral transmission. They were believed to be a revelation (S. *śruti* –

"what is heard") given to the **rishi**s, or ancient seers, and passed on to the **brahmin**s. The four Vedas are: the *Rig Veda*, the *Sama Veda*, the *Yajur Veda*, and the *Atharva Veda*. They are each comprised of four strata, beginning with the **mantra**s and hymns that are collected into the Samhitas and the three subsequent commentaries on the hymns and rituals which are the Brahmanas, the Aranyakas, and the Upanishads.

Verses Praising Rebirth in the Pure Land: (J. *Ōjō-raisan-ge* or *Ōjō-raisan*; 往生礼讃偈 or 往生礼讃) A work by **Shandao** describing the teachings and practice of the **Pure Land school** of Buddhism in verse form.

Vimalakirti: (S. Vimalakīrti; J. Yuimakitsu; 維摩詰) A wealthy layman who was the eponymous hero of the ***Vimalakirti Sutra***.

Vimalakirti Sutra: (S. *Vimalakīrti-nirdeśa*; J. *Yuima-kyō* or *Jōmyō-kyō*; 維摩経 or 浄名経) One of the typical early **Mahayana sutra**s. **Vimalakirti**, the central figure of the sutra, is a wealthy lay believer of Buddhism. Through discussions and debates between him and disciples of the **Buddha** and various **bodhisattva**s the sutra explains core Mahayana doctrines in a clever literary style. It was translated into Chinese several times. The three extant Chinese translations are the ones by Zhi Qian (fl. 220-252) between 223-228, **Kumarajiva** in 406, and **Xuanzang** in 650.

Vimalamitra, Treatise Master: (J. Muku Ronji or Mukuyū; 無垢論師 or 無垢友) A Buddhist commentator of Kashmir, India, who is said to have fallen into the Hell of **Incessant Suffering** with his tongue split into five pieces as he strongly believed in **hinayana** and vehemently slandered **Mahayana Buddhism**.
    Nichiren Shonin cites him as an example of the consequences of **slander of the True Dharma**. (WNS1, pp. 179, 246)

vinaya: (S.; J. binaya or ritsu; 毘奈耶 or 律) The Sanskrit term *vinaya* means "discipline." A general term for monastic rules, regulations, and procedures of the monastic **Sangha**. It consists of three parts: (1) the prohibitive **precept**s or binding rules for **monk**s and **nun**s, (2) the analysis of those rules, including the story of the circumstances that brought about each rule, and (3) the injunctive precepts found in the collection of rules that deal with specific procedures that should be followed by the monastic Sangha.
    By the fifth century, four different vinaya traditions of mainstream Buddhism were translated into Chinese, and a fifth was known about but not translated. These five traditions were called the disciplines of the five schools.

Virudhaka: (S. Virūḍhaka; J. Harui; 波瑠璃) The king of Koshala who ruled from the city of **Shravasti** in central India at the time of **Shakyamuni Buddha**. His father, Prasenajit, was a great protector of Shakyamuni Buddha who tried to marry a **Shakya** princess, but the Shakyas did not approve of him and deceived the king into marrying a slave woman, who gave birth to Virudhaka. Having learned the truth of his own birth after being spurned by the Shakyas during a visit to Kapilavastu, Virudhaka seized the throne from his father, King Prasenajit. He immediately waged a war against the Shakya kingdom, killing many people, for which, it is said, he fell into the **Hell** of **Incessant Suffering**. Soon after, he was burned to death during a drinking party aboard a ship on a river. He was so envious and jealous of Shakyamuni Buddha, like **Sunakshatra**, that he aggressively persecuted the Buddha.

Vishnu: (S. Viṣṇu; J. Bichū-ten; 毘紐天) In later developments of the Vedic tradition, Vishnu is a member of the *trimūrti* representing the three phases of material nature: **Brahma** the creator, Vishnu the preserver, and Shiva (S. Śiva) the destroyer (called the Freedom God or **Great Freedom God** in Buddhism). Among the Vaishnavas, he is the supreme deity.

voice-hearer: (S. śrāvaka; J. shōmon; 声聞) This term refers to those monastic disciples of a **buddha** who are able to hear the voice of that buddha in person and who then strive to attain **liberation** by listening to that buddha's teaching of the **four noble truths** and practicing the **eightfold noble path**. The goal of a voice-hearer is to become an **arhat** who is free of the **three poisons**, has realized **nirvana**, and is liberated from **samsara**. Traditionally the **ten great disciples** are listed as the primary voice-hearer disciples of the Buddha who were **monk**s, though there also other lists in the sutras of the most prominent **nun**s, and most prominent **laymen** and **laywomen** who were practitioners and supporters. The state of being a voice-hearer is one of the four highest of the **ten realms**.

Mahayana Buddhism considers voice-hearers and **privately-awakened one**s the practitioners of the **two vehicles** who are barred from being able to **attain buddhahood** because they seek only their own liberation from samsara. In East Asian Mahayana Buddhism, the **final nirvana** sought by the arhats and privately-awakened ones is pejoratively looked upon as a lowly aspiration to reduce the body to ashes and annihilate consciousness.

According to the ***Lotus Sutra***, however, even the voice-hearers are on the path of the **One Vehicle**. It is in the first half of the **sutra**, known as the **Trace Gate**, that **Shakyamuni** Buddha reveals the **attainment of buddhahood by adherents of the two vehicles**.

In the *Lotus Sutra*, the voice-hearers fall into three groups of **superior capacity**, **average capacity**, and **dull capacity**, depending on which of the three cycles of expounding the Dharma they were able to finally understand the **One Vehicle teaching**. **Shariputra** represents the superior category. He can understand the Buddha's direct teaching of the Dharma of the **true reality of all things** and the declaration of the One Vehicle in chapter two, "**Expedients**." He receives the assurance of future buddhahood in chapter three, "A Parable." **Maudgalyayana, Mahakashyapa, Mahakatyayana,** and **Subhuti** comprise those of average capacity. They respond to the parables, such as the parable of the burning house in chapter three, in order to comprehend the One Vehicle teaching. They receive the Buddha's assurance of future buddhahood in chapter six, "Assurance of Future Buddhahood." **Purna, Aniruddha, Ananda,** and **Rahula** represent those of **dull capacity**. They must learn the One Vehicle teaching in the context of stories of their past lives in chapter seven, "The Parable of a Magic City," showing their connection to the One Vehicle before they believe that it also applies to them. Purna and Aniruddha receive their assurance of future buddhahood in chapter eight, "The Assurance of Future Buddhahood of the Five Hundred Disciples," while Ananda and Rahula receive their assurance in chapter nine, "The Assurance of Future Buddhahood of the Shravakas Who Have Something More to Learn and the Shravakas Who Have Nothing More to Learn." Of the ten great voice-hearer disciples, all but one receives the assurance of future buddhahood. Only **Upali** is not mentioned in the *Lotus Sutra*.

voice-hearer vehicle: (S. śrāvakayāna; J. shōmanjō; 声聞乗) In the **parable of the burning house** told in the third, "A Parable," chapter of the *Lotus Sutra*, the teachings and practices taught to the **Buddha**'s disciples are compared to **three vehicles**. The teachings or vehicle for **voice hearer**s, such as the **four noble truths**, are represented in the parable by a goat-cart (or sheep-cart).

vow: (S. praṇidhāna; J. hotsugan or seigan; 発願 or 誓願) The Sanskrit term *praṇidhāna* can also be translated as "aspiration." In **Mahayana** Buddhism, the making of vows as a **bodhisattva practice**, includes the vow to attain **awakening** (i.e. to **attain buddhahood**) and the vow to bring **benefit** and happiness to others.

Walking on Flowers of Seven Treasures: (S. Sapta-ratna-padma-vikrāntagāmin; J. Tōshippōke; 蹈七宝華) The name of the **buddha** that **Rahula** will become according to the ninth, "The Assurance of Future Buddhahood of the Shravakas Who Have Something More to Learn and the Shravakas Who Have Nothing More to Learn" chapter of the *Lotus Sutra*.

way leading to the cessation of suffering, the truth of the: (S. mārga-satya; J. dōtai; 道諦) The fourth of the **four noble truths**. The way leading to the **cessation** of **suffering** is described by **Shakyamuni Buddha** as the **eightfold noble path**.

(LD 22.21, pp. 348-349; CD 56.11, p. 1844)

Way of the Buddha is unsurpassed; I vow to become it, The: (J. butsudō-mujō-seiganjō; 仏道無上誓願成) The fourth of the **four great vows** of a **bodhisattva**. It is a vow to attain **unsurpassed, complete, and perfect awakening**.

Wei Yuansong: (fl. 567; C.; J. Ei Gensū; 衛元嵩) Also called Songling (J. Sūryō; 嵩靈). A Buddhist novice who submitted a memorial in 567 criticizing Buddhism to Emperor Wu of the Northern Zhou, claiming that the Buddhist **Sangha** should be purged of corrupt **monk**s and **nun**s, that the building of **stupa**s was wasting the treasury of the empire and should be stopped, and that statues and images were not worthy of worship and should be destroyed. He went on to suggest that the distinction between monastic and householder should be abolished, that Buddhism and secular virtue were no different, and that the emperor should be considered as the **Buddha**. Emperor Wu had been looking for an excuse to rein in the power of the Buddhist establishment, and so the memorial was quite timely. Wei Yuansong was rewarded with the title Duke of Sichuan, and he left the Sangha and returned to the fold of Taoism. Wei Yuansong and a Taoist priest named Zhang Bin continued to advocate the suppression of Buddhism and in 574 Emperor Wu issued a decree proscribing Buddhism. Throughout the region ruled by the Northern Zhou, from 574 until Emperor Wu's death in 577, countless stupas, statues, and shrines were destroyed, more than forty thousand temples were confiscated, and millions of monks and nuns were laicized. Ironically, Emperor Wu also proscribed Taoism because it had come to his attention how much the Taoists had modeled themselves on Buddhism.

Nichiren Shonin cited Wei Yuansong as a vivid example of a Buddhist monk returning to Taoism, using the **Dharma** to further his own agenda, and then turning upon Buddhism itself.

Wen, King: (1152 – 1050 BCE; J. Bun-ō; 文王) Also known as the Count of the West (J. Seihaku; 西伯). The father of King **Wu**, who overthrew King **Zhou Xin** and established the Zhou dynasty. King Wen is sometimes considered the second of the **Three Kings**(1).

wheel-turning king: (S. cakravarti-rāja or cakaravarti-rājan or cakravartin; J. tenrin-ō or rinnō; 転輪王 or 輪王) An ideal king who rules by the **True Dharma** and is believed to have **thirty-two marks** of physical excellence (though not as perfect as the **buddha**s) and the **seven treasures**(1), including the wheel-treasure. Wheel-turning kings represent the highest state of virtue and power that one can attain in the **human** realm. They rule through peace, justice, and diplomacy rather than by violence and force of arms.

There are four kinds of wheel-turning kings according to the qualities of the wheel treasure: a gold-wheel-turning king who rules all **four continents** of a Mt. **Sumeru world** after the other kings spontaneously offer their kingdoms to him, a silver-wheel-turning king who rules three continents (all but the northern one) after he approaches their rulers and they peacefully submit to his rule, a copper-wheel-turning king who rules two continents (the eastern and southern) after he approaches their rulers and they peacefully submit to his rule despite having prepared to resist, and an iron-wheel-turning king who rules over the southern continent of **Jambudvipa** after he approaches the other rulers and they peacefully submit to his rule despite an initial show of resistance. In none of these cases does the wheel-turning king have to resort to violence. As rulers they revere, protect, and uphold the Dharma and cause people to practice the **ten virtuous precepts**. The reign of the wheel-turning kings end when the wheel-treasure disappears and a king fails to rule as did his predecessors by failing to give to the needy, which gives rise to poverty, which leads to people committing theft, then murder, and eventually all ten evil acts. This begins the process that leads to the degeneration of humanity. (AKB2, pp. 484-487, see also LD 26, pp. 395-405)

Like buddhas, there can only be one wheel-turning king per Sumeru world at a time. (e.g. ND 1.278, p. 114) Also, they only appear when the lifespan of **human**s in Jambudvipa is eighty thousand years. (e.g. LD 26.14 and 26.24, pp. 399-400, 403)

In the fourteenth chapter, "**Peaceful Practices**," of the *Lotus Sutra*, **Shakyamuni** Buddha tells the parable of the brilliant gem in the topknot that is about a wheel-turning king who bestows the ***mani*** jewel upon those who served him, just as the Buddha bestows the *Lotus Sutra* upon his own followers.

wheel-turning noble king: (J. tenrin-jō'ō; 転輪聖王) See **wheel-turning king**.

wholesome: (S. kuśala; J. zen; 善) The Sanskrit term *kuśala* can also be translated as "auspicious," "salutary," or "virtuous." Wholesome **karmic actions** or **cause**s (not **effect**s or **ripening**s) are those that lead to good consequences and bring about **merit** in present and future lives. (DCOT, p. 155; CWL, p. 349) It can also refer to that which departs from **birth** and **death**, is peaceful, knowledgeable, and extremely skillful, and opposed to the **unwholesome**. (DCOT, pp. 358-359; CWL, p. 789)

wholesome root: (S. kuśala-mūla; J. zengon/zenkon; 善根) The Sanskrit term *kuśalamūla* can also be translated as "good root." Wholesome roots are the accumulation of **merit**orious **action**s and attitudes, and in particular the **three wholesome roots**.

wisdom: (S. prajñā; J. e or chie or hannya; 慧 or 智慧 or 般若) The Sanskrit term *prajñā* can also be translated as "cognition," "discernment," "gnosis," "**knowledge**," or "understanding."

In **Mahayana** Buddhism, wisdom is the sixth of the **six perfections** of a **bodhisattva**. As a **bodhisattva practice**, wisdom includes the non-discriminating wisdom of the **emptiness** of **self**, the non-discriminating wisdom of the emptiness of **dharma**s, and the non-discriminating wisdom encompassing both kinds of emptiness.

wisdom eye: (S. prajñā-cakṣus; J. e-gen; 慧眼) One of the **five kinds of eyes**. It is the "eye" or perspective of **voice-hearer**s and **privately-awakened one**s that can perceive the principle of **emptiness**.

wish-fulfilling gem: (S. cintā-maṇi; J. nyoi-hōju; 如意宝珠) A gem which is said to have the supernatural power to produce as much treasure and necessities of life as one wishes and helps remove disease. It is likened to the **merit** of having **faith** in the **Buddha** and his **Dharma**.

Nichiren Shonin likened each Chinese character of the *Lotus Sutra* with the wish-fulfilling gem. (WNS1, p. 189)

without the nature: (S. agotra; J. mushō; 無性) The Sanskrit term *agotra* literally means "having no spiritual lineage," though the ideograms 無性 mean "without the **nature**." According to the **Dharma Characteristics school** it is one of the **five natures**, pertaining to those **sentient beings** without any **capacity** for attaining **liberation** from the **six destinies**. Such beings are said to lack the **seed**s that could develop into the **awakening** of an **arhat**, a **pratyekabbudha**, or a **buddha**. The *icchantika* would be considered to be without the lineage or nature for awakening. However, the *Lotus Sutra* and *Nirvana Sutra* teach that even the *icchantika*, who does not have **buddha-nature**, can **attain buddhahood**.

Nichiren Shonin stressed the attainment of buddhahood by *icchantika* without the buddha-nature through the great compassion of the **Eternal Shakyamuni Buddha**.

Womb-realm: (S. Garbhakoṣa-dhātu; J. Taizōkai; 胎蔵界) Also called the Matrix-realm. According to the *Mahavairochana Sutra* it is a graphic representation of the aspiring **awakening mind** to save all **sentient beings** that is born in the mind of a **bodhisattva** and assisted by the **compassion** of **Mahavairochana Buddha**, just as an unborn child is protected in its mother's womb.

wonderful: (S. sat; J. myō; 妙) The Sanskrit *sat* can also be translated as "correct," "true," or "right." The ideogram 妙 can also be translated as "fine," "marvelous," "sublime," "subtle," or "wondrous."

For **Zhiyi**'s interpretation of "wonderful" or "subtle" in reference to the name of the ***Sutra of the Lotus Flower of the Wonderful Dharma*** see **Wonderful Dharma**.

Wonderful Dharma: (S. saddharma; J. myōhō; 妙法) The Sanskrit term *saddharma* can also be translated as "Correct **Dharma**," "Fine Dharma," "Right Dharma," "Subtle Dharma," or "**True Dharma**."

According to the explanation of the name of the ***Sutra of the Lotus Flower of the Wonderful Dharma*** in the *Profound Meaning of the Lotus Sutra*, "wonderful" or "subtle" means that which is inconceivable and refers to the provisional and true **phenomena** of the **ten realms** and **ten suchnesses**. (CSQI, p. 1815) More specifically, the Dharma taught in the *Lotus Sutra* is "subtle" as opposed to "coarse" or "rough" because it is the **perfect teaching** of the **One Buddha Vehicle**. (PMLS2, pp. 5-8)

The *Lotus Sutra* is also "subtle" because its teaching is vast in **entity**, superior in position, and long in function. In terms of the **cause** of buddhahood, it is vast in entity because of the **mutual possession of the ten realms**, it is superior in position because the first nine realms are integrated with the realm of buddhas, and it is long in function because the ten realms exemplify the perfectly interfused threefold truth. In terms of the **effect** of buddhahood, it is vast in entity because the true reality that the Buddha awakened to pervades everywhere, it is superior in position because of the Buddha's **attainment of buddhahood in the remotest past**, and it is long in function because the Buddha appears throughout the past, present, and future to **benefit** all **sentient being**s. The *Lotus Sutra* teaches all of this without any recourse to coarse teachings about the causes and effects of buddhahood. In terms of contemplation of the mind, it is vast in entity because the mind includes the minds of sentient beings and the Buddha, it is superior in position because one's mind is identical to the Buddha, and it is long in function because the mind exemplifies the perfectly interfused threefold truth. It is also vast in entity, superior in position, and long in function because the realm of the Buddha encompasses the other nine realms, so that the principle of the ten realms is one, the teaching of the **five flavors** is one, the practice of the contemplation of mind is one, and the person who attains a deepening sense of identity with the Buddha is one. (FTP, pp. 175-177; PMLS2, pp. 64-67)

The "Dharma" of the *Lotus Sutra* refers to three types of dharmas: the dharma of sentient beings, the dharma of the Buddha, and the dharma of the mind.

The dharma of sentient beings is subtle because it must include buddhahood, otherwise the one great purpose for the buddhas to appear in the world to open, show, obtain, and enter the insight of the buddha for them could not be fulfilled.

In addition, since sentient beings can obtain the **five kinds of eyes** that includes the **buddha eye**, they must be able to attain buddhahood. The dharma of sentient beings also refers to the workings of **cause and effect** of the ten realms. In more detail, the dharma of sentient beings is also explained through a careful analysis of how the ten suchnesses are operative in each of the ten realms. (FTP, pp. 177-196; PMLS2, pp. 68-69, 70-80)

The dharma of the Buddha is subtle because it is inclusive of both of the two truths of ultimate truth and provisional truth. It also refers to the effect of buddhahood which is the realm of the buddhas. The Buddha's wisdom encompasses all the ten realms and all ten suchnesses and all their combinations and permutations, so that he thoroughly understands himself and others. (FTP, pp. 178-179, 196-197; PMLS2, pp. 68-69, 80-81)

The dharma of the mind is subtle because it not distinct from the dharmas of sentient beings and buddhas and through contemplation of the mind one can attain buddhahood. It also refers to the causes of buddhahood which encompass the other nine realms other than the realm of the buddhas. Finally, though the dharma of sentient beings is vast and that of the buddhas is exalted, both can be realized through contemplation of the mind which contains all realms and suchnesses and the reality of the threefold truth of emptiness, provisional existence, and the **middle way**. (FTP, pp. 179, 197-199; PMLS2, pp. 68-69, 81-82)

Subtlety is also described in terms of **relative subtlety** and **absolute subtlety**. In even greater detail, it is explicated in terms of the **ten subtleties of the Trace Gate** and the **ten subtleties of the Original Gate**.

Words and Phrases of the Lotus Sutra: (J. *Hokke-mongu*; 法華文句) Abbreviated by **Nichiren Shonin** as *Mongu*, this treatise was taught by **Zhiyi** and recorded by his disciple **Guanding** in ten fascicles. Dividing the *Lotus Sutra* into three parts of a sutra and also into the two halves of the **Trace Gate** and **Original Gate**, each of which has three parts for a total of six, Zhiyi interpreted the words and phrases of the *Lotus Sutra* through four guidelines: 1) according to **causes and conditions**, 2) according to the **four doctrinal teachings**, 3) according to the Trace Gate and the Original Gate, and 4) according to contemplation of the mind.

Nichiren Shonin drew upon the interpretations of the *Lotus Sutra* expounded in this treatise, but he also taught his own understanding of the *Lotus Sutra* through his own experiences. Also, Unlike Zhiyi who stressed the Trace Gate, Nichiren Shonin regarded the Original Gate as primary.

World Honored One: (S. lokanātha or bhagavat; J. seson; 世尊) The Sanskrit term *bhagavat* can also be translated as "Blessed One" or "Lord." The ideograms 世尊 literally mean "World Honored One." One of the honorable titles of a **buddha**.

World Honored One of Great Enlightenment: (J. daikaku-seson; 大覚世尊) A title for a **buddha**.

World Voice Perceiver: (S. Avalokitasvara and later Avalokiteśvara; J. Kanzeon or Kannon or Kanjizai; 観世音 or 観音 or 観自在) The Sanskrit name Avalokitasvara means "World Voice Perceiver" or "Regarder of the Cries of the World," but later this **bodhisattva** came to be called Avalokiteśvara, which means "The Lord Who Look Down."

In the **Pure Land school** of Buddhism this bodhisattva represents **compassion** and is an attendant of **Amitabha Buddha**.

World Voice Perceiver Bodhisattva appears among the eighty thousand bodhisattvas present in the assembly in the first, "Introductory," chapter of the *Lotus Sutra*.

World Voice Perceiver Bodhisattva also features prominently in the twenty-fifth, "Universal Gate of World Voice Perceiver Bodhisattva," chapter of the *Lotus Sutra*. In that chapter, the bodhisattva assumes thirty-three different forms (both male and female) and appears anywhere to save people from **suffering**.

Nichiren Shonin considered World Voice Perceiver Bodhisattva a disciple of the **emanation buddhas of the ten directions** appearing in the pre-*Lotus* teachings who promised to protect the **practitioner of the *Lotus Sutra*** upon listening to **Shakyamuni** Buddha expound it.

wrong views: (S. mithyā-dṛṣṭi; J. ja-ken; 邪見) An **unwholesome** mental act that is the tenth of the ten evil acts. **Shakyamuni Buddha** explained it in these words: "Or he has wrong view, distorted vision, thus: 'There is nothing given, nothing offered, nothing sacrificed; no fruit or result of good or bad **action**s; no this world, no other world; no mother, no father; no beings who are reborn spontaneously; no good and virtuous recluses and **brahmin**s in the world who have themselves realized by direct **knowledge** and declare this world and the other world.'" (MD 41.10, p. 381)

Wu, King: (d. 1043 BCE; J. Bu-ō; 武王) The son of King **Wen**, who overthrew King **Zhou Xin** and established the Zhou dynasty. Out of filial piety, he attributed the founding of the dynasty to his father. King Wu is sometimes considered the second of the **Three Kings**₍₁₎.

Xuanzang: (600/602-664; J. Genjō; 玄奘) Founder of the Chinese **Dharma Characteristics school**. Born in Sui China, Xuanzang made an overland trip to India by way of Central Asia, in order to master the **consciousness-only** doctrine in the original Sanskrit. He spent seventeen years (629-645) traveling and studying

Buddhism, chiefly at Nalanda in **Magadha**, India. There he was able to study with **Shilabhadra**, who transmitted to him the teachings of **Dharmapala**. He returned to Chang'an with six hundred and fifty-seven Sanskrit texts and translated around seventy-five of them into Chinese, including the *Demonstration of Consciousness-Only Treatise*.

Among his most influential disciples were **Kuiji**, Fabao, **Puguang**, **Shenfang**, and **Jiashang**.

yaksha: (S. yakṣa; J. yasha; 夜叉) Yakshas are lesser nature **spirit**s associated with trees, forests, or even villages; but they have a fierce side as well, and in their more demonic flesh-eating aspect they are known as **rakshasa**s. Sometimes they are classified as **god**s but other times as **hungry ghost**s among the **six destinies**. They are one of the **eight kinds of supernatural beings**. Yakshas are also included among the army and attendants of Hearing Everything, one of the **four heavenly kings**.

Yama: (S. Yama; J. Emma; 閻魔) According to the Rig Veda, Yama was the first mortal **human** to die. For this reason, he became the chief magistrate of the underworld, consisting of the **hell**s and the realm of the **hungry ghost**s where he holds his court. **Shakyamuni Buddha** says that those who fall into hell are seized by the hell wardens who present **hell-dweller**s to King Yama, who then interrogates them as to why they did not reflect on their own vulnerability and do good deeds even after witnessing so much **suffering** and the punishment of criminals in their human life. The Buddha does not say how the hell-dwellers respond but does say that King Yama is silent as the hell-dweller is then tortured by the wardens. King Yama then expresses the wish that he could be reborn as a human and encounter a **buddha** and understand the **Dharma**. (MD 130, pp. 1029-1036; ND 3.36, pp. 233-237)

According to the *Treasury of Abhidharma Treatise*, Yama is considered the king of the **hungry ghost**s and dwells with them underground. (AKB2, p. 460)

Nichiren Shonin referred to him as King Yama (J. Emma-ō; 閻魔王) or Yama the Lord of the Dharma (J. Emma-hō'ō; 閻魔法王).

Yamashina-dera Temple: (J. Yamashina-dera; 山階寺) The original name of **Kofukuji Temple**.

Yao: (C.; J. Gyō; 尭) A legendary **sage** emperor who was the second son of Emperor **Ku**. He abdicated in favor of his son-in-law, **Shun**. Yao was the fourth emperor of the **Three Sovereigns and Five Emperors**.

Yashodhara: (S. Yaśodhara; J. Yashudara or Yashutara; 耶輸陀羅 or 耶輸多羅) The wife of **Siddhartha Gautama** before he left home to become an ascetic and seek the **way** to **liberation** from **suffering**. She had a son, **Rahula**, by him. After her former husband was able to **attain buddhahood**, she became a Buddhist, becoming one of the first **nuns**.

She is one of the nuns listed as present in the assembly in the first, "Introductory," chapter of the *Lotus Sutra*. In the thirteenth chapter, "Encouragement for Keeping This Sutra," she receives the assurance of future buddhahood by Shakyamuni Buddha and told that she will become a buddha named **Emitting Ten Million Rays of Light**.

Yellow Emperor: (C. Huangdi; J. Kōtei; 黄帝) The Yellow Emperor is credited with being the inventor of clothing, boats, carts, and archery. The goddess Xuannu is said to have taught him the **five constant virtues**. The Yellow Emperor was the third of the **Three Sovereigns and Five Emperors**.

Yixing: (683-727; J. Ichigyō; 一行) A Chinese **monk** who became a **Zen master** in the Northern **Zen school**, studied the teachings of the **Tiantai school** and the **Discipline school**, and later became an **acharya** of the **Mantra school**. One list of Mantra school patriarchs lists him as the sixth patriarch.

At the invitation of Emperor Xuanzang of the Tang dynasty, Yixing moved to Luoyang where he studied **esoteric Buddhism** under **Shubhakarasimha** and assisted in the translation of the *Mahavairochana Sutra* between 724 and 725. Yixing then wrote the *Annotations on the Mahavairochana Sutra* based on Shubhakarasimha's lectures. There are stories that he may also have helped **Vajrabodhi** with his translations of esoteric texts into Chinese. Yixing was also an expert in mathematics and astronomy. He undertook an astronomical survey to revise the Chinese calendar and with the help of engineers he created a hydraulic celestial globe to show the movements of planets and constellations.

Nichiren Shonin criticized Yixing for stealing the Tiantai school doctrine of the **"three thousand realms in a single thought-moment"** and for claiming that the *Lotus Sutra* and the *Mahavairochana Sutra* were originally a single sutra in India in his *Annotations on the Mahavairochana Sutra*. (WNS1, pp. 223-224)

yojana: (S.; J. yujun: 由旬) A unit of distance in ancient India, but its length is not exactly known. The Sanskrit word *yojana* can be translated as "league," however a league is anywhere from 3.9 to 7.4 kilometers. It is said to have been the distance of a day's journey by chariot, approximately eight kilometers (five miles). Alternately, it is said to be the distance covered by the royal army in a day, which would be equivalent to thirty or forty Chinese *li* (里), which would be more than ten miles.

You, King: (795-771 BCE; J. Yū-ō; 幽王) The last ruler of the Zhou dynasty. King You was the third of the **Three Kings**(2).

Yu the Great, King: (c. 2123 – 2025 BCE; C. Da Yu; J. Dai-u-ō; 大禹王) The appointed successor of Emperor **Shun**. He is famed for having controlled the flooding of the Yellow River using dredging and irrigation canals and is considered the first ruler of the Xia dynasty. King Yu the Great is the first of the **Three Kings**(1).

zen master: (J. zenji; 禅師) See **meditation master**.

Zen school: (J. Zen-shū; 禅宗) One of the schools of Chinese Buddhism. **Bodhidharma** is credited with establishing the Zen school in China in the early sixth century. Bodhidharma was the legendary twenty-eighth of the of the **twenty-eight Indian ancestor** of Indian Buddhism and the first patriarch of the Zen school in China. The word "zen" is the Japanese pronunciation of the Chinese word *chan*, which is in turn a transliteration of *dhyāna*, the Sanskrit word for **meditative absorption**. Zen, however, refers to the unity of meditative absorption and **wisdom** and not meditative absorption alone. According to the Zen school, the **Buddha Dharma** has been transmitted from person-to-person (or **mind**-to-mind) from **Shakyamuni Buddha** through his successors all the way to the present-day **Zen masters**. In this way the true meaning of the Buddha's teachings has been passed on through the actual **awakening** of these successors and not just in the written teachings. By the tenth century there were five houses and seven schools of Zen, but only two houses have survived to any great extent: the Linji school founded by Linji Yixuan (d. 866) and the Caodong school founded by Dongshan Liangjie (807-869) and his disciple Caoshan Benji (840-901).

Zen was first brought to Japan during the Nara period by **Dosho** and Daoxuan, and **Saicho** was given transmission in the Ox Head lineage while in China, but it was promulgated as a separate teaching. During the Kamakura period a **monk** named **Dainichi Nonin** tried to establish a Bodhidharma School in 1189 after receiving a certificate of Zen transmission with a correspondent in China, but he was regarded as a fraud. Eisai succeeded in introducing the Rinzai school (C. Linji) of Zen to Japan 1191, after spending four years in China training with the Zen Masters there. Dogen introduced the Soto Shu (C. Caodong) of Zen to Japan after studying in China from 1223-1227. After the Song dynasty fell to the Mongols, Zen masters from China such as Daolong came to Japan and helped to spread Rinzai Zen. The Obaku school was introduced to Japan in the mid-seventeenth century by Yinyuan Longqi (1594-1673).

The Zen school claims to **attain buddhahood** by way of contemplation of the mind in sitting meditation. They maintain that the "treasury of the eye of the True Dharma" is transmitted directly from master to disciple without writing or teaching. It can be attained not through doctrinal study but by meditation. The Zen school claims of itself that it is "A **separate transmission outside the sutras**/not founded upon words and letters/a direct pointing to the human mind/seeing the true nature and attaining buddhahood." (See Dumoulin 1994, p. 85)

Nichiren Shonin criticized them by saying that abandoning all Buddhist **scripture**s is an act of **heavenly devil**s.

Zhang'an, Great Master: (J. Shōan Daishi; 章安 大師) See **Guanding**.

Zhanran: (711-782; C.; J. Tannen; 湛然) Also known as the Great Master **Miaole**, after the Miaolesi Temple where he lived, or the Venerable Jingqi (J. Keikei; 荊渓), after his birthplace. The sixth patriarch of the **Tiantai school** in China (or the ninth if **Nagarjuna** is counted as the first). He is regarded as the restorer of the Tiantai school.

Zhanran began to study Buddhism at the age of twenty under the fifth Tiantai patriarch, Xuanlang, but did not become a **monk** until he was thirty-eight. In his day, the Tiantai school had become moribund and was overshadowed by newer and more vital schools like the **Zen school**, the **Flower Garland school**, and the **Dharma Characteristics school**. Zhanran revitalized the Tiantai school, refuting the claims of its rivals, and wrote definitive commentaries on each of the **three major works of the Lotus School** that recorded the teachings of **Zhiyi**. Those commentaries are called: the *Notations on the Words and Phrases of the Lotus Sutra*, the *Elucidation of the Profound Meaning of the Lotus Sutra*, and the *Supplemental Amplifications on the Great Calming and Contemplation*. He also wrote the *Summary of the Great Calming and Contemplation* and other annotated editions of Zhiyi's writings.

Nichiren Shonin esteemed Zhanran highly as a legitimate successor to Zhiyi and quotes him often in written letters and treatises.

Zhidu: (n.d.; C.; J. Chido; 智度) Zhidu of Dongchun, a Tang dynasty Chinese **monk** of the **Tiantai school** who wrote *A Supplement to the Meanings of the Commentaries on the Lotus Sutra*, which is referred to sometimes as the *Dongchun* after the place where Zhidu lived.

Zhiyan: (602-669; J. Chigon; 智儼) The second patriarch of the **Flower Garland school**; generally called Grand Master Zhixiangsi. He became a **monk** at fourteen and studied the Flower Garland teachings under **Dushun**. Living at the Zhixiangsi Temple on Mt. Zhongnan, he spread Flower Garland Buddhism vigorously. He was succeeded by **Fazang**.

Zhiyi: (538-597; J. Chigi; 智顗) Also known as the **Great Master Tiantai**. The actual founder of the **Tiantai school** in China, though he is considered the third patriarch after his teacher Huisi and his teacher's teacher Huiwen. Some accounts make **Nagarjuna** the first patriarch, and then Zhiyi is regarded as the fourth. He is also called the **Shakyamuni** of China. His parents named him Dean (德安), with the family name of Chen (陳). His father's name was Chen Qizu (陳起祖), and his mother came from the Xu (徐) family.

Zhiyi was ordained as a novice at the age of eighteen, after his parents died. He was fully ordained as a **monk** at the age of twenty. From around 560 until 567 he lived at Mt. Dasu studying with Huisi.

There is a legend that when Zhiyi met Huisi, his teacher greeted him by saying that he had been waiting for him. He said that they had been together at Mt. **Sacred Eagle** where they had heard the *Lotus Sutra* from Shakyamuni **Buddha** himself. Huisi was supposedly an earthly manifestation of **World Voice Perceiver Bodhisattva** and Zhiyi was supposedly an earthly manifestation of **Medicine King** Bodhisattva. Zhiyi, in fact, is said to have attained **awakening** while reading the twenty-third, "The **Previous Life of Medicine King Bodhisattva**," **chapter** of the *Lotus Sutra*.

After studying with Huisi, Zhiyi moved to Jiankang (建康), the capital of the Chen dynasty. Jiankang was renamed Jinling (金陵) during the Tang dynasty. He spent eight years there at Waguansi Temple. In 575, he moved again to Mt. **Tiantai**, which would become his namesake and the name of the school of Buddhism that he established. In 584, he was joined on Mt. Tiantai by **Guanding**, who was later known as the Great Master **Zhang'an**, after his birthplace.

In 585, Zhiyi was persuaded to return to Jiankang to lecture on the sutras. In 587, he delivered the lectures that would become the *Words and Phrases of the Lotus Sutra*. In 589, he left Jiankang for Mt. Lu to avoid the invading forces of the Sui dynasty that was in the process of uniting all of China.

In 591, however, he visited Prince Yang Guang (who later became the second emperor of the Sui dynasty) and administered the bodhisattva **precept**s to him and gave him a **Dharma** name. In return, Prince Guang bestowed the honorary name **Zhizhe** upon Zhiyi. After that, Zhiyi returned to his homeland, Jiangling. In 593 and 594 respectively, Zhiyi delivered the lectures that would become the *Profound Meaning of the Lotus Sutra*, and the *Great Calming and Contemplation*. In 595, he returned to Mt. Tiantai and passed away there in 597. Guanding became his successor and the second patriarch of the Tiantai school.

The *Words and Phrases of the Lotus Sutra*, the *Profound Meaning of the Lotus Sutra*, and the *Great Calming and Contemplation* compiled from the notes Guanding took on Zhiyi's lectures became known as the **three major works of the Lotus School** or three major works of the Tiantai school. Together they record the core of Zhiyi's doctrine. His most important teachings include the threefold truth of **emptiness**, provisional existence, and the **middle way**; the **three thousand realms in a single thought-moment**; his comparative classification of doctrines into the **five periods** and eight teachings (consisting of the **four doctrinal teachings** and the four methods of teaching: sudden, gradual, secret, and indeterminate); and his analysis of the *Lotus Sutra* into the **Trace Gate** and the **Original Gate**. These teachings and many others gave Tiantai practitioners the ability to make sense of the vast collection of Buddhist sutras and put them into practical use in the cultivation of meditation practice. In particular, Zhiyi's commentaries enabled them to grasp the essential points and subtle teachings of the *Lotus Sutra*.

His teachings exerted a strong influence upon **Saicho** and **Nichiren Shonin** in Japan. Nichiren Shonin developed and expanded Zhiyi's concept of the three thousand realms in a single thought-moment making it applicable to the **Latter Age of Degeneration**. In his writings, Nichiren depended heavily on the three major works of the Tiantai school as well as that of the *Lotus Sutra* and the *Nirvana Sutra*.

Zhizhe: (J. Chisha; 智者) See **Zhiyi**.

Zhou Xin, King: (1105-1046; J. Chūshin-ō; 紂辛王) The last ruler of the of the Shang or Yin dynasty who was overthrown by King **Wu**. King Zhou Xin was the second of the **Three Kings**(2).

Zhuanxu: (C.; J. Senkoku; 顓項): A legendary emperor who is sometimes said to have been the grandson of the **Yellow Emperor** and the nephew of **Shaohao**. Zhuanxu was the second emperor of the **Three Sovereigns and Five Emperors**.

Bibliography

Asanga (2001) *Abhidharmasamuccaya: The Compendium of the Higher Teaching (Philosophy)*, translated by Walpola Rahula, Sara Boin-Webb, Berkeley, CA: Asian Humanities Press, 2001

Augustine, M.J. and Kondō, T. (trans.) (1997), *Senchaku Hongan Nembutsu Shu*, Berkeley, CA: Numata Center for Buddhist Translation and Research.

Blum, M. (trans.) (2013) *The Nirvana Sutra (Mahāparinirvāṇa-Sūtra) Volume I*, Moraga, CA: BDK, America, Inc.

Bodhi (trans.) (2000) *The Connected Discourses of the Buddha: A Translation of the Saṃyutta Nikāya*, Somerville, MA: Wisdom Publications.

Bodhi (trans.) (2012) *The Numerical Discourses of the Buddha: A Translation of the Aṅguttara Nikāya*, Somerville, MA: Wisdom Publications.

Bodhi (trans.) (2017) *The Suttanipāta: An Ancient Collection of the Buddha's Discourses Together with its Commentaries*, Somerville, MA: Wisdom Publications.

Buddhaghosa (1920/1) *The Expositor (Atthasālinī)*, 2 vols, trans. Maung Tin, London: Pali Text Society.

Buddhaghosa (1975) *The Path of Purification (Visuddhimagga)*, trans. Bhikkhu Nāṇamoli, Kandy, Sri Lanka: Buddhist Publication Society.

Buswell, R.E. and Lopes, D.S. Jr. (ed.) (1014) *The Princeton Dictionary of Buddhism*, Princeton, NJ: Princeton University Press.

Carter, J. R., and Palihawadana, M. (trans.) (1987) *The Dhammapada*, New York: Oxford University Press.

Cleary, Thomas. (trans.) (1993) *The Flower Ornament Scripture: A Translation of the Avatamsaka Sutra*, Boston: Sambhala Publications, Inc.

Cook, F.H. (trans.) (1999) *Demonstration of Consciousness Only by Hsüan-tsang* in *Three Texts on Consciousness Only*, Berkeley: Numata Center for Buddhist Translation and Research.

Davids, C.A.F.R. and Norman, K.R. (trans.) (1989) *Poems of Early Buddhist Nuns*, Oxford: Pali Text Society.

Donner, N. and Stevenson D.G, (1993) *The Great Calming and Contemplation: A Study and Annotated Translation for the First Chapter of Chih-i's Mo-Ho Chih-Kuan*, Hawaii: University of Hawaii Press.

Dumoulin, H. (1994) *Zen Buddhism: A History, Volume I India and China*, New York: MacMillian.

Foulk, T. G. (1999) "Sung Controversies Concerning 'Separate Transmission' of Ch'an." In *Buddhism in the Sung,* ed. by Gregory, Peter N. and Getz, Daniel A. Jr. Honolulu: University of Hawai'i Press.

Garfield, J.L. (trans.) (1995) *The Fundamental Wisdom of the Middle Way: Nāgārjuna's Mūlamadhyamikakārikā*, New York: Oxford University Press.

Giebel, Rolf W. (trans.) (2001), *Two Esoteric Sutras*. Berkeley: Numata Center for Buddhist Translation and Research.

Giebel, Rolf W. (trans.) (2005), *The Vairocanābhisaṃbodhi Sutra*. Moraga: BDK America, Inc.

Gosho Translation Committee, editor-translator. The Writings of Nichiren Daishonin. Tokyo: Soka Gakkai, 1999.

Green, R.S. and Mun (2018) C. *Gyōnen's Transmission of the Buddha Dharma in Three Countries,* Leiden/Boston: Brill.

Hakeda, Y.S. (trans.) (2005) *The Awakening of Faith Attributed to Aśvaghṣa*, Berkeley: Numata Center for Buddhist Translation and Research.

Hayashima, K. et. al. (1984) *Japanese-English Buddhist Dictionary*, Tokyo, Japan: Daitō Shuppansha.

Hori, K., (comp.) Tanabe, G. Jr. (ed.) (2002) *Writings of Nichiren Shonin: Doctrine Volume 2.* Tokyo: Nichiren Shu Overseas Propagation Promotion Association.

Hori, K., (comp.) Sakashita, J. (ed.) (2003) *Writings of Nichiren Shonin: Doctrine Volume 1.* Tokyo: Nichiren Shu Overseas Propagation Promotion Association.

Hori, K., (comp.) Sakashita, J. (ed.) (2004) *Writings of Nichiren Shonin: Doctrine Volume 3.* Tokyo: Nichiren Shu Overseas Propagation Promotion Association.

Hori, K., (comp.) Sakashita, J. (ed.) (2007) *Writings of Nichiren Shonin: Faith and*

Practice Volume 4. Tokyo: Nichiren Shu Overseas Propagation Promotion Association.

Hori, K., (comp.) Sakashita, J. (ed.) (2008) *Writings of Nichiren Shonin: Biography and Disciples Volume 5*. Tokyo: Nichiren Shu Overseas Propagation Promotion Association.

Hori, K., (comp.) Sakashita, J. (ed.) (2010) *Writings of Nichiren Shonin: Followers I Volume 6*. Tokyo: Nichiren Shu Overseas Propagation Promotion Association.

Hori, K., (comp.) Sakashita, J. (ed.) (2015) *Writings of Nichiren Shonin: Followers II Volume 7*. Tokyo: Nichiren Shu Overseas Propagation Promotion Association.

Ichishima, M. and Chappell, D.W. (2013) *A Guide to the Tiantai Fourfold Teachings* in *Tiantai Lotus Texts*, Berkeley: Bukkyō Dendō Kyōkai America, Inc.

Inagaki, H. (2001) *A Dictionary of Japanese Buddhist Terms*, Berkeley, CA: Stone Bridge Press.

Inagaki, H. and Stewart, H. (trans.) (2016) *Three Pure Land Sutras*. Berkeley: Numata Center for Buddhist Translation and Research.

Johnston, E.H., (trans.) (2015), *Asvaghosa's Buddhacaritra or Acts of the Buddha*. Delhi: Motilal Banarsidass Publishers.

Kabilsingh, C. (1991) *The Bhikkhuni Patimokkha of the Six Schools*, http://www.buddhanet.net/pdf_file/bhikkhuni_patimokkha.pdf

Keenan, J.P. (trans.) (2000) *The Scripture on the Explication of Underlying Meaning*, Berkeley: Numata Center for Buddhist Translation and Research.

Keown, D. (ed.) (2003) *A Dictionary of Buddhism*, New York: Oxford University Press.

Khantipalo (1995) "The Wheel of Birth and Death" Available online at https://www.accesstoinsight.org/lib/authors/khantipalo/wheel147.html (accessed 30 March 2020)

Law, B.C. (2014) *Geography of Early Buddhism*, Available at https://www.ancient-buddhist-texts.net/Reference/Geography-of-Early-Buddhism/index.htm (accessed 5 April 2020)

Matsunaga, A. and D. (1988) *Foundations of Japanese Buddhism: The Mass Movement*, Los Angeles/Tokyo: Buddhist Books International.

Matsunaga, A. and D. (1992) *Foundations of Japanese Buddhism: The Aristocratic Age*, Los Angeles/Tokyo: Buddhist Books International.

McCormick, R.M. (2005) *Lotus World: An Illustrated Guide to the Gohonzon*, San Jose, CA: Nichiren Buddhist Temple of San Jose.

McCormick, R.M. (2010) *Lotus Seeds: The Essence of Nichiren Shu Buddhism (Second Edition)*, San Jose, CA: Nichiren Buddhist Temple of San Jose.

McCormick, R.M. (1019) *Lotus in a Sea of Flames*, Oakland, CA: Nichiren Buddhist Sangha San Francisco Bay Area.

McCormick, R.M. (1019) *Open Your Eyes: A Nichiren Buddhist View of Awakening*, Oakland, CA: Nichiren Buddhist Sangha San Francisco Bay Area.

McRae, J. (trans.) (2004) *The Vimalakīrti Sutra* in *The Sutra of Queen Śrīmālā of the Lion's Roar and The Vimalakīrti Sutra*. Berkeley: Numata Center for Buddhist Translation and Research.

Muller, C.A. (1995 updated monthly) *Digital Dictionary of Buddhism*, http://www.buddhism-dict.net/ddb/

Murano, S. (trans.) (2000). *Kaimokusho or Liberation from Blindness*, Berkeley: Numata Center for Buddhist Translation and Research, 2000.

Murano, S. (trans.) (2003). *Two Nichiren Texts*, Berkeley: Numata Center for Buddhist Translation and Research, 2000.

Murano, S. (trans.) (2012) *The Lotus Sutra*. Tokyo: Nichiren Buddhist International Center.

Ñāṇamoli (trans.) (2001) *The Life of the Buddha*. Seattle: Buddhist Publication Society Pariyatti Editions.

Ñāṇamoli and Bodhi (trans.) (2015) *The Middle Length Discourses of the Buddha: A Translation of the Majjhima Nikāya*, Somerville, MA: Wisdom Publications.

Numata Center for Buddhist Translation and Research Editorial Staff (2003) *Buddha-Dharma: The Way to Enlightenment (Revised Second Edition)*. Berkeley: Numata Center for Buddhist Translation and Research.

Nyanaponika (2003) *Great Disciples of the Buddha: Their Lives, Their Works, Their Legacy* Somerville, MA: Wisdom Publications. Kindle Edition.

Olivelle, Patrick, (trans.) (2008) *Life of the Buddha by Ashvaghosha*. Clay Sanskrit Library.
(available at nippaku.files.wordpress.com/2017/03/life-of-the-buddha-buddhacarita-olivelle-2008-extract.pdf).

Page, T. (ed.) Yamamoto, K (trans.) (2007) *The Mahayana Mahaparinirvana Sutra*, PDF e-book created by do1@yandex.ru.

Pruden, L. (trans.) (1994) *The Essentials of the Eight Traditions by Gyōnen* in *The Essentials of the Eight Traditions and The Candle of the Latter Dharma*. Berkeley: Numata Center for Buddhist Translation and Research.

Pruden, L. (trans.) (1995) *The Essentials of the Vinaya Tradition by Gyōnen* in *The Collected Teachings of the Tendai Lotus School by Gishin* in *The Essentials of the Vinaya Tradition and The Collected Teachings of the Tendai Lotus School*. Berkeley: Numata Center for Buddhist Translation and Research.

Ramanan, K.V. (1998) *Nāgārjuna's Philosophy*, Delhi: Motilal Banarsidass Publishers.

Rulu (如露), (trans.) (update 2017) *Sūtra of Aṅgulimālika*. (available at sutrasmantras.info/sutra54a.html)

Sadataka, A. (2004) *Buddhist Cosmology: Philosophy and Origins*. Tokyo: Kosei Publishing Co.

Shen, H. (2005) *The Profound Meaning of the Lotus Sutra: T'ien-t'ai Philosophy of Buddhism*, 2 vols, Delhi: Originals.

Shinozaki, M., Ziporyn, B.A., & Earhart, D.C. (trans.) (2019) *The Threefold Lotus Sutra: A Modern Translation for Contemporary Readers*, Tokyo: Kosei Publishing Co.

Siderits, M. and Katsura, S. (trans.) (2013) *Nāgārjuna's Middle Way: Mūlamadhyamikakārikā*, Somerville, MA: Wisdom Publications.

Stone, J. (1999) *Original Enlightenment and the Transformation of Medieval Japanese Buddhism*, Honolulu, HI: University of Hawai'i Press.

Swanson, P.L. (1989) *Foundations of T'ien-t'ai Philosophy: The Flowering of the Two*

Truths Theory in Chinese Buddhism, Berkeley: Asian Humanities Press.

Swanson, P. L. (trans.) (1995) *The Collected Teachings of the Tendai Lotus School by Gishin* in *The Essentials of the Vinaya Tradition and The Collected Teachings of the Tendai Lotus School*. Berkeley: Numata Center for Buddhist Translation and Research.

Swanson, P.L. (trans.) (2018) *Clear Serenity and Quiet Insight: T'ien-t'ai Chih-i's Mo-ho Chih-kuan*. Three Volumes. Honolulu: University of Hawai'i Press.

Tat, W. (trans.) (1973) *Ch'eng Wei-Shih Lun: Doctrine of Mere Consciousness*. Hong Kong: Ch'eng Wei-Shih Lun Publication Committee.

Thānissaro (2016) *Udāna: Exclamations: A Translation*, Valley Center, CA: Metta Forest Monastery.

Thurman, R.A.F. (trans.) (1988) *The Holy Teaching of Vimalakīrti: A Mahayana Scripture*. University Park: Pennsylvania State University Press.

Vasubandhu (1988-1990) *Abhidharmakośabhāṣyam* [trans. into French by L. de la Vallée Poussin], English trans. L.M. Pruden, 4 vols, Berkeley, CA: Asian Humanities Press.

Vasubandhu, and Ninth Karmapa Wangchuk Dorje (2012) *Jewels from the Treasury: Vasubandhu's Verses on the Treasury of Abhidharma and It's Commentary Youthful Play by the Ninth Karmapa Wangchuk Dorje*, translated by David Karma Choephel, KTD Publications.

Walshe, M. (trans.) (1995) *The Long Discourses of the Buddha: A Translation of the Dīgha Nikāya*. Boston: Wisdom Publications.

Warner, W. (2018) *The History and Teachings of Nichiren Buddhism: From Śākyamuni Buddha Through Nichiren Shōnin to the Present*. Tokyo: Head Office of Nichiren Shu.

Willemen, C. (trans.) (2009) *Buddhacarita: In Praise of the Buddha's Acts*. Berkeley: Numata Center for Buddhist Translation and Research.

Williams, P., and Tribe, A. (2000) *Buddhist Thought: A Complete Introduction to the Indian Tradition*, London/New York: Routledge.

Made in the USA
Las Vegas, NV
07 November 2021